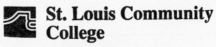

Television Myth and the American Mind

Hal Himmelstein

SECOND EDITION

Westport, Connecticut
London

Library of Congress Cataloging-in-Publication Data

Himmelstein, Hal.
    Television myth and the American mind / Hal Himmelstein. — 2nd
ed.
        p.   cm.
    Includes bibliographical references and index.
    ISBN 0-275-93156-0 (alk. paper).—ISBN 0-275-93157-9 (pbk. :
alk. paper)
    1. Television programs—United States—History and criticism.
2. Television advertising—United States.   3. Television
broadcasting—United States.   I. Title.
PN1992.3.U5H55   1994
302.23'45—dc20   93-43796

British Library Cataloguing in Publication Data is available.

Library of Congress Catalog Card Number: 93-43796
ISBN: 0-275-93156-0
        0-275-93157-9 (pbk.)

First published in 1994

Praeger Publishers, 88 Post Road West, Westport, CT 06881
An imprint of Greenwood Publishing Group, Inc.

Printed in the United States of America

The paper used in this book complies with the
Permanent Paper Standard issued by the National
Information Standards Organization (Z39.48-1984).

10 9 8 7 6 5 4 3 2 1

Copyright Acknowledgments

For my father,
Jack Himmelstein

Contents

Preface to the Second Edition

I completed work on the first edition of *Television Myth and the American Mind* in December 1983. In the ensuing decade, significant changes have occurred in the television industry in the United States. Among these has been a marked increase in viewing options, in terms of both the absolute number of available channels and the level of their penetration into American homes. The "Big Three" commercial networks (CBS, NBC, and ABC) had dominated national program distribution in prime time throughout the medium's history. Now they found themselves under siege by a proliferation of cable/satellite channels and the growing use of the VCR. In 1980, 15.5 million U.S. households subscribed to cable television; by 1993, 57.7 million households (62 percent of all U.S. television households) were cable subscribers—nearly a fourfold increase. Basic and pay cable services combined captured an 8 percent share of the prime-time audience in 1982; by 1993, these cable services commanded a 26 percent share of the prime-time audience (while pay cable's share dropped slightly, from 5 percent to 4 percent during this period, basic cable's audience grew rapidly, from 3 percent of prime-time audiences in 1982 to 22 percent in 1993). The rapid growth of basic cable cut directly into the Big Three's combined share of prime-time audience, which decreased from 81 percent in 1982 to 63 percent in 1992. In 1980, only one million U.S. television households had VCRs; by 1993, that number had risen to 70.8 million households (76 percent of all U.S. television households).

Remote-control devices allowed viewers to "graze" through programs, assembling a variety of short audiovisual bites into their "own" programs, and to employ the magical "mute" button to block out the sound of annoying commercials. Critic Raymond Williams's prophetic 1974 description of television as comprised of a "flow" of audiovisual information rather than a sequence of discrete programs had, for many young viewers at least, become a reality.

By the mid-1980s, paternalistic rule at the Big Three gave way to the era of the bottom-line managers. The much-publicized corporate mergers and acquisitions, beginning with the Capital Cities Communications acquisition of ABC in January 1986 and shortly followed by Lawrence Tisch's seizing control of CBS and General Electric's takeover of NBC that same year, led to downsizing of network staff and major changes in the corporate cultures of the three networks.

This was particularly evident in the networks' news divisions, where substantial layoffs resulted in a noticeable diminution of the quality of news coverage, especially in international stories. The "new kid on the block"—Cable News Network (CNN), at first ridiculed by the Big Three's news doyens—proved a formidable challenger. By the early 1990s, CNN's 24-hour global presence, its extensive network of foreign bureaus, and its live continuous coverage of Tiananmen Square and the Gulf War lent it a prestige that far surpassed its audience share.

Downsizing at the Big Three, combined with the deregulation initiatives of the Reagan administration during the 1980s, had a significant impact on the networks. All had departments charged with monitoring program content for its adherence to standards established by the networks within the framework of government regulation designed to delineate broadcasters' public trust obligations. The staffs of these departments (called Program Practices at CBS and Standards and Practices at NBC and ABC) were reduced by nearly two-thirds during this period, as management began to shift primary responsibility for monitoring program content and maintaining program standards to network program executives and the creative community—the Hollywood television studio producers.

Independent local television stations (those not affiliated with any of the Big Three national broadcast networks) increased their combined prime-time audience share during the 1980s, from 11 percent in 1982 to 14.6 percent in 1988. Many of these stations had, on occasion, formed "ad hoc networks" to simultaneously carry special programs but did not represent a consistent audience threat to the Big Three. This, however, changed in the late 1980s as Fox Television began a serious move to form a fourth commercial broadcast network in the United States. Consciously programming to a young target demographic audience with such hits as *The Simpsons, Married . . . with Children,* and *Beverly Hills, 90210,* by the early 1990s Fox had become commercially competitive in certain prime-time slots.

Public television continued to offer important current-affairs programming such as the *Frontline* and *P.O.V.* long-form documentary series that provided the in-depth investigative and advocacy journalism increasingly eschewed by the Big Three as the latter sought to capitalize on the ratings success of short-form "magazine" journalism, best exemplified by CBS's *60 Minutes* and the "great moments" topical journalism of *48 Hours*. One of the major accomplishments of PBS was the series *A World of Ideas with Bill Moyers*, which offered viewers the all-too-rare television experience of insightful one-on-one conversations with many of the world's most respected scholars, intellectuals, scientists, and artists regarding crises in contemporary social, political, and cultural life.

Performing-arts offerings on public television, such as *American Playhouse, Live from Lincoln Center*, the Texaco Metropolitan Opera broadcasts, and *Alive from Off Center*'s celebration of the avant-garde, highlighted the almost total absence of this genre on commercial broadcast television. But as the 1980s came to a close, cable/satellite program services such as Arts & Entertainment, Discovery, and Bravo were siphoning off public television's historically small audiences (on average comprising only a 4.5 percent share of the prime-time audience during the 1980s).

The scope of the television critic's job, in terms of the sheer number of programs available for analysis, has thus increased dramatically in the past decade. Many newspapers have responded by expanding their television beats. The *New York Times*, for example, frequently pre-reviews two or three programs every day and provides extensive coverage of the business aspects of entertainment television in its business section. For the academic television critic, however, while the quantity of programs has increased dramatically, the focus of critical analysis remains the same. The interpenetration of the domains of culture, society, economy, and politics forms the ground for such a critical analysis.

During the intervening decade between the two editions of this book, significant shifts in critical theory have occurred. These are reflected in my own writing during this period, which has been incorporated in the second edition. Most important, in two articles published in the *Journal of Film and Video* in 1989 (the second coauthored by Bernard Timberg), I have broadened the analytical horizon to incorporate both the "structuralist" position dominant in the first edition, which implies that social relations, to a significant extent engendered by and reflected in the ideology of televisual discourse, are symbolically constituted, generally not of the viewers' making, and out of their control, and a more open-ended "post-structuralist" position that moves away from a determinist textual analysis of ideology to a consideration of the presence of the television text in the everyday lives of viewing subjects. The latter position, informed by the writings of French sociologist Michel de Certeau and recent studies of viewing by television scholars such as David Morley, James Lull, and Ian Ang, admits both the complexity of subject formation in this domain and the possibility of deriving "pleasure" from the viewing experience. I do not find these critical frames to be mutually exclusive, and I have been careful not to abandon the structuralist ground, for it continues to offer a powerful explanation of attempts by the dominant culture to *regulate* social behavior, although it is clear that the nature of these attempts and the ideological formations employed change as social conditions themselves change.

My recent writings, incorporated in this edition, argue that critical television scholarship must attempt to explicate the larger process of discursive exchange by integrating studies of creation and production (the creative process), distribution, marketing and promotion of programs (the business of television), and reception (the viewer as object of commerce versus the viewer as negotiating subject).

The growth of cable/satellite channels and independent local broadcast stations in the past decade has not only challenged the commercial dominance of the Big Three but also has permitted the development of a "living museum" of television program history. Many of the "old" series discussed in this book can be viewed repeatedly on these channels. Young viewers, not born when *The Beverly Hillbillies, Leave It to Beaver,* or *East Side/West Side* were first aired on the networks, can now watch these programs repeatedly. How these programs are decoded by teenagers and preteens 30 years after their original runs and how they are seen today by middle-aged adults from an "adult's" rather than a child's perspective surely would be of interest to researchers.

Cable networks are programming "marathons," such as the E! network's 1993 *Smother's Brothers Comedy Hour* marathon featuring 24 one-hour episodes of the controversial late-1960s series. Tom and Dick Smothers, the series hosts, taped wraparounds for the episodes, providing viewers with sociohistorical context for the programs.

Many viewers videotape episodes of their favorite series, compiling their own personal archives through which they can study changes in the lifestyles, culture, humor, and politics of post–World War II America. Some programs have achieved the status of "cult" favorites, and fan clubs have been formed for actors—some now deceased, others no longer involved in the television industry.

The medium of television, although often criticized as banal, is nevertheless acknowledged by most critics to be a powerful cultural institution that increasingly frames the "universe of discourse" in American society (and throughout the world). As the medium evolves, so too does the critical project that seeks to understand both its power and influence and the individual strategies employed by viewers struggling to make meaning in their personal worlds—worlds increasingly overdetermined by the televisual discourse. This book attempts to challenge the reader to reconsider his or her attitudes, not only about television but also, and perhaps most important, about American society and culture.

I owe a sincere debt of gratitude to three colleagues whose insightful critiques of sections of the manuscript have led to what I believe is a more focused and balanced work. Bernard Timberg, Radford University, conceived the idea of a reception study related to my essay on the Kodak "America" commercial. The result of that effort originally appeared in a coauthored essay in the *Journal of Film and Video* and is presented here in chapter 3 in a slightly abridged form. Timberg's enterprising work in this area encouraged me to reexamine the relationship between production and reception of the television text. Timberg also offered many useful suggestions regarding the social significance of television talk (chapter 10). George Dessart, a long-time CBS broadcast group vice president and vice president, program practices at CBS, who is now a colleague at Brooklyn College, provided great insight into the management culture at the highest levels of network broadcasting, with which he is intimately familiar, especially the daily pressures broadcast executives face as they attempt to balance public trust obligations and profit imperatives. His critique of a late draft of chapter 2, on the business of television, was both fair-minded and cogent. Loomis Irish, formerly vice president at Batton, Barton, Durstein and Osborne and also a Brooklyn College colleague, provided a discerning assessment of the current state of the advertising industry in the United States, which proved invaluable in framing my analysis of the Kodak "America" commercial. I thank all three for their wise counsel. Responsibility for the material ultimately presented herein, of course, rests with the author.

Finally, I wish to thank two first-rate editors at Praeger—Ron Chambers and Peter Coveney. The final version of this revision and update has benefitted greatly from their enthusiastic support and substantive suggestions.

Hal Himmelstein
August 1993

TELEVISION MYTH AND THE AMERICAN MIND

1

□ □ □ □ □ □

Television Myth and the American Mind

BRAVE NEW WORLD?

In Aldous Huxley's dystopian vision of industrial civilization and mass society, *Brave New World*,[1] written over five decades ago, the brilliant, solitary Bernard Marx and the vapid, highly socialized Lenina Crowne journey from the Other Place—a sterile civilization of eternal youth, endless platitudes, indiscriminate sex without love, and the narcotizing drug *soma*, all controlled by leaders who fear that the "primitive" urges and the potential social power of the masses might undermine the smoothly operating industrial system they have built. Marx and Crowne arrive at the Reservation—a dirty, dusty world of Indians, religious human sacrifice, ragged clothes, starving dogs, old age, maternal love, and monogamy. There they encounter a white woman, Linda, and her son, John, who have been living with the Indians for years, although they have never been fully integrated into the tribe because they exhibit qualities of the Other Place the Indians find reprehensible. Bernard and Lenina return to the Other Place with Linda and John, the latter becoming fondly known as "Mr. Savage," and they share in John's celebrityhood (John, young and virile, is clearly star material, while his haggard toothless mother is a pariah in the land of beautiful people). But John's disdain for the shallow, plastic world of the Other Place leads to his eventual ostracism and suicide.

The Other Place was none other than Television Land. The Other Place eased the pain of physical and psychic dying with the "television box." "Television was left on, a running tap, from morning till night." Huxley's world of the future, in which industrialists are deities (substitute Ford for Lord) and citizens are drugged and contented, is an elaborately constructed metaphor for today's electronic world—a pastiche of psychic dreamscapes offering its citizens reassurance that through the purchase of the correct commodities and the proper respect for capitalist traditions and dominant authority life can be painless. As critic Neil Postman put it, "People will come to love their oppression, to adore the technologies that undo their capacities to think."[2] In the Huxleyan world, Postman wrote, "People are controlled by inflicting pleasure."[3]

Today, in advanced capitalist America, our television screens thrust an unending stream of commodities at us and assure us our way of life is both morally defensible and materially secure. Those in the middle and lower-middle classes live out their dreams in such a world, occasionally challenging the mythology when their economic self-interest is at stake but rarely questioning the social structures that reproduce the mythology. And, while many among the underclass reject the mythology as a cynical construction of their oppressors, they nonetheless are enticed by the appealing images, often employing means outside the dominant culture's accepted behavioral conventions as they seek psychic release, however transitory, from the pain that defines their everyday lived experience.

Huxley warned us of a world in which there was "no leisure from pleasure, not a moment to sit down and think . . . safe on the solid ground of daily labor and distraction."[4] How close have we come to living out Huxley's vision? In what ways does television seek to shape Americans' consciousness? Who exercises control over television's production and distribution apparatus, and to what ends? What strategies of individual and group resistance are employed to counter the "running tap" of television?

This book seeks possible answers to these questions by attempting to map the contemporary electronic landscapes of American life through an interpretation of our dominant myths, which provide the conceptual frames for today's television images. By understanding the construction of these myths we will come to a clearer comprehension of the social formations that are constantly reproduced by and are in turn reproducing the myths, for myths come from the culture and refer both to its present constitution and to its history. And though myths seem natural and inevitable to those under their spell—"this is how life was, is, and *should be*"—a careful deconstruction of the myths will cast doubt on their inevitability and simultaneously open up the possibility of oppositional conceptions of social formation.

THE TWILIGHT OF REALITY/FICTION

Psychoanalyst Erich Fromm once described the world of the commercial as "a kind of sacred land in which [the] image of the beautiful, successful, energetic young man [and woman] is never touched." We live, said Fromm, in the "twilight of reality/fiction."[5] Images of eternal youth achieved through the consumption of miracle products and the glamorous life that is the reward for personal success won through a combination of hard work and the right connections are the stuff of the television dream world that provides the compensatory distractions necessary to make the mundane work routines and the inherently unequal social power relationships of everyday living seem more tolerable. The frames that delimit these waking dreams exist somewhere outside the realm of our control. They exist "out there," in the "twilight" of culture, manufactured for us. Fromm argued that we accept these frames despite our desire to resist: "We want to believe [the images] and we don't." There is much of value in Fromm's analysis; however, as we shall shortly see, it is far from a complete picture of the psychology of viewership and of the relationship of that psychology to the dominant culture's ideological constructs embedded in our culture's mythologies.

The refinement of psychoanalytic techniques, beginning in the late nineteenth century, has made many in the academic community increasingly aware of some important connections between the individual's dream life and the culture's myth life. According to Fromm, both the dream and the myth are highly creative acts; both employ symbolic language; and both are reactions to significant experiences in the waking world. Most dreams reflect a significant personal experience of the preceding day, while myths reflect a significant cultural experience in the "timeless past"—the culture's prehistory—that is always present in the contemporary manifestation of the myth. Recurrent dreams and recurrent myths express a leitmotif, or a significant main theme—the former in one's life and the latter in the collective life of the culture.[6]

To understand the myth life of our television culture, we must first consider the construction of the television message and the social, political, and economic nature of the processes of construction as they are reflected in the powerful visual and verbal symbols produced and perpetuated by the "diversified commercial entertainment companies" of advanced capitalism—first and foremost financial institutions, and only tangentially culture producers. We must then examine the nature of reception—the social positioning of the message receiver and his or her struggle to make meaning as he or she confronts the culture's powerful symbology.

Most of us are unaware of the highly politicized nature of the process by which our electronic information is conceived, produced, and disseminated before it directly engages our personal worlds. Yet the acts that constitute this process are a powerful, although largely unnoticed presence in the imagery given us. To understand the process, we must focus not only on content—the visible and audible manifestations of messages—and the technologies through which the messages are delivered; we must also understand the institutional apparatuses that both structure content and establish parameters for the admission or exclusion of producers. These institutional apparatuses function according to the imperatives of (1) an economics of information manifested in the complex financial practices of entertainment companies as they demarcate the social boundaries of electronic discourse according to the bottom lines of profit formulas and of (2) a politics of information manifested in battles over content, as government sanctions particular economic postures and social stances taken by dominant media organizations while public-interest advocates on the fringes of the cultural debate put up a comparatively weak challenge to those sanctions they deem inequitable. Central to this ongoing process of cultural negotiation is the continuous reproduction of visual, verbal, and gestural language that constitutes a system of deep cultural meaning that is advanced, from a position of economic and political power, by our dominant communications institutions and is intended to circumscribe the nature of the social relations within our society.

How is television's language organized? Television first of all organizes the sale of a product—its audience—to advertisers or, in the case of public television, to program underwriters. The audience is therefore implicit in the characters presented on the small screen. Television imagery is appropriated from other public arts, including the cinema, still photography, music, fashion, the speech, the novel, and drama. At the same time, television's imagery appears more real or lifelike than the imagery in other public media because of its heavy reliance on human conversation in restricted naturalistic settings and on the conditions of its reception on small screens in private spaces. Television is thus ideally suited to the needs of mercantile interests because it is able to convincingly relate products—decor—to pedestrian characters in a believable context. However, television's realism camouflages its clever appropriation of a dreamlike symbolic language to suggest to us that the path to everlasting happiness is the unending competitive expansion of our already highly charged acquisitiveness. By a continual transforming of complex inner experiences, desires, and feelings into unidimensional sensory experiences in the outer world, viewers are coaxed into believing they must, at any cost, be au courant. Lifestyle packages are quickly adopted and just as quickly discarded (being is equated with belonging through the purchase of ephemeral decor). Clothing, jewelry, fashions, cosmetics, and luxury automobiles (e.g., *Dallas*); interior-design schemes (of all the daytime soaps); and exotic vacation spots (*The Love Boat, Hart to Hart,* and *Lifestyles of the Rich and Famous*) are the talismans of glamour, status, power, and respect created by an ecology of competitive consumption. The television programs themselves become ads for the commercials, highlighting "contemporary lifestyles" and reinforcing, through the artificially accelerated flow of action, editing, and incessant program interruptions, the frenetic pace necessary to reinforce the notion of "turnover," a concept crucial to today's world of product and human-relationship impermanence.

Television, through its use of a powerful language comprising images, words, gestures, clothing, settings, music, and sounds, has become one of our society's principal repositories of ideologies/ideology. At this juncture, it is important to distinguish between the two general uses of this term—its plural and singular forms. First, the plural. As Stuart Hall writes, "Ideologies are the frameworks of thinking and calculation about the world—the 'ideas' which people use to figure out how the social world works [and] what their place is in it."[7] Hall's definition admits a "plurality of discourses" (of "frameworks of thinking") and thus implies that the making of social meaning is to a degree at least framed by people's struggles to position themselves in the spectrum of competing "ideas" about their world.

Among the ideologies to which Hall alludes exists what many theorists term "the dominant ideology." (This "dominant ideology" is often misleadingly described as "ideology," which may lead to lexical confusion.) While Hall stresses the notion of people "figuring out" *for themselves* how the social world works, theorists who emphasize the existence and operation of a dominant ideology in a society stress the persuasive power of that dominant view of society and, more important, its coercive effect (i.e., dominating by nullifying individual will). In this latter, more restricted sense of the term, ideology is thus defined as a constructed belief system that *explains economic, political, and social reality to people* and establishes collective goals of a class, group, or, in the case of a dominant ideology, the entire society. In short, the dominant ideology is an "image society gives itself in order to perpetuate itself."[8] More precisely, society *gives over* to its leaders (e.g., business executives and government officials) the power to determine this "image." Dominant ideology is normative—it succeeds (through powerful suggestion and, if need be, through force) in persuading us that the way things are now is the way they should remain. The constructed meanings of our dominant ideology operate as "givens." The "way things are" appears commonsensical. And the ways things are is a product of the actions of the dominant class; in an advanced capitalist system such as that of the United States, that dominant class is the finance-capitalist class with global ties and little national or interpersonal loyalty. The members of that class have a responsibility to gain profits for each other. They respond to people as "markets," not as people, despite their attempts to describe markets in anthropomorphic terms such as "audience."[9] Notions of efficiency, rather than morality, tend to define such a responsibility and response.

Myth transforms the temporal common sense of the dominant ideology into the sacred realm of cultural prehistory and thus of eternal truth. Myth thereby serves an important political or organizational function. As Sheldon Wolin has argued, myth is, above all, a discourse about power, about founding and maintaining a way of life, about a fundamental order of being.[10] It defuses at the outset any oppositional ideology that attempts to posit an alternative world of social relations. Myth's work results in oppositional ideologies appearing merely disruptive and counterproductive, in a functionalist sense, in an inherently stable system of social relations.

At this point, it is necessary to clarify this narrow use of the term "myth"—a term which has, over centuries of scholarship, taken many meanings. The term has been most widely applied in the disciplines of anthropology and literature. In an anthropological sense, myths are derived from a potentially infinite series of historical, or supposedly historical, events from which a society draws a few relevant incidents that provide a broad outline of its cultural heritage. Myths are generally expressed through the narrative form of storytelling. They contain recurrent themes, references to and parallels with other myths.[11] Myths are objectified in works of literature and in representational visual art; they are also actualized in ritual performances.

Myth is humankind's oldest creation, comprising a key element in the development of oral culture. When myths were made respectable as part of religion (e.g., the various myths of creation), they were acknowledged as representative of a venerable tradition. However, when they lacked this traditional authority (e.g., in dramatic presentations such as Sophocles' Oedipus trilogy), they were relegated to the category of prescientific fantasy. In the latter case, while the aesthetic merits of the work embodying the myth might be acknowledged, the power of the myth to orient us to certain economic, political, or social realms of experience was largely discounted or ignored. Many Western commentaries continue to labor under the restricted and misleading conception of myth as outside the realm of real experience. Even the *Oxford English Dictionary* falls victim to such a reading when it defines myth as "a purely fictitious narrative usually involving supernatural persons, actions, or events, and embodying some popular idea concerning natural or historical phenomena."[12] The OED preceeds to distinguish myth from legend, the latter implying a "nucleus of fact." This narrow positivist definition of myth holds that what is not true is that which cannot be empirically verified.

In traditional societies, myth played a central role in socialization. In many patriarchal societies, during secret initiation ceremonies, young boys would be told of the group's sacred myths describing the origins of the cosmos, the earth, man and woman, their tribe. According to philosopher Mircea Eliade, myth

narrates a sacred history; it relates an event that took place in primordial Time, the fabled time of the "beginnings"; . . . myth tells how, through the deeds of Supernatural Beings, a reality came into existence, be it the whole of reality, the Cosmos, or only a fragment of reality—an island, . . . a particular kind of human behavior, an institution. Myth, then, is always an account of a "creation"; ... the myth is ... a "true history," because it always deals with *realities*.[13]

For commentators such as Eliade, the distinction of facticity is moot in myth's case, for myth is always here, always alive; its very existence as communication between people within a culture demonstrates its essential "truth."

In traditional societies, myth was sacred social discourse. When one knew the sacred myth, one knew the origin of things and people and had the potential to control them. The knowledge of origins was traditionally experienced by enacting the myth in a ritual or ceremony that involved the active participation of tribal members in an extraordinary space set apart from everyday lived space and within a carefully structured time frame, often commencing as night fell. The enactment of the myth was framed by singing or chanting; intense, often trancelike movement; and the wearing of sacred masks and/or elaborate costumes. The reciter of the myth and the listeners were forbidden to fall asleep or to sit down.

The ritual in which the myth was enacted both engaged the individual's emotions and intellect and directed the individual toward the group, its past and its future. Myth thus became a "living tradition," supplying a model for human behavior and giving meaning and value to life. Myths are human phenomena, creations of the human mind and spirit; at the same time they are sociocultural phenomena: they effectively organize the way we, as a group, view portions of our world. Myths "live" in the sense that they enter what Eliade termed "sacred time"—a time that is both "primordial" and "indefinitely recoverable."

Contemporary Marxist social analysis, such as that in the early writings of French critic Roland Barthes, clearly situates myth in the realm of the *political* by demonstrating the ways in which myth works to depoliticize ideology and to intentionally camouflage social inequities existing within a culture. According to Barthes, "Myth has a double function: it points out and it notifies, it makes us understand something and it imposes it on us."[14] To Barthes, myth has an intentionality. Myth does not hide anything from us; rather, it distorts its subject and deceives us. Myth's meaning is grounded in history. It postulates "a kind of knowledge, a past, a memory, a comparative order of facts, ideas, decisions."[15] But, according to Barthes, myth "distances" this history by converting historical reality into an illusory image of the world as "nature." The natural order is produced by myth's making historical reality "pure" or "innocent" and thus unchallengeable (e.g., espousing the eternal character of empire, its sanctity, to counteract signs of its present visible internal decay). According to Barthes, myth "organizes a world which is without contradictions because it is without depth."[16] Myth is thus employed in the service of ideology—

the process of transforming history into nature for the sake of the constant renewal of the dominant class.

Myth is not "action," as is revolution; rather, according to certain Marxist perspectives, it is "gesture" that seeks to camouflage, among other things, the human inequities evident in the history of the relationship of labor to capital. Myth, wrote Barthes, is essential on the political "right," especially as it legitimizes the value of order. The ultimate goal of myths "is to immobilize the world: they must suggest and mimic a universal order which has fixated once and for all the hierarchy of possessions. . . . Myths are . . . this insidious and inflexible demand that all men recognize themselves in this image, eternal yet bearing a date, which was built of them one day as if for all time."[17]

While much "value-neutral" anthropological investigation of traditional cultures has attempted to elucidate the ways in which the individual is clearly linked to the culture through symbolic exchange, the main goal of which is to maintain the entire ecosystem rather than the individuals who constitute it, contemporary Marxist culture criticism has instead focused on basic values inherent in capitalist institutions that constitute an industrial or postindustrial culture whose "idealistic absolutes," as expressed through the culture's dominant media, obscure basic material facts of inequitable social relations in everyday lived experience.[18]

THE DILEMMA OF HUMAN AGENCY

Cultural Marxism, such as that espoused by Barthes in his early writings, has been criticized as discounting the essential factor of *human agency*. As noted earlier, in discussing the formation of ideologies, Hall stresses that people figure out for themselves how the social world works, and they struggle to position themselves in that world—to make personal meaning through a process of "negotiation" with, among other things, mass media texts. Furthermore, as Volosinov has posited, people do not do this in isolation, for ultimately meaning-making is a social activity, a concrete "conversation" about culture. Volosinov writes, "Language acquires life and historically evolves . . . in concrete verbal communication, and not in the abstract linguistic system of language forms, nor in the individual psyche of speakers."[19] Newcomb argues, from Volosinov, that hegemony theory (such as that espoused in the early Barthes) ignores cases of clear textual multivocality by enclosing language within discourses-in-dominance. One must not ignore, continues Newcomb, the "attempt on the part of dominant groups to consciously or unconsciously impose meaning, to restrict usage and interpretation, to frame the terms of communication process and content, or to manipulate access to interpretive ability. That attempt is important." However, Newcomb concludes, the attempt is not always successful (i.e., people resist).[20]

The resistance of which Newcomb writes has perhaps been most imag-
inatively described by French social theorist Michel de Certeau:

He [the reader or viewer] insinuates into another person's text the ruses of pleasure
and appropriation: he poaches on it, is transported into it.... Ruse, metaphor,
arrangement, this production is also an "invention" of the memory.... This mu-
tation makes the text habitable, like a rented apartment. It transforms another
person's property into a space borrowed for a moment by a transient. Renters
make comparable changes in an apartment they furnish with their acts and memories.... In the same way the users of social codes turn them into metaphors and
ellipses of their own quests. The ruling order serves as a support for innumerable
productive activities, while at the same time blinding its proprietors to this creativity.[21]

De Certeau's idealistic celebration of individual freedom to "poach" on
another's text—to "transform another person's property"—taken to its
logical conclusion, is ultimately an untenable proposition. For, as Hall
argues, one must guard against an undue "emphasis of difference—on
the plurality of discourses, on the perpetual slippage of meaning ... on
the continuous slippage away from any conceivable conjuncture."[22] Or,
as John Berger puts it, "The precise meaning ... depends on the quest or
need of the [viewer]. ... The one who looks is essential to the meaning
found, *and yet can be surpassed by it.*"[23] The potential of the text to transcend mere "appearance"—to "reveal"—while dependent on the individual perceiver, is ultimately delimited by his or her social positioning.
According to Richard Dyer, "One cannot conclude from a person's class,
race, gender, sexual orientation and so on, how she or he will read a given
text (though these factors do indicate what cultural code she or he *has
access to)*" [emphasis added].[24] The question of "access" is extremely important, for while it admits potential difference in subject positioning in
mass media discourse, it also acknowledges that subjects are ultimately
circumscribed by group affiliation (which, in "class" society, is characterized by inequality of access to the means of decoding).
   Immanuel Wallerstein has, in my view, best sorted out this conundrum
of human agency and meaning-making:

The issue of agency is not a simple one. It plagues the social sciences. As those
who denigrate generalizations in the name of idiographic uniqueness never tire of
saying, any structural analysis implies that an individual, a group is caught in some
web not of their making and out of their control. And so it does, except that this
web is in turn formed by the sum of wills that are in turn formed by the structural
conditions (constraints)—a perfect circle.[25]

So we face a challenge. "Caught in a web" that is a "sum of wills ...
formed by structural ... constraints," we struggle to break free. Or, to use

Morley's paraphrase of Sartre, "It is a question of what we make of what history has made of us."[26] We shall examine this struggle in a case study of *reception* in chapter 3, on advertising, and in the domain of the struggle for control over the *production* of symbols, in our discussion of "oppositional television" in chapter 11.

THE MYTHIC FRAME

What exactly are we struggling against?

In spite of their important differences, we do find a common thread that links the traditional sacred myths, with their function of keeping alive and carrying to the future certain cultural traditions, and the secular myths that Barthes described as insidious vehicles employed to consolidate the power of the dominant capitalist class, namely, their conservative social function as powerful cultural binding agents. They speak to us, openly or not, of tradition—of the proper order of institutions and people and, in the case of bourgeois myths, of hegemonic domination—of control of entire ways of thinking and being according to a capitalist imperative presented as commonsensical.

When we examine television texts and viewer social positioning in the chapters that follow, we will use myth analysis as the central critical strategy, in an attempt to locate both the constructed meanings television produces for us and our individual struggles, as viewers, to make these texts "our own" through a process of "negotiating meaning" through appropriation of the texts offered up. Central to this analysis will be an attempt to explicate the interpenetration of several contemporary myths through their "reciprocal intelligibility."

We can begin this explicative project by isolating six well-ordered and potent ideological constructs that pervade television programs.

1. *The sanctity of the "ordinary" American family.* This is offered up either ideally, in the strong family bonds evident in the rural-middle-landscape melodrama and the 1950s and 1960s suburban-middle-landscape comedy, or cynically, by contrast, in the 1960s rural-middle-landscape comedy where the oddball family, while loving, is outside the mainstream and therefore not to be taken seriously or in the suburban-middle-landscape families of the daytime soap opera who, while generally upscale, are alienated and miserable, their American Dream turning into a nightmare. The traditional urban comedy found it necessary to substitute the work-family for the biological family as a socializing agent in a world where the urban dweller seemed cut off from the security of marriage and family. Even the contemporary single-parent divorced families of today's urban comedies portray the parent constantly searching for a new partner (whether in marriage or outside) and the stable life of the ordinary family.

2. *The triumph of personal initiative over the bureaucratic control and inefficiency of the state.* This is offered up in police melodrama in which the police hero,

often out of uniform (undercover) and beyond the police bureaucracy, may himself violate the law or police practice and also may violate the rights of the suspect, in order to produce quick results. It is also evident in the private-investigator melodrama, in which the svelte private detective shows up the bumbling, incompetent police. Not only in the tense world of the urban frontier does the individual transcend the legal arm of the state. In the distant, allegorical world of the western frontier, bourgeois cattle barons such as the Cartwrights of *Bonanza* and bounty hunters such as the romantic Paladin, the heroic knight of *Have Gun, Will Travel*, take the law into their own hands when the law is found wanting. In these cases, however, the legal apparatus itself is not being challenged; rather, the property interests of the wealthy and the police interests of the state are being more efficiently protected by the bold actions of the individual protagonist.

3. *One's gain at another's expense.* This is constantly and blatantly reinforced in game shows, and insidiously in electronic religion. In the latter instance, it is manifested in the electronic preacher's dicta that people must depend for truth on God's revelation and that God has revealed that viewers shall give part of their food and rent money to His "servants" here on earth, the televangelists.

4. *The elevated status of quiet authority in the status hierarchy of power and social control.* This is clearly seen in the contrasting forms of the television news interview as it is conducted with management and government officials in quiet television studios and management offices (most of which seem to be corporate reading rooms, judging from the shelves of hardbound books in the background) in an atmosphere of deference punctured now and then by the dramaturgically necessary "tough" question; and as it is conducted with blue-collar workers during strike actions and work disruptions and with ghetto residents and dissident students during public protests in a person-on-the-street format amid noise and confusion, featuring the halting language of heated extemporaneous speech.

5. *The celebration of celebrity.* This is most visibly manifested in television talk shows, sport interviews, and celebrity roasts. A perfect embodiment of Huxley's dual notions of respect for dominant authority and of "distraction," such celebration functions in the larger arena of social discourse to deflect attention from the economic, political, and cultural control of America's corporate-owner power elite.

6. *The mystification of history and the deflection of questions of social structure into the "personal."* This is evident in television news, documentary, and docudrama; and although not so apparent, it also frames much television social comedy. Corporate greed is most often portrayed not as reflective of the value system of a flawed social structure, but rather as a *character flaw*—the "bad egg" in an otherwise smoothly functioning, legitimate sociocultural milieu. Prejudice is portrayed as individual ignorance circumscribed by familial upbringing, existing outside the domain of "official" prejudice that pervades the broader culture. Conversely, resistance to oppressive social structures is most often presented as an act of the enlightened individual will rather than as the embodiment of organized group social action.

These ideological constructs, which seamlessly traverse a variety of genres or program types, organize what appears at first glance to be the random, cacophonous psychic landscape of American television and are offered up through a powerful, controlling mythology. By looking at the interrelationships of these constructs, we will be able to reconstruct a more comprehensive system of ideological meaning. Our goal is to demythologize the dominant ideology. This will reveal the constructed nature of the representations of reality given to us by television, as well as highlight their suppressed ideological functions. In the process, an outcome of this demythologization will be the opening up of alternative realities—representations rejected outright or coopted by the dominant television apparatus.

NOTES

1. Aldous Huxley, *Brave New World* (New York: Harper and Row, 1939).
2. Neil Postman, *Amusing Ourselves to Death* (New York: Penguin Books, 1985), p. vii.
3. Ibid., p. viii.
4. Huxley, *Brave New World*, p. 134.
5. Erich Fromm, comments from an interview included in *CBS Reports: You and the Commercial*, CBS Television Network, April 26, 1973.
6. Erich Fromm, *The Forgotten Language: An Introduction to the Understanding of Dreams, Fairy Tales and Myths* (New York: Rinehart and Co., 1951), pp. 156, 192ff.
7. Stuart Hall, "Signification, Representation, Ideology: Althusser and the Post-Structuralist Debates," *Critical Studies in Mass Communication* 2:2 (1985): 99.
8. Bill Nichols, *Ideology and the Image* (Bloomington: Indiana University Press, 1981), p. 1ff.
9. Richard J. Barnet and Ronald E. Muller, *Global Reach* (New York: Simon and Schuster, 1974). A fascinating, detailed account of the role of the transnational corporation in contemporary world society.
10. Sheldon Wolin, "The Modern Political System: Myth without Ritual." International Conference on the Presence of Myth in Contemporary Life, New York City, October 12, 1983.
11. Claude Levi-Strauss, *The Raw and the Cooked*, trans. by John and Doreen Weightman (New York: Harper and Row, 1969), pp. 16-17.
12. *Oxford English Dictionary*, 1933 ed.
13. Micrea Eliade, *Myth and Reality* (New York: Harper and Row, 1963), pp. 5-6.
14. Roland Barthes, "Myth Today," in *Mythologies* (New York: Hill and Wang, 1972), p. 117.
15. Ibid.
16. Ibid., p. 143.
17. Ibid., p. 155.
18. Nichols, *Ideology*, pp. 34-35.

19. V. N. Volosinov, *Marxism and the Philosophy of Language* (London: Seminar Press, 1973), p. 95. Although Volosinov is often given full credit for this work, it is probably jointly authored with Mikhail Bakhtin. For a discussion of this, see Katerina Clark and Michael Holquist, *Mikhail Bakhtin* (Cambridge, MA: Harvard University Press, 1984).

20. Horace Newcomb, "On The Dialogic Aspects of Mass Communication," *Critical Studies in Mass Communication* 1 (March 1984): 38.

21. Michel de Certeau, *The Practice of Everyday Life,* trans. by Steven Rendall (Berkeley: University of California Press, 1984), pp. xxi–xxii.

22. Hall, "Signification," pp. 92–93.

23. John Berger, *Another Way of Telling,* with Jean Mohr (New York: Pantheon, 1982), p. 118.

24. Richard Dyer, "Victim: Hermeneutic Project," *FilmForm* 1:2 (Autumn 1977), quoted in David Morley, *Family Television: Cultural Power and Domestic Leisure* (London: Comedia Publishing Group, 1986), p. 43.

25. Immanuel Wallerstein, "Walter Rodney: The Historian as Spokesman for Historical Forces," *American Ethnologist* 13:2 (May 1986): 332.

26. Morley, *Family Television,* p. 43.

2

□ □ □ □ □ □

The Biz: *Caution! Mythmakers at Work*

ART AS "CULTURAL HISTORY"/ART AS "MARKET"

In traditional societies, men, women, and children formed a collectivity in which their behavior was regulated to conform to rigid cultural tradition. Physical survival was the paramount goal of such societies. The collectivity was responsible for the physical well-being of its members. Spirituality was inexorably linked to the surrounding natural environment: The unknown, the mysterious, occupied much of the thinking and guided the acts of the group; over the next ridge, late at night at full moon, lies a new sensory experience, the unanticipated. The precariousness of life could not be ignored. The "art" of the time, embodied in ceremonial masks, rhythmic chants, totems, cave paintings, and other forms, reflected the anxieties of the age and offered a common symbology through which the social unit might cohere and make it to the future. Nature was to be feared, to be marvelled at, and, above all, to be respected, for in nature was the key to understanding the origins of the group itself and to understanding the necessary and proper relations among group members and between the clans that constituted the larger groups. Those charged with interpreting and transmitting the sacred stories or myths of the group to future generations through their formulaic art were more like cultural historians than artists in any contemporary sense of the term.

As societies settled onto fixed territories and took up husbandry, increasingly hierarchical social, political, geographic, and economic constraints were placed on the group by ruling elites, both secular and religious; at certain levels of the society, semiautonomous "free" relations between individuals existed. Such relations, however, were generally class-bound.

An interesting relationship developed in feudal society between the artist and the art patron, whether king, pope, or wealthy noble. In return for the enhancement of his or her prestige, the patron would employ and give nearly total creative freedom to an artist who provided the patron with the totems of power—works of art. The artist received ongoing financial support and a guaranteed audience for his or her works. The artist, however, was no longer making works for the collectivity. Rather, the works were intended for an elite community, whether the church or the secular rulers. The artist created visions of "the beautiful" that announced to the world the material wealth and/or spiritual status of the patron and put all others in their class-bound places. The artist as culture worker in this less-than-symbiotic relationship, however, was continually short-changed by relinquishing, to the patron, equity in his or her work.

As the bourgeois mercantile class emerged from feudal society, a new system of patronage developed. The artwork became a commodity—a means of economic exchange. This relationship continues today in a modified form in the artist-gallery owner-collector system. Its basic premise is the notion that spirituality—culture, refinement, or the cultivated mind—can be vested in the powerful, wealthy individual who rises above the mediocrity of the collectivity through the possession of art. The artist often becomes an ideological vehicle or tool to be bought in the quest for prestige and profits.

Today, in a corporate society fueled by the drives of advanced capitalism, art increasingly becomes a function of management. When corporations become art patrons, supplying the capital by which art is produced and distributed, prestige is measured less in terms of elitist art-circle membership and social status than in the bottom lines of financial statements. Art is plugged in institutional image-enhancing advertisements. Corporate art patronage is equated with such values as trust and sincerity and, most important, tradition. This association is embodied in the underwriting and sponsorship of the more significant works of narrative art broadcast or cablecast on mainstream television.

Beyond such visible displays of corporate culture, the contemporary art/business relationship is clearly manifested in the institutional world of television, where media entrepreneurs and creators—the latter comprised of both the fictional-entertainment creators and the news/documentary/ public affairs–entertainment creators who produce, direct, write, and star in the unending flow of programs that fuel the television apparatus— coexist in an uneasy but generally stable atmosphere of conflict and compromise.

At the highest ranks in the communications-business hierarchy are extremely powerful owners and executives whose names and faces, with notable exceptions (e.g., Ted Turner) are not easily recognized by the general public. These include the broadcast-network and local-broadcast-television and radio-station executives; the telefilm production company executives in Hollywood; the program packagers or syndicators; the management of large cable-television corporations, both the distributors of packaged program services such as Home Box Office and the multiple-system operators (MSOs) of cable-television franchises; the advertising agency executives and advertisers' marketing communications executives; and not least important, the bankers who loan the whole system the necessary capital to keep it afloat. These men and women's careers are inextricably linked to their ability to demonstrate to shareholders and investment analysts an ever-increasing corporate return on investment.

We may not recognize the other group of businesspersons, many of whom seldom wear a tie or a three-piece suit but instead wear work shirts and jeans to their offices—spaces strewn with papers, videotapes, film cans, beat-up old typewriters, and good reviews. These are the producers, writers, directors, and actors who must reconcile their art and their mercenary interests; these are members of the Hollywood "creative community." With the help and the hype of their agents, these creative men and women operate in a commercial zeitgeist in which they try to sell their talent and ideas to the highest bidder in the popular-arts marketplace.[1] They describe their profession as "the entertainment business" rather than as "the television arts" and their creative output as "product" rather than as "works of art." Their terminology reveals the core values of the world in which they have chosen to operate, a world in which the benchmarks of success are all too often monetary.

While business is common to both groups, so too is a consideration of art, at least as it joins the two major electronic-communications domains of content and profits. The inherent ambiguity in the relationship between art and commerce in the marketplace has created an ideological battleground on which questions of First Amendment rights and public responsibility are often heatedly debated.

Program creators and writer/producers, who conceive program ideas and oversee their execution, have often found themselves at odds with those who commission and distribute their work—the broadcast television networks' program development departments, who attempt to tailor series, serials, and "one-offs" (e.g., made-for-television movies) to fit the programming concept of an overall schedule.

As the programs enter production, their creators may find themselves confronting the networks' departments of standards and practices, who are charged with the daily monitoring of program ideas, story treatments, series scripts, daily rushes, and finished programs, prior to airing, for adherence to the distributors' established guidelines of public acceptability.[1] The networks, whose owned-and-operated television stations are subject to periodic license-renewal proceedings by the Federal Communications Commission, have developed these guidelines in response to government regulation delineating the broadcasters' public trust obligations. Evaluative criteria are often selectively educed from social-scientific research studies—many of which have been conducted in-house—of viewers' attitudes toward public media portrayals of violence, sexuality, and stereotyping and of possible linkages between questionable program content and human behavior.[2] Although most of the disputes between creators and networks involve questions of sensationalism, gratuitous violence and gratuitous sex, on occasion the disputes become struggles over ideology. From a critical perspective, these sites of struggle over ideology within the broadcasting community warrant detailed scrutiny.

Broadcast network decisions regarding appropriateness of content for a mass audience are frequently denounced as "censorship" by hostile program creators, who argue that the networks, while employing the rhetoric of safeguarding a "compelling public interest," are in reality protecting their profits (i.e., by not alienating advertisers, who are frequently targets of threatened consumer boycotts engineered by citizens' groups offended by certain content). The more outspoken creators take the position that the First Amendment right of the viewer to have access to the widest range of creative expression outweighs the potential offensiveness of content to certain groups. They further argue that social-scientific research results have not conclusively demonstrated any direct cause-effect relationship between certain questionable content and subsequent individual behavior.

The public rhetoric from both sides in this debate over First Amendment interpretation masks the fact that since the mid-1980s creators and distributors have been able to exercise considerable freedom in content decisions, as government deregulation of broadcasting and the emergence of new corporate cultures at the networks have marginalized the traditional functions of the networks' standards and practices departments. According to George Dessart, formerly vice president, program practices at CBS:

When the ownership of the three networks changed [in 1986], control passed, in the case of two of the three, out of the hands of professional broadcasters and into the hands of businessmen or investors with no prior experience in operating media and no demonstrated commitment to the public trust that those institutions had historically been obliged to serve. This change came about at a time when the economy in general, and the advertising-dependent businesses in particular, were in great turmoil. Deregulation and downsizing both characterized the business climate and became the rallying cries of the new media managements.[3]

In this new milieu, the television spectator is increasingly perceived as a "target" at which programming is directed. The spectator is measured by A. C. Nielsen ratings that, wrote television critic Les Brown, "have neither point of view nor soul: they are merely static data dispassionately presented."[4] Data and people merge in bottom lines as markets. Their program-selection decisions are tabulated and fed back into the production apparatus as justification for the continuation of a currently dominant program formula. Mainstream television operates according to principles of audience familiarity and reassurance. It works overtime to maintain the loyalty of its existing markets and generally equates innovation in programming with potential viewer alienation (and loss of revenue). The tales it tells are most often cautious tales.

The mythmakers are at work, constructing the endless flow of program material we see and hear. These mythmakers are bound to our culture's mythologies, reciting our myths to us, in television time and space, throughout the day and night. However, it would be naïve to conclude that these storytellers and their distributor colleagues are engaged in a conscious conspiracy to "manipulate" us for their personal profit. For, as Stuart Hall has noted, "Just as the myth-teller may be unaware of the basic elements out of which his [or her] particular version of the myth is generated, so broadcasters may not be aware of the fact that the frameworks and classifications they were drawing on reproduced the ideological inventories of their society."[5] In today's daily commerce of electronic entertainment and information, there is simply little if any time (and perhaps no desire or financial incentive) to contemplate the more profound questions regarding the impacts of television storytelling on individuals, their culture, or their society.

Here, then, we begin our quest to unravel the tightly woven core of myth that envelops us. As the reciters of the myths have achieved a special status in the society by virtue of some valued quality or skill, it seems only proper to focus first on the nature of that quality or skill.

THE MYTH OF ETERNAL PROGRESS AND THE GREAT AMERICAN DREAM

From downtown Burbank to midtown Manhattan, television is the work of extremely competitive, very clever urbane men and women whose careers are made or broken in a highly volatile atmosphere involving, in the words of social scientist George Comstock, "the assembly of ideas and capital in pursuit of public adoration."[6] It can be convincingly argued that these television people, both business executives and program creators, become what they behold. Television work is done in New York City and Los Angeles; the images, sound, and pacing of television tend to reflect the distinctive auras of both urban ecologies, which are subsequently embedded in our collective consciousness and which promise excitement, financial success, mobility, visibility, and emotional fulfillment—in short, the Great American Dream—the "good life" as described in the myth of eternal progress and characterized by the perpetual economic expansion of the society and the growth of personal material compensations. George Comstock astutely describes what he termed the "tales of two cities":

New York is a convergence of elites—fashion, finance, communications, the great corporations, and embodies . . . traditions of achievement and excellence. Los Angeles, filled with as competitive, ruthless, hard-working a citizenry as any modern city in the world, nevertheless stands for the belief that there must be more to life. . . . Los Angeles is the capital of the conversion of personal vision to commerce.[7]

Like Comstock, critic Ben Stein sees the Los Angeles creative television community as comprising "a highly articulate, well-heeled, highly motivated class on the move."[8]

Yet the myth of eternal progress has another, more human side, which is characterized by the desire for personal fulfillment that transcends material possessions. Both Stein and Comstock are quick to note, in this regard, the gulf separating the Los Angeles creative type and the New York corporate broadcast executive. According to Stein, "All of them [i.e., Hollywood producers and writers], even those with millions of dollars, believed themselves to be part of a working class distinctly at odds with the exploiting classes—who, if the subject came up, were identified as the Rockefellers and multinational corporations."[9] While Stein's assessment is overgeneralized and simplistic, it is not without some merit. Comstock, in a more lucid assessment of the creative/business relationship in television, pinpoints the differences between the two groups as they relate to perceptions of art:

The atmosphere exacerbated the dissension between network broadcasters and the Hollywood "hyphenates"—so-called because their jobs so frequently combine some portion of being a producer-director-writer—over the quality of programming. The Hollywood community, already beset by restrictions on violence, fiercely deplored the confinement of serious drama to luxury display, such as in *Holocaust.* . . .

The 1970s were new in the intensity of competition, but the values and interests of those who broadcast and those who create what is broadcast have never been in perfect congruence. The broadcasters are businessmen in the end even if they do not begin that way; anything else, given the way television is organized in America, would be gratuitous schizophrenia. The Hollywood people, however, bring to their jobs a residue of literary and journalistic intentions that have nothing to do with profits. They would like a system that provides opportunities to exercise originality, social concern—in short, a chance to parade themselves in the manner of poets or novelists. Whether rightly or wrongly, they believe that such opportunities have declined sharply over the past years. Of course, television does not encourage poor or clumsy work; the point at which these camps divide is whether what it does encourage is respectable, however skillfully executed. By the end of the 1970s, the Hollywood community, although turning out shows as steadily as ever, was bitterly saying no.[10]

Abby Mann, a highly acclaimed member of the Hollywood creative community, was outspoken in his denunciation of the business/creative relationship. Mann, who won both the Academy Award and the New York Film Critics Award for his first film script, *Judgment at Nuremberg*, developed the concept and the first three hours of script for the 1980 Lorimar/NBC ratings-dud *Skag*. He also created *Medical Story*, won a national Emmy Award in 1973 for "The Marcus Nelson Murders," from which the series *Kojak* emerged, and directed the miniseries *King*, about the life of the Reverend Martin Luther King, Jr., which, like *Skag*, was a ratings failure. Mann, obviously a person with an abundance of talent by commercial standards, was drawn to television's potential power as a medium of significant social statement, yet worried about its correlative power to promote blandness. He discussed his motivation for working in television after a highly successful film career:

I suppose I'm one of the very few writers that write both in motion pictures and in television. I get paid about five times as much for writing a motion picture script than for writing a television script. Now why do I do it? I do it because overnight something can become part of our culture. And I think . . . that television is crowded from morning to night with so much pap, I think it's a national disgrace. I think of my own experiences, and I can understand why people leave television.[11]

Mann was sharply critical of NBC's treatment of *Medical Story*. In an interview with columnist Dan Lewis, Mann said, "I wanted it to be a hard-hitting, uncompromising series about the medical profession, but it wound up watered down."[12] In another interview, Mann talked at length about his experiences with *Medical Story*:

Medical Story became a cop-out and stilted and a bore. And it's very curious to me because the series did not only differ from the intention that I had. Somehow, in this inexorable stream of our society, it became the antithesis of the reasons I wrote them for. I was first approached by Columbia to do a medical anthology and call it *Medical Story*. Usually I shy away from those things, but a personal experience that had happened to myself and my wife made me want to do a story about doctors as they really are. You know, we've never really seen them as they really are. . . . This show is supposed to tell the truth. If you have an audience turning on a show, and it's not going to be that comforting father figure or Marcus Welby or the guy in *Medical Center*, then you need to have the truth. Nor do you have a show that gives them the comfort they need or the panacea that they're looking for. And perhaps one of the worst things that I saw was a piece done on malpractice which was fudged. . . . I felt I had an unknown collaborator in the AMA.[13]

Here is an excerpt from the show to which Mann referred:

Doctor: In a way I'm kind of glad that you're here. It gives me a chance to say something about what happened.

Mother: We don't have anything against you, Doctor. That's why we're here: to say that we think you're a good doctor, a very good doctor. We don't have anything against you at all.

Girl (22): I want to be independent. I want to get a dog. I want to go it on my own. I learned braille, but things being what they are, what kind of job do you think I could get?

Mother: Good worker, doctor. She really is.

Girl: But you know what? For a blind person to get a good education, unless you have money. . . . Only thing I've got going for me is I'm blind. But it's the wrong minority. If you're a lousy WASP, you're last in line.

Doctor: O.K. I understand. You've got to do what you think is right. And you should be compensated. I don't argue that. But to say that it was malpractice when it wasn't—I've got to stand up and argue that.

Girl: You think I don't know that. You saved my life. But this lawyer, he said we should go ahead and sue anyway. He said that the hospital is going to pay your insurance; you won't get hurt none really.

Doctor: No. He's all wet. It's more than just money that's at stake here.

Girl: But it's a way for me to get ahead.

Mother: He made it all sound very . . . , he made it sound very attractive.

Mann commented on this excerpt from *Medical Story:*

Instead of a hard-hitting, searing thing, there emerged a middle-of-the-road, bland, muddled, confused piece. Now when people talk to me and they say, "Isn't it a pity that *Medical Story* has gone off?" I say I'm surprised it didn't go off before this. And I don't want it to be used as a whipping boy against other anthologies. It wasn't what it should have been. It deserved to go off.

Although Mann may have felt this particular show was "confused" or "muddled," there is in fact a clarity of ideological purpose in the segment described above, a purpose not unlike that of the television apparatus itself. The segment revealed the truth behind the Great American Dream: The doctor makes big dollars, even if a few people are unintentionally injured in the process. The victims (and their attorneys) make money, even if the doctor is not at fault. The system, with its pecuniary mechanisms, frames the transaction. There is no individual responsibility, no individual accountability. This is especially true at the nexus of institutions and people who best represent success, including physicians, lawyers, and even television producers themselves.

The *Medical Story* segment in question advances still another form of conservative political ideology. In the dialog, the blind "Girl" (who is after all a 22-year-old woman) states: "Only thing I've got going for me is I'm blind. *But it's the wrong minority. If you're a lousy WASP, you're last in line*" [emphasis added]. This not-so-subtle complaint regarding perceived reverse racial discrimination is a foreshadowing of the reactionary political discourse that gained ground throughout the 1980s.

Mann was also unhappy with the treatment of *Kojak* by Universal Television, the series producer. Universal, he argued, produced the police melodrama as a formulaic cops-and-robbers potboiler, whereas he had intended it "originally to show that cops should be watched." Elaborating on this theme, Mann said:

I wrote [the *Kojak* pilot] "The Marcus Nelson Murders" because I wanted people to understand how vulnerable we all are and that cops are human beings like everybody else. Now it's very interesting that *Kojak*, which is a show that I enjoy watching, has become exactly the reverse of what I intended. *Kojak* has become a series of programs, very entertaining, very professionally done, which I love to watch, but in which Kojak is imperturbable. He's always right, he's constantly disenfranchising blacks and minorities of their rights. . . . I just wonder . . . : If we presented the real life of cops in their many sides, would it be any less successful?[14]

The answer, unfortunately, is yes, as Mann's other television work demonstrates. The miniseries *King* and the ill-fated series *Skag* are prime examples.

About *King*, Mann noted with sadness: "It bothered me that for so many years, I couldn't get financing for a movie based on the life of King, and I had to tell him no one was willing to spend money to film his life. My great regret was that it finally materialized, but not before his death."[15] With *Skag*, Mann was given "complete freedom" by then NBC President Fred Silverman. Starring Karl Malden, *Skag* became the depressing but honest portrait of a middle-aged steelworker who, stricken by illness, can no longer take care of his family. The family begins to disintegrate as it struggles to survive. Mann was attempting to draw attention to a class of Americans who until recently were grossly underrepresented on the home screen and who, when they were allowed entry into television's dominant world of white, white-collar, middle-aged male protagonists, were generally seen either as bumbling bigots spouting malapropisms or as the unintelligent inhabitants of smoke-filled bowling alleys.

It is noteworthy that one television work Mann condemned as being compromised by network/production-company subterfuges, *Kojak*, was a big ratings success, while the television projects he held most dear and over which he had substantial creative control and could exercise and maintain artistic integrity, *King* and *Skag*, were ratings flops. Godlike physicians and macho law-and-order police live on in the mythic world of television's Great American Dream, where the dying are heroically brought back to life and wrongs are simplistically and quickly righted, while black leaders and blue-collar workers struggling in a realistic, untidy world of social injustice die quick video deaths, no matter the poignancy of the story or the skill of the storyteller.

It is ironic that this writer-director of "realistic programming" dictates his scripts to three secretaries in a hilltop retreat in the Hollywood Hills area of Los Angeles, where his meals are prepared by a personal chef and his drinks are served by a butler. One can thus live the American Dream while tangentially questioning its underlying structure. Television easily accommodates such contradictions.

David Rintels, past president of the Writers Guild of America, West, has frequently written courtroom and political dramas. His television credits include the critically acclaimed 1975 television movie *Fear on Trial*, recounting the blacklisting of John Henry Faulk; episodes of *The Senator* on *The Bold Ones* series, for one of which he won the Writers Guild 1971 award for the best dramatic television script; and cowriter credits for the 1977 miniseries *Washington: Behind Closed Doors*. Rintels coordinated the successful campaign, led by the Writers Guild and producer Norman Lear, to have the courts overturn the FCC's "family-viewing-hour" rules.

Since the early 1970s, Rintels has been a very vocal critic of television networks' timidity in their prime-time programming. In 1972 he condemned commercial-television executives for rejecting scripts dealing with such topical, sensitive subjects as venereal disease, possible amnesty for Vietnam draft evaders, the U.S. Army's storing of deadly nerve gas near large cities, antitrust issues, and drug companies' manufacture of drugs intended for the illegal drug market.[16] In a 1977 interview Rintels did not see any great improvement in prime-time entertainment television: "That's the television most of the people watch most of the time—seventy-five to eighty million people a night. And it is for many people a source of information about the real world. But the message they are getting is, I think, not an honest message."[17]

Rintels could point to numerous examples of this dishonesty from personal experience. He described one such experience, at once both poignant and laughable:

Five or six years ago, while we were still in the Vietnam War, my collaborator and I wanted to do a show about a photographer, a Robert Capra type, a war photographer, one of those fellows who so loves to be at the scene of the action that you wonder what makes him tick. We went to a production company and to a network with the idea of doing a show about a photographer who follows some young soldiers, eighteen or nineteen years old, into their first combat. To boil a very long story down, a uniquely cocky kid—the photographer keeps a close track on him, and this young man gets separated from the rest of the platoon—he's a couple hundred yards away—and they run into a little trouble, and the photographer's taking pictures of him with a long lens. When they get back to camp— nobody was wounded or killed—the photographer develops the pictures, and the pictures show that the soldier was in fact behaving very bravely. The pictures were real, but he looks terrified. So the next day when they go out into combat and they get in more trouble, this time the guy was doing his job. He turns around to see where the photographer is, whether he is taking more pictures, and he turns once too often and gets killed. I'm boiling a more complicated story down. We sent that in to the network, which liked the story and wanted to do it as a ninety-minute show, but they said that Vietnam was terribly controversial, and we couldn't set the show in Vietnam. We didn't think there was anything controversial about the show—it was just a character study. They realized that it had to be a contemporary story, so "just relocate it in Spain." We weren't aware that there was a war being fought in Spain that week. We asked them what they had in mind and they said, "Well, very simple—we just change the soldier into a matador and when the bull charges, he'll look to see where the photographer is, and he'll do it once too often and get gored." That was television's way of dealing with the Vietnam War.[18]

Perhaps it is inevitable that, in market-driven popular entertainment fiction, the concept of struggle is thus divorced from political reality and from history. Rintels's proposed work was more than what he himself termed a "character study," for the background in which the drama was to have been enacted—a background called Vietnam—could never be politically or ideologically neutral. The political context of Rintels's story idea—that of personal and national vanity, conquest, and the human consequences of their confluence—has much greater ideological resonance than the network's unmessy, distancing metaphor of the bullfight, for the Rintels's idea situates the individual's actions in a social history in which a particular set of value priorities is ascendant. Neither the soldier nor the cameraperson who documents the soldier's acts can escape history. Politically, the ideology of the successful conduct of a jingoistic war to contain "Communist expansion"—of the civilized overcoming the savage in the steamy jungles of Southeast Asia—must not be exposed and thereby subverted by the watchful, objective eye of the journalist's camera. One can see the collusion of the photographic apparatus and the war it covers as images of intense action and death are abstracted from their social contexts and used to sell newspapers and news magazines.

Today, the constructed image and the myth of eternal progress seamlessly merge as scenes from the battlefront are instantly transmitted to us via communications satellite for our edification. "Live" emphasizes the visceral at the expense of the cognitive. The myth, through video images and sounds in the natural and seemingly unmediated context, is thereby enhanced by the apparatus of contemporary electronic communication.

The struggle between producers and distributors over appropriate portrayals of highly charged "political subjects" in dramatic programs continues today. One recent example, involving ABC's hit series *thirtysomething*, involves a subject geographically much closer to home than Rintels's Vietnam. Marshall Herskovitz, co-executive producer of the series, was upset by ABC's broadcast standards and practices department's refusal to permit a character involved in a political debate to say that the government cut safety regulations "so the car companies can make more money." Herskovitz claimed that network executives told him the line was not true and was in fact irresponsible. Herskovitz sent ABC a newspaper article documenting the 15-year delay in installing air bags in automobiles. In response, ABC backed off a little, allowing criticism of Washington, but eliminated the comment about the auto manufacturers' greed. According to Herskovitz, "Broadcast standards said the line might be true, but it would upset advertisers and had to be cut."[19]

The ABC vice president of policy and standards, Alfred R. Schneider, told the *New York Times* that an entertainment program "was not the forum for such a debate." Schneider justified his decision by arguing that "Unlike book publishing, in which there is a library where you can choose various reference books, a television program may be the only book on the shelf. . . . I don't believe that all people will make the effort to . . . educate themselves to all points of view, so I err on the side of conservatism."[20]

David Rintels counters Schneider's rationale: "I understand that television is a business far more than an art, but that attitude is death to the spirit of writers."[21] Rintels adds, "There are arguments in life that have winners and losers."[22] Some arguments, however, are clearer than others. It is in those cases, drawn from real events open to various plausible interpretations, that creators and standards-and-practices editors and executives often near the breaking point in their relationship.

A case in point is the acrimony surrounding the production of *Shootdown*, a 1988 drama-based-on-fact (DBOF, or docudrama). *Shootdown* focused on the efforts of Nan Moore, a mother who goes on a crusade to learn the truth behind the Soviet shooting down of Korean Air Lines Flight 007 on August 31, 1983, in which her son John, along with 268 other passengers and crew were killed. Flight 007 was pursued by Russian fighter jets as it entered Soviet airspace over the militarily sensitive Kamchatka peninsula and was eventually shot down over Sakhalin less than two minutes before it would have reentered international airpsace on its way to Seoul, South Korea.

Nan Moore became increasingly skeptical of Reagan administration explanations of the tragedy, namely, that the crew had made innocent navigation errors and that no one on the ground knew the plane was dangerously off course. Instead, she became convinced that Moscow's version of the incident, which held that 007 was on a spy mission designed to activate Russian air-defense networks and thus reveal Russian military secrets, was the more plausible explanation.

Shootdown was based on a book written by R. W. Johnson—one of 12 books written about the incident between 1983 and 1988—which accused the U.S. government of a cover-up. A key figure in the DBOF was Robert Allardyce, a former T.W.A. flight engineer who, after studying radar tapes, flight patterns, and the type of navigational equipment aboard KAL 007, concluded that the official Reagan administration explanation was highly suspect. In the DBOF, Allardyce tells Nan Moore that he does not believe the crew members flew the plane as though they were "innocently lost." He also informs Moore about evidence that claims to show that a radar controller knew that 007 was straying into Soviet airspace and thought something should be done. This evidence was contained on a barely audible air-traffic control audiotape. (*Shootdown* did not refer to other anomalies in the case, in particular the allegedly inadvertent erasure of radar tapes by the U.S. Air Force.)[23]

The driving force behind *Shootdown* was executive producer Leonard Hill, who purchased the Johnson book and hired two *Cagney and Lacey* writers, Judy Merl and Paul Eric Myers, who wrote the script based on interviews they conducted with Nan Moore and her daughter Charlotte and on independent research. Allardyce was hired as a consultant on the project.

The primary thrust of the script was that "a Congressional inquiry should be conducted to clear up inconsistencies in the official [U.S.] version of what happened."[24] Hill's intention was to raise strong criticisms of the U.S. government's role in the incident. According to Hill, "We were not saying that 007 was a spy plane. . . . We *are* saying there is a danger of creating a secret government in this country."[25]

The DBOF that finally emerged, following an intense struggle between Hill and NBC's broadcast standards department, was significantly changed from the original conception. Some criticism of the Reagan administration remained in the script, although much criticism in the early script drafts was deleted by NBC. In addition, the network insisted that a scene in which Nan Moore appears on a radio talk program include a fictional airline captain who debates her (according to the writers, there were no other guests on that radio program). Dialogue accusing the government of using the incident to further its own political agenda was deleted. At a re-creation of a meeting of the victims' families, the network required the addition of a character who affirms his belief in the American government.[26]

Perhaps most damaging to the production was NBC's insistence that equal time be given in the script to Pulitzer Prize–winning journalist Sey-mour M. Hersh. Hersh appeared on *The Phil Donahue Show* in 1986 to discuss his book, *The Target Is Destroyed*, also about the 007 disaster. In the book, and on *Donahue*, Hersh argued that the flight could not possibly have been on a spy mission because U.S. intelligence sources told him they had no advance notice of the flight. Hersh, known for his exposés of government, carried added credibility in this instance, especially be-cause in his book he discloses that while the administration was accusing the Russians of knowing that the target was a civilian airline, in fact Air Force intelligence acknowledged the Russians had not positively identified the plane and were confused.[27]

At stake in *Shootdown* was more than the dissemination of information about an international incident shrouded in mystery and contradictory claims; at the time of its airing, hundreds of U.S. government documents about the incident were still classified. A more profound question here is that of a producer's desire to make a "film of political advocacy weighed against the network's commitment to balance and fair play."[28] The even-tual outcome suggests one incontrovertible conclusion, that while the net-works' broadcast standards departments have been severely downsized, "the network censors continue to be vigilant when it comes to overseeing the political content of television films."[29] *New York Times* television critic John J. O'Connor summed up the case well.

[The producers] clearly wanted to offer one provocative reading of the situation. With interference from the network the result is confusion. The viewer is led to expect one conclusion, but the dramatic waters are muddied by a strongly-implied endorsement of other viewpoints, some of them shown on clips from the talk show "Donahue." What chance does Mrs. Moore, clearly portrayed by an actress, have against the "reality" of Phil Donahue? The device is subtle. Some might even say insidious.[30]

Teleplay writers and producers, who draw their story ideas from the well of contemporary culture, are deeply affected by television distribu-tors' cautious posture. Gene Roddenberry, writer-producer of *Star Trek*, expressed his own frustration with television's reluctance to face honestly the world in which it operates with such potential impact:

Drama, of all the forms of communication, is the one thing that reaches out and . . . makes you . . . feel, identify, hurt. Had we been able to write a drama of that type about what was happening to a Vietnamese peasant, or an American boy over there, and forced [the audience] to become that dirt, that mud, that earth, I think the War in Vietnam probably could have been shortened.[31]

Roddenberry made the inevitable connection among the money, success, and "artistic freedom" that frame the television transaction:

Most of the improvements [in network acceptance of content] have been in sexual areas. . . . But really, on basic things like the industrial-military complex, morality of the United States, the selling of weapons to other countries all over the world— the things that writers want to talk about—you really can't get that on television, . . . at least in drama. Of course, if you get what [Norman] Lear had and you get a show [that's] number one in the ratings, you can push the network around, because you've got a threat. . . . God help you, though, if you've got a show that's just hanging on the edge.[32]

Instances when creators clearly have the upper hand in their negotiations with network management are rare enough to deserve special attention. One such case involved novelist Herman Wouk, whose *Winds of War* was turned into a blockbuster miniseries by ABC in 1983, attracting an average 50 percent share of the television audience. ABC thus enthusiastically pursued a sequel with Wouk. The reasons were clearly economic—a successful major television event brought prestige to a network and provided momentum for its other prime-time programming.

The result of ABC's negotiations with Wouk was *War and Remembrance*, a 30-hour, $104 million miniseries aired on ABC during the 1988– 89 season. It was the longest and costliest miniseries ever mounted for television. The deal was concluded three years before Capital Cities' acquisition of ABC in 1986 and must surely rank as containing the most unusual conditions in any television contract with a program creator.

Wouk insisted, and the "old ABC" agreed, that a broad range of product commercials would not be permitted to air during the program—commercials that are staples of television advertising, including bathroom products such as toilet cleansers, personal hygiene products, and toilet paper. Also banned from the miniseries were commercials for fast-food chains, retail stores, perfumes, and food companies. The presumption was that such ads would be inappropriate to the World War II drama, a major focus of which was the Holocaust. The Wouk/ABC deal also prohibited the selling of 15-second spots. These commercial restrictions left ABC seeking mostly upscale sponsors.

The contract also affected program promotions. Under the terms of the agreement, ABC was banned from broadcasting promotions for its other network programs during the miniseries. It had to run promos before and after each episode.

When Capital Cities took over ABC, it was "startled" by the terms of the deal but decided to proceed with *War and Remembrance* "as a gesture of goodwill," although the miniseries stood to lose an estimated $20 million.[33]

War and Remembrance was an archetypal television event for the Reagan 1980s, featuring macho American war heroes doing good deeds and saving the world for democracy. It was thus "politically correct" for its time and worth the investment despite the restrictive conditions imposed by Wouk.

On television in the 1990s, sex, unlike political discourse, "sells"—and to the right viewer target demographic. Few advertisers today pull commercials from programs because of their sexually oriented content; when they do, other advertisers pick the programs up. The more popular programs can easily replace skittish advertisers with their competitors. A prime example was an episode of NBC's popular comedy *Seinfeld* that dealt obliquely (and hilariously) with the subject of masturbation. Nine of the ten scheduled advertisers, acting on the report of a screening company without actually seeing the episode, dropped out of the episode. Within a few hours, NBC replaced all the advertisers with no loss of revenue. *Seinfeld*'s target audience, the most desirable "younger, sophisticated urban viewers," was attractive to the replacement advertisers. In addition, when they prescreened the episode, the advertisers "perceived [the episode] as not pandering to build audience."[34]

Paul Schulman, who heads the Paul Schulman Company, a media time buyer, said that content is almost always perceived through the prism of audience ratings and shares. He noted, "Sex and violence become love and adventure if a show has a 25 share or higher."[35]

Alan Alda, actor, writer, and director of *M*A*S*H*, put the issue a bit more philosophically: "A very big problem for us as a group, as a nation, as a culture, has been the idea that success in life equals monetary success; that aggression is always at someone's expense; that you only succeed through someone else's loss."[36] In the television microcosm of advanced capitalism, profundity is correlated with profitability. Television's "intellectuals" are its marketing executives.

Safety is the key in all this. Through observation of Hollywood story conferences—from which television scripts are converted to formulas to feed the insatiable demand for programming—critical scholar Paul Espinosa deduced a number of rules or "text-building practices" related to the ways producers perceived their audiences. One of these rules is particularly instructive: "Don't divide the audience," that is, don't debate issues in the work. Espinosa observed, "Any issue which is likely to divide, and thus diminish the audience, is viewed as a topic to be avoided."[37] As television has been so reluctant to engage important social issues in its dramatic-program fare, it should come as no surprise to anyone that it abhors the thought of addressing its own problems in any meaningful way.

The writer-producer team of Richard Levinson and William Link— whose credits include the highly successful *Columbo* detective series as well as the critically well-received television films *My Sweet Charlie, That Certain Summer*, and *The Execution of Private Slovik*—conceived, wrote, and produced an important 1977 television movie titled *The Storyteller*, which addressed the basic value system of Hollywood entertainment fiction, particularly those programs that employ violence—the so-called action shows. The central character of *The Storyteller*, television writer Ira Davidson (played by veteran actor Martin Balsam), writes a world-premiere movie in which a series of fires is set. Immediately after watching the movie, a 12-year-old Seattle boy sets fire to his school building, is trapped in the flames, and burns to death. The press pursues the story; and Davidson, who came from a poor family, who never went to college, and who began his career as a writer of radio drama, is forced to deal with the issues of televised violence, his role and responsibility as a television writer, and his personal value system as a wealthy but hard-working creative type with a $200,000 house and a $10,000 swimming pool, who has come to perceive art as a job.

On one level, this telefilm unfolds as a highly articulate video essay examining the role of televised violence in our culture. On another level, it questions the entire structure of the civil society. Levinson and Link intercut Davidson's attempts to cope with his responsibility as a television worker with a series of staged interviews in which a variety of persons— academicians, police, electronic journalists, housewives—share their personal, idiosyncratic perspectives on the impact of televised violence on society. After lengthy and tortured soul-searching, Davidson is forced to concede that his television work may indeed have deleterious effects on some people. His moral awakening is a painful, slow process. Immediately following the boy's death, when asked, by a reporter at a news conference, where he thinks his responsibilities lie, Davidson replies, "To write as well as I can [about anything] within the bounds of good taste." Later, however, he is not so certain about the social implications of his creative freedom. Could his "little ideas," his stories that seemed so harmless to him, of good guys always winning and bad guys always losing, really kill people, that is, trigger violent responses in disturbed viewers?

The recurring theme of responsibility is raised in a poignant scene later in the drama as Davidson visits the home of the dead boy's mother, Mrs. Eberhardt. Ira refuses to shoulder the blame, arguing that television is a corporate art involving writer, director, actor, studio, and network. If responsibility must be accepted, it should be shared. Davidson attempts to position the problem in a *temporary human failure* of the system, not in the system's inherent structural flaws. Questions of individual responsibility are easily deflected—no one person is to blame, but rather an anonymous collectivity of technicians, who are just doing their jobs. But Mrs. Eberhardt will not accept this rationale. She frames the problem succinctly. The show *begins* with the writer, she points out. It is *his* show.

The Storyteller, aired on NBC, was inspired by the controversy surrounding a 1974 NBC television movie, *Born Innocent*, in which a teenage girl in a detention center was gang-raped with a broom handle by other inmates. Four days after the TV rape, a nine-year-old girl was sexually assaulted with a bottle by four children. The victim's parents brought suit against NBC, charging that the assault was a direct result of the airing of *Born Innocent*.[38]

The Storyteller was a highly unusual instance of television's questioning itself in public. Ira Davidson, a fictional embodiment of the Great American Dream—the self-made man—represented the sellout. In the end, having come to grips with his own personal values, Davidson was forced to recognize the emptiness of the Dream and acted to salvage what was left of his own self-respect.

How did this film ever make it to the small screen in the first place? According to *New York Times* television critic John J. O'Connor, "They [Levinson and Link] simply hung around the network corridors long enough to wear down program executives into giving them exasperated approval."[39] In fact, NBC was the second network to be offered the project. When Levinson and Link brought the idea to another network, "They were told that perhaps the program could open on a raging fire instead of an interview about violence, or failing that, perhaps the boy could simply shoot someone and, then, there could be a terrific scene with Ira visiting him in jail."[40] Levinson and Link stood their ground and provided viewers with a rare, honestly self-reflexive examination of the routines and rationalizations that undergird the system.

The system operates in a constant tension as viewers' needs for basic information, which helps ground us in a comprehensible social reality, collide with the economic constraints of profitability. Nowhere more clearly is this manifested than in the news-gathering process. In many ways the Hollywood entertainment producer and the New York network news producer face the same battles of access to the dominant channels of distribution. Both must constantly face the inevitable compromises between communication ideals and pecuniary realities. Though the news-gathering-and-reporting process is hypothetically sacrosanct by virtue of its First Amendment free-press protection and though the television networks provide insulation for their news operations by appointing a corporate officer, at the presidential level, to oversee the news division, there can be little doubt that entertainment values constantly creep into both the determination of what is newsworthy and the actual presentation. Not so rare is the electronic journalist who lambasts his or her own corporate organization for its sacrificing the high principles of journalistic practice to the gods of profit. Fred Friendly's story is a provocative case in point.

From 1964 to 1966, Friendly (a pioneer, with Edward R. Murrow, in TV-news documentaries) was president of CBS News. He resigned on February 15, 1966, in a dispute with CBS management, when it decided to broadcast a rerun of *I Love Lucy* instead of carrying, live, former Ambassador to the Soviet Union George Kennan's testimony before the U.S. Senate Foreign Relations Committee during its hearings on the Vietnam War. The background to this incident is recounted at length in Friendly's book *Due to Circumstances beyond Our Control.*

Friendly called the Kennan testimony "an event of overriding national importance."[41] Although, according to Friendly, CBS President Frank Stanton believed CBS reporters were doing too much editorializing about the Vietnam War, he did sanction four CBS *Vietnam Perspective* broadcasts in August 1965. In a major CBS reorganization in 1966, the president of CBS News was informed he would no longer report directly to corporate President Stanton or to Board Chairman William Paley but, rather, would answer to John Schneider, president of the newly established CBS broadcast group. News judgment, traditionally made at the news-division level or at the highest corporate-management echelons, would now be made at CBS by people with entertainment or sales backgrounds. Friendly was understandably concerned with this switch in internal corporate policy. Schneider refused to carry the Kennan testimony live because, Friendly wrote, of the probable loss of about $175,000 in advertising revenues and Schneider's assessment that housewives wished to see their soap operas and game shows. NBC did carry the Kennan testimony (ironically covered by CBS's pool cameras) live at ten o'clock on the morning of February 10, 1966. CBS carried reruns of *I Love Lucy, The Real Mc-Coys,* and *Andy of Mayberry.* CBS News was offered a nighttime slot to present a summary of the hearings. Friendly insisted on a 90-minute prime-time special, but he received no reply from Schneider.

Friendly noted with bitterness, "Of course, the truth was that if we'd had a sponsor willing to pick up the bill for the Vietnam hearings or if the soap operas' sponsors had agreed to stay with us, there would have been no problem."[42] Friendly quoted from a 1958 speech by his old journalist colleague Murrow, delivered to the Radio-Television News Directors Association:

One of the basic troubles with radio and television news is that both instruments have grown up as an incomparable combination of show business, advertising, and news. . . . The top management of the networks, with a few notable exceptions, has been trained in advertising, research, sales, or show business. But, by the nature of the corporate structure, they also make the final and crucial decisions having to do with news and public affairs.

Frequently, they have neither the time nor the competence to do this.[43]

Ultimately, Friendly was to lay the blame on something larger than Jack Schneider: "The system," Friendly wrote, "had made the decision; Schneider was merely in charge of the stoplight."[44] He added, "Given their choice as responsible citizens, Paley, Stanton, Schneider and every member of the board . . . would have elected to broadcast the hearings. But a system designed to produce profits to respond to the stock market, which in turn responds to ratings, was governed more by concern for growth and earnings than for news responsibility."[45]

Business judgment has triumphed over news judgment, as it has over dramatic judgment. As Friendly noted, "The yield from the detergent, deodorant, bleach or food advertisers who possess the daytime schedule . . . is the principal reason why no serious programming can be sustained for any length of time during those hours."[46] According to *Forbes* magazine, while the commercial broadcast networks' daytime programming reaches smaller audiences than their prime-time fare and thus generates less advertising revenue, more of that revenue is clear profit because daytime programs are significantly less expensive to produce.[47] In the 1980s, for example, a network could produce a full week of hour-long episodes of a soap opera for the cost of a single prime-time drama episode.

A major breaking national or international crisis (especially one with high visual and/or emotional drama, such as an assassination of a political leader) will cause the networks to break away from their profitable daytime schedules. So too will the titillating investigations of possible government wrongdoing, such as the Iran-Contra hearings or sex scandals, as evidenced by the gavel-to-gavel coverage of the Senate Judiciary Committee's public hearings to consider Anita Hill's charges of sexual harassment against Judge Clarence Thomas. But crucial, often lengthy, and generally "unsexy" public political discourse, such as Ambassador Kennan's testimony during the Vietnam hearings, is rarely given the national attention it deserves. It is true that, unlike the late 1960s about which Friendly wrote—when the Big Three networks were the only national television news game in town—today's milieu finds new entrants such as C-Span that will surely carry such hearings. Still, viewership will most likely be limited to a relatively small group of politically active citizens. (For a detailed discussion of C-Span, see chapter 7.)

A new definition of the informed citizenry, it would seem, is emerging from the mythic world of television—a citizenry who will scramble to a neighborhood shopping mall to swoon over a macho soap opera hero whose amorous exploits they have memorized from *Soap Opera Digest* but who won't walk around the corner to participate in a debate on issues of political import. Network and local broadcasters perceive this and program accordingly. Yet they deny any culpability in the outcome.

In the Great American Dream, the notion of personal freedom transcends the notion of social responsibility, even when that freedom is really the "unfreedom" to be blithely entertained while being simultaneously ill- or misinformed. Ironically, what emerges as the Great American Dream is freedom from responsibility—either as a voter, as an assembly-line worker, as a political media manager, or even today as an electronic journalist. Our media reap great profits from violent popular entertainment, much of which has the very real potential to create lasting negative social effects. And they offer us entertainment and call it news. As a result, we may register our vote in an election but not comprehend the policy implications or ideological ramifications of that vote.

Barthes called this general state of affairs "the quantification of quality." Qualitative elements of a life give way to quantity; substance, to technique and effect. Barthes wrote, "Bourgeois dramatic art rests on a pure quantification of effects: a whole circuit of computer appearances establishes a quantitative equality between the cost of a ticket and the tears of an actor or the luxuriousness of a set: what is currently meant by the 'naturalness' of an actor, for instance, is above all a conspicuous quantity of effects."[48]

CBS News correspondent Charles Kuralt, critically acclaimed for his "On The Road" segments on the CBS evening news program and who has so successfully anchored *CBS Sunday Morning,* is certainly no Marxist, yet he would nevertheless agree with Barthes's assessment, at least as it applies to contemporary television-news gathering and reporting. Kuralt wrote:

The "quick news" idea has been preached for years by the shabby news consultants who have gone about peddling their bad advice to small television stations. They have never given a thought to the needs of the viewer, or to the reason the news is on the air in the first place—namely, that this kind of country cannot work without an informed citizenry. The ninety-second news story does not serve the people; neither do the thirty- and twenty-second stories, and that's where we're headed. Fast. With bells and graphics.

In this sort of journalism there is something insulting to the viewer. . . . We are saying to this person, "You are a simpleton with a very short attention span," or "You are too much in a hurry to care about the news anyway. . . . " The networks are in the news ratings race. . . .

The best minds in television news are thinking more about packaging and promotion and pace and image and blinking electronics than about thoughtful coverage of the news. I have worked in the field for twenty-five years and every year I thought we were getting better. Suddenly, I think we're getting worse.[49]

So far we have documented the thoughts of a few highly respected television veterans in both the Hollywood creative community and the New York national broadcast news community. We now shift our focus to the Big Three networks' staff of professional editors, whose main task from the 1950s to the late 1980s (when the networks' new owners greatly reduced their staff and responsibilities) was to examine "every entertainment program before it aired, negotiating changes to bring them into line with network standards."[50] The "negotiations" occurred on a daily basis between the networks' editors and the program producers and were arbitrated by senior network managers—vice presidents of "Program Practices" at CBS and of "Standards and Practices" at ABC and NBC. The negotiations over content were often marked by tension and frustration on both sides. As noted, both parties considered the battles over "values" extremely important. Both felt the positions they staked out best served the public interest, although the concept was defined by the parties in very different ways.

NBC's vice president of standards and practices, Jack Petry, who held his post from 1970 to 1981, told the *New York Times*, "There's no subject that the industry should avoid, as long as it is handled tastefully."[51] What is "tasteful"? To Mr. Petry, speaking in 1981, the words "hell" and "damn" were acceptable for broadcast television. Other four-letter expletives, such as those in George Carlin's "Dirty Words" monologue, were clearly not (in this instance, the U.S. Supreme Court unambiguously circumscribed the definition of acceptable speech). In other areas of "speech," such as the visual depiction of sexual activity, the demarcation of acceptability is not as clear-cut. Although it went against his personal moral standards, Petry considered showing "two people in bed in an adulterous situation who have obviously just finished or are just starting to make love" acceptable if tastefully done, that is, "two people in a double bed can embrace and we'll fade out and go to a sunset."[52]

That was 1981. Clearly, times change. As a former CBS vice president of program practices, George Dessart, has noted, "What is or is not acceptable language varies greatly from culture to culture and, within a culture, from class to class. It also changes from time to time."[53] How, then do the broadcast networks take into consideration individual and class differences in "taste," and how do they chart and respond to the more broadly based value shifts in the larger culture? Dessart argues that

Bad taste is that which is, by definition, what is unacceptable or offensive to most people. Mass media, by definition, depend for their survival on mass audiences. Failing to be sensitive to societal norms of language and portrayal will inescapably result in turning away a significant proportion of the mass audience. As audiences continue to fractionate, the networks and other distributors who aspire to capturing the largest and most diverse audience possible, must not provide a climate in which most of the time, most people are gratuitously made uncomfortable by what they see and hear, particularly in the company of other family members.

. . . The economics of primetime television require that every single hour is the subject of such intense head-to-head competition among the networks that none should consider alienating any significant portion of the audience.[54]

The industry economics argument, of which Dessart writes, is clearly an important one from the *broadcast television networks'* standpoint. Yet, Dessart also offers a social argument for monitoring broadcast language and portrayals of violence and sexuality. This argument, alluded to previously, centers on the fact that broadcasting enters the home and is frequently viewed there by parents with their children and other family members. Programming, writes Dessart, should not create individual discomfort in such viewing conditions: "Every society tolerates certain activities, speech or images, in places set aside for particular forms of amusement, while, at the same time, decreeing that those activities, speech or images, cannot be brought into the home."[55] Because viewing broadcast television is often not a private activity and because viewing does not generally occur in specially designated places outside the home selected by spectators themselves, broadcast programming, argues Dessart, must be subject to especially careful scrutiny by those charged with its distribution:

[M]ost Americans have long recognized that someone must serve as surrogate, assuring us . . . that the program selected over all others available will be that which was most likely to generally please, and will not gratuitously offend. . . . And until recently, we have mandated that government oversee this process by making sure that those who are permitted to operate the industry, understand our wishes.[56]

It is difficult to separate a discussion of "values" related to gratuitous use of language and portrayals of violence and sexuality from the "political ground" on which these values rest. Dessart admits that language varies "from class to class." At the same time, he notes broadcasters' pragmatic desire to reinforce societal norms in their programming. Whose "norms" are reinforced? Clearly not those of the "classes" whose discourse is excluded. What is "gratuitous"? One might argue that what is gratuitous is that which is not normative. If broadcast programming seeks not to offend in areas of language and portrayals of sexuality, yet tolerates gratuitous violence, have we not by definition entered the domain of political discourse? And if broadcast programming tries to minimize controversy in social and political dramas, is this not in itself "political"? Sheldon Wolin's comment, noted in chapter 1, that myth is above all "a discourse about power, about founding and maintaining a way of life, about a fundamental order of being," is apropos here, for any discussion of "class difference" can be neither politically nor ideologically neutral; such discussion must by definition assume power relationships.

Beginning in 1985, with the networks' downsizing of their standards and practices departments and the federal government's deregulation initiatives, responsibility for monitoring content in broadcast network programs has been increasingly turned over to network program executives and studio producers. According to Dessart, "Many programs went on (and continue to go on) network television without any responsible exec-

utive, from either programming or practices, ever seeing them."[57] Dessart
sees this development as problematic:

In today's climate, with the greatly reduced role those who set and enforce standards have been given, we will see the producers having more and more control
over what is seen. But not all producers understand what is happening in the
society at large, or even what the difference is between network television and
cable.[58]

Who does understand what is happening in the society at large? The more
contentious producer/writers, among them Rintels, Mann, and Herskovitz, all believed they understood, yet repeatedly found their work subjected to what they believed to be unwarranted demands for excision of
potentially controversial "political" material from their scripts. They dared
to challenge the dominant ideology. Still, they are the exceptions in the
Hollywood creative community.

Despite the philosophical differences between those who make the programs and those who distribute and promote them, the fact remains that
members of both communities engaged in the lucrative television enterprise serve quite well as examples of the Great American Dream of acquisition of material goods, power, and status. A decade ago, CBS
President Thomas Wyman reportedly earned $920,000 a year in salary,
plus a $1 million bonus he received for joining CBS.[59] Chief executives'
pay soared during the Reagan era of the 1980s. American bosses today
generally receive a base salary, a bonus tied to short-term profit targets,
and long-term incentives tied to a company's share price. In 1990, Daniel
Burke, president of Capital Cities/ABC the highest-paid network boss,
reportedly earned $1 million in salary and bonus, plus $5.6 million in long-
term compensation. While impressive, Burke's pay pales in comparison to
that of the chiefs of the major Hollywood film companies and American-
based global communications conglomerates. Walt Disney's Michael Eis-
ner reportedly received $11.2 million in salary plus bonus in 1990;
Paramount Communications' Martin Davis received $3.7 million in salary
plus bonus and $2.6 million in long-term compensation; and Time Warner
Chairman Steven Ross, the highest-paid American corporate executive,
reportedly received $3.2 million salary plus bonus and an astonishing $74.9
million in long-term compensation.[60]

Television writers are themselves no paupers. In 1993, the Writers'
Guild contract minimum for an original half-hour situation comedy story
and teleplay was $14,519; for a one-hour series episode, $21,354; and for
a 120-minute nonepisodic program, $43,206. These guaranteed minimums
do not include residuals, which can be quite substantial if a series is successful in off-network syndication. The television director—more "traffic
cop" than auteur—earned a union minimum of $11,644 for directing

a half-hour episode in 1989, with experienced directors earning nearly double that amount. These people, who may think of themselves as hard-working "regular folk," are by no means members of the proletariat. Their attitudes and values, reflected in their everyday lives and in their television work, are reflections of the dream they help to define—evidence of which can be seen as they cruise Malibu in their Rolls Royces and emerge from Fleetwood limos on the Avenue of the Americas.

Is it any wonder then that the central myth that reveals the traditions and guides the destiny of the television community is the myth of eternal progress? According to this myth, anything is possible. Opportunities for success are available for the taking. All that's needed is talent, a lot of hard work, a dash or two of chutzpah, a stiff upper lip in the face of rejection, some intuition about the entertainment tastes of the "average American," and a willingness to compromise with network program executives and standards-and-practices editors. But the myth deflects the ethical question of *personal responsibility* alluded to repeatedly above; it allows for the acknowledgment of poor judgment in an occasional instance, but immediately offers a return to "business as usual." This is a form of what Barthes termed "the inoculation," that is, "admitting the accidental evil of a class-bound institution the better to conceal its principal evil."[61] In the case of *Born Innocent*, the evil is portrayed as an "errant programming decision." In reality, *Born Innocent*, although itself critically acclaimed, signalled a trend in television to garner large profits through a depiction of titillating violence. As it is manifested in its worst form in contemporary television and other popular entertainment, the myth of eternal progress offers us "a demented carnival of topping acts [and] hustling hype"[62] under the rubric of progress.

The Great American Dream of material quantity is held out to all, but achieved by few (whose ranks, incidentally, include the television elite who reproduce the Dream). According to Larry Gelbart, the highly successful former writer and coproducer of CBS's *M*A*S*H*, the creative community cannot be held blameless, as much as it would like to be, if television falls far below its creative potential, for television's creative community, "year in and year out, for its own reasons, plays ball. They do not—and I don't know how they could—insist on diversity in programming, on quality in programming. I think we all have our narrow interests, and we find ourselves doing things we don't necessarily like for wages which we very much do like."[63] Ed. Weinberger, who wrote for *The Mary Tyler Moore Show* and created *Taxi* in 1978, was even more pointed: "By any normal, decent standards the money is absurd, but I suppose I'm the product of the worst aspects of our society. No matter how much it is, it never seems enough."[64]

In the end, the creators play ball in a game in which the rules are devised and enforced by the owners and managers of large corporations that specialize in the distribution of entertainment to mass audiences for profit. And the profitable view is the prevailing view.

BUSINESS, SCIENCE, AND ART—THE FORMULA

On July 17, 1982, *New York Times* correspondent Sally Bedell revealed that CBS programming executives had for five years been using an audience-research technique, devised by a British research group, called TAPE (television audience program evaluation).[65] The TAPE formula used a detailed list of factors to evaluate one-paragraph descriptions of ideas for television movies submitted to the network. These factors included the race, sex, and occupation of the protagonist, the setting, and the program genre. They were developed by a firm, TAPE, Ltd., over a long period through an analysis of telefilms that achieved high ratings. Three trained TAPE analysts in London translated their evaluations of television-movie ideas into success scores, with a score of 100 as a median. CBS dropped the TAPE research following reports that Hollywood telefilm producers complained to CBS executives that such a formulaic determination of content would stifle creativity. Although ABC and NBC did not buy the TAPE service, they both conduct audience surveys, using random-sampling techniques, by telephone and at shopping malls, to elicit viewer response to film ideas. All three networks test series pilots among selected audiences in theater settings such as Preview House in Burbank, California. CBS tests its programs among subjects in its New York City headquarters; its tests are conducted by in-house researchers.

While CBS executives played down the use of the TAPE formula, they did admit to Bedell that "it had been a generally reliable guide to the success of films made for television."[66] What, exactly, did the TAPE formula tell CBS about the most-and the least-desirable central characters, settings, and genres of movies made for television? Bedell gleaned the following description from a 12-page CBS memorandum distributed to management regarding the use of the service: The most desirable/successful central characters in the made-for-television film are white Anglo-Saxon Protestant males, followed by ethnic types such as American blacks, Mexicans, Jews, and Italians. Blue-collar workers and the "little guys" fighting the system are seen as desirable character types (tell that to Abby Mann). Orientals are undesirable central characters (i.e., viewers won't watch them). Another undesirable character type is the person of superior intellect who is portrayed as cunning and able to manipulate others without "getting his hands dirty." A somewhat curious representative of this character type is the "serious" composer. Desirable settings include islands where fantasies can be fulfilled and settings related to World War II, while England is among the settings seen as undesirable (although might England in World War II be seen as moderately desirable?). A highly

desirable genre is reportedly the "action-adventure" based on some thrill-
ing tale that often involves revenge as a motive for murder. Undesirable
genres include the musical and the science-fiction tale.

While it is disturbing that such a research regime is used to judge program ideas in the first place, what is more problematic is the encouragement of closure—its delimitation of the creative space in the medium. It
can be argued that such research activity produces a "chilling effect" in
the creative community. If you know which ideas have very little chance
of passing the initial network-screening procedure, which is, to a degree
at least, predetermined, you will bury those story ideas, perhaps subconsciously, before they ever find their way onto a piece of paper.

Conversely, the ideas that do make it are likely to be those rather vacuous formulaic story lines, with the requisite action or sexual innuendo,
that have registered strongly among a test audience—a sample audience
that previews a pilot episode of a network series in a screening theater
such as ASI (Audience Survey Institute) Market Research's Preview
House.

In 1977, ASI's executive vice president, Roger Seltzer, described the
consumer-research organization's conception of the testing apparatus:

In the television industry, the consumer product is a television program. And what
we're doing is providing for members of the industry some response from the
consumers, and allowing consumers to have an input, allowing [a response by]
television viewers who always complain that they have no say as to what goes on
and what goes off the air.[67]

Writer David Rintels argued that the previewing process does not admit
a cognitive response:

Preview House institutionalizes popularity at the expense of quality. Four-hundred
people a night are given tickets to come here, and they sit with dials in their
hands. The dials go from "very dull" to "very good" as if dull is the opposite of
good, and they twist the dials as the show comes on. Their visceral responses are
channeled into a computer which then gives a rating, and the higher the rating,
the more likely it is that the show will get on the air.[68]

The dial provides quantitative information, on second-by-second basis,
as to how the sample audience is reacting to the image/sound combination flashed on the screen in front of them. It provides a measure of
"flow," according to Seltzer, that allows the creative people to adjust the
show's pacing if needed. Information about characterizations is generated
from responses on questionnaires administered following the screening
and by monitoring the small-group discussions that ensue.

Danny Arnold, creator, writer, and producer of *Barney Miller*, scoffed at the purported aesthetic value of such testing, recounting a personal experience at Preview House:

We were testing a show, and on the chart that came out, the graph, the numbers showed the peaks where a laugh was present. Suddenly the needle took an enormous swing like an electrocardiogram that had reached a peak, and then after the laugh it would fall off and there would be some dialogue and then another laugh, and so forth. And he showed me this chart and he said, "You see all these peaks and valleys; . . . now if you could only take out the valleys, you'd have just one enormous peak." And I said, "But you don't seem to understand that in order to reach that peak, you must have the valley." The fundamental lesson of this is there is a straight line preceding a joke. They wanted to remove the straight lines. Now it's difficult for a writer or a creator to talk to somebody whose total orientation is numbers and peaks and valleys and lines and . . . you know, a thirty-five-year-old who's got turned-up toenails and this kind of economic area—he wants that; and here's a lady with a red hat who has three children, two of whom have left home! I can't deal with that. A creator has to write what he thinks is either funny or dramatic or whatever it happens to be, and then it's your job to convince the people at the networks that a show like that belongs on the air.[69]

Seltzer's answer to Arnold's complaint is an expected one:

Whoever buys a television program, whether you consider it to be the network or a sponsor or whoever it is, they're using that program as a vehicle [to make money]. It may be unfortunate that television isn't totally an artistic medium; you have to consider it a commercial medium that makes use of art. The art that is successful on television has to be art that is acceptable to large numbers of the viewers.[70]

Star value perhaps best defines the commercial nature of television "art," and television executives are sensitive to the popularity ratings of the performers who appear on the small screen. These ratings are reflected in the "Q score"—the quotient of people recognizing a name of a television personality who rate that personality as one of their favorites. Q-score popularity ratings have been taken since the early 1960s by Marketing Evaluations/TV Q, a Long Island, New York-based company.

Marketing Evaluations/TV Q polls about 6,000 Americans on their favorite actors, series, cartoon characters, and consumer products. The survey sample is matched with U.S. Census Bureau statistics. A questionnaire is mailed to each household that agrees to participate in the survey. The questionnaire asks the respondent whether he or she recognizes the name (in 1988, 1,450 personalities were included) and, if so, whether the performer or television series is "one of your favorites, very good, good, fair or poor." According to a TV Guide report, the networks paid $70,000 for the complete TV Q package in 1988.[71]

All network series are rated seven times each season. Supporters of TV

Q argue that a low-rated series may have a high Q score (i.e., high likeability among viewers who have seen the series), which may save the series from cancellation and buy time for audience building. The rationale for this argument is that word-of-mouth of loyal fans might eventually increase the series's ratings. According to David Poltrack, senior vice president, planning and research at CBS, "Without the TV Q ratings, *Tour of Duty* and *Wiseguy* would not have been on this season's [1988] schedule. Their Q scores helped to get them renewed despite low Nielsen ratings."[72]

Producers of critically acclaimed series that gather low Nielsen ratings and low Q scores are not unexpectedly upset with the networks' use of Q score results. Jay Tarses, creator of *The Days and Nights of Molly Dodd* (NBC) and *The "Slap" Maxwell Story* (ABC), argued, "Network television is ... disenfranchising so many people by using these bogus, insidious polls. It makes me think my work is being judged by a system of numbers that don't accurately represent the audience."[73]

Tarses may have a point, especially regarding series and performers that appeal to a white adult upscale demographic audience, for Q scores do tend to skew to certain audience segments. For example, while the average Q score for performers is 18, children six to eleven years old give an average score of 31, while people 18 and over give an average score of 15. Poor people give slightly higher Q scores than wealthier individuals. Blacks give much higher Q scores on average than nonblacks. And southerners give higher Q scores on average than northerners.[74]

According to *TV Guide*, "Network executives insist they do not use Q scores for casting. . . . But producers remain unconvinced."[75] And, while some actors may have benefitted from very high Q scores, others are concerned that a high Q score may damage an actor's chances for a role not in character with the role for which the actor scored high in the Q ratings (the problem of "typecasting"). Some actors also note the likelihood of the Q rating's confusion between an actor and the character he or she portrays.

This entire question of art versus data is eloquently expressed in a scene from *The Storyteller*. Writer Ira Davidson and production company executive Arthur Houston are screening an action show at the fictional TV Sampling Center. They are standing in a darkened screening room overlooking the theater. A standard mystery-type sound track drones in the background. Closeups of hands turning dials, as suspense builds on the screen, are intercut with scenes in the pilot episode—an extreme closeup of a hand putting a silencer on a gun barrel, taking aim at a player on a tennis court below. Of the 400 people watching this pilot, 149 are actually hooked up to the data-gathering system. Ira, noting that the network research people in the screening room are not watching the show, is informed by Arthur that they are only concerned with the data displayed on printouts that register the sample audience's "like-dislike" responses.

Ira finds this insulting. We cut to a point of view, Ira watching a typical car chase complete with the requisite loudly screeching tires. We cut to a needle on a graph rising to the "very good" level. Ira is somber. He acknowledges that "people like it."

Arthur defends both the data-gathering "marketing tool" and the action sequence that turns the audience on. Neither, he argues, is immoral. They simply represent "legitimate dramatic conflict involving an audience."

Ira, his journey toward self-realization nearly complete, is not buying Arthur's traditional Hollywood rationalization for profiteering. Instead, Ira offers the analogy that kids love candy, which is nevertheless bad for their teeth. But Arthur's retort is, for the moment, the last word: "Unless I run for King, I'm not sure I have the right to decide what's good for them."

Arthur's notion of quantitative democracy admits no personal responsibility, no clearly articulated personal values. It is an impersonal vision ultimately lacking in compassion.

To use "scientific" tools in the service of art under the umbrella of big business is to determine future ideas from the limited ideas that proved commercially acceptable in the past, rather than to explore new creative directions. To accept the profitable past as the future is no doubt a safe stance from a businessperson's viewpoint, and an unimaginative one.

The TAPE formula, Q Ratings, and the Preview House experience reflect an even deeper symptom of our contemporary cultural condition, namely, reliance on technique to bring an artificial order to an otherwise vital, disorderly world. As TAPE is a formula for evaluating television movies, so too are the movies themselves formulas—success breeds imitative success, while technique breeds more technique. The ultimate effect of technique in the service of entertainment is the legitimation of the existing relations of production in our society. Technique, a manifestation of the Great American Dream, is in the end intentionally stultifying and controlling. In the eyes of the mythmakers, the viewer is not a spectator but a consumer, the object of the transaction is not art but product, and the benefit is not enlightenment but profitability. Power is vested not in the art object but in the capitalist institution that profits from the sale of product.

The hard technical facts of our subservience to the stifling regime of profits and aesthetic dullness are camouflaged by mythical constructions of freedom as expressed in the notions of democracy and decentralization of decision making. While it may appear that we have an input into the programming decisions that determine the nature of our daily dose of television, the individual is in fact united with the collective television audience through the conscious planning of efficient corporations, including production companies, network programmers, and audience research firms. As social critic Jacques Ellul put it, the individual "is no longer a man in a group, but an element of the group."[76] We are data, incorporated into the formula. This is the enduring legacy of our electronic mythmakers.

NOTES

1. At local television stations, managers in charge of continuity acceptance perform similar functions for programs and advertisements submitted for local airing. At cable MSOs, an executive at the headquarters level or, in some instances, a regional manager will make decisions regarding the advisability of carrying potentially controversial cable-program services, such as the soft-core pornographic channels, on their system; those decisions may vary from community to community or may be instituted companywide.

The categorization of producer and distributor used in this discussion is admittedly generalized. Local stations, cable companies, and television networks produce some of their own program material as well as distribute other program services; and many large independent program producers syndicate their own programs to both domestic and overseas markets. Nevertheless, the philosophical tendencies toward one or the other basic position (large profits versus artistic integrity) can be distinguished according to one's perceived role in this process. However, in a commercially dominant system such as that existing in the United States (which is fast becoming the model throughout the industrialized world) the boundaries become increasingly blurred. In the business environment of the popular arts, in which an artist is allowed to work within certain confined creative parameters and, as the old showbiz saw goes, "is worth only as much as his last picture," if your work doesn't sell, you don't work.

2. See George Gerbner, "Science or Ritual Dance? A Revisionist View of Television Violence Effects Research," *Journal of Communication* 34 (Summer 1984): 164–173. Reviewing Willard D. Rowland, Jr.'s book *The Politics of TV Violence: Policy Uses of Communication Research* (Beverly Hills, CA: Sage, 1983), Gerbner argues that the "received history" of viewer choice that frames uses and gratifications research and the theoretical constructs of intervening variables and "selective perception" shifted the burden of effects from the broadcasters who distributed programming with violent content to the viewers themselves.

3. George Dessart, "Of Tastes and Times," *Television Quarterly* 26:2 (1992): 34.

4. Les Brown, *Televi$ion: The Business behind the Box* (New York: Harcourt Brace Jovanovich, 1971), p. 58.

5. Stuart Hall, "The Rediscovery of 'Ideology': Return of the Repressed in Media Studies," in *Culture, Society and the Media*, ed. Michael Gurevitch et al. (London: Methuen, 1982), p. 72.

6. George Comstock, *Television in America* (Beverly Hills: Sage Publications, 1980), p. 71.

7. Ibid., p. 76.

8. Ben Stein, *The View from Sunset Boulevard* (New York: Anchor Press/Doubleday, 1980), p. 113.

9. Ibid., p. 10.

10. Comstock, *Television*, p. 24.

11. A conversation with Abby Mann on the program *You Should See What You're Missing*, produced by television station WTTW, Chicago, 1977.

12. Dan Lewis, "Abby Mann Ponders Fate," *Athens (Ohio) Messenger, Fun Magazine*, July 20–26, 1980.

13. Conversation with Abby Mann on *You Should See What You're Missing*.

14. Ibid.

15. Lewis, "Mann Ponders Fate."

16. David W. Rintels, "Not for Bread Alone," *Performance* 3 (July/August 1972): 53.

17. Conversation with David Rintels on *You Should See What You're Missing*.

18. Ibid.

19. Stephen Farber, "They Watch What We Watch," *The New York Times Magazine*, May 7, 1989, p. 44.

20. Ibid., p. 62.

21. Ibid., p. 64.

22. Ibid., p. 62.

23. Richard Witkin, "Some Facts of the Flight 007 Matter," *New York Times*, November 28, 1989, p. C24.

24. Ibid.

25. Stephen Farber, "Why Sparks Flew in Retelling the Tale of Flight 007," *New York Times*, November 27, 1988, sec. 2, p. 35.

26. Ibid., p. 42.

27. Witkin, "Some Facts," p. C24.

28. Farber, "Why Sparks Flew," p. 35.

29. Ibid., p. 42.

30. John J. O'Connor, "The Mystery of the Korean Airliner," *New York Times*, November 28, 1988, p. C24.

31. Conversation with Gene Roddenberry on *TV for Better or Worse*, produced by television station WCVE, Richmond, Va., 1976.

32. Ibid.

33. Peter J. Boyer, "Unusual Deal Burdens ABC in Selling 'War' Mini-Series," *New York Times*, September 5, 1988, p. 30.

34. Bill Carter, "Advertisers Less Skittish about Explicit Programs," *New York Times*, December 7, 1992, p. D8.

35. Ibid.

36. Conversation with Alan Alda on *TV for Better or Worse*.

37. Paul Espinosa, "The Audience in the Text: Ethnographic Observations of a Hollywood Story Conference," *Media, Culture and Society* 4 (1982): 77–86.

38. NBC v. Niemi, 435 U.S. 1000 (1978). The U.S. Supreme Court refused to review a California court decision dismissing the suit brought by Niemi against NBC. However, the case and the television movie *Born Innocent* are credited with prompting the networks to establish family viewing time in 1975.

39. John J. O'Connor, "TV: Violence—'Storyteller' Asks 'What Is a Writer's Responsibility?'" *New York Times*, December 5, 1977, p. 76.

40. Ibid.

41. Fred Friendly, *Due to Circumstances beyond Our Control* (New York: Random House, 1967), p. 213.

42. Ibid., p. 239.

43. Quoted in ibid., p. 251.

44. Ibid., p. 243.

45. Ibid., p. 257.

46. Ibid., p. 263.

47. Steven Flax, "Staying Tuned to Tomorrow," *Forbes*, July 19, 1982, p. 69.

48. Roland Barthes, *Mythologies* (New York: Hill and Wang, 1972), p. 154.

49. Charles Kuralt, "The New Enemies of Journalism," *Channels*, April/May 1982, p. 61-62.

50. George Dessart, "Of Tastes and Times," p. 34.

51. Diane Wagner, "He's Kept Pace with America's Mores, Almost," *New York Times*, March 29, 1981, p. D31.

52. Ibid.

53. Dessart, "Of Tastes and Times," p. 37.

54. Ibid., p. 38.

55. Ibid., p. 35-36.

56. Ibid., p. 36.

57. Ibid., p. 35.

58. Ibid., p. 39.

59. Stratford P. Sherman, "CBS Places Its Bets on the Future," *Fortune*, August 9, 1982, p. 72.

60. "Bosses' Pay: Worthy of His Hire?" *The Economist*, February 1, 1992, p. 22.

61. Barthes, *Mythologies*, p. 150.

62. Geoffrey Wolff, "Where the Action Was," *New York Times Book Review*, July 4, 1982, p. 72.

63. Conversation with Larry Gelbart on *You Should See What You're Missing*.

64. Linda Blandford, "Anatomy of a Sitcom," *The New York Times Magazine*, April 2, 1989, p. 57.

65. Sally Bedell, "CBS Drops a Formula Involving Race for Evaluating TV Film Ideas," *New York Times*, July 17, 1982, p. 44.

66. Ibid.

67. Conversation with Roger Seltzer on *You Should See What You're Missing*.

68. Conversation with David Rintels on *You Should See What You're Missing*.

69. Conversation with Danny Arnold on *You Should See What You're Missing*.

70. Conversation with Seltzer on *You Should See What You're Missing*.

71. Dan Hurley, "Those Hush-Hush Q Ratings—Fair or Foul," *TV Guide*, December 10, 1988, p. 3.

72. Ibid.

73. Ibid., p. 6.

74. Ibid.

75. Ibid.

76. Jacques Ellul, *The Technological Society* (New York: Vantage Books, 1964), p. 335.

3

□ □ □ □ □ □

Advertising: *The Medium Is the Mirage*

The institution of advertising involves individuals working within organizational cultures whose routines are grounded in an often uneasy alliance of creative freedom and the imperatives of business. The creative end-product is a message intended to reach specified types of viewers on both a conscious and unconscious level. Conceiving an idea for an advertising campaign; defining the lifestyles of people who would be most receptive to the messages in the advertisements; actualizing a number of spots of 15, 30, and occasionally 60 seconds in duration (a type of program-length television advertisement, called an "infomercial," may run to 60 minutes); determining the best distribution channels, programs, and times of day in which to run the spots; and calculating the cost effectiveness of the campaign (in terms of dollars spent per thousand people of a certain demographic characteristic reached by the ad)—these are all salient components of the larger pecuniary mechanisms that fuel capitalist culture. The commercial that we see on our television screens is a fascinating admixture of creative energies and intuitions and highly sophisticated market research.

As art, the television commercial is an anomaly. Unlike the premiere of a Hollywood film or a gala opening of a one-person show at a SoHo art gallery in Manhattan, the premiere of a television commercial is a very quiet affair (with the exception of the unveiling of a campaign during a blockbuster sport event such as the Super Bowl); it certainly couldn't be classified as an "event." Yet that premiere may be viewed by as many as 100 million people. If you asked the relatively culturally literate person on the street, "Who directed the film *Apocalypse Now?*" the person would likely respond "Francis Ford Coppola." If you asked that same person, "Who directed AT&T's 'Tap Dancing' television commercial?" the person would look at you as if you were quite crazy. Yet Coppola and Steve Horn—one of the advertising industry's most sought-after commercial directors—both work very hard at their art, both claim to have a style they feel marks their films, and both have presented image/sound combinations that have reached tens of millions of people (in Horn's case, hundreds of millions). Both work in a business in which the "bottom line" is the key to the next job; with a disastrous bottom line, there may not be a next job.

The making of a television commercial is a complex communal affair involving the client, the advertising agency, a director of commercials, a cinematographer, performers, a film editor, and a variety of other creative individuals. The average budget for creation of a nationally broadcast spot in 1989 was $190,000. Budgets often exceed this by a substantial amount, with some major efforts, such as the Pepsi-Cola extravaganzas featuring singer Michael Jackson, costing over $600,000. The shooting ratio—the amount of film footage shot compared to the amount of footage actually used in the final version of the spot—often exceeds 200-to-1. (Director Greg Weinschenker shot at an estimated 450-to-1 ratio for the 60-second Kodak "America" commercial.) The period of gestation for a commercial—from its initial conception by a senior producer in an ad agency's creative group to its ultimate emergence as a finished print—may exceed one year. Some spots, such as the "America" commercial, may consume as much as six weeks of location shooting (equivalent to the shooting schedule of a two-hour "made-for-TV" movie). Television commercials are so big—and yet so small. As reflections of both the sociocultural and the aesthetic grounds of television, they are unmatched by any other genre and thus are deserving of very careful critical scrutiny.

ADVERTISING'S ROLE IN CONTEMPORARY CULTURE

Nothing serves the cause of advanced capitalism more effectively and with more apparent humility than does advertising. In print, on television and radio, and on billboards, sandwich boards, and T-shirts, the mythic character of the combination of words, images, and sounds and the various ideologies employed in these advertisements fuel the machines and stimulate the psyches of a highly acquisitive people. Ads cajole, boast, aesthetically massage and assault us, whisk us away through time and space on a magic-carpet ride to exotic cultures, offer us their approximations of eternal youth, and promise us "relief." Ads are not only selling us a product or service or politician, they are selling us a style of life. And they have become the engines that drive our way of life. As such, they point explicitly and unambiguously to our culture; they do not apologize for either their presence or their behavior. They are self-assured and secure.

No clearer conception of the role of advertising in contemporary American culture has been presented than that of anthropologist Jules Henry in his seminal book *Culture against Man*.[1] In this book, Henry argues that "advertising is an expression of an irrational economy that has depended for survival on a fantastically high standard of living incorporated into the American mind as a moral imperative."[2] Henry ascribes a didactic intentionality to advertisers: "As a quasi-moral institution, advertising, like any other basic cultural institution anywhere, must have a philosophy and a method of thinking. . . . I have dubbed this method of thought *pecuniary philosophy*."[3]

Henry proceeds to develop an entire lexicon to describe advertising as an institution and as an art form. We will briefly examine that language and its rationale below.

Henry claims that a new conception of truth emerges through advertising—that of "pecuniary pseudotruth"—by which a false statement is made to sound or look or read as if it were true but is not intended to be believed. It is true if it sells products or services; it is false if it does not. For example, is it literally true that "a woman in Distinction foundations is so beautiful that all other women want to kill her?"

Henry dubs one specific type of pecuniary pseudotruth "parapoetic hyperbole." Hyperbole is exaggeration. Parapoetic hyperbole is an exaggerated claim employing high-flown figures of speech that resemble, but are not, poetry. As a pecuniary pseudotruth, no reasonable person is expected to believe such a claim, but merely to purchase the product or service. Revlon's 1960s campaign for Pango Peach lipstick and nail polish provides a good example. This sensuous color, said Revlon, comes from "east of the sun, . . . west of the moon, where each tomorrow dawns." It is "succulent on your lips" and "sizzling on your fingertips . . . and on your toes, goodness knows." It promises to be a woman's "adventure in paradise."

Another advertiser truth claim, writes Henry, relies on "pecuniary logic." Here a person is asked to judge the value of a product on the basis of questionable evidence. Examples abound. One example of pecuniary logic is found in the 1991 television ad campaign of Northwest Airlines. Chosen by the Center for Science in the Public Interest as one of the most misleading ads for 1991, the commercial opens with a fast-paced montage of the process of checking in for an airline flight. The voice-over states, "There's a new idea at Northwest Airlines. A new dedication to service." Cut to a shot of a television screen as line after line of "ON TIME" scrolls up the screen and the voice-over continues, "You can see it in our on-time performance." Superimposed on the bottom of the screen are the words, in white lettering, "FOR DOMESTIC FLIGHTS BASED ON REPORTS ISSUED BY D.O.T. (JAN-APR 1990)." Quick cuts follow of a shot of a pilot walking, a male passenger walking to the-boarding area, ticket in hand, and a head-on shot of a Northwest jumbo jet, as the voice-over continues, "The best of the top seven U.S. airlines." The commercial is not patently false. Northwest Airlines did have the best on-time record, as indicated in the commercial. However, the reason the airline had the best on-time record is not revealed. The reason? Northwest schedules its flights to take longer than its competition. If you give yourself twenty minutes longer to get to your destination, that would predictably increase the chances of your getting there on time. The commercial's graphic design reinforces the voice-over claim: The prominent "ON TIME" scroll is combined with the superimposed graphic reference to the "official" D.O.T. (Department of Transportation) report results, lending the claim the aura of "scientific" credibility.

Pecuniary logic asks us to be, in Jules Henry's words, "fuzzy-minded and impulsive." Henry adds, "If we were all logicians the economy could not survive, and herein lies a terrifying paradox, for in order to exist economically as we are, we must try by might and main to remain stupid."[4]

If the "product" being examined is a political candidate, one could argue that the diminution of our logical faculties may, in the longer term, prove disastrous. The following well-known example of pecuniary logic was employed during the 1988 U.S. presidential campaign.

The Bush election campaign's infamous "revolving door" commercial ("First Degree Murderers on Furlough") attacking opponent Michael Dukakis's record on crime while he was governor of Massachusetts has been criticized by some observers as factually misrepresentational and by others, notably CNN's special assignment correspondent Ken Bode, as representing a species of negative political commercials "filled . . . with invitations to inferential inaccuracies."[5] The furlough spot was aired on national television from early September 1988 until just before the November election. In the spot, a group of prisoners are shown entering and leaving a prison through a prison turnstile (appearing to be marching into our living rooms) as the narrator's voice-over says, "[Dukakis's] revolving door prison policy gave weekend passes to first-degree murderers not eligible for parole." The words "268 escaped" then appeared on the screen. Enterprising journalists checked the statistic used in the commercial and discovered that of the 268 escapees mentioned in the graphic, only four were first-degree murderers. Further, many of the "escapees" actually returned to the prison a few hours late. Yet the spot leaves the "fuzzy-minded" viewer with the impression that the "268" who escaped were first-degree murderers, still at large.

The "revolving door" furlough ad proved even more effective when connected, in many viewers' minds, with the equally infamous "Willie Horton" spots produced by a group not formerly tied to the Bush election campaign. The Horton spots, condemned by many critics as overtly racist, featured pictures of Horton, a black convict who kidnapped and raped a woman while on furlough from a Massachusetts prison. Surveys revealed that many viewers thought the "revolving door" spot actually featured Horton, when in fact it never mentioned him.

Where is truth in the language of advertising? According to Henry, "The heart of truth in pecuniary philosophy is contained in the following three postulates: Truth is what sells. Truth is what you want people to believe. Truth is that which is not legally false."[6]

Herein lies a significant moral question raised by this convoluted conception of truth. When the gurus of Madison Avenue try to sell health or any other human services, where the issue is relief from human suffering—an inviolable value—there must be no deceit, no pseudotruth, no pecuniary logic. Likewise, when the "product" being marketed is a candidate for political office, whose judgments and actions will directly impact our individual and social well-being, there is no room for deception. Especially in these instances must the institution of advertising be held accountable to the most stringent rules of responsible behavior.

Ultimately the issue is more than whether advertisers intentionally attempt to hoodwink the public with specious imagery or spurious claims. (Advertisers have argued for years with genuine conviction that they do not engage in such practices, although evidence suggests otherwise.) The larger question is, in Henry's words, that of the "moral imperative" of acquisitiveness in American culture—a culture increasingly guided by a preoccupation with quantity rather than quality. Ask any child to show you his or her collection of broken, discarded toys and games collecting dust in the attic corner. Therein lies a compelling clue to the answer.

The moral imperative of acquisitiveness in contemporary advanced capitalist societies is manifested in such strongly held values as private property, security, competition, and achievement (often at the expense of others). This imperative is evident not only in adult life, but also in children's preparations for that adult life. Advertising provides children with pecuniary acculturation—teaching them how to grow up to be good consumers within the gender boundaries/social roles embedded in a patriarchal discourse. This concept is actualized in the interminable parade of toys that are miniature versions of adult products, such as domesticated dolls with their dollhouse kitchens containing miniature brand-name appliances and products and "swinging-singles" dolls (who are nevertheless going steady) that trigger the purchase of lifestyle accessories such as race cars, townhouses, swimming pools, and high-fashion wardrobes.

Advertising has radically affected the very structure of traditional adult-child relationships. The traditions of patriarchal and matriarchal cultures in which adults provided role models and moral direction for their children have been subverted and even reversed. According to Henry, "Advertising ... has ... forced its way into the family, an insolent usurper of parental function, degrading parents to mere intermediaries between their children and the market. This is indeed a social revolution in our time!"[7] Parents become "imps of fun," competing with one another to satisfy their children's insatiable appetites for products.

Henry's conception of the individual in contemporary society is not flattering. The responsibility for our subservience to this pecuniary system rests entirely, in Henry's view, with the institution of advertising:

Insatiably desiring, infinitely plastic, totally passive, and always a little bit sleepy; unpredictably labile and disloyal (to products); basically wooly-minded and non-obsessive about traditional truth; relaxed and undemanding with respect to the canons of traditional philosophy, indifferent to its values, and easily moved to buy whatever at the moment seems to help his underlying personal inadequacies—this is pecuniary philosophy's conception of man and woman in our culture. Since it is a very contemptuous one, it appears that Madison Avenue is not so much "the street of dreams" . . . but rather the Alley of Contempt, housing thousands who, through the manufacture of advertising, pour their scorn upon the population.[8]

While there is much of significance in Henry's conception of the role of advertising in our culture, there exists in his reasoning a questionable presupposition. Henry assumes, I think a bit simplistically, that the advertiser stands somehow outside the culture in which he or she is operating and is thus able to manipulate the rest of us—a hypodermic model of direct cause and effect that implicitly ascribes both an intellectual superiority and an evil intentionality to the efforts of the advertiser. A more reasonable approach to the question would view the advertiser, like the television executive and the television program producer, as successfully immersed in the culture and guided, often unconsciously, by its dominant myths and ideology that those myths service. The advertiser may be the dungeon master, but, like the rest of us, he is also one of its hapless inhabitants, himself driven by the rules of the dungeon.

Contemporary American culture seems to be guided in large measure by three interrelated concepts—fear, greed, and "the miracle"—that advertising, as part of that culture, draws upon and actively promotes for its own purposes. Erich Fromm, discussing the role of advertising in our culture, highlighted the significance of these concepts. Fromm noted that fear was most apparent in the deodorant ads, which focus our collective attention on the stigma of body odor. (It is important to remember that we have always had body odor, and in many cultures that odor is a sexual stimulant. Personal-hygiene product manufacturers launched a massive advertising campaign to transmute that naturally formed odor into an artificial, synthetically produced odor and to sell a product in the process. A side effect of this transmutation is the emission of fluorcarbons into our atmosphere.) Fromm added that fear operates "in a more subtle way through the general fear of not being loved."⁹ This general fear operates primarily on an unconscious level.

Employing paleosymbolic images stressing the fear of rejection, ads show us products that will make us loved (e.g., Ultra-Brite toothpaste and Certs breath deodorant). The solution to our potential rejection comes in the form of "the miracle." We are saved not by human power or human effort, but rather by the external power of the miraculous product. In Fromm's words, "Love is dependent on a gadget." The ultimate symbolic relationship between fear and the miracle is the fountain of youth—a major guiding concept in contemporary television advertising, according to Fromm.

The miracle is both qualitative and quantitative. We come to believe that the "good life"—the secure life without fear—will be ours if we consume a variety of goods and services that cumulatively will resolve all our human weaknesses (most of which are related more to our appearance than to our essence). The irrational links between monetary accumulation and the purchase of release, in the guise of miracle products, from culture-bound anxiety are thereby solidified.

Are ads responsible for this general condition, or do they merely reflect this condition? Erich Fromm provided a well-reasoned response:

It would be foolish to accuse the advertising people of poisoning the minds of the American public. They do what they *have* to do under the given rules and mechanisms of our mode of production and consumption. With our mode of consumption and production, especially [in the case of] big corporations, the taste of the public must be manipulated, must be made foreseeable. Otherwise the big, mammoth enterprise couldn't exist. And advertising is one of the means to do this.¹⁰

It becomes more apparent, as the analysis continues, that we must ultimately look to the ideological bases for the use of the system of advertising in promoting a particular way of life. Both Henry and Fromm have alluded to this. Henry's concept of the "moral imperative" of a "fantastically high standard of living," sought through the accumulation of products, and Fromm's concept of advertising's questionable coopting of basic human concerns and needs both point to the advanced state of acquisitiveness in which we exist. An advanced industrial economy with a large middle and lower-middle class finds it in its best interests to channel the free time of its workers into areas of intellectually unproductive leisure, characterized by unbridled consumption of products linked to play, which does not threaten, but rather reinforces the given structure. The advertiser helps the entire system achieve closure by always looking forward toward the Great American Dream—the rosy future of the land of plenty and the promise of "the good life," embodied in the product-purchase-to-come.

TV ADS: A BRIEF HISTORY OF THE ART

We've briefly examined some of the broader philosophical questions raised by the presence of the institution of advertising in contemporary society. We now consider the status of the television commercial as "art."

Television spots have been an integral part of the commercial medium from its public inception in the United States in the 1940s. There is little doubt that many of our earliest television memories are of ads (especially those with jingles). Those who are old enough recall the classic 1950 Old Gold cigarettes "Dancing-Packs" spot featuring a long-legged beauty and a little girl, dressed in cigarette packs, tap-dancing their way into living rooms across America to the tune of "Bicycle Built for Two" and the 1951 Muriel cigar campaign with that sexy voice-over cooing (in a reference to Mae West) "Why don't you pick me up and smoke me sometime?" The global "Marlboro Man" phenomenon began in 1955 with spots featuring a rugged western cowpuncher riding his noble steed across the majestic panorama of the American West to the beat of staccato bass rhythms. The year 1956 brought the Pepsodent toothpaste campaign featuring the bouncy selling theme "You'll wonder where the yellow went, when you brush your teeth with Pepsodent." The history of television spots is also a history of the technological advancement of the medium.

In its early years, dating from the late 1940s, television advertising was clearly derivative of radio's stylistic conventions, the most important of which was a stand-up announcer extolling a product's virtues. On television, of course, we could see the product as well as listen to the description of the miracles it could perform. To build credibility, the advertisers used recognizable stars to hawk their items—Dennis James for Old Gold Cigarettes, Bing Crosby for Philco refrigerators, and Red Skelton for J-wax. The ads were static, straightforward sales pitches. Most were done live, as were the television programs into which they were inserted.

Television soon became more tightly structured and more controlled as well as controlling. As the medium began using filmed programs much more extensively in the mid-1950s, so too did it encourage filmed advertisements. Some ad agencies set up film studios in their own offices, but production activity became chaotic. The agencies turned to industrial filmmakers to produce their commercials. These production companies were entire units like the Hollywood "major" producers, but on a much smaller scale. Many ads were shot on location, and ads began to incorporate forms from theatrical-film genres such as dramas and musicals. The television ads were abbreviated versions, lasting no more than two minutes. They were generally balanced, resembling a traditional melodramatic structure—a problem was quickly set up and solved in approximately equal amounts of time. Music signaled cuts and moved the action along. The talent in filmed ads appeared in naturalistic settings or dressed in surreal costumes such as giant models of the products being advertised. In many cases, memorable animated characters (Speedy Alka-Seltzer, the Ajax dwarfs, Colgate's Mr. Tooth Decay) were used.

The ads became more aesthetically complex with more concise structures and richer visual and aural textures. The agencies began drawing upon the talents of successful commercial still photographers who were intrigued with the potential of camera motion. Experimentation in new visual techniques began around 1964. We began to see wide-angle close-ups, with resultant distorted faces that echoed sensations of discomfort. Directors began shooting into the sun, producing a bleached-out, overlit effect. Layers of gauze were placed in front of the camera lens to create a sense of the past—of remembering Grandma (the "universal mother") and a saner, more peaceful time. The late 1960s spots were visual fantasies that walked a very thin line between the serious and the absurd. They were undoubtedly influenced by contemporary art movements such as the Theater-of-the-Absurd writings of dramatists Eugene Ionesco and Samuel Beckett, by surrealism in painting, and by existential literature. And they were conceived during an historical moment, the Vietnam War, during which absurdism seemed particularly resonant. According to art critic Bruce Kurtz, "It is not a large leap of the imagination from Beckett's absurdity to a dancing hamburger or a man dressed as a giant Clorox bottle."[11]

While this ad art was receiving rave reviews from critics, the agencies and clients were slow to question mounting evidence that while viewers may have loved the ads, they didn't necessarily flock to the stores to buy the products. Marshall McLuhan noted in the mid-1960s that "advertising is substituting for product, because the consumer today gets his satisfaction from the ad, not the product. This is only the beginning—more and more the satisfaction of all life will come from the ad and not the product."[12] While McLuhan may have made a conceptual leap of faith in concluding that we would all *become* the ad, his initial observation was borne out.

By 1970 recessions had become an unfortunate economic and social fact of life. Clients tightened their belts. Agencies began testing ads before they were produced. Many of the new campaigns consisted of brand-name product-oriented ads with a single selling theme extolling a single major product benefit; research had demonstrated that viewers could not remember ads that say two or more things. The soft-sell art commercial of the late 1960s gradually gave way to the return of the hard-sell ad.

The late 1970s saw the reduction of the standard length of the ad from 60 seconds to 30 seconds. Accompanying this was a change in the ad's time signature and its formal structure. The "vignette commercial" emerged during this period. Instead of a generally coherent traditional narrative that takes longer to present, the vignette commercial was a "free-style" sequence of associated scenes and situations. There was often no dialogue, but rather a musical theme line that moved with the scenes. The vignette commercial tightly packed visual and aural information in a structure that heightened emotions through rapid visual cutting. Shots averaged three seconds in length (some vignette ads, such as those for McDonald's "You, You're the One" campaign, averaged one cut per second). Even when the traditional narrative structure of progressive action was used, in the 30-second spot there was absolutely no time for frills. Jonathan Price noted that "by using a kind of ellipsis . . . commercials have trained us to grasp what gets left our when we see someone open his front door, then—in a quick cut—get into his car; . . . you had to snap, shock and jolt."[13]

The vignette commercials constituted a relatively small share of the total number of spots produced for national broadcast. Other, less-expensive commercial forms dominated the field. These included the "basic-monologue" form—using an on-camera narrator or voice-over narration behind images—and the "consumer-interview or testimonial" form.

Meanwhile, aesthetic explorations in the high-budget "song and dance" commercials continued throughout the 1980s. An even greater condensation of narrative was developed in the 15-second spot; often two 15-second spots for products manufactured by the same company were piggybacked in a form known as the "split-30". There was a visual consensus (some would call it a redundancy) in fashion ads employing the black-and-white, shaky-cam, grainy image look. The "artsy" soft visual images of the 1960s reemerged in the mid-1980s in nostalgia spots extolling American values and traditions (and patriotism, which coincided with the 1984 Reagan reelection campaign, which used similar images and themes in its political campaign commercials).

One aesthetic form of image condensation emerging in the 1990s is represented in the "Energizer" battery spots, in which a parody of a standard commercial is punctured by an animated rabbit moving through the final image of the parodied commercial, playing a bass drum. The tag line, "They keep going . . . and going," refers both to battery life and the rabbit's continual reappearance in subsequent "pseudospots" in the campaign. This entrance into mainstream commercial culture of postmodernist sensibility, with its playful referentiality to standard commercial campaigns of the past, marks a new and interesting aesthetic direction of the form.

Other commercial forms evolving in the early 1990s include highly composed live-action "realism" resembling Hollywood feature films, live-action integrated with imaginative graphics, and comic-book-influenced animation. Offbeat humor seems to be a major connecting thread in many of these spots.

Just what kind of art is the television commercial? One television critic, Jonathan Price, observed, "If commercials are artful, then the art is objective, not subjective; capitalist, not rebellious; part of a social activity rather than a personal search for expression; more like a Roman road than a lyric poem. Their beauty is economic."[14]

Price is correct in evaluating commercials as a mainstream art and "not rebellious." In their most basic sense the ads must be safe. They are artistic vehicles whose purpose is to move both people and merchandise. They must be popular. Therein lies one, but certainly not the only, measure of their artistic significance. According to art critic Bruce Kurtz, "Popularity is a condition of quality for popular art. . . . And today there is no art form more popular than television spots."[15] An important element of these works of popular art is their conscious connection of formal conventions with certain motifs—themes or concepts drawn from our collective cultural experience (in the form of images, stories, allegories). A good example of such a connection is the concept of the youthful, healthy, active American, reflected in the overlift visualization of the blond, aggressive, tanned California surfer (boy/girl) bathed in blue sea water and golden sunshine. This motif has been employed in many television spots (from McDonald's "Hang Ten" to ads for Coca-Cola, orange juice, milk, and many other products). We want to believe these connections. Recall that Erich Fromm noted our preoccupation with seeking the "fountain of youth."

Price, however, is incorrect when he asserts that commercials do not represent a "personal search for expression," for beyond the standard motifs lies the domain of the commercial artists' personal touches—the techniques used to create a style that marks a commercial director's works. This personal style enables many commercials (especially the high-budget ad intended for national distribution) to transcend the domain of hackneyed, formulaic selling tools and become legitimate contemporary works of art.

Personal style, or aesthetic individuality, is taken very seriously by the advertising community. The Clio Awards, advertising's answer to the Academy Awards and the Emmys, are considered highly prestigious within the industry, especially among commercial directors who can proudly point to the Clio winners on their reels, and also among the agency creative groups. This is a mark of their personal achievements in their specialized work of art making. A Clio in a way separates the artist from the competitive business environment in which he or she works.

Every highly successful director of commercials is recognized by the agency creative people for using specific techniques that mark his or her personal style. The ads shot by these individualistic directors have a certain "look" or "feel" about them. The work of some of the most influential commercial directors of the past two decades has been examined at length in books by Michael J. Arlen (*Thirty Seconds*, 1980), Bruce Kurtz (*Spots: The Popular Art of Television Commercials*, 1977), and Jonathan Price (*The Best Thing on TV: Commercials*, 1978). What emerges from these examinations is a strong sense that the commercial director considers himself first an artist and then a member of the mercantile community. However, as they try to reconcile their dual roles as creative people in the service of a business institution, an undercurrent of uneasiness emerges in the commercial directors' deeper feelings regarding their cultural influence, social responsibility, and self-image.

Elbert Budin is a master of the cinematography of food. His reel includes Sunkist, Nabisco, and Breyer's Ice Cream. Budin uses precise lighting that he drags across his subjects, emphasizing their tactile or textural quality. He uses a "scanning" camera choreography that gently plays over the food. An 18mm, wide-angle lens brings the eyes closer to the food than they would be in real life and makes the food seem larger than life. Budin also occasionally manipulates the film speed, using slow motion to produce heightened emotion or tension (e.g., the explosion of bubbles from the opening of a bottle of beer or the seismic splash of a saltine breaking the surface of a bowl of soup). Budin emphasizes the lyricism of his work, comparing it with Stanley Kubrick's film *Barry Lyndon*, in which beautifully articulated visuals dominate the story line. Budin also consciously works with the associations of eating and eroticism. On that subject he told Bruce Kurtz, "The sexual part of eating, the erotic part of it has to be put on to film. You have to enhance it. You have to bring it further than reality, . . . going past the reality of food, getting sexual, getting suggestive; . . . it's stylized."[16]

Budin's description of the sexuality of the commodity fits well in an advanced capitalist system in which the sensual, with its connotations of joy, appreciation, love, and being, is reified. Food, like other material goods, becomes a possession, perhaps an obsession. Budin sees the potential power of his transcendence of reality through art:

It's a tremendous propaganda force . . . and I guess I have to think about the moral issue of my . . . influencing so many people. . . . I've given myself certain taboos that I will not use my power for. When cigarettes were still advertised on television I refused to do cigarette commercials and I was really ostracized from a few agencies.[17]

Mike Cuesta is known for his warm human characterizations and his work in narrative structure. Many of his images take on the appearance of an informal documentary even though they are all carefully blocked and shot. His reel includes "The Hill" for Alka Seltzer, "Desk Sergeant" for Sanka coffee, and "Grandfather" for AT&T. Like Budin, Cuesta recognizes the power of the well-conceived and well-executed ad. As a pragmatist, Cuesta has built a self-defense mechanism into his concept of social responsibility. The commercial, Cuesta told Bruce Kurtz, "does exploit. It can push things down people's throats that they don't want. . . . We live and work within a system; we have to do things that rot out your gut. That's why you become an executer. You get involved on one level and you don't get involved on the higher [ethical] levels of it."[18]

Dan Nichols, a main driving force behind McDonald's "You, You're the One," campaign, specializes in creating an accelerated sense of time through rapid cutting, sweeping camera movements culminating in freeze frames, and by interrupting action with a series of cuts of related actions, with an eventual return to the original action. In his work, Nichols emphasizes upbeat, youthful lifestyles and the joys of family life. He sees ads as a potentially uplifting force in our culture. He told Kurtz:

There's so much pessimism; . . . all you have to do is flip on the news. . . . There's nothing that's going to lift you up before you go to sleep and make tomorrow seem like, "Hey! It's worthwhile getting up." That's the kind of thing I'd like to try to put in my own work—without forsaking the product. . . . When people are out [McDonald's] is like a treat, . . . a respite, . . . an oasis of sorts, and people are high just being together; . . . and the food almost becomes secondary to that.[19]

Nichols seems to live in his ads, and he may even bear out McLuhan's proposition, mentioned earlier, that "the satisfaction of all life will come from the ad."

Steve Horn, the director of "Tap Dancing" for AT&T, Miller Lite beer spots, and spots for Coca-Cola, is a master of the vignette commercial. His personal style favors interiors and the telephoto, or narrow-angle lens, which he believes is "less commercial and more real. Not really real, but more real than commercial."[20] Horn hints at the degrees of realism in the dream world of the ad. "Reality," it seems, has become both an elusive and illusive concept in his attempt at a definition.

TV ADS AS MYTHS

Nowhere is the "living tradition" of secular capitalist mythology more evident than in the advertisement. On television, sacred time is selling time (most visibly and powerfully during the sacred commercial break). The programs become ads for the commercials, depicting lifestyles for which the commercial has a product or service to plug in. Programs are prefatory statements that herald the commercials; they surround, but cannot intrude on the sacred time of the commercial break. In television culture, demands on the spectator are not nearly so great as those made on the participant in traditional rituals. Nevertheless, many interesting parallels can be drawn with traditional myth recitation. The commercial jingles and background musical scores of television may substitute for traditional chanting. Jingles and chants are both mnemonic and diachronic devices. They etch, in individual and collective consciousness, the rhythms of the public imagery with which they become forever associated; and they produce a common memory of traditions within the culture. The television icons are pictorial representations that, like traditional ritual masks and sacred religious icons, are drawn from the world of everyday lived experience and at the same time transcend that world. Television's internally structured visual and aural time signature is analogous to the rules for a traditional ritual; the segments, and particularly the commercials, "announce" themselves and demand our attention. Through the advertiser's recitation of the myth (which recurs throughout the broadcast day and night) and the spectator's subsequent performance of the ritual of purchase (reenactment of the creation of an acquisitive society), the audience is "steeped in the sacred atmosphere in which these miraculous events took place."[21]

All of this, of course, is too abstract to be believed in terms of its own logic without some verifiable evidence. What miraculous events are we witness to in the contemporary televised world? Critic Jonathan Price described the "sacred atmosphere" of the television commercial:

This mythic world is magic. Voices in the air, not attached to bodies, regularly order us around in commercials, take care of us, and give us advice, just like spirits. In this realm we can change the shape of people who have indigestion, make a package of gum as big as a tree, or slice apart a car in an instant. We can fly over golf courses, . . . we can drive on water, . . . we can make a wild deer eat Oreos and go where we want. . . . Commercials resemble the dreams of a primitive hunter or child in their faith in magic.[22]

These "dreams" in the mythic world of television advertising are no less "real" than those of traditional mythology, with its emphasis on cosmogony (the origin or creation of the world or the universe); both speak to us of entire ways of life and canonize patterns of organization of society that regulate behavior, ensuring a continuity of values and beliefs.

We examine below a few of the more powerful myths that frame contemporary American life. These myths are repeatedly employed by advertisers in the service of consumption.[23]

The myth of "manifest destiny" is one of our most powerful contemporary myths. It is employed in one form or another by societies bent on expansion and empire building. The phrase, coined in 1845, quickly became a political doctrine used by American politicians to subjugate Native Americans in the settlement of the American West. The myth was revived in the 1890s as the United States went to war against Spain in Cuba and the Philippine Islands. Today, although the phrase is no longer common currency, the notion is very much alive in the sense that America is the most powerful nation in the world; it insidiously undergirded President George Bush's political philosophy of a "New World Order" following the dissolution of the Soviet state. Advertisers appeal to our belief in the myth by focusing on the themes, "Buy this to keep America strong" or "Support us to keep America strong." The former selling theme has been used for the past decade (in desperation, some say) by U.S. automobile manufacturers, to discourage the purchase of imported Japanese automobiles. The latter selling theme is most evident in institutional commercials from our leading oil companies, who justify the rise in costs of petroleum products and environmental damage by telling us that we must drill into the ocean floor at great expense to find our own crude and thereby break our dependence on Third World oil. This myth is driven by fear of weakness and in certain manifestations has invidious racialist overtones.

Take recent U.S. advertisers' direct attacks on Japan. In certain cases, the boundaries between business competition in commercial culture and blatant nationalism and even racism seemed to have been crossed, raising serious questions regarding advertisers' social responsibility. The trend began in the winter of 1989 with a Chrysler national ad campaign featuring company president Lee Iacocca complaining on camera that American consumers refused to believe that American automobiles could be as good as Japanese cars. To its credit, the Chrysler campaign focused on specific product attributes and held up Japanese cars as a standard of excellence.

From this rather innocuous, low-key beginning, many auto ads turned increasingly nasty. Unlike the Chrysler spots, the commercials in question tended to be spots produced for local or regional markets. It should be noted that local automobile dealers' associations in the United States operate independently of the auto manufacturers and are generally free to hire their own ad agencies and develop their own campaign strategies without interference from the auto manufacturers themselves. Further, local clients and agencies often exercise less restraint in their thematic approach. This may range from a more overt "Gonzo" style of advertising (e.g., a Columbus, Ohio, Chevrolet automobile dealer in the early 1980s made a commercial showing a group of men using sledgehammers to destroy a Japanese car on camera) to a more clever approach to the problem.

Of the more recent spots, one, produced for General Motors Pontiac automobile dealers in the metropolitan New York area, began with a warning from an announcer: "Imagine a few years from now. . . . It's December, and the whole family's going to see the big Christmas tree at Hirohito Center. Go on. Keep buying Japanese cars." The spot concludes with the words "ENOUGH ALREADY" in bold white letters against a black background. The spot's oblique reference is to Mitsubishi's purchase in 1989 of a 51 percent share of New York's Rockefeller Center, perhaps the single most significant traditional symbol of American industrial greatness. The driving force behind the ad is that Japanese automobile makers continue to cut into U.S. auto manufacturers' domestic sales. Japan produced 28 percent of all cars sold in the United States in the first half of 1990, up from 24 percent in the comparable 1989 period. This reflects the continued erosion of U.S. auto manufacturers' position in their own market vis-à-vis the Japanese.

Another spot in the New York metropolitan area—this one for the Tri-State Oldsmobile Dealers—compares the average height of Japanese men with the greater average height of American men. The spot concludes: "That's why our car is built for *our* size families, not *theirs*."

The creator of the Oldsmobile spot defended it by arguing "We think it is legitimate to bring in the different heights because we did it with a sense of humor." The executive director of the New York–New Jersey Pontiac Dealers Association argued that the "Enough Already" campaign was not anti-Japanese but rather pro-American. The Pontiac dealers' ad agency's director acknowledged that the Pontiac spots were intended to appeal to American "nationalism" and claimed that this approach's success was evident in sales figures for the Pontiac dealers in the market in which the spot was shown.

Critics, however, are not so sanguine about these spots, seeing current American mass media portrayals of the Japanese people as somewhat reminiscent of American World War II propaganda depicting the Japanese as "lesser human or superhuman." Such depictions are capable of being revived by both sides in times of crisis and tension. In addition, some observers within the automobile industry itself have questioned the sales effectiveness of such negative ads, insisting that consumers want positive, not negative, messages about products and services.

In another campaign launched in the spring of 1990 by a group of Bell Telephone operating companies in newspapers around the country, an ad called for legislation that would allow the telephone companies to enter the information-generation field, from which they were excluded by law. The headline read: "First it was consumer electronics. Then it was the automobile industry. Is our telecommunications industry next?" Below the headline was a photograph of a crouched Samurai warrior apparently ready to leap into action. The Bell companies pulled the ad after a complaint by the Japanese Embassy and dismissed the agency from the account.

The myth of the frontier seems peculiarly American and has its roots in the Hollywood-cinema genre of the Western and in innumerable 1950s and 1960s Western series on television. This is the myth of freedom, virility, and ruggedness associated with the West. The frontier mentality continues to thrive in the "urban frontiers" of crime melodramas (police and private detective series). This myth is male dominated; men become comrades in their quest to conquer the harsh frontier elements. Women, where they exist in the myth at all, are relegated to the status of objects: the prostitute with the heart of gold or the "nice lady" who wants the free male to settle down, marry, raise a family, and give up killing (the woman is seen as castrater or confiner). According to John Cashill, the frontier man becomes "the American Adam"—an archetypal hero whose "absolute rootlessness and his essential innocence, his lack of moral dilemma" suggest a purity of spirit in the context of the surrounding evil.[24] Commercials frequently employ this myth to sell automobiles, beer, blue jeans and other western gear, tires, gasoline, and, in print, cigarettes and cigars. The frontier is associated with automobiles, motorcycles, and pickup trucks aimed mostly at downscale blue-collar workers. Ford has been the main auto manufacturer to employ the myth, although General Motors and Chrysler (Dodge trucks) have also created spots on this theme. Among the beer commercials, Schlitz and Miller associate the man-to-man camaraderie in the frontier work environment (and, after work, in the leisure environment) with their "full-bodied, robust" beers. According to one critic, these beer ads are beautiful, lyrical tributes to the romance of the working class and to the dignity of the work ethic.[25] However, while theirs is a rugged world, the heroes never get dirty or exhibit any frustration with the conditions of their work. Women enter the frame as barmaids serving the men or as fawning hero-worshippers. Television cigarette ads of the 1950s and 1960s were major purveyors of the myth. Especially prominent was the "Marlboro Man" campaign, which still exists in print in the United States and on television and in print throughout the world. Clearly this myth has played a significant role in American television hucksterism.

The taming of the frontier brings civilization and, with it, sanity and compromise. Nowhere is this more evident than in the myth of the "country" or "rural middle landscape." This mythic locale occupies the space between the frontier and the urban megalopolis. People who exist "out there" are not isolates, as in the frontier, but members of families in which companionship, human warmth, and happiness are central defining characteristics of human relationships. Nostalgia and nonurban purity are central feelings evoked by the presentation of this psychic landscape on television. The myth is evident in many comedic and melodramatic series (examples include *The Beverly Hillbillies, Green Acres, The Andy Griffith Show, Little House on the Prairie,* and *The Waltons*). In TV advertising we find the myth operating in the Hugh Puppies "Henry and Pa" and Country Time Lemonade spots; in certain AT&T long-distance campaigns; in several Chevrolet campaigns, including the long-running "baseball, apple pie, and Chevrolet" campaign and the more recent "heartbeat of America" campaign.

A variation of the rural-middle-landscape myth can be found in many corporate image-enhancing ad campaigns (those intended to boost the corporation's image rather than to directly sell products or services). IBM is not a giant transnational corporation, according to an ad campaign from the early 1980s. Rather, it is "people [read "plain folk"] helping to put information to work for people." Ramada Inns and Holiday Inns are not mass-produced motel chains, but "nice people taking care of nice people" and "people pleasin' people." And General Motors is no corporate behemoth. No, it is merely "people building transportation to serve people."[26]

The rural middle landscape has become a favorite myth with our politicians. Jimmy Carter, a president whose roots are clearly in the rural middle landscape, exploited the myth fully in his 1976 election campaign and caught the imagination of a country reeling from the debacle of the Nixon/Watergate era and skeptical of urban politicians (defined as Washington "insiders.") We saw Carter in one spot kneeling down to pick up Georgia dirt at his peanut farm; the blue jeans and the cultivated land spoke of farming and associated values. People wanted a return to purity and warm values of family and friendships. Within four years, however, the childlike innocence of the media hype proved incapable of dealing with the harsh international realities of Iran—a frontier far from home and desperately in need of taming. It was inevitable that a gunslinger riding tall in the saddle would come to town to clear up the confounding mess. The rural middle landscape quickly regressed to the frontier and the myth of manifest destiny. Ronald Reagan promised to lead the "fight for survival" in 1980. More bombs were built, and the "waste" of social programs was cut to help pay for them. By 1984, with the country "strong" again, Reagan's reelection campaign media handlers were able to effortlessly shift mythic motifs from the frontier to the rural middle landscape in the "It's Morning Again in America" spots. Images of Reagan the family man and of Reagan peacefully riding his horse (part of a campaign-produced documentary) were intended to assure Americans that the turmoil of the 1960s and 1970s was now behind us, that he had led the country back to greatness on the world stage and prosperity and domestic tranquility at home.

It is interesting to note that both the rural middle landscape and the frontier myth as used by politicians imply a certain resentment of the intellectual or at least a skepticism that abstract political discourse can resolve social problems. This attitude was made most evident in contemporary politics by right-wing populists such as George Wallace.

The myth perhaps closest to the sociocultural meaning engendered by the entire advertising system itself is that of the Protestant ethic. At its heart is the cliché, "God helps those who help themselves." This myth powers our drive for success and the acquisition of ever-greater quantities of goods. We can hide behind the false religiosity that encourages personal financial gain while ignoring the traditional ethic of working on behalf of others (redistributing the wealth gained through one's labors to others less fortunate). This myth is applied to a social strategy that isolates the individual as a consumer from his or her role as producer of the common store of goods and services that involves the society. The most devastating use of the myth can be found in certain luxury-automobile ads. Perhaps the most powerful of these is the Cadillac campaign targeted at upscale men during prestigious golf tournaments. Here we find combined the myths of the Protestant ethic, the suburban middle landscape, and manifest destiny, with its racialist overtones. The Cadillac slowly drives up to the country club, the suburban version of the middle landscape whose pioneers have worked hard to transform the scruffy terrain in the midst of the megalopolis into a well-manicured tamed paradise. As they worked so hard to build their paradise, it is only fair to exclude others who are unable to afford or who are socially unworthy of membership in the private society; the Cadillac represents this exclusion. Behind the purity of the images, in the locker room, sit black men who hand out towels to the members and scrape the mud from their golf spikes. They have their own dreams, which may also include Cadillacs.

A myth that is universal, but particularly potent in American television advertising, is the myth of eternal youth. Erich Fromm analyzed this myth:

There's really no limit to what a gadget can do. The product promises us the fountain of youth—eternal youth. There's a great deal of narcissism involved; the self-image of the beautiful person—good looking, strong, attractive—who never changes, who lives in a kind of sacred land in which this image of the beautiful, successful, energetic young man is never touched; the pretension must be that he never changes.[27]

The myth also applies, of course, to women. Oil of Olay promises youth (if not "eternal," certainly long lasting) to the woman who uses the skin cream with regularity. Geritol, which once was the antidote to "tired blood," now is intended for young marrieds and even college students, to keep them feeling young. Youth becomes enmeshed in a confusing web of envy, love, and sex appeal.

Beyond the mythic order of signification lies a dominant ideology that infuses all of the secular myths. Ideology, wrote Roland Barthes, explains how a mythical schema "corresponds to the interests of a definite society" and thus becomes a matter of "general history."[28] It is to an examination of that general history, seen through the distorting lens of a television commercial, that we now turn.

KODAK'S "AMERICA": IMAGES FROM THE AMERICAN EDEN

During 1984 and 1985, the J. Walter Thompson U.S.A. advertising agency conceived and produced the "Because Time Goes By"[29] national television advertising campaign for the Eastman Kodak Company. J. Walter Thompson had serviced the Kodak account, its second-oldest account, since 1930.

The campaign comprised nine spots. Five were produced in 1984: "Reunion," "Music Makers," "Baseball," "Olympics," and "The Gift." Four others were produced in 1985: "America," "Henry, My Best Friend," "Old Lovers," and "Summer Love."[30] The campaign was "transitional" for the client. It marked a return to Kodak's tradition of warm, often lyrical "emotional appeals" commercials without completely abandoning the "product benefits" focus of recent campaigns.[31] Among those featured in the new spots were young lovers on the beach sharing their memories in photographs as their summer of love comes to an end, elderly couples expressing their continued love, a little boy whose puppy quickly grows to a giant dog while the boy grows only slightly, and a Chistmas commercial featuring a young child giving a gift to an elderly black man.

The following discussion focuses on one of these spots, "America," which was first aired in the spring and summer of 1985 in both a 60-second and a 30-second version. "America" represents a dominant strain in television commercials from the period that employed themes of American patriotism and restoration. The apparent rupture between its seamless aesthetic and its socially provocative imagery opens up an important discourse on the process and power of symbolization and mythification in our contemporary public imagery.

This analysis is grounded in both a close reading of the text of "America" and a series of telephone interviews conducted in 1987 with key individuals in the agency's creative department and the client's Consumer Products Division's Marketing Communications Department who were intimately involved in the creation of the spot.[32] The interviewees were very open in their responses to all questions regarding the creative and administrative aspects of the commercial's production. At Kodak's request, financial information regarding the cost to produce the commercial was not forthcoming.[33] Although the interviews provide important insights into the "mind" of the commercial and the minds of those who conceived it, one must be careful to separate creator intentionality and the text itself as viewed.

The Social Context of "America"

The "America" spot was part of an advertising trend. The advertising industry's success is dependent in large measure on its ability to interpret

a "complex, multi-layered, fast-changing society" and to follow the society's emotional mood as quickly and accurately as possible.[34] This is especially true for commercials seeking a heterogeneous national audience.
When an ascending mood is perceived, agencies and their clients jump
on the bandwagon; when it passes, they jump off. Themes and symbols
representative of those themes are appropriated from the store of existing
public imagery to tap the perceived mood. The confluence of two national
events in 1984—the Summer Olympic Games in Los Angeles and Ronald
Reagan's presidential reelection campaign—provided advertisers a clear
signal that a patriotic mood was sweeping the country.

The swell of national pride surrounding the 1984 Los Angeles Games
was an extension of the patriotic fervor generated by the American ice
hockey team's unexpected victory over the Soviet team four years earlier
in the 1980 Winter Olympic Games in Lake Placid. Olympic competition,
always a source of nationalistic display among competing countries, had
for years been a forum for Cold War ideological warfare between the
United States and the Soviet Union. The U.S. boycott of the 1980 Summer Olympics in Moscow following the Soviet invasion of Afghanistan
and the Soviets' reprisal boycott of the Los Angeles Games are clear examples of the intrusion of international politics into sports.

The 1984 Los Angeles Games provided Americans an opportunity to
promote the American way of life in relation to the Soviets. In this case
the ideological frame was economic. Rather than massive government support for the construction of sport facilities for the Games, American private enterprise contributed large sums of money for such construction.
Corporate public relations considerations aside, the privatization of the
Los Angeles Games provided a convenient symbol of the contrast between
the Soviet athletic program, with its well-financed yet subservient athletes
carrying out the goals of the state on the playing fields, rinks, and arenas,
and the American program in which athletes are autonomous "free spirits" nurtured by free enterprise. This contrast became a subtext of many
products' advertising campaigns saluting America's Olympic athletes.

The Reagan political spots drew heavily on the theme of national re-
vitalization reflected in the American entrepreneurial spirit. The campaign's optimism seemed myopic to many, given evidence to the contrary
of America's waning economic empire. Americans continued to lose jobs
in the heavy-manufacturing and high-technology sectors of the economy
to overseas competitors, foremost among them the Japanese; and, ironically, the farm crisis in America's heartland was reaching devastating proportions just as the Reagan commercial campaign was presenting images
glorifying rural American life. Compounding the individual despair caused
by unemployment in the industrial and high-technology sectors and the
increasing loss of family farms was a general perception of America's loss
of international prestige. Viewed in the context of the American mil-

itary defeat in Vietnam and its embarrassment in the Iranian hostage debacle, America's economic decline took on added psychological importance. The central theme of the Reagan advertising campaign, that "Life is better . . . America's back . . . and people have a sense of pride they thought they'd never feel again,"[35] became the anthem for a nation gripped by malaise and apprehensive of its future.

Suddenly product campaigns extolling patriotic values cluttered the electronic landscape. Notable among them were Chrysler's "The pride is back, born in America" and Miller Beer's "Made the American way, born and bred in the U.S.A.," both of which drew directly on the Reagan campaign theme. Kodak's "America," while eschewing the overt symbolism of Chrysler's giant American flag and the equally overt lyrics of both the Chrysler and Miller spots, nonetheless drew heavily on the Reagan message—and for good reason, as we shall see.

Conceiving the Spot

In 1984, according to a J. Walter Thompson account supervisor, Eastman Kodak "was feeling somewhat vulnerable" because 10 percent of its film business in the United States had been taken away by Fuji Photo Film USA Inc., a Japanese film and videotape manufacturer that had entered the U.S. market in 1970.[36] Fuji had developed a film stock with color reproduction characteristics different from Kodak's. While Kodak had maintained its emphasis on the faithful rendition of skin tones, Fuji emphasized the bright colors (some people at Kodak called them "garish") to which the viewers of color television had become accustomed. Fuji had also taken the lead in product marketing, introducing multiroll packages of film and huge, brightly colored point-of-sale advertising displays.

There was a difference of opinion in two camps within Kodak's Marketing Communications Department as to whether a new campaign should stress product benefits or brand image.[37] Kodak's top management historically "had a clear prejudice for brand image maintenance. It was proud of its image."[38] Central to Kodak's decision to stress brand image in the campaign was the reality that Fuji had a more successful product on the market—"Quite honestly, Kodak wasn't in a position to make grand product performance claims because Fuji, at the time, had surpassed Kodak in product quality"—and the agency's belief that "nine out of 10 Americans shoot film to save their memories, not to worry about the industrial quality of film stock."[39]

Kodak decided to take the high ground, a smart move as its major competition was Japanese and the campaign coincided with the political window during which a patriotic theme would be well received. The "America" spot would "ride the tide of the new patriotism, a place that only Kodak could be."[40] The patriotic approach would allow Kodak to capitalize on the "heritage" of the brand.

Market research indicated that viewers had come to expect emotional appeal advertising from Kodak, spots with themes such as a mother's love for her son. At the same time, Kodak was trying to avoid the "trap of being [perceived as] a sentimental brand." It was committed to "moving its image forward without becoming high-tech or punk."[41]

Kodak's headquarters are located in Rochester, New York, a "stable environment out of the cultural 'firing line' of New York City," which may account in part for its conservative mindset. According to a former advertising agency executive and long-time observer of the industry, Kodak has a "deeper sense of responsibility about the country as a whole" than a company headquartered in New York City or Los Angeles, which tends to be "more cynical." "A company's personality," he added, "is the key to the way commercials are [ideologically and aesthetically] constructed."[42] An account director for J. Walter Thompson, who was assigned the Kodak account after "America" had been shot, described Kodak's corporate philosophy:

The company has a Midwestern mentality, a general outlook on life and conception of American society that is safer than most New York City-based companies. Kodak takes a more conservative approach. It is willing to be a little more provocative in terms of shooting style, but not in terms of politics. It reminds me of my Dow Chemical account in Indianapolis. It's not New York City.[43]

Kodak's director of marketing communications for consumer products agreed with this assessment, saying Kodak "goes out of its way not to be controversial." If controversy arises, he added, it is "by accident."[44]

Not only does Kodak eschew the high-tech look that has become a signature of many contemporary brand image commercials; it also does not want to be perceived as a "funny" company. A telling example offers proof of this mindset at work. In 1985, J. Walter Thompson shot a spot called "Ostriches" as part of a campaign for Kodak's 400 film. The spot opened with a close-up shot of jockeys lining up for the start of a race. As the race began, the shot widened to reveal the jockeys astride ostriches, not horses. While the spot post-tested very well, Kodak's director of marketing communications for consumer products insisted that "humor is not an emotion" in Kodak's lexicon. The spot never aired.[45]

Kodak's cautious corporate philosophy is reflected in its formal, highly structured commercial approval process. It was through this process that the "Because Time Goes By" campaign and the "America" spots were transformed from ideas to completed commercials. Kodak's formal approval process, while rare in the advertising milieu of the 1970s,[46] became far more common in the 1980s where, with increasing conglomeration, there was "a less clear [corporate] attitude toward larger visions of America" and an increased bottom-line consciousness.[47] In Kodak's case, television advertising is "so important for presenting an image of the company" that all the various levels of Kodak's management are involved in deciding the thrust of a campaign.[48]

In developing television spots for its film products, Kodak's first decision-making level is that of the marketing communications director for film,[49] who oversees the advertising production process for commercials, print, and outdoor advertising of all film products. Generally in attendance at the initial meeting between client and agency staff are, for the client, the marketing communications director for film and "communication specialists" who will oversee the actual production of the spots and monitor costs and, for the agency, several key members of the creative team. This meeting is intended to narrow down a number of ideas for the proposed spots to those that have special merit.

The marketing communications director for film makes a recommendation to Kodak's director of marketing communications for consumer products (including, but not limited to film products). This stage is "the most important buy-in. Management above [this level] will usually buy the Marketing Communications Director's judgment."[50] It was at this level that the debate between brand image and product-benefits approaches for the campaign took place, with brand image carrying the day.

The next level of decision-making resides with Kodak's marketing general manager for film. Here we move from marketing communications to overall marketing management. Storyboards and related creative materials are presented by the agency. A "go-ahead" is given for the shoots. The succeeding stages of Kodak management decision-making are generally "for review only." These include Kodak's general manager for the Consumer Products Division and the group executive vice president for the Photographic Products Group. Once the spot is completed, it is presented to Kodak's chairman, vice chairman, and president for *pro forma* approval. This is often done the day before the spot is scheduled to premiere on television. The purpose of the review is to familiarize the corporate officers with the spot or spots so that they can intelligently respond to any feedback they might receive from viewers. Of course, "a look from the Chairman" is worth a thousand words. If he doesn't like it, it won't air.[51]

The team assembled by the agency to produce a spot generally includes a vice president and creative supervisor, primarily an administrator, who assigns creative people to the account and acts as liaison with the client; an account supervisor; a group creative director who develops ideas for the spot (in the case of "America," the group creative director was selected to direct the shooting of the spot; J. Walter Thompson often goes outside the agency to hire commercial directors); another group creative director who writes music and lyrics for the spot; an executive producer

who supervises the production, hires a production house to do the shooting, and monitors production costs (on the "America" shoot, the executive
producer functioned as the Second Unit director and also shot stills that
were used in the spot); and an art director who does most of the casting
for the spot.

It is difficult to credit any individual in a group creative effort such as that
which resulted in "America" as the sole originator of an idea or theme. We
know that in a collective endeavor ideas are generated by numerous informal
dialogues among key participants as well as in more formal meetings. This is
especially true in the creative departments of advertising agencies. According to one observer with many years of firsthand agency experience as an executive of one of the country's leading agencies:

One probably won't get an answer as to the exact process in which an idea is
constructed, because decisions get made in a non-decisional way at most agencies.
The crystallization of the decision-making process is announced in a very brief
memo from the agency's account executive: "We've decided to go forward with
this idea." No one knows exactly who "we" was.[52]

Recognizing this difficulty, the author conducted telephone interviews,
ranging in length from 20 minutes to an hour-and-a-half, with seven key
players involved in the creation of "America" in an attempt to develop as
clear a picture as possible of the gestation of the images, music, and lyrics
that constitute the finished product. These interviews occurred two years
after the spot's completion and may suffer to some extent from the problem of participant recall of specific details and the exact sequence of
events. In addition, as with any highly successful group creative effort,
some participants may claim credit for others' ideas. The author sought
to avoid this potential problem by cross-checking participant accounts and
asking follow-up questions. In each instance of an unresolved discrepancy,
and there were but three such cases, the author accepted as the accurate
account that on which two or more participants concurred. Through this
process a clear portrait of the spot's development emerged.

The J. Walter Thompson creative team was in California working on
another project when word came from New York to develop an idea with
a "patriotic theme" for the "America" spot. According to Greg Weinschenker, who had been assigned to direct "America," "They sent back
an idea with people saluting the American flag." Weinschenker found that
idea "boring." He suggested instead a motorcycle journey across the
United States. His suggestion was autobiographical. In 1970 Weinschenker
had travelled across the country on a motorcycle from New York City to
Albuquerque, New Mexico, with his dog. Unlike "America," Weinschenker's journey "was not that romantic. In fact it was physically painful. It
took two or three weeks."[53] According to Weinschenker, because Kodak

wanted the spot to show more color than the previous spots in the campaign, most of which were shot indoors, the idea of an outdoors shoot was appealing.

Kodak's marketing communications director for film at the time, Bruce Wilson, was clear from the outset of discussions with agency staff as to the "concept and feeling" Kodak sought to achieve with "America," as well as its style. It was to be a "vignette" spot. Rather than a coherent narrative, a vignette commercial is a sequence of "slightly interlocking little scenes and situations."[54]

The agency's creative team went to work developing a storyboard based on Weinschenker's and Kodak's conceptions. Weinschenker sat down with Linda Kaplan, an agency group creative director and lyricist, to flesh out the idea. Kaplan and Weinschenker had worked closely on many projects prior to "America." Kaplan proposed the idea of a Vietnam draft evader returning from Canada following years of exile to see his family and reunite with his old girlfriend. Not only did Weinschenker find this idea too controversial, but he said, "The rider would be too old." He wanted the rider to be "youthful, not jaded." According to Weinschenker, "The character was to have no preconceived notions about anything."[55] Had the agency proposed the draft-evader idea to Kodak, it would never have entertained such a storyline, according to Kodak's Bruce Wilson.[56]

The "board" that emerged showed a young motorcycle rider going across the country, meeting different people (Figure 3.1). One original concept had the cyclist coming into a big city, Los Angeles, at the end of his journey. In contrast to the warmth and friendliness of the "country" he had seen, Los Angeles was a "cold place." Sitting on Hollywood Boulevard with tears in his eyes, the motorcycle rider internalizes the contrast.[57]

The precise storyboard for the spot was not that important to Kodak in giving the go-ahead to begin production. Director Weinschenker's "loose" shooting style, developed in many successful Kodak spots prior to "America," was well known to the client, who voiced no objection to such an approach. Kodak allowed the agency creative group sufficient latitude to pick up shots on location as opportunities for unplanned scenes became available. Because "America" was part of a larger "marketing package"— stills from the shoot were to be used for print advertisements in magazines in addition to their use in the commercial—the precise budget for the shoot was not of critical concern to Kodak.[58]

Shooting the Spot

Director Greg Weinschenker emphasized seeking "real people" rather than actors for the vignettes that would comprise the spot. The motorcycle-rider protagonist would be a professional actor. The people he encountered on his journey across America would for the most part be cast from nonactors who lived in the places he visited.

Casting began. Greg Blanchard, the actor chosen to play the cyclist, was cast in Los Angeles. He "had the right spirit,"according to Weinschenker. Blanchard's youthful, clean-cut appearance was ideally suited to the "depoliticized" image both agency and client sought. The "clean cyclist" would maximize the viewers' identification and provide a functional hero, an ego-ideal.[59] Conversely, the viewer's potential anxiety and defensive response to the iconography of the cyclist-as-anarchist, cultivated through decades of B-grade motorcycle-gang movies and culminating in the antiestablishment pot-smoking antiheroes of *Easy Rider*, would be minimized. A professional motorcycle rider was cast as Blanchard's double. He would appear in panorama shots picked up by the Second Unit, headed by Executive Producer Sid Horn.

Sites for shooting were selected by agency art directors Kathy McMahon and Marisa Acocella. Primary sites were Oregon, Arizona, and Los Angeles. The rural locations would provide the palette of outdoor colors that Kodak desired—the lush greens and golds of the Oregon countryside and the earthy browns and reds of the Arizona desert and mesas. Los Angeles would provide the contrasting image of big-city "coldness."

These West Coast locations offered additional economic benefits. Agency Executive Producer Sid Horn had hired Ron Dexter, of Dexter, Dreyer and Lai, a Los Angeles–based film production house, as director of photography for "America." Art directors McMahon and Acocella went out into the field two weeks before the crew to do the initial precasting of the "real people" Weinschenker sought. Weinschenker asked them to "just find the right people and the right look" for the scenes he had planned. Most of the final casting decisions were made by the director on site.

Weinschenker and Dexter headed the First Unit, which shot all the scenes featuring interactions between Greg Blanchard and the characters he encountered in Oregon, Arizona, and Los Angeles. Kodak Marketing Communications Specialist Ann Winkler, the client's representative on the shoot, worked with the First Unit. Executive Producer Sid Horn headed the Second Unit, which travelled south from Oregon to Monument Valley, Utah, picking up shots of Blanchard's double riding through the countryside. In addition to the film footage shot for the spot, Weinschenker, Horn, and a Kodak photographer shot stills, which were subsequently used in the spot and in magazine advertisements.

The persons appearing in the spot and those who were cast and shot but did not appear in the final version (the "outgrades") were paid between $300 and $600 a day, depending on the length of the shooting day. Because the spot was so successful, airing over the course of many months

Figure 3.1
The Kodak "America" Commercial

"America"
Client: Eastman Kodak
Agency: J. Walter Thompson U.S.A.
Director: Greg Weinschenker
Executive Producer: Sid Horn

<table>
<tr><td colspan="2">VIDEO</td><td>AUDIO</td></tr>
<tr><td colspan="3">FADE IN:</td></tr>
<tr><td colspan="2">EXT. DAY</td><td>MUSIC FULL</td></tr>
<tr><td>WS CYCLIST RIDING SCREEN LEFT.
SUNRISE IN BACKGROUND. (SLO-MO)</td><td>:05</td><td>Settin off to find</td></tr>
<tr><td>(SUPER: KODAK LOGO WITH "AMERICA")</td><td></td><td></td></tr>
<tr><td colspan="3">DISSOLVE TO:</td></tr>
<tr><td>MS CYCLIST TOWARD CAMERA (SLO-MO)</td><td>:03</td><td>America.</td></tr>
<tr><td colspan="3">DISSOLVE TO:</td></tr>
<tr><td>M 2-SHOT CYCLIST & OLD WOMAN BY
MAILBOX. CYCLIST ASKS DIRECTIONS.
OLD WOMAN POINTS DOWN ROAD.(SLO-MO)</td><td>:06</td><td>Gonna take my own sweet
time to find America.</td></tr>
<tr><td colspan="3">DISSOLVE TO:</td></tr>
<tr><td>M 2-SHOT CYCLIST ON BENCH IN FRONT
OF COUNTRY STORE. BEARDED MAN ON
BENCH. CYCLIST SHAKES A COLLIE'S
PAW. (SLO-MO)</td><td>:03</td><td>And everywhere I see</td></tr>
<tr><td colspan="3">DISSOLVE TO:</td></tr>
<tr><td>3-SHOT CYCLIST & 2 YOUNG BLACK MEN
ON BED OF PICK-UP, TOSSING HAY.
(SLO-MO)</td><td>:03</td><td>People smilin back at
me.</td></tr>
<tr><td colspan="3">DISSOLVE TO:</td></tr>
<tr><td>2-SHOT CYCLIST GREETING COWBOY AT
ROADSIDE. (SLO-MO)</td><td>:05</td><td>So glad to be in
America.</td></tr>
<tr><td colspan="3">DISSOLVE TO:</td></tr>
<tr><td>SUPER. MS CYCLIST TOWARD CAMERA/
OVER WS ROAD w/ CAR AWAY FROM
CAMERA TOWARD MOUNTAIN. (SLO-MO)</td><td>:02</td><td></td></tr>
<tr><td colspan="3">DISSOLVE TO:</td></tr>
<tr><td>2-SHOT CYCLIST SHAKES HAND OF
BEARDED MAN, IN VIETNAM-ERA ARMY
FATIGUE JACKET & HAT, IN WHEEL
CHAIR. (SLO-MO)</td><td>:04</td><td>So come take my hand
and let's discover</td></tr>
<tr><td colspan="3">DISSOLVE TO:</td></tr>
<tr><td>MS CYCLIST TOWARD CAMERA, MOUNTAINS
IN BACKGROUND. (SLO-MO)</td><td>:01</td><td></td></tr>
<tr><td colspan="3">DISSOLVE TO:</td></tr>
<tr><td>2-SHOT CYCLIST AND NATIVE AMERICAN,
ON CHAIRS, IN TALL GRASS. LAUGHING
& GESTURING. MTS. IN BACKGROUND.
(SLO-MO)</td><td>:04</td><td>The love that we share
brother to brother.</td></tr>
</table>

Figure 3.1 *(continued)*

<table>
<tr><td align="center">VIDEO</td><td></td><td align="center">AUDIO</td></tr>
</table>

DISSOLVE TO:

WS FARMER ON OLD TRACTOR DRIVING DOWN ROAD TOWARD CAMERA, CYCLIST LEADING IN FOREGROUND. (SLO-MO)	:02	(VO: Bring America home

DISSOLVE TO:

CU DISPLAY, KODAK FILMS	:03	on Kodacolor VR films.

DISSOLVE TO:

BEARDED MAN ON BENCH w/ COLLIE, LOOKING AFTER DEPARTING CYCLIST. (STILL)	:01	Films as vibrant and

DISSOLVE:

OLD WOMAN w/ LETTER IN HAND, LOOKING AFTER DEPARTED CYCLIST. (STILL)	:01	as sensitive as the faces

DISSOLVE TO:

COWBOY w/ SADDLE BY ROAD, LOOKING AFTER DEPARTED CYCLIST. (STILL)	:02	and places that bring this land together.)

DISSOLVE TO:

SUPER WS CYCLIST OVER BIRDS FLYING. (SLO-MO)	:02	

DISSOLVE TO:

MCU CYCLIST LYING AGAINST CYCLE, FEEDING A PUPPY. (SLO-MO)	:03	And as far as I can see.

DISSOLVE TO:

MWS CYCLIST TOWARD CAMERA, ON TREE-LINED ROAD. (SLO-MO)	:02	There's no place I'd rather be.

DISSOLVE TO:

MS CYCLIST STOPPED ON ROAD. FOUR YOUNG GIRLS EXITING SCHOOL BUS & CROSSING IN FRONT OF HIM, FOLLOWED BY YOUNG BOY WHO STOPS AND TURNS TOWARD CYCLIST. CYCLIST SALUTES. (SLO-MO/FREEZE FRAME)	:06	Than ridin free in America.

SUPER:

KODAK LOGO w/ "BECAUSE TIME GOES BY" CAPTION.	:02	(VO: Kodak film. Because time goes by.)

FADE OUT VIDEO   FADE OUT AUDIO

in the national market, those appearing in major roles in the spot's final version made between $15,000 and $20,000 with residuals.[60]

The motorcyclist's first human encounter in the spot, with an elderly woman, was not storyboarded. While the crew was shooting the Oregon school-bus scene (which became the spot's concluding vignette), an elderly woman wandered out of her house to see what was happening, then disappeared back into the house. Weinschenker spotted her, stopped the shoot, and ran after her. Her daughter, who lived in the house, talked with the director and got her mother to play in the spot. The elderly woman was totally deaf. As it turned out, the elderly woman's great-granddaughter was one of the children getting off the school bus. Weinschenker set up a two-shot of Blanchard and the elderly woman at a rural mail box. Blanchard began to point, and the elderly woman, picking up the cue, also pointed. The shot was in the can. According to Weinschenker, the elderly woman "never did know what was going on."

The scene of the motorcycle rider sitting with a bearded man on a bench in front of a country store and reaching out to shake a collie's paw was shot in an old Arizona town fallen on hard times. This town, once thriving because of its proximity to the mining industry, was now a virtual ghost town. The shot had the archetypal look of the "Old West" we have come to expect in our popular imagery of the area.

The pickup-truck scene with Blanchard and two black men was storyboarded before the shoot began. It was shot in Oregon. The original concept for this vignette had the three men sitting in the truck bed filled with hay. One of the black men was playing a harmonica, while Blanchard played guitar. This was shot, but Kodak's Winkler did not like it. She felt that "portraying blacks as musicians was a cliche."[61] Kodak was very careful not to represent groups in ways that some might consider stereotyped or demeaning. The scene was reconceived at the site. Weinschenker had the three men begin to unload the hay, which quickly turned into the playful hay-tossing scene used in the completed spot. Another version of the scene was shot but not used. In this version, some black teenagers had gotten their pickup truck stuck in the mud. Blanchard stopped to help them free the truck. The consensus among the crew was that this shot didn't work.

When asked about the appropriateness of casting blacks in such a setting, Weinschenker replied "We had to have blacks in the commercial. If you have six people in a spot, one has to be black."[62] This statement should not be taken literally as evidence that racial quotas are employed by the agencies or their clients. It does, however, generally reflect agency and client sensitivity to demographics. One long-time agency insider noted that "everyone in the ad business is very familiar with and sensitive to demographics" and that there is a "racial mind set" at the agencies today.[63]

The question of the portrayal of blacks resurfaced a year later at Kodak. J. Walter Thompson had cast a black saxophone musician in one of the spots in Kodak's "The Color of Life" campaign. Before giving the go-ahead for the shoot, Kodak insisted that the role be recast with a white musician in the role, arguing, as had Winkler on the "America" shoot, that the black musician was a cliché.[64]

The scene of the cowboy greeting the motorcycle rider along the road-side was shot in Arizona. The cowboy was a real cowboy cast at the site.

Three Vietnam veterans were lined up at a veterans hospital in Port-land, Oregon, as possible actors in the scene where the motorcyclist offers a friendly handshake to a disabled veteran confined to a wheelchair. (None of the veterans who were physically disabled would agree to appear on camera in a wheelchair.) As it rained constantly in Oregon during the time scheduled to shoot the scene, the veteran's shoot was moved to Arizona.

The First Unit found Richard, the veteran who appeared in the scene, in a Phoenix, Arizona, veterans' clinic. He was the only veteran who wanted to do the shot. Though not physically disabled, he did have emo-tional problems. Like the other veterans, Richard didn't want to appear in a wheelchair, but, said Weinschenker, "He needed the money." Wein-schenker added, "He was a nice guy who couldn't cope with society. He had done drugs." Winkler was not comfortable with placing a veteran who was not physically disabled in a wheelchair. The contradiction between the artifice of such a representation and Weinschenker's professed desire to use "real people" in the spot was all too transparent; the veteran was "real," the nature of his injury was not. Winkler suggested that the scene be shot two ways, one in the wheelchair and one not, and that the decision on which to use be made in editing. Weinschenker did a number of takes of Richard in the wheelchair, but before he could get the second shot without the wheelchair it started to rain and that shot was never done. Winkler said, partly in jest, partly with conviction, "Greg must have planned it that way."[65] During the shooting of the scene, Weinschenker said, the veteran started to cry, although this version is not the one used in the completed spot.[66]

The Native American was cast in Arizona. McMahon wanted to use Will Sampson, the powerful Indian who starred in the film *One Flew Over the Cuckoo's Nest*, but he was unavailable. Instead, she found an Indian actor friend of Sampson's. The Indian was the head of an entertainment family who travelled the world doing tribal dances. He also worked with Indians with alcohol problems. During the shoot, Weinschenker wanted the Indian to hug the motorcyclist, but he discovered that Indians "don't like to hug." Instead, the scene as shot became a lighthearted animated conversation between the two men seated on a grassy hilltop.

The scene of the farmer on the old tractor following the cyclist down the two-lane rural highway was shot in Oregon. The final scene in the spot is a shot of the motorcyclist stopped on a country road as children alight from a yellow school bus and cross in front of him. The last child off, a small blond-haired boy carrying a lunch pail, stops in the middle of the road and turns toward the cyclist, who gives the boy a military salute. This scene, like the one featuring the elderly woman, was not story-boarded. The idea for the scene was generated by Ann Winkler, Kodak's marketing communications specialist, during the shoot. At that point in the shoot, Winkler pointed out to Weinschenker, no kids had been cast for the spot. Winkler and Kodak "wanted kids and dogs."[67] Weinschenker and the crew hated Winkler's suggestion but shot the scene anyway. Wein-schenker set up the scene with the children crossing in front of Greg Blanchard, the motorcycle rider. While they were shooting, one little boy stopped on his own to look at the cyclist. Weinschenker liked that image and recreated the scene, directing Blanchard to salute. At the time of the shoot, the scene did not particularly stand out from the others, and it was not being considered as an ending. According to Kodak's Bruce Wilson, the agency creative people "felt the image was 'hoakey,' but during editing it turned out to be a very powerful ending."[68]

Two alternative endings were shot, but neither was used. Weinschenker felt that the Hollywood Boulevard ending described earlier was poignant but not right for the spot as it developed in editing, where the decision was made to confine the vignettes to the "country" with the possibility that the city footage shot, including the Hollywood Boulevard scene, might comprise a totally separate spot. (This, however, never material-ized.) The other ending, which was not storyboarded, was shot in the same Arizona "ghost town" as the scene featuring the bearded man and collie. In it, the protagonist-rider meets an aging biker. After they circle one another, Blanchard catches up with the aging biker and the two exchange greetings. According to Executive Producer Sid Horn and Kodak's Ann Winkler, although the scene was shot in numerous takes, upon viewing the dailies it was obvious that the scene "did not click."[69] It was discarded.

Lyricist Linda Kaplan, working separately from Weinschenker while he was on the shoot, wrote the lyrics for "America," then waited for the footage to see if the lyrics and images worked well together. If they didn't, Kaplan would adjust the lyrics to fit the images. According to Kaplan, they ended up matching well. Kaplan chose to establish a "Christopher Cross" feeling in the music, rejecting rock and roll.[70]

The First and Second Units together shot "between 40 and 50 thousand feet of film" for the spot.[71] This resulted in a shooting ratio of about 450 feet shot for every foot actually used—a very high ratio by normal na-tionally distributed commercial standards.

The respective skills of director Weinschenker and director of photog-raphy Ron Dexter, who led the First Unit, complemented one another. Weinschenker, who generated the ideas for most of the scenes shot, was particularly adept at working with actors. Dexter, who had an excellent sense of color and composition, was very good at picking up the perfect shot, and brought the "look" of the spot together.[72] Sid Horn's Second Unit brought in many very effective panorama shots.

Editing was done in New York City, with Weinschenker in charge. Kodak's Ann Winkler watched the editing for a few days. She had become emotionally involved in the spot, as had the other participants on the crew, and was reluctant to "let it go" at that time. At various points Weinschenker asked her for "suggestions" as to which scenarios she preferred, but she stayed out of the decision-making process.[73]

The edited spot was post-tested. According to Kodak's Bruce Wilson, Kodak "was trying to be a little more contemporary than in previous campaigns." "America" appeared to achieve this. The spot "tested more positive among younger people than older people, yet it did not test as more 'emotional.' " According to the research, the youth and patriotism theme of "America" was relevant to younger, single viewers who saw the spot. "They could relate," added Wilson.[74]

The spot began airing during Kodak's peak advertising period, the time of year most Americans take their vacations, in the spring and summer 1985. "America" won numerous creative awards, including a 1986 Clio award for Best Original Music with Lyrics; a 1986 *Advertising Age* award for Best Commercial, "Leisure Entertainment" category; Mobius awards for Best Direction, Best Music, and Best Cinematography; an Art Directors Club Certificate of Merit; and a Silver award for Best Original Music with Lyrics at the 1985 International Film and TV Festival.

Viewer Responses

According to Kodak's Bruce Wilson, "The motorcycle community was absolutely ecstatic" about the portrayal of the motorcyclist. Kodak "received hundreds of letters in appreciation of the spot."[75] Ann Winkler noted that Kodak received "less than five negative letters."[76] The response received at the agency was similar. According to Vice President and Creative Supervisor Geraldine Killeen, more letters were received on "America" than for any spot she can remember. Especially praiseworthy were motorcycle riders and motorcycle magazines, who noted the clean-cut image of the cyclist, which "reflected the majority of weekend motorcycle enthusiasts."[77]

Although Bruce Wilson indicated Kodak did not receive "a single letter regarding the Vietnam veteran image," agency lyricist Kaplan noted that the agency did receive a few letters expressing the feeling that viewers did not want to be reminded of the war.[78]

Interpretive Contexts

The "story" embedded in the images, lyrics, and music of "America" may appear at first glance to be seamless. Its lush greens and highly saturated golds and reds, its majestic panoramas, its slow-motion action and slow lap-dissolves, its "kids and dogs" and other warm, friendly, compassionate, fun-loving denizens of rural America, all produce an almost hypnotic, transcendental vision of an American Eden in which the proud "American family" celebrates the sacrosanct American value of individual freedom, represented by the cyclist's journey of personal and geographic discovery. Nonetheless, as John Berger wrote:

No story is like a wheeled vehicle whose contact with the road is continuous. Stories walk, like animals and men. And their steps are not only between narrated events but between each sentence, sometimes each word. Every step is a stride over something not said.[79]

Though "America" director Greg Weinschenker insisted that there was "no story" in the spot and that the motorcycle rider "was to have no preconceived notions about anything," it is clear from the creators' own descriptions of the spot's gestation that narrative "strides" were taken; specific, conscious decisions were made regarding what to include in the spot and what to withhold. On one level, these decisions in practice appear to be more "negative reactive" than active. For example, the alternative ending, with the motorcycle rider sitting on Hollywood Boulevard, tears welling in his eyes as the stark contrast between the purity of the countryside and the coldness of the big city comes to consciousness, was rejected in favor of the theme of the celebration of the heartland.

The conceptualization process in commercial-making is essentially inductive, with the creators troubleshooting individual scenes, rejecting representations that might offend subgroups within the commercial's target audience. On another level, however, the decisions can be seen as ideologically grounded. For example, Weinschenker rejected the possible draft-evader scenario at the outset. However, he subsequently made reference to Vietnam in the scene, filled with pathos, in which the cyclist meets and shakes hands with the "disabled" Vietnam veteran. In what was to become the concluding vignette in the spot, the scene Kodak's Bruce Wilson called the spot's "central image," Weinschenker directed the motorcyclist to throw a military salute to the young boy, last off the school bus, who stopped to stare at the rider.

The inclusion of the Vietnam veteran vignette and the image of the cyclist's military salute in the final version of the spot is significant when considered in the context of the experiences of the two men most responsible for the spot's creation: director Weinschenker and Kodak's marketing communications director for film, Bruce Wilson. Weinschenker characterized himself as a "protester during Vietnam." He did not go to war; his draft lottery number never came up. A friend of Jeff Miller, one of the students killed at Kent State, he had "animosity toward the establishment." He felt his 1970 motorcycle journey across America, the basis for his idea for the spot's theme, produced a change in him, resulting in "a great love for the country and its people."[80] Wilson, who felt the veteran image was "powerful and appropriate" and was concerned only that the handicapped person be presented in a "natural way," served in the Army for four-and-a-half years, although not in Vietnam, and indicated he was in favor of the war.[81]

The "things not said" are part of the story of "America." So too are those things that, having been said, are then wrenched from the hands of their creators and entered into the larger cultural discourse. "Cultures are dramatic conversations about things that matter to their participants, [arguments] about the meaning of the destiny its members share."[82] The creators never have the final word. Their work is alive in the culture, part of its "constituted narrative," appropriated by professional critics and regular viewers alike. It is therefore both intensely personal and political.

One of the most significant applications of themes and symbols by the advertising and public relations storytellers is "the power to create support for ideas and institutions by personalizing and humanizing them."[83] Advertising, like all fictional narrative,

is a mode constantly susceptible to transformation into myth. The creation of a narrative almost always entails the shaping of awkward materials into a smooth, closed structure. And this is the essence of myth. Like bourgeois ideology most narrative . . . denies history, denies material reality as contradictory, and denies the fact of its own production.[84]

The apparent seamlessness of "America" may be interpreted in such a mythic context.

Shortly after "America" began its run in the national television market, one critic, reviewing the spot in *Advertising Age*, the industry's most respected trade publication, undertook to demythologize the spot. The review begins by comparing "America" with a scene from the film *Cabaret*, in which a blond-haired German youth, wearing a Nazi uniform, sings the song "Tomorrow Belongs to Me." The review continues:

What distinguishes the Kodak campaign, entitled "Because Time Goes By," [from other patriotic commercials] is that it manipulates the concept of time as a means of political propaganda. . . .

If the definition of a reactionary is one who tries to reconstruct a romanticized past for an uncertain future, then the Kodak campaign is the most ultraconservative selling job of the '80s. . . . "America" . . . shows a young white man on a motorcycle "setting off to find America." Set in the present, the spot shows little but rustic surroundings and human symbols of a sanitized past.

It's bad enough to show our grinning Everyman encountering a fluffy collie, a weatherbeaten cowboy and a little old lady at a roadside mailbox. But when he starts shaking hands with a crippled Vietnam veteran or yukking it up with a deliriously happy Indian, the spot crosses the line from mere nostalgia to pure demagoguery.

The implication that all past ugliness can be whitewashed for a brighter future is driven home by the final image: As the cyclist stops for a little boy carrying a lunch box, he raises his hand to his forehead and flashes the boy a military salute. It's as if he is saying to his diminutive comrade: "Tomorrow belongs to us."

. . . Freezing moments in time has less to do with sentimental glory than precisely documenting the past. Tomorrow has never belonged to those who misremember yesterday.[85]

The critic, Michael McWilliams, had been reviewing spots on a freelance basis for *Advertising Age* for about a year prior to his review of "America." McWilliams was a conscientious objector during the Vietnam War. He had been drafted and performed two years of alternative service. The issue, argued McWilliams, is "Simply that fifty-five thousand men died there. And that's what's important. Nothing else."[86]

The *Advertising Age* review prompted a strong rebuttal in the "Letters" column of *Advertising Age* from Stephen G. Bowen, at the time executive vice president and general manager, New York, J. Walter Thompson U.S.A. (Bowen was appointed president of J. Walter Thompson U.S.A. in May 1987.) Bowen wrote that McWilliams "has an extraordinarily fertile imagination reminiscent of the defeatists' laments of the national Democratic party during the past two elections." Bowen implied that McWilliams was out of touch with American values that helped elect Ronald Reagan, who campaigned on a platform of optimism and "for a healing of the wounds that kept our society from living up to its promise in the 60s and 70s." Bowen concluded that if McWilliams became enlightened and had an insight, "He should be sure to get it to Ted Kennedy first. He needs it. . . . "[87]

Kodak would have preferred that Bowen not respond to the review. Kodak's own public position was not to respond, a company policy regarding any public debate in reference to one of its commercials. Internally, "No one [at Kodak] understood" how McWilliams could interpret "America" in this way. The Marketing Communications staff thought McWilliams was "a crackpot."[88] Director Greg Weinschenker expressed anger at the review, indicating he could not see how the spot could be interpreted as "Nazi propaganda."[89]

According to McWilliams, "Not a word or a comma was ever changed in any of my *Ad Age* reviews. My editor, Fred Danzig, who had been with

Ad Age for many years, stood behind me in the whole affair."[90] Shortly after the appearance of his "America" review, McWilliams found his work was no longer being accepted for publication by *Advertising Age*, and he began writing about television for *Rolling Stone*.

The deeply personal nature of the varied responses to the images of the Vietnam veteran and the cyclist's military salute in the spot's final scene were brought into clearer focus by a colleague to whom the author showed the 60-second version of "America." The colleague, himself able to avoid military service through a student deferment, found the imagery in the spot "profoundly troubling, calling into question one's own actions and decisions made during the war. It revives unresolved conflicts about personal ethics."[91]

These varied responses to the Vietnam War in particular and to militarism in general point to the power of public imagery to evoke cultural discourse that is profound, contentious, and psychologically complex. In a commercial, as in a photograph, "The *seen*, the revealed, is the child of both appearances and the search. . . . appearances . . . go beyond, they insinuate further than the discrete phenomena they present, and yet their insinuations are rarely sufficient to make any more comprehensive reading indisputable."[92]

Multiple readings must be acknowledged and respected as representing differences in individual perspective. At the same time, the mythology in "America" surpasses these readings—not only the cursory readings of McWilliams and Bowen but also the intentions of the spot's creators. A closer examination of the signification, representation, and ideology embedded in the mythic constructs of "America" will reveal the discursive practices in the text, its "ideological work."

Kodak is "about" photography. "Photographed images do not seem to be statements about the world so much as pieces of it, miniatures of reality that anyone can make or acquire."[93] Kodak's vision, to create a nation of casual snapshooters and "serious amateur" photographers, relies heavily on this distinction between "making statements" and the capturing and preserving of raw "reality." The photograph "seems to have a more innocent, and *therefore more accurate*, relation to visible reality than do other mimetic objects" like paintings and drawings [emphasis added].[94] Beyond this appearance of the accurate reporting of reality, "Photographs actively promote nostalgia. Photography is an elegiac art, a twilight art. Most subjects photographed are, by virtue of being photographed, touched with bathos."[95]

The combination of the seemingly real and the sentimental mystifies that which is photographed. The camera "can bestow authenticity upon any set of appearances, however false. The camera does not lie even when it is used to quote a lie. And so this makes the lie *appear* more truthful."[96] In advertising "The lie is constructed before the camera."[97]

The mystifying power of the photograph is ideally suited to the construction of mythology. The elegiac quality of "America," its bathos, is firmly rooted in the mythology of the American Eden. Kodak celebrates the Jeffersonian ideal of the honest ordinariness of the rural American, whose "good" labor and desire for community are morally superior to the vices of idleness, diversion, and intemperance of his urban brothers. Jefferson's ideal citizen was the diligent democratic husbandman, who could earn an independent living and participate in the civic life of a community of self-governing relative equals. Like the Puritans, Jefferson feared and abhorred the utilitarian individualism associated with the economic man of cities and industrialization and characterized by the "spirit of enterprise and the right to amass wealth and power for oneself."[98]

The mythic hero in American culture "must leave society [the Metropolis], alone or with one or a few others, in order to realize the moral good in the wilderness, at sea, or on the margins of settled society."[99] Though Kodak's hero, the cyclist-wanderer, sets off to find America and to "realize the moral good in the wilderness," he comes from nowhere. Existing outside history, he does not bear the taint of the Metropolis, of the American technological and military hegemony that was used for class subordination in the industrial city, projection of class war outward into racial war against Native Americans on the borders, and subsequently for creation of a vast international economic and political empire following World War II.[100] References to the city as a "cold place" with its implicit sociopolitical implications of unbridled commercial power, class and race warfare, and lack of community were removed from the spot by eliminating the Hollywood Boulevard ending.

The history of the nineteenth-century conquest of Native Americans and the mythic ideological frame that rationalized it is glaringly absent from the discourse of "America." This complex mythic ideological system, consisting of two dominant readings of history, agrarianism and progressivism, provided an intellectual justification for American expansionism. The agrarian ideology of the Jeffersonians was "an antidote to the class anthipathies generated by industrialization," substituting "the cultivation of the land, the interaction of man with pure and inanimate nature, for the human conflict of Indian dispossession."[101] The accompanying literary mythology of agrarianism saw the brutal Indian wars of the eighteenth and nineteenth centuries as an unpleasant prelude to the story of clearing and cultivating the soil by democratic farmers. The literary mythology of the Progressives, on the other hand, saw "the naturalness and inescapability of violence arising when two countries or races compete for the same territory."[102]

In either case, Native Americans' claims to the vast frontier and wilderness lands were invalidated in the name of progress and "manifest destiny." True, Jefferson promised Native American leaders in 1809 that:

We will never do an unjust act toward you. On the contrary, we wish you to live in peace, to increase in numbers . . . and furnish food for your increasing numbers. . . . We wish to see you possessed of property, and protecting it by regular laws. . . . all our people . . . look upon you as brethren, born in the same land and having the same interests.[103]

But there was a price. Native Americans would have to shift from hunting to farming, thereby reducing the landholdings they would need to support their own increasing population while opening frontier lands to accommodate the increasing white-settler population.[104] Jefferson's desire to accomplish this land transfer justly and nonviolently ignored both Native Americans' sacred ties to the land and the drives of the Metropolitan machinery of capitalism for continual resource exploitation.

Native Americans' status as marginal people living on the social and cultural periphery of Anglo America continues to the present. In the mid-1950s, under a U.S. government policy of "relocation," Native Americans began moving en masse from the reservations to selected cities, among them Los Angeles, Seattle, San Francisco, and Minneapolis, in anticipation of receiving education and job training. Many of those who signed up for these programs were placed in rundown Army barracks and given little or no training. Many didn't speak English. The problems of the reservations—poverty, poor health, alcoholism, and suicide—followed Native Americans to the cities. Today, over half of the 1.4 million Native Americans live in metropolitan areas, where they have assumed the status of an urban underclass. There are great fears in the Native American community that these displaced persons are losing the "spiritual path" as they become assimilated into urban culture.

The nineteenth-century visual representations of Native Americans portrayed them as the colorfully primitive, gloriously doomed uncivilized.[105] Kodak's "America," in its own mystifying construction, portrays the Native American as an ideal Jeffersonian citizen living in Edenic bliss, unproblematically anchored in the vast space of the American wilderness.

"America" is equally mystifying in its representation of the American farm. Images of lush farmland are combined with a shot of a farmer sitting high atop an anachronistic tractor, following the cyclist down a winding two-lane country road. The images evoke memories of the family farm and a simple agrarian life. These images belie not only the contemporary economic and political struggles of family farmers but also the social history of American agriculture. In fact, the images of the farm and the farmer offered by the spot accomplish their ideological work by mythologizing a preexisting myth.

The continued expansion of the "corporate farm" and its subsumption of the small family farm, excluded from Kodak's vision of the heartland, is not unique to the twentieth century. Nineteenth-century American bourgeois development belied the extant mythology linking national prosperity with the pioneer farmer. In reality, according to historian Richard Slotkin, "The special environment of some frontiers . . . gave . . . agricultural enterprises a particularly monopolistic and tyrannical form that was inimical to the 'individualism' of entrepreneurs."[106] This was especially true of farmers in regions dominated by railroad land companies and small ranchers on range land desired by landowning "oligarchies." Not only did the railroads sell land at vastly inflated rates to individual settlers or organized colonies, they also controlled the best land of the plains region and kept farm holders continually in their debt through manipulation of freight rates. In the South, the main cash crop, cotton, was instrumental in the organization of farming into a system of large plantations. The work of harvesting cotton was accomplished through the institution of slavery. Today's rural working class, among them tenant farmers and migrant farm workers, is largely ignored in contemporary accounts of the "farm crisis." Also ignored is the exploitative relationship between migrant workers and the family farmers glorified in populist mythology. This relationship was exposed more than a quarter-century ago in the CBS Reports documentary "Harvest of Shame."

In the process of reproducing the mythology of the American Eden, Kodak's "America" falls victim to "the general impulse toward . . . malignant possessiveness [which] shows signs of being stronger than ever in American life." According to psychiatrist Robert Jay Lifton, this impulse

is populist in its rural, common-man, anti-cosmopolitan tones, nativist in its easy rage toward whatever is "foreign" and "alien," chauvinistic in its blindly "patriotic" distinction between "us" and "them." It is an impulse that not only runs deep in the American grain but in the universal grain as well. For it is associated with a broader image of restoration—an urge, often violent, to recover a past that never was, a golden age of perfect harmony during which all lived in loving simplicity and beauty.[107]

The need for restoration is grounded in "symbolizations around national virtue and military honor."[108] One of the most powerful of these is that of the "warrior as hero" who functions as "a repository of broad social guilt. Sharing in his heroic mission could serve as a cleansing experience of collective relief from whatever guilt had been experienced over distant killing, or *from the need to feel any guilt whatsoever*" [emphasis added].[109] The insistence on "the continuing purity and guiltlessness of American warriors"[110] is transferred to American society as a whole.

The American ethos has always contained a strong strain of self-righteousness. "In matters of war and national destiny," Lifton wrote, "Americans have always felt themselves to be a 'blessed' or 'chosen people.' "[111] America's post-World War II economic, technological, and military power rendered unpalatable our defeat in Vietnam at the hands of a "third-rate" military power. Those who called into question the American warrior-hero's "purity of mission" were considered by many if not most Americans as disloyal to the American vision.

The draft-evader scenario rejected by Weinschenker at the outset of the conceptualization process would likely have reawakened guilt associated with its conduct. The scenario that did evolve substitutes a recruit for warrior-hero symbolization. The symbolization functions in the spot on both levels described by Lifton. The first level—the cleansing experience of collective relief from the guilt that has been experienced—is contained within the scene featuring the cyclist and the Vietnam veteran in the wheelchair. This scene presents the cyclist's mission as one of reconciliation. He becomes the agent of adjustment, restoring harmony to a country torn apart by the war, welcoming the tainted veteran back into the company of "good men."[112] This scene is placed at the temporal center of the 60-second spot (0:27 – 0:31). The second level—the cleansing experience of collective release from the need to feel any guilt whatsoever—is contained in the spot's final image, the freeze-frame of the cyclist's military salute to the young school boy. Is this young boy another echo of the "warrior-hero-to-be," carrying the American purity of mission into the future? Was the Persian Gulf War, occurring six years after the airing of the Kodak spot, the apotheosis of this system of signification, representation, and ideology?

The warrior images in "America" are a far cry from the narrative of revenge exploited in mainstream theatrical films such as *Rambo*, in which the soldier-hero's retributive actions are decidedly individualistic and ultimately antisocial.[113] Nonetheless, in its quiet way the iconography of redemption in "America" seeks to build ideological consensus around the notion of the retrieval of America's greatness, a legacy of power and control reestablished. By implication, war in general and the Vietnam War in particular are legitimized.

The warrior-hero iconography is a distinctly male iconography. Pure, rational, and strong, the male is the culture's source of stability. His journey is that of the "straight path." "America" is a commercial about the actions of men. The only women in the spot, the elderly woman and the young girls in the school-bus scene, signalize the spot's main action but are not integral to it. The elderly woman's pointing gesture directs the cyclist to the various men with whom he subsequently connects in the remainder of the spot. The four young schoolgirls who run past the cyclist prior to the little boy's entrance in the frame do not acknowledge the cyclist's presence and therefore cannot bond with him. On the other hand, the schoolgirls' presence in the shot serves to announce and frame the subsequent military bonding that does occur between the young boy and the cyclist.

The restorative impulse that motivates "America" is inscribed, in the "Because Time Goes By" caption, over the spot's final image. According to Walter Benjamin,

"The illiterate of the future," it has been said, "will not be the man who cannot read the alphabet, but the one who cannot take a photograph." But must we not also count as illiterate the photographer who cannot read his own pictures? Will not the caption become the most important component of the shot?[114]

Benjamin focuses on the power of captions to direct meaning and thereby to liberate the photographic object from its aura. For me, the "Because Time Goes By" caption works against the mystifying and depoliticizing practices inherent in the commercial, while appearing at first reading to reinforce them. For a critical viewer in post-Vietnam America, the images in this commercial are not innocent ones.[115] This is so precisely because, in spite of the passage of time, the real social relations and human connections evoked in the mythology of the spot are haunting. They refuse to be turned entirely into "art." Benjamin views history as a process of mourning, not in the elegiac sense, but rather as the history of the oppressed brought to present consciousness. Here the dialectic of official or dominant ideology and the "other" history of oppression becomes the source of emergent oppositional ideology. The photographer, a soothsayer predicting the future from remnants of the past, uncovers guilt and names the guilty in his pictures. "America," in spite of its massive, corporate attempt to cover and sanitize the past, ultimately succeeds, for a critical viewer, in doing just the opposite. The restorative impulse in "America" runs counter to the model of "transformation" proposed by Lifton: a model according to which we *confront*, through sustained questioning, the values and symbols that lead to acts of violence; *reorder* our values; and *renew* ourselves through the creative exploration of alternative social forms.[116] These "animating" principles both expose and refute the denial associated with the restorationist impulse.

LIFE UNDER THE COMMERCIAL MICROSCOPE

According to Stanford Research Institute (SRI) senior economist Richard Carlson: "The whole concept of one general ad and one general audience is already dead, and advertisers are just starting to figure that out."[117] The fact is that advertisers "figured that out" some time ago and consequently developed relatively sophisticated audience-testing procedures that have been in use for decades. Critics often assail these procedures as voyeuristic and manipulative, while advertising executives defend them as tools that provide important information about human needs in a rapidly evolving society. The procedures and their ideological implications warrant our closer scrutiny.

On the most basic audience-research level, the advertising agency will test for audience recall—the determination of whether people remember an ad they have recently seen. One method of testing recall is "copy pretesting." On location for a shoot, a member of the production team will shoot still pictures that highlight the progression of the action in the spot. These stills are then transferred onto videotape with some zooms and dissolves used as transitional devices (a still-in-motion technique also frequently used in the historical documentary). This videotape is called a "photomatic." The agency then contracts with an outside supplier to test the photomatic with a target audience. A spot will be bought on a particular show for the photomatic to be aired (usually on UHF television stations in a small number of selected test markets). On the day prior to the show, research people make telephone calls and get a sample of viewers to agree to watch the show. The researchers call back after the show and ask the viewers whether they remembered the ad (a test of unaided recall). If they can't respond yes, the researcher will prod them a bit, asking, "Do you remember the ad for . . . ?' (aided recall). There is another approach, referred to as related recall—the viewer's being able to remember specifically what he or she saw in the ad. If at least 22 to 24 percent of the interviewees have related recall, the ad is considered a success. Obviously this method of analysis is subject to some researcher distortion, for the very nature of the questions asked implies that the researcher must prompt the interviewee to obtain an answer.

A more direct and diagnostic research approach often used by agencies is the mobile-van interview. A van will be driven to a shopping center. People will be asked to enter the van to watch an ad, a screening of the photomatic. Afterward, researcher will ask them diagnostic questions about the ad, such as, "Was the ad humorous? Rate on a scale of zero to five."

Other research approaches widely used in advertising research are motivational research (MR), psychographics, and values and lifestyles (VALS) research. While each has its advocates, psychographics and, more recently, VALS are the dominant approaches in effect today.

In the 1960s Ernest Dichter, who pioneered motivational research in advertising, counseled corporations on the Freudian meanings of products. Dichter and his associates relied on in-depth interviews with individuals or small groups. They administered word-association tests to their interviewees to elicit these deeper psychic meanings. Examples of MR results include people's association of prunes with old maids and of drinking tea with sickness.

Some ad agencies do their own MR by using "focus groups." A therapist/researcher talks to "regular people" around a table, trying to determine their deeper feelings about a product.

These methods have some significant drawbacks for the advertiser. First, they are primarily intuitive; they are not predictive of audience behavior in regard to the actual product being marketed. Second, the sample is so small that it is hardly predictive of the behavior of the population.

In the 1970s another research approach was applied to advertising. Called psychographics (sometimes also termed segmentation research), this approach recognizes that the television audience has split into many disparate segments and tries to identify a particular market segment—members of a specific group of consumers—according to a lifestyle common to or a psychological makeup of that market segment. The ultimate goal of this research approach is to develop a group's so-called psychographic portrait, consisting of generally applicable personal values, attitudes, and emotions. Psychographics moves beyond such often unreliable demographic information as income, age, sex, and place of residence, all of which are incomplete descriptive data rather than interpretive information.

Psychographics employs personal interviews or mail questionnaires as research tools. These are administered to a large sample of the population, which allows a statistical analysis of the responses and ostensibly results in a more objective assessment than does MR.

The results of this research can be presented in a form similar to the following example of the toothpaste market, supplied by Daniel Henninger.[118] According to Henninger, toothpaste buyers can be separated into four distinct psychographic segments: worriers, sociables, sensory people, and independents. Worriers are usually families with children and are concerned about cavities. Crest toothpaste has traditionally positioned its campaigns to reach this group. Crest campaigns are serious, stressing Crest's cavity-prevention record. Sociables are generally young marrieds or singles who are very active and who often are smokers. Ads appealing to this segment are upbeat, light, often use fast cutting, and stress the sex appeal of the active young person with white teeth. Ultra-Brite campaigns are good examples of this approach. Sensory people are generally children who want a pleasing flavor and appearance in their toothpaste. Ad campaigns aimed at this segment may be animated and will likely stress tingly taste or colorful stripes or specks in the toothpaste itself. Finally, there are the independents—price-conscious adults who will listen only to rational arguments and who will buy the least expensive brand of toothpaste that they believe will do the job, often "house brands" that cost less because their manufacturers and distributors don't spend a great amount of money on ad campaigns.

The Stanford Research Institute, after many years of in-depth interviews with consumers, created VALS, a psychographic-type emotional-, social-, and economic-profiling approach to the analysis of American society. Based on extensive SRI interviews, VALS attempts to understand the consumer's general attitude toward life itself. VALS segments adults into eight groups, each with special character-typing. These groups include (1) belongers, who tend to be patriotic, traditional, and stable, who are of all ages, and who are generally quite happy with their lives; (2) achievers—prosperous, middle-aged materialists; (3) emulators—ambitious young adults; (4) sociables—impulsive, narcissistic young adults; (5) experientials—generally young, people-oriented, inner-directed adults; (6) societally conscious, mission-oriented people who have chosen to live simply; (7) survivors—elderly people with little optimism; and (8) sustainers—resentful poor people.[119]

Ad agencies use these categories to develop campaign strategies that will appeal to a combination of these groups. For example, Young & Rubicam, a major user of VALS, prepared a campaign for its personal-computer client, Atari, that would address both the needs of achievers, who want the computers for their children to learn faster, and of the intelligent and committed societally conscious, who have entered the market with the idea of trying to establish computerized cottage industries and who might get turned off if they perceived the machines as taking over from people.

Is psychographic and VALS research a gimmick? Does it tell the ad people anything more than they would have intuited? Is it an invasion of collective privacy?

On the most general level, psychographics and VALS are attempts to predict changes in the scope and direction of our culture's "moral imperative of acquisitiveness," described by Jules Henry earlier in this chapter. According to Henninger, "psychographics is the product of statisticians, sociologists, and psychologists trying to figure out how a shifting market of finite consumption capacity can absorb an endless proliferation of goods and services. For them, computers have replaced the couch."[120]

On a more insidious level, psychographics and VALS appear to be a high-stakes game played by people whose dual objectives are accumulating wealth and possessing others' psyches. Henninger reported a conversation he had had with Shirley Young, director of research for Grey Advertising, in which Young candidly told him "the personality and lifestyle data . . . allow us to become voyeurs into the psyche of the consumer."[121]

Do these researchers need to pry into our very souls for the purpose of profit? Jonathan Price argues no:

For all the research that corporations have done to find out who buys their products and why, . . . for all the sociological jargon that has been Xeroxed, the resulting advertising strategies are often little more than what a good salesman would suggest after a year on the road. Market research prospers simply because people like the obvious to be confirmed before okaying a $3 million ad strategy.[122]

Price's statement should not tempt us to discount the deeper meanings of the very act of conducting this type of research in our society. For the act itself indicates the existence of highly skilled individuals, with advanced degrees from respected educational institutions, who are using relatively sophisticated measurement techniques against the general populace so as to promote a way of life that many of our most respected scholars have argued is ultimately suicidal, as it rapidly depletes natural resources and turns family member against family member and neighbor against neighbor in the struggle to consume and enjoy the elusive "good life." At the very least, the researchers know as much and perhaps more about us than we do about ourselves, which, of course, calls into question our personal control over our own destinies.

TELEVISION COMMERCIALS AND THE CONTRADICTIONS OF EVERYDAY LIFE

As noted earlier, television commercials may, on a deeper level, evoke cultural discourse that is profound, contentious, and psychologically complex. Instrumental audience research, such as that described in the preceding section, is not organized to reveal such discourse. One gets at these "deep structures" of our public commercial symbology only by "close readings" of the texts of advertising in discursive circumstances conducive to such readings, such as formal group discussions framed by specific critically informed questions. The following section recounts such a discussion centered on the images in the Kodak "America" commercial.

The way we position ourselves as subjects within our culture is often complex, with varying degrees of expressed or suppressed ambivalence towards images of desire in that culture. Family values, religion, social class, professional goals, how we express ourselves in certain settings (a university setting, for instance)—all play a part in how we talk about social issues. All of these factors came into play in two focus-group discussions of the Kodak "America" commercial led by Bernard Timberg and this author with student volunteers from Timberg's Broadcast Criticism class at Rutgers University, Newark, during the spring of 1989.[123]

In the discussion of the focus groups we see different sources of influence, thought, and value in conflict. The dialogue and debate over the Kodak imagery and its meaning creates, in Volosinov's terms, an ideological terrain bridged by the words and actions of the participants. This is the way Volosinov describes verbal communication:

A word is a bridge thrown between myself and another. If one end of the bridge depends on me, then the other depends on my addressee. A word is a territory shared by both addresser and addressee, the speaker and interlocutor. . . . Any *utterance*, no matter how weighty and complete in and of itself, *is only a moment in the continuous process of verbal communication.*[124]

The domain of individual and social meaning, according to Volosinov, is dialogic—contested and continually in the process of being created. There is no hard-and-fast boundary between psyche and ideology from this point of view.

A thought that as yet exists only in the context of my consciousness, without embodiment in the context of a discipline constituting some unified ideological system, remains a dim, unprocessed thought. But that thought had come into existence in my consciousness already with an orientation toward an ideological system and it itself had been engendered by the ideological signs that I absorbed earlier.[125]

Ideologically conditioned thinking in its rawest form Volosinov terms "inner speech."

Closer analysis would show that the units of which inner speech is constituted are certain *whole entities* somewhat resembling a passage of monologic speech or whole utterances. But most of all they resemble the *alternating lines of dialogue.* There was good reason why thinkers in ancient times should have conceived inner speech as *inner dialogue.*[126]

In the dialogue of the students' focus groups we see social speech in the making: thought (inner speech) coming to the fore. As we shall see, certain determinations structure the opinions of the students. These embody, or at times override, "problems" brought to the surface in analytically confronting the commercial's images in a university setting.

To better understand the different "subject positions" from which the students speak, descriptions of the backgrounds of some of the students who played a vocal role in the discussions are provided here.

Enrique began one of the focus-group discussions with a series of strongly held opinions about the Kodak commercial. He was born in 1970 in the United States, six years after his parents and sister had arrived in this country as refugees from Castro's Cuba. He is one of three children and is a biology major at the university. He works in a medical laboratory and would like to go to Yale for graduate school. Enrique's mother is a pharmacist. His father is a quality control inspector. Enrique described his family as "working/middle class." During the focus group discussion, he defined this class fraction:

I consider a lot of middle class working class. I figure if you can take a year off and not work and be happy, well then you're not working class. But if you can't afford to take a year off, then obviously you're working class, and pretty much all of us here are working class.[127]

Though both of Enrique's parents make "good money," after 25 years in this country "they're still struggling." The family's traumatic departure from Cuba in 1964 still marks the family, particularly through the father's memories.

My father, and his parents and my sister, lost their country. They had to leave. They were kicked out. They left because it got worse. But in a real way they were kicked out at their own will. So he [Enrique's father] knows what happens when people don't respect their government.[128]

Enrique describes his father as being "pro-Reagan all the way."

I don't agree with him, but I have to take his word for it when he says what Reagan does with anti-Communism and building up the arms. Even though I don't agree with him, something inside tells me I agree with him because he *does* know better. He always says, "I've seen it happen."[129]

Patriotism, in particular that of a first-generation American citizen, is a very real issue for Enrique. He cites an example.

When I was a child growing up, I used to like to watch baseball [on television] with my dad. In the beginning of the game, when the national anthem was being sung, my father would tell me to stand up. I didn't understand why he insisted on this. I could remember as a child having this "customary ritual" performed before every game I watched. Even today, when the national anthem is being sung, played, or hymned, whether it be in a baseball game or the Olympics, I stand erect and proud until it is completed. People ask me: Why? I simply reply, "Love and respect for your country and freedom." I really believe acts like his helped me become a "proud American."[130]

Even though Enrique's *emotional* identification with his father's patriotism is strong, he does not, as he says, "agree with" many of his father's political positions. He demonstrated a clear understanding of the difference between "dominant" and "oppositional" values in the media. Writing of the Kodak commercial as a discourse in dominance, Enrique noted:

The Kodak commercial is a very good example of dominant imagery. It depicts a motorcyclist's voyage to what seems to be the western United States: a place where things are pure and natural. He symbolizes the great, brave American pioneer in a covered wagon searching for a better life. . . . Symbolic sites of the U.S.

such as mountains, prairies, and fields are being flashed on the screen. Accompanying these sites are stereotypical "honorable Americans": Boy Scouts, Indians, and farmers; all with smiles on their faces. . . . All of these dominant images cause the viewer to get a feeling of security and stability. Good feeling overcomes the viewer. These natural values give Americans pride in themselves and their country. . . . These values lead us to believe there are no opposing images. Everything seems all right. This is what everyone wants to believe, so they do. . . . [These images run counter to] the real world where things aren't always the way they seem.[131]

Throughout the focus group dialogue we see in Enrique the emergence of a clear conflict of two values in the outward articulation of his "inner speech": his analytical awareness of the manipulation of patriotic emotion to cover (and cover up) issues of social injustice and his belief in patriotic emotion (engendered in his close relationship with his father) as a good in itself, as something that builds the nation.

Another student, Adam, takes a very different position regarding the emotion-laden patriotic images of the commercial. Adam was 24 when he attended the focus groups. He comes from an upper-middle-class family of German and Polish Jewish extraction (his parents are second-generation Americans). The family lives in an affluent New Jersey suburb with one of the best educational systems in the state. Adam lived away from his family for four years in New York. During this time he openly acknowledged to his family and friends that he was gay. He returned to live with his family for economic reasons, an arrangement he made with his father until he finished his B.A. degree in theater arts at the university. Adam describes himself as largely unaware, until recently, of the educational and economic privileges he grew up with.

Clearly alienated from many of his parents' values, at the same time he is a high achiever at school (he was a National Merit Scholarship finalist in high school). If anyone in the group represented a consistent "oppositional" response to the images in the Kodak commercial, it was Adam. He responded sharply to the comments of two other students (Carlos, an Ecuadorian, who had been in this country from the age of nine, and Raymond, a black Haitian American) that *they* were able to identify with the motorcyclist despite his blond, WASP looks.

Carlos: You can't tell what income family this guy [motorcycle rider] comes from. He could be a regular guy working in a factory, and he takes off for a month and he's going through the country on a bike. Or he can be a regular rich guy. No, I just don't see him as a dominant white American. Just a regular person.[132]

Raymond: It seems like this is a man—it could be any man—that's trying to make a conscious effort to understand different people. I think that's why they show you that Indian, and he's playing with the black guys on the barn, and all that. So I think he's trying to get a general idea of what the American people are like, and not so much into the pride thing and all that. I don't really see any point in the pride. But the image that this commercial is trying to project is that he's always moving.[133]

Adam: Raymond and Carlos don't feel alienated at all by the image of the blond guy on the motorcycle. On the other hand, I feel very alienated by him personally, because I feel that all my life I grew up thinking that I should grow up to be him. And I can't be him. There are various aspects of what he represents that I won't be. And in a way, I feel conflicted because I can't be that fantasy Nordic blond California type with that kind of background. . . . That's Hollywood, and it's trying to sell me some ideals which aren't my own. It's going to make me feel insecure.[134]

Adam is questioned by Carlos, the Ecuadorian who is now a naturalized American citizen and working toward a marketing degree, and Jackie, a first-generation Haitian-American.

Carlos: But that's what the commercial is there for, to manipulate people in any way.

Adam: Yes, it's there to manipulate people, and the way they want to do it is to get people to identify with it, and say, "Oh, yeah, I really like this." Immediately I see that guy and I go "It's him again." I mean, I can't be him.

Jackie: Why do you want to be him? Do you want to be that blond-haired free spirit travelling through the country?

Adam: Do I want to be? There's part of me that wants to be.

Jackie: It's your own personal conflict with the image.[135]

From the start of the discussion, Jackie has been a consistent defender of the commercial against those, like Adam, who attack its constructed images. Adam, Jewish and gay, sees these images of an "ideal" America as taunting and manipulative. Jackie, a black female Haitian-American who is as objectively removed from "being" the motorcycle rider in the commercial as Adam, sees it entirely differently.

I see it as a positive image, a typical America. You don't know if he's rich or poor. He's just an American. He's with the people. You get a feeling of peace and harmony. . . . Throughout the whole commercial, you see him on the same level with everybody . . . All the people that are oppressed in this country: the Indian, the veteran, the elderly . . . and are treated like they are lower than everybody else, you see him interacting with them. . . . So when other people are saying that this is a big blond promoting white supremacy, when you look at it, it's not.[136]

Others in the group press Jackie on this point:

Timberg: But these are happy images.

Jackie: When you look at the vet, it's not like he's overjoyed. He's just there.

Timberg: The vet's not [happy]. Everyone else is super friendly. . . . I would be suspicious, just in a logical way, of everyone beaming and smiling and welcoming you.

Jackie: That's a positive image. What do you want, for them to show you a commercial where they are negative?

John: It is really strange that they're all smiling at you.[137]

Ultimately, what Jackie appears to be defending, in addition to the underlying values of community, equality, and interracial and interclass harmony the commercial celebrates, is the right to escape into an ideal world, a world of unquestionable "ideals." An exchange between Jackie and Ruth, a Haitian-American in her mid-twenties, in the first focus group meeting underlines the issue.

Ruth: Here I am living in Newark, and I witness the opposite of what is on the commercial every day. Coming to school, I see homeless people in the streets, drugs, and pregnant teenage mothers. All these things. But it didn't hit me until we started analyzing the commercials.

Jackie: Being that I live in New York City, I see the homeless in trains every day. I don't want to come home and turn it on on my TV. I don't want to think about it any more. It's just depressing. That's why I don't really see anything wrong with that commercial. Why do you have to look at depressing things? You can leave it outside. Why can't you come home and just enjoy a nice commercial?[138]

Jackie, 18, is the youngest of four children and a freshman at Rutgers-Newark. She is Haitian on her mother's side, Italian-Haitian on her father's. She describes her family as working middle class, her parents having worked their way up from the "lower class" status of her grandparents' generation. Jackie is described by a classmate as "very ambitious and determined to reach goals set out for herself," the principal one of which is to become a lawyer. At the same time she defends the patriotic, pastoral values of the Kodak commercial ("they [the makers of the commercial] know that parents aren't instilling values of nationalism and patriotism, so they're trying to represent this through the commercial"[139]), she is well aware that television is selective in its portrayals. This is especially important to her when those portrayals focus on black experience in America.

They don't want to advertise Malcolm X because a lot of politicians didn't agree with what he was saying. Showing a picture of him would be like they were promoting . . . his views. They would rather show Martin Luther King, because he

was passive, he was a Reverend, he was for the people. But you don't see Martin
Luther King's pictures or speeches on TV. Only during black history month.
They'll start showing a few McDonald's commercials or Coke commercials [fea-
turing blacks]. That's when you'll see images of black politicians. Aside from that
you won't.[140]

But then, in the next sentence, Jackie seems to justify commercial television's exclusion of black culture and black political expression in a
white-dominated culture. "Aside from black history month, you'll never
see Jessie Jackson, because they don't want to promote that. . . . The country's not run by blacks. Why would they promote black imagery?"[141]

When she is pressed, yet another side of Jackie's thinking emerges: "It
doesn't have to be that way. It's really annoying when you sit down and
think about it. When you sit down and watch TV things like that don't
come to mind. But when you sit down and *really* think about it."[142]

Which side is the true Jackie? The one that acknowledges the exclusion
of black experience from commercial television? The one that feels that
such exclusion is perfectly natural in a dominant culture forged, primarily,
by whites? Or the one that is outraged by this exclusionary policy when
she stops to "think about it"? All these voices, to one degree or another,
"speak" within a matter of minutes—in contradiction, in conflict with
each other.

Meaning, "inner speech" externalized, sets itself forth here in a process
of negotiation. In Enrique's case, the voice of first-generation patriotism
(instilled and reinforced by his family, particularly by his father) is in direct
conflict with the voice of a second-generation political analysis. Adam has
clearly spent time analyzing and coming to terms with the contradictory
voices in his head. He details rather clearly the cultural forces that often
place him in a contradictory and, as he puts it, impossible-to-obtain relationship to the social ideals and values placed before him. Some of the
"trying out" of social positions Jackie engages in could be attributed to
the university setting in which students are expected to try out ideas.
Viewing in a family context, as Morley points out, may be quite different
and creates another range of possibilities for trying out social positions.[143]

Jackie's defense of the Kodak commercial can be seen not only in terms
of a simple defense of "escape," but also, on another level, as a defense
of the imagination itself. She relishes the ability to, in de Certeau's words,
"poach"[144]—to take and rearrange the "furniture" (i.e., symbology) of the
commercial, as Raymond and Carlos have done, and make it uniquely
hers. No one else's analysis (rearrangement) should be able to supersede
hers.

Ruth's pattern of viewing is quite different. She also "poaches" on
mainstream imagery in the media but tends to relate it immediately and
directly to her own experiences of the world. Although she is Haitian-

American, Ruth's early childhood was spent in West Africa. Her father's parents are from southern Haiti, and her mother's parents are from Peru and the Dominican Republic. She is the oldest in a family of four, the second generation on her father's side to attend college. A single mother of a one-year-old child, Ruth moved in with her family after separating from her husband. She describes her socioeconomic background as "middle class, but now that I've become a single mother things are different; my financial and economic situation places me in the lower class."

In the focus group discussions, Ruth was often relating or contrasting images from the screen to people she had known, places she had been, and things she had seen or experienced. In response to the image of the Vietnam veteran in "America," for instance, she said:

I used to date somebody that was a Vietnam veteran. He was discharged. I skimmed [the image] and didn't even look at it. But now that you bring it up, it does make me angry. He told me in detail what they went through. They kept asking themselves what am I here for? They killed other human beings. And the fact that they were doing this for the people *here*. And they didn't know what reaction they were going to get once they arrived home. And when he got home, he was totally isolated by his whole family, his friends. Coming home was the biggest disillusion for him. He thought he would have people welcoming him home. Plus the fact that he was handicapped. He was blinded in one eye. Another day I was with my daughter in New York, and this veteran in a wheelchair was passing out rainbow puzzles to little kids . . . saying "God loves America, God loves me."[145]

Ruth's compassion, based on her personal experience, could lead one to interpret her reading of the veteran vignette in "America" as essentially sympathetic. However, the anger in her voice belied this. It was as if she was saying the image is too "easy," that much has been left unspoken in the history of images dealing with the survivors of Vietnam.

Most of all Ruth notices and thinks about children on television, relating them to her own position as a single mother.

Children are one of the most oppressed groups in society. They show these little white kids [in "America"]—they're all white—and they're running out of this bus, all carefree. And I think to myself—all of these images start coming up to my mind—about children being abused, child abuse. The fact that many children in this country do not get a decent education. A lot of kids don't get to go to school. A lot of children are malnourished. This whole bit about patriotism, with children being brought up in American society where they don't really know where they are heading. We're not quite sure of where we're going. Children are also the poorest members of our society. So, Kodak is not showing the "real" child or children of America.[146]

Ruth's response here seems clearly "oppositional." But she too harbors contradictory feelings. She describes herself as having gone through a process that opened her eyes to the falsity of "America" and other commercials, coming to see (in part as a response to issues raised in Timberg's Broadcast Criticism class) social and political divisions in society that gave certain groups vested interest in the imagery.

Ruth: If I hadn't taken this course, I probably would have felt pretty wonderfully (about the commercial). But this course has sort of enlightened me on this, and right now I'm just sort of turned off by it. When we started analyzing this commercial and started asking questions. . . . I noticed the whole class's reactions. There was always some sort of conflict in the class over certain things.

Himmelstein: Defending class and race positions?

Ruth: Yes. The class was divided into cliques. One side was sort of "all American." . . . The other side of the class was minorities. And then we had "liberal-minded" people in the middle.

Timberg: The battle really surfaced [when the class watched *Consuming Hunger*, a documentary criticizing Western broadcast news reporting of the 1984 Ethiopian famine and the "Live Aid" and "Hands Across America" media events] when the African diplomat made his statement that "We don't want your charity. We want to speak for ourselves. We don't want to be used as images." And there were some people who got really mad.

Ruth: You know, I don't blame them at all. They're expressing their own opinions. But it is society's fault that they are conditioned to think that way.[147]

At the end of the statement, Ruth shifts ground. She moves to the level of an analyst, and ends up empathizing, interestingly, with the "all-American" students in the class. Ruth also speaks in several voices, then. One analyzes the unreality of dominant imagery and condemns it for its neglect of the suffering, struggling children of the world; another voice steps back and analyzes the divisions of the class sociologically; another empathizes with the students who have been "conditioned" to see Africans (and by extension African-Americans and other blacks) as victims and wards of society.

Clearly, the students profiled in this study see and understand the Kodak commercial through a series of different filters and through a series of contradictory views that they themselves sometimes acknowledge. Simple categorical terms that classify decoding practices—dominant, negotiated, oppositional—begin to break down in the praxis of this discussion. We begin to see how much more complicated decoding is—that these students can support oppositional and dominant impulses at the same time and that the negotiation of meaning is a constant and ongoing process.

Contradictions, not one-to-one correspondences between race, class, and social position, are central to the construction of meaning. The struggle detailed in the production history of the making of the Kodak "America" commercial, presented earlier in this chapter—a struggle for a cohesive world of institutional and artistic symbols that would resonate with a mass audience—has a flip side: a struggle to accept, adapt, confront, inhabit, or poach upon these images when they appear on the television screen at home or in a classroom setting. Clearly the focus-group discussions recounted here activated, sharpened, and clarified contested areas of meaning. By speaking these inner voices and airing contradictions, participants in the discussion assumed a little more power over the images in this commercial, and, by implication, over the ur-images of American popular culture in general.

The study of this one small group of viewers is but one step along a path that demands a much deeper and fuller appreciation of cultural and political contradiction, of how meaning is worked out dialogically. Direct observation in lived environments and interviews *en famille*, for example, can add valuable sketches of family role playing in viewing situations.

This discussion concludes with an exchange that occurred in the middle of the second focus-group discussion. The exchange centered on Enrique and Adam, but others also contributed to it.

Timberg: Does the patriotism of this commercial affect you in a different way?

Enrique: Yeah. I'm glad it exists, because I think it's important to put that into the people. Because we're all Americans. And when someone asks you what you are, I say "American." Then they say, "Hey, where're your parents from?" "They're Cuban." We're Americans, and yet you probably say, "Oh, I'm Irish" or "I'm Italian." And I think that these commercials will bring that out. But I'm glad *I* don't see it that way. I'm glad that I look at it differently. But I'm glad that *other* people look at it to get that pride, because I think that's important. But I'm glad I'm not fooled.

Adam: So you're saying you're glad other people believe what it says, but you're glad you don't believe what it says.

Enrique: It's a false pride.

Adam: Why should other people get pumped up on false pride?

Enrique: Because it's better to have them believe those lies than have them believe other things that . . .

Adam (interrupting): So you're saying that the people aren't smart enough to figure out that they're lies . . .

Enrique (interrupting): No, not smart enough. Maybe not informed enough. Because I wasn't smart enough to see that either until we had the class.

Adam: So in other words you're saying that the great mass of people in this country are ignorant enough to believe this artificial . . .

Enrique (interrupting): No, not ignorant. You're calling me ignorant because I was not informed.

Adam: I use ignorant as the "not informed" meaning of the word. You're glad that they all don't know enough, or don't have enough information to see that this is all just hype and a media message. And you're glad that they are taken in by this, and that they believe it, but you're glad that you do have enough information to realize that . . .

Enrique: I'm glad that there's some way to put pride—whether you want to call it pride or beliefs or faith—into the people. Whether this is true or not is not as important as the fact that the purpose is carried out, which is obvious in everything. Whether it is true or not, the point of the commercial gets carried through. That's more important than whether it's true or not. But I'm glad that I don't see this, because maybe if I saw it beforehand, and I realized it beforehand, I would say "How could anybody believe this? They're stupid." But no. The first time I saw the commercial, I said, "Wow! That's good." But now, after all these discussions, I see what it's really about. I'm glad that I can see it differently, because next time it happens I'll know what to see, what to expect, and what not to believe. I'm not trying to say that I'm better than people out there.[148]

In Enrique's steadfast maintenance of two opposing sets of ideas and values at the same time we have the daily experience of many Americans. If we accept that the first step to living with or resolving a contradiction is to bring it squarely to consciousness, to acknowledge our possession of different "subject positions," then Enrique has taken that first step. What the next step is, how the contradiction is or is not resolved, will depend ultimately on which subject positions are "more powerful or generative."[149]

SOME FINAL THOUGHTS ON COMMERCIAL CULTURE

Erich Fromm perceived the cumulative impact of commercial culture as intensely negative.[150] He believed that ads mold one's personality, just as do the institutions of school, church, and family. Ads do this, according to Fromm, through an insidious process of "semihypnotic" suggestion that is "demogogic." It attempts to break down a person's rationality and critical sensibilities and then in essence to force the person to accept anything. He saw this as the opposite of the act of convincing—providing rational arguments as to the value of something.

In the previous section we underscored the struggles of students to negotiate meaning in the texts of television commercials in an attempt to answer the question "Do people really *believe* what the ads tell them?" Fromm's response to this question is, "Yes and no." People know the claims "are all nonsense," but at the same time, "They would like to hope that there might be something to [them], and so we have an experience which is not clearly that of differentiating between reality and fantasy, but reality and fantasy become mixed up."[151]

This semihypnotic magic land located on the edge of the real is brilliantly revealed by Marshall McLuhan in his seminal 1951 discussion of print media, *The Mechanical Bride*:

The ad agencies function in relation to the commercial world much as Hollywood does in respect to the world of entertainment. In his cogent study, *The Hollywood Hallucination*, Parker Tyler summed it up in a sentence: "The movie theater is the psychoanalytic clinic of the average worker's daylight dream." That is, the spectator dreams in the darkened theater. He dreams the dreams that money can buy but which he can neither afford nor earn in the daylight world. . . .

So Hollywood is like the ad agencies in constantly striving to enter and control the unconscious minds of a vast public, not in order to understand or to present these minds, as the serious novelist does, but in order to exploit them for profit. The novelist tries to get inside his characters in order to tell you what is happening on the invisible stage of their minds. The ad agencies and Hollywood, in their different ways, are always trying to get inside the public mind in order to impose their collective dreams on that inner stage. . . . The ad agencies flood the daytime world of conscious purpose and control with erotic imagery from the night world in order to drown, by suggestion, all sales resistance. Hollywood floods the night world with daytime imagery in which synthetic gods and goddesses (stars) appear to assume the roles of our wakeaday existence in order to flatter and console us for the failures of our daily lives. . . .

The ad agencies and Hollywood turn themselves unwittingly into a sort of collective novelist, whose characters, imagery, and situations are an intimate revelation of the passions of the age. But this huge collective novel can be read only by someone trained to use his eyes and ears, and in detachment from the visceral riot that this sensational fare tends to produce. The reader has to be a second Ulysses in order to withstand the siren onslaught. . . . Without the mirror of the mind, nobody can live a human life in the face of our present mechanized dream.[152]

McLuhan, as did Jules Henry and Erich Fromm, appealed to our rationality as adults in the effort to stem the tide of increasing fantasy invading our workaday world. Unfortunately one must begin to resist in childhood—no easy task.

Jonathan Price summarized social science findings regarding children's cognitive development and its relation to advertising. When the child is five or six years old, he has difficulty distinguishing fantasy and reality, make-believe and lying. He does not doubt adults. He often confuses the programs with the commercials but does not seem to be particularly harmed by the commercials. Between seven and ten years of age, the child is most vulnerable to televised manipulation; by age seven he can usually distinguish reality and fantasy; by age nine he has asked for many products, received them, been disappointed in their performance, but still has high hopes; he might suspect deception in the commercials, based on his personal experience with the product, but cannot articulate the exact nature of that deception; by age ten many children decide that commercials lie. Thus, commercials become harmful because they turn the child into a cynic. By ages 11 and 12, the child develops more balanced views; he begins to understand the purpose of commercials and seems more willing to tolerate adults' lies in commercials. This is the real birth of the adolescent's acculturation into a system of social hypocrisy.[153]

According to social theorist Jacques Ellul, a human environment is good or natural when it satisfies man's basic material needs if it also leaves him free to use the environment as a means to fulfill his individual spiritual needs.[154] We have noted in this chapter how the institution of advertising in our advanced capitalist society appears to be continually usurping those individual spiritual needs through a substitutional process that equates human worth with material goods. At the same time, we have noted the individual's struggles against such usurpation.

Advertising has become one of our culture's primary educational tools; according to Jules Henry, "The function of education has never been to free the mind and the spirit of man, but to bind them . . . for where every man is unique there is no society . . . for originality, by definition, is different from what is given, and what is given is the culture itself."[155]

The genres of television programs discussed in succeeding chapters will reveal themselves to spring from the culture, as does advertising, using a particular language to develop a secular mythology guided, often unconsciously, by our culture's dominant ideology. And programs, like the commercials they frame, reveal much more about our own lives than we are normally willing to admit.

NOTES

1. Jules Henry, *Culture against Man* (New York: Random House, 1963); see especially chap. 3, "Advertising As a Philosophical System," pp. 45–99.

2. Ibid., p. 45.

3. Ibid.

4. Ibid., p. 48.

5. Ken Bode, "Guidelines for Covering Ads As News Stories," *Electronic Media,* February 17, 1992, p. 28.

6. Henry, *Culture against Man*, p. 50.

7. Ibid., p. 76.

8. Ibid., p. 79.

9. Erich Fromm's comments were taken from an interview included in CBS *Reports*: "You and the Commercial," aired on the CBS television network, April 26, 1973.

10. Ibid.

11. Bruce Kurtz, *Spots: The Popular Art of American Television Commercials* (New York: Arts Communications, 1977), p. 10.

12. Marshall McLuhan, "Television in a New Light," in *The Meaning of Commercial Television*, ed. Stanley T. Donner (Austin, TX: University of Texas Press, 1967), p. 104.

13. Jonathan Price, *The Best Thing on TV: Commercials* (New York: Penguin Books, 1978), p. 6.

14. Ibid., p. 2.

15. Kurtz, *Spots*, p. 30.

16. Ibid., p. 27.

17. Ibid., p. 28.

18. Ibid., p. 55.

19. Ibid., p. 108.

20. Michael J. Arlen, *Thirty Seconds* (New York: Farrar, Straus and Giroux, 1979), p. 158. In this book, Arlen presents a fascinating look at the making of a single television commercial.

21. Mircea Eliade, *Myth and Reality* (New York: Harper and Row, 1963), p. 18.

22. Price, *Commercials*, p. 161.

23. John R. Cashill has skillfully described many of these secular myths operating in television advertisements in an informative essay, "Packaging Pop Mythology," in *The New Languages*, ed. Thomas H. Olgren and Lynn M. Berk (Englewood Cliffs, NJ: Prentice-Hall, 1977), pp. 79–88.

24. Ibid., p. 84.

25. Ron Rosenbaum, "The Hardsell: How TV Ads Talk Tough in the New Troubled Times," *Mother Jones*, December 1981, p. 30.

26. Ibid.

27. Fromm, from "You and the Commercial."

28. Roland Barthes, "Myth Today," in *Mythologies* (New York: Hill and Wang, 1972), p. 128.

29. The "Because Time Goes By" theme is an appropriation of a memorable and still resonant older popular culture coding, the nostalgic "As Time Goes By" lyric in the film *Casablanca* (1942). The lyric evokes the memory of a brief, passionate love affair between Rick Blaine (Humphrey Bogart) and Ilsa Lund (Ingrid Bergman) in Paris just prior to the Nazi occupation. As Prefect of Police, Capitaine L. Renault reminded Rick, "Under that cynical shell, you're at heart a sentimentalist." A similar appropriation, but with a sardonic twist, is the theme song of the 1970s social comedy *All in the Family*, "Those Were the Days."

30. Conversation with Sid Horn, former Executive Producer, J. Walter Thompson U.S.A., and Second Unit Director, "America," October 8, 1987. (Horn left the agency at the end of 1987.)

31. Conversation with Ann Winkler, Marketing Communications Specialist, Eastman Kodak (1980–1986), October 14, 1987. Since these spots were introducing Kodak's Kodacolor VR film, the product-benefits approach could not be completely ignored.

32. The only key person directly involved in the spot's creation who declined an interview was the director of photography, Ron Dexter. Dexter indicated his busy production schedule prevented his participation in the study.

33. "America" is clearly a very high cost commercial by contemporary stan-

dards. Its six-week shooting schedule and approximately 450:1 shooting ratio led the author to estimate the cost to produce the spot in excess of $500,000.

34. Richard W. Stevenson, "Red, White and Blue Is Out," *New York Times,* March 16, 1987, p. D4.

35. Ibid.

36. Conversation with Warren Milich, Account Supervisor on "America," J. Walter Thompson U.S.A., May 8, 1987.

37. Bruce Wilson, at the time Kodak's Marketing Communications Director for Film, believed that the political climate in the country was right for an emotional approach. His immediate supervisor, Jack Powers, at the time the Director of Marketing Communications for Consumer Products, felt on the other hand that a product-benefits approach would be more successful. Wilson's view prevailed in the ensuing discussions. The spots would be produced to appeal more to emotions, with less emphasis on touting the specific benefits of Kodak films.

38. Conversation with Warren Milich.

39. Ibid.

40. Ibid.

41. Ibid.

42. Conversation with Loomis Irish, Professor of Television and Radio, Brooklyn College of the City University of New York, and an executive for many years with Batten, Barton, Durstein and Osborne, April 29, 1987.

43. Conversation with Mitchell Brooks, Account Director on the Eastman Kodak account, J. Walter Thompson U.S.A., May 6, 1987.

44. Conversation with Bruce Wilson, Director Marketing Communications and Support Services for Consumer Products, Eastman Kodak, May 8, 1987. Kodak's marketing philosophy should not be generalized to all "heartland" companies, however. Some practitioners note that certain heartland companies, such as 3M and B. F. Goodrich, have supported controversial programs on Vietnam and China, while more "urban" East Coast companies such as General Electric and DuPont have scrupulously avoided controversy.

45. Conversations with Sid Horn and Ann Winkler.

46. Traditionally in the advertising business, an idea on how to proceed with a campaign often was agreed upon by agency executives and clients over a game of golf or on a fishing trip. This was particularly true with family-owned clients and publicly owned companies with a very secure senior management that had a clearly articulated company philosophy on the perception of the American "reality."

47. Conversation with Loomis Irish.

48. Conversation with Bruce Wilson.

49. Kodak's organization of its marketing division is highly unusual for a large corporation. The division is divided into two distinct units, marketing and marketing communications. Marketing's primary functions include pricing of products, developing sales programs, and financial planning. Marketing communications, on the other hand, employs "communication specialists" working solely on advertising for all "paid communication." These communication specialists are involved in overseeing the advertising production process.

50. Conversation with Bruce Wilson.

51. Ibid. In *Thirty Seconds,* an eyewitness account of the "Reach Out" cam-

paign for American Telephone and Telegraph (AT&T), author Michael J. Arlen indicates that final approval of the spots was given by an AT&T corporate vice president in charge of public relations. Although the lines of decision-making authority may differ from corporation to corporation, it is clear that the ultimate decision to air or not air a spot is made at the highest level of the client management structure—in Kodak's case, at the very top.

52. Conversation with Loomis Irish.

53. Conversation with Greg Weinschenker, Director, "America," J. Walter Thompson U.S.A., April 11, 1987.

54. Arlen, *Thirty Seconds*, p. 7.

55. Conversation with Greg Weinschenker.

56. Conversation with Bruce Wilson. In all fairness, it is hard to imagine that any client would accept such a draft-evader scenario.

57. Conversation with Sid Horn.

58. Conversations with Bruce Wilson and Ann Winkler. The client pays the cost to shoot the commercial. Kodak Marketing Communications Specialist Winkler was on the shoot and monitored production costs along with J. Walter Thompson Executive Producer Sid Horn. Horn was highly regarded by Kodak as being "very budget-conscious."

59. Dan Steinbock, *Television and Screen Transference* (Helsinki: Finnish Broadcasting Company, 1986), pp. 64–66.

60. Conversation with Sid Horn.

61. Conversation with Ann Winkler.

62. Conversation with Greg Weinschenker.

63. Conversation with Loomis Irish.

64. Conversation with Sid Horn.

65. Conversation with Ann Winkler.

66. Conversation with Greg Weinschenker.

67. Conversation with Ann Winkler.

68. Conversation with Bruce Wilson.

69. Conversations with Sid Horn and Ann Winkler.

70. Conversation with Linda Kaplan, Group Creative Director and Lyricist, J. Walter Thompson U.S.A., March 4, 1987.

71. Conversation with Greg Weinschenker.

72. Conversation with Sid Horn.

73. Conversation with Ann Winkler.

74. Conversation with Bruce Wilson.

75. Ibid.

76. Conversation with Ann Winkler.

77. Conversation with Geraldine Killeen, Vice President and Creative Supervisor, J. Walter Thompson U.S.A., April 13, 1987.

78. Conversations with Bruce Wilson and Linda Kaplan.

79. John Berger, *Another Way of Telling*, with Jean Mohr (New York: Pantheon, 1982), pp. 284–85.

80. Conversation with Greg Weinschenker.

81. Conversation with Bruce Wilson.

82. Robert N. Bellah et al., *Habits of the Heart: Individualism and Commitment in American Life* (Berkeley: University of California Press, 1985), p. 153.

83. Doris E. Fleischman and Howard Walden Cutler, "Themes and Symbols," in *The Engineering of Consent*, ed. Edward L. Bernays (Norman, OK: University of Oklahoma Press, 1955), p. 144.

84. Gil Davies, "Teaching about Narrative," *Screen Education* 29 (Winter 1978–79):70.

85. Michael McWilliams, "Kodak Ads Strain Credulity," *Advertising Age*, August 26, 1985, p. 52.

86. Conversation with Michael McWilliams, April 29, 1987.

87. Stephen G. Bowen, "Letter to the Editor," *Advertising Age*, September 23, 1985, p. 20.

88. Conversation with Ann Winkler.

89. Conversation with Greg Weinschenker.

90. Conversation with Michael McWilliams.

91. Conversation with Drewery McDaniel, Professor of Telecommunications, Ohio University, October 10, 1986.

92. Berger, *Another Way of Telling*, p. 118.

93. Susan Sontag, *On Photography* (New York: Delta, 1977), p. 4.

94. Ibid., p. 6.

95. Ibid., p. 15.

96. Berger, *Another Way of Telling*, pp. 96–97.

97. Ibid., p. 96.

98. Bellah et al., *Habits of the Heart*, p. 28.

99. Ibid., p. 144.

100. Richard Slotkin, *The Fatal Environment: The Myth of the Frontier in the Age of Industrialization, 1800–1890* (Middletown, CT: Wesleyan University Press, 1985), pp. 51–52.

101. Ibid., p. 52.

102. Ibid.

103. Thomas Jefferson, "Speech to the Chiefs of Various Indian Tribes," in *Modern Eloquence: Political Oratory*, vol. 13, ed. Thomas B. Reed (Philadelphia: John D. Morris, 1903), p. 1267.

104. Advocating the westward expansion of white settlers and recognizing its inevitability, Jefferson nevertheless vowed to protect the Native American against the exploitation of unscrupulous whites, who made a practice of plying Indians with alcohol and getting them to sign over their land. Unlike the Puritans, who saw armed conflict with Native Americans as the inevitable struggle between God-fearing Christians and immoral heathens according to divine order, Jefferson, echoing French policy, envisioned the Indian and the Caucasian intermarrying and forming a single community of noble farmers.

105. Michael Dorris, "Mythmaking in the Old West," *New York Times*, September 21, 1986, pp. 27, 36. See also Slotkin, *The Fatal Environment*, p. 12. Slotkin explores the "industrial and imperial version of the Frontier Myth whose categories still inform our political rhetoric of pioneering progress, world mission, and eternal strife with the forces of darkness and barbarism."

106. Slotkin, *Fatal Environment*, pp. 43–44.

107. Robert Jay Lifton, "Introduction," *America and the Asian Revolutions*, ed. Lifton (New York: Aldine, 1970), p. 4.

108. Robert Jay Lifton, *Home from the War: Vietnam Veterans—Neither Victims nor Executioners* (New York: Simon and Schuster, 1973), p. 132.

109. Ibid.

110. Ibid., pp. 132–33.

111. Ibid., p. 158.

112. The symbolization of reconciliation is firmly rooted in American history. In *The Fatal Environment*, p. 5, Slotkin describes the Fourth of July celebration held in conjunction with the 1876 Centennial Exposition in Philadelphia, which

carried these themes of [national] growth and reconciliation into the realm of civic ritual. ... The great parade ... included a prominent contingent of former soldiers and officers of the Southern Confederacy—a display that was meant to symbolize the binding up of the wounds from the terrible Civil War that had torn the nation apart in four years of battle and twice that many of rancorous and uneasy peace.... But the imagery was a mask, the oratory hollow. The United States in 1876 was in the midst of the worst economic depression in its history, and of a crisis of cultural morale as well. The reality outside the fairgrounds put the Exposition's triumphant pageantry in a context that was corrosively ironic.

113. Daniel C. Hallin, "Network News: We Keep America on Top of the World," in *Watching Television,* ed. Todd Gitlin (New York: Pantheon, 1986), p. 22.

114. Walter Benjamin, "A Short History of Photography," *Screen* 13:1 (1972): 25.

115. My own reading is informed by my experience of six years in the U.S. Army Reserve during the period of the Vietnam War. That experience was marked by my disapproval of the war, a critical awareness of the contradictions of my role in the army, and the resultant feelings of guilt that I had not taken alternative action, such as evading the draft by going to Canada or claiming conscientious objector status and thereby refusing to participate in any manner, no matter how tangential, in the machinery of killing.

116. Lifton, *Home from the War,* pp. 388–406.

117. John S. DeMott, "Going after the Mightiest Market," *Time,* September 14, 1981, p. 56.

118. Daniel Henninger, "Worriers, Swingers, Shoppers, 'Psychographics' Can Tell Who'll Buy Crest, Who'll Buy Ultra-Brite," in *New Languages,* ed. Thomas H. Olgren and Lynn M. Berk (Englewood Cliffs, NJ: Prentice-Hall, 1977), pp. 70–77.

119. William Meyers, "Of Belongers, Achievers, Survivors et al.," *New York Times,* December 5, 1982, p. F29.

120. Henninger, "Worriers," p. 73.

121. Ibid., p. 72.

122. Price, *Commercials,* p. 62.

123. The following discussion first appeared in Bernard Timberg and Hal Himmelstein, "Television Commercials and the Contradictions of Everyday Life: A Follow-Up to Himmelstein's Production Study of the Kodak 'America' Commercial," *Journal of Film and Video* 41:3 (Fall 1989):67–79. It appears here in an abridged form.

124. V. N. Volosinov, *Marxism and the Philosophy of Language* (London: Seminar Press, 1973), p. 86.

125. Ibid., p. 34.

126. Ibid., p. 38.

127. Focus Group II. Audio tape transcript, May 9, 1989, p. 2.

128. Ibid., p. 4.

129. Ibid.

130. This quote is from an essay written in Timberg's Broadcast Criticism class at Rutgers University, Newark in April, 1989.

131. Ibid.

132. Focus Group II, p. 9.

133. Ibid., p. 7.

134. Ibid., p. 10.

135. Ibid.

136. Ibid., pp. 10–11.

137. Ibid., p. 11.

138. Focus Group I. Audio tape transcript, January 12, 1989, p. 7.

139. Focus Group II, p. 12.

140. Focus Group I, p. 9.

141. Ibid.

142. Ibid.

143. David Morley, *Family Television: Cultural Power and Domestic Leisure* (London: Comedia Publishing Group, 1986).

144. Michel de Certeau, *The Practice of Everyday Life*, trans. Steven Rendall (Berkeley: University of California Press, 1984), pp. xxi–xxii.

145. Focus Group I, pp. 1–2.

146. Ibid., pp. 4–5. The last sentence in the quote comes from written comments Ruth made at the beginning of the focus group session.

147. Ibid.

148. Focus Group II, pp. 4–5.

149. Morley, *Family Television*, p. 42.

150. Fromm, from "You and the Commercial."

151. Ibid.

152. Marshall McLuhan, *The Mechanical Bride* (New York: Vanguard, 1951), p. 97.

153. Price, *Commercials*, pp. 144–45.

154. Jacques Ellul, *The Technological Society* (New York: Alfred A. Knopf, 1964).

155. Henry, *Culture against Man*, p. 286.

4

□ □ □ □ □ □

TV Comedy and Contemporary Life: *Mayfield, Mayberry, Minneapolis, and Manhattan*

Joseph Campbell defined comedy as "the wild and careless, inexhaustible joy of life invincible."[1] Philosopher James K. Feibleman wrote of comedy that it "is one kind of exemplification of the proposition that nothing actual is wholly logical."[2] Life—never entirely logical, sometimes joyous, perhaps more often confusing, with its infinite variety of complicated predicaments resulting from the unpredictability of human interaction—is the proper subject of comedy.

Comedy, both in its traditional literary and theatrical modes and in its contemporary cinematic, radio, and televisual forms, is grounded in both time and place—it addresses the immediate life conditions of the society in which it is produced. It may do this through lovable, if often absurd individual characters who prompt us to ask, "How will this impossible misfit react to a situation with which we are all familiar?" The viewer, in this instance, is allowed a superior position vis-à-vis the performer in that the viewer knows the situation and the accepted codes of behavior. Or comedy may confront us, through satire or irony, as it addresses our collective fears and concerns regarding the constraints placed on the human spirit by oppressive institutions or outmoded customs.

The term "comedy" presumably originated with the Greek *komos*—a village revel—and was associated with an ode sung at a feast in honor of Dionysus, god of fertility. These revels were crudely phallic and involved a *gamos*, or sexual union.[3] By the time of the Greek Aristophanes (fourth century B.C.), the gross lyrics, jokes, and rustic satire had given way to an almost lyrical comedy with a chorus criticizing contemporary events and in the end celebrating the unity achieved among the characters upon the successful resolution of their conflicts.

The Aristophanic comedies were in turn replaced by a form of comedy that flourished in the Roman era and that was more realistic; the dramatic plots usually involved young lovers being deceived by their parents, guardians, or other worldly-wise antagonists. The society's absurdities were ridiculed as they interfered with the natural order of things, namely, mating and procreation.

While medieval comedy, like medieval visual arts, often strived to present a high moral religious tone, this was offset by the tendency to poke fun at man's earthy weaknesses; the buffoon became a central character in the later comedies of the period. The Italian *commedia dell'arte*, which developed in the first half of the sixteenth century and declined after about 1750, is cited by many critics and artists as an important model for television comedy. This form was a racy mixture of rapid-fire satirical dialogue, slapstick, earthy buffoonery, music, and sometimes dancing. Characterized by the use of masks or stock characters (Harlequin, Scaramouche, etc.), there was little coherent drama, but rather a sequence of sideshows, not unlike the British music-hall and American vaudeville traditions.[4]

In the sixteenth- and early seventeenth-century Renaissance comedy, especially that of the Elizabethan master William Shakespeare, humanism predominated. These comedies often focused on man's complexities and contradictions. Themes ranged from escape from actuality to bitter satire. The comedy of Ben Jonson dealt with the ridiculousness of the emerging middle class's preoccupation with acquisitiveness. The seventeenth-century dramatic comedy of the French master Moliere focused even more critically on contemporary social abuses—the excesses of the pretentious manners of the middle class, religious hypocrisy, and the general lack of moral scruples in the society.

Victorian comedy of the late nineteenth century employed nonsense to emphasize the confusion of the conventional modern world, bound by artificial class distinctions and stultifying manners. Twentieth-century dramatic comedy, especially that of the modern comedic genius Bernard Shaw, pinpointed the growing conflicts between the individual and the dominant capitalist/industrial social order. Shaw realized that while man was not perfectible, man's societies were capable of reform. Shaw, like other great writers of comedy, was able to transcend the unidimensional limitations of farce to produce comedy that became a powerful instrument of social criticism.

It should be apparent from even such a brief and limited historical survey of the types of comedy that have developed in Western cultures that the art form has served and today still serves a very important social function. According to Feibleman, "Comedy is always . . . realistic . . . it gets to handle . . . the traditional and ever-present irritations which people know as evils but which they also find themselves powerless to eradicate."[5] The feeling person finds it difficult to cope with actuality's defects and needs a sense of order superimposed on the chaos of daily life. Such order emerges as we recognize and admit to the limitations of actuality itself. Comedy, which reveals to us ludicrous and ridiculous aspects of our existence, represents the logical order of the ideal. Comedy, "in its broadest sense is the appeal away from things as they are and toward things as they ought to be."[6]

Comedy, especially dramatic comedy, is a crying out for human improvement; it thrives during troubled times, when it is possible for both the artist and the spectator to note the contradictions and value conflicts of society. In the twentieth century it has flourished, most notably in the cinematic artistry of Charlie Chaplin; in the provocative comedy-dramas of Samuel Beckett; in the biting satire of Bernard Shaw and the Russian master Mikhail Bulgakov; in the powerful television comedies of Norman Lear, especially *All in the Family* and *Mary Hartman, Mary Hartman*; and in Robert Altman's and Larry Gelbart's *M*A*S*H*.

STRUCTURAL AND INSTITUTIONAL CHARACTERISTICS OF THE TELEVISION COMEDY APPARATUS

While television comedy is grounded in the forms of theatrical comedy, it exhibits unique formal-structural characteristics. The situation comedy, television's staple comedic vehicle, is a 22-minute, two-act playlet comprising 40 or more script pages. It generally revolves around a single "umbrella" plot or situation. Episodes are usually self-contained. There are three or four scenes per act. Some sitcoms use a "teaser"—a short scene that transpires before the program title and production credits and the first commercial break. Some sitcoms use a "tag"—the final joke after the last commercial break in the program. Some, like *The Beverly Hillbillies*, open with a "backstory"—images and a theme song with lyrics that provide details on the characters' lives prior to their first appearance in the sitcom. There is a regular cast of core characters who are generally stereotypical ones and who engage in ritualistic humor through the repetition of action or "running gags"—physical comedy of gestures and one-liners. The main characters' stance toward the world of social relations is generally illogical or irrational.[7]

A situation or domestic comedy is today frequently videotaped, using four cameras, before a live studio audience, although more traditional techniques such as single-camera film-style shooting on a soundstage persist (significant examples of the latter include *Cheers* and *M*A*S*H*). Action is generally shot on two or three regular sets, with a special "swing set" available to be used, probably just one time, to meet the needs of a specific episode. As a rule, a single director is employed to direct all or most of the episodes of a comedy series; stylistic consistency in production elements is thereby achieved (e.g., in choice of shots, style of lighting, and methods of blocking the action).

The typical workweek for situation comedy rehearsal and shooting generally includes three days of rehearsal, including actor improvisations and setting of stage business; one day of blocking out camera angles; and one day of shooting. The first meeting of a new episode is held Monday morning. At this crucial "Monday morning reading," the first draft of the script is unveiled (white paper for the original and various colored pages for redrafts). By Wednesday, the episode is in run-through rehearsals. Writers continue to rewrite each line. The script is now in its third complete rewrite. Thursdays are generally set aside for the director to block out camera angles. The program is performed and taped in a charged atmosphere on Friday night before a live audience of as many as 300 people. Because this is a costly business, deadlines must be met.

Long-form comedy/sketch formats, such as that for NBC's *Saturday Night Live*, are generally more elaborate. *Saturday Night Live* often has as many as 11 sets on the studio floor. Five video cameras move from set to set during the course of the production, with no more than three cameras used in a single sketch. All sketches are written in two days and blocked out in two more days, and a run-through rehearsal and a dress rehearsal are done the same day as the airing of the program. The chaotic pace of the work process, tempered by the professionalism of the writers, directors, actresses and actors, and crew, provides the controlled aesthetic edge so necessary for good comedy. The live character of the production allows for a topicality that is critical to television satire, given our expectations of instant analysis.

An analysis of the production apparatus of television comedy reveals much about the look of this work—lifelike characters are seen in enclosed spaces, and are revealed in tight two- or three-shots and close-ups, acting out the mundane, everyday world manifested in incongruous if not bizarre configurations. Situation and characterization are crucial to the success of this work. But beyond the aesthetics of television comedy lies its relationship to the real world of social relations.

Scholars have offered a variety of analytical schemes to elucidate the broad range of television comedy, including a breakdown of types of television comedy according to genre characteristics and a typology of the social roles of the central characters in comedy series. James W. Chesebro's scheme of narrative television "communication strategies" includes, but is not limited to, comedy.[8] This scheme, which owes an acknowledged debt to the work of critic Northrop Frye, is based on the relationship between a central character and the viewing audience, with intelligence and ability to control one's circumstances seen as the key variables determining the relationship.

Chesebro isolated five strategies: (1) the "ironic," in which the central character is intellectually inferior and less able to control circumstances than is the audience—"the rhetoric of the loser"; (2) the "mimetic," in which the central character is as intelligent and in control as is the audience—the character is "one of us"; (3) the "leader-centered," in which the central character possesses superior intelligence because of some specialized training but deals with events similar to those in which the audience is involved; (4) the "romantic," in which the central character remains "human" but superior to the audience in both intelligence and control over circumstances; and (5) the "mythical," in which the central character transcends the mundane world of the audience and is confronted with a mystical experience.[9]

According to Chesebro, television comedy most frequently employs the mimetic strategy, with a few notable comedies employing irony and an occasional comedy using a leader-centered strategy. The mimetic strategy, "used to crate the *impression* that typical behaviors and values are being reflected,"[10] becomes an agent for reinforcing traditional dominant value orientations and thus becomes a primary mechanism for socialization. Problems that arise in this type of comedy are treated as the result of "misunderstood intentions"—a principal ingredient of traditional television situation comedy. The basic underlying questions of the relationship of intentionality to social control remain, on the surface of the comedic text at least, unexplored. Among the more aesthetically and financially successful of the mimetic television comedies over the past few decades are *The Mary Tyler Moore Show, The Bob Newhart Show, Happy Days, Barney Miller, The Cosby Show,* and *Roseanne.*

The ironic strategy has two distinct sides: what Chesebro terms "Socratic irony," in which the central character pretends to be ignorant so that his or her adversaries will be forced to reveal their false ideas as they try to explain them to the central character (the melodrama *Columbo* used this strategy quite effectively), and "unknowing irony," in which the central character reveals his or her own ignorance and social powerlessness to the audience. Examples of the latter character type in television comedy include Archie Bunker of *All in the Family* and Al Bundy of *Married . . . With Children.* Archie's malapropisms and inability to interpret clearly and accurately his world frame the comedy of *All in the Family,* which, unlike *Married . . . With Children,* has frequent pathos. Still, both Archie and Al, according to this strategy, are eternal losers.

The leader-centered strategy, which produces central characters who exhibit moral courage and strength, who are articulate, and who face easily identifiable situations, is not a strategy often used in television comedy, according to Chesebro. There are, however, occasional notable exceptions to the rule. Chesebro cites both *M*A*S*H* and *Maude* as examples. Maude and many of the members of the 4077th flaunt conventions; they are authentic in that they thoughtfully consider and actively attempt to change their less-than-perfect world.

The romantic strategy, in which legendary central characters exhibit tremendous courage and endurance, and the mythical strategy (at least as Chesebro defines it, which is inadequate for purposes of this book) of ritual, dreams, and universal struggles to achieve a new social order are the proper domains of heroic/epic adventure melodrama rather than of television comedy.

Other critics point to thematic statements about social relations that, their authors argue, cut across the subgenres of television comedy. Here, the analysis attempts to relate television characters to broad social movements.

According to Sylvia Moss, the comedy of "ingroup-outgroup" emerged in the mid-1960s.[11] Pioneered, in her view, by *The Beverly Hillbillies* and followed by *Bewitched, The Munsters, The Addams Family,* and *My Favorite Martian,* this comedy relied for its laughs on the "clash of social conventions" that clearly differentiated the two groups. Each group adhered to its own code of conduct. As the "small, alien culture," the ingroup was enclosed by the "modern society" of the outgroup, and thus the accepted societal norms were reinforced. The ingroup never affected the outgroup's basic value system; and the audience, which is "apprehensive of healthy, happy, uninhibited rustics," was never threatened or challenged.

This ingroup-outgroup scheme remains useful in discussing television comedy. Today, however, we must reconsider the scheme in light of the shifting social ground of the family institution itself, reflected both in the characterizations on the small screen and in the everyday lived experience of the viewing audience.

In contemporary television comedy, ingroup members (as defined by Moss) remain laughable because their actions are circumscribed by dominant ideology and the life ways it sanctions through its mythology. More importantly, however, these ingroup members have become the objects of the humor of alienation.

This trend began in the late 1970s and early 1980s. The ingroup was no longer the family unit comprised of easily contained "supernatural" social misfits such as Martians and witches but rather the parents of the "normal" family unit. In the post-*All in the Family* world of television comedies, the adult had become a "dolt" and being wise was "square." Father no longer "knew best." His *children* did.[12] Wisecracking children lectured their parents on sexual matters and personal values. Working-class people were not only reconciled to the low social status of their class fraction but felt themselves to be morally superior to the white-collar well-to-do. The ingroup (the object of humor), in short, comprised mature, intelligent white-collar parents—long-standing symbols of the stable family unit in television situation comedy—who had lost control of their personal lives and their families. This dramatic shift in television comedy reflected the rapid and major change in the family's role and composition in advanced capitalist society, as it took on a variety of new forms, many of them "makeshift" and destabilized. The family as labile social unit is ideally suited to the comedic form, for the greater the instability of the basic family unit, the greater the potential for a variety of disruptive human interactions.

By the late 1980s and early 1990s, the image of suburban family bliss was further eroded by two highly popular comedies aired on the emerging Fox television network—*Married . . . With Children* and *The Simpsons* (the latter an animation). In the new comedies, however, while the parents continue to be "tormented by children who gleefully disrespect them," the parents are now *blue-collar* and are also tormented "by status symbols that remain far beyond their grasp."[13] The "ingroup" in these comedies has shifted to working-class adults caught in a miserable web of disrespectful children, a vague, politically defocused awareness of their socioeconomic marginalization, and a general feeling of helplessness and inadequacy.

Newsweek critic Harry F. Waters concluded that when the television entrepreneurs decide to court what he termed an "adolescent" audience, "the small screen is bound to reflect a distorted image of the culture as a whole."[14] But does it? The demystification of the American family in the television comedy may instead reflect, although in the exaggerated form endemic to the comedy genre, what we have become or are becoming. More importantly, this cultural shift may be due in no small measure to television's presence in the culture. Perhaps both white-collar and working-class adults have become egocentric children, demanding that the culture satisfy their insatiable desire to consume their way to happiness, as Jules Henry and Erich Fromm argued in the preceding chapter.

If we are to come to terms with television comedy's relationship to the social reality it both reflects and shapes, we must acknowledge television for what it is—an extremely powerful vehicle for storytelling, a medium whose intimate presence in our lives lends its stories a sense of truthfulness that tends to obscure their status as fiction. Comedy series and serials, like other television forms, express through their myths the dynamics within the collective American mind at a moment in history. These myths not only live in the imagination. They immediately find their way into the attitudes and behaviors of the culture—into the practical everyday lives of the people.

Figure 4.1 includes those television comedies that I believe are particularly significant examples of the comedy types they represent. In this chapter we will examine the mythic constructs in television comedy, using selected examples from various series in each category as examples of the myths at work. The examination will point to both an aesthetic reality— why these works make us laugh—and a sociocultural/historical reality— what these works reveal about the nature of social relations in contemporary American society.

Figure 4.1
Television Comedies

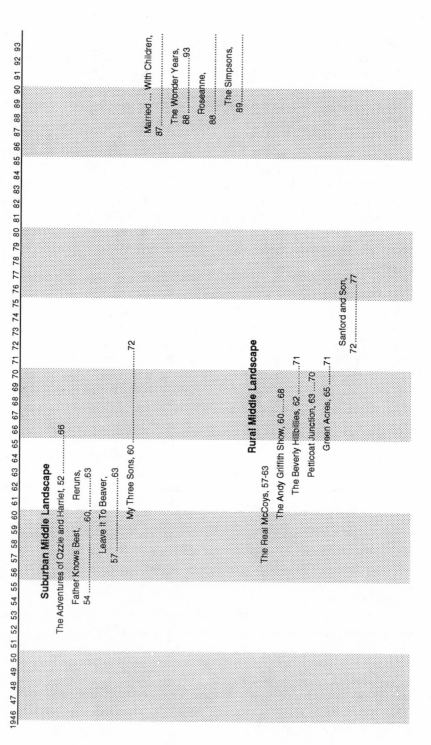

Urban Comedy

1946 47 48 49 50 51 52 53 54 55 56 57 58 59 60 61 62 63 64 65 66 67 68 69 70 71 72 73 74 75 76 77 78 79 80 81 82 83 84 85 86 87 88 89 90 91 92 93

I Love Lucy, 51............57

Make Room For Daddy/The Danny Thomas Show, 53.............64

The Honeymooners, 55 56

The Dick Van Dyke Show, 61............66

The Mary Tyler Moore Show, 70.............77

Sanford and Son, 72............77

The Bob Newhart Show, 72.............78

Barney Miller, 75.............82

The Jeffersons, 75.............85

Taxi, 78............83

Cheers, 83.............93

The Cosby Show, 84.............92

Murphy Brown, 88 ....

THE SUBURBAN-MIDDLE-LANDSCAPE COMEDY

Americans are proud of their heritage as a nation that reveres the "common man." This heritage is related to a variety of ambiguous political, social, and economic constructs, among them plebiscitary democracy, in which the vote of each citizen is presumed to have equal status in the policy-mking arena (thereby confusing concepts of representative and direct democracy and the domains of politics and policy-making); majority rule, with its inherent notion of a compromise of principles in the name of consensus; and marketplace economics, in which the relatively under-educated, unskilled worker, through personal determination, upright moral values, and a bit of luck can become a highly successful entrepreneur—a case of the highly valued Horatio Alger "rags-to-riches" dream that incorporates the myths of the Protestant ethic and eternal progress. This mythology suggests, although obliquely, that success exacts a high personal price unless it is tempered with humility, for the American must never forget his/her roots in the common people. We are constantly reminded of this through our highly developed folklore, which includes as central characters George Washington and Thomas Jefferson, "farmer"-presidents; Ben Franklin, thrifty, level-headed publisher/statesman; Abe Lincoln, woodcutter and small-town lawyer/president; and Dwight D. "Ike" Eisenhower, midwestern country boy/military hero/president.

It is this highly intriguing mixture of the drive for personal gain and status through hard work and the need to acknowledge the humble roots of the common person that represents the archetypal American character. This archetype is reinforced through the way Americans perceive and use space. The United States has a geography characterized by vast empty space and a history characterized by expansion and conquest—the myth of manifest destiny has operated for the past century, in particular, to legitimize that expansion. In our language, we tend to refer to those who established settlements in the western territories as "pioneers," from the French word for foot soldier, rather than as "settlers," a term with more peaceful connotations.

Nineteenth-century American expansionist strategies that incorporated the vast western wilderness were pursued because of a need to expropriate the natural resources of those areas to fuel a furiously expanding industrial economic base. Railroads were built, often at great human expense, to transport raw materials and people over great distances in the name of progress and commerce. Native Americans who got in the way of this progress were expendable. Once an advanced industrial economy was firmly established in the early twentieth century in the United States, another form of geographic dispersion was inevitable. Advanced industrialization required internal mobility within the work sector, both within an organization and between organizations and within a geographical area and between geographical areas, and encouraged new-home building and the concomitant strategy of increasing consumption of identical durable goods for the detached single-family home (one of the most powerful symbols of the Great American Dream—the conquest and possession of space). People were encouraged, through commercial culture, to "move up" in their home and durable-goods purchases; as they were promoted within their companies, more spacious and elegant accommodations, "deluxe" consumer durables, and more luxurious leisure pursuits requiring sophisticated specialized equipment and personalized training became the mark of status. Aided by advances in automotive technology, President Eisenhower's interstate highway program (a primary intention of which was to facilitate the rapid transport of military equipment in a national emergency), the widespread availability of television as a means for decentralized entertainment and outside information, and the development of efficient air-conditioning systems, workers found it desirable (and in fact were encouraged by the hegemonic demands of an advanced industrial economy reflected in corporate behavioral norms) to fan out from overcrowded, polluted, multiracial urban industrial inner cities into the overwhelmingly white suburban developments that sprang up to accommodate the rapid family formation in the post-World War II era.

In the suburb, space, while personal in the sense of separating one family from other families, was not necessarily individualized. The spaces and the dwellings occupying those spaces were often equivalent, with houses of essentially the same basic design with minor structural variations on identical quarter-acre parcels of land. The repetition of suburban-tract homes was both an acknowledgment of the myth of eternal progress (through the glorification of efficient technique) and a personal acquiescence to America's heritage of the common man.

The era of what social critic Raymond Williams termed "mobile privatization" had arrived. Mobile privatization, according to Williams, is characterized by the confluence of "two apparently paradoxical yet deeply connected tendencies of modern urban industrial living: on the one hand mobility, on the other the more apparently self-sufficient family home."[15] The American suburb was clearly a new social form, signifying increased middle-class geographical and social mobility; but its roots could be clearly traced to American ideological traditions and material history.

Television's version of suburban life was most clearly presented in the situation comedy. An idealized vision of suburban living, the myth of the suburban middle landscape, reinforced basic American notions of progress tempered by humility. The suburb was the mythical space between two untamed rugged frontiers: the wilderness and the chaotic, dangerous inner city (the urban frontier). It was a place where sanity prevailed, a place of full employment; conventional white, white-collar corporate families; clean streets, well-kept weedless lawns, neatly trimmed hedges, and, in the older suburbs, an occasional freshly painted white picket fence. People there were not rugged isolates, as in the myth of the frontier, but neither were they exactly oriented to the world of the close neighborly bonds in the traditional rural community. There were "neighborhood associations," but their activities seemed to focus mainly on prescriptions for inclusion in the "club," such as pressuring homeowners delinquent in their yard-care activities. The invidious converse of such inclusion was racial and ethnic exclusion. The Protestant ethic dominated the mental landscape of television's suburban dweller. Success was measured by its visible material manifestations. Since neighbors generally minded their own business, with occasional limited interaction when some problem arose (usually a case of parents trying to sort out their children's misbehavior or social crises), conformity to community values was signified more through these material possessions and less through the more traditional moral and ethical codes of conduct. In fact, the ultimate moral imperative in the myth of the suburban middle landscape was acquisitiveness; the inhabitants were comfortable, having built an insular world of material objects within which they found security. While a feeling of humanity surfaced in the interactions of the central characters within the nuclear family in the suburban-middle-landscape comedies of the 1950s and 1960s, underlying the entire genre were notions of complacency and exclusion. This was a surface world cut off from the larger social environment with its racial tensions, its decaying urban industrial centers (most suburbanites, it could be presumed, worked in the inner-city business centers), and its Cold War between the United States and the Soviet Union, with the constant threat of nuclear annihilation. Television's myth of the suburban middle landscape became an idealized representation of the quality of life of upwardly mobile white Americans divorced from the social infrastructure that allowed that mobility (we are inevitably upwardly mobile at another's expense). We see the results of progress limited to the privileged, but we are denied access to the broader social reality in which that "progress" occurs.

The suburban-middle-landscape television comedy was a comedy of reassurance. Beneath its funny situations, involving the often inexplicable, illogical actions of cute kids who refused to become adults, was a very nearly uniform world view that television executive Sprague Vonier once termed the "urban outlook."[16] The urban outlook framed a world in which principles of fair play prevailed; judges were sober; lawyers were intelligent and honest; police were calm, understanding, brave, and, above all, incorruptible; everyone had a right to freedom of speech; everyone was entitled to the best possible education; the able, hard-working person would, with a bit of luck, do well financially; everyone should be kind to children and animals; and society will come to the aid of the individual in a personal crisis.[17]

This was the comedy of the true nuclear family. Sons and daughters struggled to grow up while their parents, who tended to smother them in piety and sociological wisdom, were constantly faced with their children's fantasies and nonsense, which, while illogical from an adult's point of view, were nevertheless refreshing and adventurous in a world of conformity and of fear of deviation from norms. We all know that when Beaver Cleaver says "Sure, dad," what he really is saying is, "I'll do what you want me to do because you're a grown-up, but I really would rather have fun." This universal generational difference defines the basic comedic structure of the genre in its 1950s and 1960s manifestations. It also simultaneously points, albeit indirectly, to a social reality in which the archetypal adult says to us, all children at heart, "When you grow up, you too will find it necessary to conform to the dominant ideology so that you may be successful like us." Our laugh is a knowing one—we apprehend the irritations of our own constraints and admire the idealized freedom of Beaver, a little boy with buckteeth and an explorer's psyche.

Of all the suburban-middle-landscape television comedies of the 1950s and 1960s, four stand out as significant examples of the genre: *The Adventures of Ozzie and Harriet* (1952–66), *Father Knows Best* (1954–60, with reruns in 1960–63), *Leave It to Beaver* (1957–63), and *My Three Sons* (1960–72).

Of these four comedy series, only *Ozzie and Harriet* featured a real-life family as central characters. Ozzie, Harriet, David, and Ricky Nelson resided in a television house modeled on their real Hollywood home. On television, Ozzie was never acknowledged to have a job. He just seemed to hang around the house all the time, although we all knew he was an actor. Harriet was a housewife. Ricky sang pop songs on the series and soon became a real-life rock-and-roll star. Both David and Ricky grew up on the show. When they married in real life, their wives joined the cast of the show as regulars, becoming part of the entire enterprise. The medium of television became our kitchen window as we curiously peeked at the goings-on of our next-door neighbors, the Nelsons. Success abounded: The Nelsons were successful television stars, acting out their successful suburban lifestyle—the Hollywood dream—on the small screen before millions of viewers.

The other three series assembled adult and child actors and actresses to play families. *Father Knows Best*, which launched Robert Young's highly successful television acting career, featured Jim and Margaret Anderson (Young and Jane Wyatt) and their three children—Betty, 17 when the series began; Bud, 14; and Kathy, nine—who lived in the comfort of Springfield (in the Midwest). Jim, an agent for the General Insurance Company, and Margaret, a housewife, played the roles of thoughtful, responsible parents. As in all suburban-middle-landscape comedy of the time, family members never raised their voices to one another. Problems were resolved quietly and sensibly, according to the wisdom of the parents and the dominant ideology of the day, to everyone's satisfaction. The children, while generally toeing the line, occasionally successfully asserted their independence. The Andersons so well epitomized the middle-American character of their time that the U.S. Department of the Treasury commissioned the series' producers to film a special episode to promote the 1959 U.S. Savings Bond Drive. Called "24 Hours in Tyrant Land," this episode showed the Anderson children trying to live for a day under a fictional dictatorship. This was late-1950s-television comedy's contribution to the Cold War. Other television personalities, most notably *Dragnet's* Jack Webb, had made similar anti-Communist propaganda statements on celluloid. While the "24 Hours" episode was distributed to schools, churches, and meetings of civil organizations to promote the maintenance of democracy, American style, it was never aired on television.[18]

My Three Sons began its long run (five years on ABC, followed by seven on CBS) in 1960. The family was guided by widowed patriarch Steve Douglas, a consulting aviation engineer. Played by veteran actor Fred MacMurray, Steve was strictly upscale, white collar. An avid golfer, he personified the pace of the myth of the suburban middle landscape—slow, deliberate, quiet, and, above all, even tempered. Steve's office was cramped, signifying either that he was not at the top executive echelon or that he was not given to posturing or ostentation. The limited space of his office was in marked contrast to the spaciousness of the Douglas home—an elegant standard-issue two-story upper-middle-class abode of the mid-1960s. Its early-American furnishings and leather chairs bespoke tradition and success. In 1960 the Douglas brood included 18-year-old Mike, 14-year-old Robbie, and seven-year-old Chip—Steve's three sons. After five years on the show, Mike married and left the series, and Steve adopted Chip's next-door pal Ernie, an orphan. "Bub" O'Casey, Steve's father-in-law and surrogate housewife for the first four years of the series, was replaced by his brother, "Uncle Charlie," a crusty old sailor. "Bub" and "Uncle Charlie" reinforced the portrayal of the basic decency of the upscale Douglas family. They were gruff, undereducated, yet decent common men. They both were taken in by the highly successful yet humble son-in-law. Their social position, however, was confounded as they functioned in the household as tireless, if willing, servants and as the boys' grandfathers.

The Douglases began their television life in a "medium-sized midwestern city" but moved to North Hollywood in 1967 because of Steve's job. Robbie had married Katie Miller in 1967, and they had triplets, all boys of course. In 1969 Steve married the widow Barbara Harper, one of Ernie's teachers, and in 1970 Chip eloped with his college girlfriend Polly. By this point in the series run, all the men except O'Casey and Ernie had married and the premise of bachelorhood that had sparked much of the series comedy was gone. The series was fading fast in the ratings, and a new era in television comedy, marked by the premiere of *All in the Family*, was beginning.

Like its predecessors, *My Three Sons* posited a clear view of the authority of the adult, especially the male, and stressed the sanctity of traditional American values such as the nuclear family, with its bonds of trust and concern, the importance of hard work, and the drive for success tempered with humility. This comedy also very clearly represented the myths of eternal progress and manifest destiny that were exemplified by the 1960s "space race" initiated by President John Kennedy at the beginning of the decade. When the scene shifted to Steve, the aviation engineer, at work at his desk, we see, in a medium-shot, on the wall immediately behind him, neatly framed photographs of powerful guided missiles exploding from their launch pads. These missiles, with their phallic signification, subtly reinforce notions of competition, a drive toward conquest (of space via the moon, and of the Soviet Union), and, ultimately, patriarchal control of both the nuclear family and (perhaps through "nuclear deterrent") the larger and more problematic global family. In both "families" the patriarchal figure, exercising the quiet use of power, promotes social stability through inhibition. The presence of missiles in the suburban middle landscape of the 1960s reveals the true colors behind the myth's camouflage.

The most enduring example of the myth of the suburban middle landscape can be found in *Leave It to Beaver*. While the series' first run lasted only six years (1957–63), an average run for a successful television comedy, it seems destined for television immortality in syndication. Its 234 episodes, all shot in black and white, provide us with a glimpse of a deceptively simple moment in our recent history that ironically reemerged in the Reagan era. *Leave It to Beaver* framed a sociocultural milieu immediately preceding the social upheavals of the Vietnam era, the free-speech movement, the revolt against the traditional authority of the family and state ideological apparatuses, and the ascendence of women toward equal partnership in the work experience. The quiet, idealized, insulated life of the suburban middle landscape would soon be confronted with a harsher reality outside our television screens. But the myth, though shaken, would live on.

The show's creators and principal writers, Joe Connelly and Bob Moser, had 12 children between them and were, by virtue of that statistic, qualified to write on the subject. Many of the rather mundane incidents and crises on the series were drawn from their own life experience. The ensemble acting of Hugh Beaumont, Barbara Billingsley, Tony Dow, and

Jerry Mathers was of consistently high quality. *Leave It to Beaver* rang true as a work of realist fiction. As the embodiment of the suburban-middle-landscape myth, it speaks to us of an attitude, a world view with which we are now quite familiar: In the suburban town of Mayfield lived a nice couple—a handsome, rugged-looking, but gentle accountant in his late thirties or early forties, his beautiful, pert, almost sexy housewife with blond hair and a marvelous wardrobe, and their two sons. One, 12 years old and entering puberty, was showing the initial signs of interest in girls and dating, while the other, five years his junior, hated girls and was interested in pet frogs. This was the quiet world of the Cleavers: Ward, June, Wally, and Theodore, "The Beaver."

In the 1957 premiere episode of *Leave It to Beaver*, titled "Captain Jack," we fade in from black to a close-up of a pair of shoes resting on a curb, then slowly tilt up to reveal a policeman in a black uniform. He is twirling a nightstick and, from this low-angle shot, he looks somber and menacing. Throughout this opening shot, we hear Ward Cleaver delivering his opening lecture in a voice-over; Ward lectured a lot. He told the viewers: "Children and adults look at the world through different eyes. When you're young, a policeman stands ten feet tall. And if you see it in print, it's supposed to be true." Thus is established the series' basic premise—that in this world, the authority of adults and societal institutions is sacrosanct; skepticism has no space reserved for it in the suburban middle landscape.

The scene shifts to Beaver and Wally sending away for a "genuine Florida alligator" advertised for $2.50 in the *Robot Men of Mars* comic. Ward and June of course know nothing about this, nor is it clear where the boys got the money, a tidy sum in 1957, to purchase the reptile. An illustration in the comic book shows a handsome man in a pith helmet wrestling an alligator. From the relative sizes of the man and the alligator in the illustration, the scaly creature appears to be eight feet long. The boys trust the ad, but when their gator arrives at the Mayfield Post Office, they are chagrined to discover it is a baby alligator no more than six or seven inches long. There is no discussion of suing the company for false representation or of demanding their money back. Rather, accepting the deception, they visit their local "alligator farm" to learn more about their new pet. A crusty old man with the moniker Captain Jack operates the farm. He is every boy's dream of adventure—unshaven, wearing a soiled pith helmet and a striped boat-neck shirt, his gruff voice exhibiting his many years of experience in the jungle. His demeanor, however, betrays a periodic nip or two from the bottle—something adults would understand, but not little boys. He is exotic but unthreatening. Captain Jack gives the boys a regime for caring for their alligator, including feeding it a bizarre mixture of brandy and milk and raw eggs and massaging it with beauty cream. The boys swear fealty to the Captain and appropriately name their baby gator after him. They return home elated. Then the fun begins.

To hide their alligator from their parents, yet keep it in or near water, Wally and Beaver place the gator on a sponge and float it in the toilet tank. (The producers had to fight for this scene with CBS censors, who had to that point prohibited the showing of toilets on the air. The producers won their battle.)

In the second act, we fade in to the Cleavers' substantial two-story home in what was an older suburban neighborhood; its white picket fence spoke of tradition, of an almost rustic serenity. (Later in the series, the fence disappeared and the house seemed more urban than rural.) We cut to Ward sitting calmly at the breakfast table while June serves him breakfast; she was seemingly chained to her toaster and skillet, although in 1957 the bondage appeared natural. Minerva, the Irish maid, enters the kitchen. In late middle age, white, and frumpy, if not dumpy, Minerva signifies suburban affluence—a Cleaver "possession" emblematic of the difference between their and her class status—yet avoids the racism attached to having a black maid working for whites. June turns to Ward and matter-of-factly states "I told Minerva to come three times a week now to help with the cleaning and the laundry." Ward says to June: "That's fine with me." June's statement implies Minerva has worked for the Cleavers before, but her duties and, one assumes, the Cleavers' income are presently increasing. Following this verbal confirmation of the Cleavers' bourgeois status, Ward notices that certain items are disappearing from around the house, most notably his brandy (Ward is no beer drinker). June confirms that her eggs and beauty cream, items associated with woman/wifehood, are also rapidly disappearing. Ward suspects Minerva of sipping his brandy; we know Wally and Beaver are mixing it with milk and feeding it to their pet, who has grown ever larger. A traditional comedic device is employed here, by withholding important information from some of the core characters and thereby placing the audience in a privileged position of superior knowledge vis-à-vis those characters. Ward, seeking an explanation for Minerva's alleged transgression, combines the patriarchal sexist attitudes of his generation with the distinctions of class as he says to June: "Maybe after a few nips, she begins to feel romantic." Middle-aged, unattractive Minerva, representing the drabness of proletarian woman, is portrayed as incapable of love or romance in her real conditions of existence; only when inebriated can she begin to dream of the mysteries of romance withheld from her. This is reminiscent of many video and print ads from the period for such items as lipstick and hairspray, which, when used, transport the drab, lifeless woman to exotic lands to share her newly found sexuality with some muscular nut-brown lover who lives in a grass hut on stilts. Today, these housewifely fantasies are pandered to by Harlequein romance novels. The Cleavers, exemplifying the suburban middle landscape, can, of course, transcend the need for fantasy and escapism and find romance in their luxurious surroundings. Ward Cleaver is on the inside track, using the distinction of his class fraction to disdain the "have-nots." His status and, by implication, his control over his own life admit the sensual under normal material conditions of existence.

The materialism built into this episode is further revealed in a scene in which Wally and the Beaver play the role of youthful entrepreneurs, charging their school chums ten cents apiece to see the alligator as the boys regurgitate Captain Jack's inflated discourse on the lives of alligators in the wild. As we watch a line of satisfied young customers filing out the Cleavers' front door, we know that Wally and Beaver have made a good return on what began as a pet and has subtly changed into an investment.

Later, when Minerva goes down to the Cleavers' basement to get the laundry, she discovers the alligator, which the boys have moved from the toilet tank to the basement sink because the beast outgrew its initial habitat. Extremely agitated, Minerva informs Ward and June of the pet's presence. However, Ward, thinking Minerva is once again drinking, commands her to go home and dry out before returning to the Cleaver household. June goes to the basement, discovers the alligator, and informs Ward, who, still unbelieving, takes a skeptical look for himself. The alligator bites Ward on the finger, thus providing his punishment for his insensitive treatment of Minerva while at the same time deflecting the more basic issue of Ward's distrust of blue-collar workers.

Naturally, the gator must go. Ward, the rational, gentle family patriarch explains to Wally and Beaver that he is proud of them for raising the alligator, an act that implied responsibility, an adult quality stressed throughout the series. He adds, "Someday you boys are going to grow up, leave your mother and me, get married, and have a family of your own." Such a cycle was of course never questioned in 1957. Captain Jack, the alligator, would certainly want the same opportunity. So the understanding mother and father, and the acquiescent boys return Captain Jack to Captain Jack's alligator farm. Even this scene stresses the Cleavers' bourgeois status, for while all the other tourists at the alligator farm wore shirts or plain dresses, Ward, Wally, and Beaver all wore coats and ties and June wore an expensive, well-tailored dress that could have been purchased in Beverly Hills.

The inferior role of women and the status of adults as the agents of social control in this mythic world were continually represented in the series. In a 1962 episode, near the end of its run, *Leave It to Beaver* tackled the evils of sloth, a character trait condemned by the myths of eternal progress and the Protestant ethic. Ward entrusts Wally and Beaver, who are now 17 and 12, respectively, with the job of cleaning up the front yard and the garage. It is a beautiful Saturday morning (it rarely rains on the suburban middle landscape) and the boys' fancies turn to lighter matters than raking leaves. They end up doing "goofy" things like taking target practice with Beaver's old bow and arrow, which are due to be discarded with the other trash, and playing catch. Time passes fast when you're having so much fun, and the boys finally finish their yard work later in the afternoon, too late to have Mr. Peck, the local trash hauler, take the refuse to the Mayfield city dump. Wally's friends, Clarence "Lumpy" Rutherford and Eddie Haskell (the latter the prototypical con man), happen to be driving through the neighborhood in Lumpy's jalopy. They agree to haul the trash for half of what Peck would charge. Lumpy and Eddy drive off with the trash, but, being lazy, dump it on a vacant lot in the middle of town instead of at the dump. The lot owner, a Mr. Hill, finds a magazine with Ward's name on it among the refuse and lambastes Ward for being a litterbug. Irate that his reputation has been tarnished, Ward commands all four boys to clean up Hill's vacant lot the following morning. In an exchange following the incident, Wally admits, "If we hadn't goofed around all day, then this whole mess wouldn't have happened." Ward, angry but reserved as always, replies: "That's exactly what it means Wally. So the next time you fellows just do what you're told when you're told, and we'll all avoid a lot of trouble." The episode, like most other episodes, represents an event that helps initiate the boys into the adult society as defined in the dominant ideology. The woman in this society, while not lazy, as are the children, is represented instead and vacuous. In the episode just described, Ward makes small talk with June, a device often used as a bridge between the scenes that involve the boys. Ward says to June: "How is the news today?" June responds, "Well, I started to read the paper. I found that sewing was much more restful." The woman does not think in this milieu and is not part of the events that frame the world outside the house; in other words, in a world in which the woman's place is in the kitchen or at the beauty parlor, the woman is not a socially relevant being.

The signs of the material existence of the suburban middle landscape are manifold in *Leave It to Beaver*, as in the other comedies of the genre during this period of television history—June wears white cotton gloves to go shopping; Ward eats breakfast in a tie and a buttoned sports jacket; the Cleavers' two-story brick home has carriage lamps outside; and Ward's study resembles a library in a mansion, with hardwood, floor-to-ceiling bookcases containing innumerable leather-bound books (the "Great Books" series and encyclopedias were big door-to-door sales items at the time). The Cleavers, as were the other television suburban-middle-landscape families, were upscale, socially conservative, politically inactive, essentially kind to one another and their neighbors, and generally dull.

The P.T.A. Magazine praised *Leave It to Beaver* as showing children and adults how "to value each other more truly and to set up worthy standards for their life together."[19] With its emphasis on everyday life and on learning lessons, Beaver was a product of the times, which were changing even as Leave It to Beaver was being produced. The suburban middle landscape was the epitome of comfort, where the values of family support are portrayed amidst the reassurance of modest wealth. It is here that an entire generation of the middle class grew up and purchased its happiness. Yet the material wealth rested on a thin base of pretension. The wealth was accumulated at others' expense, a matter left unexplored in these suburban-middle-landscape comedies. We rarely saw our television protagonists even remotely acknowledge these social facts or question their own social status outside their nuclear-family existence. The outside world was a vague abstraction providing the background for a didactic morality play, with comedic elements inserted to hold the viewers' attention.

Suburban-middle-landscape comedy in the late 1980s and early 1990s reflected a world decidedly different from its 1950s and 1960s predecessors. The Great American Dream, as portrayed in its mythified earlier television comedy version, had soured. Many of the problems of the inner city that the suburbanites had fled—drugs, pollution, traffic congestion, noise, the disintegrating family unit—followed them into their tree-lined enclaves. A small group of highly popular contemporary situation comedies, reacting against the condensation symbology employed during the Reagan era to deny the existence of these nagging social problems, frequently focus on this suburban social breakdown; but, in the tradition of the form, the comedic frame is restrictive—the problems are transformed into the everyday "irritations" that plague the comedies' central characters and propel the comedic vehicles, while any pointed "social" reading fades into the background (unlike the social comedies discussed in chapter 5).

Three suburban-middle-landscape comedies of recent vintage, all set in the present—Married . . . With Children (1987–), Roseanne (1988–), and The Simpsons (1989–)—are prime examples of new directions in this form. A fourth—The Wonder Years (1988–93)—is a softer, nostalgic look at the late 1960s, albeit with a small dose of late 1980s "realism."

Married . . . With Children premiered on the Fox Network on April 5, 1987. After a slow ratings start, it became Fox's most popular series and the first of Fox's programs to achieve a double-digit Nielsen rating—a 10 for the November 27, 1988, episode. The series was created by Ron Leavitt and Michael M. Moye, former writers for The Jeffersons.

Married has been described as a "delightfully raunchy"[20] comedy that has "all the warmth of a boa constrictor."[21] According to Les Brown, it signals "a marked departure from the idealized, suburban domestic comedy, ... center[ing] on a quarrelsome working-class family in an unkempt household."[22]

Married's setting is suburban Chicago. Its central characters include Al and Peg Bundy, their two children Kelly (15 when the series began) and Bud (11), the Bundy family dog Buck, and from 1987–89 the Bundy's neighbors Steve and Marcy Rhoades (Marcy remarried in 1991). Leavitt and Moye chose the name Bundy after King Kong Bundy, one of their favorite professional wrestlers.

Al and Peg had been married for 15 years when the series began. Al, a prototypical "working-stiff" male chauvinist, is a "hapless shoe salesman with bad breath, armpit stains and smelly feet. Peg [wears] lots of spandex and teased hair, and loathe[s] housework and cooking."[23] Their "less-than-wholesome" children, Kelly, a "sexy airhead," and Bud, a "budding young con-man," are constantly bickering with one another. Topics of argument (there is rarely a "civilized" conversation in the Bundy household) include money, the children's activities, and Al's sexual prowess (or lack thereof) and Al and Peg's habitual sexual dissatisfaction.

Steve and Marcy Rhoades, the Bundys' neighbors, begin the series as wholesome newlyweds. Both are white-collar accountants. They are deeply in love until Al begins to explain the "real world" to Steve, and Peg likewise to Marcy.

Steve authorizes a bank loan to finance one of Al's get-rich-quick schemes, which, like everything in Al's life, seems doomed to failure. When Al fails to repay the loan, Steve loses his job at the bank. After months of unemployment and depression, he leaves Marcy to become a park ranger at Yosemite. Marcy subsequently meets Jefferson D'Arcy during a drinking binge at a banker's convention, and the two are married (yes ... Marcy D'Arcy!).

Although the program's ratings were steadily growing, Fox refused to air the fall 1988 premiere episode, "A Period Piece." In it, the Bundys and the Rhoadses go camping together, and Peg, Kelly, and Marcy all start their menstrual periods. The episode was aired later in the season, following numerous script changes. Later in the 1988–89 season, an episode in which Al and Peg are videotaped having sex in a sleazy motel was axed and has never been aired.[24]

In 1989, Michigan housewife Terry Rakolta attempted to organize a boycott of advertisers on the program. She was outraged by a January 15, 1989, episode involving Peg shopping for a new bra. Rakolta had been watching the episode with her children. While the boycott ultimately failed, Fox nevertheless moved the program from 8:30 to 9:00 P.M. EST. Rakolta—and the series and its network—received much publicity in the media, including a front-page story in the *New York Times*. The program's ratings continued to improve as the curious tuned in.

Cocreator Leavitt said, "We'd always hated the typical family on television. It just makes us sick, basically."[25] *Married . . . With Children* was clearly not *Father Knows Best* (Al didn't). Neither did anyone else in this anomic suburban family.

We can always laugh at the ignorance of hapless losers, celebrating our own enlightened superiority. Many can also find pleasure in the sexual humor of such comedies. After all, *Married*'s reference point was one of the original comedic forms, the early Greek *komos.*

Still, the series's treatment of the working class as buffoons with few if any redeeming qualities is highly problematic. If the "typical family" of the suburban-middle-landscape comedy made Leavitt "sick," his 180-degree swing creates an equally unrealistic and ultimately unacceptable stereotype.

Another working-class suburban-middle-landscape comedy premiered on ABC in October 1988. *Roseanne* was an audience hit from the outset. Roseanne Barr (later Arnold) and John Goodman, as Roseanne and Dan Conner, were, according to *Washington Post* television critic Tom Shales, the ideal television couple because their "chubby compatibility" transcends the glamour thought necessary for good male-female chemistry. Shales added, "Like Ralph and Alice Kramden [of *The Honeymooners*] they're wonderful to watch together."[26] The Conner brood included boy-crazy daughter Becky (13), tomboy Darlene (11), and D. J. (6), who idolized Dan.

Critic Les Brown attributed much of the success of the series to its honest portrayal of the family, who is "imperfect, unglamorous and somewhat vulgar."[27] Although much of the verbal comedy of *Roseanne* revolves around Roseanne's harsh criticism of her wisecracking children, in the end she always demonstrates her love.

The series's story lines often focus on "little people" (working class) against the system. But these are not the "helpless" folk of *Married . . . With Children.* Rather, as critic Walter Goodman points out, the series "bespeaks a comfortable acquaintance with and a sly superiority toward upper-class ways" and pretentions.[28] When Roseanne and Dan go to a "fancy" restaurant, they use a discount coupon and are not embarrassed. The hostess informs them, "This is Charles and he'll be your waiter," to which Roseanne sarcastically retorts, "Hello, Charles, this is Dan and I'm Roseanne, and we'll be your customers."

The "other" in Roseanne is often represented by institutions such as the Internal Revenue Service and the school system. In one episode, Darlene's teacher calls Roseanne to report her 11-year-old has a habit of drinking in class. The teacher interprets this behavior as rooted in the Conners' family problems and perhaps even child neglect. She asks Roseanne how much time the family spends together. Roseanne knowingly inquires, "You mean *quality* time?"[29]

All the tokens of working-class life are here: the Conners are chronically short of money. Dan, a building contractor, is intermittently employed at the outset of the series and eventually opens a motorcycle shop in their hometown, Lanford, Illinois. Roseanne and her younger sister Jackie begin the series working at Wellman Plastics. In 1989 Roseanne was shampooing and cleaning up at a beauty salon. In 1990 she became a waitress at the Lobo Lounge. Jackie became a policewoman. From the beginning, many of Roseanne's coworkers have been prominently featured in various episodes. But the working-class world of the Conners has an important twist. Roseanne is so much "smarter" than earlier working-class characters. How, Goodman asks, is this accomplished, since Roseanne rarely reads books or travels? His answer: she watches television, through which she keeps abreast of topical subjects and becomes "such a shrewd psychologist of her friends' neuroses and the antics of the kids."[30]

Goodman sees *Roseanne* as a situation comedy for its time:

The Conner family is wonderfully free of bigotry. . . . "Roseanne" is not aimed at stirring up the sort of commotion that "All in the Family" did when it began back in 1971. . . . Despite appearances, the Conners are a throwback to a kinder, gentler sitcom. They represent inoffensiveness with a dirty face. . . . Nobody's political or religious sensibilities are offended. . . . These creatures of television have to know what is in so that they can continue to be out in a reassuring way, offering viewers the satisfaction of seeing class differences mocked but never challenged.[31]

Roseanne presents a much more positive image of the working-class American than that represented by *Married . . . With Children*. It does so in part because it is aired on one of the Big Three commercial television networks, all of which recognize the increasing importance of attracting the working-class target demographic, who comprise a growing share of their audiences as the economically well-to-do seek alternative programming options on specialized cable television services. It also reflects the growing dissatisfaction of the working class with traditional institutionalized politics, which became clear in the populist response to Ross Perot's presidential candidacy in 1992. In the end, however, as Goodman notes, this is still a traditional suburban-middle-landscape comedy of reassurance that focuses on the strength of family bonds.

The Simpsons is an animated series that premiered on the Fox Network in December 1989, after being introduced as a series of short vignettes to fill the time between skits on Fox's *The Tracey Ullman Show* in 1988. The program was created by Matt Groening, whose comic strip "Life in Hell" had achieved a cult following since its appearance in 1977. Groening calls *The Simpsons* a "mutant Ozzie and Harriet.[32]

The Simpsons features an interesting admixture of character types found on *Married . . . With Children* and *Roseanne* as well as numerous intertextual televisual references. The setting for the series is the "idyllic" town of Springfield—also the fictional setting for *Father Knows Best*. The "modern" Springfield contains certain features missing from its predecessor, most notably a prison, toxic waste, and a nuclear power plant, where Homer Simpson, the family patriarch, works as a safety inspector.

Homer is a lazy, balding, not very intelligent slob who spends a good deal of time after work drinking beer at Moe's tavern and bowling at Barney's New Bowlerama (a reference to the 1960s prime-time animation hit *The Flintstones*). In many ways, Homer is an animated version of Al Bundy, with one notable exception—he has compassion for his family. Like Al, he personifies the beleaguered perennial loser. He is constantly broke. In one episode, Homer's Christmas savings went to remove a tattoo from his son Bart. He tried to get money by gambling his last $13 at the dog track. He wound up instead with one of the losing dogs.

Homer's wife Marge, the woman under the huge blue beehive hairdo, assumes a role not unlike Edith Bunker of *All in the Family*. She is gentle and caring—the "family peacemaker."

And she has her hands full with her spiky-haired son Bart, the star of the show—an archetypal hip, cynical, under-achieving fourth-grader who is extremely appealing to a 12-to-17-year-old target audience. The rebellious Bart is the "obnoxious misfit" who skateboards around Springfield grossing out his friends and tormenting his teacher, Mrs. Karbappel.

Homer and Marge have two other children. Lisa, who is 8, is a baritone saxophone prodigy and the family "brain," but the Simpsons fail to notice her abilities. The youngest child, Maggie, is constantly sucking a pacifier.

While Homer and Marge have their share of arguments and while the wisecracking Bart provides a constant source of irritation, like Roseanne and Dan Conner (and unlike Al and Peg Bundy) they seem genuinely to love each other and their children—a love that occasionally borders on sentimentality. This fact is significant, for it holds the sardonic comedy within the reassuring frame of the traditional suburban middle landscape.

Critic Les Brown called the program a "genuine breakthrough show."[33] Brooks and Marsh assert that *The Simpsons* is "arguably the most subversive" of the new suburban-middle-landscape television comedies and that the program's humor and "anarchic message" were admissible on television "largely because it was a cartoon."[34] This is hyperbole. Bart's hip lingo—"Don't have a cow, man," "Eat my shorts, man," "Watch it, dude," or "Underachiever, and proud of it, man"—is neither "anarchic" or "subversive." And while the series's general attitude to contemporary life is indeed cynical, it is difficult to find anarchy or subversion in characters whose likenesses are featured on more than 70 spin-off products, from T-shirts and sweatshirts to Bart bubble gun, Butterfinger candy bars, Simpsons shoes, snow boots, sandals and moon boots, dolls, napkins, laminated magnets, license-plate frames, beach towels, and air fresheners.

The Wonder Years is the final suburban-middle-landscape comedy considered here. The series premiered on ABC in a preview episode following ABC's January 1988 Super Bowl telecast, had a limited run in the spring, and entered full-time production in the fall. *The Wonder Years* was generally a "whimsical" look back at suburban life in the late 1960s, seen through the eyes of an adult Kevin Arnold, the program's central character. The omniscient narrator device—looking over the shoulder of the adolescent Kevin struggling to establish his self-identity—is the series's principal "cognitive" vehicle.[35] Its television forerunner was John Boy's voice-over narration in *The Waltons*.

Kevin was 12 years old in 1968, the youngest of the three Arnold children. His older brother Wayne loved to tease him. His older sister Karen, a flower child and social protester, was immersed in her own world. His father, Jack Arnold, seemed distant and disagreeable, coming home from work tired and constantly arguing. His mother, Norma, was distracted.

As the series begins, Kevin is about to enter John F. Kennedy Junior High School. When the series ended, in May 1993, the 17-year-old Kevin quits a summer job at his father's furniture factory and leaves town on a journey of "self-discovery." In between, Kevin and his best friend, the nerdy Paul Pfeiffer, try very hard to fit in at school. The Vietnam War protests, Beatles music, and the race to land a man on the moon are depoliticized backdrops to Kevin's road to adulthood (like many who grew up during this period, he was immersed in a cultural, not a political revolution). News clips and music from the era are frequently employed. The program's theme song was "With a Little Help from My Friends," sung by Joe Cocker.

What connects this comedy-drama to its three suburban-middle-landscape comedy contemporaries (and distinguishes it from the early examples of the genre) is the "remarkably unglamorized" family. And, like *Married . . . With Children* and *The Simpsons*, the family appears "foolish, inarticulate, even mean-spirited on occasion. . . . They fumble through life."[36]

The contemporary suburban-middle-landscape comedy dares to show the warts that its progenitors ignored. The series use different aesthetic devices (or "strategies," as Chesebro defined them at the beginning of the chapter) to accomplish this—*Roseanne* employs a "mimetic" strategy wherein the central characters are intelligent (in this case "TV intelligent") and in control—they are "one of us"; *Married . . . With Children* and *The Simpsons* both employ an "ironic" strategy—the central characters are less able to control circumstances than is the audience; and *The Wonder Years* employs a "leader-centered" strategy—the adult Kevin possesses superior intelligence through his adult hindsight.

In the final analysis, all these comedies, despite their occasional pretentions to the contrary, are depoliticized—lacking the trenchant political discourse of the social comedies examined in chapter 5.

THE RURAL-MIDDLE-LANDSCAPE COMEDY

A certain sanctity existed in the suburban-middle-landscape comedies of the 1950s and early 1960s; it was characterized by the gentle authority of the patriarch and the strength of warm family relations exemplified by the loving, if often vacuous, mothering activities of the homemaker that overcame such personal character defects as the slothfulness, lying, and unbridled greed hidden just beneath the surface of respectability. At the same time, a barely detectable undercurrent of class separation and tension framed the human transaction in this mythic milieu. In contrast, in the rural-middle-landscape comedies of the late 1950s and the 1960s, especially in two extremely popular series—*The Beverly Hillbillies* and *Green Acres*—we find class separation and tension surfacing; however, because class distinction is expressed by bizarre central characters interacting in unbelievable situations, the class tensions are thereby defused. Unlike the suburban-middle-landscape comedies, in which the children were often ridiculously illogical by adult standards (to which they were always expected to adhere), in the rural-middle-landscape comedies, that character trait shifts to the naïve yet noble adults who inhabit a world filled with urban con men and pretentious middle-class boors reminiscent of Moliere's characters.

In the suburban-middle-landscape comedies, the adult central characters are motivated by drives for success and material acquisition tempered with humility, tacitly acknowledging the humble roots of the common man. This traditional rags-to-riches dream incorporating the myths of the Protestant ethic and eternal progress surfaced throughout the entire subgenre. In this mythic world, conformity to community values was signified through the reification of traditional moral and ethical codes of conduct (e.g., clean living—a clean front yard free of dirty old leaves, dandelions, and scraggly bushes; employed in this project was a battery of bourgeois implements such as electric hedge trimmers, weed eaters, mulchers, and fertilizer wagons or, if one wished to flaunt one's bourgeois status, a lawn-care service). In contrast, in the rural-middle-landscape comedies, the central characters either have inadvertently achieved wealth and simply have no interest in the status related to possession of money (e.g., Jed Clampett, out hunting for food, struck oil); have worked hard for wealth and subsequently rejected it for a purer, more spiritual existence in the countryside (Oliver Wendell Douglas deserting Park Avenue for the "serenity" of Hooterville); or have transcended the very notion of material wealth through upbringing and staunchly held traditional values (Amos McCoy and Andy Taylor). In all cases, the central characters of the rural middle landscape, rooted to their humane ecosystems by the warmth of their biological families, safe from the perils of the isolation of the frontier and from the deception in the city, speak to us of basic human values. Yet, their portrayal as children outside the mainstream of contemporary technicized culture condemns their actions to the status of antitechnical responses to a society they do not understand and cannot keep up with. The rustic, in questioning the entire milieu of advanced capitalism and its principal bourgeouis and petit bourgeois actors, is rendered both quaint and unthreatening because he or she operates outside the guiding myth of eternal progress. We can therefore laugh at the hillbilly without heeding his or her warnings dealing with questions of morality and ethics in advanced capitalism.

The Real McCoys, the pioneer rural-middle-landscape comedy, began its six-year run in 1957. Financed by Danny Thomas Productions, the series barely made it to the small screen: NBC turned it down, but ABC, then with a very weak schedule, was finally convinced of its potential. ABC would not be sorry for its decision. Production began. Writers Irving and Norman Pincus created an ensemble of simple, folksy characters who were nothing short of stereotypical. The patriarch of the McCoy clan, Grampa Amos, played by three-time Academy Award–winning actor Walter Brennan, walked with a limp, and spoke in a high-pitched, broken voice verging on a hoarse shout. Amos, a repository of country wisdom and a constant meddler, was a wily old codger, careful with what little money he had, and ready to stand up for his rights; the wisdom of experience had taught Amos to be wary of strangers, especially city slickers. Amos's grandson Luke, played by Richard (then known as Dick) Crenna, was the prototypical young male hillbilly—strong, angularly handsome, naive, gullible, kindhearted, and a bit slow to catch on. His devoted wife Kate was a simple country girl who was comfortable in the kitchen and had few material wants. Luke's 11-year-old brother Little Luke, a relatively docile youngster, understood the meaning of respect for adult authority. Pepino, the guitar-playing Latino, referred to in the show's theme song as "the Hired Hand," was happy-go-lucky, always smiling, and complacent in his position of subservience.

The McCoys (their namesakes could be the McCoys who feuded with the Hatfields) were an Appalachian mountain family who moved to a ranch in California's San Fernando Valley in search of the American Dream. While they had yet to realize that dream of prosperity, the family bonds—"together they share all the sorrows and joys" (again from the theme song)—were very powerful and compensated for their material wants. It is true that the family bonds of the suburban-middle-landscape comedies were also strong. Yet, in *The Real McCoys*, as in the other rural-middle-landscape comedies, the bonds, exemplified in both the geographical and psychic space of the rural environment, were constantly threatened by the encroachment of the city—a common motif in this comedic subgenre. We saw this theme considered but ultimately rejected in the conception of the Kodak "America" commercial nearly 30 years later. The city indeed became a psychic threat. Its residents exhibited such character traits as greed, deception, and vanity—the traits of the bourgeois and petit bourgeois classes in an advanced capitalist economy. The rural residents, who held to their more traditional agrarian/populist values (at least in the *mythology* of rural America) of honesty and a sense of sharing, at first seemed no match for their cunning urban counterparts. But, in the end, the purity of the peasants won the day. Of course, the characterizations of both classes were so exaggerated that it became difficult to accept the results of the conflict of values as meaningful.

A 1962 episode of *The Real McCoys* provides striking evidence of the use of this class conflict to garner laughs. By this point in the series, Luke is a widower and Amos is trying to find him a wife. Amos and neighbor George MacMichael take off in George's car for a convention, leaving Luke to mind the house. An old ranch-style home, well kept but sparsely furnished, it signifies a basic "dignified" poverty, reflected in the kitchen cabinets covered with curtains instead of cabinet doors. Before he left, Amos had asked Luke to fix the leaky roof while he was away. We cut to a sign on the side of a modern shiny automobile that reads "New Age Building Materials." In the car sit Jack Masters and Sally Burton, both sharply dressed, their neatly coiffed hair resembling that of local news anchors. They exude the veneer that clearly announces their status as city-type travelling salespersons. Watch out! The stage is set for the con. Masters sends the beautiful, well-proportioned Miss Burton ahead to the McCoy ranch in an effort to sell Luke some roof coating. Luke, the shy, gullible adult-child, is easily taken in by Sally's appearance and tight sweater. Sally describes her product to Luke—a "new miracle plastic spray" that gives "100 years of worry-free roofing." (Sally was clearly a harbinger of the cable television per-inquiry "miracle"-product advertising campaign.) In a feeble attempt at humor, Luke responds, "Imagine that! You can still have a roof after the house is gone." Sally grimaces. She continues the pitch, "Our company has developed this material for weatherproofing of missiles." Although Luke buys this (to us) obvious nonsense, he is still reluctant to commit himself to the project because of its cost. Masters, the fast-talking con man, must use pressure to make the sale. He appeals to Luke's "manliness," his need to take charge, to fix his house, to make an adult decision. At the same time, Masters appeals to Luke's compassion, asking him to help Sally, a damsel-in-distress, to keep her job, which will be lost if she doesn't make some sales in the neighborhood. Luke, unsure of his status as man or child, wavers. Sally begins to cry. Luke empathizes, "Now don't go gittin' yourself all onionized." Moved by this display of womanly frailty and feeling guilty for her plight, Luke agrees to buy the roofing treatment and to help sell the product to his neighbors, for 2 percent of the gross.

Act two finds Luke conducting a meeting on his front porch. In the foreground is an old beat-up pickup truck, its tailgate lowered and a hay bale in the truck bed, signifying the poverty of the area and framing the entire scam in progress. Luke, completely caught up in the headiness of the role of entrepreneur, is the proverbial "snake-oil salesman." He's now a "man," in charge of a meetin', and moving his neighbors through his oratorical powers. Luke shouts to the assembled crowd: "As you all know, us McCoys is just poor dirt farmers like all you. Why to us, money is practically just a word in the dictionary. So when we spend it, we got to get double value. . . . I'm going to give you a demonstration that's going to open your eyes to the wonders of science." Luke proceeds to demonstrate a sample of a shingle supposedly treated in the miracle plastic spray, which he describes as "treated with all them chemical goodies" and "satchumerated with all them chemicals." The neighbors are impressed, and they all buy. By now, Luke is feeling very proud of his efforts. Sally turns to Masters and comments, "His head's starting to swell up like our shingles in the rain."

When Amos returns from the convention, Luke tells him of all the activity. Amos is quickly skeptical. Luke demonstrates their newly coated roof by turning the garden hose on the shingles. Amos, sitting in his living-room rocking chair, is drenched. Luke, despondent and admitting he was "the Judas goat" leading the lambs to slaughter for a bag of gold, helps Amos bait a trap. They call Masters and Burton back on the pretense that George MacMichael wants to have his roof coated. They all meet at the McCoys'. Amos pretends to get his painful "weather knee," which signals rain. Masters and Burton are visibly nervous. Amos describes other "swindlers" who have come to the valley, especially the "magic-fertilizer swindlers."

Amos: Remember them?

George: I bet they haven't forgotten us either.

Masters: What happened to them?

Luke: They recovered . . . eventually.

Amos: They was young and healthy to start with. They recovered quickly. But the crooks with the miracle stock feed.

George: That was pitiful. Just pitiful.

Luke sprays the roof with the hose. Masters, sitting in Amos's chair, is drenched. The neighbors, who have been waiting outside, angrily con-

verge on the two city con artists. Masters reluctantly returns all their de-
posits. Luke turns to Sally and notes, "Miss Burton, you have just set the
cause of the American business woman back 50 years." Masters says to
Amos, "You tricked me. And I trusted you."

In this last scene, we find a key story element that has often been
employed in the rural context, although generally in melodrama—the city
dweller's fear of the evil that lurks just beyond the bend in the country
road. For while the rural middle landscape in its comedic form is full of
rather gentle, charming, if simple-minded characters—misfits with pure
values—beneath this idyllic surface lives a seething rage that emerges
when the fast-talking city slicker stumbles into the town, bringing his contemptible values.

The adult masculine iconography representing the materialization of
this basic value conflict is clearly established: the muddy or dusty jalopy,
the floppy hat, the rumpled clothing, and unshaven face representing the
purity of the country, the earth, and the common heritage; and the highly
polished, chrome-plated sedan with whitewall tires, the fedora (or, absent
a hat, the shiny, slicked-back hair), and the neatly pressed suit and clean-
shaven face representing the jaded wealth of the bourgeoisie. The adult
female icons follow the same general patterns: the honorable rural woman's neatly pressed but very simple, loose-fitting cotton print dress and a
minimum of makeup and the urban woman's snug-fitting business suit or
sweater and skirt and her heaviness of makeup and hair spray.

The Real McCoys broke television ground. The series's high rating—
number eight in the 1958–59 season and number five in the 1960–61
season—opened the door for the other rural comedies that were to rule
the airwaves in the 1960s as the suburban-middle-landscape comedy cycle
faded.

One of the most successful television comedies of the 1960s, *The Andy
Griffith Show*, would bring to the rural-middle-landscape comedy a true
human warmth exemplified in the character of Sheriff Andy Taylor of
the small town of Mayberry, North Carolina. Andy, a widower with a
young son, Opie, played by Ron Howard, later of *Happy Days* fame, lived
with his Aunt Bee. At work, Andy was faced less with the problems of
preserving law and order than with the difficult task of preserving his own
sanity in the presence of his incredible, bumbling deputy, Barney Fife,
played to perfection by Don Knotts, who won five Emmy Awards as best
supporting actor in the role. (Knotts left the series in 1965 to pursue his
own series.) Andy was philosophical, a kind father to Opie and to the
denizens of Mayberry. The show's opening reflects this relationship between father and son as we see a two-shot of Andy and Opie quietly
strolling along a lake, fishing poles on their shoulders, Opie barefooted
and Andy with a comforting hand resting on Opie's shoulder. Andy's gentle masculinity was in sharp contrast to the skinny, nervous, pip-squeakish

Barney—a man without an original thought but with plenty of opinions, a man who constantly tried to imitate Andy but who simultaneously was possessed by an overwhelming drive to be macho. His totally laughable attempts at masculinity through constant posturing and bravado provided many of television comedy's finest moments. Aunt Bee provided the womanly warmth in the series. The epitome of the countrified "mother hen," Bee, who always wore her hair in a bun, was eternally good-natured, jovial, and generally very slow until she got excited, at which point she would scurry around in total confusion "like a chicken with her head cut off." However, Aunt Bee broke the stereotypicalness of the countrywoman character in one way—she was a lousy cook.

Mayberry was generally unthreatened and unthreatening. There was hardly any crime in this peaceful setting. The jail's occasional occupants were mostly town drunks like Otis, who seemed to be a permanent resident. Once in a while, a city criminal would pass through town and cause a momentary uproar. The conflicts that arose in Mayberry were motivated not so much by greed or jealousy or vanity as they were by individuals' needs to maintain their sense of self-esteem, to demonstrate that they were of some value to the community. Pride was based not on a neighbor's defeat or on assuring someone else's lower social status but rather on one's own sense of accomplishment or contribution to the goals of the community. An early-1961 episode provides a clear example of the human warmth and sense of caring that define this version of the rural-middle-landscape comedy.

Each year for the past 11 years, Aunt Bee and Clara Edwards entered the pickle contest at the county fair. Clara had won the contest every year. She feigns humility, but we can tell she is very proud of her success. She is the town "pickle expert," as is reflected in her confident explications of the proper combination of ingredients and the techniques of pickling necessary for the successful pickle-making endeavor. Her success in pickle making compensates for her shortcomings in other areas. Aunt Bee, on the other hand, makes terrible pickles, to which Andy, Barney, and Opie will quickly attest. Act one begins with Clara tasting Aunt Bee's latest batch of pickles and offering Bee expert advice on possible modifications of the recipe. Bee, while at first graciously admitting Clara's pickling accomplishments, soon becomes tired of Clara's barely hidden condescension. In this "little world," success, while limited in its larger social impact, is nevertheless important in an interpersonal context.

Aunt Bee brings a jar of her new pickles to the sheriff's office for Andy and Barney to sample. Their faces drop in despair. To please Aunt Bee, they bite into the pickles and pretend satisfaction. Meanwhile, a fly lands on a pickle on Andy's desk and promptly expires. After Aunt Bee's exit, Barney turns to Andy and declares, "I don't know how I can face the future when I know there's eight quarts of these pickles in it." Thus is the stage set for the complication and confusion that frame so much action in the situation comedy genre. Andy and Barney decide to replace the "bad old home pickles" in Aunt Bee's jars with "good old store pickles." Andy explains this deception to Opie as father, son, and deputy Fife surreptitiously carry out the deed in Aunt Bee's kitchen: "Opie, I want you to understand. Ordinarily I don't approve of doin' things behind folks' backs. Now you know why we're doin' this?" Opie answers "Yeah, 'cause we don't want to hurt Aunt Bee's feelings." Opie has learned his values well. Having pulled the switcheroo, the boys must dispose of Aunt Bee's pickles. Barney takes them to the highway and begins to stop cars with out-of-state license plates, giving their drivers a "safe driving award"—a jar of Aunt Bee's deadly pickles. At dinner, everyone can comment on Bee's delectable (store-bought) pickles. But the deception backfires, as it must. Aunt Bee had decided that the pickles were to be her last batch and she would not enter the contest. But since the boys seemed to like them so much, she changed her mind and decided to enter them in the fair. The joke was beginning to go as sour as her pickles. What if Clara got beat by a store pickle?

We cut to a scene in which Clara shows Andy her pickle scrapbook with its 11 blue ribbons. Clara confides in Andy: "Whenever I get lonely or discouraged, I take out my book and look at my ribbons." Her eyes light up as music swells in the background: "I don't know how to explain it, but it's a great comfort to know that there's something I can do. Well, I suppose I'm just a foolish old lady." Andy, obviously moved, responds, "Oh well, now, I wouldn't believe that for a minute." Clara answers, "You probably think I'm just putting on airs. But I do try to make my pickles better every year. It means so much to me." Here we have a clear clue to the true meaning of the rural middle landscape as conceived in the myth. Clara, the traditional artisan, is not alienated from her work; she has direct control over it and it thus reflects and in fact is a part of her being—Clara and her pickles are inseparable. Andy relates the encounter to Barney in the following aphorism: "What's small potatoes to some folks can be mighty important to others." He continues, "Barney, that poor soul just lives for that contest, and if she got nosed out by a store pickle, I'd never forgive myself."

Barney and Andy are forced to eat all eight quarts of store pickles in a hurry so that Aunt Bee will make a new batch of homemade pickles and enter those in the contest. This she does, and we cut to the judging at the fair. The judges, barely able to continue their work after tasting one of Aunt Bee's homemade pickles, suspect that the pickles were dipped in kerosene. Clara wins again. Aunt Bee is a very gracious loser: "As long as my family likes what I make, that's blue-ribbon enough for me." Because the boys liked the pickles so much, she made 16 more quarts.

In the epilog, Barney comes over to Aunt Bee's to pick up Andy, who is eating breakfast. He sits down to eat a piece of toast, opens the jelly jar. They both sniff.

Barney: You been doin' some paintin' in here?

Andy: No. Probably just some glue Opie's usin' on model airplanes.

Barney: Don't smell like glue to me. Smells more like ammonia.

Andy: You don't think that gas stove's leakin', do ya?

Barney starts to eat his toast with the jelly on it, but nearly passes out; it's Aunt Bee's homemade marmalade. They just can't win.

Aunt Bee's "family" and Clara's blue ribbons are their respective "small potatoes," very personal concerns related not to the larger questions of social relations but rather to the immediacy of everyday experience in the insulated environment of the rural middle landscape.

The problem of self-esteem is raised throughout this series. In a 1966 episode, Andy and Goober, who runs the local gas station, go to an evening continuing-education class to study American history. The men of Mayberry all wear suits and ties to class, reflecting the importance they have placed on this activity. Goober feels inadequate because of a self-perceived limited cognitive capacity, which is in truth a lack of educational background. He lags far behind the class, although he has studied hard. With no confidence and with a vocabulary inadequate for the discussion of the history of political thought, Goober drops out of school, goes on a three-week hunting trip, something he is very skilled at doing, and returns to Mayberry sporting a beard (he forgot to take his razor). The people of Mayberry think Goober, with his new facial hair, looks like a scholar. They refer to Goober as a "deep thinker," a "scientist," an "ambassador," or a "philosopher." Goober wastes little time taking these compliments to heart, grows a full beard and, with confidence or a swelled head—the line between the two is often a fine one—returns to class toting a briefcase and an unstoppable mouth. A veritable fount of knowledge, Goober develops a country analogy for every political event involving U.S. domestic and international policy making. His grammar and syntax are still pure rural middle landscape, but his ideas are generally sound. As he stands to discourse in the foreground of the frame, a picture of Abe Lincoln on the back wall of the classroom is shown over his left shoulder.

Soon Goober becomes the town boor. People begin avoiding him in the street. One day he stops at a fruitstand, picks up a red apple, and addresses it: "One time you was a seed." He visits his chum Floyd, the barber, and exclaims with authority, "A man's best friend is not his dog. It's people." Andy, who can stand no more, ultimately takes responsibility for ending both Goober's pontifications and his isolation, which is now almost complete. Andy says to his old friend, "Confidence is something that's on the inside. . . . It doesn't hurt to listen once in a while." Goober subsequently regains his humility, shaves his beard, and with renewed confidence returns to the evening class as himself.

The Andy Griffith Show, which ran from 1960 through 1968, was immensely popular. It was never lower than seventh in the ratings, and in its final year it was the highest-rated series on television. By 1968 the Vietnam conflict was well along; the free speech movement at Berkeley had signaled a new student awareness of political and social inequity; we were about to come to grips with Tet and napalm in a rural context halfway around the earth; and our urban slums were about to burn following the assassination of Martin Luther King, Jr.; but we took refuge in the television security of Sheriff Andy Taylor of Mayberry, North Carolina, deeply embedded in the rural middle landscape, where there was no war, no crime, and no deep division in our social fabric.

If *The Andy Griffith Show* stressed warm human values within the generally isolated cognitive and geographical space of rural America, *The Beverly Hillbillies* and *Green Acres*, each in a distinct way, brought the rural middle landscape face to face with the greed and vanity of the city. In this dialectic of rural purity and urban seaminess, we find positive values of the rural area such as familial love and support, honesty, and humility emerging victorious, although the victory is a hollow one, for the human manifestations of rural purity—the charming, oddball central characters— in all their naïveté, manage to deflect and thereby subvert the significance of the confrontation.

The Beverly Hillbillies was one of those rare television phenomena—an immediate smash hit. Created and produced by Paul Henning, it was the highest-rated program in its first two television seasons (1962-64). However, its charm began to wear thin by its third season as it fell to twelfth in the ratings and stabilized between the eighth and twelfth spots for the next four years. Featuring the actor-dancer Buddy Ebsen in the title role of Jed Clampett, the Clampett clan included Granny (Irene Ryan), Elly May (Donna Douglas), and Jethro Bodine (Max Baer, Jr.)—a motley group of kind, nature-loving Ozark Mountain hill people who strike oil on their property, instantly become enormously wealthy, and move to a Beverly Hills mansion on the advice of their relatives. Jed, the clan's patriarch, is a widower. Full of native intelligence if not book learning, Jed is the voice of compromise and restraint, who must constantly arbitrate between the quick-tempered ancient countrywoman, Granny—a feisty hellcat whose character was the exact opposite of Aunt Bee of *The Andy Griffith Show*—and Mrs. Drysdale, the Clampetts' next-door neighbor and wife of Milburn Drysdale, president of the Commerce Bank of Beverly Hills, an institution deeply indebted to the Clampetts for their business. The two "younguns," the beautiful blond-haired virgin Elly May and the large-framed, boneheaded country oaf Jethro, provide innumerable causes for guffawing as their seemingly total ignorance of urban customs and lack of formal education get them into awkward situations. Both have been educated in the woods and commune much better with "critters" than with city folk. Jed must constantly rescue Granny, Elly, and Jethro by humbly apologizing to the city folks who have been "wronged" by the naïve Clampetts' actions. It seems as if the Clampetts are always begging forgiveness for their status as outsiders. This, of course, makes their superior values easy to write off.

As with *The Real McCoys*, California seemed to hold the key to the American Dream for the Clampett clan. However, Jed and the rest did not go to California in search of a living wage, as did the McCoys, but rather because, as the theme song tells us, it "is the place ya oughta be"— a beckoning mecca complete with movie stars and swimming pools. The Clampetts are more observers of than participants in the American Dream. Their fascination with the status that seems to come naturally to the wealthy in advanced capitalist America is reflective of the attitudes of many viewers. However, the Clampetts, while millionaires, are indeed on the periphery because of their unkempt appearance and country ways, and they intend to remain there, observing from a position of moral superiority. They steadfastly maintain their heritage of self-sufficiency, for while they could easily afford a mansion full of servants, they have none, preferring to perform all household duties themselves. It is, of course, possible that had they desired servants, none would agree to live and work in such an eccentric, low-status atmosphere and to cook possum bellies for Granny.

The Beverly Hillbillies is highly dependent on physical comedy and gestures. Jethro's herculean strength, Elly's awkward shyness, Jed's country amble and bowlegs, and Granny's militant duck walk give the characters distinctive movement qualities and dictate much of the theatrical "business" in which they engage. This ranges from Jethro's lifting automobiles and airplanes off the ground and moving them around to Granny's charging after the Drysdales, shotgun thrust forward, as she prepares, as she says, to "feud 'em." The objects of civilized society become properties used in this physical comedy. For example, in one episode the Clampetts confuse a beautiful old billiard table that came with their mansion with what Granny called an "eatin' table." The pool cues become "pot passers"—the table was so large that four people could not conveniently pass food around it without inserting the pool cues through the pot handles and gently easing the precariously suspended pots across the green expanse. Jed sharpened a few of the pool cues—"turkey stickers"—which were used to pass whole parts of a turkey from serving platter to the hungry Clampetts. The table rail was a bit unusual for an eatin' table, but

Granny surmised its function as preventing plates from slipping off onto the floor. The green felt was a sign that the previous owners were bad housekeepers; Granny, thinking the tablecloth was stuck to the table underneath, tried in vain to peel it off but finally gave up in frustration and disgust. While we must really suspend our disbelief when faced with such ridiculously illogical situations—after all, what rural county doesn't sport at least one bar or, if dry, a meeting hall with a pool table in it—the Clampetts' total isolation from the modern world becomes the series's consistent comedic premise. As physical comedy it works very well, although after a while, such comedy grows stale if not accompanied by complex characters who develop as the series progresses.

Beyond the physical comedy of *The Beverly Hillbillies*, the dialectic of rural and urban values is a frequent theme in the plot lines. These values are directly tied to socioeconomic class difference. The Clampetts are an amalgam of the rural hick and the nouveau riche, with their rural values controlling the use of their wealth. Milburn Drysdale is a callous bourgeois banker, putting capital to work for the Clampetts; he is conservative to the point of being overly cautious as the Clampetts try to give money away or help finance their rural friends' rather odd entrepreneurial ventures. Drysdale is portrayed as an angry, shameless, and ruthless parasite. He underpays and verbally abuses his employees, most notably Miss Jane Hathaway, his personal assistant. Yet he always looks the fool as he must humble himself before his main depositors, the Clampetts, whom he can barely tolerate. Drysdale's wife, a fat, lazy woman with no wit, represents the decadent blue blood. Her family having fallen on financially hard times, she married the commoner Milburn to regain the pride that comes with material wealth. Her voice, rising in a cracking falsetto, reveals her unbearable pretensions. The Clampetts, while finding her insufferable, nevertheless are willing to accept her character defects if only because she is their neighbor.

In one particularly revealing episode early in the series, Drysdale's 35-year-old stepson Sonny (played to perfection by Louie Nye), comes home to visit from Harvard, where he has been "trying to find himself" as an undergraduate student for 17 years. Effeminate, immature, vain, and slothful, Sonny is a fop—the archetypal "blue blood-on-the-skids." Sonny hates his stepfather's low caste. His mother consoles him: "I know it was wrong of me to marry a common bank president, but I wanted you to have everything, and all I could give you was the heritage of a fine old family. But it takes money too, darling." Sonny would have none of this: "Money. I hate that word. It makes the rich the social equal to us." "Oh no, dear," responds Mrs. Drysdale, "it would never do that."

Milburn, who constantly seeks ways to please the Clampetts, has decided that Sonny should date Elly May. Having never seen Elly, Sonny is reluctant to participate. He informs his stepfather, "I refuse to date a strange girl just to benefit your economic situation." When Milburn warns Sonny that his and Sonny's economic situations are inseparable, Sonny retorts, "Money doesn't interest me; who steals my purse, steals trash." This reference to Shakespeare's *Othello* (act III, scene iii), in which Iago urges Othello to think of his good name ("Good name in man and woman, dear my lord,/Is the immediate jewel of their souls:/Who steals my purse steals trash; 'tis something, nothing;"), while seemingly out of place in such a "low-brow" program, exemplifies the moments of "play" by which writers enrich the popular culture text. Sonny, after all, attended Harvard.

Returning to the class theme of this episode, Mrs. Drysdale disdainfully notes: "I've heard the most disturbing reports about the Clampetts. I understand they're no better than peasants." Appalled at the thought of dating a peasant, Sonny is quickly won over, however, when he spots Elly lounging by her backyard swimming pool. Sonny, the fallen aristocrat, lacks any sense of principles and has no commitment save to the pursuit of ephemeral sensual pleasure. He is a 35-year-old child, as much outside the world of meaningful adult social relationships as are the Clampetts.

In act two, Jed and Granny prepare Elly for her date with Sonny. Totally unaware of her own sexuality and knowing nothing about the customs of dating or of the phrase "the birds and the bees" (which she believes refers to critters in the woods), Elly is about to begin her initiation. Jed describes "courtin' and sparkin' " to her, and it seems as though she gets the general drift of that activity. Sonny, meanwhile, prepares for his date, admiring himself in the mirror. We cut to Sonny's arrival at the Clampett mansion: Dressed to kill in a double-breasted blazer, he arrives in his Mercedes-Benz 190 convertible, parks next to Jed's dilapidated truck, gets out, and saunters to the Clampetts' front door. Jethro enters the frame; dressed in a coat too small, his pants held up by a rope and falling a little below midcalf, his black socks and gigantic brogan shoes calling attention to his status as country clown, Jethro is mistaken for an eccentric servant. Referring to Jed's truck, Sonny asks Jethro to move that "weird thing." Jethro of course thinks Sonny is talking about the Mercedes, and after Sonny is admitted to the mansion by Granny, Jethro and Jed (who has arrived on the scene) store the Mercedes behind some bushes, safely out of sight. Elly comes down the stairs to meet Sonny. She is dressed in a pretty, promish dress, but she is not wearing shoes. After some preliminary niceties, including Sonny's presentation of a gift to Elly—a framed picture of himself—he tries to kiss Elly's hand. Thinking Sonny is trying to bite her, Elly flips him. Sonny lands on his back and, dazed, picks himself up and flees. Jethro, having hidden Sonny's automobile, has returned to the front of the mansion. Upon learning that his Mercedes has been so disposed of, the irate and feeble Sonny begins pummeling Jethro in the chest with karate chops. Jethro, feeling no pain, stands immobile as Sonny finally hurts his hand and runs off.

Following this incident, we cut to the Clampetts arriving at the Drysdales to apologize for their actions. Sonny's car is returned, Elly is sorry
she misunderstood Sonny's intentions, and Jed regrets not greeting Sonny
at the front door, "as a proper pa should." Granny, who has nothing for
which to apologize and who wouldn't have apologized if she had, reluctantly invites the Drysdales over for Thanksgiving dinner. In the final
scene, following Jed's saying grace, we see the pot passers in action as we
note the looks of consternation on the faces of the Drysdales, who are
"slumming" so that they can continue to benefit from the Clampetts'
wealth.

Throughout this episode and the entire series, the humor is produced
both by the Clampetts' ignorance of urban customs and language, which
generates much of the physical comedy, and by Drysdale's constant grov-
eling at the feet of these humble millionaires, who would seemingly not
even consider withdrawing their money from his bank. The folksy Clampetts seem firmly tied to tradition, to the family as an institution, and
warm human values such as sharing one's good fortune with the less fortunate; at the same time, as outsiders, their acts seem anachronistic, gestures to be laughed at rather than emulated. The Drysdales, on the other
hand, seem lost. Mrs. Drysdale deludes herself about maintaining her aristocratic heritage; and Milburn has no tradition, living from day to day,
fearing the loss of his wealth, which could occur by virtue of a single
act—the Clampetts' removal of their assets from his vault.

In retrospect, this rural-middle-landscape comedy appears quite cynical,
admiring but ultimately discounting basic human values associated with
the mythology of the pure spirit of rural life and condemning yet tacitly
accepting the life of Beverly Hills, a jaded version of the American Dream.

One additional version of the rural-middle-landscape comedy gets brief
treatment here, if only because of its basic premise and the fact that *The
Beverly Hillbillies* creator, Paul Henning, created it, too. *Green Acres*, an
exact reversal of the major premise of *The Beverly Hillbillies*, had a successful six-year run on CBS (1965–71). It featured Eddie Albert in the role
of Oliver Wendell Douglas, a highly successful Manhattan lawyer who
wanted to "get back to nature"; his urban-chic wife Lisa was played by
Eva Gabor. Oliver bought a 160-acre farm, sight unseen, just outside
Hooterville, the setting for yet another rural comedy, *Petticoat Junction*.
The Douglases got conned, this time by a rural wheeler-dealer, Mr. Haney.
They bought an old shack on a rock pile, but that notwithstanding, Oliver
was determined to make a go of the rural life. While Lisa was never able
to adjust to being a rustic, she did become quite fond of their farm animals, naming each of the chickens and cows. There was frequent interaction between the characters of *Green Acres* and *Petticoat Junction*
because of the common Hooterville setting. The old-timers, skeptical of
Oliver's motives, constantly laughed at his farming ineptitude; he was

outside the outsiders, yet he persevered. Lisa constantly lobbied for their return to Park Avenue, but Oliver would have none of it. Instead, he felt at home among his neighbors, who included pig farmer Fred Ziffel and his highly intelligent pet pig Arnold, who watched television and did tricks; handyman Eb Dawson, who helped fix up the rundown property; and country-store owner Sam Drucker. What one remembers most clearly about this series was its portrayal of rural people as generally plain, un-attractive, and not above an occasional deception if it meant making money off a city slicker. Rather than the purity of rural values transcend-ing the evil influence of civilization and city ways, a basic characteristic of the myth of the rural middle landscape, here we see a transparent version of the myth in which many of the town's inhabitants are wily, shrewd entrepreneurs hiding behind the guise of the country bumpkin. We are reminded here of the fear of having our automobile break down in some small town in the middle of nowhere and of being charged an exorbitant price for what should have been a minor repair. The "ugly face" of the myth, like its converse, is generated by the Hollywood cultural production machine itself.

Rural-middle-landscape comedy introduced America to black protago-nists on a television series in 1972. Norman Lear's *Sanford and Son* (im-mediately following Lear's success with *All in the Family*), brought America's Deep South to life on the small screen. The setting was actually transplanted to the black Los Angeles ghetto, the site of an urban seam-iness different in character from the Clampett's Beverly Hills environs, but seamy nonetheless.

Junk dealer Fred Sanford (played brilliantly by Redd Foxx) and his son Lamont (played by Demond Wilson) represented positive rural values—deep familial love and support and an underlying honesty. Fred's shrewd, rural-entrepreneurial character traits were motivated less by the desire to acquire wealth than by the pleasure of the game and were effectively counterbalanced by Lamont's guilt and moral suasion. A panoply of charming rustic eccentrics inhabited this urban version of rural America—Fred; Aunt Esther, the Bible-toting southern-Baptist proprietor of the di-lapidated Sanford Arms boarding house; and Fred's dear old buddies, the slow-moving, gentle Bubba and the kind-but-confused Grady Wilson.

While Lear's social satire would, on occasion, emerge as Fred, the black racist, derided Julio Fuentes, his Puerto Rican neighbor and Lamont's friend, this was a minor subtext to the comedy's essentially rural aesthetic. Fred's constant verbal assaults against Rollo Larson, another of Lamont's friends and clearly a cynical, streetwise urban con artist, placed Fred squarely in his rural milieu, in which shrewdness exuded a peculiar charm—a charm unknown to the likes of Rollo.

As in most rural comedy, in which business is conducted at home or within walking distance of it, Fred and Lamont's junk business was carried on in the living room, in the yard, and in the kitchen.

Perhaps most significantly, the main character, Fred, was a cantankerous old geezer reminiscent of Amos McCoy of *The Real McCoys*. Like Amos, Fred was a widower with a grown son living at home. Also like Amos, Fred's gruffness obscured, but not completely, an underlying naïveté and compassion. *Sanford and Son* demonstrated that, according to the myth of the rural-middle-landscape comedy, blacks, like their rural hillbilly counterparts, were not to be taken seriously in our culture.

This brief journey through the comedic rural middle landscape has attempted to expose the mythic realm of seemingly pure traditional values that paradigmatically reveals the ways in which those values are rendered meaningless through the characterization of those who hold such values as quaint childlike actors in a contemporary situation they can neither truly comprehend nor change. These comedies, while often hilarious by virtue of their physical comedy, their use of malapropism, and their absurd characterizations, ultimately reinforce the marginalization of real social groups. And while we, like the rustics in these comedies, can escape to a less complicated, less threatening physical and psychic landscape, we will always be subjected to the dominant cultural visions of eternal progress being projected just beyond the boundaries of the rural middle landscape. After all, Andy Taylor did eventually move to the city.

URBAN COMEDY—ETERNAL PROGRESS

If there is a television comedy form that develops most naturally from the life experience of those creative television workers who represent the New York–Hollywood nexus, it is the urban comedy. According to Arthur Hough, who, in the early 1980s, did an extensive traditional content analysis of the television comedy, of the 400-plus situation comedies that appeared on television from 1948 to 1978, 211 casts lived in a metropolitan setting, 93 series were set in New York City alone, and 67 of the couples involved lived in apartments.[37] These data don't reveal much about the character of the urbanity of these series, but they do provide quantitative evidence of the pervasive presence of this comedic type on our prime-time screens. This trend has continued and even intensified in the 1980s and early 1990s as *Cheers*, *The Cosby Show*, and *Murphy Brown* have made the urban comedy increasingly popular.

Work has played a significant role in the social relations depicted in urban comedy. Whereas to the protagonists of the suburban-middle-landscape comedies, work was an occasional digression from the main business of raising a family and whereas to the protagonists of the rural-middle-landscape comedies, work was occasional and done somewhere else (e.g., Oliver Wendell Douglas, the gentleman farmer of *Green Acres*), not done at all (e.g., Jed Clampett, the millionaire patriarch of *The Beverly*

Hillbillies), or simply a way of leisurely passing the day (Sheriff Andy Taylor of Mayberry), work in the urban comedy is truly a way of life around which other activities revolve.

Some of the urban comedies are mildly cynical. *Barney Miller's* 12th Precinct in New York City's Greenwich Village employed a broken-down old cop named Fish, who always seemed to have one foot in the grave and who constantly griped about everything—the classic case of urban burnout. *Taxi's* characters, mostly part-time moonlighters, consisted of a frustrated actor waiting for the big break, a boxer who never won a fight, and a lost student searching for meaning, all of whom were dominated by a tyrannical dispatcher. *The Honeymooners* unfolded in a sparsely furnished, claustrophobic kitchen/living-room setting, with a window looking out on the brick facade of another building. The main characters, blue-collar workers, seemed trapped but nevertheless dignified. *The Bob Newhart Show* featured a variety of wealthy, urbane professionals who, in spite of their material comfort, seemed lonely and insecure.

Other urban comedies, for the most part, border on the euphoric. *I Love Lucy, Make Room for Daddy, The Dick Van Dyke Show,* and *The Mary Tyler Moore Show* all celebrate the excitement and glamour of show-business lifestyles. Lucy's plight as a frustrated actress, whose husband wanted her to remain a housewife in their Manhattan apartment, was perhaps only vaguely understood by an audience locked in the context of social relations of the 1950s (today, her subtextual struggle for liberation would likely be read in a much different way by many women and men). Only in the final episode of *The Mary Tyler Moore Show* did the euphoria collapse as the television station, which framed the action of the series, was sold and the entire news team fired, except, ironically, the incompetent news anchor Ted Baxter. *The Cosby Show,* featuring a successful professional couple, an obstetrician and an attorney, brought the long-overdue celebration of the Great American Dream to the black community.

Whether mildly cynical or bordering on euphoria, at the core of all these comedic works is the myth of eternal progress. From the New York City bus driver Ralph Kramden and his sewer-worker sidekick Ed Norton of *The Honeymooners,* to the Ph.D.-level psychologist Bob Hartley of *The Bob Newhart Show,* and the dry-cleaning entrepreneur and social climber George Jefferson of *The Jeffersons,* the social construct of the good life is manifest in these works—an urban American vision framed by the achievements of commerce and the ideology of equal opportunity. The protagonists, even those in the mildly cynical urban comedies, are not fatalists; they are always searching for the way forward, whether by opening one's own business and thereby shifting one's status from worker to entrepreneur (e.g., Ricky Ricardo's opening his own nightclub, the Ricky Ricardo Babaloo Club, on *I Love Lucy,* and Sam Malone's repurchasing his beloved downtown Boston bar Cheers); or by searching for the fool-proof get-rich-quick scheme (Ralph Kramden of *The Honeymooners* was constantly on the lookout for the fast buck, but his efforts were always thwarted by his inept neighbor and lifetime buddy Norton); or by working hard and being pliant in order to win a promotion within the group (e.g., Mary Richards's promotion from her initial position as assistant producer to associate producer and finally to producer and Lou Grant's concurrent promotion to news director at Minneapolis's WJM-TV). From show busi-ness to broadcast news and police business—from Ricky Ricardo, Danny Williams, and Rob Petrie, whose lives in show biz continually interfered with their lives at home; to Mary Richards, who had little home life as a single career woman and apartment dweller; to Murphy Brown, whose career as a star reporter rendered remarriage problematic if not unthink-able; and to Captain Barney Miller, whose family was written out of his world not long after the series debuted—the quest for personal status outside the traditional confines of the nuclear family became increasingly important.

The protagonists' human frailties and their frustrations with the various pressures of everyday urban life have provided the context for both laugh-ter and empathy. The outcomes, however, were never in doubt; in the words of Mary's theme song, "You're gonna make it after all." Or would she? Bob Hartley, week after week, ministered to the emotional castoffs of an ungrounded urban social milieu. Ted Baxter would have been a perfect candidate for Bob's therapy. It was inevitable that television's ur-ban comedy would achieve many of its finest moments on the couch of a wealthy Chicago psychologist.

The biological families of the suburban-and rural-middle-landscape com-edies are generally either supplemented or replaced in the urban comedy by the nonbiological work family that provides the protagonists with the support needed to survive and progress in a chaotic, constantly reforming world. The need for community, in these comedies and seemingly in our own everyday lives as well, is increasingly satisfied through office or work-place relationships. There are, of course, notable exceptions. *The Cosby Show*, which often resembled a traditional suburban-middle-landscape comedy in an urban setting, increasingly focused on the warm, supportive family relationships in the Huxtable household as the series developed.

According to critic Janet Maslin, writing in 1980 in the *New York Times*: "The workplace has grown especially popular with television writers at a time when family life is particularly hard to explain. Besides, as it is pre-sented on television, the shared experience of a group of people working together can be as important as family life—in some ways, even more so."[38] Maslin is correct, as far as her argument goes, in her assessment of the social importance of the new work family as a group of people co-operating to resolve common difficulties and offer mutual support in a familylike setting in times of personal crisis. The relationships of these television characters, especially the archetypal boss/worker relationship, provide the viewers with a comprehensible social context so that they can laugh at the limitations of power in the persona of the boss/father-figure, while recognizing the basic humanness that frames the television version of work life. In *The Dick Van Dyke Show*, Melvin Cooley, the balding, pompous producer of the fictional *Alan Brady Show* (and the brother-in-law of the show's star) was made the constant fool by Rob Petrie and coworkers Sally Rogers and Buddy Sorrell. Lou Grant, Mary Richards's newsroom boss on *The Mary Tyler Moore Show*, possessed a gruff exterior, underneath which was a heart of gold; he was never the fool but would, on occasion, be forced to retract some epithet or rash judgment made at a moment of hotheadedness as we laughed at his discomfort while still admiring his basic humility. On *The Bob Newhart Show*, Bob Hartley's understated manner and the constant frustrations of his work were the source of amusement, as his bizarre patients and his sassy receptionist Carol seemed always to have the upper hand in the social transactions around the office; at the same time, sanity prevailed, in large measure because of the maturity of Bob's wife Emily and Carol's underlying respect for Bob's professionalism. Sam Malone, *Cheers*'s lothario owner/bartender may not have been very smart or heroic. But he (or rather his bar) provided stability for his coworkers, and his regular customers, who would rather be at Cheers than anywhere else. It really was "home" for them.

The increasing difficulty in explaining family life as seen in the contemporary biological family and the presentation of the work family as a significant social institution often functioning as a surrogate nuclear family providing comfort and security in many ways reflect an actual confusion regarding the social importance of the nuclear family in the everyday activities of today's consumer economy. Is the family becoming an institution whose raison d'être is the provision of leisure commodities for its anomic individual members, a group wherein parents, in the words of cultural anthropologist Jules Henry, have become "imps of fun," struggling to please their children by providing unlimited opportunities for material gratification at the expense of human contact? Over the past two centuries, as work was separated from the range of activities in which the nuclear family engaged as a unit, it was inevitable that the power of the family as a socially binding institution would wane. Yet, the essentially conservative television apparatus cannot let the family appear to be dying or relinquishing its larger social role. The medium's constant pull toward the center, through its espousal of the dominant ideology (which stresses individual opportunity within the context of benevolent social control), predetermines certain motifs, among them the power of the "family" group to enforce social norms through "education." The naïve Mary Richards is educated to the ways and rituals of the newsroom by her surrogate father Lou. The naïve Rob Petrie is educated to the sometimes sordid ways of the production of television comedy by his worldly-wise "older brother and sister," Sally Rogers and and Buddy Sorrell.

In these comedies, success outside the world of nuclear-family relationships seems assured, if temporary, and in most cases it comes very easily. Success in the biological-family unit is often more difficult to achieve. Lou Grant was separated from his wife Edie in the 1973–74 season of *The Mary Tyler Moore Show*. Mary's news work began following the breakup of a four-year relationship. Critic John Phelan argues that the difficulty in achieving stable family relationships is in part due to a lack of "moral clarity from enduring values" in both the television world itself and the real world upon which the television world comments.[39] In the primary world of our everyday lives, which television appropriates in its series of "realistic" plays in settings that convey the appearance of authenticity through the intimacy of a small enclosed space, the fragmentary and the temporary have become the rule. Contemporary television narrative, especially evident in urban comedy, often reveals a world of "multiple real alternatives, . . . the plurality of self-worlds [and] the fragments of unconfident sub-cultures."[40] We are offered a world of "plurality without purpose," according to Phelan. Bob Hartley's patients would surely agree. Urban comedy offers us transient togetherness in a highly competitive white-collar work context best described as professional-entrepreneurial. As Phelan notes about modern narrative, it

neither promises nor delivers transcendent meaning. It does afford companionship, the universalism of vulnerability, the venting of vicarious rage or lust, however banal in motive and meaning. In modern narrative, one is offered a peek into another room of the enormous modern mansion where there are others, in different clothes, with different jobs, just like oneself in age, or values, or expectations. Everyone can observe a media counterpart, . . . command an episode. There are no . . . ideals or models for inner emulation. Rather, there are representative figures which attract universal attention and thus give meaning to various self-worlds.[41]

It was precisely this dilemma—the lack of transcendent models—that motivated Bill Cosby to structure *The Cosby Show* around the dual notions of providing positive role models for what blacks could achieve and lessons for everyone in humane child-rearing practices. This, in turn, prompted some critics to label the series as myopic and unrealistic, given the contemporary socioeconomic status of most blacks in America and the tensions in black-white relations (*The Cosby Show* all but ignored this latter issue).

Transcendent meaning, especially that clearly grounded in "the political" as defined in this book, is not something most members of the Hollywood creative community and few if any members of the business world of television entertainment feel very comfortable with. While such meaning may emerge through insightful critical analysis of a television work, in no way is such transcendent meaning intended as part of urban comedy's meaning-bearing systems. This is certainly true if we consider the absence of any truly alternative or oppositional strategies in these comedies. James L. Brooks, one of the most respected writer-producers in television, whose credits include *The Mary Tyler Moore Show*, *Lou Grant*, and *The Simpsons*, noted in particular about *Mary Tyler Moore*: "We try not to get into right and wrong. I don't know what's right or wrong. I'm personally distrustful of anything political. We don't get into much conservative-liberal argument. It's never an issue with our show."[42] Brooks's statement may serve as the credo for urban comedy on television.

Brooks pointed to an episode of *The Mary Tyler Moore Show* in which Mary was faced with the very difficult decision of claiming a journalist's privilege, that is, the right to protect the identity of her news source, which would likely lead to her being tossed in jail for contempt of court or perhaps to her revealing the source and breaking the trust established in the journalist-source relationship (this dilemma is of great importance in the "real world" of journalism). Viewing the treatment of this very volatile issue regarding the freedom to gather news, Brooks termed it "a very human" show about "someone who didn't want to get caught up in issues."[43] Mary didn't want to be thrown in the slammer with prostitutes— an understandable reaction, but one that negated the possibility of a meaningful personal and professional ethical commitment. Of course, the comedy emerges as Mary reverts to the persona the audience came to love—the beautiful associate news producer whose veneer of professionalism is stripped back to reveal her true vulnerability (the "emotional" woman). This dilemma is revealed to us as, in a two-shot, we see Lou Grant, dressed in a rumpled white shirt, his tie loosened, sitting behind his plain, uncluttered desk and Mary, in her neatly tailored beige business suit with a white turtleneck and fashionable pumps, sitting in an office chair facing Lou:

Lou (*in a close-up*): The whole concept of freedom of the press will be destroyed, and, with it, democracy as you and I know it and cherish it.

Cut to:

Mary (*reaction shot, looking very sad*).

Cut to:

Lou and Mary (*two-shot*).

Lou: But don't let that influence you. (Laugh track.)

Cut to:

Mary (*close-up*): Well, I'll just have to go to jail. That's the right thing, it's the honorable thing, it's the only thing.

Cut to:

Lou (*reaction shot, approving*).

Cut to:

Mary (*close-up*): There's just one problem . . . (*Tears well up in her eyes as she cries out*). I don't wanna go to jail! (Laugh track.)[44]

The audience track laughs at Lou's encomium on the "sacred trusts" of press freedom and democracy as he tries to make Mary feel the slightest bit of guilt about her ambivalence regarding her professional journalistic commitment. This is in keeping with the series, which stresses the social life of the television newsroom against the hazy backdrop of issues that cross the news desk. This was a comedy of character rather than of issues, a "joyous" comedy rather than a comedy of irony, satire, or sarcasm.[45]

Eleven years after *The Mary Tyler Moore Show* ended its network run, another equally well-written urban comedy focusing on broadcast journalism, *Murphy Brown*, would present a more realistic view of this workplace and its inhabitants. The title character, a star reporter on the fictional CBS-TV weekly news magazine program *F.Y.I.* is (unlike Mary Richards) opinionated, sarcastic, overbearing, driven, and somewhat neurotic. Murphy spent a month at the Betty Ford Clinic to kick her smoking and drinking habits. Murphy's character is in many ways reminiscent of Maude Findlay of the mid-1970s Norman Lear comedy *Maude*, the independent, even dominant woman.

Maude's abortion drew heavy protest mail. Murphy's decision to have a baby conceived during a brief fling with her ex-husband became a controversy during the 1992 Presidential election campaign as Vice President Dan Quayle charged the series with subverting "family values."

Murphy's strong professional ethical sense would most certainly have produced a quite different response to the question of journalist's privilege than Mary's.

Murphy Brown represents a strain of contemporary hard-edged urban comedy that can be read as a "liberal" reaction against the restorationist values that came to frame the ideology of Reaganism. *The Cosby Show*, the most popular series in all 1980s television, on the other hand has been criticized as the embodiment of those Reaganite values despite its creators' admirable intentions. According to Jack Hitt, senior editor at *Harper's Magazine*, who moderated a 1988 roundtable of television writers and producers:

What replaces *All in the Family* as the top show in the country? *The Cosby Show*—a sitcom that taps into the Reganesque reaffirmation of the American Dream. The show is a symbolic welcome by the middle class to a historically oppressed group, blacks. We laugh while we think this is really a great country.

Sally Lapiduss, a freelance television writer, responds to Hitt's comment: "It certainly is Reaganesque. America can deal with a black family only if it poses no economic, social, or racial problems."[46]

This critique is arguably not directed against *The Cosby Show* per se. Rather, it can be interpreted as a critique of the cautious nature of the medium's programmers generally. As noted in chapter 2, a basic rule in commercial broadcast network television's text building practices is, "Don't divide the audience." The outcome, in situation comedy as in most other television program forms, is the avoidance of the overtly threatening. *The Cosby Show*, like almost all the examples offered in this chapter, has profited immensely by adhering to this dictum.

Taken as a whole, television's urban comedy occupies an intermediate position between the self-deceptive naïveté of the early suburban-middle-landscape comedies and the rural-middle-landscape comedies of the 1960s that represent cultures cut off from the real world of social relations, and the self-reflexive comedy-drama (discussed in chapter 5) that grounds both the individual and the family unit firmly in that world—a world in which social relations are inexorably, if often somewhat ambiguously, connected to "the political."

NOTES

1. Joseph Campbell, *The Hero with a Thousand Faces* (New York: Pantheon Books, 1949), p. 28.

2. James K. Feibleman, *In Praise of Comedy* (New York: Horizon Press, 1970), p. 178.

3. Henry Ten Eyck Perry, "Comedy," in *Collier's Encyclopedia*, vol. 7 (New York: Macmillan, 1980), p. 44.

4. Elton Hocking, "Commedia Dell'Arte," in *Collier's Encyclopedia*, vol. 7 (New York: Macmillan, 1980), p. 59.

5. Feibleman, *Comedy*, p. 272.

6. Ibid., pp. 134–5.

7. Arthur Hough, "Trials and Tribulations—Thirty Years of Sitcom," in *Understanding Television*, ed. Richard P. Adler (New York: Praeger, 1981), p. 204. Also see Linda Blandford, "Anatomy of a Sitcom," *The New York Times Magazine*, April 2, 1989, pp. 34–37, 56–57.

8. James W. Chesebro, "Communication, Values, and Popular Television Series—A Four Year Assessment," in *Television: The Critical View*, 2d ed., ed. Horace Newcomb (New York: Oxford University Press, 1979), pp. 16–54.

9. Ibid., pp. 21–22.

10. Ibid., p. 31.

11. Sylvia Moss, "The New Comedy," *Television Quarterly* 4 (Winter 1965): 42–45.

12. "Lexington: Responsibility and the American Teenager," *The Economist*, March 28, 1992, p. 28.

13. Ibid.

14. Harry F. Waters, "TV Comedy: What It's Teaching the Kids," *Newsweek*, May 7, 1979, p. 68.

15. Raymond Williams, *Television: Technology and Cultural Form* (New York: Schocken Books, 1975), p. 26.

16. Sprague Vonier, "Television—The Urban Outlook," *Television Quarterly* 3 (Winter 1964): 24–29.

17. Ibid., p. 25.

18. Tim Brooks and Earle Marsh, eds., *The Complete Directory to Prime Time Network TV Shows 1946–Present* (New York: Ballantine Books, 1979), pp. 196–97.

19. Quoted in Jack Behar, "On TV Criticism," *Television Quarterly* 4 (Summer 1965): 60.

20. Alex McNeil, *Total Television*, 3d ed. (New York: Penguin Books, 1991), p. 474.

21. Tim Brooks and Earle Marsh, eds., *The Complete Directory to Prime Time Network TV Shows 1946–Present*, 5th ed. (New York: Ballantine Books, 1992), p. 557.

22. *Les Brown's Encyclopedia of Television*, 3d ed. (Detroit: Gale Research, 1992), p. 338.

23. McNeil, *Total Television*, pp. 474–75.

24. Ibid., p. 475.

25. Ibid., p. 474.

26. Ileane Rudolph, "Chemical Attractions," *TV Guide*, February 15, 1992, p. 11.

27. *Les Brown's Encyclopedia*, 3d ed., p. 469.

28. Walter Goodman, "Roseanne Is No Cousin to Archie Bunker," *New York Times*, January 1, 1989, sec. 2, p. 29.

29. Ibid.

30. Ibid.

31. Ibid.

32. N. R. Kleinfield, "Cashing in on a Hot New Brand Name," *New York Times*, April 29, 1990, sec. 3, p. 6.

33. *Les Brown's Encyclopedia*, 3d ed., p. 509.

34. Brooks and Marsh, *The Complete Directory*, 5th ed., p. 805.

35. Peter Kaufman, "Closing the Album on 'The Wonder Years,' " *New York Times*, May 9, 1993, sec. 2, p. 31.

36. Ibid.

37. Hough, "Trials and Tribulations," pp. 201–23.

38. Janet Maslin, "In Prime-Time, the Workplace Is Where the Heart Is," *New York Times*, February 10, 1980, sec. 2, p. 1.

39. John M. Phelan, *Disenchantment: Meaning and Morality in the Media* (New York: Hastings House, 1980), p. 35.

40. Ibid.

41. Ibid., pp. 35–36.

42. Conversation with James Brooks on *TV for Better or Worse*, produced by WCVE-TV, Richmond, Va., 1976.

43. Ibid.

44. Excerpt from *The Mary Tyler Moore Show*, shown on *TV for Better or Worse*.

45. Feibleman, *Comedy*, p. 205.

46. "Forum: Lay Pipe, Add Heat, Get Laughs!" *Harper's Magazine*, November 1988, p. 47.

5

□ □ □ □ □ □

Television's Social Comedies

THE SELF-REFLEXIVE COMEDY-DRAMA: TELEVISION
TOPICALITY AND THE CLASS STRUGGLE

As we enter the "real world" of social relations depicted in television comedy, we recognize television's peculiar ability to present us ostensibly significant social commentary that, in its deeper layers, reinforces traditional values and thereby makes the threatening unthreatening and incorporates potentially emergent oppositional social strategies into the social fabric as demanded by the dominant values of the culture.

Such is the case with television comedy's most substantial "dramatic" form, the self-reflexive comedy-drama. Significant examples of this form as well as the satiric comedy-variety form are represented in Figure 5.1. Here the thin line between laughter and despair is crossed again and again; but, finally, the ambiguity of everyday experience is resolved—usually, although, thankfully, not always—with predictably sanguine results. In this comedy we see the emergence of clearly drawn class distinctions. The false consciousness of the working class clearly emerges in *All in the Family* through the principal character of Archie Bunker. The pathos of the helpless working-class rural "children" completely narcotized by the television dream life reveals itself through Mary and Tom Hartman of *Mary Hartman, Mary Hartman*; their American Dream is a composite television commercial. Socioeconomic-class confrontation is represented, albeit often crudely, in *Soap*, as the anomic bourgeois characters, Jessica and Chester Tate, collide with Jessica's sister Mary and her foolish, macho, working-class husband Burt Campbell. The Tates' black servant, Benson, takes great joy in Jessica's and Chester's miserable marriage and their constant bickering—the archetypal fall from grace. In the most enigmatic of all television series, *M*A*S*H*, we find the ultimate sardonic "working-

Figure 5.1
The Self-Reflexive Comedy-Drama

1946 47 48 49 50 51 52 53 54 55 56 57 58 59 60 61 62 63 64 65 66 67 68 69 70 71 72 73 74 75 76 77 78 79 80 81 82 83 84 85 86 87 88 89 90 91 92 93

Self-Reflexive Comedy-Drama
(television topicality and the class struggle)

All in the Family, 71.........79

Maude, 72.........78

M*A*S*H*, 72.........83

Mary Hartman,
76-77

Soap, 77.........81

The "Slap" Maxwell Story,
87-88

Satiric Comedy-Variety

TW3,
64-65

The Smothers Brothers Comedy Hour
67.........69

Rowan and Martin's Laugh-In,
68.........73

Dream Machine,
71-72

Saturday Night Live, 75.........

The Richard Pryor Show,
77

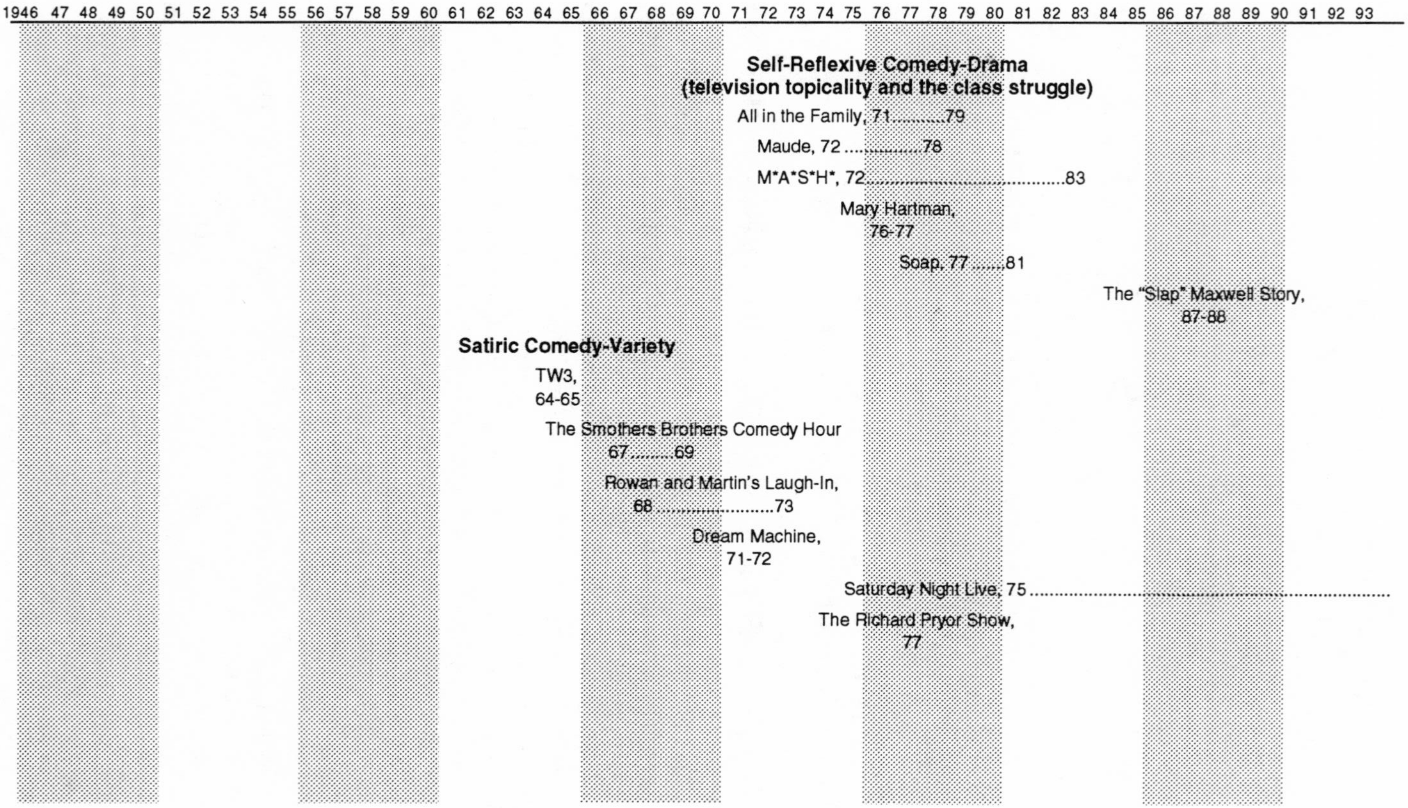

class" comedy—highly skilled draftee-surgeons working in the assembly-line repair-shop atmosphere of the wartime operating room. The "damaged goods" are not broken stereos but people who are patched up and shipped back to the front line to be reconsumed or returned to sender "unrepairable." This is black humor, associated with the eternal progress of an increasingly sophisticated technology that can find more efficient ways to kill. Doctors become the "white-collar proletariat." War is ultimately the equalizer of all people as well as the ultimate metaphor for advanced capitalism.

These self-reflexive comedy-dramas give us room to examine the human foibles that constitute our contemporary everyday lives: ethnocentrism, warlike posturing and war making, and subservience to cultural production in our media that trades on the most blatant condensation symbology encouraging self-centeredness, fear, and envy. Through these works we can see in ourselves the human results of our most ill-conceived thoughts and actions. Yet, curiously, these same works tell us that in spite of our foibles, the strength of biological or work-related family bonds will help us endure our darkest moments. This is television's traditional answer to the bewildering complexity of contemporary social relations. Further, the mythic geography of the comedy-drama is not the real world, as we might at first have believed, but rather the geography of the television screen itself.

All in the Family, which premiered in January 1971, brought millions of American viewers face to face with the television version of the harsh realities of urban working-class existence in the culturally isolated, multiethnic, and racially mixed Corona section of Queens, New York. At 704 Houser Street, the Bunkers—Archie and Edith—and their son-in-law Michael (Meathead) and daughter Gloria, Archie's "little girl," grappled with all manner of social and personal issues television had ignored during the 1960s—issues that had polarized an entire nation, dividing what was once naïvely considered a country united into a society of intolerant subcultures. *All in the Family*'s structure employed the grossest oppositions to make its social comments. In the Archie/Michael pair, for example, we find value conflicts organized as conservative/liberal, WASP/ethnic, prejudiced/open-minded,   undereducated-worker/overeducated-student-professor, and pseudo-religious/atheist-humanist dichotomies. In the Archie/Edith pair, dichotomies include dominant employed male/ subservient woman-housewife, and boisterous male/quietly emotional female. In the Edith/Gloria pair, we find the naïve mother/worldly-wise daughter and the traditional husband-centered woman/new-liberated-woman oppositions. True, the roles transmuted when the occasion and dramatic license warranted; Michael would become an irrational, babbling idiot, just like his father-in-law, when provoked by the latter's enormous prejudice and hatred, although Michael did so in the best of the bleeding-liberal tradition. Edith could overcome her guilt and embarrassment regarding the discussion of sexual matters when Gloria and Michael needed the warm family counseling of a mother. Gloria could break down and cry, just like daddy's little girl, when accosted on the subway. Of all the characters, Archie maintained his dominant role as family patriarch and tyrant, the defender of the flag and the traditional values for which he believed that flag stood—values such as the use of religion in the service of jingoism; the sanctity of the police state over the civil rights of individuals, except of course himself, when he felt personally wronged; and the state sanction of ethnocentric, exclusionist social practices. Archie Bunker, television representative of the contemporary American working-class "stiff," was a living, breathing anachronism. And the audience loved him.

Why was this put-down of the American working-class lifestyle and value system the incredibly popular number-one television series from 1971 until 1976, with ratings exceeding 30.0 for the entire period? Was it because in the end, Archie was damned to eternal torment, could not escape from the ethnically and racially "inferior" people he so despised? Was it because many viewers subscribed to the same value priorities as he did? Was it because All in the Family was a superb comedy of gestures, relying on the extremely powerful small-screen aesthetic device of the reaction shot, so sensitively executed by all of the cast members, but especially by Carroll O'Connor? Or was it because the Bunkers were survivors, weathering the social storms of the times, secure in their tiny piece of the American landscape, marked out as "private property"? Each viewer brought a personal perspective to All in the Family, as they do to every viewing experience, allowing for a multiplicity of readings, none of them privileged. However in this case, it can be argued, the series's intensity—its playing with extreme characterizations in a highly charged social milieu—brought a special poignance to the viewing experience.

The multiplicity of readings were quick to emerge. Two months following its premiere, All in the Family was both soundly condemned and fervently defended by certain of our journalist-critics of television. Life's John Leonard wrote of the premiere of the series: "All in the Family is a wretched program. . . . [It] is not merely insulting to minorities: it is insulting to Mr. O'Connor, Miss Stapleton, Miss Struthers, Mr. Reiner, the American workingman, CBS and everybody who watches the program. Bigotry becomes a form of dirty joke."[1] Leonard looked into the series's ideological signification and discovered "a double-edged lie . . . [that] tells us that workingmen are mindless buffoons: their opinions, unlike ours, are unrelated to social, psychological or political conditions; . . . [and] that . . . Archie is, anyway, charming. Forgivable."[2] Thus, Lear, CBS, and the audience are pandered to; all are better than Archie, who is ridiculous and not to be taken seriously. In this way, our antihero comes to represent a vision of America not unlike the adult-child of the rural middle landscape;

the main difference between the two character types is that Archie's blue-collar workingman is naïvely bigoted while Jed Clampett's kind rural folk hero is simply ignorant.

Saturday Review's Robert Lewis Shayon took a decidedly different view of the series, although his endorsement was not without an important qualification. Writing in the same month as Leonard, Shayon found the novelty of the series in view of the 1971 television milieu, "exhilarating, . . . a unique experience in television viewing."[3] Shayon believed the value of the series was its ostensible power to reinforce the values of those who came to the series already convinced of the evils of prejudice and ethnocentrism. As to the argument that *All in the Family* would reinforce bigotry, Shayon concluded that bigots would feel threatened by the series and would tune out. The major flaw in the series, Shayon perceptively noted, was Archie's utter inability to recognize his own sinful ethnocentrism. Shayon concluded, "If Archie did know—if he were, even in the smallest degree, self-critical and willing to engage in dialogue about his hostility to all groups but his own— . . . he would be . . . a powerful vehicle toward the remedying of prejudice."[4] Maybe so, but then the comedy-drama would sacrifice its "unknowing irony" and become not a biting artistic revelation of bigotry, but rather a popularized group-therapy session.

Writing some four years after the premiere of *All in the Family*, the *New Yorker*'s television critic, Michael Arlen, noted that the series was not primarily focused on its central character's prejudice; rather, as in Lear's other television comedies, it revealed "a curious, modern, undifferentiated anger."[5] While Arlen gave Lear credit for introducing viewers to television comedies that deal with serious contemporary social problems such as racism (*All in the Family*), alcoholism (*Maude*), the intersection of class and race exemplified by the inferior social status and immense personal struggles of poor urban blacks (*Good Times*), and sexual taboos (*Hot L Baltimore*), he also pointed out the tendency in Lear's work for this "angry" humor to be transformed into "an accepted form of stage business" and thereby to relinquish its deeper social and political meaning as it deflected its focus from the outside world to the narrow world of the central characters. What is meaningful in these works, according to Arlen, is their status as "our first true 'media' dramas," which are more like television talk shows than traditional narratives. They provide viewers with "a commonality, . . . created largely by television itself, . . . of casual worldliness and [of television's] ability to propel . . . vast, undifferentiated quantities of topical information, problem discussions, psychiatric terminology, and surface political and social involvement through the national bloodstream."[6]

All in the Family is ultimately "mainstream." It makes us feel connected to "social change" while simultaneously defusing any truly emergent oppositional ideology that could clearly posit strategies for such change. As Arlen so perceptively discerns, beneath its surface tension, *All in the Family* is all talk.

Despite this basic mainstream character of the series, there are moments of ironic brilliance that the critic would be remiss to ignore and that highlight the major value conflicts inherent in the social relations of this Queens family and their neighbors—conflicts that frequently involve the sanctity of institutions versus human dignity and individual autonomy. Two particularly memorable scenes from *All in the Family* demonstrate the sensitivity with which the series's creators could treat human problems in drama tempered with comedic overtones. One scene explored the obligation of the individual to submit to the demands of his government regardless of the perceived injustices of the state's cause. The other focused on the son's unquestioned acceptance of his father's teachings and actions despite the son's vague doubts as to their ultimate wisdom.

"The Draft Dodger" episode of *All in the Family*, written by Jay Moriarty and Mike Milligan, was aired on December 15, 1976. The scene was the Bunkers' dining room, Christmas Eve, 1976. Mike's friend David, a draft dodger living in Canada, has come to dinner. Archie has invited his good friend Pinky, whose son Steve had been killed in Vietnam. David's presence was too much for Archie to handle. Mike and David are dressed in sport jackets and neat but casual trousers; Archie is bedecked in his usual open-necked white shirt; Pinky has on traditional Christmas colors of red and green. The scene follows:

Archie: How do you like that, Pinky, huh? We got a draft dodger here who writes a snotty letter to the Commander in Chief. I mean, what the hell do you do with that?

(*Wide shot—all around the table, we see ARCHIE, EDITH, GLORIA, MIKE, PINKY.*)

David: Look, Mr. Bunker. I don't want to spoil your Christmas dinner, so maybe I should go.

Edith and Gloria: Oh, no! Don't make him go.

Archie: Certainly he's got to go! What are you talkin' about. (*A beat.*) If the FBI was to find him here, we could all be havin' Christmas dinner in the hoosegow.

Gloria: Daddy, it's Christmas Eve. Now don't go making a big crisis out of this.

Mike: (*Slams his napkin on the table and bolts out of his chair.*) Arch. What David did took a lot of guts.

Archie: What do ya mean, a lot of guts?

David: (*to MIKE.*) My own father doesn't understand. Why should he?

Mike: (*extreme close-up shot, screaming—to ARCHIE.*) When the hell are you going to admit that the war was wrong?

Archie: (*in a three-shot with MIKE and DAVID looking on; he is shouting at the top of his lungs.*) I ain't talkin' about the war. I don't wanna talk about that rotten damn war no more.[7] I'm talkin' about somethin' else. And what he done was wrong. Sayin' he won't go. (*To DAVID.*) What do ya think, that all the people in this country can say whether or not they wanna go to war? (*Beat.*) You couldn't get a decent war off the ground that way. All the young people would say no. Sure they would. Cause they don't wanna get killed. (*Beat.*) And that's why we leave it to the Congress, 'cause them old crocks ain't gonna get killed. (*Beat.*) And they're gonna do the right thing and get behind the president and vote yes.

Pinky: (*stands.*) Arch. If my opinion is of any importance, . . .

Archie: (*calming down.*) Certainly your opinion is important. (*Beat.*) A Gold Star father. Your opinion is more important than anyone else's in this room, and I wanna hear that opinion. You tell 'em, Pinky, you tell 'em.

Pinky: (*in a two-shot, over ARCHIE's shoulder, speaks calmly but with obvious pain as the camera slowly zooms in to a close-up.*) I understand how you feel Arch. My kid hated the war, too. But he did what he thought he had to do. (*Beat.*) And David here did what he thought he had to do. But David's alive to share Christmas dinner with us. And if Steve were here, he'd wanna sit down with him. And that's what I wanna do.
(*PINKY reaches out to shake hands with DAVID. DAVID holds back his tears.*)

Pinky: Merry Christmas, David.
(*PINKY, still shaking hands, places his left hand on DAVID's shoulder.*)

David: Merry Christmas sir.
(*Wide shot of dinner table. DAVID, PINKY, MIKE sit down. ARCHIE remains standing, shocked. He walks away, alone. EDITH, faithful as always, gets up to attempt to console him.*)

Edith: Archie, please. Sit down and eat.

Archie: Aw, no, no, no.

Edith: But Archie, it's Christmas.

Archie: I can't. I gotta work this out, Edith. I can't think about that.

Edith: But Archie, you asked Pinky what to do and you see what he's doing. You oughta do the same. Come on.
(*Silently, EDITH and ARCHIE move back to the table.*)

Edith: There's a drumstick for ya.

Archie: Oh Edith, I ain't thinkin' about eatin'.

Mike: I'll take it, Ma.

Archie: (*immediately snaps back.*) Leave it on the plate. (*Beat. ARCHIE is sweating profusely.*) Well, I don't wanna stop none of youse from eatin' Edith's nice Christmas dinner here. So you might as well eat it. But I'll tell you one thing:

when dinner's over, I still gotta work this out. (*Beat.*) You better remind me
to do that, Edith.

Edith: I will. (*She kisses ARCHIE on the cheek.*)

In this scene, we see emerging, in a very powerful form, the beginning
of an attempt to articulate the restorative impulse following the war, about
which psychiatrist Robert J. Lifton has written. But, unlike the Kodak
"America" commercial, discussed in chapter 3, this poignant scene does
this without resorting to "symbolizations around national virtue and military honor."

On a personal level, Archie was never able to "work it out," nor did he
really seem to want to. His pride was hurt, but his dogmatic view of militarism was essentially unshaken, as the audience would expect and as the
comedic aesthetic would demand if his character was to remain the well-
spring from which irony would continue to flow.

Also unshaken was Archie's belief in the correctness of his upbringing,
which included his father's severe disciplinary measures and bigotry. Archie was not in the habit of reading Piaget or of attempting to deal with
questions of the relationship of a child's later aggressive and belligerent
behavior to his parents' child-rearing techniques. Instead, the curiously
"romantic" Archie chose to remember only the vague, distanced scenes
of his father's love for him. And above all, he respected his father's manly
power. This is revealed in a touching scene from the February 8, 1978,
episode "Two's A Crowd," written by Phil Sharp. Archie and Mike acci-
dentally lock themselves in the storeroom in Archie's bar. It's getting cold
outside, but there is plenty to drink to keep them warm. The two men
crawl under a piece of an old awning they find in the storeroom and
proceed to get potted. The conversation leads to Archie's lack of trust in
Mike and slowly the scene takes on a melancholy air. Archie describes his
school days during the Great Depression and reveals his incredible cynicism:

Archie: The hell with the world! The world out there, kid, ain't up to no good.
You don't trust nobody out there except for your own kind, and you remember that, Meathead.

Mike: (*A beat.*) There's another thing. Meathead. Why must you always call me
Meathead?

Archie: What the hell? Why does that bother you so much? I bet I wasn't the first
one to call you Meathead.

Mike: You were the only one to call me Meathead. They never called me Meathead in school. In school they always called me Michael.

Archie: That's all they called you?

Mike: Well, Mike, or Mikey.

Archie: What a sweet little school you went to. No wonder you grew up thinkin' the world was beautiful.

Mike: Why? What did they call *you* in school?

Archie: (*ad lib resistance*) Oh . . . different things.

Mike; What? Tell me. What'd they call you in school? Tell me what they called you.

Archie: (*takes a drink*) Well, I remember one winter during the depression, we didn't have no money 'cause the old man lost a job, and we was all busted . . . and I couldn't go to school with only one shoe; but my mother, she found a boot, so . . . I had a shoe on one foot there and boot on the other. A shoe and a boot; shoe, boot. So the kids called me Shoebootie.

Mike: Kids all made fun of you, huh?

Archie: (*his voice becoming increasingly slurred*) Yeah, they all made fun, well, . . . all except one little black kid by the name of Winston.

Mike: (*incredulous*) A black kid liked you?

Archie: Oh, no. The black kid beat the hell outta me.

Mike: Why?

Archie: (*mumbles*) I don't know. Nothin'.

Mike: He musta had a reason.

Archie: Well, he said that I said he was a nigger.

Mike: Well, did you?

Archie: Yeah.

Mike: Well then, that's the reason.

Archie: What the hell reason was that? That's what all them people was called in them days there. I mean everybody we knew called 'em people niggers. That's all my old man ever called 'em there.

Mike: Did you ever think that possibly your father just might be wrong?

Archie: Wrong, my old man? Don't be stupid. My old man, let me tell you about him. He was never wrong about nothin'.

Mike: Yes he was, Arch.

Archie: (*barely able to articulate*) Huh? Your father who made ya? Wrong? The breadwinner of the house there, the man who goes out and busts his butt to keep a roof over your head and clothes on your back; you call your father wrong? Your father, the man who comes home bringin' candy. Your father's the first guy to throw a baseball to you and take you for walks in the park, holdin' you by the hand. (*Holds up his hand.*) I'll tell you. He busted that hand once, and he busted it on me to teach me to do good. My father. He shoved me in a closet for seven hours to teach me to do good 'cause he loved me. (*Beat.*) Don't be lookin' at me. (ARCHIE *gets up, moves away, leaving* MIKE, *seen in a close-up, looking sad and bewildered.*) Let me tell you somethin', you're supposed to love your father. 'Cause your father loves you. (*Beat.*) Now, how can any man who loves you tell you anything that's wrong? What's the use in talkin' to you?

(*Beat. ARCHIE lies down on a tablecloth that is spread on the floor. He falls asleep. After a few beats, MIKE rises, crosses to ARCHIE, carefully covers him with the awning, and looks down at him.*)

Mike: Good night, Shoebootie.

Archie, drunk and uncomprehending, has fallen into the existential void. His physical awakening will not correspond to any cognitive or moral awakening. Mike's sad, bewildered look brilliantly reveals Archie's permanent state of unfreedom; Archie is helpless against the world, trapped in his own personal history.

These scenes, brilliantly acted and carefully scripted and shot, transcend the general comedic level of *All in the Family*, a series with high-pitched insults that Archie continuously and indiscriminately flings at outsiders and insiders alike. There were, of course, many other poignant scenes, including one showing Archie's despair at losing his job, Archie's genuine display of love for his grandson, and the family's tender good-byes as Mike and Gloria left Queens for a new life in California. This last scene was particularly revealing as Archie, wanting to express his love for his son-in-law, could not utter the words. The power of Archie's closed cultural tradition dominated one final time. Archie, a "real man," was not permitted to express his softness in public.

While many television critics continued to praise the series for its effort at "breaking down old taboos," the cultural climate, of which television was but one part, had in fact already sanctioned that breaking-down. Television, as always, through its most persuasive creators, followed. "The Draft Dodger," taped in late 1976, confirmed the growing sentiment that Vietnam was a colossal mistake. Only Archie and those diehard jingoists whom he represented were blind to that fact. "Two's a Crowd," shot in 1978, alluded to the pressures that signalled the breakdown of patriarchal authority long underway, as the changing nature of family relations had manifested itself in postindustrial social systems. Blue-collar children such as Mike had come to know the advanced education their fathers (represented by Archie) could never achieve. The fathers encouraged this education so that children could improve their relative material status in the dominant social and economic structures, not so that they would become enlightened about the social inequities inherent in advanced capitalism or about misguided ethnocentrism. The American Dream, as lived by second- and third-generation blue-collar immigrants, cut both ways, and the changes brought about by opening higher education spoke to both. *All in the Family* uses this value conflict as a major focus of its action and characterization.

We should not expect anything revolutionary from entertainment television. Sociologist Todd Gitlin noted the difficulty, if not impossibility, in having truly controversial material enter our public electronic media: "Alternative material is routinely *incorporated*: brought into the body of cultural production. Occasionally oppositional material may succeed in being indigestible; that material is excluded from the media discourse and returned to the cultural margins from which it came, while *elements* of it are incorporated into the dominant forms" (emphasis in original).[8] The "The casual worldliness" and "topicality" Michael Arlen attributed to the series provides us with an outline of our contemporary world of social relations. The substance inside that outline, however, could benefit from additional, more pointed explication.

While *All in the Family* used Vietnam as a vehicle to discuss larger political and social conflicts in America, another comedy-drama used a different, though not dissimilar, war of containment to reveal the personal tragedy brought about by the abstractions of politics. *M*A*S*H* took on nothing less than the human condition in the age of mechanization and its ultimate manifestation in efficient warfare. Such material is an appropriate subject for the logic of the ridiculous as best expressed through black comedy.

On September 17, 1972, America was still mired "waist deep in the Big Muddy" of Vietnam, as the Pete Seeger song went; we were desperately searching for a way out. The bombing of Cambodia had precipitated a national outcry for disengagement. The outcry, most visibly manifested on our nation's university campuses, triggered confrontations between au- thority—the National Guard protecting what was fast becoming a police state, the goal of which was the securing of bourgeois property and the prolonging of a war that had brought an economic recovery and material prosperity—and the student rebels who were seriously and continually deconstructing this country's dominant cultural value priorities. When the smoke from the tear gas cleared from the battleground at Kent State, students lay dead. The war had at last truly come home. The small screen, on which the actual footage of this distant war had been shown to a packed house on the evening news for nearly a decade, now trembled with scenes from northern Ohio, scenes far more difficult to explain and harder to swallow.

The setting for a new television comedy series (and for the Robert Alt- man theatrical film, based on a novel by Richard Hooker, from which the series was derived) was Korea. The time was the early 1950s. The protag- onists were U.S. Army Surgeons, nurses, and corpsmen assigned to the 4077th Mobile Army Surgical Hospital—a frantic tent city five miles from the battlefront. All the doctors at the series's beginning were draftees (later, an army lifer would assume command of the unit). We knew that this was more than just Korea—it was all war, and, more immediately, it was Vietnam.

M*A*S*H's main contribution to television comedy-drama was the sincerity with which it tackled the more existential questions of the quest for personal meaning in an anomic culture. Throughout the series's 11-year-run, there was revealed a nagging sense of futility and insanity about war. Humor was a key ingredient for survival—it highlighted despair and provided a temporary respite from the hopelessness of war by ridiculing war's basic modus operandi.

The doctors—Captain Benjamin Franklin "Hawkeye" Pierce; Captain "Trapper John" McIntyre; company commander, Lieutenant Colonel Henry Blake; and, later, Captain B. J. Hunnicut—were always breaking regulations, asserting, in whatever feeble attempts they could mount, their independence from an inhumane, unforgiving system that inexorably ground forward as it ground up young men in the quest for highly questionable political ends. The central protagonist, Hawkeye, offered the most consistent voice that questioned the moral validity of war. His role was that of the philosopher who always seemed to be burdened with the understanding of the conflict's ultimate meaninglessness. His understanding carried with it a rage, a frustration, and a cynicism just beneath the mask of calm professionalism. Hawkeye's character, as it developed over the life of the series, is one of the most complex in television comedy— that of the "bitter idealist,"[9] whose ultimate optimism is continually challenged by the realities of the wartime operating room. The role was brilliantly revealed to us by actor, writer, and director Alan Alda.

M*A*S*H was accessible to a television audience searching, although perhaps unknowingly, for a framework to help explain the meaning of the Vietnam War and of the domestic social confrontations of the 1960s. How could a sensitive observer reconcile an enlightened domestic policy that was making serious attempts to correct the sordid living conditions of racial, ethnic, and economically impoverished subcultures—conditions exacerbated by decades of governmental neglect—with the fact that the sons of these groups were being urged to enlist or were disproportionately drafted as cannon fodder for a jingoistic war? The irony of this policy confusion was all too apparent to the privileged middle-class child who was demonstrating on his or her college campus, exempt from the draft through a student deferment; it was perhaps not so apparent to the inner-city youth who had not been provided with the proper education with which to see the sham. The American Dream had soured. Some people recognized the fact and grieved. Others used the occasion to question the basic tenets of that dream.

M*A*S*H provided clear-cut characterizations that defined much larger cultural issues framing contemporary value conflicts. The war was the backdrop for the definition. We find, on its most basic level, the confrontation clearly presented in the dichotomous characterizations of Hawkeye and Major Frank Burns. Hawkeye represented individualism, the right to rebel, peace, and skilled professionalism in the service of life. His was the existential voice crying out in the wilderness of social control, ultimately manifested in the hierarchical social relations of the military apparatus. Frank, Hawkeye's opposite force, represented the authority, bureaucracy, war, and butchery that easily accepted death as a given. His character struggled to uphold the sanctity of institutions and their ostensibly legitimate claims to power. The classic confrontations of *M*A*S*H* were acted out in the naturalistic theater of the operating room, the one place where life, both physical and emotional, constantly hangs in the balance.

Characters were allowed to grow throughout the life of the series. Maxwell Klinger, hairy-chested son of a Lebanese immigrant family from Toledo, Ohio, was constantly seeking a discharge for a mental disability. His cross-dressing was to no avail. In 1979, following the departure of Corporal Radar O'Reilly, Klinger was appointed company clerk and was subsequently promoted to sergeant. His new responsibilities overshadowed his strong desire to exit from the war; in one sense, his promotion within the hierarchy also represented his cooptation. This theme in *M*A*S*H*, of the conflict between the deep feelings of responsibility for the welfare of the 4077th "family" and the desire to escape the horror, was a constantly recurring motif. In the end, Klinger became a team player, as we expected he should; the renegade was subsumed into the family unit. Ironically, Klinger married a young Korean woman at the war's conclusion and stayed in Korea to search for his new bride's parents. He would be the last of the unit to leave.

Margaret "Hot Lips" Houlihan gradually transcends her initial stereotypical role as an army brat-sexpot with questionable morals who loves to have affairs with superior officer-doctors. Through inner development brought about by her marriage, subsequent divorce, and the painful process of reconciling her strong passions with an understanding of the authentic human communication of love, she matures as the series unfolds. The series's writers increasingly shifted our attention to Margaret's function as a paraprofessional, highly skilled nurse, and generally effective administrator as the drive in the United States for the passage of the Equal Rights Amendment to the constitution intensified. Thus, two historical milieux are intertwined—1970s values are successfully implanted in the social relations of the 1950s.

The company-commander role changed during the series as well. Lieutenant Colonel Henry Blake, the kind but bumbling and weak-willed commanding officer of the unit, who just wanted to get by until the conflict faded away, was killed in a plane crash on his way home following his discharge (another ironic twist). In his place came Army lifer Colonel Sherman Potter, a veteran of World Wars I and II—a compassionate man, as was Henry, but also a strong-willed soldier who believed in at least a modicum of discipline, although he knew the value of good surgeons even when they were as wacky as Hawkeye and B. J.

Hawkeye changed in more subtle and profound ways throughout the series than did the others. Early in the series we saw Hawkeye following the model established in the Altman film. Dressed in a Hawaiian floral-print shirt, the swinging bachelor wooed the nurses and used his quick wit, ribald humor, and imitations of Groucho Marx to provide the people of the 4077th, except for Frank Burns and Margaret Houlihan, with the needed release and a sense of optimism. Gradually, however, the optimism gave way to Hawkeye's bitter cynicism. He tried to maintain his comic demeanor, but the audience felt the substantive emptiness the jokes unintentionally revealed. We see and hear hints of the tenuous nature of the relationship between sanity and insanity as expressed through dark humor even in the series pilot. Hawkeye and his tent mate at the time, Trapper John McIntyre, are walking slowly through the camp reflecting on their roles as doctors in the war:

Hawkeye: I keep telling you: We gotta give up this preoccupation with keeping people alive or we'll never get outta here.

Trapper: It's no use. We're doomed.

Hawkeye: Maybe we should start using rusty instruments.

Trapper: Or not washing our hands.

Hawkeye: Or raising our prices.

Hawkeye's bitterness clearly surfaced in a 1978 hour-long episode modeled on the Edward R. Murrow (CBS-TV) *See It Now* documentary episode titled "Christmas in Korea" (1953). Correspondent Clete Roberts (a fictional Murrow) interviews the members of the 4077th in the fictional early winter of 1952. His questions, as did those questions posed in the Murrow documentary, probe the soldiers' feelings about their "work," attempting to reveal the war in human terms. The war is more than a series of scenes revealed in the newsreel footage shipped back to the United States—it is people with expressions, voices, and reflections. At the beginning of the interview, Hawkeye still manages to maintain his basic optimism as he responds to Roberts: "I'm very impressed now with the ... terrible fragility of the human body, and the unbelievable resiliency of the human spirit." However, later in the episode, Hawkeye reveals his inner torment in a voice-over accompanying a scene of choppers descending from the heavens, bringing in more wounded, and of ambulances hurtling down the dusty road into the camp: "The wounded keep coming and coming. The common denominator is blood. It's all red. And there's an awful lot of it leaking out around here." We cut to a scene in the operating room. Shells are exploding all around the camp. Lights are flickering on and off as the surgeons attempt to continue their work. Hawkeye looks beyond the war to the social relations that encourage such activities. His soliloquy is among the most direct ever offered on commercial entertainment television:

I just don't know why they're shooting at us. All we want to do is bring them democracy and white bread, transplant the American Dream—freedom, achievement, hyperacidity, affluence, flatulence, technology, tension. The inalienable right to an early coronary sitting at your desk while plotting to stab your boss in the back.

Later, Hawkeye comes to a clear and incredibly simple understanding of the meaning of all this—the powerlessness of the individual worker to affect the apparatus of production—as he notes with sadness, "They keep coming whether I'm here or not."

Hawkeye is a philosopher whose real milieu is the 1960s and early 1970s. Indeed, Korea, as recognized in a graphic overlay in the pilot episode, was "1950: a hundred years ago." The war issues, in their human terms, were the central focus of the series. The war came home to the central protagonist in *M*A*S*H*'s 255th and final episode: Hawkeye is locked in a mental ward of an army hospital. He has finally cracked. He had tried to operate on a patient without using an anesthetic because he believed the anesthesiologist was trying to smother the patient with a mask. Hawkeye relates a story to his psychiatrist, Sidney Finkelstein, of a dark journey on a bus returning members of the 4077th to camp following a day of rest and relaxation at a beach. The bus had stopped along the way to pick up some refugees and wounded soldiers (one could never really escape the war). The bus was forced to stop that night before reaching camp because it was feared that there were Chinese soldiers in the area who would be attracted by the engine noise and the headlights. A Korean refugee woman with an infant was riding at the back of the bus. The infant began to cry and would not stop. Hawkeye made his way to the woman and yelled at her to keep the child quiet. The situation was desperate. The woman, looking fearfully at Hawkeye, responded by smothering her baby to death. Hawkeye went mad. The gin mill to which he and B. J. and Trapper and Henry and Sherman had so often turned for solace would do him no good here, for he was in uncharted territory. His recovery was painful as he had to move beyond his guilt. In a way, Hawkeye's recovery was more rapid and the questions less resolved than artistic probability will allow, given the years of inner turbulence and soul-searching suffered by this sensitive surgeon. He is, quite visibly, emotionally scarred for life, although he continues to work upon his return to the unit. A very highly skilled surgeon, he has chosen to shun the rat race of big-city surgical practice and the wealth and status attached to such a position in order to return to the small town from which he came and start a quiet practice in family medicine. Yet the enigmatic Hawkeye will bring his emotional scars to this rural middle landscape. We sense he will live out his life in character, always on or near the edge, filled with compassion yet haunted by the bitterness and guilt engendered by "his" war.

The motif of the personalness of the war experience is *M*A*S*H*'s primary artistic strength as well as its primary ideological shortcoming, although the latter is not by any means a fatal flaw in the series. The profundity of war lies in the inevitable fact that a great many individuals die, are maimed, or survive physically unscathed yet emotionally scarred. The intensity of the war experience makes it an ideal subject for art, especially allegory. On the other hand, the personalness of war is framed, in reality, by the ideology of war. Wars are conducted by generals and presidents and emperors in response to disagreements in basic social, political, and economic principles neatly abstracted from the daily fighting and the daily deaths. Wars are plotted in rooms, often below ground. The ultimate victory or defeat or stalemate resulting from the successful or unsuccessful or marginally successful conduct of war produces some shift in ideology and in the system of material and social relations in those states who are engaged in that war. The soldiers in the trenches and the civilians on whose land the war is fought are impacted by these shifts but do not control them—they simply live or die in defense of one or another ideological position that they are led to believe is "sacred" or natural. *M*A*S*H* offers a pointed critique, on an allegorical level, of all war. This critique stresses the impact of war on the individual—the impact of war's utter barbarity, its lack of discrimination between soldier and civilian, and its seeming unendingness. Yet the conflicts, Korea and, by implication, Vietnam, that provide the specific social context for the series become mere settings—backdrops for the personal struggles that unfold. Ideology, as it directly impacts the modern question of the justifiability of wars of national liberation as opposed to wars of foreign intervention, is conspicuous by its absence here. This led critic Roger Hofeldt to suggest that within the structure of comedy, *M*A*S*H* presented controversy while at the same time reinforcing traditional institutions and values and acting as a "bulwark against change and social criticism."[10]

However, when its corpus of 255 episodes is considered, it can be argued that the series clearly transcends Hofeldt's critique. Artistically, *M*A*S*H* pioneered a new approach to television comedy. Many episodes were singular attempts to structurally revise the television-comedy form. One episode was shot as a black-and-white documentary; another hour-long episode, described above, drew upon the Murrow documentary style of the *See It Now* series; another episode featured a "subjective camera" that became a character; many episodes were aired without a laugh track (including the final, two-and-a-half hour "Goodbye, Farewell, and

Amen"); and a real-time episode was aired in which the doctors had 20 minutes to successfully treat a soldier before he became paralyzed for life—a clock in the frame ticked inexorably onward, showing the viewer how much time was left.

The comedy in this comedy-drama occasionally, though fortunately not often, lapses into rather stale army jokes most of us have repeatedly heard. Perhaps those who have served in the military justifiably take some small pleasure in reminiscing about the seemingly pointless little events that distanced them from the more immediate gravity of the larger situation in which they suffered and many of their friends died. Such events include the constant revulsion at the thought of eating the same soggy meals day after day—overcooked liver, runny mashed potatoes, coffee that tastes like iodine—and the incredibly frustrating military bureaucracy. One scene in *M*A*S*H* features an arrogant officer in the Quartermaster Corps who is authorizing the 4077th's request for a jukebox and a pizza oven but withholding the incubator the unit had requested, while another scene features Henry Blake signing redundant forms for a requisition. In the same scene, Henry asks Radar, "Tell me, Radar. Do you understand any of this?" Radar responds, "I try not to, sir. It slows up the war."

Likewise, the series sometimes slips into self-indulgent melodrama, as in the final episode, in which Major Charles Winchester, the New England blue-blood thoracic surgeon inadvertently "captures" five Chinese musicians who are trying to surrender. He teaches them a favorite Mozart piece they slowly master during the course of their detainment in the camp. Here we are presented with the simplistic old saw that calls music the "universal language" that transcends the differences of war. The musicians are taken away, despite Winchester's protestations, to another holding area, but en route their truck is shelled and they all die. Winchester, grief-stricken, smashes a recording of the Mozart piece he kept in his tent. Music, said Winchester, would no longer be "a refuge from this miserable experience, but now it will always be a reminder." The naïve notion of music's transcending the sordidness of everyday experience is played out through Charles's hyperbolic romantic character. While the acting makes the scene indeed touching, the underlying cliché points awkwardly to itself and to standard television-melodrama convention.

The general level of comedy, however, transcends the one-liners and physical comedy that often keep the individual episodes moving; and the drama generally reveals complex characterization in which the protagonists must search for deeper meanings as they face their eventual return to civilian life, realizing their experiences in Korea will have measurably changed them.

As Joseph Campbell wrote, "The divine comedies of redemption . . . in the ancient world were regarded as of a higher rank than tragedy, of a deeper truth, of a more difficult realization, of a sounder structure, and of a revelation more complete."[11] M*A*S*H's portrayal of the strength of family bonds as a "transcendence of the universal tragedy of man," in which "enduring being is made manifest,"[12] reveals the comedy's ultimate focus beyond the immediate life-and-death struggle to the larger question of the value of a life itself in a desensitized world in which bureaucracy, with its charts, data, and strategies, controls basic human actions, a world in which control is vested in unapproachable, powerful institutions. The battle was waged and concluded; the results were recited over the radio playing in the operating room as the surgeons of the 4077th operated as a team for the last time:

The cost of the war to the United States has been placed at $22 billion [*The camera tilts down to reveal pools of blood on the operating room floor.*][13] . . . In human terms the cost was much greater. The UN forces have suffered the following casualties: killed in combat, 71,500; missing and captured, 82,263; wounded, 250,000. . . . On the Communist side, 1,347,000 people were killed and wounded; . . . also killed [were] 400,000 Korean civilians. If you add it all up, it comes to more than 2,000,000 people killed or wounded.

In the era of the "bottom line," the money spent on this war of containment became the headline, followed by the tally of bodies. The atmosphere of the assembly line was revealed everywhere. War was surely nothing more and nothing less than work. As Hawkeye had once bitterly noted, "You just do your job and try to forget there's a war going on outside the window." In another scene, he told Sherman Potter, "Maybe we should charge them piecework."

M*A*S*H brought to an audience of 125 million viewers (60 percent of all homes with television) in its final episode a sense not so much of closure, of a merciful end to a terribly depressing condition, but of openness to a future where reasonably sane and sensitive people could see through the camouflage of such absurd myths as those of manifest destiny (assuming the role of the world's policeman) and of eternal progress (the glorification of technique and its deployment in the service of foolish military escapades). M*A*S*H, to the credit of its creators, writers, directors, and actors, of whom Larry Gelbart, Alan Alda, and Bert Metcalfe stand out, had on numerous occasions the courage to be oppositional—a rare act in contemporary commercial television.[14]

Perhaps the most clearly oppositional work in television comedy, and perhaps in all of television, was Mary Hartman, Mary Hartman. While its television life was short (January 1976 to July 1977), and its audience small by network standards (it was turned down by all three networks, although CBS had financed the pilot, and instead ran in syndication in about 100 markets), this work made a significant impact on the critical community and established a cult following. Part legitimate soap opera and part spoof, the serial, produced by Norman Lear and T.A.T. Productions, was able to slide effortlessly between sardonic humor and pathos via the hesitancy of its incredibly ambivalent characters. *Mary Hartman, Mary Hartman* aired for a half hour Monday through Friday, on most stations either in late afternoon or late night. The program was losing about $50,000 a week because its initial 26-week "charter contracts" negotiated with station groups had a minimal try-out fee—a necessity for oppositional work that could not secure immediate network financing. The serial was so popular in some markets that two major station groups, Kaiser and Metromedia, offered to renegotiate their contracts at higher fees to keep the serial alive. This was a revealing commentary on the willingness of business interests to ignore the oppositional nature of material when it is highly profitable. Its popularity seemed to operate on two levels: One audience, in all likelihood, took the serial as pure entertainment—a soap-opera spoof—while another audience reveled in its biting social satire.

Part of the serial's popularity was undoubtedly due to its very frank treatment of contemporary problems of sexuality, including impotence, extramarital affairs, and lechery. Unlike the prime-time soaps featuring wealthy anomic meanies such as *Dallas*'s Ewings, the Hartmans—Mary and Tom—and their friends Charlie and Loretta Haggers, were essentially honest blue-collar, middle-American working folks from fictional Fernwood, Ohio, with good intentions and a strong sense of underlying morality. But Tom's and Mary's total dependency on the television world, their low self-esteem brought about by a sense of inferior socioeconomic status, and their increasing inability to communicate with one another led to the breakdown of their marriage, their desperate search for human contact in extramarital affairs (Mary with handsome police-sergeant Dennis Foley, with whom she makes love in his hospital bed; and Tom with Annie, an upper-middle-class culture snob), and their eventual separation.

The odd assortment of characters lends the serial a surreal quality while, at the same time, the marks of the rural blue-collar proletariat force the viewer to acknowledge the realism of the scenes played out in Mary's kitchen, her true domain, and in the lunchroom of the Fernwood Assembly Plant, Tom's workplace. This dichotomy provides *Mary Hartman, Mary Hartman* with unusual artistic power.

The characters in the serial are among the most memorable on television. Mary Hartman, played by Louise Lasser, is the prototypical blue-collar housewife—unfulfilled and constantly dreaming of the glamorous life she has seen enacted far too often on television, especially in television advertising. Her inability to achieve the American Dream is a constant source of frustration and leads to ultimate confusion and a eventual mental collapse. This confusion is not of the mindless variety so often seen in the domestic situation comedies of *I Love Lucy* and the like; it is a gnawing substantive inner confusion—a confusion of values. Mary's braids

and bangs, her buckteeth, and her little-girl clothes reveal her basic innocence and lack of emotional development. Her personality is "uninte-
grated."[15] Mary's 13-year-old daughter Heather is a miniature version of
her mother. We can see the sad inevitability of her future, a potentially
capable child burdened with circumstances beyond her control. Mary's
husband Tom is pure rural blue-collar proletarian with all the marks of
small-town insularity. Like Mary, he has never really grown up, as evidenced by his ever-present blue-and-white Fernwood High School jacket
and baseball cap. His lunch pail is filled with Twinkies. He drinks too
much, although he is miraculously cured during the course of the series.
His personal problems lead to his impotency; and when Mary offers herself, body and soul, to him, he angrily proclaims that the male determines
when to have sex with his wife. Mary's and Tom's best friends, Charlie
and Loretta, represent the naïve optimism of rural workers. Charlie and
Loretta are sexually active and presumably very happy with one another
as the serial opens, in marked contrast to Tom and Mary. Charlie is much
older than Loretta, balding, physically unattractive, yet a powerhouse in
bed, or so Loretta says. Loretta is young, pretty, vivacious, and a talented
country-western singer. She believes in her Bible-belt religion and displays
a strong moral character in public. Other, less prominent characters in
the serial are even more bizarre than Mary. These include Chester Mark-
ham, who plans to blow up the entire state of Ohio; Mary's 80-year-old
lecherous Grandpa Larkin, out of jail on probation, who is dating his
young woman social worker; Mary's ignorant parents, George and Martha
Shumway; and eight-year-old Reverend Jimmy Joe Jeeter, a Marjoe Gort-
ner type, and his con-man father Merle. With all of these characters, and
their glaring human weaknesses, levels of frustration pile on top of one
another and in the end become oppressive to the residents of Fernwood.
This is television's true theater of the absurd.

The worker is presented as generally inarticulate, with low self-esteem,
and unable to hold a job (Tom lost his at the assembly plant, which has-
tened his emotional decline). The protagonists seem out of control. This
is ingeniously reflected aesthetically in the serial's structure as the rotating
and periodically suspended plot-line structure of the traditional soap opera
is convoluted—*Mary Hartman, Mary Hartman* (even the redundancy of
the title evokes this) gives the viewer a strange sense of the "haphazard,
without a conspicuous overall plan or consistent development."[16] The
viewer is engaged in the "ordinary" disjointed world of the residents of
Fernwood, a world of shallow topicality framed by the god of topicality
itself, television.

Our heroine, Mary, seems the character most taken in by the televised
American Dream. In values-and-lifestyles-research terms, by which so
many advertisers live and breathe, Mary is a cross between the patriotic
and sentimental "belonger" and the "sustainer," who has a hard time

making ends meet and is resentful of her condition.[17] Such an anomaly is appropriate as it propels this artistic vehicle forward. Mary wants desperately to be a "belonger," but she does not have the necessary educational background or social status and has a difficult time coming to grips with this sad fact. Critics Tamm, Hanson, and Gordon perhaps best described Mary's unenviable state:

In all her glory [Mary is] one of the most pathetic figures of our era: the modern housewife—who really believes what advertisers and media simplifiers have told her, because she *wants* to believe them. Eventually this fiction disclosed its premise: a reverse analogy of Ibsen's *Doll House*: Mary, outside the house, wanted to get *in.* The delusion annihilates Mary—or drives her mad—because she has been so cruelly victimized by the shallow cultural ideals she worships.[18] (emphasis in original)

Almost everything in Mary's world has a pointed relationship to television; here the emphasis is on commodities and surface appearances at the expense of authentic human communication. In Mary's world, household items take precedence over human relationships. While a police detective questions Mary in her kitchen about Heather's possible sighting of a mass murderer in their neighborhood, Mary is more concerned with whether her kitchen floor has a "waxy yellow buildup." In another scene, Mary engages in a serious debate with a neighbor regarding the pros and cons of freeze-dried versus perked coffee, rather than worrying about her physical safety, which is indirectly threatened by the presence of the mass murderer in the vicinity. When a reporter for the *Fernwood Courier* comes to the Hartmans' house to take a photo of Heather, who is becoming an instant celebrity because of her sighting of the mass murderer, Mary says no, not because of considerations regarding Heather's privacy but because Heather's hair is out of place and covers the "beautiful bone structure" of her face—the normal reaction of an ideal "media mother." All of Mary's food has an advertising jingle attached to it, which she dutifully recites when the opportunity arises: "Want some sausage, brown and serve?" or, "I usually buy mountain grown."

Television has intimate ties to both death and insanity in this self-reflexive serial. The child minister Jimmy Joe Jeeter is electrocuted while watching TV in the bathtub. Zoning Commissioner Rittenhouse is strangled to death on a television talk show. (A "real-life" version of an attempted TV strangulation—life imitating art—occurred on *Geraldo* 11 years later; see chapter 10.) Mary herself mentally collapses under questioning from three so-called experts—a women's liberationist, a sociologist, and a sexologist—on the *David Susskind Show*. Ironically, the television audience thinks her breakdown is part of the entertainment (a reminder of Paddy Chayefsky's *Network*). Mary's relationship to television does not end here. She is admitted to the mental ward of the Fernwood Receiving Hospital, whose chief administrator wants to keep her locked up, despite her doctor's recommendation that she be released, because her celebrity status is bringing attention to the hospital. When Mary wants out, she is told to "sit and look at television to show them that you are normal."[19]

Perhaps no bit of dialogue better sums up the underlying ambience of *Mary Hartman, Mary Hartman* than Charlie's last words to Mary and Tom as he and Loretta leave for Nashville to cut Loretta's first country-western album: "We'll send you a pecan log from Stuckeys." The mundane then merges with the bizarre to produce a disquieting tableau of America— scenes from a poorly printed, out-of-focus four-color postcard showing a restaurant by a four-lane interstate.

Mary Hartman, Mary Hartman went voluntarily silent in July 1977 "because of the strain of producing five shows a week," according to critic Les Brown.[20] It was succeeded by *Fernwood 2-Night*, a short-lived fictional talk show involving many of the *Mary Hartman, Mary Hartman* characters. The serial had provided television viewers with a rare and none-too-flattering glimpse of blue-collar life permeated by doubt, low self-esteem, the trivial topicality of television itself, and the harsh reality that the American Dream, manifested in the myth of eternal progress, was more fantasy than substance. This mythic rural middle landscape was not at all like the one we witnessed in *The Beverly Hillbillies, The Andy Griffith Show,* or *Green Acres.* It was, instead, a rural middle landscape that we fear, not cherish—a psychic landscape that reveals the darker side of human nature and holds it up to careful, critical evaluation. *Mary Hartman, Mary Hartman*'s creators had the insight to provide their audience with an amalgam of two forms—soap opera and black comedy—that brilliantly revealed the uneasy relationship between the emptiness of ordinary workers' lives and their desperate need for fantasy, which is so cleverly provided by our most accessible public art form.

The disappearance of the self-reflexive comedy-drama from the small screen during the Reagan 1980s reflects in large measure the movement of the society away from critical self-examination. The form's hard-edged social critique was alien to the ideology of the feel-good zeitgeist and the celebration of greed that came to dominate commercial culture's discursive structures during this period.

Among the few notable attempts to revive the form was *The "Slap" Maxwell Story,* created by Jay Tarses and starring Dabney Coleman. The series enjoyed a brief run on ABC during the 1987–88 season.

"Slap" Maxwell was a depraved, egomaniacal sports writer for a second-rate southwestern newspaper, *The Ledger.* His acrimonious column, "Slap Shots," was full of innuendo and rumor and provoked open hostility and frequent lawsuits from Maxwell's targets. He was despised by *The Ledger*'s editor, Nelson Kruger, and was repeatedly fired. But he always came crawling back.

The 50-year-old Maxwell's personal life was as stormy as his professional life. His relationship with *Ledger* secretary Judy Ralston—a woman half his age—seemed doomed to failure. His ex-wife Annie, whom he left 15 years prior to the start of the series's action, was still hanging around, adding to his misery.

Maxwell lived in a "dumpy motel-apartment." His wardrobe—a battered fedora and outlandish ties—was as anachronistic as his social attitudes, among which was his denial of the existence of women's liberation. "Slap" was constantly looking backward—the best athletes existed in the past, most notably baseball hero Ted Williams.

Each episode opened with Maxwell being deservedly slapped around by someone he had offended. Some of his one-liners, which provoked these angry responses, are classics in insensitivity and mean-spiritedness.

In one episode "Slap" interviews a nun and her championship basketball team. He makes a ridiculous charge about the team using steroids. As he is leaving, he shouts to the nun, "I'll tell you one thing Sister, you're not going to be able to hide behind that moustache forever."

In another episode, "Slap" is punched in the face by a poker partner. He whines, "Why didn't you tell me about your wife's hysterectomy before I told the joke."

"Slap" yells out the window at a neighbor: "You're lucky you have a wheel chair and a ramp. I have to walk up those stairs."

A young Japanese girl, asked to guess "Slap"'s age, replies "106." He snaps back at her, "Go back to Korea."

New York Times television critic John J. O'Connor praised *The "Slap" Maxwell Story* for introducing a character rarely seen on television—the "ironic comic misanthrope in the distinctive [W. C.] Fields mold."[21] O'Connor noted that prime-time television has traditionally transformed its "few curmudgeons into sweet old softies." He offers as examples George Jefferson—"an angel under the interminable ranting"—and Archie Bunker—"the loveable bigot." On the other hand, Maxwell, like Fields in the cinema, both have "a decided element of seriousness to [their] nastiness."[22]

The program's premise—"*survival* in a world that is basically unfriendly"—is articulated by Maxwell: "We can't all lead the idyllic Reader's Digest life. Some of us get a little tired of giggling."[23] The intertextuality of Maxwell's lament is clear as a critique of the television sitcom formula, against which the program consciously rebels. It can also be read as a pointed challenge to the images in the 1984 Reagan reelection advertising campaign, "It's Morning Again in America," and to the patriotic commercials discussed in chapter 3. On a deeper level, perhaps the "mean-spirited" insensitivity of the backward-looking "Slap" can be seen as self-reflexive—an archteype for the American character of its time.

THE SATIRIC COMEDY-VARIETY SERIES

Another hybrid televisual form that has provided an arena for the occasional expression of emergent oppositional ideology is the comedy-variety series. Over the 45-year history of television in America, a few series in this genre stand out as exemplary—*That Was the Week That Was* (NBC, 1964–65), *The Smothers Brothers Comedy Hour* (CBS, 1967–69), *Rowan and Martin's Laugh-In* (NBC, 1968–73), *The Great American Dream Machine* (PBS, 1971–72), *Saturday Night Live* (NBC, 1975–present), and *The Richard Pryor Show* (NBC, 1977). These programs combined satirical sketches often lambasting the spokespersons for the dominant ideology, occasional protest songs, and acerbic commentaries on such sacred cows as television commercials and network television news programs. The programs were uneven, ranging from the devastating political protest ballads of Pete Seeger on *The Smothers Brothers Comedy Hour* at the height of the war in Vietnam to the nonsensical mugging in John Belushi's "Samurai Warrior" sketches and the perverse if intriguing "Mr. Bill" short films on *Saturday Night Live*. Like all good satire, the strongest of the shows dealt directly with topical issues and social irritations produced by inequities in the extant system of social relations. They did so, however, within a larger structure—the eclectic variety-show format—that tended to diminish the potential overall impact of the satiric and even sardonic work that emerged, work that frequently provoked public controversy. Television would always find a way to make the potentially unpalatable somehow palatable; if it could not do so, it would simply cancel the offenders, that is, unless the said offenders were gaining substantial ratings. Comedian George Carlin, whose "Dirty Words" monologue sparked the WBAI/Pacifica case that established the government's definition of "indecency," put it this way: "If truth and candor are proved to be hot items in the rating game, the networks will jump all over them."[24] Steve Allen, who directed his satire against the television medium itself, noted, "You can get away with anything on television if you have a big enough rating. Network executives may wince, but . . . they would much rather have a vulgar or politically offensive show with a 30 Nielsen than a tasteful, inoffensive program with a 15."[25] Both Allen and Carlin tend to exaggerate the networks' willingness to accede to any content if it is profitable, as we shall shortly see.

Contemporary American satire, especially on television, traces its heritage to the coffeehouse worlds of Lenny Bruce and Mort Sahl in the mid-to-late 1950s. Bruce's ribald humor and sardonic wit were reminiscent of the formal comedy in the theater of classical Greece in which risqué "religious" exercises celebrated Dionysus—a comedy of rebellion and revolution against constraining social systems. Bruce and Sahl were "creator-comics," as Carlin terms them, who, unlike traditional stand-up comics, wrote their own material and brought with them a sense of strong personal social commitment. They cut through the camouflage of the dominant ideology to reveal the harsh realities of American politics in an era that witnessed the emergence of the powerful corporate state. Their comedy was ultimately more about personal freedom, however, than about politics.[26] The coffeehouse satirists appealed to the growing number of American college-educated youths who had become increasingly skeptical about the dominant institutions of corporate America. They opened the creaky, conservative doors of our dominant electronic communications medium to the satiric comedy-variety series of the 1960s and 1970s. Bruce and Sahl were experts in using their characters, voices, paralanguage, and informal modes of dress to cloak their biting satire in personality and make it acceptable not only to those seeking an emergent counterculture but also to those on the fringes of the social debate who were curious but not yet committed. Bruce and Sahl chose a carefully orchestrated performance stance to make their points; they represented the universal motif of the angry young artist. The time for their comedy was right. Civil rights confrontation and, soon, a highly questionable war would merge with the feelings of anomie and alienation that had come to characterize the corporate 1950s—a bland era in which white people were consumed with the idea of "belonging." Sahl and Bruce led the walk away from the suburban middle landscape and into an urban world in which social revolution would seem a meaningful response.

Television itself would intensify this atmosphere through the power of incessant imaging. Carlin himself perceptively summed up the atmosphere in which television satire emerged:

The extended coverage of recent assassinations and their aftermaths, the daily Viet Nam battle film, campus rebellion, the extraordinary political year 1968, including Chicago's police riots— . . . all of these events documented nightly on the home screen have served to convince the viewer that the little box is more than a vehicle for escape.[27]

Carlin added that the audience "can accept social satire as a logical extension of the absurd reality viewed on news and information programs. The frame of reference . . . (the very medium which provides our yardstick of the norm) is perfect."[28] In fact, as Carlin noted, "The very use of the satiric form supposes respect for audience awareness."[29] The audience watched the two wars at home—the Freedom Riders and the famous 1963 civil rights march on Washington highlighted a domestic war, while the Tet offensive brought a foreign war into clearer perspective. After Walter

Cronkite's reassuring image faded from view on the *CBS Evening News*, the debate would often rage on among those who remained gathered around the screen as scenes were recalled; the screen would light up again, in prime time, for the satiric follow-up—a forum for a continued questioning of our nation's basic value priorities.

That Was the Week That Was enlivened our television screens from January 10, 1964, to May 4, 1965. It would serve as a model for subsequent television-news satires. The previous week's top news items were subjected to pointed and often brutal satire through comedy sketches, blackouts, musical-production numbers, and news reports. The series introduced David Frost to an American audience. Frost had hosted a British series upon which *TW3* was modeled, and he hosted the second and final season of the American series as well. The most memorable participant in the series was writer-composer Tom Lehrer, whose scathing songs condemned racism, political cronyism, chemical pollution, nuclearism, the abuses of organized religion, and a variety of other social irritations. These songs included "National Brotherhood Week," "Whatever Became of Hubert?" and the infamous "Vatican Rag" and "Pollution." The latter song followed the publication of Rachel Carson's book *Silent Spring* and a subsequent *CBS Reports* television documentary that chronicled the controversy involving Carson's basic challenge to the corporate chemical giants and the U.S. Department of Agriculture over the environmental dangers and health hazards of the uncontrolled use of pesticides. *That Was the Week That Was*, with moments of true oppositional ideological expression, never broke into the top 25 Nielsen programs. According to Steve Allen, the series failed because it came five years too early for the American audience and many of its actors, who included Henry Morgan and Phyllis Newman, weren't very engaging small-screen personalities.

While *TW3* never achieved popularity with America's mass audience, a comedy-variety series that was aired two years later was able to find that large audience, particularly the younger demographic group. In the interim, America had been exposed, via television news, to the possibility of a cruel hoax ten thousand miles from home. Vietnam had entered the national debate; young men were being drafted and were dying there. The emotional fires ignited in August 1965 in Los Angeles by the Watts riots were still smoldering and would soon be rekindled in urban ghettos throughout the United States. It was February 5, 1967, and an important milestone in television was achieved as *The Smothers Brothers Comedy Hour* premiered on CBS. For the next two-and-a-half years, the series, with its many artistic ups and downs, its constant battles with network standards-and-practices executives, and its status as legitimizer of the counterculture, would highlight the social and political crises that seemed to rock this country almost daily. The series was hosted by brothers Tom and Dick Smothers and featured comedian Pat Paulsen. Tom, the "dull brother," played the guitar; his older and much wiser brother Dick played the bass violin. Tom's famous line, "Mom liked you best," provided the series with a distinctive personality—the codes of sibling rivalry were a comic dodge used to keep the audience open to the more serious fare that emerged in the series. The two brothers would open each show with a song that never quite went right. Keeping in character, Tom would always mess the song up by forgetting either the lyrics or the tune, or he would become recalcitrant and childish and want to change the entire routine. But beyond the internicine quarrels, *The Smothers Brothers Comedy Hour* satirized almost every hallowed American institution, especially its political institutions. Tom and Dick, it seems fair to say, did not themselves often "do political or social satire. It is more correct to say that political and social satire are presented on their show."[30] They had, however, a strong social consciousness—a personal commitment to exposing social ills—and that was the crucial element that carried the series through its roughest tests in CBS corporate boardrooms. Sketches on the series included a highly controversial antireligion polemic aired early in 1969; an antiwar ballad titled "Waist Deep in the Big Muddy," sung by Pete Seeger, a frequent guest on the program, who had long been blacklisted on television; and a bizarre campaign for the presidency of the United States, waged by the droll deadpan comedian Pat Paulsen. In the summer of 1968, Paulsen attempted to take his campaign on the airwaves via the *Comedy Hour*, but CBS, fearing demands for "equal opportunities" from other political candidates under Section 315 of the Federal Communications Act, kept Paulsen's campaign off the air until after the November elections. Paulsen's campaign slogan, "If nominated I will not run, and if elected I will not serve," was drawn directly from Civil War general William Tecumseh Sherman. It became a rallying point for dissatisfied college students throughout the country who had lost faith in our national political leadership (Lyndon Johnson, himself buried waist deep in Vietnam, had declined to seek reelection, and the specter of Richard Nixon loomed ominously on the national political horizon).

One of the most controversial *Comedy Hour* segments was never seen by viewers.[31] Shot for the first show of their third season, which aired September 29, 1968, the segment featured a song by Harry Belafonte, an outspoken champion of civil rights and critic of Vietnam. The calypso tune, titled "Don't Stop the Carnival," was sung by Belafonte against a visual backdrop featuring a montage of images from the recently concluded Democratic National Convention in Chicago. As Belafonte sang "Lord, don't stop the carnival . . . carnival's an American bacchanal," viewers saw footage of the violent confrontations between Chicago police and antiwar demonstrators outside the convention hall, images of military police herding up journalists inside the hall, and, most striking of all, the image of Chicago Mayor Richard Daley clapping as an obese woman delegate, wearing a Hubert Humphrey placard on her back, danced the night away. Belafonte's intentionally ironic lyrics, which suggested that the American people just want to be entertained, no matter what political issues were swirling around them, was too much for CBS, which cut the five-minute song from the show. To fill the dead air created by the CBS cut, Tom and Dick attempted to insert a studio audience "question and answer" segment they had shot, but CBS rejected that plan and instead aired the show in its shortened version. Adding insult to injury, CBS, with the five-minute gap to fill, sold the time to Republican presidential candidate Richard Nixon.

Although Tom and Dick lost this particular battle, they continued to engage not only the dominant political institutions but also the powerful media institutions they depended on for survival. They often failed to deliver their completed programs early enough for network editing (the Belafonte episode was evidence of the potential outcome). While this tactic helped them sneak their more oppositional material past wary network officials and traditionally conservative affiliate-station managers, it also so angered CBS executives that the series was replaced in June 1969 with *Hee Haw*, a rural-hillbilly takeoff on the highly successful NBC series *Laugh-In*.

The Smothers Brothers Comedy Hour achieved solid ratings in both its spring 1967 run and its full 1967–68 season (it ranked sixteenth and eighteenth of all rated series aired in those respective periods), but it slid in the ratings in the 1968–69 season, which certainly contributed to its cancellation. Its oppositional material was no longer achieving a significant payback where it really counted—the financial balance sheet. The series received an Emmy Award in 1968–69 for "outstanding writing in comedy, variety or music." For those who struggled through this volatile period in American cultural and social history, *The Smothers Brothers Comedy Hour* provided a needed satiric perspective on the incredible events unfolding daily.

Another comedy-variety series of the time, *Rowan and Martin's Laugh-In*, ran on NBC from January 22, 1968, to May 14, 1973. While not as overtly political as either *TW3* or *The Smothers Brothers Comedy Hour*, it nevertheless poked fun at many of America's bourgeois social codes while at the same time seeming to revel in that social milieu. The series format was anchored by the individual performer's sketch, which became a personal trademark. The series's roots were in the fast-paced, seemingly unstructured action comedy of such early film comedians as the Keystone Cops and in the news satire of *TW3*. With *Laugh-In*'s huge cast of 40 or more regular players delivering rapid-fire catch phrases such as "sock it to me," "velly intellestink," and "look that up in your Funk'n Wagnalls" and with the frenetic pacing of the regular features—the go-go-dancer-filled cocktail-party scene, the "Flying Fickle Finger of Fate Award," "Laugh-

In Looks at the News," and the show's concluding segment, the "Joke Wall"—the program became a frenzied hour of tomfoolery that reflected the confusing mosaic of everyday experience of the late 1960s and early 1970s, a period in which events and personal relationships seemed far from the ordered state of things as reflected in the suburban middle landscape of the 1950s and early 1960s.

Laugh-In was a smash hit. It was the top-rated television series in both the 1968 and 1969 seasons. One reason for such success may have been the series's ability to get even the most famous national figures to do guest appearances on the show. Who can forget a perplexed Richard Nixon, in close-up, saying to the camera, "Sock it to *me?*"

Laugh-In's cohost, Dan Rowan, is firmly convinced that comedy is, above all, visual, and the series reflects that philosophy. It is a visual three-ring circus without magicians, bears, or acrobats, more the province of traditional variety shows, which were so successful in television's early period (e.g., *The Ed Sullivan Show*). Rowan saw his series as distinct from *The Smothers Brothers Comedy Hour*, about which he noted, "[They] have a definite direction and philosophy and are simply using comedy as a platform for a doctrine. Whether or not we agree with the Smothers (and we generally do), we aren't doing *that thing*" (emphasis in original).[32] The dirty-old-man sketches and other sexual innuendos that pervaded *Laugh-In* were allowable in a period in which the youth audience was becoming increasingly important to the networks; demographics had become a relevant analytical tool employed by advertisers to help them target their audience. In 1970, for example, CBS performed a major housecleaning, removing its rural-middle-landscape comedies and middle-aged variety stars—its staples for decades—in favor of what it called relevant urban-oriented works it felt would appeal to younger city audiences comprised of recent college graduates who would soon be decidedly upscale, once the social protests subsided. It was clear, at least to Rowan, that the mainstream audience, to which *Laugh-In* appealed, would accept a raucous mixture of topicality, slapstick, sex, violence, and the portrayal of the human idiot. Rowan disclaimed any comedic "revolution" here, asking, "What's new?"

Indeed, *Laugh-In* was not as polemical as were the Smothers Brothers or as consistently acerbic as *TW3*. But it did at least expose the outlines of irreverent comedy to a larger audience. The much smaller audience that in 1971 could tune through the UHF snow to find the local public television station might have been treated to one of our finest, yet most short-lived, satiric comedies—*The Great American Dream Machine*. Produced at WNET/13 in New York, this series, whose executive producers were A. H. Perlmutter and Jack Willis, aired from January 1971 to February 1972 (for the first nine months in a 90-minute format and thereafter for 60 minutes). *Dream Machine* featured some memorable television mo-

ments as satire, serious political documentaries, drama, and music segments were blended into a coherent and often scathing attack on
American values. It seemed to many people that the Great American
Dream had run amok. The "Machine," whether political, economic, or
cultural, kept cranking out products—public condensation symbols behind which cowered questionable value priorities. Etched in memory is
the mustachioed, plump, frumpy, and brilliant Marshall Efron, who, in
his consumer segments, would meticulously demystify the apparatus that
actualized our pecuniary philosophy, psychology, and biology. Of all the
great moments, none stands out more to me than Efron's incredible revelation that the trash compactor, seen lurking lifelessly in the background,
ready to grind away on call and which sold for a mere $400, could "turn
25 pounds of trash [Efron holds up an unwieldy trash bag] into 25 pounds
of trash [he holds up compacted bag of trash]."

Dream Machine ran into serious political trouble late in its run as it
aired a documentary segment alleging that the Federal Bureau of Investigation had planted its agents as "terrorists" whose job it was to convince
college-student radicals to sabotage public facilities, to help them build
bombs for that purpose, and then to arrest them. The series was dis-
banded after one year for lack of funding, according to television critic
Les Brown.

In 1975 a new series emerged, modeling itself in many ways on both
TW3 and *Laugh-In*. The series, *Saturday Night Live*, was to serve as a late-
night NBC showcase for young comedians, and it did precisely that. Live,
90 minutes in duration, and transmitted from New York City originally
three Saturdays each month (the fourth Saturday was devoted to Lloyd
Dobyns's excellent documentary magazine *Weekend*), *Saturday Night Live*
premiered October 11, 1975. Its first guest host was George Carlin. The
resident cast in those early years included Chevy Chase, Dan Ackroyd,
John Belushi, Jane Curtin, Garrett Morris, Laraine Newman, and Gilda
Radner, all of whom became household names among America's youth.
Each comedian, as was the case with *Laugh-In*, developed his or her own
trademark character. Chase became famous for his satirical newscast and
impressions of President Gerald Ford stumbling around. He left the series
in 1976 to pursue a highly successful film acting career. Ackroyd and Belushi remained with the series for four years before leaving for Hollywood
to make films as a comedy team. Belushi's samurai-warrior routines (not
considered "Japan-bashing" at the time) lent a classic touch of the absurd
to the show.

Highlights from the series are difficult to cite in a limited space, but
the most imaginative work often emerged in the commercial spoofs that
were ingeniously built into the program's flow so that the audience was
never immediately certain whether the real thing or a takeoff was unfolding (the current "Energizer" battery ad campaign has its roots in this

form). This aesthetic device pointed clearly and self-reflexively to the perceptual stance ingrained in television viewers over time—we had unconsciously become part of the flow of television. *Saturday Night Live*, at its best, jerked us out of that flow. A memorable example was Jerry Rubin's pitch for "Yippie Wallpaper," something to help the now-upscale, former radical-revolutionaries of the 1960s remember the glories of the "good old days." Rubin, himself a revolutionary-turned-stockbroker, was the ideal absurd pitchman in the new era of the "me generation."

Saturday Night Live has been extremely uneven throughout its nearly two-decade run. Some sketches boardered on the puerile, such as "The Killer Bees," but other recurring sketches, notably the "Cone Heads," did insightfully address contemporary social issues such as parochialism and prejudice in suburbia. Segments such as the "Mr. Bill" filmed narratives simultaneously appealed to our odd cultural sense of morbidity and titillated us, creating an uneasy ambiguity. These sketches often stretched the bounds of acceptability, which in itself tests the fiber of the dominant ideology.

Unfortunately, today's *Saturday Night Live* has become decidedly establishment. George Bush invited *SNL* star Dana Carvey to the White House to do his scathing George Bush imitation. Even the occasional provocative moment is quickly coopted. When the Irish singer Sinead O'Connor unexpectedly concluded her appearance on the show by tearing up a photograph of the Pope—a pointed reference to the Church's Neanderthal views on women—NBC was deluged by angry telephone calls from viewers. *Saturday Night Live* responded by ridiculing O'Connor in a subsequent program.[33]

The Richard Pryor Show premiered September 13, 1977, and died a quiet death October 20 of that same year. It was the controversial black comedian's first regular television series. Pryor had originally committed himself to a minimum of ten shows with NBC, but censorship problems with the network reduced his quota to five. Pryor got off on the wrong foot with the network brass; in what was to be the opening segment of his first program in the series, he appeared on camera nude from the waist up. As the camera slowly tilted down revealing what appeared to be a nude Pryor (he was really wearing a body stocking), he was delivering a monologue on his relationship with NBC, stating he had "lost nothing" in his censorship battles. This segment was cut from the show. Another memorable sketch was a bitter and poignant attack on guns, especially handguns that seemed to kill a disproportionate number of inner city blacks. The impassioned attack and plea for sanity was, of course, directed by implication at the National Rifle Association and at its blind adherence to the myth of individual freedom, as expressed in its libertarian/conservative politics. This was strong stuff for prime-time network "entertainment" television. But ultimately there was little for NBC to worry about.

The network had conveniently counterprogrammed *The Richard Pryor Show* against ABC's smash hit *Happy Days*, which drew an audience twice as large as Pryor's.

While it is impossible to adequately sum up the discussion of the wide variety of comedic presentations described and interpreted in this chapter, a few common threads are worth noting. Works of television comedy are contemporary, that is, they are culturally relevant because of their temporality. Television comedies reflect, and occasionally call into question, the predominant operational myths of the culture. Television comedies tend to lag slightly behind the broad social movements that produce subtle yet large-scale cultural shifts; as such, the comedies, while seemingly oppositional, are in fact more like cautionary tales whose confrontational quality is at best mildly provocative. There can be little doubt that those who produce, write, perform, and direct television comedy are among the best talents working in the medium today. And of all the genres of television, comedy, especially satiric comedy and comedy-drama, provides us with the clearest opportunity to express emergent oppositional ideology. At the same time, the institutional apparatus that might permit such occasional forays into the deep waters of social criticism can easily pull the plug on the maverick producer through counterprogramming, prior censorship, or outright cancellation. And, although the networks will stay with a controversial comedy series that sells very well, it is apparent that the more truly oppositional series, with the notable exception of *M*A*S*H* and, to a lesser degree, *The Smothers Brothers Comedy Hour*, are never great audience successes. In the end, the television networks and their corporate shareholders have the last laugh.

NOTES

1. John Leonard, "Bigotry as a Dirty Joke," *Life*, March 19, 1971, p. 10.
2. Ibid.
3. Robert Lewis Shayon, "Love That Hate," *Saturday Review*, March 27, 1971, p. 20.
4. Ibid.
5. Michael Arlen, "The Media Dramas of Normal Lear," *The New Yorker*, March 10, 1975.
6. Ibid.
7. Archie's voice was dubbed over the video. The actual line Archie delivered in live performance of the scene was, "I don't wanna talk about that goddam war no more."
8. Todd Gitlin, "Prime Time Ideology: The Hegemonic Process in Television Entertainment," in *Television: The Critical View*, 4th ed., ed. Horace Newcomb (New York: Oxford University Press, 1987), p. 527.
9. Roger L. Hofeldt, "Cultural Bias in M*A*S*H," in *Television: The Critical*

View, 3d ed., ed. Horace Newcomb (New York: Oxford University Press, 1982), p. 161.

10. Ibid., p. 164.

11. Joseph Campbell, *The Hero with a Thousand Faces* (New York: Pantheon Books, 1949), p. 28.

12. Ibid.

13. The amount of blood shown during the course of the series increased dramatically in sync with the overall increasing levels of cynicism and anger expressed by the protagonists.

14. It should be noted that, as was the case with *All in the Family*, one can take risks if one is profitable. The final episode of *M*A*S*H*, while costing more than $1 million to produce, earned CBS in excess of $10 million, according to published news reports. Thirty-second spots sold for about $450,000.

15. Robert Craft, "Elegy for Mary Hartman," in *Television: The Critical View*, 3d ed., ed. Horace Newcomb (New York: Oxford University Press, 1982), p. 153.

16. Ibid., p. 149.

17. William Meyers, "Of Belongers, Achievers, Survivors et al.," *New York Times*, December 5, 1982, p. F29.

18. Goran Tamm, Hans Ingvar Hanson, and George N. Gordon, *Man in Focus: New Approaches to Commercial Communications* (New York: Hastings House, 1980), p. 26.

19. Craft, "Elegy," p. 151.

20. Les Brown, *Encyclopedia of Television*, 3d ed. (Detroit: Gale Research, 1992), p. 340.

21. John J. O'Connor, "Two New Sitcoms Forgo Musty Formulas," *New York Times*, October 25, 1987, p. 31.

22. Ibid.

23. Ibid., p. 32.

24. George Carlin, "Made for Each Other: TV and Satire," *Television Quarterly* 8 (Winter 1969): 25.

25. Steve Allen, "The Revolution in Humor," *Television Quarterly* 8 (Winter 1969): 11.

26. Ibid., p. 12.

27. Carlin, "Made for Each Other," pp. 25–26.

28. Ibid., p. 26.

29. Ibid., p. 24.

30. Allen, "Revolution," p. 8.

31. David Hinckley, " '60s 'Smothers' No-no Finally Gets Its Airing," (New York) *Daily News*, March 18, 1993, p. 93. After 25 years, the censored Belafonte song was at last seen by viewers, on the E! cable network, which ran a reprise of the best of the 71 episodes of the original *The Smothers Brothers Comedy Hour* with commentary on the series' production history provided by Tom and Dick Smothers and guests on the original episodes.

32. Dan Rowan, "What Revolution in Comedy?" *Television Quarterly* 8 (Winter 1969): 24.

33. John J. O'Connor, "A Prosperous 'Saturday Night' Grows Tame," *New York Times*, March 14, 1993, sec. 2, p. 29.

6

□ □ □ □ □ □

Television Melodrama

The intentional ironic comedy of *Mary Hartman, Mary Hartman* played off the journalistic realism of television soap opera, one of television's most significant traditional melodramatic forms. The realism of the television soaps constitutes one pole of the melodramatic continuum. At the other extreme are the romantic epics of loner-heroes and wanderers whose mystical experiences reveal a mythic dream world of fear and conquest. Like melodrama generally, both the soap opera and the romantic epic take a centrist sociocultural position. In the former instance, the protagonists and antagonists operate within a highly constrained code of conduct in which erratic/anarchistic behavior is punished; in the latter instance, the loner-hero, while suffering numerous tests of physical and moral strength along the journey, prevails and is incorporated back into society.

Television melodrama has its roots in the early-nineteenth-century stage play in which romantic, sensational plots and incidents were mixed with songs and orchestral music. The word melodrama evolved from the Greek *melos*, meaning song or music, and from *drama*, a deed, action, or play, especially tragedy. In tragedy the hero is isolated from society so that he may better understand his own and the society's moral weakness; but, once enlightened, the hero cannot stave off the disaster embedded in the social structure beyond his control. In contrast, melodrama finds the hero's acts constantly reinforcing the dominant ideology. The melodramatic hero is a normative character representing incorporation into society. Critic Northrop Frye described a central theme in melodrama as "the triumph of moral virtue over villainy, and the consequent idealizing of the moral views assumed to be held by the audience."[1] Since melodrama, according to Frye, exists squarely within a mass-cultural framework, it could easily become "advance propaganda for the police state" if it were taken seriously.[2] Frye sidesteps this fear by positing that the audience does not take such work seriously.

Peter Brooks, in contrast to Frye, finds melodrama acting powerfully in society, reflecting the socialization of the deeply personal. Brooks finds the heightened dramatization and excess of enactment of melodrama reflected in psychoanalysis: "Psychoanalysis can be read as a systematic realization of the melodramatic aesthetic, applied to the structure of dynamics of the mind."[3] Brooks sees in the melodramatic aesthetic unremitting conflict, possibly disabling, excessive enactment, and clarification and cure. Brooks elaborates:

Melodrama regularly stimulates the experience of nightmare, where virtue, representative of the ego, lies supine, helpless, while menace plays out its occult designs. The end of the nightmare is an awakening brought about by confrontation and expulsion of the villain, the person in whom the evil is seen to be concentrated, and a reaffirmation of the society of "decent people."[4]

Melodrama demands strong justice—"a perfect justice of punishment and reward, expulsion and recognition"[5]—while tragedy, in contrast, often includes the ambivalence of mercy in its code. Melodrama is highly significant in an age of surface complexity and contradiction (which we experience in our everyday lives), for it provides us with models of clear resolution for highly personalized, intensely enacted conflict. As Brooks notes, contemporary television melodrama substitutes for the traditional forms of social control—the rituals of organized religion and, before that, of "primitive mythologies"—that provided easily understandable models of "primal, intense, polarized forces."

Melodrama is thus powerfully conservative. Like the ceremonial ritual that bound tribesmen together, melodrama today, repositioned in politics and economics, draws us into the prescriptions of the dominant culture.

THE HERO AS CULTURAL SYMBOL

The hero is central to melodrama. The dominant concept of the hero in Western culture dates from the heroic period of Grecian history that preceded the return of Greek soldiers from their conquest of Troy in Asia Minor (early twelfth century B.C.). Hero was the name given to a man of superhuman strength, courage, or ability who was favored by the gods. In antiquity, the hero was regarded as an immortal intermediary between the gods and people—a demigod who was the offspring of a god or goddess and a human being.

Later, the heroic class came to include mortal men of renown who were deified because of great and noble deeds or for firmness or greatness of soul in any course of action they undertook. These men became national or local heroes. They included men distinguished by extraordinary bravery and martial achievement—the illustrious warriors—and men who wandered in quest of adventures—the heroes-errant (called knights-errant in medieval culture). Many heroes were boldly experimental or resourceful in their actions. Heroic actions were not always pure, however; cunning became a characteristic of the hero as he used his wit to outsmart the enemy (as exemplified by Homer's epic hero Odysseus's invention of the wooden horse, his encounter with the sirens, and his beggar's disguise that tricked his wife's suitors). Punishment of those who disturbed the proper order of things was harsh. Odysseus slaughtered all 108 of his wife Penelope's suitors in order to restore decency to the court of Ithaca. Women as well as men possessed heroic qualities such as valor, resourcefulness, intelligence, and moral strength (although she had no knowledge of Odysseus's fate, as he was forced by the gods to wander the Mediterranean for ten years, Penelope nevertheless remained faithful and put off all her suitors with courage and moral conviction).

The world in which the classic hero operated was a world of heightened emotional intensity—a harsh world in which the norm included unending tests of both physical and moral strength and the constant threat of death. The hero represented a carefully defined value system in which good triumphed over evil in the end and in which the actions of the hero, with the assistance of the gods, produced order and stability out of chaos.

Stylistically, the classic Greek epic poem, composed in the oral, mnemonic form that favored recurrent themes and motifs and flexible rhythms, presented to the listener an accessible form in which to deal with the complex narrative development. Structurally, Homer's *Odyssey* is the precursor of the modern television "backstory" or flashback—the narrative begins near the chronological conclusion of the story and Odysseus's ten years' wanderings are recounted later in the story.

Scholars date the creation of the *Odyssey* in the eighth century B.C. Almost 2,700 years later, the German composer Richard Wagner wrote a series of musical dramas that stand as modern epics. *Der Ring des Nibelungen,* four operas that address the relationships between humans and gods, was written between 1853 and 1874. The *Ring* presents in epic terms the destiny of men determined by supernatural agents—a common theme of most heroic epic poetry. However, at the *Ring*'s conclusion, Wagner posits a new condition in which responsibility for the future is placed in the hands of mortals—heroic man must bravely explore and shape the future without the help of the gods. Wagner's *Ring* thus reflects a broad artistic concern of the late nineteenth and twentieth centuries, namely, a move from the primitive mythic realm toward social realism.

While Homer's *Odyssey* and Wagner's *Ring* deal in legend, one cannot ignore their ultimate grounding in cultural reality. The sociopolitical resonance of the heroic epic is evident in the critical debate that often surrounds such work. Plato condemned Homer's poetry as morally corrupt, while Aristotle praised it as the height of brilliantly crafted lies. The ambiguity of Wagner's philosophy in the *Ring* opened the mammoth work to a variety of social interpretations. Bernard Shaw saw the heroism in the *Ring* as symbolic of a socialist struggle, with the gods representing the decadent bourgeois capitalists defiled by their greed. Supporters of Adolf Hitler used the *Ring* as a rationalization of their aggressive twentieth-century ambitions.

Heroes are ultimately "social types," which, according to sociologist Orrin Klapp, represent "roles which, though informal, have become rather well conceptualized and in which there is a comparatively high degree of consensus."[6] Social types are drawn from a cultural stock of images and symbols. They provide models people try to approximate and, perhaps more important, act as "a kind of photograph" of the society's previous activities.[7] A close examination of the character traits of our heroes thus reveals much information about our cultural traditions. Distinguished from stereotypes—inaccurate popular concepts that are applied indiscriminately to individuals without regard for those individuals' actual characteristics—social types are both accurate and revealing. Klapp posits, correctly I believe, that social types represent "basic dimensions of social control in any society."[8]

Heroes cannot exist without one or the other of two additional social types—villains and fools. Heroes are praised, followed, set up as models, and given a central part in our dramas (both fictional and real); they are ultimately better than societal norms. Villains are negative models of evil to be feared, hated, and ultimately eradicated or reformed by the actions of the hero; villains are dangerous to societal norms. Fools are models of absurdity, to be ridiculed; they fall far short of societal norms.[9] A special category of fool is the so-called holy fool of tragedy, who is mocked by society but may have superior insight or special knowledge developed from a vantage point as an "outsider." The holy fool's role is often that of a commentator.

Within the television melodrama, these social types operate as signs, constructed according to our society's dominant values, reinforcing commonly held concepts of the "proper order of things." The hero, villain, and fool are therefore ideological, representing an ensemble of social relationships and social constraints, and an operational mythology—the images a society presents to itself in order to perpetuate itself. A closer look at melodramatic heroes, villains, and fools—at their words, gestures, interactions, and institutional affiliations—reveals, through the basic transparency of their characterizations, the locus of social control in contemporary American society.

THE STRUCTURE OF TELEVISION MELODRAMA

The essential feature of orally composed, lengthy epic poems such as Homer's *Iliad* and *Odyssey* is the use of verbal formulas—groups of two or more poetic words that fit metrical positions in the poetic line or extend over several lines. The key element is repetition. Homer employed alternating long and double-short syllables to build a rhythm and to help hold the listener's attention—to draw the listener into the poetry.

In grand opera, of which Wagner's *Ring* is one of the great examples, a series of distinct acts, each generally signifying a change either in time or place, is linked by orchestral transitions. Superfluous exposition is eliminated. We see a series of intense highlights of the lives of the protagonists and antagonists. Orchestral music introduces action, provides a background for plot movement, and reinforces moments of heightened dramatic intensity. Opera is generally constructed to formula. As in literary melodrama, plot dominates, initiating excitement and suspense by raising for its protagonists questions of self-preservation. Characterization is secondary.

In nineteenth- and twentieth-century literature, melodrama came to signify "democratic drama." Harsher critics condemned the form as sensational, sentimental entertainment for the "masses." Rural-type melodrama—with its beautiful, virtuous, poor heroine, its pure hero, its despicable villain who ties the heroine to the railroad tracks, and the rustic clown who aids the hero (wonderfully satirized in the television cartoon "Dudley Do-Right of the Royal Canadian Mounties," originally a segment of *The Bullwinkle Show*)—gave way to city melodramas focusing on the seamy underworld and to suspenseful crime-dramas such as those of Agatha Christie.

Television melodrama has drawn freely from all these precursors, both structurally and conceptually. Highly-segmented plots developed in four 12-minute acts, each with a climax, and a happy ending, are carried along by background music and stress peaks of action and emotional involvement. Suspense and excitement are heightened by a sense of realism created through sophisticated, if formulaic visualizations (car chases being obvious examples). Characterizations are generally unidimensional, employing eccentric protagonists and antagonists who are made credible by good acting. Ideologically, the plot elements reinforce conventional morality.

The rhythm of the commercial television melodrama depends on a predictable structure, as did the rhythm of the Homeric poems. In television melodrama, the structure is motivated by the flow of the program segment–music-commercial sequence. A typical structure might be sketched as shown in Figure 6.1. This plot structure beautifully combines aesthetics and ideology. As suspense builds and the plot thickens, we are carried forward at various crucial junctures by a combination of rapid visual cutting and an intense buildup of the background music and ambient sound that create the smooth transition to the often frenetic, high-pitched ads. The rhythm produces a flow with which we have become quite com-

Figure 6.1
The Structure of Television Melodrama

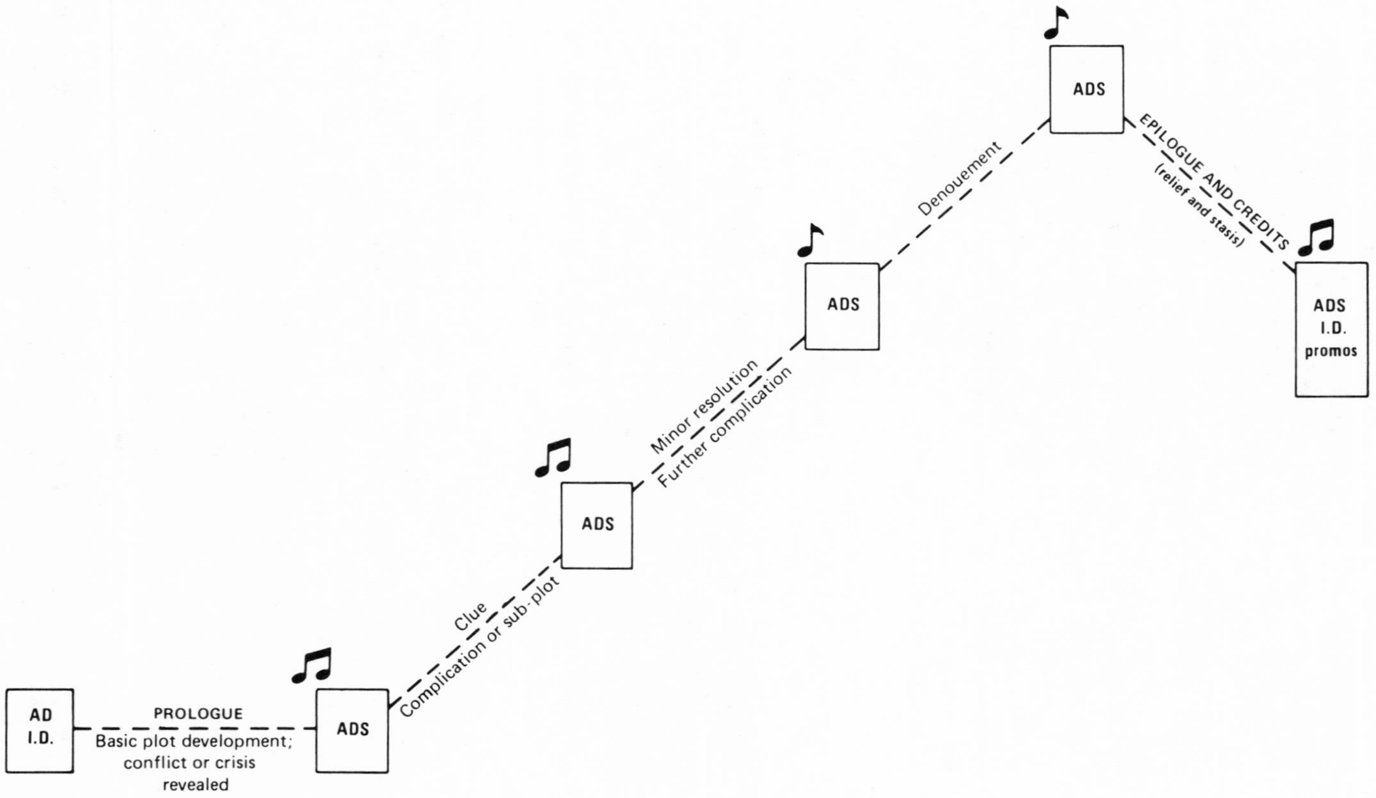

| AD I.D. | PROLOGUE Basic plot development; conflict or crisis revealed | ADS | Complication or sub-plot Clue | ADS | Minor resolution Further complication | ADS | Denouement | ADS | EPILOGUE AND CREDITS (relief and stasis) | ADS I.D. promos |

fortable. In fact, it can be argued, we have come to both understand and accept the genre conventions in the context of the production mechanisms that define the regime of commercial television.

Critic David Thorburn described the structure of television melodrama according to what he termed a "multiplicity principle," by which a particular television melodrama will

> draw . . . many times upon the immense store of stories and situations created by the genre's brief but crowded history. . . . By minimizing the need for long establishing or expository sequences, the multiplicity principle allows the story to leave aside the question of how these emotional entanglements were arrived at and to concentrate its energies on their credible and powerful present enactment.[10]

Thorburn is correct in locating the dramatic power of the television melodrama in a series of powerful if somewhat isolated scenes that highlight intense interpersonal confrontations. Taking this interpretation of melodramatic structure one step further, we discover that much more than dramatic power is involved. Pecuniary philosophy is also operating, for by cutting down on exposition or establishing sequences that tend toward lengthy and deliberate characterizations, the purveyors of melodrama are able to break their little tales into shortened, fast-paced, and often disconnected simple sequences that make commercial breaks feel natural to viewers.

Culture critic Raymond Williams, with characteristic insight, related the concept of what he called "planned flow" to both the medium and the institutions that sustain it:

> What is being offered is not, in older terms, a programme of discrete units with particular insertions, but a planned flow, in which the true series is not the published sequence of programme items but this sequence transformed by the inclusion of another kind of sequence [incorporating advertisements], so that these sequences together compose the real flow, the real "broadcasting." Increasingly, in both commercial and public-service television, a further sequence was added: "trailers of programmes . . . or more itemized programme news [program promos]. This was intensified in conditions of competition. . . .
>
> But this flow is planned: not only in itself, but at an early stage in all original television production for commercial systems. . . . There is a characteristic kind of opening sequence, meant to excite interest. . . . In American television, after two or three minutes, this is succeeded by commercials. . . . What follows is apparently quite unconnected material. It is then not surprising that so many of these opening moments are violent or bizarre: the interest aroused must be strong enough to initiate the expectations of (interrupted but sustainable) sequence. . . . Some part of the flow offered is then directly traceable to conditions of controlled com-

petition, just as some of its specific original elements are traceable to the financing of television by commercial advertising.[11]

Thus, we often describe our experience as "watching TV," not as watching *The CBS Evening News* or "the ballgame." The flow is always there, easily accessible—the central organizing principle of the medium.

The production imperatives of television-series melodrama reinforce Williams's concept of the commodification of flow. Producers Richard Levinson and William Link described these production procedures. The network commits itself to a new television series in mid-April. The series premieres in early September, leaving four-and-one-half months lead time for producers to hire staff, including writers and directors, prepare scripts, and begin shooting and editing. It takes four weeks, under the best conditions, to complete an episode of a melodrama; with luck, four shows will be "in the can" by the season's premiere, with others in varying stages of development (at any time during the process, many series episodes will be in development simultaneously, one being edited, another shot, and another scripted). By October, the initial four episodes will have been aired, and the fifth will be nearly ready. If the show is renewed at midseason, the producer will need as many as 22 episodes for the entire season. By December, there will be but a matter of days between the final edit and the airing of an episode, as inevitable delays shorten the turnaround time. In addition to normal time problems, there are problems with staff. Levinson and Link cite the frequent problem of having a good freelance writer in demand who agrees to write for one producer's shows as well as those of other producers. The writer with a track record will be juggling an outline for one show, a first draft for another, and a "notion" for a third.[12]

In the frenzied world of the daytime soap opera, actors get the script the night before the taping, begin run-through rehearsals at 7:30 the next morning, do three rehearsals before taping, and tape between 3:30 and 6:00 that afternoon. This hectic ritual is repeated five days a week.

The prime-time-melodrama production process is ruled by shortcuts, scattered attention, and occasional network interference in content, created by the fear of viewer response to potentially controversial material that may range from questionable street language, however dramatically appropriate, to sexual taboos. Simplicity, predictability, and safety become the norm.

Planned flow, the melodrama's highly symbolic heroic ideal, its formal conventions, and its reinforcement of the society's dominant value systems render the genre highly significant as a centrist cultural mechanism stressing order and stasis.

Examples of television melodramas discussed in the following section are presented in Figure 6.2.

TELEVISION MELODRAMA AND CONTEMPORARY SOCIAL
RELATIONS: A HISTORICAL VIEW

C. Wright Mills observed that American society of the 1950s was increasingly controlled by the heads of large corporations, the warrior-chieftains in the Defense Department, and professional celebrities. Mills focused on our mythology's glorification of the chief executive as an individual who makes it to the top with "an element of luck."[13] Mills interpreted the myth to mean, rather, that the chief executive made it to the top with "an accumulation of corporate success," corporate executives choosing one another for promotion to ever-higher corporate positions within a closed system of entry and advancement. This was a world in which the rise to the top depended in large measure on the corporate achiever's "beginnings," especially educational tracking and gender.[14]

This was clearly not the world of the 1950s suburban-middle-landscape comedy in which the handsome professional father from humble beginnings exhibited humility and compassion for his family, neighbors, and occasional coworkers, if not his domestic servants. Nor was it the world of the socially myopic "kitchen dramas" of the "Golden Age" of television—so called because of their limited interior settings and their personal, narrow focus, which kept out social and political issues. Presented in weekly anthology programs such as *Kraft Television Theatre* (1947–58), *Studio One* (1948–58), and *Playhouse 90* (1956–60), such television classics as "Marty," "Requiem for a Heavyweight," and "Twelve Angry Men" zoomed in on what teleplay writer Paddy Chayefsky labeled "the remarkable world of the ordinary." This was a world characterized by individual problems and struggles against injustice in many guises. Problems were frequently created by ethnicity. In many of Chayefsky's more powerful tales, such as "Marty," the conflict between Old World social customs and the contemporary values of "modern" American society was accentuated. Family relations were examined in this context, as "modern" children deserted their parents, leaving them to grow old without the family support characteristic of more traditional European society. Other work focused on the narrow-minded provincial attitudes of undereducated Americans towards race, religious difference, and progressive ideas. Reginald Rose's 1954 drama "Thunder on Sycamore Street," produced for *Studio One* and sponsored by Westinghouse, was based on a real racial incident in Chicago in which a black family moved into an all-white housing project and the whites stoned them. Westinghouse refused to allow the family portrayed in the drama to be black. Rose converted the blacks to the family of a white ex-convict to satisfy the advertiser's demands. While many of these little dramas dealt with working-class life, such as Chayefsky's "Marty," the story of a homely, lonely Italian butcher who has never been married, and Rod Serling's "Requiem for a Heavy-

Figure 6.2
Television Melodramas

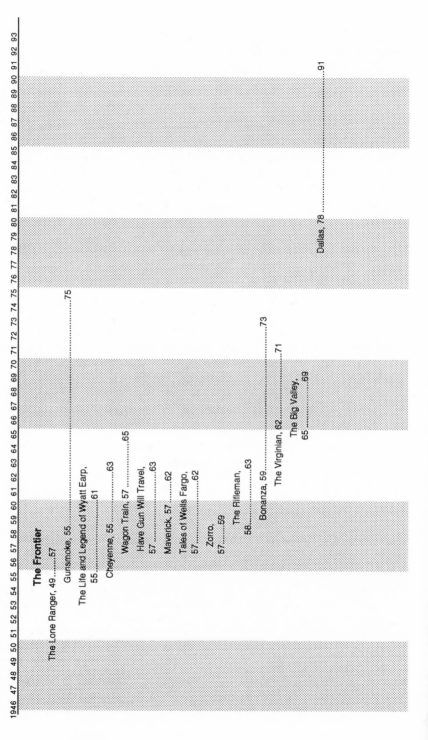

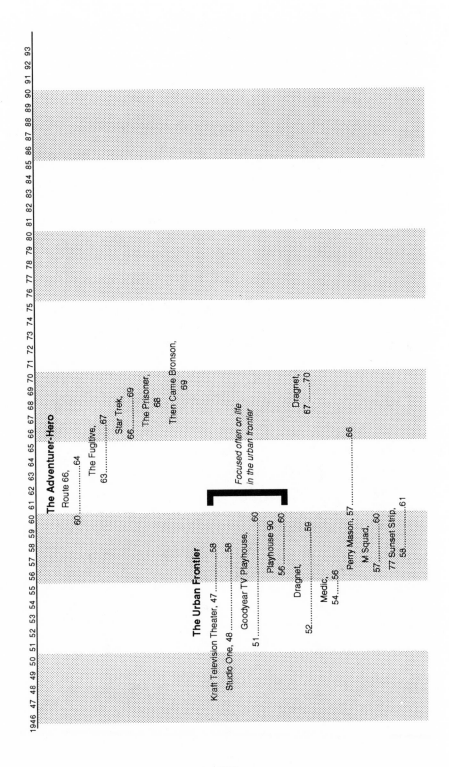

The Adventurer-Hero

Route 66, 60—64

The Fugitive, 63—67

Star Trek, 66—69

The Prisoner, 68

Then Came Bronson, 69

Focused often on life in the urban frontier

Dragnet, 67—70

Dragnet, 66

The Urban Frontier

Kraft Television Theater, 47—58

Studio One, 48—58

Goodyear TV Playhouse, 51—60

Playhouse 90 56—60

Dragnet, 52—59

Medic, 54—56

Perry Mason, 57—66

M Squad, 57—60

77 Sunset Strip, 58—61

Figure 6.2 *(continued)*

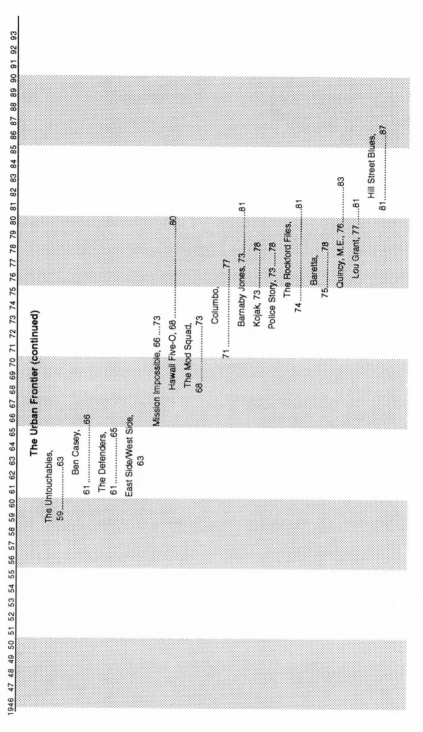

The Urban Frontier (continued)

The Untouchables, 59....63
Ben Casey, 61....66
The Defenders, 61....65
East Side/West Side, 63
Mission Impossible, 66 73
Hawaii Five-O, 68....80
The Mod Squad, 68....73
Columbo, 71....77
Barnaby Jones, 73....81
Kojak, 73....78
Police Story, 73....78
The Rockford Files, 74....81
Baretta, 75....78
Quincy, M.E., 76....83
Lou Grant, 77....81
Hill Street Blues, 81....87

1946 47 48 49 50 51 52 53 54 55 56 57 58 59 60 61 62 63 64 65 66 67 68 69 70 71 72 73 74 75 76 77 78 79 80 81 82 83 84 85 86 87 88 89 90 91 92 93

The Urban Frontier (continued)

Skag, 80

St. Elsewhere, 82 88

Miami Vice, 84 ...89

Crime Story, 86 88

L.A. Law, 86 ....

The Street, 88

Shannon's Deal, 90 ...91

Dallas, 78

Knots Landing, 79 91

Dynasty, 81 89

Falcon Crest, 81 90

thirtysomething, 87 91

Twin Peaks, 90..91

Northern Exposure, 90 ....

The Suburban Middle Landscape

Daytime Soaps

Marcus Welby, M.D., 69 ..76

The Rural Middle Landscape

Waltons, 72.........81

Little House on the Prairie, 74 ...83

weight," the story of an over-the-hill fighter, they never really approached the important economic questions of working-class subservience in the capitalist social order. This was not unexpected, for the anthology drama flourished during the era of blacklisting of members of television's creative community. Hundreds of actors, writers, and producers in Hollywood and New York were marked as Communist sympathizers by groups such as Aware, Inc., which received encouragement from politicians, most notably Senator Joseph McCarthy of Wisconsin. Sponsors of anthology drama were pressured to disapprove certain actors and writers with alleged Communist connections. In such an atmosphere, the kitchen dramas were careful to avoid the potential stigma of social controversy.

The nonanthological television melodrama of the 1950s, framed by the TV Western in the mid-1950s and by the private-detective/G-man series in the late 1950s, likewise refused to examine a contemporary social milieu in which the corporate capitalist establishment joined in a partnership with the huge postwar military apparatus in a Cold War against the Soviet Union. Melodrama would not acknowledge the impact of advanced capitalism on the personal lives of both those who were allowed to ascend the corporate hierarchy in exchange for the sacrifice of their individuality and oftentimes their moral values and those who, as unskilled laborers, semi-skilled operatives, or intelligent-but-female clerks, powered the corporate profit centers but were relegated to second-class citizen status. Even after McCarthy's Communist witch-hunts were exposed, our distrust of the Soviet Union did not diminish. McCarthy's escapade was treated more as a fatal flaw in his individual character than as a general systemic over-reaction. As the Soviet Union launched Sputnik in 1957, Americans were rudely awakened to their technological shortcomings and we needed re-assurance—a sense of control and order and power—in an international atmosphere of nuclear tension and superpower mutual distrust. We were in no mood for self-critique.

What television melodrama gave us during this period of global uncertainty was a predictably highly simplistic ideological frame in which petty criminals were quickly and easily apprehended by the authorities—law-and-order cops whose crime-solving methods, often excessively violent, went unquestioned. From the realistic routine of police work so effectively portrayed in *Dragnet* (1952–59), the melodrama of the urban frontier moved to the excesses of *M Squad* and to the ultraviolent *The Untouchables*, men who fought the violence of organized crime with a retribution unparalleled in television history and backed by the authority of our federal government. When the police establishment proved incapable of solving the crime, private detectives such as Peter Gunn and the boys from *77 Sunset Strip* would step in. They were often better police than the "real" police and provided viewers with an interesting ideological perspective, that is, what was to be valued above all was the maintenance of order, whether that order was maintained by the duly constituted and brutal authorities or by private citizens in positions of police power sanctioned through extralegal relations with civil authority—in effect, the condoning of a system of vigilante justice. This theme would reemerge in the Reagan 1980s, especially in the Hollywood cinema.

On the western frontier, the duly appointed authorities kept the peace at the fringes of civilization where the id bubbled over each weeknight. *Gunsmoke's* Matt Dillon, the fictional marshal of rugged Dodge City, Kansas, and Wyatt Earp of *The Life and Legend of Wyatt Earp*, the real-life marshal of Dodge, kept the frontier town safe for white pioneers to live out their lives and build a future for America's heartland. *Tales of Wells Fargo's* hero-agent Jim Hardie made certain the money to finance this growth got through to the bankers. As was the case in the urban frontier, when the authorities in the wild West could not cope, justice was brought in by the vigilante-cowboys—ranging from the wanderers of *The Lone Ranger* and *Cheyenne* to the more sedentary characters of *The Rifleman* and *Zorro*. These archetypal loner-heroes in the myth of the frontier were pure, their motives clear and unassailable; and their relation to a real West in which the myth of manifest destiny fueled the Anglo culture's conquest of the Native Americans was often confused. To these pure heroes, "Injuns" merely got in trouble a lot through their inability to handle alcohol, burned log cabins, raped white women, and practiced queer religious ceremonies, while in actuality Native Americans got in the way of American expansion and occupied valuable land by declaring it sacred territory.

An unusually sophisticated Western wanderer was the hired gunman Paladin, played superbly by Richard Boone in *Have Gun, Will Travel* (1957–63). The character of Paladin was drawn from the Charlemagne romances, in which one of the 12 famous warriors of Charlemagne's court, Count Palatine, was the foremost warrior, a knight-errant and renowned champion. Palatine's television counterpart Paladin was a college-educated (West Point) man of culture and ethics who lived at the Hotel Carlton in San Francisco and took on assignments, if the price was right, that led him from his opulent, courtlike surroundings into the uncivilized countryside. His business card featured a white chess knight, an emblem of his goodness, and contrasted with the sinister appearance of his black duds and black mustache. Paladin's character was certainly more complex than the traditional sheriff or cowpoke-errant. He would turn on those who hired him if he believed they were guilty of some crime. He showed little mercy to the prey he was hired to get. The dialectic of culture/violence, white/black, and mercenary/defender of justice lent dramatic credibility to this television Western hero. On the other hand, Paladin's pecuniary motives remained unquestioned.

The 1960s were ushered in by the optimism of John F. Kennedy's New Frontier. A mood of youthful exuberance, expansionism, and, however, briefly, of compassion swept the nation. Kennedy offered hope to minority cultures that they could achieve equal status with Anglos. The 1962 Cuban missile crisis had managed to dispel the sour taste of the 1961 Bay of Pigs debacle in Cuba. In the wake of the missile crisis, Americans seemed less preoccupied with Soviet domination of the world or with impending nuclear annihilation. Perhaps the significant change in attitude was a result of the dramatic catharsis that had occurred, with the Kennedy-Khrushchev missile showdown, itself, interestingly, conjuring images from the opening sequence of *Gunsmoke*. Feeling strong and just as a nation, America exported the Peace Corps and began to prop up an ailing and corrupt South Vietnamese regime. Television melodrama meanwhile was reinforcing this decidedly upbeat, if self-delusory, mood.

In the urban frontier, the tough cop of *Dragnet* and the implacable government agent of *The Untouchables*—the unidimensional, self-righteous defenders of the dominant order—were waning in popularity. These superheroes were replaced by the socially concerned lawyers and physicians.

In contrast to the courtroom dramatics of *Perry Mason* (1957–66), framed in the standard murder mystery/private-investigation motif, teleplay writer Reginald Rose ("Twelve Angry Men" and "Thunder on Sycamore Street") created *The Defenders* (1961–65)—a dramatic series that provided, for its time, a rare fictional television exploration of controversial subject matter, including the ethics of capital punishment, abortion, euthanasia, and blacklisting.

In the urban frontier, two lawyers, Lawrence Preston and his son Kenneth, whose youthful exuberance and idealism were tempered by his father's experience and wisdom, sought a human-justice system that accounted for the underdog and acknowledged prevailing social conditions. Their compassion and total dedication to the causes of their clients attracted a loyal viewership whose criticisms of capitalist America were given voice. In *The Defenders*, the justice system on television appeared to be working for the benefit of all, equally. Of course, life was nothing like that. The Cook County jail and Attica prison are testimonies to the realities of the justice system. While *The Defenders* was a significant departure from the melodrama's seemingly inherent fear of taking on the world of real social relations, the talkative legal atmosphere in which these problems were addressed tended to abstract the seamier side of life and to deflect consideration of the urban crises about to explode.

Not only in the courtroom but also in the operating room, melodramatic heroes were attempting, in their limited fashion, to address social issues. *Ben Casey* (1916–66) was a highly popular medical melodrama highlighting life in an urban hospital. It was not the real hospital we were to shudder at a decade-and-a-half later during the provocative documentary series *Lifeline*, but it at least attempted to portray the system of hospital care in an essentially honest manner. Like *The Defenders*, *Ben Casey* featured a "father/son" relationship of youthful idealism and elder rationality. Casey's mentor, chief of surgery Dr. David Zorba, acted much as did Lawrence Preston, urging Ben to use caution and patience. Ben, like Kenneth (and the public media image of John Kennedy) boldly moved ahead. While dwelling excessively on its virile young doctor-hero's surgical exploits and love interests, *Ben Casey* did on occasion tackle the medical establishment, which was shown to be highly conservative and not always concerned with the rights of patients. Still, the profession was always finally vindicated by Casey's seemingly superhuman technical skills.

One bold attempt was made during this period to explore the urban social reality that would erupt in the mid-1960s riots in Watts, Newark, Detroit, Washington, D.C., and many other American cities: Premiering in 1963, *East Side/West Side* was a powerful study, both visually and dramaturgically, of the daily routine of a social worker in the New York City slums. Its visualization was rooted in the realist medical melodrama *Medic* and Jack Webb's *Dragnet*. The viewer was provided a view of urban life at once stark and gloomy. Social worker Neil Brock, played by George C. Scott, was faced day after day with unremitting grimness revealed in the human disasters that were the result of a system of gross social inequity. Stories focused on child abuse, welfare, drug addiction, aging in the ghetto, and included one particularly wrenching episode in which a black ghetto child died from a rat bite. Produced by Talent Associates/David Susskind, *East Side/West Side* conjured memories of Lincoln Steffens's long late-night walks through the streets of New York in the late nineteenth century. *East Side/West Side* lasted one year on the small screen. It was not to disturb the mythic geography of television's generally sanitized urban frontier.

In television's mythic world of the frontier, the gunslingers of the 1950s gave way to the warm, compassionate father-figures of Ben Cartwright and Matt Dillon—the Western heroes of the early 1960s. These weather-beaten frontiersmen resembled Ward Cleaver, Steve Douglas, and Jim Anderson, of the suburban-middle-landscape comedy, more than they did the tough-as-nails pioneer of the traditional Western. By 1963, most of the television Westerns so successful in the 1950s had played themselves out. *Gunsmoke*, *Bonanza*, and *Wagon Train*, all very successful and all developing the family motif, remained.

Bonanza (1959–73), with its powerful, wealthy, mature, and humane patriarch, Ben Cartwright, and his three sons, who formed a composite character at once witty (Adam), powerful but gentle (Hoss), and young, handsome, and impetuous (Little Joe), became an ideal reflection of the American spirit of the times. While they lived in baronial splendor, old-West style, the Cartwrights nevertheless worked hard to acquire and maintain their possessions. They were far removed from the aristocratic snobs of Europe whom the Americans had always disdained even while trying to emulate their cultural gentility; but they did represent a peculiarly American aristocracy whose emblem was the accumulation of vast amounts of territory (the Ponderosa Ranch encompassed about 100,000 square miles), but whose celebration of manifest destiny was tempered with humility. And they had a vision for the future—a vision of civilization, namely, the consolidation of their wealth and their continued status as respected patrons of Virginia City, Nevada. The Cartwrights would quarrel internally on occasion, for dramaturgic purposes, but they would rarely if ever clash over questions of ethics. They lived according to the democratic code of the West—each man could dare to be different. Daring to be different was accepted so long as one's actions remained within the scope of the law (a law established to protect the interests of men of property like the Cartwrights). If a man chose to live alone in the wilderness as a vagabond, the Cartwrights respected that decision, so long as the vagabond didn't end up squatting on the Ponderosa.

Women in this world were conformists, almost always sedentary, and waited for their men to return; furthermore, women did not seem to live long—a result of the harsh environment and the difficulty of childbirth— Ben's three wives, each of whom had given birth to a single Cartwright son, had all died, leaving Ben a perpetual widower.

Bonanza presented an American history whose contradictions were smoothed out by its mythology—a nation in which the heirs of the aristocratic Tidewater society of Thomas Jefferson could coexist, however uneasily, with the heirs of Andy Jackson and the independent earthy men of the Piedmont. It was an America that held firmly to visions of geographical expansion, the sanctity of privately held property, polite exclusion, and male domination.

The Big Valley, which premiered in 1965, drew upon the success of *Bonanza*. While the characters were not as well developed as the Cartwrights, Victoria Barkley, the hard-nosed matriarch, her three handsome sons, and a beautiful daughter were all quite well off at the Barkley spread in the San Joaquin Valley of 1870s California. The series's premise was quite simple: successful pioneers continually fought off lawless elements to preserve their large landholdings. The Barkleys faced the standard set of Western antagonists, including schemers, murderers, bank robbers, and even Mexican revolutionaries. The America of the Cartwrights and the Barkleys was also the America of modern-day sons of nouveau riche aristocrats, such as John F. Kennedy, and of middle-class self-made "country boys" such as Lyndon Johnson, Richard Nixon, Jimmy Carter, Ronald Reagan, and Bill Clinton.

As the frontier and urban-frontier cycles spent themselves, a new public symbol of America's preoccupation with space emerged. The romantic motif of "the journey" emerged in television melodrama in the 1960s.

Two parallel developments in American culture encouraged this preoccupation—the growth of the American suburb and exurb, with their dependence on the automobile and the superhighway, and America's
reassertion of its technological leadership, manifested in President Kennedy's challenge to land a man on the moon before the decade's end.

The Western adventurer-hero, a mystified historical and legendary type,
à la Paladin, was locked in time. The new adventurer in television melodrama was our contemporary, "one of us." This new adventurer, searching for pleasurable experiences, was emblematic of the growth of the
suburban "superkids" whom Tom Wolfe described in *The Electric Kool-
Aid Acid Test*:

But of course!—the *feeling*—out here at night, free, with the motor running and
the adrenaline flowing, cruising in the neon glories of the new American night—
it was very Heaven to be the first wave of the most extraordinary kids in the history
of the world—only 15, 16, 17 years old, dressed [in] the *haute couture* of pink
Oxford shirts, sharp pants, snaky half-inch belts, fast shoes—with all this Straight-
6 and V-8 power underneath and all this neon glamour overhead, which somehow
tied in with the technological superheroics of the jet, TV, atomic subs, ultrason-
ics—postwar American suburbs—glorious world! and the hell with the intellectual
badmouthers of America's tailfin civilization. . . . They couldn't know what it was
like or else they had it cultivated out of the them—the feeling—to be very Superkids! The world's first generation of the little devils—feeling immune, beyond
calamity. One's parents remembered the sloughing common order, War & Depression—but Superkids knew only the emotional surge of the great payoff, when
nothing was common any longer—The Life! A glorious place, a glorious age, I tell
you! A very Neon Renaissance.[15]

Cut off from history, the superkids would come to reject their parents'
struggles. The parents, happy to have escaped the "sloughing common
order," would do everything in their power to insulate their children from
such a state of existence.

While the family Western of the early 1960s, à la *Bonanza*, was providing viewers with a mythic psychic geography remarkably similar to that
of the suburban-middle-landscape comedies of the period—what adults
wanted to believe was the new order of pecuniary security and family love
and warmth—the new adventurer, first seen in *Route 66* (1960–64), was
providing the young viewer perhaps unintentionally with a more accurate
version of that psychic landscape—a version in which the transcendent
values were materialistic and in which our protagonists seemed to be trav-
eling nowhere in particular at very high speeds.

Route 66's protagonists were Tod Stiles, born to wealth, but whose father squandered his money, and Buz Murdock, who grew up in New York
City's Hell's Kitchen area and who had been employed by Tod's father
prior to his death. The young men set off in Tod's Corvette in search of

adventure and romance. *Route 66* played off two universal themes. Tod and Buz bear a striking resemblance to the priests-errant of Carl Orff's secular cantata *Carmina Burana*. The cantata is based on texts of 200 sacred and secular poems dating to the thirteenth century and discovered in 1903 in a Bavarian monastery. The poems were written by earthy vagabonds called goliards—defrocked monks and minstrels who delighted in the pleasures of the flesh. Orff divided his work into three motifs: spring, the tavern, and love. There are poems of fortunes lost, of spring and youthful virility ("And over all the boyish god rules"), and of heavy drinking in the tavern ("On the broad road I move along as youth is wont to do. I am entangled in vice, and unmindful of virtue. Greedy more for lust than for welfare; dead in soul, I care only for my body"). Tod and Buz, as the new youthful television priests-errant of the 1960s, show only the vaguest hints of vice. They are not above fistfights and romantic encounters. Yet their wanderlust is tempered with a certain undirected compassion. While Tod and Buz had no particular destination in mind, they were drawn, like Odysseus, along a predetermined path, in their case Route 66 —named by John Steinbeck "the mother road." In *The Grapes of Wrath*, the highway becomes "the path of a people in flight." Stretching from Chicago to Los Angeles, established in 1926 by the National Highway Act, Route 66 has entered our folklore. It carried the "Okies" and the "Arkies" of the dust bowl on their escape to find a new life in California. It was a symbol of despair, but more a symbol of hope. By the 1950s it had become a symbol of America's neon roadside culture—the emblem of a mobile society. In 1960 it still retained its mystique, although very soon it would be replaced by our superhighway system of monotonous four-lane interstates, Holiday Inns, and McDonalds—the new streamlined, high-tech America. Unfortunately, Route 66 became a meaningless backdrop for the adventures of our young melodrama protagonists—just another concrete slab in the open spaces that allowed the Corvette to move out. Like Wolfe's superkids, Tod and Buz were divorced from social history. Theirs was a road traveled but not really understood.

Another wanderer, Dr. Richard Kimble, was forced to give up his comfortable suburban environment for a life as *The Fugitive* (1963–67). In the traditions of the epic wanderer-hero Odysseus, Kimble was forced by fate to wander, enduring trials and tests to prove his inherent moral strength. The melodramatic premise was simple: Kimble, a physician, is wrongly accused and convicted of murdering his wife (shades of the Dr. Sam Sheppard murder case, a cause celèbre at that time), is sentenced to death, but escapes while being taken to death row. For 120 episodes, Kimble is relentlessly pursued by Lieutenant Gerard, who was accompanying him when he escaped, while Kimble himself pursues a mysterious one-armed man who Kimble knows was the actual murderer. Throughout his ordeal, Kimble is reduced to a common man, taking odd jobs to support himself as he searches for the killer and assuming new identities at each stop. He learns much about regular folks from these encounters and in turn impacts those with whom he comes in contact. In the final episode, a two-parter, Kimble finds the one-armed man and places himself in great danger; but he is saved by Lieutenant Gerard, who has come to admire Kimble's resourcefulness and resiliency and now even believes in Kimble's innocence. Gerard shoots and kills the one-armed man. Kimble is exonerated. And while Kimble, the good doctor, has grown from experience, we get the distinct feeling that he can now, like Odysseus, return to his home—in Kimble's case, the suburban middle landscape—and reclaim his material wealth and his medical practice.

The television adventure moved from the suburban middle landscape to outer space in 1966 as *Star Trek* premiered. The warts on America's self-complacent expansionist politics had barely begun to show in Vietnam. Journalists such as David Halberstam of the *New York Times*, Neil Sheehan of United Press International, Malcolm Browne of the Associated Press, and Morley Safer of CBS News had, since 1962, pointed out the political and moral quagmire that was Vietnam, but they were a small minority in the news community. America still saw the war in just terms outlined by the late President Kennedy—that "we will fight any foe" to protect the world for democracy. Gene Roddenberry's *Star Trek* offered the American television viewer a variety of relatively abstract antiwar themes, among them the impersonal quantification of the results of war—the body counts that had become the nagging "facts" of America's Vietnam involvement, recounted with numbing regularity on the nightly news. One episode of *Star Trek* dealt with a society that fought war with a computer. Everyone who was listed as "killed" was forced to step into a disintegration machine. Unlike Vietnam, there was no property damage (the episode foreshadowed the absurdity of the idea of the neutron bomb). The star ship "Enterprise," a metaphor for the hard work of the myth of the Protestant ethic, was piloted by "all-American boy" Captain James Kirk; it was the ultimate cosmic policeman/meddler. Living with a pseudoreligious fervor, as befitted the myth of manifest destiny, Kirk and crew spread truth, justice, and the American way of life, including a life of high technology and eternal progress. In one episode, "A Private Little War," Kirk was forced to introduce high-technology warfare to a planet where the evil klingons had interfered. There was now no turning back. Vietnam, and more recently the Persian Gulf War are contemporary real-world analogues.

Ultimately the goals of Kirk and the international crew of the "Enterprise" were never seriously and consistently questioned. *Star Trek*'s liberal abhorrence of war deaths was undermined by the series's implicit jingoism.

Two other adventure series of the late 1960s seriously questioned contemporary social relations although, like *Star Trek*, they ultimately defused the issues they raised. *The Prisoner,* created for British television by Patrick McGoohan and aired in the United States in the summer of 1968, presents a hero on an inward journey into a mental landscape in which he is trapped by a materialistic, totalitarian state apparatus. In McGoohan's first television series, *Secret Agent,* he played British intelligence agent John Drake, a rather violent character. The premise of *The Prisoner* builds from the backstory of *Secret Agent*: Drake comes to question the morality of his work. He resigns from the intelligence service as *The Prisoner* begins, an act which will lead him into the uncharted dystopian hell of technology and the repressive nature of the corporate state. Over the course of 17 episodes, Drake is imprisoned by the state in a mental landscape known simply as "the Village" (reminiscent of the "Other Place" in Huxley's *Brave New World*). Drake becomes "Number Six." The Village appears harmonious, but this is a bizarre illusion. "Number Two," the Village's main authority figure, is clearly not the person at the top (the mysterious "Number One"). This is a metaphor not only for the invisibility of the corporate chieftains, as described by C. Wright Mills in *The Power Elite*—the true leaders use their managers and professional celebrities as fronts, choosing to run things from the shadows—but also, in the case of the character Number Two, for the interchangeability of the managers (Number Two is different in each episode). Number Six, the representative of individual freedom, is subjugated to the will of the state. He should think he is free, for the Village is idyllic and all his material needs are easily satisfied; but he resists the initially subtle but finally not-so-subtle attempts at brainwashing. He is euphemistically described as a "guest" of the Village, not the prisoner that he is. Number Six's dual desire to escape and to understand the forces that have captured him frames the ongoing struggle. In the final episode of the allegory, Number One is revealed as the prisoner's alter ego, the side of the repressive authoritarian. Like everyone else in the Village, the prisoner cannot be trusted. This cynical view of human nature in the end deflects responsibility for social conditions into the murky realm of psychologism, where all seems hopeless. As *The Prisoner* concludes, we see Drake driving down the road in a sports roadster, his hair blowing in the breeze; he is at last free from totalitarianism and the corporate state, yet not free from the darker side of his own nature. Nothing has really changed, and although he now "understands" his condition, he seems incapable of any action other than personal escape, the only solution to his alienation.

With *Then Came Bronson* in 1969, Americans had an adventurer-hero who clearly reflected the times. Jim Bronson was a newspaper reporter. His buddy, a Vietnam veteran, committed suicide. Bronson wanted to do a story on the suicide and its social meaning. His editor refused, saying it was not newsworthy. Outraged, Bronson quit the paper, leaving behind a life filled with drudgery and lack of autonomy, and headed out on the open road on his fallen friend's motorcycle to search for meaning in life. Scarcely seeming to understand his own motives for wandering, in a modern political sense Bronson is ineffective. He cannot resolve other people's dilemmas, as could Richard Kimble and Captain Kirk. He does not come to the self-realization of McGoohan's Number Six. What *Then Came Bronson* revealed was its hero's sense of inner dissatisfaction, emptiness, lack of commitment, frustration, and lack of direction coupled with an underlying goodness and tolerance of those around him—in short, here is the archetypal "flower child." Yet, while Jim Bronson seems awkward and powerless, his character is in the initial stages of a progressive transformation from the low-mimetic to the traditionally mythological, in which outward deeds of the hero are less important than inner realization. As Joseph Campbell wrote of the traditional hero of mythology, "the passage of the mythological hero . . . fundamentally . . . is inward—into the depths where obscure resistances are overcome, and long lost, forgotten powers are revivified, to be made available for the transfiguration of the world."[16] Bronson has vanished into the American wilderness—has gone to the mountaintop—seeking a clearer understanding of the rhythms of nature and of people. He had not reemerged with any answers as the series was canceled after one year. The series's slow pacing, introspection, and anti-acting did not lend itself to Williams's concept of commodified planned flow essential to "successful" television. While many young Americans—so-called cultural radicals who tuned in, turned on, and dropped out—may have empathized with Bronson's antipolitical response of noninvolvement, others were engaged in active political protest in the streets of Chicago and Berkeley and on the campuses of Columbia and the University of Wisconsin. Television melodrama was not the principle forum in which the heated political discourse of Vietnam and American interventionism generally was aired. Although his acts lacked overt political motivation, Jim Bronson was nevertheless rare for series-television heroes—his ethics of nonpower spoke to larger issues of social control and personal states of unfreedom.

For a brief period at the end of the decade, commercial entertainment television made its "politically correct" response to Vietnam and the civil rights movement by airing so-called social-relevance melodrama, such as *The Mod Squad* (1968–73) and *Storefront Lawyers* (1970), which featured hip youthful protagonists fighting for justice and equality. A far remove from the artistic sensitivity of *The Defenders* and the social commitment and grit of *East Side/West Side*, these programs were blatant in their exploitation of the "Movement" of the 1960s. Their hipper-than-thou attitude and handsome stars and starlets rang false.

In 1968, the year *The Mod Squad* premiered, another new television series signaled the shift in direction of television melodrama from the adventurer motif to a return to the sedentary world of the suburban and rural middle landscapes. *Marcus Welby, M.D.* reintroduced the father figure to television melodrama. Welby, who practiced family medicine, was the community patriarch—kind, gentle, competent, and humble. For seven years, this wise physician diagnosed the most bizarre ailments known to medical science (his wisdom went far beyond his medical training), offered informal psychiatric advice to his patients, and made house calls. He was revered by millions of American viewers. Welby brought stability to an external world reeling from the horrors of Tet and the Martin Luther King, Jr. and Robert Kennedy assassinations. The show was performing the true popular melodramatic function, acting as a force pulling the society toward its center—the peace, affluence, optimism, and myopia of the suburban middle landscape.

Another highly successful melodrama, premiering in 1972, served the same function. *The Waltons*, focusing on the rural middle landscape of Appalachia, was a humane celebration of the values of strong family bonds and of the inherent goodness and seriousness of country folk. Fighting their way through the Great Depression, the Waltons were survivors. This message rang true to an America painfully working its way out of Southeast Asia, trying to forget Kent State, and shortly to be faced with an economically devastating Arab oil embargo—another stark realization of the limits of American power in the world.

The inherent conservatism of melodramatic television series on occasion admitted a made-for-television movie that might question, in a limited fashion, the dominant ideology. Levinson's and Link's 1969 telefilm *My Sweet Charlie*, a personalized story of race relations in the South, and their 1972 telefilm *That Certain Summer*, a story about the coming out of a homosexual father, both broke television taboos. As a "one-off," a television movie can risk mildly controversial material without any long-term negative impact on ratings. The network can choose to publicize a piece it believes will draw big numbers and not be terribly offensive (as ABC did when it promoted the 1983 television movie *The Day After*, whose conservative premise was that people will survive an all-out nuclear conflagration and carry on). Or it can air its more controversial work during a traditionally light viewing period such as late summer, satisfy the more vocal among the Hollywood creative community who call for artistic integrity, fend off a few irate telephone calls from viewers, and continue with its standard reassuring *Marcus Welby* fare. The Levinson and Link teleplays, while opening doors to controversial contemporary social material in a melodramatic context, did, however, manage to come down firmly on both sides of the debate on both race and homosexuality—under pressure, the creators insist, from network censors. Levinson and Link admit, in their own analysis of *That Certain Summer*, that they would rewrite the speech of the homosexual father in the final scene, in which, having come to terms with his life as a gay, he reintroduces the guilt he has successfully overcome by saying to his son, "If I had a choice it's not something I'd pick for myself."

While a television movie now and then would brush up against a difficult contemporary social problem in the early 1970s and while Norman Lear was turning out pointed social comedy, American television series melodrama was by comparison tame. *Gunsmoke* and *Bonanza* neared the end of their runs, both having lost much of their artistic drive. *Marcus Welby* was immensely popular. The proletarian cop in *Columbo*, created by Levinson and Link, premiered in 1971. *Columbo* was steeped in the classic murder-mystery tradition of Ellery Queen and Agatha Christie. It was good entertainment, well written, and television's best adaptation of the literary murder-mystery (Levinson and Link, along with Peter S. Fischer, would follow with *Murder, She Wrote* in 1984 featuring Jessica Fletcher, a woman, as the central character). Viewers were led by Columbo through a world of elegant, wealthy criminality. What on the surface seemed to many critics to be a celebration of the working cop was also a skillful voyeuristic journey into the land of the rich and infamous which reinforced the moral superiority of the common viewer, a motif that emerges again a few years later in *Dallas*.

In 1974 America almost came apart at the seams. Watergate had bubbled away in the American conscience for two years, as television slowly and painfully revealed the grimy underside of American politics. The facial contortions of Richard Nixon, the cold distance of John Dean, and the smug arrogance of John Erlichman and H. R. Haldeman were seen in television news stories and during the Senate's televised public hearings. This display demonstrated to Americans television's potential as a recorder and transmitter of the inner voices of those upon whom it turns its gaze. The unblinking lens of the camera sits in judgment—a neurosystem linked directly to almost every American. Watergate seemed to drain every last ounce of optimism from the American public. Kennedy's mythified Camelot had turned first into Johnson's Oriental quagmire and now Nixon's Last Stand—like Custer, their egos and blindness to reality led to their demise.

Television's response to this malaise was threefold. The relevant social comedies of Norman Lear continued as strongly as ever. Nixon became a legitimate target. While questions remained as to the social impact of the Archie Bunker character on ultraconservative and liberal viewers, there is little doubt that the Lear comedies of the period, especially *All in the Family* and *Maude*, attempted to grapple with contemporary social problems. Television melodrama, on the other hand, chose its traditionally conservative response. This was manifested in two ways. One was a return to the frontier, but a frontier with decidedly rural-middle-landscape characteristics. *Little House on the Prairie*, which premiered in 1974, involved a loving family surviving hard times in the 1870s in Minnesota. The Ingalls family—the father, Charles; the wife and loving mother, Caroline; and daughters Laura, Mary, and Carrie—were good people. Charles was a pioneer farmer who had come from Kansas. The Ingalls struggled against natural disasters and the eventual collapse of their hometown, Walnut Grove. They were forced to move to a city in the Dakota territory, but they hated city life and headed back to their Minnesota farm—a prototypical rural-middle-landscape journey, away from contemporary social problems, a return to the garden and to grace. A second melodramatic response was more insidious: the recognition of contemporary evil and its subsequent punishment via a system of summary justice. Such a typical melodramatic response had appeared in the late 1950s and early 1960s television melodrama and now reappeared with some modifications.

As the 1960s stumbled to an end, America's technological superiority could not compensate for its untenable ideological position in Vietnam. Television's creative community, contrary to Ben Stein's arguments in *The View from Sunset Boulevard,* was in touch with public opinion in America in the later years of the decade. Many, though certainly not all or even a numerical majority of Americans, were disillusioned with the militaristic exploits of a nation that continually sought its way out of economic recessions by engaging in foreign military adventures, manifested in the formation, during and immediately after World War II, of a military-industrial complex. Yet the resistance to this politics was vocal, committed, and persuasive. Further, many Americans had come to despise their highest public officials, who were corrupt or corruptible and who maintained ethically questionable connections with wealthy business interests. This growing public cynicism was at last reflected on our television screens in the police melodrama of the mid-1970s, which included an assortment of protagonists, from the private detectives of *The Rockford Files* and *Barnaby Jones* to the undercover cop in *Baretta,* the detective in *Kojak,* and coroner in *Quincy.* A central antagonist for all these law-enforcement types was the evil businessman. Writers and producers began to define this character as the "true criminal," whose criminality was directly reflected in murder, maiming, extortion, and drug smuggling—in short, in felonious activities that smacked of organized crime. Unlike the investigation of organized crime, the drama would ultimately lead to the arrest and conviction of the criminal businessman; he never got away, unlike the president and many of his Watergate associates. The game of clear-cut avarice and subsequent punishment became a unidimensional ritual dance ignoring or bracketing the more relevant and prevalent contemporary business problems of white-collar abuses, committed against workers, that resulted not only in their physical deaths (when safety hazards went uncorrected) but, on a much larger scale, their psychic deaths.

By the end of the decade, the memories of Vietnam and Watergate were receding (in the age of television, history is ephemeral), and television melodrama refocused its gaze on corporate life. Now, instead of images of evil—of corrupt businessmen as felons and common thugs—we were given the conservative celebration of business success manifested in the myth of the individual. One hero type, the individual winner/smart operator, predominated in the prime-time soap-opera cycle. This hero—a captain of finance who outsmarts other smart operators but does not swindle innocent people—lived in a world of intense competition. We returned to a belief in the American system of laissez-faire capitalism that favors such a portrayal.

The frontier world of *Dallas*, like the frontier world of *Bonanza*, is framed by achievement. However, this achievement is manifested in different ways. Ben Cartwright represented, in his uniquely American-frontier way, the old values of the traditional aristocracy—a sense of civic responsibility, charity, and warm family relations. In an equally American vein, he succeeded through hard work and investments made after careful consideration combined with superior intuition and mature judgment. His frontier wisdom substituted admirably for his lack of intellectualism. In contrast, Jock Ewing, the modern patriarch of South Fork, represented a more contemporary version of the American upper class. He succeeded through a cynical mixture of common sense, hard work, and often questionable business practices. In Jock's wife, Miss Ellie, the Ewing matriarch, we are presented with an aristocratic model of old values and standards. But these values are under constant assault as Jock's sons, J. R. and Bobby—the two sides of their father's ambivalent personality—constantly battle for supremacy. Sweet yet hard-nosed Bobby tries hard to win honestly, while J. R. employs every shady business tactic known to man, including bribery, duplicity, and spying, to succeed. On a deeper level, Jock's two sons are warring at the ideological edge of the advanced capitalist system. To the question, "Is it worth winning at any cost?" J. R., representing the reality of advanced capitalist relations in contemporary America, answers an unqualified yes. Bobby, on the other hand, representing a mystified America (as it once was before it lost its innocence), is not sure at what price success comes.

The audience is given a backstory in which in the process of becoming rich, the Ewings are characterized as "smart operators," hard-working entrepreneurs who built a huge oil-and-cattle empire in Texas, the new land of opportunity. However, staying rich, in the world created by the Ewings, means the villainous rogue—a flouter—is in control, but just barely. The latter character type is ably represented by J. R. Ewing, the often hilarious antagonist who operates in the melodramatic tradition of the ambivalent evil buffoon, always on the edge of self-destruction, yet always making a comeback. Nonetheless, the viewers are led to sense J. R.'s ultimate doom. He almost is killed, but recovers. There is, of course, a clear ideological rationale for this characterization both in contemporary American life and in melodrama.

Dallas's success on television throughout the world is a triumph of the symbolic world of the vainglorious new upper class over that of the traditional old upper class in America. The old American upper class, which acquired money through ancestors, has generally been defined as those families who, for at least five generations, have been accepted in the society of the Metropolitan 400 and other such elitist symbols of social status. Having turned their attention to other matters such as philanthropy (an excellent tax shelter), civic responsibility (through contributions to elitist arts institutions), and elegant play, they have been pushed aside in the status game by the nouveaux riches, who have little sense of community values, use social relations to accumulate ever-greater wealth, which they need to prove their status to the world, and thrive on cheap publicity (often gained not through their donations of works to the permanent collections of art museums, but, rather, through their purchase of professional sports teams, gambling casinos, television networks, or airlines, which instantly catapults them into the public spotlight). This is their only way to encroach upon the status relations established by the old upper class in America.

C. Wright Mills is provocative on this battle for status:

"Conspicuous consumption," as [Thorstein] Veblen knew, is not confined to the upper classes. But today I should say that it prevails *especially* among one element of the new upper classes—the *nouveaux riches* of the new corporate privileges—the men on expense accounts, and those enjoying other corporate prerogatives—and with even more grievous effects on the standard and style of life of the professional celebrities. . . . And, of course, among recent crops of more old-fashioned *nouveaux riches* dramatized by the "Texas millionaires."[17]

These new upper-class groups—the high-level corporate managers, professional celebrities, and Texas cattle and oil barons—whom Mills labeled "the power elite" are now celebrated as our popular leaders. The Ewings are the ultimate public symbol of this power elite—the new upper-class "Texas millionaires" with a thirst for ostentation and cheap publicity (which provides them status they do not possess by virtue of either educational or cultural capital) and a total lack of concern for the values of community. The Ewings operate in a Texas version of the café society, with its increasingly popularized motif of ostentation via, not the garden party, but the big Texas-style barbecue. The glamour of the Sunbelt, with its elaborately coiffed cowgirls and strangely un-Western-looking cowboy-entrepreneurs, provides viewers with an atmosphere of the suburban middle landscape to which they can easily relate, while simultaneously offering viewers the dream life of the new frontier—of the rugged cowboy making his way alone in the corporate boardrooms of the latest office tower in the international style, doling out his personal, eccentric version of corporate justice. As viewers could relate to the fictional Ewings, so too could they relate, in 1992, to a real-life analog, H. Ross Perot, as they came to reject the "old wealth" represented by a Texas transplant, the Yankee George Bush. Mills was clearly on to something 35 years earlier.

The new frontier of *Dallas* is a reflection of our social conservatism and of the "me generation" of Americans. It is the celebration of "doing one's own thing," except that, rather than the 1960s anthem, which signified an inner quest for meaning accompanied by a rejection of suburban-middle-landscape conformity (a prevalent theme of *The Wonder Years*), the 1980s anthem signaled a search for personal wealth and status at the expense of others.

Dallas is a world in which a government energy-department representative reveals oil-lease secrets to the Ewings in exchange for family favors, including a trip to the annual Ewing barbecue. And no one flinches. Critic Michael Arlen saw in *Dallas* a revelation of the breakdown of rules of conduct in American society generally (rules for so long framing and providing logical order to the chaotic, often despicable social relations of daytime soap opera) and the resultant loss of any clear sense of ethical behavior or social responsibility. Arlen wrote:

In the audience, our citizens reconstitute themselves ever more rapidly according to fashion "looks" (proletarian, Russian, Chinese, Navaho, cowboy, preppy). . . . Meanwhile, our new television favorites float free above their glossy plots. . . . In other words, ourselves aerodynamically advanced, we cheer the streamlined, destabilized characters we so resemble.[18]

This can be said of our upper-middle-class achievers who see the glow of the new suburban middle landscape and who find this selfish, anomic behavior acceptable and even desirable. But what of the others—the white- and blue-collar proletarians who are alien to this world of celebrity, casual sex, and corruption but who are negatively affected by such a system every day of their working and leisure lives, as the surplus value of their labor is converted to the profits that support the ostentatious lifestyle of the protagonists represented in these melodramas? As Mills wrote:

The idea that the millionaire finds nothing but a sad, empty place at the top of society; the idea that the rich do not know what to do with their money; the idea that the successful are poor and little as well as rich—the idea, in short, of the disconsolateness of the rich—is, in the main, merely a way by which those who are not rich reconcile themselves to the fact. Wealth in America is directly gratifying and directly leads to many further gratifications.[19]

Workers are thus encouraged to take on an attitude of moral superiority while accepting their financial and general inferiority. This deception has its counterpart in the traditional argument of wealthy organized religion, that is, of "the righteousness of the poor." Beyond the realm of the personal relationship of the viewer and the melodrama character is the social domain of the melodrama in which one sees the central characters' personally and socially destabilizing actions as not met with external sanctions from the dominant social authority but, rather, internalized as personal discomfort and unhappiness. *Dallas* and similar contemporary melodramas do not question institutions but instead focus on individual misconduct—on the corporate executive as duplicitous, not the corporate apparatus itself. The consequences of the Ewings' actions are not social but personal—turned inward on themselves. Further, because of the general atmosphere of individual destabilization, the consequences of their acts seem random—not clearly linked to behavioral proscriptions. Viewers can revel in both the Ewings' wealth (which creates the condition of desire in viewers) and their discomfort (which provides the viewer with a sense of moral superiority while he acknowledges his economic and social inferiority) and simultaneously not feel at all threatened by the Ewings' fictional power.

David Jacobs, creator of *Dallas* and its more middle-class spin-off *Falcon Crest*, called *Dallas* "a singular expression" of the 1980s. J. R. Ewing, who quickly became the serial's linchpin, was neither ethical nor decent, but dramaturgically he functioned as a protagonist. Jacobs wrote of J. R., "His unapologetic commitment to self-interest, his unabashed belief in the corruptability of others linked him to a generation that would soon be told that greed was O.K. and read on bumper stickers that Jesus wanted people to get rich."[20]

If *Dallas* "was about the quest for money," wrote Jacobs, then *Dynasty*, which replaced *Dallas* in the mid-1980s as the world's most-watched television drama, "was about the things money could buy."[21] Jacobs saw *Dynasty* as more reflective of an American attitude prevalent during the second Reagan administration. *Dynasty*, premiering in 1981, was an excess in extravagance. Its ostentatious lifestyles, opulent sets, and expensive clothes—its characters wore jewelry with lingerie—were perceived not as "vulgar," but rather as "classy." "The pleasure of watching 'Dynasty' and 'Dallas,'" Jacobs wrote, "was voyeuristic.... I don't think that [they] would have had a prayer of succeeding in any other era, save perhaps the Harding or Coolidge Administrations."[22]

By the late 1980s many viewers in the suburban middle landscape were turning to melodrama closer to their own lived reality. Network programmers were eager to attract the highly desirable target demographic of young upwardly mobile professionals. These viewers became the loyal fans of their own melodrama of "suburban yuppie angst."

thirtysomething examined the lives of seven principal characters—two couples and three singles—all friends, all in their thirties, and all upwardly mobile. Like the Ewings and the Carringtons, all of their relationships seemed to lack stability. However, unlike the Ewings and Carringtons, *thirtysomething's* protagonists constantly fretted over the meaning of their lives, loves, and marriages.

The series addressed many personal issues that clearly resonated with its intended primary target audience. Some critics called the characters, and by implication those in the audience whose lives resembled the fictional world of the series, "pampered" and "self-indulgent."

Michael Steadman and Elliot Weston had once worked together in a large advertising agency. Both left it to open their own agency, which eventually went bankrupt. They were then forced to find employment at a large agency run by the cold Miles Drentell. In VALS terms, Michael and Elliot were a combination of "emulators" and "experientials"—ambitious, yet inner-directed young adults. They lived well but suffered from lingering doubts about the direction their lives had taken. Like the other characters in the series, they were introspective, longing for the innocence of a lost youth (only in their thirties, they felt "old").

Michael's wife Hope Murdoch, a beautiful overachiever educated at Princeton, had her career goal—to be a successful freelance writer—put on hold while she raised a young daughter and later in the series an infant son. She became increasingly unhappy in her role as wife and mother. Elliot's wife Nancy wanted to be an artist, but she too found herself raising two school-age children.

Elliot and Nancy went through a painful separation but eventually reconciled. Nancy was diagnosed with ovarian cancer just as her first children's book was about to be published.

Michael's best friend, Gary Shepherd, an assistant professor of classics, lost his position after he and his wife Susannah had their first child. Gary was killed in an automobile accident on his way to visit Nancy in the hospital.

Hope's best friend Ellyn Warren and Michael's cousin Melissa Steadman were continually involved in unsuccessful relationships with men and were worried about their futures as single women.

The American Dream of the late 1980s for these suburban-middle-landscape inhabitants was less about greed and more about maintaining their sanity and their families. The series's core message—that although children created certain burdens, especially for well-educated women who were forced to make painful career decisions, they were an integral part of family life—played perfectly into the upper-middle-class consumerist lifestyle so important to advertisers. Michael and Elliot, archetypes of the "new male"—sensitive and introspective—still, after all, worked for the company.

With *Hill Street Blues* (1981–87), we leave the sheltered but troubled suburban middle landscape and return to the urban frontier of overt violence and lawlessness. The series was cocreated by Steven Bochco and Michael Kozoll (Bochco wrote many *Columbo* episodes, and *Hill Street* benefited from his emphasis on intelligent dialogue). Aesthetically, its structure was complex for television, although it still fit very comfortably into the commodified planned flow of commercial television. Scenes constantly shifted; plot strands were left hanging in its open-ended, serial format. Contrasty lighting, reminiscent of *The Untouchables*, and hand-held, remote camera work lent it a sense of realism and immediacy. Overlapping conversations, as in Robert Altman films, enhanced the feel of everyday experience. Its 13 major characters—led by inner-city precinct Captain Frank Furillo; his lover, and by 1983 his second wife, attorney Joyce Davenport; Sergeant Phil Esterhaus, Lieutenant Howard Hunter, and Officers Lucy Bates and Andy Renko—formed a complex web of personal stories that moved the series along. The characters were archetypes of the constantly shifting status positions in today's social system. Furillo, a divorced father, suffered from guilt because he was so happy in his torrid (for television at that time) bathtub love affair with gorgeous Joyce, while his plain-looking ex-wife Faye was decidedly unhappy. The residual ideology of the nuclear family was still an ideal for Frank. He eventually married Joyce, although he was resentful of Faye's happiness with another man.

On the job, Frank was tough but compassionate. Work at the precinct house centered on Phil, a working man's working man with a good heart—the model of the kind, understanding shop steward who has the interest of his men and women at heart. Lieutenant Hunter was intentionally unidimensional—a caricature of the SWAT mentality of the post-Vietnam era. Lucy Bates was liberated, but wanted to be loved; however, her work was very important to her, and she did "a man's job" very well. Andy Renko was a white racist at heart, but his work with his black partner deflected the prejudice of his upbringing (blacks are O.K. if they save your life).

In *Hill Street Blues* the correspondences to the myth of the frontier, Western style, are evident. The cowboy-Indian confrontation translates into the white-black/Hispanic confrontation. Indians were nature-oriented and had the advantage when the game was played on their field. Blacks and Hispanics (and in *Hill Street*, Irish as well) are streetwise and, like Native Americans, have the home-court advantage. Whites (cowboys-cavalry and police) invade their territory to bring civilization, setting up forts/police precinct houses and attempting to control the neighborhood and its social transactions. Whites—the products of enlightenment rationality—use law-enforcement tactics and strategies, and eventually the power of education, to civilize the more body-oriented primitive ghetto residents. However, *Hill Street* astutely points out another parable that counters the traditional presentation of the confrontation of savagery and civilization, namely, the parable of Vietnam. The blacks and Hispanics may be seen as the Vietcong (certainly Howard sees them as such, as does Renko, although it is more difficult for him to admit this)—guerrillas in the urban frontier, hanging on despite all odds in a war of attrition. The ambiguity in *Hill Street Blues* is that while the social-worker mentality is obviously inappropriate in these circumstances, do we then resort to force after all? *Hill Street*'s weakness lies in its failure to transcend personalness to reveal the ideological underpinnings of a system of social, political, and economic dominance and subordination.

As *Hill Street Blues* was attracting a devoted audience who found pleasure in its multidimensional characterizations, quality writing, and gritty style, two other urban frontier police melodramas, both created by Michael Mann, took the form in a decidedly different direction. *Miami Vice* (1984–89) focused on formal innovation rather than sophisticated content. Its core concept was "MTV cops," a phrase coined by NBC Entertainment President Brandon Tartikoff, who commissioned the series.

Detectives "Sonny" Crockett and Ricardo Tubbs, two well-dressed undercover vice cops, chased bad guys (often drug dealers) around pastel Miami in their hip automobiles (Crockett drove a Ferrari and Tubbs a vintage Cadillac, not bad on a police officer's salary) to the accompaniment of contemporary rock songs. Dialogue was sparse—this program was about color and music—and the action fast-paced.

The program represented the genre stripped to its bare essentials, and these were extremely well presented. *Miami Vice* cost an estimated $1.2 million per episode to produce, which was very expensive for its time. When the transparency of the plots wore thin, the producers would inject life into the series through the appearance of guest stars, including singers Phil Collins and Sheena Easton (who married Sonny in a highly rated 1987 episode), singer/poet Leonard Cohen, G. Gordon Liddy of Watergate fame, who was his sinister self, and auto president and head of the Statue of Liberty bicentennial restoration committee Lee Iacocca.

Miami Vice was an unabashed celebration of style, wealth, and celebrityhood. It also fit neatly into the rhetoric of the Reagan administration's war on drugs. Perfectly ideologically positioned, it was truly a show for its time.

The other Michael Mann series, *Crime Story* (1986–88) cost even more to produce, an estimated $1.5 million per episode, much of it spent on meticulous recreation of authentic settings and props of its era, the 1960s. Like *Miami Vice*, *Crime Story* used rock music (in this case, music of the 1960s; the theme song was "Runaway," sung by Del Shannon). The pacing and shooting style of the two shows was similar. But unlike *Miami Vice*, *Crime Story* is noted for its introduction of quirky comedy elements, mainly through characterization, into this otherwise excessively violent melodramatic form.

The basic story line involved the head of Chicago's Major Crime Unit, Lieutenant Mike Torello, in the pursuit of a rising young Chicago gangster, Ray Luca, and his bumbling side-kick Pauli Taglia. No matter what Torello did, he couldn't get Luca behind bars. When Luca moved his operation to Las Vegas during the first season, Torello followed, now as an agent of a federal strike force against organized crime. In the final episode of the first season, Luca is wounded in a breathtaking gun battle with the federal agents on the streets of Las Vegas (violence never looked this good on television). Then, in a classic comic scene, the boneheaded Pauli drives Luca into the Yucca Flats to an isolated house to recover. Seated at a table are a group of mannequins. Pauli is a bit slow on the uptake—they had arrived at the site of an atomic bomb test! As they prepare to flee, the program ends with a big question mark flashed on the screen.

The following season, Ray and Pauli were back. They had miraculously escaped, although both were suffering the effects of nuclear radiation. In the first episode of the second season, "Pauli's Bad Dream," both are under guard in a hospital. American intelligence agents believe they are Russian spies who infiltrated the nuclear test site. The interrogation takes place through Pauli's point of view, with the intelligence agents shot in distorted extreme close-ups. Through a series of flashbacks, Pauli relives the good and bad times with Ray, including Ray's beating and rape of Pauli's girlfriend. In one surreal scene, he hallucinates, imagining he is a rock singer at a nightclub, dressed in a ridiculous sequined jacket and sporting a pompadour, singing "I Fought the Law and the Law Won." After much soul-searching and after learning from a nurse that the Army is about to give him a large dose of LSD to make him talk, Pauli declares his loyalty to Ray and leads their violent escape from the hospital. Following more comic misadventures, a Mafia airplane whisks them away to Latin America, where Torello's pursuit continues.

While *Crime Story* never achieved great success in the ratings, it did attract a loyal following. The series was an anomaly. The level of violence and its gratuitousness were problematic. At the same time, the violence was often highly stylized and framed by comic characterization and a nostalgic music bed. In a sense, *Crime Story* was an extremely elaborate and well-crafted cartoon—a pleasurable viewing experience with a repugnant sociocultural subtext. Like the violent cinema of the time (e.g., *Rambo*), it was symptomatic of the values confusion that seemed to permeate American society.

The Street (1988) was a world away from the stylized police of *Miami Vice* and *Crime Story*. Produced for first-run syndication, its 65 half-hour episodes aired five nights a week at 11 P.M. in most markets (because of its raw language).

The setting was inner-city Newark, New Jersey. The series was shot direct video style with handheld cameras (see the discussion of *The Police Tapes* in chapters 7 and 11) and featured "the kind of conversation people make when they're on duty and passing the time; its language is realistically profane."[23]

The main characters were two pairs of patrolmen whose stories alternated each night. One pair—Scolari and Peluso—grew up together, attended the same parochial school, and remain close friends. They work the 3–11 P.M. shift. The other pair—Runyon and Scott—are clearly mismatched. Runyon tells racist jokes, has a drinking problem, doesn't mind beating up an innocent person if that person is black, and is more concerned with being killed than doing efficient police work. Scott, who is black, attends law school and is "on the way up," unlike his colleagues. Runyon and Scott work the 11 P.M.–7 A.M. "graveyard" shift.

These are not the glamorous *Miami Vice* protagonists. Rather, they are balding, confused, and occasionally tormented by the nature of their work. And they only occasionally catch the suspect. The sound track is urban noise, not rock music. And while the cost to produce an hour of *Miami Vice* and *Crime Story* was well over $1 million, *The Street* logged in at $50,000 per half hour, over a quarter of which was spent on writing. This is not an "action" show. According to Jim Korris, senior vice president of MCA-TV, the series syndicator: "The reality of their lives is generally mind-numbing tedium punctuated by abject terror."[24]

Among the ironies of the production history of *The Street* was its creative staff. Executive producers John Mankiewicz and Daniel Pyne were both *Miami Vice* veterans. The series was produced by Quantum Media, whose chief executive officer was Robert Pittman, founder of MTV. The producers felt that the audience, especially the young target demographic, had tired of the slick police melodramas.

An interesting sidebar to the production history of *The Street* involves the producers' use of writers. Thirty different writers were used for the first 40 episodes, including poets, playwrights, journalists, fiction writers, a physician, and a criminal attorney.[25]

In the end, however, the mundanity of everyday police work portrayed in the series may have contributed to its demise. By comparison, the successful syndicated documentary series *Cops* features real police and is shot in direct video style; the difference is that almost every act in the latter incorporates a heightened dramatic element, such as an investigation of a violent crime with bodies and blood at the scene or a drug raid.

After decades of melodramatic violence, the four commercial broadcast networks finally agreed, in the summer of 1993, to place parental warnings on programs they deemed excessively violent. The action followed Congressional hearings on this issue and continued expressions of outrage from vocal audience segments who threatened advertiser boycotts. Some critics felt that the networks' reluctant step did not go far enough and were pressuring for an actual reduction in the levels of violence. Other critics questioned why children's Saturday-morning cartoons were not included in the networks' plans to label their programs.

CBS President Howard Stringer, speaking at a press conference during which senior network executives announced the move, addressed a core issue regarding television's portrayal of violence, namely, that this violence did not "evoke emotions like grief or remorse."[26] Series like *Miami Vice* and *Crime Story* are prime examples of this problem, which is compounded by such programs' framing both police work and criminality in an ambience of glamour and high fashion.

St. Elsewhere (1982–88), created by Joshua Brand and John Falsey, was a "doctors and nurses version of 'Hill Street Blues' " with handheld cameras, multiplot episodes, and overlapping dialogue.[27] And like *Hill Street*, it "brought a new urban edge to a programming genre that had become fossilized."[28]

The setting was St. Eligius—a rundown and offbeat teaching hospital in a poor Boston neighborhood. The idea was based on the experience of a childhood friend of Brand's in a Cleveland teaching hospital and also bears a striking resemblance to Paddy Chayefsky's theatrical film *The Hospital*. The series premise—"whimsical doctors in a hospital's solemn hallways"[29]—allowed for an intelligent exploration of the pathos of ministering to the indigent and homeless tinged with black humor frequently connected with sexuality and serving as a release for the staff, who were pushed to the emotional edge by the unremitting grimness of the hospital's environment.

St. Elsewhere, a derisive moniker for St. Eligius, was clearly "a big city dumping ground for patients not wanted by the higher class (and more expensive) medical facilities in Boston."[30] The series, in its finer moments, was able to foreground this ideological question, especially as St. Eligius was taken over by the profit-oriented Ecumena Hospitals Corporation, which proceeded to introduce "business principles" of medicine, to which the highly professional and socially conscious staff offered strong resistance.

Never a major television audience hit, *St. Elsewhere* began near the bottom of the ratings in its first season, winding up in 86th place out of 98 prime-time series. Nevertheless, NBC renewed it, and the series gradually developed a loyal following, finishing near the middle of the ratings during the remainder of its run.

Gradually, according to *New York Times* critic John J. O'Connor, the focus of *St. Elsewhere* shifted away from social commentary to self-conscious glibness:

The hospital staff members became more important than the patients. Grab-the-audience gimmicks turned more obvious. Rape, both heterosexual and homosexual, got an especially big play. Fey humor was encouraged, complete with elaborate fantasy sequences. . . . increasingly the show seemed to be more interested in proving that everybody connected with it was far too yuppie-hip to take a hospital television formula seriously.[31]

St. Elsewhere, like Crime Story, was pushing the edge of postmodern "play," using among other devices intertextual humor (St. Eligius's loudspeaker would frequently page other TV doctors) to signalize that this drama was not to be taken all that seriously.

As St. Elsewhere was a world removed from the decorous urban County General Hospital of Ben Casey and the suburban middle landscape gentility of Marcus Welby, M.D., so too were two very different 1980s lawyer melodramas—L.A. Law and Shannon's Deal—far removed from the cerebral and somber atmosphere that permeated The Defenders.

L.A. Law (1986–) focuses on the private lives and professional work of a group of attorneys employed by McKenzie, Brackman, Chaney, and Kuzak, a powerful Los Angeles legal firm.

Steven Bochco, who cocreated Hill Street Blues, and Terry Louise Fisher, herself an attorney and formerly producer of Cagney and Lacey, cocreated the series. Both left shortly after its first season in an internecine dispute, which appropriately ended in a lawsuit.

According to Brooks and Marsh, L.A. Law "looked like Hill Street Blues in a law office."[32] Like Hill Street, it employed multiple story lines and a set opening (in the firm's conference room). It has often featured cases dealing with contemporary social issues, such as insurance companies refusing to cover AIDS treatment and sexual discrimination. In keeping with the emerging melodramatic tendency to mix seriousness and humor, the series explored a variety of cases, from the thought-provoking to the outrageous. An example of the latter involved "a businessman with Tourette's syndrome—causing him to blurt out obscenities at the most inopportune moments."[33] Unlike Perry Mason, the firm's attorneys occasionally lost a case.

Late 1980s television melodrama, reacting against the excessive self-interest of the early 1980s, was prone to engage in a bit of consciousness raising, and L.A. Law was no exception. So, although the firm generally charged high fees for its work, its attorneys did occasional pro bono work. The cast included a "token" Hispanic attorney who knew it, a hotshot young black lawyer, and a developmentally disabled office worker (a character rarely featured in a continuing role on series television). Women were prominently featured as high-powered attorneys.

As in the other "hip" melodramas of the 1980s, sex played a significant role in the lives of the series's protagonists.

If L.A. Law celebrated the upper stratum of the profession, Shannon's Deal (1990–91) mocked it as inherently unscrupulous. Shannon's Deal was created by filmmaker and novelist John Sayles, who directed the theatrical films *Return of the Secaucus Seven* (1980) and *Matewan* (1987), the latter a story of beleaguered West Virginia coal miners. Sayles's "sensitivity to working class Americans"[34] is evident in *Shannon's Deal.* The series is clearly aware of the issue of class in America, and of "the relation of class to money and power,"[35] especially as reflected in the legal system. Sayles is clever enough to foreground the complex issues surrounding the existence of class difference without becoming polemical or sentimental.

The central character, lawyer Jack Shannon, grew up in a working-class Irish family in 1960s Philadelphia. He missed the "revolution" because he had to put himself through Temple law school, in part by gambling at poker. He made law review. Upon graduation, he joined a prestigious law firm, Coleman and Weiss, with numerous corporate clients. Shannon worked for the firm for 15 years, specializing in representing chemical companies. In the process, he became "the object of his own contempt."[36] This led to his eventual self-destruction, as he amassed substantial debts from gambling at poker, to which he had been addicted since college (hence one meaning of the series title). His wife left him and took their daughter with her. He was fired from the law firm.

According to Sayles, "I was interested in . . . a guy who thought of himself as a failure. This is such a success-oriented country. He's trying to come back doing something slightly different and trying to find out what's important to him."[37]

The pilot for the series begins with Shannon moving into his new office—a shabby room in a rundown professional building. Sayles seamlessly works the backstory into the pilot. Rather than run from his guilt and sense of loss, Shannon confronts it. By understanding his failure, he may be able to use his painful experience to benefit others abused by the system.

Coleman and Weiss, his former law firm, becomes Shannon's most formidable enemy. With energy and a commitment to justice, Shannon pursues a "low-echelon brand of general practice."[38] He understands that the working class and the poor are at a decided disadvantage in the court system, that consumer laws favor landlords over tenants, creditors over debtors. Thus, lawyers like Shannon, who seek to defend the poor, try to cut deals and settle cases out of court (the second meaning of the title). Shannon never enters a courtroom in the first three episodes of the series. Instead, he negotiates settlements with other lawyers, gets district attorneys to drop cases, and trades favors with court clerks for postponements of trials. His is not sleazy, but necessary business. Like a poker game, which he knows so well, a player must often "bluff" and "stall."

Shannon was a realist. The series pilot was careful to satirize not only his former law firm but also a self-righteous reporter for an alternative newspaper. Shannon knew that one had to get down in the dirt to fight the inequities of the system—that not words alone, but words combined with concrete social action might make some difference.

Shannon's Deal was melodrama that intelligently explored the underbelly of the urban frontier, much as *East Side/West Side* had done nearly 30 years earlier. And like its predecessor, it barely lasted the year. Critics loved it. The audience didn't.

The rural-middle-landscape melodrama also assumed a decided contemporary edge in the early 1990s. The caring, trusting, and stable nuclear family unit struggling for economic and physical survival, featured in *Little House on the Prairie* and *The Waltons*, was replaced in the "new" rural middle landscape by a loose-knit community of eccentric individualists whose relationships to one another and to "reality" were labile and often bizarre. In this sense, the "new" rural-middle-landscape melodrama, exemplified by *Twin Peaks* (1990–91), is an intriguing amalgam of the rural-middle-landscape comedy of *Green Acres* and the contemporary urban frontier melodrama of *Hill Street Blues* and *St. Elsewhere*. We are encouraged to enter a world where people are both strange and strangers, both protean and disconnected. It is a world filled with contradiction and ambivalence, humor, and extreme violence. In many ways it is symptomatic of our contemporary condition.

Filmmaker David Lynch made his commercial television debut in *Twin Peaks*, originally a seven-part miniseries "about the corruptions of sex, drugs, politics, and maybe even psychiatry in an all-American lumber town near the Canadian border."[39] Coproducer and cowriter Mark Frost, who also directed an episode, was formerly a writer and executive story editor for *Hill Street Blues*.

Lynch, who had directed such theatrical films as *Eraserhead* (1978), *The Elephant Man* (1980), and *Blue Velvet* (1986), was known for his "surreal sensibility . . . partial to gore and violent comedy."[40] He favored degenerate behavior and odd characters. Critic John Leonard elaborated on Lynch's aesthetic, clearly evident although toned down in *Twin Peaks* to meet the constraints of network broadcast television, noting:

the sinister fluidity, the absurd detail, the shocking relief, the elegant gesture, the deadpan jokes, the painterly pointillism, the bad puns, the erotic violence, the lingering close-up camera, the rampaging of non-sequiturs, the underlining and italicizing of emotions, the warping of the light, the appetite for all that's grotesque and quirky, a sense of unconscious dreaming . . . moon thoughts . . . sadness . . . demonic possession.[41]

In short, Lynch and Frost, in *Twin Peaks*, took to an extreme (for television) the melodramatic tendencies already explored in *St. Elsewhere*, *Crime Story*, and the fantasy sequences of many daytime soap operas.

The complex plotting of *Twin Peaks* can be summarized as follows. The body of 17-year-old Twin Peaks homecoming queen Laura Palmer washes ashore in a plastic bag near the Twin Peaks sawmill. Before local sheriff Harry S. Truman can begin his investigation, another victim of torture and rape is discovered. FBI agent Dale Cooper, who one writer called "a mystical loner," arrives on the scene to take charge of the case. Everyone in the town of Twin Peaks is suspect, including Laura's boyfriend Bobby Briggs, occasional lover of Shelly Johnson, a waitress at the local diner who is married to Leo, a sadistic truck driver and drug dealer. Laura, it is subsequently discovered, was addicted to cocaine, appeared in porno-graphic magazines, and had stashed away a sizable amount of money. Along the path to the discovery of Laura's killer (her father, who is pos-sessed by an evil spirit and turns into a homicidal maniac), agent Cooper dreams of a singing red dwarf, talks with a sentient old lady who constantly cradles a log ("the log lady"), eats doughnuts, and talks into his microcas-sette recorder to his secretary: "Diana, I'm holding in my hand a small box of chocolate bunnies." The dialog is often amazingly and intentionally banal. AGENT COOPER to SHERIFF TRUMAN: "Who's the lady with the log?" TRUMAN to COOPER: "We call her the log lady."

Mark Frost recounted his discussions with ABC, who had reason to fear the outcome, while hoping that *Twin Peaks* would engage the desirable young target demographic. According to Frost,

We told them we were going to give them a two-hour moody, dark soap-opera murder mystery set in a fictional town in the Northwest, with an ensemble cast and an edge. . . . And . . . they said . . . that what we'd done was so foreign to their experience that they couldn't presume to tell us how to do it any better or any different.[42]

ABC's worst fears were well founded. The heavily promoted pilot, which was directed by Lynch and cost about $4 million, captured a 33 share, but the first episode dropped to 27. The first episode ended with a long fade-out on a wife beating, which apparently angered many women 35 years old and up (a crucial audience for prime-time soaps). They de-serted the serial; and the second episode, which was also directed by Lynch and featured the bizarre dwarf who sang backward, dropped fur-ther to a 21 share.

Critic John Leonard, who has traditionally searched for deeper meaning on the small screen and has generally found its program fare wanting, made an exception in this case:

Though beautiful to look at, there isn't much of anything inside [Lynch's and Frost's] soft labyrinth except an unimportant secret. Unlike, say, *The Prisoner*, with Patrick McGoohan . . . *Twin Peaks* has nothing at all in its pretty little head except the desire to please. In this, and only in this, it resembles almost everything else on television. But beautiful is better. Must we, like the Deconstructionists, moisten everything with meaning?[43]

In the end, however, it appeared that many viewers found Lynch's and Frost's vision of the rural middle landscape too confusing, or perhaps too unsettling, even by early 1990s melodramatic standards.

Northern Exposure (1990–) is a "kinder and gentler" version of *Twin Peaks* more suitable for general viewership. While it eschews *Twin Peaks*'s overtly erotic violence, its characters are also decidedly eccentric. Its humor resides in the interpersonal interactions resulting from a clash of cultures, which is most clearly drawn in the central character of Dr. Joel Fleischman, the only doctor in the isolated town of Cicely, Alaska. Fleischman, a young neurotic recent graduate of Columbia University medical school in New York City, is assigned to Cicely for four years to repay his educational expenses (he thought he would be stationed in Anchorage, but was sent to Cicely, in the middle of nowhere, when Cicely's only doctor died). Fleischman is gradually and reluctantly initiated into "a rustic setting rich in folklore."[44]

Cicely is populated by a rich assortment of "characters." Fleischman and his landlady, the beautiful and independent air-taxi pilot Maggie O'Connell, are constantly bickering but seem to be gradually falling in love. This may have significant ramifications for the young doctor, as Maggie's five previous boyfriends all died in bizarre fashion—the last, Rick, was killed by a falling satellite. Many in Cicely feel that Maggie has a love curse.

Maurice Minnifield, president of Cicely's chamber of commerce, is a blustering and boorish ex-astronaut. His young Native American assistant Ed is a popular-culture expert and fledgling filmmaker. In one memorable episode, Ed makes his own "avant-garde" home movie about the residents of Cicely, which receives raves at its premiere at the local cinema. The townsfolk couldn't imagine what in Cicely would make a worthwhile subject for a film . . . until Ed provided the answer.

Chris Stevens is Cicely's erudite disc jockey on radio station KBHR (K-Bear)—host of "Chris in the Morning." An autodidact, Chris is also an ex-convict. He discovered Walt Whitman when in jail and is thoroughly familiar with the writings of Hegel, Kierkegaard, Kant, Nietzsche, Tolstoy, Jefferson, and Tocqueville. "Chris in the Morning" rejects format, playing everything from Irish folk music to Italian opera to "Louie, Louie." While *Miami Vice* limited its use of music from the outside world to recent rock hits and *The Wonder Years* and *Crime Story* used 1960s "oldies," *Northern Exposure* ranges far and wide for its appropriation of music genres.[45]

Holling Vincoeur, about 60 years old, was an adventurer who settled in Cicely and opened a bar, which is a primary gathering place for the town residents. Holling is embarrassed by his lack of a high school diploma and

begins a personal quest to achieve a GED. His 18-year-old lover, Shelly
Tambo, works at the bar. Their relationship is tender and accepting and
is reminiscent of *Mary Hartman, Mary Hartman*'s odd couple, Charlie and
Loretta Haggers.

Ruth Anne runs Cicely's general store. She bears a striking resemblance
to the "log lady."

One of the most intriguing characters in the series is Marilyn, Fleischman's quiet, self-appointed Eskimo assistant who raises ostriches in her
back yard (why not?). Fleischman constantly (and patronizingly) worries
about Marilyn's well-being, but she repeatedly demonstrates her ability to
take care of herself.

Northern Exposure's creators, Joshua Brand and John Falsey, also created *St. Elsewhere*. Falsey sees *Northern Exposure* as a "nonjudgmental
universe" of unconventional characters.[46] Its essential optimism is perhaps
its primary strength. It encourages tolerance and, more important, acceptance of "the other" in an age in which intolerance seems to frame social
relations in everyday life. In this sense, *Northern Exposure* moves beyond
the self-conscious hipness of the later episodes of *St. Elsewhere*. At the
same time, it reminds us of the essential goodness of the Clampetts of
Beverly Hills without, however, resorting to the portrayal of rustics as
naïve children.

SOCIAL AWARENESS IN DAYTIME SOAPS

As an aesthetic vehicle, a soap opera, according to one critic, is "an
ingenious symbiosis of intimate and frequently mundane details of daily
life and plots laced with unbelievable flights of fancy and much dramatic
license [which] indulges the eavesdropper in most viewers."[47] Beyond this
description of soap opera's dramaturgy and its connection with its intensely loyal viewership, who often refer to the soaps as "our stories," lies
the domain of the ideological, which may not be so innocent.

According to critic Dennis Porter, writing in the early 1980s, daytime
soap opera presents the viewer "a country without history, politics or
religion, poverty, unemployment, recession or inflation, and only with
minimal references to class and ethnicity." We are given instead problems
of character, such as "sexual identity, family situation, . . . romantic love,
or sexual dysfunctions." Soap opera, Porter concludes, presents "decor in
the absence of an historical or socio-economic frame of reference, commodities in space."[48]

A decade later, while some noticeable changes have occurred in the
daytime dramatic serials that deflect some of Porter's criticisms, many of
his charges remain valid.

While the soaps continued their virtual exclusion of the lower socioeconomic strata of society and while rites of passage in characters' per-

sonal lives, such as weddings, births, and deaths (often violent) remained central dramaturgical elements, by the early 1990s the soaps had introduced a range of "serious issues" in their story lines. This move toward the topical was reinforced by the seemingly endless discussion of such issues on the morning and late afternoon talk programs that bracketed the soaps in the networks' program schedules.

Although rape and incest have been addressed on the soaps for many years, certain subjects—most notably abortion—were still taboo (despite the fact that *Maude* had boldly introduced the issue on prime-time television in the mid-1970s). By the early 1990s less inflammatory subjects, which had rarely been presented, if at all, on the soaps in the past found their way into the form. Among these were illiteracy (*The Young and the Restless* and *One Life to Live*), alcoholism presented as a disease (*All My Children*), interracial love stories, almost always featuring a black woman and a white man (*As the World Turns*), homosexuality, explored from the perspective of homophobia (*One Life to Live*), the battered-wife syndrome (*All My Children*), child abuse (*Santa Barbara*), child custody battles (*Loving*), and HIV testing (*The Young and the Restless*).[49] *Generations*, a short-lived NBC soap (1989–91), introduced daytime soaps' first black family as a central and ongoing focus.

The introduction of these heretofore largely ignored topics may be in part a response to feedback from committed soap opera viewers, who have expressed a desire to see more realistic portrayals of contemporary life in "their stories." Research indicates, for example, that the audience want women characters "to be stronger, more independent and self-sufficient."[50]

An additional factor driving many of the changes in soap opera story lines is the changing demographic composition of the soap opera audience—certainly a key to any consideration of content areas in this traditionally profitable program form. By the late 1980s, A. C. Nielsen was reporting a drop in daytime soap operas' household ratings (perhaps due in part to the increase in unbelievable fantasy sequences that pervaded the serials, a trend also noticeable in prime-time melodrama). In November 1978, the average household rating for soap operas was 6.8, representing an average viewership of 5.06 million television households. In November 1988, this had declined to a 5.0 rating, or an average viewership of 4.48 million television households. Combined with declining audiences were steadily falling advertising revenues and rising production costs.

Much of the decline in audience was occurring in nonblack households. A 1988 Nielsen report, "Television Viewing among Blacks," indicated that 12.7 percent of all black households with television sets watched daytime dramatic serials, compared with 6.3 percent of "all others." Although only about 10 million of the 88.6 million television households in 1988 were black, the proportions of soap viewers was still considered noteworthy.

Furthermore, viewing trends recorded by Nielsen during the mid-1980s indicated that black viewers' soap viewing was increasing, while that of "all others" was declining.[51] In early 1988, black viewers watched an average of 14.7 hours of daytime television a week (including soaps and game shows), while "all others" watched an average of 9.5 hours of daytime television each week.

At the networks, numbers talk. This in large measure explains the attempt to include more black characters in major roles in the daytime soaps. By the late 1980s more than half of the eleven network daytime soap operas featured story lines with prominent black characters. Still, however, with the notable exception of *Generations*, "black characters in soap operas, numerous as they are, generally exist in a kind of vacuum. They arrive in town, have a brief moment in the sun (which in soap operas can mean several months) as part of a specific story line, then fade into the background or disappear as suddenly as they came."[52]

And despite the soaps' recent willingness to address certain social issues and admit more blacks as temporarily prominent characters, certain soap demographics remain essentially unchanged. Soaps remain largely populated by upper-middle-class whites, with very few truly wealthy characters and still fewer operatives, laborers, or clerical workers, whose lives are considered too mundane to sell the commodities of the suburban middle landscape, even though in actuality these workers today constitute much of the population of that domain.

TELEVISION DOCUDRAMA: TRUTH AT WHAT PRICE?

We introduced our discussion of docudrama, or drama-based-on-fact (DBOF) in chapter 2, describing the contentious production history of *Shootdown*, which examined the 1983 downing of Korean Air Lines Flight 007 by Soviet fighter aircraft in Soviet air space. Among the issues raised in the debate over *Shootdown* were the creators' selective use of evidence to advance one viewpoint regarding the event (which was at the time still shrouded in mystery) and the network's requirement that fictional characters and events be included in the story line to produce balance. The controversy surrounding *Shootdown* raises important questions about the nature of truth claims in this program form, in which historical events are melodramatically recreated.

A precise definition of the docudrama form is elusive. Yet, for purposes of this discussion we can divide the form into two broad subgenres. In "biographical" docudrama, which has its roots in literary biography, actual historical characters and events are dominant (*Shootdown* falls in this category). In "novelized" docudrama, which corresponds to historical fiction, invented characters dominate but events are real or historically situated

(*Washington behind Closed Doors*, discussed below, is representative of this category).

Defenders and detractors of the docudrama form most often focus their debate on the creator's desire to insightfully portray character in any dramatic form versus the creator's responsibility to provide journalistic or historical accuracy when recounting actual events to a vast audience whose knowledge and understanding of political and social history may be significantly and perhaps irrevocably influenced by the viewing experience.

Television producer-writers Richard Levinson and William Link adapted the television docudrama *The Execution of Private Slovik* (1973) from a book of the same name written by William Bradford Huie. The docudrama is a moving recreation of the events leading to the only American execution, by a firing squad, of a World War II deserter—the first such execution since the Civil War. Levinson and Link believe the debate over the docudrama's truth claims is spurious. Their defense of the docudrama form echoes most members of television's creative community:

Shakespeare put words in the mouth of Julius Caesar, as did Shaw and Thornton Wilder. Playwrights and novelists have pillaged history for centuries, turning the quick and the dead into spokesmen for their own philosophies. . . . The objections to these liberties have been minimal. But television brings with it a strong element of credibility that historians and other critics of the medium feel changes the perception of the audience in a significant way; . . . there are those who are convinced that the TV viewer cannot easily distinguish between reality and dramatic truth, especially when they cohabit the same piece of furniture; . . . is it only permissible to play hob with the truth when a suitable number of centuries have intervened and none of the actors wears business suits?[53]

Critic Michael Arlen, writing about *Washington behind Closed Doors* (1977), a 12-hour "novelized" docudrama focusing on the Nixon administration during Watergate, disagrees with Levinson and Link. Arlen notes that this docudramatic serial, created by David Rintels and based in part on John Erlichman's insider novel *The Company*, clearly represented the Nixon administration even though its characters bore fictitious names (Jason Robards played the fictitious President Richard Monckton). It thereby "lays deliberate claim to authenticity," which it should not do. Arlen nevertheless concedes the work was the best in the genre's history to that date and, as a form of psychobiography, may have revealed much more about the personalities of Nixon and his White House associates than could any straight documentary. Arlen's way out of this conundrum seems to be to clearly label the work "fiction." He wrote,

There should be room in our historical narrative for such a marvellously evocative (though perhaps not precisely factual) interpretation as Robards' depiction of

Nixon-Monckton's strange humorous humorlessness, where an actor's art gave pleasure, brought out character, and took us closer to truth.[54]

Critics of docudrama who claim a "distortion of history" treat history as if it can somehow be separated from ideology. It cannot. History is always naturalized and therefore ideological; it is what those in control wish it to be. Political analyst Richard Reeves was correct when he argued that docudrama should be treated as a political event.[55] For, as with all television, what is given and what is left out offer a distinction of major importance. Television production is expensive. All presentations of history are not equal in terms of their impact. Oppositional history—Walter Benjamin's parallel stream of the history of the oppressed, which counters official history—is rarely presented on television. Exceptions include an occasional public-television series such as *Visions*, which presented controversial docudramas, among them one about life in a U.S. World War II internment camp in which Japanese-Americans were forced to live in intolerable conditions. Ultimately, the critic must examine the choices made in docudramatic presentations for their ideological consequences and engage dominant culture producers in a dialogue regarding those choices. As Michel de Certeau wrote, "There will be *facts* that are no longer *truths*. The inflation of the latter is controlled, if not shut off, by criticism of the places of authority in which facts are converted into truths."[56]

The world of the docudrama, which until the mid-1980s tended to focus on the more significant problems and issues of our time, has in recent years turned toward the lurid, following the lead of the late-afternoon television talk programs, the local evening "Eyewitness News" presentations, and the syndicated tabloid "news" magazines such as *Hard Copy* and *A Current Affair*. One argument advanced for this shift in focus is that it is easier to get people to watch DBOFs about stories they have seen on their local newscasts than to sell them on a story they know nothing about. The news stories thus act as promotional vehicles for the docudramas, assuring higher ratings. Because there are so many reality-based programs in various television genres on the air in the early 1990s, docudrama must literally scream at viewers to grab their attention.

In 1992, the story of Amy Fisher, nicknamed "the Long Island Lolita," whose love for Joey Buttafuoco led to her shooting Buttafuoco's wife Mary Jo, was front-page news in all the New York City tabloid newspapers and often the lead story on the city's local evening newscasts. The 17-year-old Fisher was a member of the local chapter of an after-school call-girls' club. Her story was clearly profitable docudrama material, and the Big Three networks were quick to buy in. The Fishers reportedly received $80,000 for film rights to Amy's story from KLM Productions, which was to appear on NBC, and used the money to pay their daughter's bail. Tri-

Star paid the Buttafuocos between $200,000 and $300,000 for rights to their version of the story, which was to appear on CBS. ABC took the high road in this instance, basing its docudrama, *Beyond Control: The Amy Fisher Story,* on news accounts and court records.[57]

The film producers' and networks' scramble to get Amy's story to the larger public as quickly as possible is referred to by one critic as "media-in-heat madness." Such material is not new to television. However, the frequency with which it appears and its immediacy have increased. "Television . . . has long harbored a special place in its heart for criminal activity, dangerous obsessions and sociopathic behavior . . . high-profile, true events (the stranger the better)."[58] In the early 1980s a docudrama would appear on television an average of four to five years after the event's occurrence. By the early 1990s, the turnaround time averaged four to nine months.

Network executives defend the airing of these stories and advance two criteria for their acceptance: first, that they explore an aspect of our lives that asks a question people would normally ask, and second, that they offer some insight into the event itself—a "window" into behavior.[59]

Critics see a window and, peering through it, a voyeur.

NOTES

1. Northrop Frye, *Anatomy of Criticism* (Princeton, NJ: Princeton University Press, 1957), p. 47.

2. Ibid.

3. Peter Brooks, *The Melodramatic Imagination* (New Haven, CT: Yale University Press, 1976), p. 201.

4. Ibid., p. 204.

5. Ibid.

6. Orrin E. Klapp, *Heroes, Villains, and Fools: The Changing American Character* (Englewood Cliffs, NJ: Prentice-Hall, 1962), p. 19.

7. Ibid., p. 8.

8. Ibid., p. 17.

9. Ibid., pp. 16–17.

10. David Thorburn, "Television Melodrama," in *Television as a Cultural Force,* ed. Richard Adler and Douglass Cater (New York: Praeger, 1976), p. 85.

11. Raymond Williams, *Television: Technology and Cultural Form* (New York: Schocken Books, 1975), pp. 86–94 passim.

12. Richard Levinson and William Link, *Stay Tuned* (New York: Ace, 1983), pp. 74–75.

13. C. Wright Mills, *The Power Elite* (New York: Oxford University Press, 1956), p. 138.

14. In a survey of top corporate executives and members of boards of directors of six leading electronic-media corporations—RCA/NBC, CBS, ABC, Time, Inc., Westinghouse, and Warner Communications—conducted by the author and colleague Allen Lichtenstein in 1983, we were able to isolate and profile 76 members

of the boards. This limited survey confirmed the description offered by Mills a quarter of a century earlier. Of the 76 board members, 38 held undergraduate, advanced, or professional degrees from Ivy League universities. One-sixth held degrees from Harvard, and one-tenth from Yale. Of the remaining 38 directors, a significant number attended prestigious midwestern and western private educational institutions, notably Northwestern, the University of Chicago, and Stanford. Of the 76 directors, only six, or 7.9 percent, were women, with no more than one woman on any board. This was an educated, genteel, and clubbish man's world defined by conservative politics, social elitism, and the tight economic control of the interlocking directorate. At the lower levels of control, it was a world in which a corporate "team" was really a set of cliques among which, as Mills put it, "the prideful grace of individuality is not at a premium." One learns the art of conformity well before advancing to the upper reaches of the powerful organization— one is, above all, a corporate man, with a proper birthright and education.

15. Tom Wolfe, *The Electric Kool-Aid Acid Test* (New York: Bantam Books, 1969), pp. 34–35.

16. Joseph Campbell, *The Hero with a Thousand Faces* (New York: Pantheon Books, 1949), p. 29.

17. Mills, *Power Elite*, p. 59.

18. Michael J. Arlen, "Smooth Pebbles at Southfork," in *The Camera Age* (New York: Farrar, Straus and Giroux, 1981), p. 50.

19. Mills, *Power Elite*, p. 163.

20. David Jacobs, "When the Rich and the Powerful Were Riding High," *New York Times*, April 15, 1990, sec. 2, p. 33.

21. Ibid.

22. Ibid.

23. Leslie Bennetts, " 'The Street' Is Miles from 'Miami Vice,' " *New York Times*, April 10, 1988, sec. 2, p. 39.

24. Ibid.

25. Ibid.

26. Walter Goodman, "About the New Labels On TV Violence: Meanings and Motives," *New York Times*, July 7, 1993, p. C17.

27. John J. O'Connor, "For 'St. Elsewhere,' It's Goodbye (or Is It?)," *New York Times*, May 25, 1988, p. C26.

28. Ibid.

29. Mark Shapiro, "How a Couple of Bookish Guys Made Good on TV," *New York Times*, January 12, 1992, sec. 2, p. 29.

30. Tim Brooks and Earle Marsh, eds., *The Complete Directory to Prime Time Network TV Shows: 1946–Present*, 5th ed. (New York: Ballantine Books, 1992), p. 774.

31. O'Connor, "For 'St. Elsewhere,' " p. C26.

32. Brooks and Marsh, *The Complete Directory*, 5th ed., p. 490.

33. Ibid.

34. Amy Taubin, "Full House," (The Village) *Voice*, April 17, 1990, p. 50.

35. Ibid.

36. F. Scott Fitzgerald, quoted in Samuel G. Freedman, "How John Sayles Shuffled 'Shannon's Deal'," *New York Times*, April 15, 1990, p. 33.

37. Taubin, "Full House," p. 50.

38. Freedman, "How John Sayles Shuffled," p. 33.

39. John Leonard, "The Quirky Allure of Twin Peaks," *New York*, May 7, 1990, p. 34.

40. Richard B. Woodward, "When 'Blue Velvet' Meets 'Hill Street Blues,' " *New York Times*, April 8, 1990, sec. 2, p. 31.

41. Leonard, "Quirky Allure," p. 36.

42. Ibid., p. 34.

43. Ibid., p. 39.

44. Shapiro, "How a Couple of Bookish Guys," p. 29.

45. Jon Parales, "Radio Days in Cicely, Alaska: Anything Goes," *New York Times*, May 3, 1992, sec. 2, p. 29.

46. Shapiro, "How a Couple of Bookish Guys," p. 29.

47. Mimi Torchin, "Black Family Shares Spotlight in a New Soap Opera," *New York Times*, March 26, 1989, p. 27.

48. Dennis Porter, "Soap Time: Thoughts on a Commodity Art Form," in *Television: The Critical View*, 3d ed., ed. Horace Newcomb (New York: Oxford University Press, 1982), pp. 125–26, 130.

49. John J. O'Connor, "The Young, the Restless and the Socially Aware," *New York Times*, July 19, 1992, sec. 2, pp. 1, 23.

50. Ibid., p. 23.

51. Torchin, "Black Family Shares Spotlight," p. 27.

52. Ibid.

53. Levinson and Link, *Stay Tuned*, pp. 146–47.

54. Michael J. Arlen, "Getting the Goods on President Monckton," *The New Yorker*, October 3, 1977, p. 115ff.

55. Richard Reeves, "How I Became a Supporter of and Appalled by Docudrama, and a Fan of the Talented, Frustrated, Confused Men and Women Who Would Like to Make Television Better If Only So They Wouldn't Have to Apologize for What They Do—Write and Produce the Stuff America Loves," *Panorama*, March 1980, p. 39.

56. Michel de Certeau, *The Practice of Everyday Life*, trans. Steven Rendall (Berkeley: University of California Press, 1984), p. 11.

57. Jeff Silverman, "Murder, Mayhem Stalk TV," *New York Times*, November 22, 1992, sec. 2, p. 1.

58. Ibid.

59. Ibid., p. 28.

7

□　□　□　□　□　□

Television News and the Television Documentary

THE TELEVISION-NEWSGATHERING APPARATUS

Much has been written regarding the ideological frames that determine news selection and packaging. One especially important consideration for critical scholars is the extent to which news organizations' work routines and individual journalists' social, economic, cultural, and educational backgrounds determine news content.[1] We will examine this and related questions within the context of myth analysis.

As a starting point, consider the following definition of news—one that many critics argue reflects today's realities, although not the ideals of electronic journalism—"News is what the television news department covers and airs on a given day." One should not be deceived by the apparent ideological neutrality of this definition, for, as Tuchman explains, "The framing of news is subservient to the industrialization of time through the coordination of the processes of newswork with the 'business day' of legitimated agencies, especially centralized government bureaucracies."[2] News frames, according to Tuchman, are seen by newsgathering organizations as "problems in temporal processing and how the identification of facts is tied to organizational deadlines."[3]

The coordination of the work routines of the newsgathering process with the "bureaucratic phase structures" of government and major corporations is not a new phenomenon. However, following the acquisitions, in 1986, of the three major television networks, the new ownership has placed increasing pressure on network news managers to become both efficient and profitable.[4] This in turn has led to the downsizing of the network news divisions that has resulted in a decline of "enterprise journalism," which is time-consuming and expensive, requiring extensive backgrounding of stories and cross-checking of sources, and in an increased reliance on the packaged press release, news conference, public speech, and "photo-opportunity"—routinely covered stories, often of questionable news value, whose principal value to the news organization is their low cost and easy availability. An additional benefit is their pre-dictable delivery in time to be processed for the evening news broadcast.

One particularly questionable newsgathering shortcut is the use of the video news release (VNR) supplied by a public relations firm and incor-porated into the news broadcast. In one telling example, the *CBS Evening News* of June 13, 1991, aired a report, narrated by CBS correspondent Mark Phillips, in which he reported that safety belts are "a labor-saving device that may be costing lives instead of saving them."[5] The videotape used in the report shows an automobile being turned on its side, the door opening, and a dummy falling out and being crushed by the car. CBS's "eye" logo ran throughout the piece, and the viewer had no indication as to who actually conducted the demonstration. The videotape, it turned out, was not shot by a CBS News crew, but rather was supplied to CBS News by the Institute for Injury Reduction (IIR), a lobbying group sup-ported by lawyers whose clients often file lawsuits against automobile manufacturers for crash-related injuries. IIR's opponents claim that IIR lawyers often show news reports like CBS's to win cases in court. They argue that juries find reports aired on network newscasts to be more cred-ible than a taped test conducted by someone with an obvious vested in-terest in the case.[6]

The Radio-Television News Directors Association (RTNDA), an indus-try trade group, urges news divisions to include a label on the screen noting that such material has been supplied by non-news organizations. However, as in the CBS report, this recommendation is often ignored. According to critic David Lieberman, the irony is that news directors don't want to alert viewers that the news organization didn't gather the footage, for that might lead viewers to perceive the journalists as lazy and thereby "compromise the believability" of the newscast.[7]

Even when offered an opportunity to do enterprise journalism, network correspondents have often refused. According to Ken Auletta, in 1988 ABC began a special segment, titled "American Agenda," on its evening newscast. The segment was given extra time during the newscast and featured more in-depth reporting. ABC News executive producer Paul Friedman assumed that ABC reporters would welcome the opportunity to spend days or even weeks to prepare a single story. To his dismay, he discovered instead that few of the reporters were interested in these as-signments, preferring rather to be seen on the air every night doing the more routine stories. "The system has become so corrupt," Friedman told Auletta, "that your success as a correspondent is ... measured by how often you get on the air."[8]

Economic pressures have also forced the network news divisions to close many foreign bureaus and to turn increasingly to freelance producers and international news services to provide news footage for overseas-breaking stories. In the end, this may lead to the loss of network news's most important asset—its "credibility." According to Auletta, by the end of 1991, CBS News had only four full-sized foreign bureaus (London, Moscow, Tokyo, and Tel Aviv) and two "minibureaus" (Rome and Johannesburg, South Africa). The network thus has to "parachute someone in" to cover a breaking story outside the normal bureau territory. This person may not speak the local language, may lack knowledge of the politics and culture of the area, and may not have ready access to credible, knowledgeable sources.[9] More often than not, this person is the network's evening news anchor. Despite the drive for efficiency at the networks, and the news divisions' cost-cutting initiatives, when a major breaking foreign story occurs, all three networks rush to send their star anchors and their retinues to the scene even though, according to one senior network executive, the news division saves about $70,000 a day by covering a foreign event with a regular correspondent on the scene.[10]

The network news divisions' increasing tendency to "wallpaper" stories with dramatic pictures has led to the purchase of news footage from outside sources when their own news crews cannot get to the scene. The result can be quite problematic. A case in point involved the accident at the Soviet nuclear power plant in Chernobyl in April 1986. Two weeks after the accident, ABC and NBC ran film footage claiming to show the damaged reactor amid smoke and ruins. The networks had purchased the footage from Albatross, an Italian news photography agency. It turned out that the pictures that purported to be the Chernobyl reactor were in fact those of a damaged cement factory in Trieste, Italy. Within two days of the discovery, both ABC and NBC issued apologies to viewers during their evening newscasts.[11]

Increasingly, it would appear, the quality of the information in the news stories is of less importance than the dramatic impact of the stories and the performances of the news anchors and the few star (or "bigfoot") correspondents whose faces and voices appear with regularity during the newscast. The messenger, not the message, becomes the news.

In the highly competitive and increasingly lurid world of local television news, the stories are essentially the same from station to station in a given market and reflect "a developing blur between the local news and 'reality' programs like A Current Affair and Hard Copy. And that energy is transferred back and forth daily between television stations and the tabloid press."[12] Catherine S. Mangold offers an account of a typical evening's local news broadcast:

Another night, another nightmare. The teen-age killer gives way to the subway slasher. The mob slaying segues into a spot on kids with guns. The face of a weeping mother dissolves into a close-up of a blood-stained shirt. House fires become 'raging infernos.' Traffic snarls. Kids fall out of windows. Babies die in random shootings. . . . Did Princess Diana almost kill herself? Then, the weather. Welcome to New York.[13]

To distinguish itself from its competitors and make it the market leader, a station's newscast must therefore project an instantly recognizable and engaging style. Thus, "packaging"—the news anchors' personalities, appearance, repartee, and ethnic/racial/gender mix; the newscast's theme music and graphics; the design of the news set—comes to represent a newscast's competitive edge. Most major-market station owners hire news consultants who test and market formulas for successful local news packaging. The fact that a few dominant news-consultant companies provide their services to local stations throughout the country explains why local newscasts in Kansas City, Dallas, and New York City, with minor variations reflecting differences in market area demographics, essentially look and sound the same.

Surely there is a higher purpose to the journalistic project than economic efficiency or being a profitable market leader. Defining that purpose has preoccupied scholars and critics of journalism throughout this century.

University of Chicago sociologist Robert E. Park defined news as a part of our communications that calls for a change of attitudes concerning events of importance to a community—events whose significance is still under consideration and discussion. Journalism historian Frank Luther Mott defined news as an accurate, unbiased account of the significant facts of some timely happening. A synthesis of the definitional frames leads us to the definition of news as the provision of significant facts relevant to the formation of an opinion or to the change of attitude on some current public issue of importance to a community of persons. That community may be a group of workers, a neighborhood, city, county, state, region, nation, continent, or the world. A public issue is one about where there already exists some division of opinion. Mott's call for an "accurate, unbiased account" is, of course, moot if one acknowledges the influence of ideology in the structuring of public discourse—accuracy and lack of bias will be claimed by different positions within the public debate in an effort to enforce or counteract an ideology. No journalist can divorce him or herself from the community of persons and thus cannot, in reality, stand apart from the world he or she covers. The resolution of the debate is really a matter in which whoever disseminates news either directly or indirectly determines its ideological slant.

In contrast to news, this traditional definitional scheme views human-interest content as that which describes, in a dramatic narrative style, some human experience in a manner that enables the viewer to make a sympathetic personal identification with the subject.

In this dichotomous definitional construct distinguishing news from human-interest content, we find a forced separation of the truth claims of the accurate news report, which presents facts and lets us decide which side we will support, from the probing, interpretive psychobiographical reportage that may be engaging but is subject to charges of sensationalism and questions regarding its veracity. As a result, public issues abstracted from everyday experience and presented by middle-class public officials with an aura of authority are treated with a certain reverence, while the depiction of everyday experience, with its chaotic images of human suffering, frustration, and despair, is open to question regarding reporters' motives (former ABC reporter/muckraker Geraldo Rivera was frequently criticized for his overtly liberal ideological bias as he reported on the disenfranchised and degraded minority cultures in American society).

This definitional framework places the journalist in an essentially subservient role vis-à-vis the dominant political institutions—as "faithful messenger" of the political elites—whose task becomes, as Walter Lippmann once described it, to simply "signalize" events about to unfold. Such a view of the newsgathering apparatus, however, is by no means shared by all critics.

Ron Powers, the Pulitzer Prize–winning former television critic for the *Chicago Sun-Times*, takes a radically different view of the journalist's role in this process. Powers describes the function of news, which he admits he is defining narrowly, as monitoring and reporting "the conduct of public officials and others who exercise power over private citizens, toward the goal of assuring openness, accountability, and the intelligent administration of community life."[14] Powers, unlike Park and Mott in their more disinterested academic definitions of news, sees the newsgathering apparatus operating to rebalance a system of social relations unbalanced by dominant-subordinate power relationships revealed in human experience. He adds that contemporary television newsgathering does not perform "the vigorous, adversary, check-on-government intervening role that American journalism has traditionally performed."[15] Far from the "signalizing function," Powers concludes that the best American journalism "traditionally proceeded from the assumption that it is mining areas that the public did not even know existed."[16]

Journalism scholar Edward Jay Epstein warned, however, of the inherent dangers of journalistic interventionism—of the journalist perceiving his or her role as public crusader, a role that can easily lead, wrote Epstein, to the myth of journalistic revelation of truth, in which the journalist, acting as "little David," punctures the "the official veil of secrecy" and, in the heightened dramaturgy of melodrama, brings Goliath—monolithic government—to its knees.[17] Epstein believes that such a journalistic mythos conceals the actual relations of the process of revealing truth—a process in which the journalist, removed by at least one step from the context in which an actual event occurred, can best function honestly as a conduit for the release of information to publics.

With this debate unsettled regarding both the definition of news and the proper role of journalistic practice in the conduct of human affairs, many of the activities of the television-newsgathering apparatus unfortunately become all too easily defensible.

Journalistic practice is significantly more complex than the tale of the "news hound" hot on the trail of a breaking scandal, although taken in by the contemporary mythology of the embattled star reporter seeking to blast through walls of government deception, duplicity, and euphemism, one might not recognize the competing pressures that delimit the journalistic endeavor. The reporter, whether in print or broadcast media, is first of all institutionalized by the very fact that he or she is hired to report for a particular organization and by subordination to the needs of that organization as determined by the decisions of editors who assign the reporter stories and particular beats and thus determine at the outset the very nature of the relationship of the reporter to the subject matter. Many reporters, especially those in electronic media, have little or no special knowledge of their subject, which insures that coverage will be limited to information from press handouts and interviewees and that reporters will not seriously challenge sources' accounts. Of course, the reporter can grow into the beat over time. On the other hand, the ambitious young reporter is trying to make a name for himself or herself—to climb the ladder of achievement, success, and public recognition.

In the struggle that ensues between the journalistic organization, whose survival instinct tells it to avoid major conflict with other powerful institutions, especially the executive branch of the federal government (which controls access to privileged information) and large corporations (actual or potential advertisers), and the reporter, who seeks a privileged and lucrative position in the status hierarchy of journalism professionals, the organization often reaches a position of wary tolerance of the superstar, superego investigative or adversarial journalist who will produce the Pulitzer Prize–winning or Columbia-Dupont Award–winning exposé of corruption. The prize is, of course, subsequently appropriated by the institution, which uses it as a mantle of prestige and respectability.

TELEVISION NEWS AND MYTH

The television medium is ideally suited to the transmission of the mythic world of news. Its combination of simplified press, which fulfills needs for rudimentary political and economic information (e.g., how much the viewer can expect to pay for a loaf of bread, given the current international monetary crisis); the photograph, which presents the world of the community, the family, and personal life to the literate and the nonliterate alike; and the motion picture, which satisfies the need for curiosity and entertainment, establishes a readily accessible and understandable (and ultimately a palatable) context for the unfolding of our contemporary social debates and struggles.[18]

In television journalism more than in print journalism, the symbol of truth often becomes the image of the journalist—the aggressive investigator or advocate willing to challenge authority—rather than the story itself. Style tends to predominate over content and context. The defender of the public's right to know satisfies the medium's insatiable demand for melodramatic personae who clearly and simplistically represent the just cause. These journalist-heroes allow viewers vicariously to question the unapproachable bureaucrat and the arrogant general and to witness their upbraiding. The journalist, like Odysseus, is an epic wanderer traversing the globe, condemned to wandering and facing continual tests of his or her ability to outwit the dangerous adversary. With the divine intervention of technology—the live satellite feed—the journalist electronically returns home to restore a semblance of order to the kingdom. The television audience revels in the myth of the individual in news, manifested in the symbology of the reporter as "independent spirit," unafraid to take on the powerful on their own turf.

The mise-en-scène of the journalistic quest reveals first the reporter, standing alone in front of a backdrop, such as the immobile, ponderous architecture of the government building signifying stasis and impenetrability (or why would the reporter be standing outside?). The reporter then moves inside to the office of the interviewee, with its bookshelves lined with innumerable specialized reports that obviously were written to obfuscate the clear and simple truth the reporter, and the viewer, are seeking. The reporter has now pierced the veil of secrecy, like Superman, who can see the enemy through concrete walls, and has brought us all closer to the correct solution to the investigative problem. At this point the reporter is "living the myth" as Tom Wolfe once said regarding his own status as star journalist.

One of the major characteristics of the myth of the individual in television news is that heroes are more efficient than villains. The individual hero-correspondent, who has used craftiness and wit to outsmart the institution and penetrate the institutional barriers that hide the conspiracy or deception, next traps the reluctant interviewee into ostensible admissions of culpability or into internal contradictions in his or her answers. If the source refuses to appear on camera, the journalist may implicate the institution in an implied cover-up, berating the institution for its sphinxlike failure to cooperate with the legitimate investigation. To underscore this point, a picture of the institution's imposing headquarters—

the physical and intellectual barrier to the truth—may frame the shot. This aggressive journalistic dance, extended to its extreme, features, in the words of critic Michael Arlen, the correspondent as "prosecutor" in a courtroom-style melodrama. Arlen described a CBS *60 Minutes* investigation of corruption in Wyoming as an example of the myth at work.[19] Arlen saw television news and especially the news magazine, of which *60 Minutes* is the most successful and critically acclaimed representative, as succumbing to the mystique of "the thrill of the chase," with the interview subjects serving as "quarry." The *60 Minutes* correspondents were increasingly drawn into "prosecutorial scenarios" in the 1970s, in which the reporter personified "judgmental righteousness." Here we find aggressive correspondents in search of a story upon which a clear-cut moral judgment can be passed. What becomes important in this realm of prosecutorial journalism is "the *appearance* of a story: the dramatic texture of televised confrontation."[20] By using a technique in which allegations of misconduct are framed as dramatic questions, *60 Minutes* reporter Dan Rather was able to "prove" that everyone, from the Rock Springs, Wyoming, police chief to the state's governor "knew about" prostitution in the energy boomtown (and by implication were "guilty" of condoning prostitution). Rather then attempted to demonstrate how the governor of Wyoming might be linked to organized crime. As it turned out, Rather relied on a questionable source for evidence to support this allegation (Rather set the source up as "a superb investigator"). However, in Arlen's subsequent investigation of the Wyoming reports, "facts" turned out to be "inaccurate, or incompletely presented or ambiguous."[21] The news-gathering process was paramount here. As Rather's inquisitorial style convinced the viewer that he was on top of the story, his findings must be correct. The efficient, provocative interrogation of sources became the key element of the story—what Arlen termed "the seductive flow of the news-gathering drama."[22]

In another television-news context—the evening news report—the myth of the individual, of the larger-than-life journalist-hero, is further established in the persona of the anchorperson. The networks' public-relations campaigns promoting their anchorpersons project an image of the anchor as nearly omniscient and omnipresent. Frank Reynolds was touted by ABC as "uniquely qualified to bring you the world"—Reynolds clearly operated on a plane considerably above that of the traditional news reader or the contemporary print journalist, at least in the world of public relations.

In American television the news anchor, through his or her introductions to every story in the newscast, assumes a central role in all stories, usurping authority from the correspondent in the field. The anchor will go on location for the big story, e.g., Operation Desert Storm, or a U.S.–Russian summit meeting, or a natural disaster such as Hurricane Andrew, further relegating the correspondent to a minor position in the news operation by implication that the correspondent is not qualified to do the really big stories. The anchor is the presence that connects the newscast, the voice that orders the chaos of the everyday world. The anchor is the mystical loner of the myth of the individual, standing outside the group of correspondents, sources, and viewers. Secure in the magical atmosphere of the television studio, the anchor diligently observes the world outside from this lofty vantage point. The news anchor does more than read us the news; he guides us through the world as his news organization has defined it that day. In the presentation of news, Raymond Williams noted, the anchorperson presents "a studied informality" with less emphasis on reading a script (a formal gesture) and more emphasis on "personal presentation" via eye contact through a teleprompter.[23] The personal gaze becomes the anchor's heroic signature as he confronts the world of danger and mystery. We live vicariously through his journey. Anchors become "arbiters of correct reactions to the news."[24] The anchor is detached one moment, skeptical, amused, folksy, or self-righteously indignant the next. After we are led through this range of emotional reactions to the world, we reach our final destination—the newscast's end, the drama's epilogue. The anchor-hero's sign-off provides closure. Walter Cronkite's famous "And that's the way it is" offered a note of finality and self-assurance, a sign that the anchor is still in control. In a nonnewscast context, Edward R. Murrow's famous "good night, and good luck" sign-off injected a more open-ended and cautious response to his world. His hero-character was not so self-assured as today's electronic journalists, perhaps because Murrow sensed, correctly, that the world of everyday experience was ultimately beyond the control of the journalistic apparatus. Murrow was the strong, worldly-wise, tired hero of the traditional epic, not today's corporate hero for whom efficiency would always overcome ambiguity.

The anchor's sign-off leads us to a discussion of another myth revealed in the television-news presentation—the myth of the Protestant ethic—for the sign-off not only works to consolidate the anchor's position of power and control over news; it also leaves the viewer with the "illusion of hard work accomplished."[25] Reporters and news anchors must believe in this myth by the very nature of their occupations. Just as their work is to order a world of dangerous events and personal confrontations, so too is the "work" of their news subjects celebrated in stories with themes such as "putting their lives back together after the disaster" or "returning to normal after the aborted coup d'état" or "mother works two jobs to put her sons through college so they can have a better life than she." Work is rarely viewed for what it is in our society—by and large, an alienating experience to many unskilled or semiskilled laborers, and increasingly to the white-collar proletariat—the clerical-information workers of the computer age. Rather, work is presented as evidence of the human will to overcome hardship and make a better life—a distinctly middle-class vision of the world. The stories are framed as highly individualized accounts of survival symbolic of the human condition and are therefore cut off from their more concrete and powerful social and ideological contexts. Rarely do we get an adequate exploration or analysis of the increased suscepti- bility of the lower socioeconomic classes to physical danger in the work- place or in inadequate housing, unsafe transportation to and from work, or lack of sufficient police protection outside the work environment—or of their desertion by the educational apparatus that teaches them at best how to cope in the technological world, while "streaming" them to ensure their marginal status in that world. On television news generally, the suc- cess of those who have escaped these conditions through hard work is celebrated, while the basic structure of oppression is largely ignored.

The illusion of hard work is reinforced in the presentational elements of the newscasts themselves. In many newscasts, both local and national (e.g., the old CBS/Cronkite set and the *ABC World News Tonight* set), the working newsroom becomes the backdrop for the report. In the back- ground of the establishing shots, we see people moving about, preparing the news. Many local newscasts present the newsroom as an exciting place where the viewer is taken for a sneak preview of upcoming stories. Weath- erpersons are seen fiddling with weather computers, the high-tech ma- chinery reinforcing the presenter's status as a hard-working expert in charge of the machinery. Anchors about to go on the air are busy at work preparing copy, jackets removed, shirtsleeves rolled up (the video equiv- alent of the green eyeshade).

The calculated presentation of the journalist as a hard worker, a direct formatting change designed to counter the critical outrage over "happy- talk" and "tabloid" news, should not be taken as a total ruse; many jour- nalists do work very hard. The issue is one of the nature of the work itself. With all that hard work done, why are television newscasts generally so stylized and devoid of cognitive substance?

A classic spoof of the working newsroom was mounted by the Los An- geles Metromedia independent-television-station KTTV in the mid-1970s. Titled *Metronews, Metronews,* the half-hour "newscast" featured two informal anchors—one in an army fatigue shirt, the other in a tie and rumpled white shirt with sleeves rolled up—who wisecracked their way through the day's events in a mock-tabloid style using what appeared to be parodies of soft news features (one was never certain just how seriously the show took itself). The show's coup was its newsroom setting, which looked like a real, although extremely low-tech, newsroom complete with a water cooler, file cabinets, old desks, teletype machines, and messages scrawled on slips of paper and tacked up here and there. *Metronews, Me- tronews* clearly confronted, through its style, the show-business world of the legitimate newscast. The informality of the *Metronews* anchors, who were *really* happy (and who seemed to border on being stoned), pointed to the contrived happy informality of "happy-talk" local news. The telephone to the newsroom (a standard set piece in a "real" newscast), into which one of the *Metronews* anchors was seen talking as we returned from a commercial break, was dead. "Nobody there," he exclaimed as he hung up.

The reward for the journalist's hard work is a combination of prestige and significant pecuniary compensation. At the highest levels of contemporary electronic journalism, the network news anchors, this reward is substantial. In television's early days, salaries were good, but not mind-boggling. In 1948, NBC paid John Cameron Swayze $25,000 a year to read the news on the nightly *Camel News Caravan*, a 15-minute newscast, while CBS paid Douglas Edwards $30,000 for his nightly news program. In contrast, in 1983, according to CBS's *60 Minutes*, ABC paid its anchor Peter Jennings about $1 million; NBC paid anchor Tom Brokaw $1.7 million; and CBS paid Dan Rather, the ratings leader in the competition at that time, $2.2 million—some 73 times as much as fellow CBSer Douglas Edwards had earned some 35 years earlier.[26] Rather had jumped from a $300,000 annual salary on *60 Minutes* in 1978. The Rather deal, negotiated by his powerful agent, Richard Leibner of N. S. Bienstock, Inc., was a ten-year contract worth $22 million, making Rather more like a Hollywood star or a super athlete than a journalist. Leibner renegotiated Rather's contract in 1985 to bring Rather's salary to more than $3.5 million a year by 1990.[27]

Rather's enormous salary increase was symptomatic of the atmosphere pervading the "old" networks in the late 1970s and early 1980s, before their acquisition by the new owners and their worsening financial climate brought on by intense competition from cable and independent broadcast stations. The bidding wars began in earnest in 1977 when Roone Arledge, president of ABC Sports, was given a mandate from his network to infuse life into the moribund ABC News operation. According to critic Ben Yagoda, "He did so by instituting the network equivalent of baseball free agency."[28] Arledge began the era of talent raids at the other networks. CBS at that time had a "second tier" of talented reporters who saw little room to move up in that news organization. Leibner noted that these reporters had no "first refusal clause" in their contracts, which would have given CBS the option to retain their services. The reporters were therefore free to move to other network news operations. Many of them did. The powerful Leibner, who negotiated many of their new contracts, could "play network against network" to get them top dollar.[29]

Even given the "new" networks' tough fiscal management policies in the late 1980s, star reporters could still command large salaries. In 1989, Leibner helped Diane Sawyer get $1.6 million a year to leave CBS's *60 Minutes* and join ABC to cohost *Primetime Live* with Sam Donaldson.[30]

After the Sawyer deal, however, the new austerity programs at the networks produced "take-it-or-leave-it" offers for most reporters.[31]

Bill Leonard, president of CBS News from 1979 to 1982, does not believe the network anchors are overpaid. However, a problem not related to money has arisen in these megacontracts, according to Leonard, who argues that the "deals for anchorpeople . . . gave them excessive authority and upset the balance of how the news was properly managed."[32]

CBS's Rather, NBC's Brokaw, and ABC's Jennings all say they take an active role in their nightly newscasts. Brokaw, the "managing editor" of the *NBC Nightly News,* works with the program's executive producer to construct the newscast and writes, he says, about 60 percent of the program; but, he noted, "It's not a big deal, . . . it's mostly lead-ins to the correspondents." Jennings, ABC *World News Tonight*'s "senior editor," says he has "an editorial presence." He helps determine the day's news coverage with his executive producer, and he writes the beginning and end of the broadcast and edits introductions to stories prepared by news-staff writers in New York.[33] These are most likely understatements of the anchors' actual influence over their news operations, for they all assume major decision-making roles in determining each night's news lineup. It is impossible, however, to determine which news executives—the news division presidents, the nightly news executive producers, or the anchor/managing editors—are ultimately responsible for the increased infusion of entertainment values in these news programs. In all likelihood, given the nature of organizational cultures generally, all bear some individual responsibility. They certainly bear collective responsibility.

In this world of megasalaries and prestige, there always exists a possibility that the network electronic journalist-superstar will lose touch with "the people" as he or she spends the preponderant amount of working, and in many cases socializing, hours with top nationaland foreign-government officials. "The people," described by Brokaw as a "large mass, looking at us in a distracted way,"[34] are the target audience for both network and local evening-news programs. Audience studies have repeatedly found network and local news viewers to be below the national average educational level and generally older. The network news image makers, most likely unconsciously, work hard to project an atmosphere that is pure upscale suburban middle landscape—the mental landscape in which the majority of newspersons themselves dwell. Network reporters and anchors appear as highly successful, self-important personages, taking themselves very seriously. This image building does, however, serve a useful purpose in the larger world of network-affiliate relations, for the rarified ambience of the national news, which exudes "responsibility," compensates for the tent-show atmosphere of so much local news, which gathers higher ratings than serious news but runs the risk of alienating government regulators. Local news generates audience carryover for the network news that follows. What is therefore of primary importance is getting the "average Joe" to turn on the set for the fires, rapes, and murders, then keep him watching while the serious world events are presented in a truncated, easily digestible form by the serious news people. The affiliates have made money and have kept the Federal Communications Commission off their case, the people have been entertained, and the networks have secured their carryover into their prime-time shows.

The suburban middle landscape in network news is reflected in news values, dress, and presentational codes. This landscape is presented in news not as a geographic place (the suburb is exceedingly difficult to locate geographically any more), but as a state of mind to which an appearance is correlated. Most of the spokespersons, both journalists and sources, seem to come from this place irrespective of their personal life histories or the nature of the story being reported. Their dress and their mannerisms point, above all, to their "belonging."

Values-and-lifestyles research would classify the successful news anchor, male or female, as part "achiever"—a prosperous, middle-aged materialist—and part "belonger"—a patriotic, traditional, and stable person generally quite happy with his or her life. Critic Edwin Diamond provided his own version of the "anchor model": "middle-aged, mid-American, white males, . . . the men the old Life magazine used to refer to as the 'command generation.' "[35] They look and sound authoritative, but not authoritarian— the Walter Cronkite persona. Edward R. Murrow was too authoritative, too intense for the night-after-night presence of news anchoring, but his intensity was ideal for the clear focus and closure of documentary work. The anchors write and report well, but not too well; otherwise they sound erudite and are relegated to providing commentary (e.g., the late Eric Severeid and Bill Moyers). They are not too young, not too old (ABC's Peter Jennings spent four years as ABC anchor in the mid-1960s, but was too young to command the necessary presence; ten years later, in 1978, now more mature, he returned to the anchor desk at ABC in their triple-anchor format, and in 1983 he took sole possession of ABC's anchor). They are good looking, but not too handsome. They are, above all, loyal to the corporation. And they have an "unceasing drive to win."[36] As CBS anchor Dan Rather said while being interviewed for a 60 Minutes segment on network-television news anchors, part of his desire to be a network anchorperson was "to run something on your own." This entrepreneurial spirit is a prerequisite for the successful anchor, who is clearly now a corporate person, but one who also maintains his individual pride and the sense of skepticism that got him to this point in his career as a serious professional. He knows the limits to which he can bend the corporate apparatus and still maintain his professional integrity and personal status.

This perfect combination of fierce competitive drive, good looks, cool controlled informality, and substantial talent, which is nonetheless unthreatening to one's associates, is rare, and makes the ideal anchor a valuable corporate commodity. Sociologist Orrin Klapp classified this classic American-hero character type as the "group servant"—a defender of the dominant order who, through tireless work, rights wrongs, and saves the weak from the strong. This hero is what Klapp terms a "compensatory type," helping people put up with a reality different from the ideal.[37] The television anchor, while he or she may not actually accomplish such feats, gives the appearance of such accomplishment. Compensation is particularly relevant, given the context of news, which so often presents to the viewer a vision of the urban frontier, which is, according to critic Tony Schwartz, "almost unbelievably dominated by film of burning buildings and smoke-blackened firemen; stretchers being loaded into ambulances and tight-lipped detectives pacing around cordoned-off crime scenes."[38] The same images are also prevalent in national and international news coverage as minor wars pop up all over the globe and American military forces and news correspondents are shipped off to become involved.

No longer the youthful independent spirit—the lone individual doing battle with the unyielding institution—but still personifying the myth of the individual in large measure, standing above the fray, guiding our view of the world, and teaching us how to react, the mature anchor now must also play a role of reasonable arbiter of reality for millions of Americans; he must be strong and fair, decisive and warm. Above all, he must be trusted by tens of millions of average people. Dan Rather's warm, middle-class gentility is reminiscent of Steve Douglas, Ozzie Nelson, and Ward Cleaver, three famous denizens of television's suburban middle landscape. But Dan didn't exude such an aura until the sweater; before the sweater, we knew Dan as the tough White House correspondent who directly challenged Richard Nixon during the famous press conferences surrounding Watergate and as the conscientious, aggressive interrogator of 60 Minutes. His image for millions of viewers was cool if not cold—a bit too hard-edged for the nightly exposure as news anchor. The sweater, a V-neck pullover, gave him, in the words of Washington Post critic Tom Shales, the "trust-me, you've-got-a-friend, hello-out-there-in-television-land sense."[39] The CBS Evening News with Dan Rather, which had lost much of its substantial ratings lead over NBC and ABC since Rather took over for the avuncular Cronkite in March 1981, surged ahead once again, regaining Cronkite's commanding lead. (By the early 1990s, ABC had assumed the ratings lead, and, wrote Ken Auletta, "claimed the mantle of respect once proudly worn by CBS News."[40] CBS responded in the summer of 1993 by initiating a co-anchor team on its evening news broadcast as Connie Chung joined Rather.) Was the sweater a tremendous public relations coup? Not to hear Rather tell the story, a story right out of Leave It to Beaver. It appears he had a cold in early winter and wore his V-neck sweater, which his wife had given him 11 years before, around the office. One night he kept it on for the newscast and his wife said it looked great on the air. The rest is history. What made the sweater so vital to Rather's image? One CBS executive hypothesized to Shales that Rather's handsomeness and perfection were putting some viewers off, making people feel inadequate by comparison. Rather, it is reported, went out and bought three new sleeveless sweaters and two long-sleeve sweaters, "off the rack."

The stories that reinforce this image of warm middle-class gentility are those that deal with culture and civility and act to set straight once again the world of bad news and human degradation. We see this clearly manifested in the lifestyle reports of CBS Sunday Morning with Charles Kuralt and occasionally on the tail end of the nightly newscast. PBS's entry into the competition, The MacNeil/Lehrer News Hour, adopted Kuralt's video-postcard motif as well as the "trip-to-the-art-gallery" report. The world of arts reportage, showing aficionados attending mainstream galleries or blockbuster museum retrospectives such as the 1992 Matisse exhibit at New York's Museum of Modern Art, serves to reinforce the power of corporate patronage under the illusion of democratic access to culture. As critic John Berger wrote,

The majority of the population do not visit art museums. . . . [They] take it as axiomatic that the museums are full of holy relics which refer to a mystery which excludes them . . . that original masterpieces belong to the preserve (both materially and spiritually) of the rich.[41]

What is set straight in the world of news and of suburban-middle-landscape culture is the dominance of the corporate elite.

There can be little doubt that the news is a middle-class corporate venture. As critic George Comstock noted:

News and public affairs programming, unlike entertainment, are the products of the disseminators. . . . The daily selection and treatment of events are the responsibility of the news staff. These decisions are made autonomously of management. Yet news cannot escape the values of management, which reside in popularity. Journalists may manufacture the news, but management manufactures the newsmen and their tools. Formats and personnel are the creatures of management, as is the budget to do the job. Thus news, like entertainment, becomes honed to the exigencies of competition.[42]

When we involve management, the critique of news must include not only matters of style but also related matters of technique, for management, not willing to trust its aesthetic or gut feel, and not prone to bold experimentation, turns to the modern-day management tools—viewer surveys and news consultants—to generate information about news presentation. Not even the sacrosanct anchor is spared such quantitative, detached scrutiny. From the use of data on what viewers want to see as their news, it is a small step to the concept of news packaging—the employment of rigid formulas to structure and order the presentation of each day's messy world according to some notion of audience acceptability.

Technique operates on many levels in television news. As a manifestation of the myth of eternal progress—of a technically sophisticated America in charge of her destiny—technique is most clearly visible in an ostensibly neutral technological context, represented by the progress of computer graphics on local weather (which lends an aura of authority to the performance of the weatherperson via an association with sophisticated machinery); live minicam reports from the field on breaking stories; computer-generated reports on battle tactics (continual graphics displays during the 1991 Persian Gulf War drew viewers into a real-life version of the video game); the incredible tumbling graphic inserts, used in many local news openings, designed to give the newscast a modern look as well as to further reinforce the notion of news control of a chaotic world, as the tumbling insert comes to rest and the anchor begins; and the promotional bumpers before the commercials—graphics that provide teasers for upcoming stories. Viewers have generally reacted very favorably to such technological wizardry in news presentation, saying that these technical effects enliven the show, making it more interesting to watch. This, of course, would be expected, given the atmosphere of entertainment that pervades today's daily news broadcasts.

Technique moves beyond simple fascinating electronic blips and live reports from Baghdad. The "human technique" of which Jacques Ellul has written is manifested in the pseudoscientism of war reportage, as war becomes body counts; of politics, as issues become poll results; and of economics, as the economy becomes indexes and graphs. The network newspersons try their best to balance numbers with stories about individuals who are included in those numbers. This "personal touch" obscures what is lost in the antinomy of data and living beings, namely, the intelligent discussion of social structures as the ground for a particular type of social relations. The world of data-as-news is a world of "unassimilated facts"[43]—of "scenes," as Michael Arlen once described television generally. Closure in this world is related more to formal dramaturgical structures and correspondingly less to conceptualization. Each story, especially if it deals in relatively difficult abstractions, must be closed that night and filed away to be discussed again at some future time. Exceptions to this type of closure are voyeuristic journeys into the violence of war and terrorism, sex crimes, murder trials, and death-row watches, coverage of which continues in a serial format until the stories reach their conclusions.

Most local newscasts use technique in their story ordering within the news hole. It is predictable and, to the viewer, comfortable. The news generally moves from a description of the grave events of the day (fires, murders, rapes, sex scandals, auto accidents, natural disasters, and acts of terrorism are grist for the local news headlines whether they are local or not) to the description of more mundane matters. To these events, which often directly affect our daily lives, few of us pay much attention because they are buried in the middle of the news, they lack exciting visuals, and they often involve conceptually complex issues—matters such as the reduction of city services due to budget cuts necessitated by a shortfall in projected tax revenue. Finally comes the human-interest wrap story, from the pathos of the "Our Block" motif, which often features hapless people, such as elderly citizens in a blighted urban ghetto, who are struggling to hold their lives together—the will-to-survive theme that tugs at so many middle-class and working-class heartstrings—to the contrived humor of "the story about the man with a winged cat."

Technique operates behind the scenes in television news as well, most notably in the activities of the audience survey and the regimes of the news consultants. Here is where most of the damage is done, out of sight of viewers and critics. As discussed in detail in chapter 2, networks use Q-ratings developed by market researchers to rate newspersons and other television personalities according to a viewer's positive response to a performer's personality. According to the Q-ratings, CBS anchor Dan Rather was found to be almost as warm, compassionate, and honest as Walter Cronkite (although not warm enough until the sweater), while Rather's major competition for the CBS anchor position, savvy veteran Washington correspondent Roger Mudd, scored "cold" in comparison. CBS executives denied that the Q-ratings played a role in their anchor decision.

Local news operations have increasingly relied on news consultants such as Frank N. Magid Associates and McHugh and Hoffman (the major competitors for consultancy supremacy in television news) to help them find ways to improve their news presentation. McHugh and Hoffman is generally credited with developing the lurid tabloid-news format featuring large doses of sex, violence, and corruption coverage, which transformed San Francisco station KGO from a loser to a striking news success in a very short time. Other news operations followed suit and San Francisco went from a city whose local news operations were nationally respected to the site of the nightly peep show. Generally, the formula for news success, the consultants determined, was reduction of the maximum story length to 90 seconds, regardless of the story's inherent news value and relative importance to the community, and an attractive newsreader.[44] The revolving-door approach to news talent resulted, as Kansas City anchorwoman Christine Craft of KMBZ discovered to her dismay and anger in 1981 when she was demoted from anchor to reporter because she was not pretty enough and not deferential to her male colleagues. Ms. Craft sued the station and was awarded damages in a jury trial.

News consultants poll viewers and tailor the news and the news personalities to fit viewers' desires. They fine-tune their clients' image through the use of technique. They are paid handsomely. Their clients, on the whole, realize increased profitability by following their advice.

As Jacques Ellul wrote, "Technique . . . clarifies, arranges, and rationalizes. . . . It is efficient and brings efficiency to everything."[45] Certainly television news is no exception. Here all is order, efficiency, and comfort as the familiar persona of the anchorperson night after night, aided by slick technical visualization and easily understood symbology, conjures up scenes of events from far and near via satellites, helicopters, microwave dishes, and minicams and entertains us while providing the barest hint of the day's happenings. That, after all, is what we have come to expect and what we have told the television news consultants we want.

THE CLASH OF MYTHS IN TELEVISION NEWS

Beneath the smooth exterior of the television-news presentation are hints of the real conflicts that exist in contemporary social relations but seem somehow to escape the watchful eye of the video camera and reporter. They are there nonetheless and can be discovered through an analysis of the complex clash of myths that subtly pervades television-news content, despite institutional attempts to present a world of clear-cut antagonisms dependent for their resolutions on the force and power of the dominant culture.

As soon as television journalists announce their professional status, namely, their "objectivity," we discover perhaps the most basic clash of myths in television news. As critic William Henry III wrote, "American TV news, like the rest of American journalism, is scrupulously 'objective'—which means it does not challenge the prevailing biases of a predominantly white, Judeo-Christian, imperial, internationalist, capitalist society."[46]

Objectivity, which many journalists prefer to define as overall fairness and balance in presenting various positions in a controversy of immediate concern to a community or the nation and an openness to correction, is in reality a subterfuge that conceals presentational inequities favoring the dominant cultural position in almost all arguments. This is most clearly evident in the clash of the myths of the suburban middle landscape and the urban frontier as represented in social conflict. Critic Jeff Greenfield described the atmosphere in which these two myths collided as television news was forced to deal with the social unrest of the 1960s:

A largely unwilling participant, . . . the medium was communicating events over which *it had little or no control*—against its clear institutional interests. . . . The cultural upheaval of fashion and taste—rooted in the power of rock-and-roll music—was an upheaval ignored on the national airwaves until its presence was un-avoidable.[47] (italics mine)

Rock and roll, political assassinations, burning cities, police brutality, and violent demonstrations on college campuses and at a national political convention—all these powerful symbolic images were manifestations of the urban frontier. The news was certainly incongruous in the context of reassurance of the suburban-middle-landscape television comedy so popular during the early years of the decade and of the rural-middle-landscape comedies of childlike escapism of the middle and late years of that same decade. Newscasts and live coverage of news events could thus easily be considered by viewers to be distorted because the predominant television-entertainment frames showed a much less troubled world. One can argue with Greenfield's conclusion that television had "little or no control" over the events it was communicating. The television-news apparatus attempted to draw clear ideological lines between legitimate authority and anarchic protest. The voice of legitimate authority was heard resonating in the suburban middle landscape in the form of "reasoned responses of the arranged studio discussion," which had greater persuasive power than "unreasoned, merely demonstrative, responses" of street confrontations.[48]

The oppositional elements who were forced to resort to protest demonstrations to make their points publicly took to the streets in the urban frontier. These political "happenings" often became violent, and the film crews provided millions of viewers with powerful scenes of the conflict shot mostly from behind police lines. The point of view the images revealed showed us an unruly mob in the urban frontier. Young people wore clown makeup, army fatigue shirts, and torn blue jeans. Some draped themselves in American flags. They threw rocks, bottles, and human feces at law-enforcement agents. When scenes of violent confrontation were presented, they provoked charges from news critics, such as Vice President Spiro Agnew, that the television networks advocated radical change in society. On the contrary, as Edward Epstein pointed out, this bias toward change was "not ideologically motivated but an inevitable outcome of the search for a mass audience" through the construction of "highly simplified melodramas, built around conflict, and illustrated with visual action."[49] Clearly Epstein is closer to the truth in this debate, but he discounts the strong pull of the network news apparatus to balance coverage to the point that order inevitably predominates. Walter Cronkite's liberal indignation at the thug tactics used by Chicago Mayor Richard Daley's police against CBS news correspondents (among them Dan Rather, who covered the 1968 Democratic National Convention) was clearly substantively motivated rather than some search for a mass audience. Cronkite's remarks set up a clear-cut conflict of ideas; yet it was quickly followed by Cronkite's invitation to the Chicago mayor to appear in the CBS anchor booth at the convention hall to respond. Cronkite, the voice of reason, had backed down. The CBS news organization appeared to be apologizing, both to the mayor and to the American people, for Cronkite's justifiably passionate condemnation of the suppression of journalistic activity the night before. Daley appeared calm and authoritative. Everything was civilized. The confrontation was defused and the antiwar demonstrators protesting in front of the Conrad Hilton Hotel—the convention headquarters hotel—appeared by contrast to be overreacting. Cronkite's attempt at fairness and balance in the end confused the entire issue. As the protesters shouted that "the whole world is watching," the television news frames were pro–law and order. By emphasizing law-enforcement activities during the 1965 urban riots in Watts, and again in its coverage of the 1967 and 1968 riots in Detroit, Newark, Washington, D.C., and other cities and by stressing interviews—many with whites in black neighborhoods—television news deflected substantive matters of blacks' "underlying grievances and tensions" and thereby failed to present a meaningful sociohistorical context for these confrontations.[50]

The myths of the individual and the Protestant ethic lead the television newsperson ever closer to the status system that contains the politician. The ultimate fusion of journalism and politics comes at times like 1968, when the journalist whose reasoned voice seemed to rise above political demagoguery was touted as a potential presidential nominee: Walter Cronkite, the "most trusted man in America," seemed capable of running the country. Indeed, on his February 27, 1968, news special, Cronkite declared that the Vietnam War was "a bloody stalemate" and that the only "rational way out" was to negotiate a settlement "not as victors but as an honorable people." Cronkite indeed sounded more like a true leader than the politicians we had elected to that position.

Regardless of the journalist's sympathy with the cause of the underdog and tendency toward the more liberal political stance, the status world of the hard-working achiever/belonger is far removed from the dirty nonstatus world of street demonstrations. The urban frontier provides visual fuel for the nightly news report. The fire is put out by the boys from the suburban middle landscape. The technique embodied in the slick package and the instant report—the myth of eternal progress—reassures the viewer that the "radical messiness of reality" is under control.[51]

The myth of the individual as it operates in television news contains subtle internal contradictions. The basic operating frame of the myth is clear: An individual meets an institution in a confrontation. The results are far more complicated and hinge on characterization. When the individual is a superstar journalist, the likely outcome is that the individual will emerge victorious. When the individual is the common man, the likely outcome is that the individual will be wronged by the institution and rendered seemingly helpless, but will be saved through the divine intervention of the journalist as moral defender of truth and justice (thus demonstrating that democracy works, i.e., that a free and unfettered press protects people from abuses of power). If the institution in question is government, the institution is likely portrayed as unresponsive, anonymous, bureaucratic, and inefficient—in short, the institution is at fault. If the institution is a giant corporation, the wrong done to the individual is blamed not on the capitalist institution itself, heartless greed, or corruption but rather on individual mismanagement. If the bad manager is fired or if a more effective management strategy is initiated, the wrong will disappear. It is little wonder that the hard-working aggressive star journalist would implicitly view the problem as one of managerial ineptitude rather than as one of basic systemic structural deficiency, for his or her success has depended in large measure on his or her corporateness—a basic belief in efficient management and the value of creative entrepreneurial solutions to human problems. Entrepreneurial flair and style will inevitably produce the better mousetrap and the better social solution; bureaucratic hesitation, bungling, and lack of imagination will produce failed social programs. Admittedly this antinomy is presented here in broad brush strokes, but it can be argued that such a frame operates in television news in the broadest sense, with notable exceptions now and then.

When things get so hot in the urban frontier that the men and women from the suburban middle landscape cannot provide reassurance that they are under control, the television-news apparatus may invoke one of its most powerful myths—the myth of the rural middle landscape—to deflect attention from the chaos. This version of the myth is "Waltonesque"— the strong mature rural citizen coping with the evil world crashing all around him by maintaining the purity of country values, including the sanctity of the extended family and the value of hard work not for achievement, but for a higher moral purpose. The rural middle landscape speaks to a moral victory. The eloquent poetics of Charles Kuralt's "On The Road" profiles of strong-willed, commonsensical country folks lent substantial credibility to the myth.

In contrast to the rural middle landscape, the urban frontier—when it is New York City—may lose morally; but its portrayal in television news assures us that it will at least win a cultural victory. The suburban-middle-landscape mind-set of the news professionals assures such victory by deflecting pressing questions of human degradation and social injustice in the name of the vibrancy of urban culture—the American melting-pot ideal that produces great authors from the slums. However, when the urban frontier is Los Angeles (the great television entertainment capital), it pales in comparison with the rural middle landscape both morally (it is portrayed as the "Hollywood Babylon"—the epitome of the self-centered egotism of the "me generation" of which Tom Wolfe wrote) and culturally (it is portrayed as inhabited by ostentatious kooks disguised as creative people; it has no urbanity in the New York sense, but rather, harbors Hollywood pretenders to the cultural throne of Broadway).

Network television news is a New York affair, with deference to the nation's political capital, for while the word *capital* denotes the seat of government, more to the point, its meaning is more clearly grounded in the value of accumulated goods, a major preoccupation of the corporate enterprise that guides the news division. Although the roots of many of the anchors and correspondents are in southern or midwestern culture, those places have become merely origins from which occasionally a strong sense of morality will well up in condemnation of a generally uncivilized world. The world in which these people now live and work is a far remove from those roots. It is a world of intense personal and organizational competition, achievement, success, public prestige, and corporate control.

THE TALKING HEADS (NOT THE ROCK GROUP)

For viewers desiring a peek into the corridors of political power inside the Beltway, network television has for decades offered the Sunday morning public-affairs talk programs during what critics referred to as "television's news ghetto"—a comment aimed at the general dearth of such programming throughout the remainder of the networks' schedules. NBC's *Meet the Press*, the networks' longest-running program, premiered in 1947 after having been introduced on radio in 1945. CBS followed with *Face the Nation* in 1954 (with Senator Joseph McCarthy as the guest on the premiere program). ABC's *Issues and Answers*, which began in 1960, was replaced by *This Week with David Brinkley* in 1981. Brinkley joined ABC after 38 years with NBC News. By 1990, Brinkley's hour-long program was attracting an audience of about 3.6 million viewers, compared to *Face the Nation*'s 3 million, and *Meet the Press*'s 2.6 million.[52] The latter two programs were then half an hour in length; *Meet the Press* expanded to an hour-long format in the early 1990s.

By the end of the 1980s, "Sunday morning news ghetto" was no longer an apt descriptor of this program form. "Political talk" on television had expanded to all hours of the day and night, throughout the week, in a variety of formats on both broadcast and cable channels.

ABC News Nightline, which premiered in March 1980 as a regular late-night public affairs discussion program, actually began in November 1979 as a special news program titled *The Iran Crisis: America Held Hostage*. Originally hosted by Frank Reynolds, an anchor on ABC's evening newscast, *The Iran Crisis* followed developments in the aftermath of the seizure of the American embassy in Tehran. In late November, ABC diplomatic correspondent Ted Koppel substituted for Reynolds and shortly thereafter took over as host. ABC News executives were pleasantly surprised that the special program, which aired opposite the first fifteen minutes of the *Tonight* Show on NBC (featuring Carson's monologue), was receiving good audience ratings and decided to make the program a permanent late-night entry. As the hostage crisis wore on and little breaking news emerged from Iran, *Nightline* began to shift its gaze to other subjects, usually focusing on a single topic. The program, like *This Week with David Brinkley,* opened with a short video backgrounder framing the topic and followed with an extended newsmaker interview (see chapter 11 for a discussion of one particularly provocative *Nightline* program dealing with Third World news coverage).

The *MacNeil/Lehrer Newshour,* which premiered on the PBS national program service in September 1983, began in 1975 as a half-hour weeknight news analysis program—*The Robert MacNeil Report*—aired locally in New York City. MacNeil, a former Canadian Broadcasting Corporation (CBC), BBC, NBC, and Reuters correspondent, was joined by Jim Lehrer, a reporter at a PBS station in Dallas, Texas, in 1976. The program was retitled *The MacNeil-Lehrer Report.* MacNeil was based in New York, Lehrer in Washington. Like *Nightline,* they focused on a single topic each night. Charlayne Hunter-Gault joined the program as a reporter in 1978, and former NBC newswoman Judy Woodruff came aboard in 1983, shortly before the program expanded to its present one-hour format and became nationally distributed. The *MacNeil/Lehrer Newshour* format begins with a brief summary of the day's news, usually featuring one or two videotaped reports, then moves to two or three discussion segments, ranging in length from 15 to 20 minutes each. A regular feature of the program is a short "political analysis" segment. There are periodic personal video "essays" by a variety of writers on politics, society, and culture.

While both *ABC News Nightline* and *The MacNeil/Lehrer Newshour* have been praised by many critics as providing "in-depth, objective analysis," others are not as sanguine. One study commissioned by Fairness and Accuracy In Reporting (FAIR), for example, analyzed 865 episodes of *Nightline* aired between January 1, 1985, and April 30, 1988, and concluded that "minorities, women and those with challenging views are generally excluded" from appearances on the program in favor of "white male elite representative of the status quo." (The *Nightline* episode described in chapter 11 is clearly an exception to this finding.) The report argued that "Plainly stated, 'Nightline' presents a picture of the world which is startlingly similar to that presented by the U.S. Government."[53] In a separate study FAIR reaches the same conclusions about *The MacNeil/Lehrer Newshour,* which MacNeil disputes.

Richard Kaplan, *Nightline's* executive producer, agreed with some of the FAIR study's findings, particularly that the program should include more points of view "not represented by officials we elect. We need to bring opposing domestic viewpoints." But Kaplan added that he believed the FAIR study was flawed in assuming *Nightline* should function as an "Op Ed Page." He submitted that *Nightline* was in fact a news program and could not "degenerate into a polemicists' forum." In the same breath, however, he added, "When you have a conservative government elected by the people of this country, as a news broadcast that's what we have to deal with."[54]

Kaplan's rather fluid conception of "polemicists" belies the ideological ground upon which *Nightline* stands. His defense of the guests and subjects *Nightline* selects reads like the argument extolling the signalizing function of journalism. At the same time, one should not, however, deny host Ted Koppel's frequent pointed questioning of the establishment government officials who *do* generally hold the floor on *Nightline*.

Critic Walter Goodman sees a potential problem with these programs, namely that "office holders and politicians have learned to use these programs to promote themselves and their causes."[55] Goodman concludes that the three network Sunday morning public affairs discussion programs—and by extension *Nightline* and *The MacNeil/Lehrer Newshour*— "would gain from more venturesome guest-selection, a reaching-out beyond the corridors of power to introduce audiences to people who are thinking about large issues in less political, less mainstream ways."[56] (An example of one such effort, *A World of Ideas* with Bill Moyers, is discussed in chapter 10.)

Given their shortcomings, these news analysis programs are nonetheless far more balanced than programs such as *The McLaughlin Group*—a half-hour weekly news analysis program with a distinctively conservative ideology—which premiered on PBS in 1982 (the program was airing in NBC's Sunday morning lineup in the early 1990s). Created, produced, and moderated by John McLaughlin, a former Jesuit priest and Nixon speechwriter, the program features as regular guests conservative pundits Patrick Buchanan and Robert Novak. McLaughlin also hosts CNBC's *Mc-Laughlin*, a *Donahue*-style program with a studio audience.

According to critic Jacob Weisberg, *The McLaughlin Group* "became intertwined with the style of opinion journalism that is a hallmark of the political culture of the 1980s."[57] Weisberg calls McLaughlin "a political entertainer" whose fame has led to guest appearances on the *Tonight* show and the *Letterman* show, where he admitted that *The McLaughlin Group* was "its own postmodern self-parody."[58] McLaughlin was parodied on a Halloween episode of *Saturday Night Live* by Dana Carvey, who appeared as McLaughlin the devil, with a trident and a tail, only to be attacked by McLaughlin playing himself. He has also appeared as himself on *Cheers*.

While all this might be seen as "just good fun," the more insidious side of McLaughlin's act is not so humorous. A prime example is the story behind the rise of *The McLaughlin Group*, reported by Weisberg.

In the summer of 1986, the program, which was in its fourth year on PBS, was strapped for cash—a normal condition in public television in the United States. McLaughlin, whose wife Ann Dore McLaughlin was then an undersecretary of the Interior Department in the Reagan administration, decided to invite the President and Nancy Reagan to their house for a private dinner. To accomplish this, McLaughlin first invited actor Charlton Heston and his wife, long-time friends of the Reagans. Finally, having received a commitment from the Reagans, McLaughlin invited Jack Welch, the chief executive officer of General Electric (the new owner of the NBC television network), and his wife. According to Weisberg, McLaughlin "had been lobbying Welch for more than a year about sponsoring his televised shouting match, *The McLaughlin Group*."[59] The dinner was held, and Welch agreed to pay more than $1 million a year to make GE the sole sponsor of the program.

McLaughlin seems to have little interest in the ethics of journalistic practice, as is evident in one incident associated with his interview program *One on One*, which premiered in 1984. In 1986, McLaughlin went to Mexico to tape an interview with then-President Miguel de la Madrid. De la Madrid, who was under investigation for vote fraud at the time, was unhappy with some of the answers he had given during the interview, which was shot by a camera crew provided by the Mexican government. He released the edited interview to McLaughlin with those answers omitted. According to Weisberg, a *One on One* staffer suggested to McLaughlin that the broadcast begin with a statement that the interview had been edited by the Mexican government. McLaughlin became very angry at this suggestion and refused, denying that he had thereby "sacrificed editorial integrity."[60]

McLaughlin exemplifies what happens when news analysis slides into the dramaturgy of entertainment. In the quest for personal celebrity status and power, journalistic ideals are thrown to the wind.

Living in the same city, yet philosophically a world away from McLaughlin is Brian Lamb, founder and chief executive officer of the Cable Satellite Public Affairs Network (C-Span), the nation's round-the-clock window on the daily activities of its federal government. Lamb, a former naval aide in the Johnson White House and for three years an assistant to the Director of the Office of Telecommunications Policy (OTP) in the Nixon administration, was Washington bureau chief of *Cablevision* magazine in the mid-1970s when he conceived the idea of C-Span. His tenure at OTP convinced him of cable television's potential to deliver a niche service such as C-Span. C-Span went on the air in 1979.

Lamb was frustrated by television news coverage of American life, arguing that "we were being unfairly treated as a society by the television news."[61] He recalled an incident in the late 1960s that convinced him that a change in television news coverage of public debate was needed. At that time, he went to a black Baptist church to hear the black civil rights activist Stokely Carmichael speak: "Well, [it was a] 30-minute speech, probably, and maybe 2 minutes was incendiary. The rest of it was thoughtful and intelligent and very well stated. What made it on [the NBC evening news with David Brinkley] was the fire and brimstone."[62]

Lamb's response has been to champion unedited political speech on C-Span. According to Thomas J. Meyer, "C-Span . . . has made the most radical breakthrough in broadcasting: showing life as it happens, without commentary, spin or editing."[63]

As part of its mandate, C-Span broadcasts live gavel-to-gavel coverage of the U.S. House of Representatives; its companion channel C-Span 2, founded in 1986, broadcasts gavel-to-gavel coverage of the Senate. This, however, comprises only about 10 percent of C-Span's total programming. It also carries political think-tank panels, Congressional committee hearings, marathon coverage of political parties' nominating conventions, presidential campaign events, and a plethora of call-in shows. A regular feature in the early 1990s has been a retransmission of the nightly news broadcast from Russia, with English translation.

C-Span, a nonprofit corporation, accepts no advertising. It is financed through payments from cable systems, which charged subscribers an average of 36 cents per year in 1992. About 90 percent of all cable systems provide the service to their subscribers. C-Span has grown from four employees and an annual budget of $480,000 in 1979 to 185 employees and a budget of $18 million in 1992.

C-Span doesn't hire on-camera talent. The program hosts for the channels' call-in programs have other full-time responsibilities at the network. Lamb himself hosts three call-in programs each week. The company's vice president and general counsel also host call-in programs. The hosts provide no commentary during these programs; only the callers are permitted the luxury of editorializing. The hosts are identified by name only in small lettering superimposed a few times during the show. And the hosts are very well prepared as moderators. They encourage viewers to seek out information in other media and often hold up relevant print journalism stories to the camera.

Lamb, who has been described as having "all the charisma of a test pattern. And none of the color,"[64] nonetheless has a fanatical following of politically active viewers. A poll taken in early 1991 found that 74 percent of C-Span's viewers voted in the 1990 off-year election, compared to the national turnout of 36 percent.[65] The callers clearly respect Lamb's intelligent handling of the discussions. Can it really be true that one doesn't need to scream and gesticulate to get the viewers' attention? Is it perhaps because Lamb and the other hosts let the callers talk and do not patronize them?

C-Span, under Lamb's direction, refuses to operate in a crisis mode, to go after the dramatic story. It doesn't interrupt its scheduled programs to cover breaking stories.

C-Span's programming decisions are often quite telling. In 1992, for example, C-Span devoted two days of coverage to the Libertarian Party's political nominating convention. And while CNN was providing extended coverage of the William Kennedy Smith rape trial, C-Span broadcast the Senate Finance Committee's hearings on tax reform.[66] During the 1992 presidential campaign, C-Span presented a weekly 90-minute series, *The Road to the White House,* which featured unnarrated documentaries about the week's campaign activities (a form of "direct video") and provided interesting insights into what happens behind-the-scenes at a "photo-opportunity."

C-Span's attempts to demystify political discourse, while lacking the critical framing of ideologically informed commentary, nevertheless provide as closely as possible an unvarnished picture of political life and trust the viewer to get the message. C-Span is a welcome relief from the cynical hysteria of the likes of McLaughlin.

LOOK WHAT THEY'VE DONE TO THE WAR, MA

So much has been written about the cheerleading role assumed by both network and local television news during the 1991 Persian Gulf War that yet another critical commentary seems unnecessary. However, one particularly striking incident bearing directly on the thesis of this chapter needs reiterating. That incident involved the now-infamous "Nayirah."

In 1990, the public relations firm of Hill and Knowlton, then headed by Craig Fuller, former chief of staff to George Bush when he was vice president, packaged and rehearsed the teary-eyed Congressional testimony of an "anonymous Kuwaiti refugee girl" identified as "Nayirah." Nayirah, it was subsequently discovered, was the daughter of Kuwait's ambassador to the United States. She spoke to a Congressional caucus about alleged atrocities committed by Kuwait's Iraqi occupiers. Hill and Knowlton's client in this case was Citizens for a Free Kuwait, an exile organization primarily funded by the Emir of Kuwait.

Nayirah charged that Iraqi soldiers had pulled newborn babies from their incubators, leaving them to die. Her testimony was given extensive coverage by network television newscasts. Later, Kuwaiti doctors interviewed on CBS's *60 Minutes* and ABC's *20/20* denied such incidents had actually occurred. This does not suggest that the Iraqi soldiers committed no atrocities during their occupation of Kuwait. However, that is not at issue here.

The Hill and Knowlton story does not end there, for in addition to its coaching of Nayirah, the company also selected and coached other Kuwaiti refugees with stories about conditions in Kuwait after the Iraqi occupation. The "most compelling" stories were made available to news organizations. Hill and Knowlton also collected, screened, and edited amateur videos shot inside Kuwait and smuggled out. The packaged videos were then distributed free of charge to the television networks, ostensibly by Citizens for a Free Kuwait.[67]

Morgan Strong, a consultant for PBS's *Frontline* documentary series and England's Thames Television, who spent extended time in Saudi Arabia during the Gulf War, claims that "the PR firm's operatives were given free rein to travel unescorted throughout Saudi Arabia, while journalists were severely restricted."[68] Because of this, the networks were placed in a position of choosing whether or not to use footage provided by outside sources (the same predicament we noted in our discussion of the Chernobyl footage). Because the footage was compelling, the chances of its being aired were great.

"It is an inescapable fact," wrote Strong, "that much of what Americans saw on their news broadcasts, especially leading up to the Allied offensive against Iraqi-occupied Kuwait, was in large measure the contrivance of a public relations firm."[69]

THE DOCUMENTARY: CONTROL AND DEMYSTIFICATION

The television documentary has taken many forms, including the television argument (Peter Davis's "The Selling of the Pentagon," *CBS Reports*, 1971); the personal television essay (*Bill Moyers's Journal*); the television history (Allistair Cooke's *America: A Personal History of the United States*, NBC, early 1970s); television exposition (Dr. Jacob Bronowski's *The Ascent of Man*, BBC, aired on PBS, 1975); the television magazine (CBS *60 Minutes*; ABC *20/20*); and direct cinema (Frederick Wiseman's many notable efforts, including *Welfare*; Craig Gilbert's *An American Family*, PBS, 1973; and Peter Davis's *Middletown*, PBS, 1982).

Most television-documentary work has used a correspondent/narrator structure that packages various scenes into a clear linear presentation. The layer of external explanation is provided in both the on-camera speech and the voiceover narration of the correspondent or narrator, who generally follows a script and an interview framework developed beforehand by the documentary's producer/writer. The tone of the documentary may be that of Edward R. Murrow's and producer David Lowe's moral indignation in "Harvest of Shame" (*CBS Reports*, 1960), a powerful exposé of the terrible living and working conditions of migrant farm laborers who feed the nation; that of cynical distrust, as in producer Peter Davis's "The Selling of the Pentagon" (correspondent Roger Mudd), which focused on the questionable motives and fiscal waste of the U.S. military's public-relations activities; or of irony, as in the controversial 1970 National Educational Television *Realities* documentary "Banks and the Poor,"

produced by Mort Silverstein, which accused the banking industry of consciously perpetuating the miserable conditions in our urban ghettos. In a
devastating indictment of governmental conflict of interest, the Silverstein
documentary closed with a superimposed crawl listing 98 members of
Congress who owned shares in or were directors of banks, over a shot of
the capital building, while the "Battle Hymn of the Republic" played in
the background.

These critically acclaimed efforts attempted to transcend the pattern of
reassurance that characterized the "soft" evening news. The best work in
the documentary form was hard-edged, clear-cut, and provocative. The
primary weakness with this narrative format, however, was the danger that
viewers might feel that once these social injustices and institutional excesses of power had been exposed and righteously condemned, the social
problems would be resolved. (Such was generally not the case; ten years
after "Harvest of Shame," NBC's Martin Carr produced "Migrant," which
documented that conditions for migrant workers had not changed despite
Murrow's passionate exhortations.) The narrative closure encouraged such
a feeling of accomplishment.

Beginning in 1959 the three commercial television networks packaged
their documentary work in competing series. *CBS Reports* was the pioneer, followed by NBC's *White Paper* and ABC's *Close-Up!* in 1960. The
progenitor of these efforts was the provocative Edward R. Murrow–Fred
W. Friendly documentary series on CBS, *See It Now*, which began in 1951.

Ratings for these programs have always been considered failures by
commercial television network executives. "The Selling of the Pentagon,"
which was aired February 23, 1971, and is considered by many as the
hardest-hitting and most exciting investigative documentary of 1970s television, was seen in 5,350,000 homes. Like most documentaries, it came
in last in the week's ratings race. In contrast, its entertainment competition, *Marcus Welby, M.D.* was seen in 17,250,000 homes. "The Guns of
Autumn" (*CBS Reports*, 1975; Irv Drasnin, producer) was seen in
8,490,000 homes. It so angered the National Rifle Association that hate
mail poured into CBS. Its ideological impact went far beyond its general
popularity level. Although these documentaries' viewership figures are
small compared to prime-time entertainment programs, they still reveal a
significant national interest in such programming despite many network
executives' assertions to the contrary.

Particularly low in the ratings are documentary works dealing with foreign affairs (e.g., the Communist party in Italy or the economic and social
decline of Britain). Most viewers seem to be turned off by discussion of
complex economic questions, especially in the international arena, where
the immediate ramifications to the individual are more difficult to inter-
polate. More successful are documentaries that broadly survey domestic
problems such as violence and crime.

In absolute numbers, long-form documentaries on the commercial television networks declined significantly during the 1980s. In 1975, for example, 61 documentaries were presented (28 on CBS, 18 on ABC, and 15 on NBC). In 1976, a presidential-election year, the total fell to 36 (15 on CBS, 13 on NBC, and eight on ABC). In the September-April period of the 1982–83 season, only 14 long-form documentaries were aired. These constituted 10.7 percent of all network specials. The average Nielsen rating for the documentary in the 1982–83 season was 8.0. The average share was 13.6 (about one in seven homes that were watching television at the time were tuned to a documentary—certainly not a negligible figure). A further analysis of the 1982–83 season's data reveals that nine of the 14 documentaries were aired in the 10:00–11:00 P.M. time slot (EST)—the last hour of prime-time, when audiences were beginning to decline. Two were aired in the early 7:00–8:00 P.M. time slot (EST) on Sunday. Thus, only three documentaries, or about one-fifth of the total, were aired in the heart of prime time. No documentaries were aired between September 22, 1982, and December 4, 1982—the "new season," when viewer interest is at its peak.[70] Documentaries have been, and are now more than ever, second-class citizens in a video world dominated by melodramatic and comedic television entertainment.

In contrast to the long-form documentary, the network news magazine, led by CBS's 60 Minutes, has been a ratings success, and sometimes a huge success (60 Minutes has been in the top ten network programs since 1977, twice being number one, in 1979–80 and 1982–83). During the six-week period from April 7 to May 12, 1983, 60 Minutes averaged a 23.2 rating and 39.75 share, three times that of the average long-form documentary during the 1982–83 season. ABC's 20/20 averaged a respectable 17.2 rating and 29 share during that same six-week period (a level considered acceptable at the time by network entertainment-program standards for renewal), or twice that of the average long-form documentary. Especially revealing is the April 1983 reading for the 20/20 time slot (ABC, Thursday, 10:00–11:00 P.M., EST). On April 7, 14, and 29, 20/20 had a 29 share each night. On April 21, ABC substituted an ABC Close-Up documentary entitled "Banking." The 20/20 audience deserted in droves—the 29 share was nearly cut in half, down to 17. This suggests that viewers may watch the television news magazine more for the personalities of the correspondent-performers than for the substance or that the substance of the magazine is less conceptually difficult and more entertainingly packaged than the traditional investigative long-form documentary.[71] While 60 Minutes and 20/20 demonstrate that audiences are not turned off by controversy, a mainstay of their reports, they may be turned off by the level of abstraction inherent in the serious discussion of economics, social policy, and ideology.

The long-form, 60 or 90-minute documentary on a single subject has suffered in competition with the news magazine. CBS's vice president for public-affairs broadcasts, John Sharnik, told critic John Culhane in 1977, "It's hard to drum up enthusiasm around here for some things when '60 Minutes' has taken off the cream."[72] By covering three stories in abbreviated form each week, the news magazine leaves the viewer with the feeling that all that need be said has been said on the subject (the same sense of closure one feels with traditional long-form narrative documentaries), while also eating up potential topics at a rapid rate.

When a long-form documentary project is undertaken, which may engage a producer and staff for a year and a half, the end result may be years of aggravation for the creative forces who worked hard to produce a meaningful piece. As one documentary producer told Culhane, "If the show is controversial enough . . . the producer finds that everything he did in the course of the film is subject to the minutest investigation. . . . The networks sometimes back you up and sometimes don't."[73]

The producer/director/writer and the correspondent of a highly controversial documentary may get pressure from outside their organization. While "The Selling of the Pentagon" was still being transmitted, CBS started getting angry telephone calls. CBS News president Richard Salant was called before the House Commerce Committee, and eventually the full House of Representatives, to answer questions about the documentary. CBS president Frank Stanton refused Representative Harley Staggers's subpoena for the outtakes of the documentary. The documentary was rebroadcast a month later with a 15-minute critical response from Vice President Spiro Agnew, Secretary of Defense Melvin Laird, and Representative F. Edward Hebert, chair of the House Armed Services Committee. Guards were placed at CBS Studios in New York and Washington as a caller threatened to assassinate correspondent Mudd. In May 1971 Marine Colonel John MacNeil, who claimed CBS rearranged parts of a speech he had given in Peoria, Illinois, to publicly embarrass him on the documentary, filed a $2 million libel suit against CBS, Inc., and WTOP-TV in Washington, D.C., which carried the documentary. The same month, CBS won an Emmy Award for "The Selling of the Pentagon." Clearly, the network backed its documentary workers in this case even though some questionable film-editing practices were employed, including the excision of qualifying phrases of some interviewees and the joining of statements made in a number of different contexts as the single answer to a question.

Eleven years later, CBS was faced with another libel suit regarding one of its investigative documentaries. This time both the circumstances surrounding the production and the network's response were markedly different. Broadcast in January 1982 on CBS Reports, "The Uncounted Enemy: A Vietnam Deception" featured a heated interview between CBS's Mike Wallace and retired U.S. Army General William Westmoreland. The 90-minute documentary's thesis was that, in 1976, Westmoreland led a military conspiracy to sustain U.S. support for a faltering war by grossly underreporting enemy troop strength. *TV Guide* reporters Sally Bedell and Don Kowet investigated the documentary and questioned CBS's evidence. CBS News president Van Gordon Sauter asked the respected former vice president of CBS News Burton Benjamin to conduct an unprecedented internal investigation. Upon receipt of Benjamin's report, which found 11 major flaws in the documentary, Sauter publicly admitted that the broadcast contained factual errors. He labeled use of the word "conspiracy" as "inappropriate." CBS set up an ombudsman to hear complaints about future newsgathering practices. Although not mentioning him by name in the public admissions of errors, Sauter found producer George Crile negligent in "combining answers from several questions on the same subject into one answer," thereby violating network news guidelines. Sauter said the documentary should have included more remarks from officials who disputed the charge against the top-level military strategists. Nevertheless, CBS publicly stood behind the basic thesis of the documentary.

Westmoreland filed a $120 million libel suit against CBS in September 1982. After prolonged and intense publicity, the libel suit went to trial in October 1984. Shortly thereafter, CBS and Westmoreland reached an agreement. Westmoreland dropped his libel suit in exchange for a CBS statement to the effect that Westmoreland had long and faithfully served his country and that CBS never intended to assert that the general was unpatriotic or disloyal in performing his military duties as he saw them.[74]

Claiming CBS News "credibility" was at stake, Sauter had publicly called into question the techniques and, by implication, the ideological motives of the CBS documentary-production apparatus. CBS News had in essence apologized to Chicago Mayor Richard Daley in 1968 before millions of Americans. Sixteen years later, CBS News apologized to the man who drove us deeper into the morass of Southeast Asia. In both cases, the newsgathering apparatus had boldly approached some real ideological issues (police as "thugs" and generals as "conspirators" in a lie that cost over 50,000 young Americans and countless Vietnamese soldiers and civilians their lives), and a heated public discourse ensued. But the network news operations, ever conscious of their status with their news sources in high places in government, backed away from the core issues. Clearly, different persons in different political climates will react differently. News generally, and Salant and Stanton in particular, were testy in the 1971 era of "The Selling of the Pentagon"—a time when Nixon's inherent distrust of journalists produced a contentiousness among the press corps and press executives. Not so Sauter and CBS News in Reagan's restorationist milieu.

If the traditional long-form network documentary, with its built-in layers of control through clear narrative structure, is exposed to charges of conscious manipulation from those whose ideological positions it challenges, the "direct cinema/video" documentary—a form in which the documentarian rejects external narration and instead ideally lets the subjects reveal themselves through their everyday activities, filmed or taped by the unobtrusive camera/observer—gives the appearance of objectivity. Of course, objectivity is impossible because the editing of thousands of feet of film or hours of videotape superimposes a structure on the work. The essential difference between the two forms is the latter's acceptance of life's complexity, ambiguity, and lack of closure. The direct cinema/video work ends, but the personal lives it revealed and the relationships among people and between people and institutions continue. Direct cinema/video thus seems to leave more room for viewer response and subsequent action because of the inherent continuation in the work itself. The form's weakness, however, is that the subsequent plan of action is often vague or nonexistent because the social relations explored in the work are not clearly explicated within a well-developed conceptual frame. While the traditional long-form television narrative documentary may leave the viewer complacent, feeling the problem is under control because the documentary producer has discovered and properly framed the problem, the direct cinema/video documentary may leave the viewer cynical and frustrated. Neither response is optimal.

The direct cinema/video documentary is, on the other hand, ideally suited to penetrating the veil of contemporary mythology, and herein lies its potential as a counterideological tool. By burrowing beneath the surface of the standardized public images of heroic character types presented in television entertainment, it can reveal the ugly blemishes that contextualize the myth. Whether focusing on social institutions, as Frederick Wiseman has done repeatedly and with often powerful results, or focusing on individuals and intimate social groups such as families, as Craig Gilbert and Peter Davis have done in their work, the myths are opened to the intense gaze of the camera's unrelenting eye. Direct cinema/video can be a provocative tool, as it cannot occur unless it is admitted into its subject's world and thereby becomes privy to the primary-source context of everyday experience—the place where mythology is manifested. Unlike news coverage or the tightly scripted traditional television documentary, in which the correspondent enters the context for a brief moment, does a stand-upper or a few prearranged interviews, and leaves the scene, direct cinema/video is, at its best, a type of cultural anthropology. While it could easily become voyeuristic, direct cinema/video's professed role is as a chronicler of and, by the very nature of its relationship with its subject, a participant in the social acts of the time.

As the direct cinema/video form is synonymous with handheld camera work, run-on scenes, and lengthy exposition, it is generally thought unsuited for commercial television network broadcast, with its time constraints and demand for careful narrative control. Most independent direct cinema/video work that has been aired has received its support from PBS, especially from the New York flagship WNET. Two important examples of direct cinema/video's ability to unmask myth were aired nearly a decade apart on public television. Both explored, in quite different ways, the reality behind the myth of the suburban middle landscape. The first, *An American Family*—a 12-part serial focusing on the Loud family of Santa Barbara, California—was produced by Craig Gilbert and aired in 1973. *An American Family* revealed the vacuousness in the anomic social relations of the suburban middle landscape. The second, the "Family Business" episode of *Middletown*, a six-part series documenting life in Muncie, Indiana, was produced by Peter Davis, whose credits include "The Selling of the Pentagon" and the theatrical release *Hearts and Minds*. Tom Cohen directed "Family Business." Aired in 1982, "Family Business" revealed the pathos of the Howie Snyder family as they struggled courageously to keep alive the Great American Dream of the successful small entrepreneur, embodied in their suburban Shakey's Pizza Parlor franchise. They were deeply in debt to the corporation and on the verge of foreclosure. The Great American Dream was nothing but an empty slogan in the hollow lives of the Louds. In the lives of the Snyders, it was something to be cherished, but its veracity was increasingly in doubt.

Conceived and produced by Gilbert, with cameraperson Alan Raymond and soundperson Susan Raymond (who were to produce *The Police Tapes* for PBS in 1976, discussed in chapter 11), *An American Family* documented the final stages of the disintegration of the 20-year marriage of William and Patricia Loud. The family was filmed from May 30, 1971, to January 1, 1972, in Santa Barbara, California, and New York City. More than 300 hours of film were edited down. The serial cost over $1 million to make. The Louds and their five children were filmed in their lovely suburban house with its lovely swimming pool; 35 Wooddale Lane in Santa Barbara became, for a few months, the stage upon which was acted out the promises and perils of the Great American Dream. It was the heart of the suburban middle landscape, a world right out of the film *The Graduate*, with heavy drinking, boredom, a twice-a-week Mexican maid, and gross materialism. When the scene shifted to New York City, 20-year-old homosexual son Lance was camped at the Chelsea Hotel on Twenty-third Street—once a haven for some of America's great artists, now an overpriced rundown boarding house for suburban avant-garde groupies. Lance constantly telephones home for money. The Louds' other children seem nondirected, bored. Eighteen-year-old Kevin seems pleasant enough but vacuous. Seventeen-year-old Grant wants to be a rock star. Bill wants him to work at manual labor, but he would rather play. Fifteen-year-old Delilah tap dances in the third episode. She is going through adolescence.

Thirteen-year-old Michele is shy, gentle—the warmest member of the family. Admittedly, the children are frozen in time in the documentary. They will change and mature. But the scenes question the shaky ground upon which they will construct their adult lives.

Bill drinks too much, has affairs, and seems dissatisfied with his children. He blames Lance's "failure" on Pat for her allowing doctors to induce labor. Pat, a Stanford graduate, is interested in fashion, manners, and money. She blames Lance's "failure" on Bill for his not being closer to his son. Bill is busy trying to keep his strip-mining machinery business from going downhill. Rather than pursuing the Great American Dream, he seems to be chased unrelentingly by its ghost.

This is a far cry from Mayfield and *Leave It to Beaver*. The Louds' reality has order, but the order has nothing to do with mutual trust. Their order is that of routine. Love, which all of these people seem so desperately to need, escapes their relationships. As Anne Roiphe wrote of the series, "The Louds have escaped the small-town mores of an earlier America" into a world with no central core of beliefs and little conscious understanding of work structures.[75]

But curiously, *An American Family* did share some of the attributes of *Beaver*. For during the filming, the Vietnam War raged on and Pakistan decimated Bangladesh, yet the Louds didn't notice. Theirs was a world, like that of Ward, June, Wally, and the Beaver, in which the view was cut off at the edge of town or at the perimeter of the front yard.

The Louds, who volunteered to be filmed and were paid no money for their participation, were bitter upon seeing the results. While critics generally were effusive in their praise of the work, Bill Loud accused Gilbert and the Raymonds of New York–leftist leanings. Pat felt easterners lived too close together and seemed to be in an unending state of psychoanalysis.[76] Pat wrote an articulate and poignant "Letter to the Forum for Contemporary History," dated February 23, 1973, 13 months after the completion of filming. In it she stresses the horror of being constantly dissected, especially when "shows are being taped for replay in class, and . . . students are assigned to play one of the various roles within the family."

Reviews were generally scornful of the Louds. Pat felt critics treated her family as "objects and things instead of people." On one level, the Louds had become symbols, examples of contemporary bourgeois America. On a more personal level, Pat Loud wrote, "It has denuded us of such honor and dignity as we owned." The mirror, she felt, was distorted. Pat continued in her letter, "Like Kafka's prisoner, I am frightened, confused and saddened by what I see. I find myself shrinking in defense not only from critics and detractors, but from friends, sympathisers and finally, myself." The Louds didn't like what they saw. Pat concluded, "We have been ground through the big media machine, and are coming out enter-

tainment . . . did we, *family and network alike*, serve up great slices of ourselves—irretrievable slices—that only serve to entertain briefly, to titillate,
and diminish into nothing?" (italics mine).[77] Fashion-conscious, status-
conscious Patricia Loud seemed to have awakened from her suburban-
middle-landscape dream. If so, the documentary effort was successful in
human terms.

Following the airing of *An American Family*, Bill and Pat Loud became
talk-show celebrities, their media "slices" not yet fully consumed.

If *An American Family* revealed the anomie of the suburban middle
landscape, Peter Davis's and Tom Cohen's "Family Business" (*Middletown*) provided a moving account of one family's struggle to hold onto the
elusive Great American Dream in an economic reality that was constantly
eating away at the outdated nineteenth-century promise of the independent entrepreneur. The protagonists, the Howie Snyder family, were part
of a new entrepreneurial class, the franchisees. They operated a Shakey's
Pizza Parlor in Muncie, Indiana—pure American middle landscape. The
ma-and-pa-and-sons operation is characterized in the documentary by
pride in their work and the dream of sharing as a family its financial
rewards. Howie, a Marine Corps veteran, is a natural-born entertainer,
singing and clowning his way through the grueling work routine of long
days and nights. Director Cohen captured the Snyders' despair in many
moving scenes, including one in which Howie is talking on the telephone
to the invisible parent-corporation's representative, asking and almost begging for an extension on credit. The corporate operative on the other end
of the line does not seem to be moved by Howie's personal stories of hard
work and dedication to the company. Shakey's is threatening to foreclose.
In the background Howie's wife is crying.

As the work at the pizza parlor drags on, we begin to feel its sweatshop
atmosphere and both Howie's courage and, in a profound way, his naïveté
emerge. At a family dinner, Howie discusses the possibility of giving up
the business, but he decides to continue. One son breaks down and sobs
as he confronts the idea that his father might be a failure. It is powerful
and revealing material, especially as it uncovers relationships between the
traditional petit-bourgeois entrepreneur and the new middle-class managers—an internal struggle for control within the suburban middle landscape. Howie Snyder, in the tradition of the small-shop owner, has roots
and affiliations with the working class of which he is proud, and he is
resentful of the efficient managerial system established in the pizza-
franchising apparatus. He can't seem to understand, however, the extent
to which he lacks control over his own business. He does not realize that
in 1980, 25 percent of retail businesses were franchises and that their
owners—businessmen such as himself—were accountable to the corporations who dictated to them how their businesses were to be run, the
prices, and the look of the product and business establishment itself. He

knows that, on a personal level, Shakey's is threatening to foreclose. But on a social and macroeconomic level, he is overwhelmed by the abstraction. But while Howie has yet to clearly articulate his status in the context of Muncie and his pizza franchise, the viewer is able to see the economics in action.

Critics of direct cinema/video argue that the difficulty with the form is that social context is sacrificed in favor of the human, personal story; that these documentaries are little more than liberal voyeurism. They argue that explanations of political economy require highly structured documentary work. "Family Business" demonstrates that direct cinema/video techniques can be effectively and profoundly used to reveal social processes by going into families' everyday experiences and by selecting families because they represent an idea. Such occasions are both memorable and rare in the world of television news and documentaries.

NOTES

1. Edward Jay Epstein, *News from Nowhere* (New York: Vantage Books, 1973) is the classic study of the organizational imperatives operating in the newsgathering process in television news. Epstein's study is based on ethnographic observations of the process, with emphasis on NBC News, which provided Epstein with substantial access to its day-to-day news operations. John Fiske and John Hartley, *Reading Television* (London: Methuen and Co., 1978), pp. 91–100, offer a clear discussion of the ideological frames that ground television news. For an excellent summary of the key academic debates regarding the nature of the newsgathering process, see Michael J. Robinson, "Future Television News Research: Beyond Edward Jay Epstein," in *Television Network News: Issues in Content Research*, ed. William Adama and Fay Schreibman (Washington, DC: School of Public and International Affairs, George Washington University, 1978), pp. 197–211. Also see Daniel Menaker, "Art and Artifice in Network News," in *Television: The Critical View*, 3d ed., ed. Horace Newcomb (New York: Oxford University Press, 1982), p. 240ff; and Raymond Williams, *Television: Technology and Cultural Form* (New York: Schocken Books, 1975), especially pp. 44–54.

2. Gaye Tuchman, "Consciousness Industries and the Production of Culture," *Journal of Communication* 33 (Summer 1983): 334.

3. Ibid.

4. Bill Carter, "Tough Job Done, NBC Is Looking Ahead," *New York Times*, March 4, 1993, p. A20.

5. David Lieberman, "Fake News," *TV Guide*, February 22, 1992, p. 10.

6. Ibid., pp. 10–11.

7. Ibid., p. 14.

8. Ken Auletta, "Look What They've Done to the News," *TV Guide*, November 9, 1991, p. 6.

9. Ibid., pp. 5–6.

10. Bill Carter, "Networks Cutting Back on Foreign Coverage," *New York Times*, June 10, 1992, p. C18.

11. Bill Carter, "CBS News Is Investigating Charges It Used Staged Film," *New York Times*, September 28, 1989, p. C20.

12. Catherine S. Mangold, "A Grim Wasteland on News at Six," *New York Times*, June 14, 1992, sec. L, p. 50.

13. Ibid., p. 41.

14. Ron Powers, "A Modest Proposal," in *The Newscasters* (New York: St. Martin's Press, 1978), p. 236.

15. Powers, "Vamping It," in *Newscasters*, p. 13. It must be noted that this "intervening role" is the exception in American journalistic history. Such journalists as James Franklin, with his editorial campaigns against the Massachusetts colonial government, the heavy-handed theocracy of Mather in his *New England Courant* in 1721–26, and Horace Greeley, with his pro-labor and abolitionist editorials in his *New York Tribune* in the mid-nineteenth century, while exemplary advocacy journalists, often stood alone in their eras as other journalists, more conservative, satisfied themselves with reprinting government and later corporate press releases.

16. Powers, "In the Palace of the Ice King," in *Newscasters*, p. 109.

17. Edward J. Epstein, *Between Fact and Fiction* (New York: Vantage Books, 1975), p. 19.

18. Williams, *Television*, pp. 22–23.

19. Michael J. Arlen, "The Prosecutor," in *The Camera Age* (New York: Farrar, Straus and Giroux, 1981), pp. 158–79.

20. Ibid., p. 159.

21. Ibid., p. 172.

22. Ibid., p. 173. A Wyoming Grand Jury, dubbed "the 60 Minutes Grand Jury," met for a year on allegations of government corruption stemming from the *60 Minutes* telecasts, but returned no indictments of top officials, including the governor, the mayor, or the state's Democratic chairman, all linked to corruption by the two *60 Minutes* reports.

23. Williams, *Television*, p. 47.

24. Tom Smucker, "Control Factors: The Legacy of Lawrence Welk," (The Village) *Voice*, November 9, 1982, p. 56.

25. Menaker, "Art and Artifice," p. 233.

26. CBS, *60 Minutes*, September 26, 1983.

27. Ben Yagoda, "When Leibner Calls, The Networks Listen," *The New York Times Magazine*, June 18, 1989, p. 50.

28. Ibid., p. 38.

29. Ibid., pp. 38, 49.

30. Ibid., p. 38.

31. Ibid., p. 52.

32. Ibid., p. 50.

33. Sally Bedell Smith, "The Great Chase in Network News," *New York Times*, November 28, 1983, p. C21.

34. Ibid.

35. Edwin Diamond, "Television's 'Great Anchors'—And What Made Them Rate," *New York Times*, March 23, 1980, sec. 2, p. 35.

36. Ibid., p. 40.

37. Orrin E. Klapp, *Heroes, Villains, and Fools: The Changing American Character* (Englewood Cliffs, NJ: Prentice-Hall, 1962), pp. 46–48.

38. Tony Schwartz, "What's Wrong with Local TV News?" *New York Times*, February 21, 1982, sec. 2, p. D1.

39. Tom Shales, "The Pull of the Pullover," *Washington Post*, February 8, 1982, p. C1.

40. Auletta, "Look What They've Done," p. 6.

41. John Berger, *Ways of Seeing* (London: British Broadcasting Company, 1972), p. 24.

42. George Comstock, *Television in America* (Beverly Hills: Sage Publications, 1980), pp. 25–26.

43. William A. Henry III, "News as Entertainment: The Search for Dramatic Unity," in *What's News*, ed. Elie Abel (San Francisco: Institute for Contemporary Studies, 1981), p. 134.

44. Marvin Barnett, *Moments of Truth?* (New York: Thomas Y. Crowell, 1975), pp. 90, 94.

45. Jacques Ellul, *The Technological Society*, trans. John Wilkinson (New York: Alfred A. Knopf, 1964), p. 5.

46. Henry III, "News as Entertainment," p. 135.

47. Jeff Greenfield, "Remembering the 1960's, as Seen on TV," *New York Times*, August 12, 1979, sec. 2, p. 25.

48. Williams, *Television*, p. 53.

49. Epstein, *Fact and Fiction*, pp. 204–5.

50. *Report of the National Advisory Commission on Civil Disorders* (New York: Bantam, 1968), pp. 369–73.

51. Menaker, "Art," p. 234.

52. Walter Goodman, "Shaking Up the Shakers and the Movers," *New York Times*, April 8, 1990, sec. 2, p. 31.

53. Jeremy Gerard, "TV Notes," *New York Times*, February 6, 1989, p. C14.

54. Ibid.

55. Goodman, "Shaking Up the Shakers," p. 41.

56. Ibid.

57. Jacob Weisberg, "American Scene: The Devil in John McLaughlin," *Esquire*, November 1992, p. 79.

58. Ibid., p. 71.

59. Ibid., p. 69.

60. Ibid., p. 79.

61. Thomas J. Meyer, "No Sound Bites Here," *The New York Times Magazine*, March 15, 1992, p. 46.

62. Ibid.

63. Ibid.

64. Ibid., p. 56.

65. Ibid., p. 57.

66. Ibid., p. 56.

67. Morgan Strong, "Portions of the Gulf War Were Brought to You by . . . the Folks at Hill and Knowlton," *TV Guide*, February 22, 1992, p. 12.

68. Ibid.

69. Ibid., p. 13.

70. On the local television level, very few individual independent stations or station groups bother to explore the serious long-form documentary as a way of fulfilling FCC public-interest obligations. The high cost and low return scare the

local broadcast entrepreneur away. Even the well-intentioned Westinghouse Group-W documentary unit—the Urban America Unit—which did a series of 20 documentaries over a five-year period under executive producer Dick Hubert, could find very few commercial TV stations outside Group-W to take the works (exceptions were WMAL, Washington, D.C.; WHEC, Rochester, New York; WISN, Milwaukee, Wisconsin; and WCBW, Buffalo, New York). Of 246 public-television outlets, only 13 put the UAU documentaries on, even when they were offered for free. See Barnett, *Moments of Truth?*, pp. 104–5.

71. Data for 1982–83 are interpolated from "Programming" reports of Petry, a station representative who distributes network ratings summaries to station clients.

72. John Culhane, "Where TV Documentaries Don't Dare to Tread," *New York Times*, February 20, 1977, sec. 2, p. D14.

73. Ibid., p. D15.

74. For background reports on the controversy, see Jonathan Friendly, "CBS Producer Defends Program on Vietnam," *New York Times*, July 17, 1982, p. 44; William A. Henry III, "Autopsy on a CBS 'Expose,'" *Time*, July 26, 1982, p. 40; John Corry, "Weighing the Facts in Westmoreland vs. CBS," *New York Times*, September 4, 1983, sec. 2, p. 19; Peter J. Boyer, *Who Killed CBS?* (New York: St. Martin's Press, 1988), pp. 218–30; and Burton Benjamin, *Fair Play: CBS, General Westmoreland, and How a Television Documentary Went Wrong* (New York: Harper and Row, 1988).

75. Anne Roiphe, "Things Are Keen But Could Be Keener," in *An American Family* (New York: Warner Paperback Library, 1973), p. 22.

76. Ibid.

77. *An American Family*, pp. 236–38.

8

□ □ □ □ □ □

Live TV: *Sport and the TV Event*

Defenders of "live" television frequently celebrate the medium's ability to present events, as they happen, in real time, and they glorify the resultant drama of the unpredictable, an open future in which anything may happen. Though there indeed may be some cause to praise live television when compared to the often stultifying formal predictability and redundancy of such television genres as melodrama, one should nevertheless avoid such a facile interpretation.

Ours is an assembly-line lifestyle in which repetition and consistency produce on the one hand the boredom of the workplace circumscribed by technique, tasks, and productivity quotients and on the other hand a sense of security, of the known in a world of increasing confusion complicated by high levels of mobility and shifting value systems. In the world of sport, the joy of experiencing the unpredictable, with little personally at stake, allows us to momentarily escape the routine, the predictable, and ride a safe psychic roller coaster of victory and defeat, of quick changes in fortune. Like the Congress sending troops off to war or the general on the ridge top, surveying the battlefield, our participation is vicarious, our personal safety assured. From the security of such a vantage point, we can dream of the glorious victory, the upset of the decade. We can transcend the predictable for a few hours, breaking the all-too-familiar pattern of much of everyday life. We hang on to the hope of a miracle finish. In nonsport contexts, we hope that the streaker who briefly derailed the gentrified Academy Awards ceremony some years ago will someday return to the small screen with some new outrage. Thus, on the surface we have a relatively clear-cut rationale for the culture's reveling in the live television event, whether it focus on sport or on the celebrity processional: We're desperately seeking an emotional catharsis, a release without personal risk from the routines and relative monotony of everyday life. Achieving this, we can return to *our own* world in which our place is as secure as it was yesterday.

In the age of television, and especially now with cable/satellite distribution and program development, the American sport fanatic can stuff him or herself with vicarious witnessing of the athletic competition of others from daybreak to daybreak, without a break, for all time. Three basic cable channels are devoted entirely to sport—ESPN, ESPN2, and MSG. ESPN reached well over 50 percent of all U.S. television households in the early 1990s. Today, every major sport has a national cable television package in addition to its traditional deal with the "Big Three" broadcast television networks. As this book went to press, the Fox network had just outbid CBS for rights to telecast professional football's National Football Conference. The broadcast networks, driven by increasing competition for advertising revenue with other television distributors, continue to expand their coverage of major sporting events, which on occasion reaches the point of absurdity, most notably in the interminable pregame reportage connected with football's annual Super Bowl ritual.

Why this voracious appetite for televised sport, especially at a time when increasingly vocal critics of both the genre and the world of corporate sport point to the incredible system of values being promoted through sport to generations of susceptible youth? The answers are complex and intriguing and can in large measure be found in the study of contemporary American mythology.

SPORT—THE MERCENARY WARRIOR MEETS THE JOURNALIST-PUBLICITY AGENT

If heroes, as sociologist Orrin Klapp defined them, are social types providing the society with models people try to approximate and further act as a "photograph" of the society's previous activities, then the public symbols manifested in our athlete/heroes bring the major shifts in our twentieth-century culture into clearer focus. These social types include the individual as adventurer/wanderer and seeker of joy and personal fulfillment through the playing of leisurely children's games and the corporate warrior as a celebrated and expendable public commodity whose legendary exploits are chronicled in business data. Further, if social types such as our public heroes represent the essential dimensions of social control— of that which is to be valued, of the proper order of things and people— then a discussion of sport, the sport hero, the sport journalist, and television must, by implication, refer to ideology and the nature of social relations outside the narrowly defined world of sport.

In our culture's mythology of the rural middle landscape, the links between the folk hero and the culture from which that hero emerged are strong and clear. The hero's special skills or calling may cause him to venture forth from the geographical confines of the community, but his exploits, while strongly individualistic, inevitably return something vital to the culture from which he emerged. Because the hero's unusual physical and/or character traits transcend the normative boundaries associated with the relatively confined world of the rural community, his actions lend themselves to the telling, retelling, and embellishing of stories. The famous pitcher who began by throwing baseballs into a bushel basket out behind the barn and who became the tobacco-chewing strikeout king, but who always came back home at season's end to sit around fishin' with the folks he never really left behind is, in its many guises, a recurring rural sport motif—"fame never spoils the country boy." While such is obviously not always the stuff of reality, especially in today's highly mobile and increasingly urbanized society, the myth serves an important function by offering a positive value frame as an antidote to a sport world seen as increasingly dehumanized and money-obsessed. ABC Sports, in its "Up Close and Personal" profiles, often draws on this mythology, featuring highly competitive star athletes at home in such bucolic settings as the wooded mountains of Vermont or a tiny Italian coastal fishing village as they enjoy life's simpler pleasures.

Today's more "modern" (and one might claim, more accurate) journalistic profiles of athletes increasingly focus on the well-organized training regimen (to improve the athlete's strength, stamina, and technique) and the role of the personal sport psychologist (to help the athlete achieve a mental edge through "psyching-up") as keys to athletic success. The athlete is seen less as belonging to (and created by) a traditional community, with its attendant values of sharing or "giving back," than as an autonomous individual served by a retinue of highly paid modern "specialists" who include both those who fine-tune the athlete's body and mind and others, such as business agents, investment counselors, and tax lawyers, who "micromanage" the athlete's life off the field. Today's dominant image, which reflects the realities of corporate sport, is that of the king and his subservient courtiers.

We have entered a new phase of sport reporting in the television era— the celebration of celebrity itself. C. Wright Mills defined celebrity as "the names that need no further identification, [who are] recognized with some excitement and awe, [and who] are the material for the media of communication and entertainment."[1] In this new world of money and power, finesse—Sandy Koufax's miraculous curveball that "falls off the table," or Tom Watson's "surgeon's touch" with the sand wedge, or Bjorn Borg's uncanny accuracy with a two-handed backhand top-spin passing shot down the line, or O. J. Simpson's wonderfully balletic quality of changing direction on his run in midair—fades into the background as the emphasis increasingly shifts to competition and ultimately to winning. As early as 1954, Mills found, in the celebration of celebrity, "the star system of a society that makes a fetish of competition. . . . It does not seem to matter what the man is very best at; so long as he won out in competition over all others, he is celebrated."[2]

The celebrants, led by the television sportscasters who specialize in what critic John J. O'Connor called the "superfluous packaged by the hyperbolic,"[3] invoke warlike, pugilistic metaphors in the service of "color." One player or team "demolishes" or "finishes off" the opponent. Because he was a superb tennis player, Borg became "the angelic assassin" who outlasted his underdog American opponent Roscoe Tanner, the folksy innocent "hillbilly from [Lookout Mountain] Tennessee," in the 1979 Wimbledon final.[4] The tennis tiebreaker, instituted to speed up the game in the television era, is ominously described by the unflappable announcer as "lingering death," a phrase sure to inject agony into the drama of the contest. These metaphors of war are far from culturally "innocent" descriptors of children's games, for they reveal the darker side of contemporary sport, with its overemphasis, both parental and institutional, on winning at all costs, even at the risk of bodily harm.[5]

This warlike and, in the case of international sporting events, jingoistic character of the television treatment artificially builds dramatic tension and solidifies allegiances. (Now that the Soviet Union no longer exists to play the role of enemy in the geopolitics of international sport, what new enemy will emerge to satisfy the demand?)

According to critic Karl Meyer, the catalyst in the "long-postponed passing of the Main Street Myth" in our culture has been the contemporary American phenomenon of marketing.[6] Television packages its audience into "metropolitan units," according to Meyer, and like the citizens of the classic Greek city-states, Americans have become possessed by the passion for urban display. In addition to such public symbols of urban wealth and eternal progress as the blockbuster museum exhibition (e.g., the 1992 Matisse show at the Museum of Modern Art in New York City), the convention center, the city magazine extolling the glory of *your* community, and the downtown rehabilitation/gentrification, our new contemporary tabernacle—the multimillion-dollar sports complex—provides the modern space for the performance of the ritual combat. Television enlarges the public ritual space to the region, and now with superstations such as Ted Turner's WTBS in Atlanta broadcasting a single team's schedule (the Atlanta Braves, which Turner also owns) to the entire country, we have, at least according to the television hypesters, "America's team." The athlete becomes a public symbol of the city's status in the competitive world of city pride and ultimately of its economic viability (by encouraging tourism). The symbol becomes so important in some instances that bizarre behavior results; however, as "fan" is short for "fanatic," one might argue that no behavior exhibited by such a class of persons could be considered bizarre. Consider, for example, Cincinnatians' attempt to have the ageless former baseball hero Pete Rose, of "Grecian Formula" fame, proclaimed a city landmark to prevent him from changing teams. He eventually left Cincinnati for the Philadelphia Phillies, who paid him significantly more money.

If cities are expendable to the mercenary warriors who wander from metropolis to metropolis in search of the golden fleece, so too are the athletes themselves expendable in this corporate sport world of winning. Sociobiologist Edward O. Wilson, in his book *On Human Nature*, posits that the contemporary citizen can easily form, break, and reconstitute alliances and accept, without lasting hostility, the annual buying, selling, and trading of professional athletes and even entire teams as mere commodity deals because he has resolved his environment into personal identity with an "aggressive" ingroup against an enemy—"an elemental physical struggle between tribal surrogates" in which "teamwork, bravery, and sacrifice" transcend the persona of the sport hero.[7]

Television has contributed greatly to both the athlete's and the city's expendability as it has created its own world of sport. The broadcast television networks and cable sports channels reportedly paid $3.6 billion to the National Football League (NFL) for rights to televise their contests during the 1991–94 cycle, or about $32 million per team per year—"the most lucrative deal in television history."[8] Thus, "Without even one customer buying a seat or a hot dog, the professional football teams will be able [to] meet all expenses, and even earn hefty profits, from television income alone."[9]

By paying huge sums of money to professional sport leagues for telecast rights, television has provided the sport franchise with the necessary capital to "hold a city hostage" by threatening a move if the city does not provide a new, ultramodern sport facility. In addition, the exponential increase in income from television rights has allowed teams to engage in a murderous bidding war for the services of the most talented players. Baseball's "free agency" rules, in effect for many years, have produced superstar megasalaries upward of $6 million per year. And although the NFL eschewed free agency during the 1980s, the 1990 contract intensified the league owners' conflict with players over salaries and free agency. Nineteen ninety-three marked the NFL's first venture into unrestricted free agency, and the results were eye-opening, with players being offered contracts to sign with new teams that were from five to as much as ten times the annual salaries of their previous contracts before free agency.[10]

For a select group of superstar athletes in a variety of sports, even the hefty salary deals or prize monies pale when compared to the fortunes they can amass from product endorsements and appearances in television commercials. The potential of brand-image enhancement through athlete product endorsements was first clearly recognized by Horst Dassler, head of Adidas and now deceased, who began paying "amateur" athletes to wear his company's shoes in the early 1960s. Thirty years later, the *Sports Marketing Newsletter* reported superstars' 1991 worldwide earnings from endorsements of products and services: basketball superstar Michael Jordan, $11 million; senior golf heroes Arnold Palmer and Jack Nicklaus, $10 million each; retired basketball star Magic Johnson, $9 million; golfer Greg Norman, $8.5 million; tennis sensation Andre Agassi, $7 million; ice hockey superstar Wayne Gretsky, $7 million; football quarterback Joe Montana, $6.75 million; retired tennis star Chris Evert, $6 million.[11] The money flows in from a variety of sources, including endorsements for products such as athletic equipment and clothing and fast foods, and services such as financial investment services. The superstars have new brands named for them (Nike's Air-Jordan sneakers). And a select group have even become cartoon characters on Saturday morning network television cartoon shows (baseball's Bo Jackson, basketballer Jordan, and ice hockey king Gretsky on NBC's *ProStars*). There are other, rather unusual income opportunities as well. A niche market has developed for athletes to collect appearance fees for attending company meetings. Former Chicago Bears superstar running back Walter Payton was paid $75,000 by the Pfizer chemical company and drug manufacturer to attend three parties at medical conventions. Doctors were photographed with Payton, and company salespersons delivered the photos to the doctors and pitched a Pfizer drug in the process.[12]

Even aging superstars in the twilight of their careers can assure "marketing immortality" with a gusty performance in a losing cause. Take, for example, the 1991 U.S. Tennis Open. Swedish tennis star Stephan Edberg, at the top of his form, won the men's singles title, a world number-one ranking, and the $400,000 first prize in the tournament. But the really big winner was semifinal *loser* Jimmy Connors. The 39-year-old aging wonder "ensured himself for the next 40 years" as a marketing celebrity, according to Martin Blackman, who advises advertisers which athletes will be the best product spokespersons.[13] "Jimbo" was a natural to launch a Nuprin pain-reliever television ad campaign targeted to the fortysomethings who can still move around the court but experience a few more aches and pains in the process.

While newspapers and radio have, for decades, created and traded on the celebrity status of the sport hero (Babe Ruth was pitching Wheaties in the 1920s), television has made the sport star truly wealthy and has transformed him or her from culture hero to commodity.

The star athlete's marketing potential today extends to the entire globe. About 4,000 companies were spending about $3 billion annually on sport marketing in the early 1990s.[14] The modern era of sport marketing was pioneered by lawyer Mark McCormack's International Management Group (IMG) in 1958. McCormack's first client, Arnold Palmer, winner of the 1958 U.S. golfing Masters tournament, remains IMG's most famous (and lucrative) client. Today, IMG is the biggest sport marketing group, with 42 offices in 19 countries. IMG and its major rivals Pro Serv and Advantage International link the sporting businesses of corporate marketing, event management, and athlete representation. The sport marketing group handles an increasingly complex web of superstar athletes' activities. The agents' services for their clients include negotiating playing contracts; overseeing investments and finances; handling tax, legal, and insurance matters; getting product and service endorsement deals; packaging their clients with other sport stars in made-for-television events such as *The Superstars*; securing a publisher for a client's autobiography; getting a magazine feature for a client; and setting up production of a home video featuring the client.[15] The reward for all this activity is substantial: Agents' fees range from 15 to 30 percent of a client's earnings.[16]

In "a business where image is everything,"[17] there is always a risk that an athlete will get into some personal trouble and tarnish the advertiser's image. However, given the profit potential of a superstar's product endorsement, this is a risk most advertisers are more than willing to take. Nevertheless, more companies are signing at least two select big names to appear in a single campaign; if one gets into trouble, the other or others are still there to enhance the company's image. "These days, any time an athlete is signed to an endorsement deal he's scrutinized like a Supreme Court nominee."[18]

While much has been gained by athlete, agent, big-league team owner, major event organizer, and television network in a pecuniary sense, much has also been lost. Minor-league baseball in the United States and lower-level Third and Fourth Division soccer in England have suffered greatly from the video overexposure of the top-level teams. Because of the constant hype of sport celebrity, community teams such as minor-league or semiprofessional teams are considered second-raters unworthy of much support. The once-mythic exploits, the dusty bus trips and stops at roadside diners from town to town, are now viewed as low class, and the underpaid struggling athletes are seen as losers rather than as eccentric characters. Only when there is a human-interest story involved do the sportscasters dip down into the minors. An archetypal story is that of the once-great major-league player, former Detroit Tigers pitcher Mark "the Bird" Fidrych, whose bad arm forced him out of the big leagues, but whose spirit and tenacity kept him fighting for a comeback. The minor leagues become places for player rehabilitation on the road back to stardom. The movement toward the development of a caste system in the modern sport and television era is increasingly evident, for television favors only the celebrity, the success, the human incarnation of the myth of eternal progress who sets the new record in yards gained or prize money won.

Television has even changed the tempo of sport. To meet the insatiable demands for advertising revenues, television has given sport the "television time-out" for commercials. This intrusion transforms the event's structure according to television's time signature (baseball, tennis, and boxing, with natural oneor two-minute breaks after short durations of action, don't face this problem, while football and basketball, two of America's most popular television sports, do).

The networks' pecuniary motives lead to pumping up even the dullest of contests—dull because one team or person is so far ahead of the other that victory, the sine qua non of contemporary sport, is assured. Viewers, who have through the years been trained by the networks to deal with ends and not means or the process of play, must somehow be induced to stay tuned for the commercials that pay for the spectacle. Some sportscasters, faced with this dilemma they themselves have helped create, resort to ridicule of individual athletes' weaknesses to hold viewer attention.

In its quest for the ultimate continuous entertainment, television surrounds the sport activity itself with a variety of other, related TV events—a Kentucky Derby special or a Super Bowl special featuring pop singers and other notables. Sport becomes a contextual element in a larger social ritual of the celebration of money, sex, drugs, and power. The dominant ideology's concepts of success are paraded before the television screen in this show of competitiveness and desire. When ninth-graders were queried some years ago regarding revelations that some of their Dallas Cowboy heroes were involved in buying, selling, and using cocaine, they became disillusioned. However, by the time they pass adolescence, many will have come to accept such behavior as the price to be paid for modern superstardom, for the trappings of celebrity as revealed on television include drug use as part of the daily video ritual. The myth of eternal progress admits the use of stimulants to improve performance—within limits, of course, as Canadian sprinter Ben Johnson discovered to his chagrin.

Atop all this activity stands the sport celebrity, the isolate, a man figuratively "without a country," whose motivation to engage in sport has increasingly become monetary, whose responsibility to the social group is the provision of a brief thrill and emotional uplift without any long-term commitment to the community. He comes into the community like the mercenary gunslinger in the mythic Western, does his business—murders the opponent—and departs for other parts and other battles.

So the star athlete moves from city to city selling his talents to the highest bidder, and the fan learns to accept this behavior as he has accepted the larger social system that produces it. The imaginary realm of the athlete-celebrity is that of the self-as-ego, the "I." The team is composed of discrete units, of interchangeable individuals, who sell their labor power for substantial sums but who, at the same time, are robbed of their surplus value by the team owners who make large profits off their players. The stars in turn cause the labor power of second-string major leaguers

and especially the minor-league players to command much less remuner-
ation than should be the case were the community supporting the local
team and not staying home, eyes glued to the big boys racing across the
television screen. The public image we have learned to accept is that of
the individual celebrity who is free to get rich through his and his agent's
initiative. This image is a mirage. Thus, when the NFL players called a
strike in the middle of the 1982 football season, the very idea of a union
of players representing the interests of individual celebrity-heroes—the
symbolic "we"—turned off sports fans and viewers, who were duped into
reverence for the abstract imaginary realm of the "I." That all those
"greatests" should have to resort to a union negotiator to gain salary in-
creases was incongruous with their telehyped status. It exposed the guile
of the club owners who exploit humans for profit. It also exposed the
spectators' confusion regarding the true locus of pecuniary power that
defines contemporary sport, namely, the fiscal arrangements made between the large television companies and the power elites that own sports
teams and players. On occasion one detects spectator cynicism seething
just below the surface, as the realization sinks in that the athlete has
become a prostitute, selling himself to the highest bidder, and further, as
the spectator realizes that the athlete can do this because club owners
and sport promoters, anxious to make large profits from their operations,
encourage this practice. The losers are the fans, who lose a proper perspective of the nature of heroism and community.

The pecuniary motif in contemporary sport is encouraged by those who
pompously refer to themselves as sports journalists or sportscasters; a
more appropriate term for the majority of these individuals would be sport
public-relations agents, whose main function is to elevate the banal.

Just as the outrageous behavior, on and off the field or court, of such
"bad-boy" sport celebrities as baseball manager Billy Martin, owner
George Steinbrenner, player Reggie Jackson, and tennis players John
McEnroe and Ilie "Nasty" Nastase, "was rewarded by even bigger fees
and commercial endorsements,"[19] so too did the outrageous behavior of
sportscaster Howard Cosell—a provocateur more than an analyst—lead
to the emergence of the superstar sportscaster as hype-artist, a celebrity
in his own right, who becomes as important as the event and players he
covers. The sportscaster's actions often become the event, creating the
controversy. Clearly situated in the age of telenarcissism, the sports-
caster-hyperbolist lives through the sports celebrities he covers. The first
important modern television tandem was Cosell and heavyweight-
champion boxer Muhammad Ali in the 1960s. In those early days, much
to his credit and prior to his rise to telecelebrity status, Cosell decried racism in sport and in the society generally as he defended Ali's position regarding the draft, a position that had alienated many in the jingoistic
U.S. sport establishment. Then, as Cosell began to build his own televi-

sion-star status through alliances with such "great ones" as O. J. Simpson, Broadway Joe Namath, and Sugar Ray Leonard, he became less and less involved with sport and social issues and more and more involved in himself.

Like so many other sport hyperbolists, Cosell became so involved in the language he used to describe the event that analysis was lost in what critic John O'Connor called "a numbing polysyllabic onslaught" that served no purpose other than to demonstrate Cosell's erudition but that, under careful semantic scrutiny, proved instead his ineptness. Examples of such linguistic pretensions abound: Reporting the content of an interview he conducted with boxer Michael Spinks, Cosell stated, "I had to ask Michael some of the key questions circumscribing his whole career."[20] That is to say, Cosell talked to Spinks about his life. Cosell once described the shift of control of a boxing contest from one fighter to another as "a sharp change in the tide of affairs of these two men." Cosell's use of English is analogous to the advertising lingo anthropologist Jules Henry dubbed "parapoetic hyperbole"—the use of high-flown figures of speech that resemble, but are not, poetry to make the subject appear more significant or important or powerful than it is in actuality. Cosell, the self-as-ego, meets the bad-boy athlete self-as-ego. Together they frame the television transaction of sport-celebrities we love to hate, the "big properties" in a web of vaudeville, propaganda, and money.[21]

The ultimate hypocrisy and the shameless use of ideology to camouflage the true social relations of contemporary professional and even amateur sport in this country are best exemplified by the high moral tone sportscasters such as Cosell take toward the other members of their profession as well as toward athletes. The following examples of such confusion of values are taken from a fascinating interview conducted by Chicago public-television station WTTW's John Callaway, with Cosell as interviewee. The interview was aired nationally on PBS on November 12, 1981. About sport journalism, of which he was the major national symbol throughout the 1970s, Cosell argued,

I thought about the hypocrisy involved in sports journalism. And I thought about Edward R. Murrow. And then I thought about sports and the sanctity given to it. And I find more personal integrity in doing a movie with [Woody] Allen than in doing a big-time college game with the bought-and-paid-for players who don't even, in most cases, belong in college and who don't ever get degrees.[22]

The Super Bowl, according to Cosell, is "another excess in the world of sports"; "a prolonged hype"; "a corporate enterprise—most of the seats and most of the suites are held by the great corporations"; and "Commissioner Rozelle's party, which now costs anywhere from eighty to one-hundred-thousand dollars for the print medium, is frankly a disgrace." Of the athletes, Cosell complained:

All athletes are heroes, to the point where they become surrogate parents in many American homes. When, as a matter of fact, an athlete may be a drug addict, he may be an alcoholic, he may be a whore-monger . . . and is hardly equipped for heroism because he can hit a baseball or catch a football. And then as wrong after wrong and corruption after corruption is exposed in the sports world, where have the media people been through all of the years? And why are they so desperately afraid of and resistant to truth in sport?

Finally, of newspaper sport journalism, Cosell complains, "The very hypocrisy and contradiction of our sports pages in this country is almost self-evident; . . . the sports pages appear now as a series of tout sheets, listing the point spreads and inviting the very gambling that leads to college scandals we talk about."

Cosell, who "symbolized within sports the rise of the television superstar over the print superstar,"[23] had numerous internecine battles with print sport journalists who claimed his bombast, combined with television's need for constant action, was wrecking the image of American sport and sport journalism. Who are we to believe? The overbearing telecelebrity Cosell we saw and heard on television, covering Monday-night football contests, the Kentucky Derby, the major league baseball playoffs, and boxing matches? Or the moralist who granted interviews about the sorry state of sport and sport journalism and their negative impact on our society? Cosell's bifurcated self represents the confusion of values evident in the larger society and manifested in attitudes about sport. Such confusion obfuscates the important social issues regarding the nature of sport and the character of those who engage in the public ritual of sport, both players and reporters.

SPORT AND IDEOLOGY—TELEVISION MYTH AND THE OLYMPIC GAMES

Amateur athletics are not exempt from the hype and the pecuniary fixations of professional sport. In fact, the boundary between the two is increasingly blurred. Recurring recruiting violations plague big-time college football and basketball as the drive toward a prestigious national championship, with the resultant increased income for the school's sports program (and increased salary for the coach), encourages coaches and recruiters to bend the rules. On the other hand, a coach need *not* violate N.C.A.A. rules to achieve success on the court and reap substantial financial rewards as a result. This is amply demonstrated by Duke University basketball coach Mike Krzyzewski, whose Blue Devils won back-to-back national basketball championships in 1991 and 1992. According to a 1993 *New York Times* report Krzyzewski, whose team wore Adidas basketball sneakers for years, agreed to switch to Nike sneakers on September 1, 1993. By switching brand loyalty, Krzyzewski reportedly will receive a $1 million signing bonus from Nike and an annual salary worth about $375,000 a year, plus stock options, for a 15-year contract.[24]

International "amateur" athletic competition, and especially its most visible manifestation, the Olympic Games, is not immune from these economic pressures. The original Greek Olympic ideal of "pure mind, pure body," of the athlete as a competitor in a game that allowed one to demonstrate grace, agility, strength, finesse, and stamina—all elements of the well-conditioned body guided by the intelligent, resourceful mind—was the stuff of legendary heroes whose praises were sung by the bards. In the spirit of civilized competition between mutually respectful people, the victor was rewarded with laurel and congratulated by the vanquished, who would redouble his or her effort in an attempt to be victorious in the next games. When the Romans conquered Greece, they weren't interested in these ideals but rather wanted gladiatorial contests and money. Events were sometimes fixed (e.g., Emperor Nero drove his own chariot in a race, which he was destined to win). In 394 A.D., the Olympics were terminated by Emperor Theodosius I, ending 1,170 years of the event.[25]

French educator and sportsman Baron de Coubertin revived the Olympic Games in 1896 with the original Greek ideal in mind, but with a twist. According to athletics historian Arthur Weston, the concept of "amateurism" promoted by de Coubertin "grew from an elitist notion that evolved in Victorian England to distinguish the 'pure' sports of the aristocracy, as symbolized by the white Olympic flag, from the professional sports of the working classes."[26]

Nationalism had entered the Olympic Games by the Paris Olympiad in 1924 and was accentuated by the geopolitics of the Cold War following World War II. This deflected the *class issues* surrounding the concept of "amateurism." Eventually, however, class issues once again came into focus, with defenders of the idea of opening Olympic competition to professional athletes arguing that such a practice would "legitimize the athletic experience" by allowing everyone the opportunity to play, unrestricted by financing that was once reserved to the leisure class. Today, professional athletes compete in the games, thus acknowledging the reality that only about 30 of the 160 or more nations whose athletes compete even distinguish between amateur and professional sports.[27] And ironically, those who continue to oppose "professional" athletes competing seem to have little or no objection to the increased corporate sponsorship and attendant commercialization of the Games.

In one sense, the Olympics are still "amateur." They offer no appearance fees or money prizes. But the competitors are not amateurs. For decades during the Cold War they were participants in a high-stakes game of international politics and transnational marketing. And while the 1992 games saw the demise of the former, the latter continued to undermine the original spirit of the Olympic Movement. As Stephen Hugh-Jones noted, "The Olympic motto *Citius, altius, fortius*—faster, higher, stronger—is meant for athletes. It applies still better to the flow of money around them."[28]

During the Cold War, the athlete became an ideological vehicle—the public token of national will. One memorable example was the 1983 Miller Beer advertising campaign celebrating athletic achievement. Miller's "This American Dream" campaign included one spot, which I shall label "that kid's out there," in which a young, handsome, muscular black runner dreams of winning the Olympic 400-meter run. After his daily job, he goes to a deserted track somewhere in urban America and runs by himself. At this point, his dream is probably just that, and will remain so, alas; however, with institutional support provided by your friendly neighborhood transnational corporate conglomerate, i.e., Miller Brewing Company, he will succeed because he is able to train at the Olympic Training Center.

How easily and conveniently this entire commercial fairy tale ignored the reality of the political-ideological fiasco of the U.S. boycott of the 1980 Summer Olympic Games, held in Moscow, in protest over the Soviet Union's invasion of Afghanistan. The institutions, who had prepared our athletes for those "apolitical international" games, deserted those athletes by capitulating to the desires of a political administration whose vaguely defined and ill-conceived foreign policy took precedence over this American Dream. NBC, which was to cover the 1980 games, recovered most of its investment through its insurance with the British firm Lloyds. The athletes were not so fortunate.

What do today's Olympic Games mean? To a nation, they may mean national pride, international visibility, or in some cases saving face. To a competitor, they may launch a professional career in some sport such as boxing or ice hockey or skiing or football (which has recruited on occasion from Olympic track stars), or they may simply be valued for the national-hero status they confer on winning contestants. To a transnational corporation, they may mean large profits through public relations. The "quest-for-the-gold" hype of American television sportscasters might lead the skeptical observer to conclude that the network sports divisions, in search of heightened dramatic tension, have turned the Olympiad and other world-championship amateur competitions into battlegrounds on which national honor and even national legitimacy are won or lost.

American television sports divisions covering the Olympic Games are not unique in their jingoistic framing of the contests. Critical scholar Michael R. Real has noted that nationalism is "common to Olympic reporting throughout the world."[29] However, a content analysis of selected newspaper coverage of the 1984 Summer Games in Los Angeles, reported by Real, found that 79 percent of Olympic coverage in U.S. newspapers concerned American athletes, "the highest percentage [of nationalistic coverage] of any of the countries studied."[30] This, according to Real "unfortunately [confirmed] many charges about American nationalism and self-centeredness."[31]

Nationalistic reporting of the Games takes many forms besides concentrating attention on the exploits of a nation's own athletes. CBS Sports' coverage of the 1992 Winter Games in Albertville, France, managed a Cold War rhetorical reprise as it focused on the potential monetary rewards offered the "professional" ice hockey players from the Unified Team (formerly U.S.S.R.)—$3,000 U.S. for a Gold Medal, $2,000 for a Silver, and $1,000 for a Bronze—implying the Unified Team's players were "bought and paid for," while ignoring the potential pecuniary benefits an "amateur" U.S. ice hockey player was likely to receive (in the form of product endorsements or a professional contract) for a victory. Yet the American sportscasters (this time NBC Sports) had no trouble accepting the presence of the professional NBA "Dream Team" at the 1992 Summer Games in Barcelona, Spain (after all, the Olympics had become professionalized). The Dream Team's mission was to recapture the basketball Gold Medal lost by the United States in 1988, when the amateur team had to settle for a third-place finish. NBC's endless hyping of the NBA superstars, as they methodically crushed their opponents, ignored the often surly on-court behavior of the basketball superstars and many of the behind-the-scenes realities reported by the more responsible print media. According to the *New York Times*, "the ultraprofessionals were set apart from the rest of the American Olympic team."[32] The Dream Team and wealthier professional tennis and track and field stars stayed in luxury apartments or in $900-a-night hotel suites, while most athletes stayed in cramped Olympic Village quarters, creating tension among the American athletes. Novelist Stephen King best summed up the Dream Team spectacle:

[T]hese high-salaried, promotion-conscious pros, with their baggage of bad court habits, loud mouths, and absolutely staggering basketball skills, can serve as a perfectly apt epilogue to the last 12 years of American life, when the almighty buck swamped just about everyone's principles, when the deal became more important than the game, and any sane discussion of athletics and what they mean disappeared into a welter of Chroma-Key effects, slow motion, and game-diagram supers, all before fading into the next beer ad, naturally.[33]

When nationalism is combined with male chauvinism, the results can be most disconcerting, as evidenced by CBS Sports profiles of American and Unified Team athletes aired during the 1992 Winter Games. When

CBS profiled U.S. speed skaters Bonnie Blair and Dan Jansen, reporters stressed the theme of "strong family ties" that provided these athletes with a solid ground that contributed to their enhanced performances and made them better human beings. In contrast, a CBS profile of Unified Team nordic skier Yelena Valbe focused on her giving up family in her quest for Olympic victory. Valbe, it was reported, left her young son behind in Siberia for six months at a time to train in Estonia. Furthermore, the report noted that her husband was divorcing her. Leaving aside for the moment the inherent jingoism implicit in these comparative profiles, the Valbe story alone represents an insensitive male-dominated discourse. Its theme, that women give up families to seek *personal* success (and by implication, that career women make bad mothers and even destroy families in the process), is not applied to male athletes, who it must be assumed are free to absent themselves from their families for long periods to pursue their athletic quests with no attendant negative consequences.

Such media framing ultimately detracts from the ideal of Olympic competition—a "compelling combination of drama, beauty, achievement, celebrity, and accessibility."[34] So, too, does the image the Games have assumed in recent years as a supermediated global business venture—an intensely competitive battleground on which large transnational corporations struggle to secure official Olympic sponsorship status. To become an official sponsor, a company must pay large sums to the International Olympic Committee (I.O.C.) and the host city's Organizing Committee in exchange for an exclusive in their industry and are thereby allowed to display both the official Olympic symbol and official mascot of the Games in their advertising and public relations materials. The benefit to the official sponsor is "a shinier public image, a bigger market share."[35]

The modern era of supersponsorship was ushered in at the 1984 Summer Olympic Games. The Los Angeles city government, host for the Games, was well aware of the tremendous financial losses incurred by the city of Montreal, Canada, host of the 1976 Summer Games. To avoid such an outcome, Los Angeles's city charter was amended to prohibit government subsidy of any cost overruns. The government turned to private industry for financial support. The Los Angeles Olympic Organizing Committee (LAOOC), a group of private business and professional people, limited sponsorship to 30 companies and required a minimum payment of $4 million for sponsorship. By April 1983, more than $116 million had been generated in corporate sponsorship and advance royalty fees.

Atlantic Richfield (ARCO) spent about $30 million in connection with the Los Angeles event, including a gift to the city of $4 million to refurbish the Los Angeles Coliseum and build practice tracks. ARCO Olympic program manager Earl McKinley frankly admitted the purpose of ARCO's participation—to "positively influence the media, politicians, and the community."[36] With businesses, especially oil companies, constantly complaining about unfair media treatment in news programs, the linking of sport, politics, and public-relations efforts in such a visible and ostensibly neutral forum is ideal.

Anheuser-Busch, America's largest brewer, contributed about $10 million in sponsorship money and planned to spend about $20 million on advertising related to the games. While it did not declare any of its beers the official Olympic beer, its ads showcased "the free enterprise system."

McDonald's, which won the race to become the official fast-service restaurant of the Olympics, built the new Olympic swimming stadium on the campus of the University of Southern California, another $4 million gift to the city.

Fuji Photo Film, an American subsidiary of the Japanese transnational corporation, beat out Kodak as the official photographic products, with a sponsorship gift of $5 million in cash. (See chapter 3 for a detailed discussion of the continuing ideological saga of Kodak and Fuji.) Fuji intended "to dispense free film to authorized media staffers."[37] Not content to rest with free gifts to photojournalists, Fuji developed a high-school photography course, the final lesson of which was a photo contest, with the winner receiving a free trip to the Los Angeles Olympic Games. Having infiltrated educational curricula, with the assumed support of educators, the task was complete.

The Los Angeles Olympic Organizing Committee reported a surplus of $150 million, ten times its projection. This was an eye-opener for the I.O.C., which, prior to 1984, had viewed sponsorships as a threat to the amateur nature of the Olympics. In 1985 the I.O.C. and national Olympic groups' managers became more businesslike and began more aggressively seeking the benefits of corporate sponsors. They began promoting a marketing plan known as "The Olympic Program" (T.O.P.) that enables corporations to buy worldwide sponsorship rights from nearly all the 167 national Olympic committees for their product categories (prior to this, a corporation had to reach agreement separately with each country). Sponsorships for the 1988 Summer Olympic Games in Seoul, South Korea, had risen 276 percent from total 1984 figures, totalling $338 million. Companies bought worldwide sponsorship rights at an average cost of about $14 million.[38]

The financial success of today's Olympic Games is dependent not only on corporate sponsorship but also (and since 1984 primarily) on the sale of television rights to telecast the event. In 1960, television rights fees provided only one of every 400 dollars of the cost of hosting the Olympic Games. In 1984, television provided more than half of the income needed to host the Los Angeles Summer Games.[39]

The bulk of the television rights fees come from the American broadcaster who secures U.S. rights from the I.O.C. in a one-bid auction. For example, the worldwide television rights contracts for the 1992 Summer

Games in Barcelona, Spain, totalled $635 million, of which $401 million (63 percent) was paid by NBC for U.S. rights, $90 million (14 percent) was paid by the European Broadcasting Union for European rights, $62 million (10 percent) was paid by Japan, and $82 million (13 percent) was paid by all other broadcasters around the world.[40] For the 1992 Winter Games in Albertville, France, CBS rights fees comprised over 82 percent of the worldwide total.[41]

Critics believe that the ferocious bidding wars for rights have gotten out of hand and ultimately disserve audiences. ABC reportedly lost about $65 million on its coverage of the 1988 Calgary Winter Games, although it sold all of its commercial slots, because the rights fee was too high and the prices for individual commercials were too low. And while NBC showed a profit from its coverage of the 1988 Seoul Summer Games, it delivered lower ratings than it had promised advertisers and had to offer advertisers "make-goods" (free spots), some of which aired during its Olympic coverage, causing commercial clutter.[42]

Why should the Olympic Games be any different from any other hyped sport event? Why shouldn't heroism on the field of sport be used to sell beer, hamburgers, gasoline, film, and the glories of the free enterprise system and to promote the program schedule of the television network covering the event? Defenders of the trend toward increasing commercialization of sport can rationalize, as does Stephen Hugh-Jones of *The Economist*:

The Olympics may reek of money, chauvinism and empty parade, but the all-amateur Berlin Olympics of 1936 reeked of parades much nastier than that. True, like any entertainment business, sport shares out its money with wild unevenness. But to be shared at all, money has to exist. Would equality of poverty be preferable? . . . today's money-driven sports are faster, higher and stronger than ever before. That is what top-level sport is about.[43]

Hugh-Jones sees "poverty" in purely economic terms. Lest one forget, the concept can be examined in a moral and ethical sense as well.

THE TV EVENT—PREDICTABLE AND UNEVENTFUL

If televised sport has become predictable as celebrity hype with attendant values, so too has the nonsport live television event, our country's contemporary ceremonial.

In the TV event, we find the stars of many different celebrity systems drawn together. It is truly a world of champions. It is also "the pinnacle of the prestige system and a big-scale business."[44] Television creates, selects, and celebrates celebrities. Celebrities are put on display. They also use media. As television has gained in both power and prestige, a class of professional celebrities has solidified its power base through continual use of the medium. Entertainers, entertainment businesspersons, champions of sport, famous artists, journalists, and commentators, through their regular appearances in a variety of television contexts, become household words, names of those we come to admire and respect. Many are anointed as "wise." We await their appearances at our public ceremonials, the televised rituals of awards presentations, national political conventions, celebrity roasts, and tributes from our hallowed national cultural institutions for those aging popular artists in the twilight of their careers.

We hope to see our celebrities, in the living-room intimacy of television, somehow unmasked—to know something of their human quality while still reveling in the mystique of their status as stars. What we now get, according to critic Michael Arlen, is a television event that is "increasingly fine-tuned and over-directed until [its] point . . . often seems to be no more (and no less) than [its] televisability."[45] The Academy Awards, in the early days of television, before the medium's tremendous visceral power to mold public opinion was clearly understood, featured cigar-smoking, visibly inebriated Hollywood celebrities dressed to the nines in often outrageous costumes, seated around tables, thoroughly enjoying the party but often losing their composure under the harsh scrutiny of the television camera, of which they surprisingly seemed either unaware or disinterested. Today's public ceremonial in Tinseltown finds well-behaved, rather conservatively dressed (for Southern California at any rate) young men and women sitting in rows of theater seats in the Dorothy Chandler Pavillion graciously applauding the awardees and "the new 'Internationale' of pop music."[46] The celebrities are confined to brief winners' speeches, the emcees read quickly from the teleprompters, and the commercial breaks are precisely orchestrated in the tightly scripted format. As in the case in the well-planned sovereign processionals for the coronation, marriage, and death of monarchs and their heirs, the event now must, at all costs, exhibit propriety.

The only time that truly "live" television emerges in these increasingly dull video spectacles is when some brazen or slightly demented soul interjects the improvisational human act into the proceedings by tearing up the script and becoming confrontational, as when a Venessa Redgrave or a Paddy Chayefsky or a Marlon Brando engages in a polemic about the Palestine Liberation Organization or McCarthy's blacklisting of Hollywood artists in the 1950s or the plight of the American Indian—and when the voices of the Hollywood establishment, the dominant entertainment culture, counter that the awards ceremonies are no place for personal politics or ideology, as if the writer, director, or actor were somehow a cipher with no ideas of his or her own or with no right to state those ideas they do have in a nonnarrative context—at least not during a program sponsored by Revlon or General Motors—and further, as if the television extravaganza itself were outside the domain of ideology and politics, a patently false conception to begin with.

What we are given at presidential tributes to the arts are visions of the café society, as the Reagans and Bushes, their invited guests, and millions of bored television viewers who have tuned in for the live event are treated to a pas de deux performed under a grotesque White House chandelier and paraded out as a celebration of American artistic genius, while thousands of progressive cultural workers have found their government-funding support evaporate like a shallow creek bed in a drought.

Our political conventions, especially those of the Democrats, were once vital, fascinating fora for the public exercise of the political process, at which party delegates would wrangle, bolt from one faction to another, stage demonstrations in the hall, and argue passionately over the language of the party platform. Since the Chicago Democratic Convention of 1968, with the riots in the streets and the rough handling of television journalists in the convention hall itself—all carried live and uncut to an incredulous nationwide television audience—party officials have done all within their power to manipulate both the delegates themselves and the television journalists to prevent any controversy from reaching the American viewers. The Republican public-relations experts have in fact succeeded in turning their conventions of recent vintage into mirror images of the Academy or Emmy Awards (one might also claim the Grammies) with songs by Donnie and Marie Osmond, dancing, polite applause, and mindless public speeches. The conventions even end on time—at the end of prime time—something the Oscars cannot even yet claim. A notable exception to these rather lifeless and irrelevant political events occurred during the 1992 Republican Convention as former candidate Pat Buchanan and televangelist Pat Robertson startled and outraged many in the nation with their exclusionary invective, delivered from the podium in prime time. While their remarks were thoughtless, they made many in the audience think twice.

If political conventions have become made-for-TV live entertainment events, so too have our national celebrations. A telling example was "Liberty Weekend," the nation's official Independence Day celebration linked in 1986 to the unveiling of the rehabilitated Statue of Liberty. The master of ceremonies was none other than our actor/president.

Portions of "Liberty Weekend" were sold on an exclusive basis for $10 million to ABC, which outbid NBC (CBS did not bid), by David Wolper, who produced the event (and who had also produced the ABC miniseries *Roots* and the opening and closing ceremonies of the 1984 Summer Olympic Games in Los Angeles, covered by ABC Sports). Liberty Weekend's official regulations stipulated that "all the proceedings except President Reagan's remarks and the actual lighting of the statue and torch are exclusive to ABC."[47] This restrictive clause drew formal protests from the news organizations at the rival networks, who asked how a bona-fide national news event could be licensed for sale.

Wolper maintained that the four-day event was an "entertainment event" even though it included ceremonies featuring President Ronald Reagan awarding the Medal of Liberty (invented by Wolper for this occasion) to 12 distinguished naturalized citizens, and Supreme Court Chief Justice Warren E. Burger swearing in 300 petitioners for citizenship on Ellis Island. Admittedly, Liberty Weekend was an unusual event:

the rededication of a national monument on a national holiday, commissioned by the private sector. The private Statue of Liberty–Ellis Island Foundation, empowered by the U.S. Interior Department to raise private funds for the restoration of the statue, was also given rein to plan the Fourth of July ceremony.[48]

And what did the private sector, with the approval of the U.S. government, come up with? Tap dancers, waterfalls, 200 Elvis Presley look-alikes. The cost, about $30 million.

ABC did pretty well by this celebration of freedom. The network spent about $14 million ($10 million in securing the exclusive rights and $4 million in coverage costs) and took in about $30 million from advertisers, who purchased 181 prime-time 30-second spots for about $165,000 each.[49]

There are larger social questions raised by the relationship of television to our reverence of the professional celebrity. As this chapter has repeatedly emphasized, the professional celebrity in the era of television, while revered by the fan, stands somehow outside the pattern of everyday social relations, although not outside the values of many citizens. Of course, this fact is endemic to the very quality of celebrityhood. The social function of celebrityhood is less apparent. C. Wright Mills found that an important function of the celebrity in contemporary social relations is the use of the celebrity by the country's "power elite"—the economic, political, and military bosses—to help them avoid the spotlight of public-media attention. In Mills's argument, the professional celebrity becomes an important and necessary media distraction, channeling the energy of the masses into hero worship. Mills suggested that for clearly defined reasons, namely, the continued consolidation of their true economic and political power, the power elite is "quite content to rest uncelebrated."[50] Karl Meyer found an essential class bias concealed in the myth of eternal progress as manifested in the worship of celebrity and fed to the flock by the latest marketing techniques, for the institutions and their workers who have achieved celebrity status appeal to the needs of demographically upscale audiences. The classic theme of the new city-statism or urban regionalism, according to Meyer, is inequality. Thus "money is available for 'blockbuster' shows but not for humdrum museum conservation; for municipal stadiums and convention centers but not services for the poor; for 'gentrification' of townhouses, while slum areas are redlined."[51]

Our distractions are expensive in a larger social context, for while we sit down to our beer and popcorn and watch the parade of telecelebrities pass before the camera lens, brought to us by official sponsors, the pecuniary system of social values is solidified and the material gap between the haves inside the set and have-nots sitting at home watching them widens. The Great American Dream is to be celebrated in living color with voice-over commentary supplied by the electronic pundits of our age.

NOTES

1. C. Wright Mills, *The Power Elite* (New York: Oxford University Press, 1956), pp. 71–72.

2. Ibid., p. 74.

3. John J. O'Connor, "On 'Chats' and Chatty Sports Announcers," *New York Times*, July 26, 1981, sec. 2, p. D25.

4. John J. O'Connor, "Sportscasting—Over-Explained, Over-Researched, Over-Hyped," *New York Times*, July 29, 1979, sec. 2, p. 25.

5. Erich Segal, "Take Me Out to the Metagame," review of Allen Guttman's *A Whole New Ball Game, The New York Times Book Review*, August 21, 1988, p. 37.

6. Karl E. Meyer, "Love Thy City: Marketing the American Metropolis," *Saturday Review*, April 28, 1979, p. 16.

7. Quoted in Meyer, ibid., p. 17.

8. Bill Carter, "New TV Contracts for N.F.L.'s Games Total $3.6 Billion," *New York Times*, March 10, 1990, p. 1. CBS paid $1 billion; ABC, $950 million; NBC $752 million; ESPN and Turner Entertainment Television, $450 million each.

9. Ibid.

10. Frank Litsky, "Around and Around These Free Agents Go," *New York Times*, March 28, 1993, "Sports Sunday," p. 8. In the 1993 free agency period, 298 NFL players (with five or more seasons in the NFL) were unrestricted free agents, and 140 players (entering their fourth or fifth pro season) were restricted free agents. A restricted free agent's team may retain his services by matching the other team's salary offer within seven days. Litsky reported that some restricted free agents were being offered three-year contracts at $4 million, or $1.33 million per year; their previous salaries averaged around $250,000 per year. Pittsburgh Steelers quarterback Neil O'Donnell, a restricted free agent who earned $250,000 in 1992, was offered a three-year $8.2 million deal by Tampa Bay, or over ten times his 1992 salary!

11. David Levine, "Image Is Everything," *Profiles*, January 1992, p. 21.

12. "The Business of Sport: What a Racket," *The Economist*, March 28, 1992, p. 78.

13. Levine, "Image," p. 18.

14. "The Business of Sport," p. 78.

15. Levine, "Image," p. 40.

16. Stephen Hugh-Jones, "A Survey of the Sports Business," *The Economist,* July 25, 1992, p. 16.

17. Edward Cone, "How to Shoot Yourself in the Foot and Still Win the Sales Race," *The European,* November 9–11, 1990, p. 22.

18. Levine, "Image," p. 42.

19. David Halberstam, "The Mouth That Roared," *Playboy,* December 1982, p. 130.

20. O'Connor, "On 'Chats,' " p. D25.

21. BBC sport coverage, like newsreading on the British network, is markedly different from American television's sport coverage. BBC commentators are less verbose, generally more insightful, and focus on analysis of the play rather than on the personalities of the players or on their status as multimillionaire celebrities.

22. Cosell did play-by-play of the assassination of a dictator in Allen's film *Bananas.*

23. Halberstam, "Mouth," p. 130.

24. "Sports People," *New York Times,* April 14, 1993, p. B10.

25. Michael Jahn, "From Sparta to Seoul: Glory and Politics at the Finish Line," *Brooklyn College Magazine,* May 1988, p. 2.

26. Quoted in ibid.

27. Ibid., p. 4.

28. Hugh-Jones, "A Survey of the Sports Business," p. 3.

29. Michael R. Real, *Super Media: A Cultural Studies Approach* (Newbury Park, CA: Sage Publications, 1989), p. 235.

30. Ibid., p. 239.

31. Ibid.

32. William C. Rhoden, "Yes, the Dream Team Romped, but Was It Worth It?" *New York Times,* August 9, 1992, sec. 4, p. 2.

33. Stephen King, "Dream Team: Just Another Horror Show," *New York Times,* August 9, 1992, sec. 8, p. 5.

34. Real, *Super Media,* p. 223.

35. Chris Barnett and Richard J. Pietschmann, "American Business Goes for the Gold," *United: The Magazine of the Friendly Skies,* April 1982, p. 77.

36. Ibid., p. 82.

37. Ibid.

38. "For Companies, Marketing Is the Main Sport of the Olympics," *New York Times,* September 12, 1988, p. D6.

39. Real, *Super Media,* p. 230.

40. Hugh-Jones, "A Survey of the Sports Business," p. 4.

41. Michael Janofsky, "CBS Given '92 Winter Games," *New York Times,* May 25, 1988, p. D25. According to the I.O.C.'s television rights distribution formula, the U.S. Olympic Committee received 10 percent of the CBS rights fee off the top, while the Albertville organizing committee received 48 percent for its general fund and 18 percent for facilities construction, and the I.O.C. itself received 24 percent of the total.

42. Geraldine Fabrikant, "NBC's Surprising Olympic Win," *New York Times,* December 1, 1988, sec. 3, p. 5.

43. Hugh-Jones, "A Survey of the Sports Business," p. 19.

44. Mills, *Power Elite,* p. 74.

45. Michael J. Arlen, "The Big Parade," *The New Yorker*, April 30, 1979, p. 122.

46. Ibid., p. 123.

47. Peter J. Boyer, "ABC's Rivals Challenge 'Liberty' Exclusivity," *New York Times*, June 14, 1986, p. C26.

48. Ibid.

49. Ibid.

50. Mills, *Power Elite*, p. 91.

51. Meyer, "Love Thy City," p. 20.

9

□ □ □ □ □ □

TV Religion and the TV Game Show: *The Great American Dream in the Late Twentieth Century*

The television preacher is this culture's most peculiar and most provocative version of the entertainer-celebrity. A truly splendid performer, his ego-driven quest for notoriety has served this country's conservative political and industrial elites well, diverting attention from their ideological regime of ever-increasing centralized control of production and capital accumulation by redirecting the barely contained anger of the exploited rural and urban working poor toward the alleged evils of twentieth-century social reformers who are, he declares, tampering with both the word of the Lord and one's inherent "right" to lead one's own life. This modern-day theocrat has updated an ideology grounded in the American Calvinist theological tradition by incorporating both the dogmatic idea of the "right ordering" of self, family, and state—of total control of every aspect of everyday life in order to glorify God—and the late-nineteenth-century conservative American socioeconomic theory of individualism, which held that the government, while providing an orderly society in which each individual can fulfill a personal destiny, should avoid unnecessary intrusion in people's lives. The television preacher has buttressed this ideology with the myth of the Protestant ethic and its promise of reward, through God, for hard work. The result is an intense video celebration of an American social ethos revealed in the mythic constructs of eternal progress, as manifested in entrepreneurial capitalism; of the frontier, with its rugged individualism; and of manifest destiny, with its single-minded philosophy of conquest, sanctioned by God, of geography, bank accounts, and souls. In short, the electronic preacher is the exemplification of the Great American Dream, television style.

A study of the electronic ministry becomes an examination of television's self-reflexivity, of television endlessly imitating itself. The video domain of power and progress is clearly revealed in the imaging system that marks the new religion. Establishing shots divulge the conspicuous splendor of the video church, more likely than not a massive television studio with live audiences supplying the background enthusiasm. In one particularly elaborate electronic church/studio, the audience dutifully and very politely applauds a pop singer's "easy-listening" rendition of some religious tune—pure Lawrence Welk from the golden age of television. Extreme close-ups of these preachers' intense, Rasputin-like gazes and their occasional wistful stares into space, evoking the vision of pioneers preparing for the conquest of the American West, captivate millions of sedentary American living-room parishioners. One electronic minister, following AT&T's advertising campaign advice to "reach out and touch someone," goes so far as to lay hands on your television screen. The viewer knows this electronic prophet is working overtime to drive away the devil as he sweats profusely under the klieg lights, exhorting God to "heal . . . heal . . . heeeeeaaaaallll!"

The fundamentalist social subculture, which today claims a very large following, estimated variously between 55 and 80 million persons throughout the United States,[1] traces its lineage to groups such as the lower-class rural Virginians of the late-eighteenth century. According to American cultural historian Russel Blaine Nye, "The small farmers of the Piedmont and the artisans of the towns were rough, proud, individualistic, turbulent people. They were Calvinist or evangelical in their religion, with little sympathy for the gentlemanly deism or Anglicanism of the Tidewater."[2] Today, Virginia boasts a concentration of electronic ministries, from Jerry Falwell's rural Thomas Road Baptist Church in Lynchburg to Pat Robertson's mammoth suburban-style Christian Broadcasting Network operation in Virginia Beach.

With this subculture's roots so closely linked with Calvinist dogma and its notions of the inherent sinfulness of humanity, is it any wonder that so many Americans tune in regularly to be reminded of their debased condition—of their fall from grace, in which the television melodrama, and especially soap opera, has specialized for decades—and to revel in the sideshow spectacle of its temporary subjugation as the preacher, resembling a combatant on all-star wrestling, puts the "atomic drop" on the devil. Television is a medium that, against its own best pecuniary interests, exposes the soul in all its banality—"up close and personal," in the words of that indefatigable sports announcer–celebrity Howard Cosell—just as it unflatteringly reveals the wrinkles, which makeup will not hide, in the aging actor's face. It is through the television minister, with his crass pecuniary motives and perspiring insincerity, that the true colors of bourgeois culture stare out at us from behind the curtain of grace.

Not far from the sacred realm of television preaching, in the root cellar of the human imagination, dwells that other modern entertainer-celebrity, the television game-show host. He wears the same ostentatious haberdashery the television preacher wears, but adds a bit of Southern California–calculated informality, such as a plaid sport jacket or an open-necked shirt and love beads or gold chain. His (almost all are men; women's roles in this domain are as sexy assistants) on-air attitude is clearly analogous to that of his televangelist counterpart—a mixture of smug condescension and used-car-salesman hard sell. He exhorts his prey, the contestants, to bare their souls to the millions in the audience by dressing up in outlandishly degrading costumes or by abandoning all public decorum by uncontrollably gesticulating and feigning excitement at the slightest provocation. Their actions are direct confessions of their abject complicity in this debasing public spectacle of greed and narcissism.

The essential difference between these two television forms is that the latter, rather than glorifying the socially conservative work ethic, celebrates instead sloth and chance, although the contestants must work hard—a new form of American work—to be noticed by the host or his agent by exhibiting some provocative or bizarre behavior and, by virtue of such behavior, to be selected to appear on the show. Yet the religious show and the game show are similar in many ways, not the least important of which is their promise of instant salvation—that money, either donated in the former instance or won in the latter, will release one from some psychic or physical suffering. These shows are the epic odysseys of our time—electronic journeys of punishment and the quest for release. As critic Edwin Diamond wrote, "On God's television one prays for God's help to get a new car or a higher paying job or a better apartment . . . and the unremitting faith in getting the world's goods makes these programs resemble 'The $20,000 Pyramid' or other television grab shows."[3] Pat Robertson told his 700 Club audience one night that Jesus would help them find parking spaces.

The dramaturgy of these shows is similar, although their formats are distinct. Miracles/clues to the merchandise behind door number two are revealed to the show's participants and the home audience at breakneck speed. There is incessant small talk, periodic singing or music background, and always selling. Don Pardo, rattling off the list of prizes "donated" for the daily jackpot, bears a striking resemblance to the born-again local bible-hour guest breathlessly speaking in tongues. Cries of joy and hallelujahs are heard from the winners, sobs from the losers (although the electronic preachers talk about losers in the past tense). There is continual tension and its subsequent release. This is great television drama.

THE GOSPEL ACCORDING TO JIM BAKKER ET AL.

The image of Jim Bakker, bent and sobbing, being led off to prison, must have been difficult for many evangelical Christians to apprehend. Bakker, son of a Muskegon, Michigan, minister, who went on the road with his wife Tammy Faye to preach throughout the South for the Pentacostal Assemblies of God and who became spiritual leader of a multimillion-dollar television ministry, had been convicted in federal court in October 1989 of twenty-four counts of fraud and conspiracy and sentenced to forty-five years in prison in connection with the sale of "lifetime partnerships"—viewer contributions of $1,000 or more to help finance the construction of Heritage USA, a Christian family resort and retreat center near Charlotte, North Carolina. (The lifetime partners would receive three nights' annual lodgings at Heritage forever.) Bakker's rise and fall is more than a morality tale. It is symptomatic of the greed that insidiously infiltrated many of this country's major institutions in the 1980s. Electronic religion was no exception.

The Bakkers began their television careers in 1964 as host and puppeteer of a children's religious show on a Portsmouth, Virginia, UHF station owned by Pat Robertson. Two years later, Robertson asked them to host an early version of Christian Broadcasting Network's *The 700 Club*. Jim interviewed guests, and Tammy Faye sang. They left CBN in 1972 and established their own television program, *The P.T.L. Club* (P.T.L. stood for "Praise the Lord" and "People That Love"), in 1976. Like *The 700 Club*, *The P.T.L. Club* employed a talk-show format. The P.T.L. Network's revenues soon rivalled those of Robertson's CBN and Jimmy Swaggart's television ministry.

Bakker's principal theme was that it was acceptable to God for Christians to be prosperous. And he set out to prove his point. The Bakkers' annual salary of $250,000 paled when set against the perks of the job. In the mid-1980s, at the height of their religious empire, the Bakkers lived in a church-owned house near Heritage USA. They owned a $449,000 house in Palm Springs, California, and a $375,000 condominium in Florida furnished with $60,000 in gold plumbing fixtures. They drove matching Rolls Royces and vacationed on an ocean-going cruiser.

The P.T.L. Club bought approximately $7.5 million worth of air time on nearly 200 broadcast television stations and 3,000 cable systems nationwide in 1979. By 1985 Bakker's programs were available on cable systems serving 13 million households. Bakker's on-air fundraising was yielding over $100 million annually (PTL reported revenue of $129 million in 1986). Bakker appeared to have the Midas touch. However, as a highly profitable television ministry was not enough, Bakker extended his entrepreneurial vision.

Bakker broke ground for Heritage USA in 1978. Located on 2,300 acres in Fort Mill, South Carolina, by 1985 the $150 million Christian theme park would include a luxury hotel, campground, private homes and rental condominiums, a shopping mall, eight restaurants, and a 1,200-seat auditorium complete with television studios. Plans were on the boards for a 30,000-seat convention center. About four million people visited Heritage USA in 1984.

The Bakkers' rise to power was not without controversy. In 1981, Bakker was under investigation by the Federal Communications Commission for possible misappropriation of funds. It was alleged that Bakker's pleas for financial support for his overseas missions had produced substantial contributions, many of which may have been diverted to domestic projects under Bakker's control. No action was taken by the FCC. Also in the early 1980s, the Internal Revenue Service questioned PTL's bookeeping practices that left $13 million in PTL revenue incompletely accounted for. Bakker suggested that "the devil got into the computer" used for P.T.L.'s record-keeping.[4]

Bakker survived these challenges. But more trouble, of a different kind, awaited. Bakker had had a sexual encounter with a church secretary, Jessica Hahn, in December 1980, which had been hushed up by a $115,000 payment to Hahn. Fearing that televangelist rival Jimmy Swaggart would break the story in an effort to take over P.T.L., Bakker suddenly resigned his ministry in March 1987 and appointed Baptist televangelist Jerry Falwell to assume the ministry's leadership. It was revealed that Tammy Faye was receiving treatment for dependency on prescription drugs. The Hahn affair soon became public. Falwell audited the P.T.L. books and discovered substantial irregularities, which he made public. Bakker was accused of cheating contributors of nearly $158 million.

In June 1987, the P.T.L. ministry sought protection from creditors in bankruptcy court. In 1988 a judge approved the sale of P.T.L.'s chief asset, Heritage USA.

Jim and Tammy Faye Bakker returned to the air in early 1988. They paid for the time with their own money and made no direct appeals for donations. *The Jim and Tammy Show* originated from a living room of a home the Bakkers had borrowed in Pineville, North Carolina. The program was sent by satellite to six stations around the country.

The Bakkers' fall from grace may best be described by the dictum, revised to meet the tenor of the times: "He who lives by TV shall die by TV." Like the Roman Empire of old, the electronic preacher, in the megalomaniacal quest for self-aggrandizement, may ignore the dangers of overextended supply lines.

The Bakkers' rise to media prominence had been the focus of pointed criticism well before the public revelations of impropriety. Critics argued that the ostentatious Heritage Grand hotel was "a monument inconsistent with its own Christian heritage." University of Chicago professor of religion Martin Marty noted that televangelists like Bakker have a "very bold transactional view of bargaining with the diety. They tell the viewers, many of whom are people who live on Social Security, that if they send money, they'll be blessed, not with meaning, but with things."[5]

One unintended consequence of P.T.L.'s success was the migration of thousands of poor and often homeless Christians who, inspired by P.T.L.'s message of hope and optimism, came to Heritage USA not on holiday, but rather looking for jobs and charity. P.T.L. officials gave them one night's free lodging but eventually turned them away. Many ended up on the public and private social agency rolls in nearby Charlotte, North Carolina.[6]

Televised religion clearly represents the confusing contemporary social milieu wherein, in the constant clash of traditional values and pecuniary drives, competition emerges victorious at the expense of community and our cultural orientation gradually and subtly shifts from reciprocity to struggle and survival at the level of the individual, for himself or herself, not for the group. This is manifested both in the attitudes and praxis of the electronic minister himself, as the survival of his ministry takes precedence over theological questions related to the nature of the Gospel, and in the electronic parishioner, whose salvation is linked to prayer inextricably tied to monetary contributions to support the ministry's regime of communication satellites and opulent university complexes—temples not to humanist education or to God, but to the persona of the electronic minister himself. The reward for the viewer's contribution is individual recognition on the air through such cunning gimmicks as inclusion of his name in a "prayer tower" subsequently sealed for eternity. This lends a sense of exclusivity to the religious act of giving, analogous to one's gaining membership in some prestigious society or country club. And, while the individual souls of the electronic church's faithful major contributors are so saved, the society as a whole, say the electronic preachers, is rapidly going to hell, courtesy of Communist sympathizers and homosexuals who undermine family values, while traditional respect for the authority of dominant institutions, such as the corporate state apparatus with its police power, diminishes.

What is ironic about this incongruous mixture of pecuniary philosophy and traditional values manifested in electronic religion is the resultant transformation of these very traditional values the electronic church extols into their opposites. As cultural anthropologist Jules Henry noted,

Since values like love, truth, the sacredness of high office, God, the Bible, motherhood, generosity, solicitude of others . . . are the foundations of Western culture, anything that weakens or distorts them shades traditional life; . . . as it embraces the traditional values, pecuniary philosophy chokes them to death.[7]

This state of affairs, termed by Henry "value deterioration through monetization," occurs when certain cultural forces, such as religion, not ordinarily considered part of the processes of production and selling are used to make money.

The electronic church is, on its most basic level, a contradiction in terms. Religious values and the hucksterism associated with commercial television entertainment can at best coexist in an uneasy alliance. While it provides an important basic service to one segment of the population—the shut-ins, who would not otherwise enjoy the sense of community offered to the mobile by the neighborhood spiritual center traditionally associated with organized mainline religion of all denominations—the electronic church, needing (or so it claims) the intensive capitalization necessary to play the big-time television game of prestige and profitability, to secure, in short, electronic cultural legitimacy, moves beyond this limited social function toward a new role as contemporary polemicist and moral watchdog in the worst traditions of 1950s McCarthyism. The motto of the electronic preacher, who has learned how to milk the dramatic possibilities of television, might well read: "First get their attention; then get their money; then save 'em." And from what are they being saved? First, from themselves, in the cynical Calvinist tradition. Second, from Communism and, according to the ideological scheme, its American offspring, evil liberal secular humanism. The electronic preachers offer hackneyed political dogma sandwiched between clean all-American entertainment, packaged in a late-night talk-show format perfected by that secular humanist Johnny Carson, but minus Carson's wit and sexual innuendo. The neatly scrubbed, racially balanced gospel singers, who graduated from the "Muzak School of Tunes and Human Factor Engineering," provide the uptempo ambience for a celebration of success—the Great American Dream of eternal progress in the suburban middle landscape (here "eternal" really means eternal). Critic Dick Dabney wrote disapprovingly that TV evangelists were "raising money by selling miracles—and hard-selling them especially to the poor, the ill, and the desperate, . . . [equating] New Testament Christianity with the worship of success."[8] The incongruity of these celebrations of winning is clear to Christian critic Virginia Owens, who wrote "The original pattern these people profess to imitate was [that of] a vagrant celibate whose own seminar on happiness elevated the mourning meek rather than the smiling success."[9] The winners in this new era of pecuniary religion, who have been saved from themselves and have subsequently come to know both Christ and King Midas, parade through the ether to testify. The stories of human degradation and ultimate salvation are the preludes to the inevitable pitch, which takes a myriad of amazingly inventive forms in the glorious tradition of television ad campaigns, but interestingly without the polish the studio acts and lavish sets seem to portend. The pitches are often made on videotape and are generally very quiet compared with the preceding razzle-dazzle. In the CBN studios, Pat Robertson asks the viewer to send him $100 or more along with "seven lifetime prayer requests." The viewer's name and requests are then put on microfilm and interred in something called a "prayer pillar," upon which rests a tabletop and a large King James Bible, in the center of the prayer chapel in the CBN building. The pillar is sealed and the donor's salvation guaranteed, at least for this year.[10] If you happened to tune in Rex Humbard's television ministry and contribute, but failed to continue your contributions, you may have received a personalized, word-processed letter, which read, "Dear . . . : Last week I knelt at the prayer altar to pray for every member in the Prayer Key Family Book, and I wanted to pray for you . . . but your name was not there." Ernest Angley, the TV faith healer who lays his hands on your television screen, offers a more modest package. For only $100, you receive 16 audio cassettes that contain the complete New Testament. This seems the best deal of the lot.

The quiet pitch for financial support becomes the preacher's down-home ruse, signifying he hasn't forgotten his roots. He thus reminds his followers of the humble rural-middle-landscape mythology that undergirds the entire electronic religious enterprise. The electronic preacher uses this poor-country-boy heritage to great advantage as he stresses his own humble beginnings in the context of his successful rise to power through hard work, single-mindedness of purpose, and prayer—a spiritual version of Horatio Alger. These are stories involving faith, love of family and children, and folksiness. There is Jim Bakker's story, recounted earlier. There is Oral Roberts, poor Oklahoma farm boy who now has a home on the edge of a Palm Springs country club. There is Pat Robertson, a seeming exception to the tale of the self-made Christian. Son of a U.S. senator from Virginia and a Yale graduate, Robertson has nevertheless made the best of his potentially problematic heritage (after all, the Piedmont farmers of 200 years ago had little respect for the likes of Thomas Jefferson and the Tidewater intelligentsia). Robertson claims he fled his posh Manhattan apartment, his wealth, and his secular emptiness to return to his Virginia roots and his Bible study. Upon conversion, Robertson claims, he gave all his worldly goods to the poor. Yet somehow he sent four children to college, has horses, a beautifully furnished house, and an office described as luxurious.[11] There is Robert Schuller, genial host of *The Hour of Power*, an Iowa farm boy who came to Southern California in 1955 with $500 and an organ in a rented U-Haul trailer, started a drive-in church on top of a snack bar of the Orange Drive-In Theater, which he used from 1955 to 1961, and now preaches from the $15 million Crystal Cathedral, designed by architect Philip Johnson.

How is it possible for these televangelists to be so visibly successful and yet continue to lay claim to their inherent humbleness? This is accomplished through the contemporary advanced capitalist mechanism of the fringe benefit or perk—that extra benefit beyond salary that freshens the deal. Indeed, if one looks at the televangelists' salaries, one gets a highly distorted view of their wealth. According to a Cable News Network special report on televangelists, aired in 1981, the average salary for an electronic minister of some note was $45,000–$60,000 per year, yet they had "considerable expense accounts" and "rent-free mansions."[12] In 1979 Robert

Schuller reportedly had a salary of but $39,000. He was driving a Cadillac Seville donated by a wealthy parishioner.[13] As C. Wright Mills wrote in *The Power Elite,* the new power elite camouflages its wealth in stock options and benefits other than "visible" salary. As the newest members of this American power elite, the televangelists are no exception.

This powerful battery of myths—of the humble beginnings and family support in the rural middle landscape; the rugged individualism of the frontier, which encourages the humble minister to venture forth unafraid into the spiritual wilderness in hopes of establishing a viable ministry; and the entrepreneurial success to be found in the suburban middle landscape—coalesce in the vision of the Great American Dream, late-twentieth-century style. To understand the power of such a sociocultural construct as presented in the lives and words of the televangelists, one must recognize that the predominant audience for television worship is rural, southern or southwestern (although there are many provincial viewers in large east-coast metropolitan areas as well), and traditional in its value orientation; these people are also the children of the camera age, with its constant imaging focused on consumption, competition, shifting values, and individual achievement. The eclecticism of the television church fits comfortably into this seemingly contradictory mythic frame. Like the characters on *Dallas,* whom we love to hate, the electronic church allows us to view ourselves—acquisitive, competitive, successful, anomic, and full of sin—and to reconcile ourselves to the contradictions we observe. We mollify our self-hate; and we send money for this ecclesiastical legerdemain.

All this is a far cry from the individual "justification by faith" of Martin Luther. Indeed, the entire apparatus of the electronic church flies in the face of the Reformation, which asserted the sovereignty of God over both the individual and the religious institution. How does the pecuniary salvation of *The 700 Club* and *The P.T.L. Club* differ in intent from the medieval Catholic papacy's sale of indulgences to the German city-states to gather money needed to build elaborate basilicas?

As was the case with the church's construction of monuments to its own power, the televangelists likewise construct vast media edifices to legitimize their authority and to spread the "word." The Christian Broadcasting Network tapes *The 700 Club* in a 400-seat studio with a live audience. The studio cameras and videotape recording equipment are state-of-the-art. The studio lighting is computerized. And the studio is but a small part of the $20 million CBN headquarters complex, which includes television studios, corporate offices, and a graduate school in Christian communication. Robert Schuller's Crystal Cathedral is pure Southern California. His weekly *Hour of Power* program is taped there. The song-and-dance extravaganza, reminiscent of the most lavish of Cecil B. DeMille sets, fits perfectly in the all-glass tower. The glass entrance features doors

80 feet high and 12 feet wide. Architect Philip Johnson, the cathedral's designer, noted that "the opening of those doors will look great on TV. Dr. Schuller knows exactly what he's doing."[14] Bakker's *The P.T.L. Club* was taped before a live studio audience in Charlotte, North Carolina, in an extravagant studio complex rivaling that of CBN. Oral Roberts's telecasts, taped at the Maybee Center television complex at Oral Roberts University in Tulsa, Oklahoma, use equipment equivalent to that used in the network television studios in New York City. The electronic preachers, being practical men, understand that the television audience has come to expect the very highest technical quality from their religious programs. The local gospel hour, with its "hot" preacher, taped either in a closet studio with faded draperies as a backdrop, cheap microphones, and uneven lighting, or in a cavernous auditorium with awful acoustics, is unacceptable to today's multimillion-dollar religious entrepreneurs. Oral Roberts, in his earlier television faith-healing days, preached in such an environment. But he has grown up with the medium. And the younger electronic preachers have followed suit.

These elaborate facilities confer status on their owners and build credibility, which allows them to continue to spread the word. And the word is "control." The most intelligent and ambitious of the televangelists, men such as Pat Robertson, who made a serious run for the Republican presidential nomination in 1988, and Jerry Falwell, who has organized a powerful conservative political lobbying group, have a clearly conceived world view of theology, economic theory, political theory, and sociology woven together to form an articulate, if highly debatable vision of human nature and contemporary social response to human needs.[15]

The world view articulated by the televangelists is grounded in their fundamentalist theological position, that is, a literal belief in the Bible. The word of the Lord dominates all discussion of lifestyle, politics, and economics. The viewer must come to know Jesus directly. Traditional theology would have this happen as one contemplated, in silence, in the presence of other worshipers, the mystery of the spiritual. Further, the hiddenness of religious meaning, according to traditional theological argument, would, upon one's participation in sacred "initiation rites," be revealed to the true believer.[16] Televangelists give this traditional theology a contemporary twist, best expressed by CBN's Pat Robertson through his so-called kingdom principles. According to this schema, one comes to know Jesus through a combination of prayer and giving. If the viewer gives to Jesus, Jesus will give back to the viewer. And the most effective and efficient way to give to Jesus in the television age is to give money to his slave, the televangelist—in this case, Pat Robertson. Through his kingdom principles, Robertson thus encourages his audience "to believe that they can buy miracles."[17] If one is in desperate financial straits and still manages to give to Jesus, through Robertson, out of one's need, that person will achieve even greater power. This, cynically translated, means you give your social-security check to Robertson and his ministry, do without heat, and eat white bread and gravy every day. To the middle class, Robertson preaches a modified version of the kingdom principles, namely, that these upwardly mobile Christians should refrain from purchasing that new house so that they might be able to maintain their contributions to his ministry, and through it to Jesus. The twist here is that by answering Robertson's call to give, economic miracles may flow. The unemployed man may get that job offer he has been desperately seeking. The struggling entrepreneur, on the verge of insolvency, may swing that big deal that was always just beyond his grasp. Hope is held out in exchange for an investment in Robertson's ministry, with salvation as a fringe benefit. These people have worked hard and fallen on misfortune but will be saved through the miracle of Jesus Christ, with the intercession of the televangelist.

While the Bible suggests Jesus will bring the believer tribulation as a test of his or her moral commitment, the new evangelical interpretation has Jesus bringing instead riches, an interpretation appropriate for its television context. The televised religious experience is, first of all, not private or communal. It is preformulated and one-way. It is immediate, rational, highly planned, and carefully budgeted—in short, it has clear secular overtones dictated in large measure by the medium that carries it and by the culture created in large measure by that medium. As such, the new television religion stands in direct contradistinction to the traditional mainline religion, a stance the televangelists are quick to defend.

The television preachers declare that mainline religious theology is at odds with today's "supposedly spontaneous spirituality," is dull, and preaches an increasingly liberal secular doctrine.[18] In contrast, they argue, they offer contemporary religion to which people can relate. They see little virtue in solitude, humility, or frugality. They are upbeat, preaching personal, if not social, optimism and the ethic of success—what one critic termed "brisk, no-apologies materialism."[19] Before he was sent to prison, Jim Bakker could say with a straight face, "Diamonds are made for Christians, not Satan."[20] Robert Schuller, the champion of "possibility thinking," a strange mixture of religion and economics, can profess the "economics of Christianity"—a doctrine aimed at middle-class Christians stressing personal pride, business success, and charisma, the latter defined by one of Schuller's guests, professor David Schwartz, as divine spirit given to mankind, which man must use to make money.[21] Schuller's program is the embodiment of this Christian ethos. The service is a mixture of pop Christian tunes, in the manner of Barry Manilow, sung by elegantly gowned soloists using wireless handheld microphones. The imaging is decidedly high-tech. Camera work is flawless and well rehearsed and relies on dissolves, through flower arrangements and gently waving palm trees, from a large choir to Schuller's son Robert A., engrossed in prayer. Schuller's son is the warm-up for dad's appearance. The transition between son and father is the inevitable pitch for money, which has included, as a gift for one's contribution, a coffee mug inscribed with Schuller's motto: "If it's going to be, it's up to me."

This new religion has a deeply troubling implicit premise, namely, "An ordinary life is contemptible and . . . there is a magical way out."[22] The premise is revealed in two highly disparate ways. In the Calvinist religious traditions of fundamentalism, we watch "the televised confessions of frailty, guilt, misdemeanor or felony," which "become inspiration events, . . . the equivalents of revivalist baptisms."[23] Bakker's The P.T.L. Club once had a children's puppet segment in which the puppets were singing, "How do you spell relief? J.E.S.U.S." This motley scene was modeled on the advertising jingle for Rolaids antacid tablets. The children were being relieved from original sin. Such analogizing of moral status and indigestion is offensive to the religious and areligious alike because it reduces higher questions of the meaning of spirituality to the level of over-the-counter drugs. On another level, in the tradition of mid-twentieth-century American individualism, the most important Christians have become the Christian superstars of the public-media world. Singers such as Pat Boone and Robert Goulet, actors such as Efram Zimbalist, Jr., athletes such as Sugar Ray Leonard, politicos such as Chuck Colson of Watergate fame and former radical Eldridge Cleaver, and chicken magnates such as Colonel Harlan Sanders have all appeared to testify on The 700 Club or another of the Christian "talkies." The world of Christian winners, like the secular world upon which it so consciously models itself, offers a world of champions to the downtrodden viewer—a media world in which the stars of a variety of systems are drawn together to celebrate their success. This is "the star system of a society that makes a fetish of competition."[24] This celebration of celebrityhood draws attention to the economic power and social prestige of the televangelist, who is able to achieve the coup of getting top-name talent on his show. And it lessens the blow of economic-class and social-class status inequality associated with celebrityhood by revealing that even these superstar heroes were once humanly weak. As always, spiritual equality is presented as transcending material inequality. This rationale sets the stage for additional requests for financial support.

The realm of superstar media Christianity is reinforced by an entire Christian lifestyle-marketing strategy, which fits nicely into the cool ambience of the suburban middle landscape of the Christian talk show and the suave elegance of Schuller's Crystal Cathedral. This new Christian lifestyle is strictly suburban middle landscape. Its psychographic profile would include achievers—prosperous, middle-aged Christian materialists—and emulators—ambitious young Christian adults. The resentful, poor sustainers, who are more likely to relate better to the heavy-handed

Elmer Gantryism of a television faith healer like Ernest Angley or Rex Humbard or any of a variety of local or regional "UHF preachers," are outside the purview of this new upper-middle-class Christianity (although these sustainers are attracted to the messages of Pat Robertson, who can successfully play both sides of the Christian scene—a tribute to his media performance skills).

The scope of Christian lifestyle marketing is far-reaching, with books on Christian cooking, diets, exercise regimens, moneymaking strategies, athletics, sexuality, and psychology—a perfect mirror of secular culture. There are conference ministries, the "retreat centers," which critic Virginia Owens calls "genial exercises in relaxation."[25] There are Christian lifestyle workshops in such areas as assertiveness training, feminism, and cooking. There is the Christian entertainment industry with its concerts, record companies, agents who book appearances and determine, through market research, the hottest-selling theology of the day, and Christian nightclubs that sell soft drinks. The mass-produced romance has "gone Christian" as Silhouette Books, a $140 million publishing enterprise, released a new line of formulaic romantic novellas in early 1984 called "Silhouette Inspirations." According to the Inspirations editor-in-chief, these romances are "entertaining stories about wholesome people who have made a commitment to God in their lives."[26] The book launch called for 24 new titles, each 192 pages long, to be released every year and sold in religion sections of secular bookstores.

In the 1990s, Christian lifestyle marketing is targeting youth culture through Christian music videos. One recent video, "Out of the Tombs," produced by the American Bible Society's multimedia program, is a contemporary translation of the story of Gadarene Demoniac, contained in Mark 5:1-20. The original version describes a man possessed by evil spirits, which Jesus casts into swine on the shores of the Sea of Galilee. In the music video, filmed in Queens and Brooklyn, New York, Jesus appears as a welder. He wanders with the possessed man through tenements and graffiti-covered urban landscapes. The evil spirit wears a turned-around baseball cap and high-top sneakers. The man is healed and transformed and is seen at the conclusion of the nine-minute video telling his story to a group of children on a tree-lined street straight out of the suburban middle landscape. A 20-page discussion guide is included with the video.[27]

The image underlying the new Christian lifestyle is "impeccable cultural accommodation"[28] to the secular world, as the televangelists seek the financial support needed to fuel their ever-expanding media machines. And it is a small step from lifestyle into direct involvement in the affairs of state. It is in this latter realm that the role of the televangelist has stirred bitter controversy, not only between television preachers and secular critics but also among television preachers themselves.

John Cotton, a seventeenth-century Puritan clergyman and a leader of the Massachusetts Bay Colony, wrote that fundamentalism prescribed "perfect rules for the right ordering of a private mans soule . . . a mans family, yea, of the commonwealth too, so farre as both of them are subordinate to spiritual ends."[29] Cotton staunchly defended the colony's policy that men were admitted to citizenship only if they were church members, irrespective of their social status. Cotton was a highly articulate spokesperson for a fundamentalist Christian aristocracy and monarchy. Cotton's dogma was attacked by Enlightenment defenders of disestablishment, most notably Thomas Paine who, in his 1792 essay "The Rights of Man," warned that "as religion is very improperly made a political machine . . . the reality of it is thereby destroyed."[30]

Today's most vociferous television ministers would agree with Cotton that the ideal form of government is a Christian theocracy. How this is accomplished, however, is open to dispute. Billy Graham cautioned that television ministers should avoid the political arena and that television transformed "staid politicians into glib media stars. The same process could devour preachers and their ministries."[31] Graham, a close friend of Richard Nixon, urged televangelists to speak to moral issues, not to endorse political causes or support political candidates. Graham's argument is, of course, specious, for morality and politics are inseparable, as Cotton knew so well.

Today, if one needs a "mandate from the people," as well as from God, to lead in the political arena, then the most prominent televangelists believe they have that mandate, based both on the sheer numbers of declared "born-agains" revealed by survey research and on the fervent commitment of these people to the born-again dogma. A 1979 Gallup survey, for example, funded by 29 religious groups, found that 34 percent of those interviewed considered themselves born-again Christians.[32] A 1982 Gallup survey, quoted by Graham, found that one-third of the Americans in the sample said they watched religious programs during the seven days prior to the survey, and most said these programs were evangelical. A 1981 Nielsen survey found that during the survey period, 1.36 million households (or about 4 million people) watched Oral Roberts's weekly program *Oral Roberts and You*; 1.26 million households watched Robert Schuller's weekly *Hour of Power*; 690,000 households watched Jerry Falwell's weekly *Old-Time Gospel Hour*; and 413,000 households watched Jim Bakker's *The P.T.L. Club*.[33] These programs were among the most successful of the evangelistic shows carried by hundreds of broadcast television stations throughout the United States. It has been estimated that more than 62 million people worldwide watch Oral Roberts's Christmas and Easter television specials. With such a potential power base, it is little wonder that Robertson, Falwell, and others believe that a political mission is an integral part of the ideology of their ministries.[34]

While each minister has his individual political goals and philosophy, there is a commonality to their basic political thought. The New Christian Right, as the political movement is called, has an implicit political platform. It adheres to the constitutional principle of freedom of speech (i.e., the church should be free to condemn the evils of misguided liberals). It believes in the separation of church and state (i.e., the state should stay out of the church's affairs). And it believes secular authority has lost control, that America is being held captive to the whims of homosexuals, prochoice advocates (whom it castigates as murderers), feminists, liberal politicians and Supreme Court justices, pornographers, and "bloated consumerism." In short, America is diseased. According to CBN's Pat Robertson, we suffer "values confusion" and seek answers for our confusion in pleasure and secular therapies that are doomed to failure. This "embattled view" offered by television ministers would have us believe that our real enemy is "secular humanism," which holds that God is irrelevant to the conduct of our everyday lives, and that secular authorities are playing God by socializing the nation's children, through amoral secular education, to believe in "moral relativism" and theories of evolution. Further, according to this line of reasoning, liberal politicians "robbed the working class to create for themselves a huge constituency of debased, supine, viscious lumpen" whose existence was destroying the moral fiber of American society.[35] This argument is not new. It was advanced in the early nineteenth century by politically and socially conservative Christians of the Christian benevolent societies. Between 1815 and 1830 nearly a dozen moral reform societies were established to counter threats to social control by irreligious democrats espousing egalitarianism. These groups— the American Tract Society, American Bible Society, American Sunday School Union, and others—dreamed of a "nonpolitical" Christian Party ensuring a one-party system open to moral talent and the natural superiority of Christian leadership.

Robertson is correct that secular education is "amoral." However, his definition is incorrect—the amorality comes in the acculturation of obedient students into a regime of consumption and unproductive leisure and in the preparation of these students for mindless work as white-collar proletarians, acculturation of which Robertson would approve so long as the children were also taught to give money to Jesus through *The 700 Club.*

To reinstall a politics of morality in the United States, Robertson offers his "earthly program," which advocates (1) Christians taking control of education from the secular humanists and fighting government attempts to impose racial quotas on generally segregated Christian schools in the South; (2) Christians deserting mainline religious denominations, which have become irrelevant; (3) Christians controlling their own media; and (4) Christians assuming power in the federal government. Redemption of individual souls is insufficient according to this program, which calls for nothing less than the redemption of amoral American institutions themselves, accomplished through the auspices of televangelism. If it takes church involvement in politics to remove bureaucrats from control of social welfare programs, that's what must happen. After all, it is argued, it is the church's duty to deal with destiny, not the secular government's duty.

In this battle for control over the destiny of America, Jerry Falwell has declared "[I will] gamble my ministry . . . on saving this country."[36] As spiritual leader of Thomas Road Baptist Church, Chancellor of Liberty Baptist College, and head of Moral Majority, Inc., a political organization approximately one million families strong, Falwell's goals include the election of conservative Christians to political office and the cleanup of television, which he calls a "vendor of perniciousness."[37] Falwell's Moral Majority has helped finance the activities of the Reverend Donald Wildmon, founder of the National Federation for Decency and chairman of the Christian Leaders for Responsible Television. The latter group initiated an organized program of monitoring television programs and rating both them and their sponsors according to the level of harmful and gratuitous sex, violence, and profanity displayed. Since 1977, they have pressured sponsors of programs they disapproved of to drop their sponsorship. These efforts have produced calls by Procter & Gamble, General Foods, and Bristol Meyers, all major television advertisers, to reduce the levels of sex and violence on programs in which they advertise. Such "hit lists" of programs and advertisers, while making a mockery of First Amendment principles, are justified by the organization on grounds of moral obligation. This vehement video crusade has been countered in the media by liberal television producer Norman Lear, who cofounded People for the American Way (PAW). PAW produced a series of television commercials featuring celebrities such as Muhammad Ali as well as "regular folks" that stressed pluralism, secular humanist individualism, and the liberal concept of the free marketplace of ideas.

The battle between the dogmatic Christians and the liberal pluralist wealthy sidestepped such core issues as the economic inequality existing throughout the society and the invidious framing of social discourse regarding the locus of control of the means of production of both material goods and culture. The debate was about abstract concepts of morality and relative freedoms. Questions of morality as it relates to actual social structures and conditions of everyday life were largely ignored.

On April 29, 1980, the "Washington for Jesus March," organized by Pat Robertson and others of the New Christian Right, attracted 250,000 born-agains to the nation's capitol. Robertson claimed the March was not political, but rather one of repentance. The fervent marchers had listened to Pat Boone sing at Robert F. Kennedy stadium the previous night. The United States hostage rescue attempt in Iran had just failed, and the country was questioning the political leadership ability of its highest elected officials. The message that a televangelist would risk his entire ministry to save America was sweet music to the ears of the disenchanted who watched America lose a war in Vietnam, saw a president resign in disgrace, heard the sitting president—a professed Christian—declare that there was a "malaise" in this country, and recalled how they sat in their automobiles waiting to buy gasoline after the Arabs had turned off the petroleum in the early 1970s. Pat Robertson had been predicting Armageddon in the Middle East both on television and in his CBN newsletter *The Perspective*. It appeared many were listening.

One wonders about the net change when one set of powerful suburban-middle-landscape entrepreneurs and actors is replaced by another set of powerful suburban-middle-landscape entrepreneurs and actors. Both groups wear three-piece pinstriped bankers suits, drive Cadillacs, live in luxurious mansions, make relatively modest salaries while garnering substantial fringe benefits that make life exceedingly comfortable, and profess to care about the rights of the poor while hiring the best lawyers to find every conceivable tax shelter and loophole and thereby increase the tax burden on these same poor who are being cared for. The difference between the two groups is that one group claims a moral imperative in civil government while the other claims a moral imperative in divine rule. In either case, the Great American Dream of eternal progress is paraded across the airwaves and false hope is encouraged. Which group is closer to the truth?

The New Christianity is cast in the image of the Great American Dream in which discourse on social inequity is excluded. The language spoken by the electronic church is increasingly pecuniary language, camouflaged by political rhetoric that preaches the need for moral equality while ignoring economic and social inequality and in many ways reinforcing that inequality. Recent events in the personal lives of a few of the most visible televangelists have, however, revealed the cynical transparency of this rhetoric of moral equality.

The Bakker scandals and admission by rival Jimmy Swaggart that he frequented prostitutes, not only fostered disdain among many of the evangelical faithful and confirmed the views of critics of televangelism but also seemed to affect attitudes toward religious leaders generally. A survey by the Princeton Religion Research Center, conducted in 1992, found that the public confidence in the nation's priests, ministers, and rabbis had reached an all-time low. Positive ratings for clergy had peaked in 1985, when 66 percent of Americans surveyed ranked them highly on standards of honesty and ethics. By 1992, their positive rating had fallen to 54 percent, far below pharmacists (66 percent), but slightly higher than college professors (50 percent). At the bottom of the list were Congress (11 percent positive ratings) and used-car salespersons (5 percent positive).[38]

THE GOSPEL ACCORDING TO CHUCK BARRIS

No one spoke pecuniary language better than Chuck Barris, the P. T. Barnum of contemporary television entertainment. His game shows delighted the perverse entertainment appetites of millions of television viewers in the 1960s and 1970s. His early works, *The Dating Game* and *The Newlywed Game*, were produced for ABC, for whom he had been a program executive. In 1987 *TV Guide* called the latter "the worst piece of sleaze on television today." In these and other shows, Barris revealed his disdain for authentic human relations. *The Newlywed Game* featured couples revealing their intimate activities on their honeymoons and in their first months together to an audience of video voyeurs. In the process, they sometimes revealed some strong reservations they had developed regarding their partner and the marriage—secret thoughts they had withheld from each other in their everyday lives, but now revealed to each other in public. Their confessions were often accompanied by embarrassed glances and occasional open hostility. Barris, whether out of sadistic pleasure or not is impossible to say, kept a scoreboard of his contestants' marriages and found that 40 percent had subsequently ended in divorce. On the surface, this is not unusual, since the divorce rate during the period in the larger culture was also high. Barris's later works, *The Gong Show* and *The $1.98 Beauty Show* featured contestants, thirsty for television exposure, making fools of themselves for the most minimal of prizes. Barris's work thus may be characterized as the purest form of exploitation of one's fellow human beings—that which preys upon their feelings of insignificance or inadequacy in their everyday lives and allows them a moment of video exposure in exchange for their naïve complicity in their own exploitation for the producer's profit. This is nothing other than a slaveowner-slave relationship, where the exploited ephemeral television celebrity is purchased and displayed as a commodity, as a fool, before the invited guests, the millions of television viewers.

Whereas the televangelist relies on the display of successful winners to make money, game show producers such as Barris rely on losers to the same ends. After watching hundreds, if not thousands, of average Americans being ridiculed on his programs and after amassing a sizable personal fortune in the process, Barris refused to acknowledge that degradation had occurred. Rather, he felt that "95%–97% of these people" were "real, not phony," and were "having a ball." He added that one cannot "purposely, knowingly humiliate somebody because a person knows in advance that it's coming and they can avoid it if they have any brains at all."[39] This cynical view of the inherent stupidity of his guests is reinforced by Barris's admission that "if I was married, and we love and respected each other, I just know that my wife and I would never go on *The Newlywed Game*."[40]

At his peak Barris, once director of daytime programming at the ABC television network, was producing 11 hours of prime-access-time programming per week through his independent production company. He is perhaps best known for *The Gong Show*, which aired from 1976 through 1980 and featured such aspiring "talent" as Murray Langston, the "Unknown Comic," one of the shows' better acts, and the infamous Popsicle Girls, which Barris said was his most memorable act. Popsicle Girls were two attractive young women who came out in shorts and halter tops and proceeded to provocatively suck away on Popsicles. The show was "knocked off the network West of Chicago," according to Barris, who was forced to apologize to the president of the television network who had vigorously complained about the show's lack of taste.

Barris went a step further with *The $1.98 Beauty Show* as women, many not very physically attractive, many without talent, and seemingly desperate for attention, competed in a "talent" contest and a bathing suit competition that was ostensibly a parody of the Miss America Pageant, but was in reality a study of female degradation. Outraged critics called for its quick death. With *The $1.98 Beauty Show*, Barris, "one of the few men who really understands the outrageously exhibitionistic, tabloid-shallow nature of what is the only art form ever devised for accountants,"[41] seemed to have burnt himself out and slithered away from television.

Barris's television of exhibitionism and sexual innuendo is rivalled if not equalled by other representatives of the genre, including quiz shows and game formats featuring celebrities on the skids, such as *The Hollywood Squares*, and the "cynical exploitations of middle-class greed,"[42] *Let's Make a Deal*, *The $25,000 Treasure Hunt*, and *The New Price Is Right*.

The suburban middle landscape lurked just behind door number two, as *Let's Make a Deal* stormed into millions of television living rooms. More than any other daytime game show, *Deal* represented what critic Karl Meyer termed "that epiphany of greed."[43] The show originated in 1965 in its daytime version on NBC. In 1968 it moved to ABC, taking with it a loyal following of nine million daytime viewers (the evening version attracted 27 million viewers), and transformed ABC's entire daytime ratings standing. Between 1965 and 1978, the total income from the show earned by its host Monty Hall, the most-kissed man in America, and producer and former symphonic oboist Stephan Hatos was about $45 million. In 1976 alone, the pair earned $11 million (a very large sum in those days). In the 13-year period 1965 to 1978, *Let's Make a Deal* distributed over $31 million in prizes over its 3,800 programs, more than any other game show, and gave product manufacturers thousands of free plugs in the process.

Structurally, the game show format required no skill, not even the rote memorization of early quiz-type programs. It did require chutzpah, however, as Hall selected 31 contestants, known as "traders," to appear on the program. Prospective contestants arrived at the studio in outlandish costumes. The more ridiculous, the greater the odds of being recognized and perhaps selected. The lucky 31 would then be given opportunities to win cash and prizes and would dutifully quake, scream, pogo, or cry upon victory or defeat. Hall would often apply the subtle torture technique to his hapless victims by describing, in the vaguest terms, the prize just won before revealing its true nature. An "automobile" might turn out to be nothing more than a replica of the Beverly Hillbillies' jalopy. A "swimming pool" might in fact be a 6-foot plastic wading pool with a rubber duck floating in it. The audience laughed as the contestant squirmed. The rudimentary video performance work by the traders was the heart of the show. However, after a few screenings, the performances seemed contrived. One could tell that the contestants had watched other contestants run through the same repertoire and had practiced the successful scream and winning leap. But millions kept watching. The show's stinger was the "big deal"; three contestants had a chance to win, but only one would eventually claim the prize. Behind one of the three doors were real cars, motor boats, trips to Las Vegas, and cash to spend for the lucky big winner. The pathos of *Deal* could never equal that of a famous 1950s forerunner in the genre, *Queen for a Day*, in which five downtrodden women would spill out their stories of misfortune to a sympathetic studio audience. The winner—the woman with the most effective tearjerker—was chosen by studio audience approbation, registered on an applause meter. She would win a mink coat to wear on that special night out and an automatic washing machine to assist her with her children's laundry. But *Deal* did provide suspense to the very end. Hall and Hatos were defensive about their show, as well they should have been, claiming that "they want the program to be seen as a symbolic statement about the glories of competition and the rewards of American life."[44] The contestants' motives were more direct—they wanted something for nothing. Everyone, it seems, was deceived, even viewers who must take a secret joy in watching the greedy contestant lose, put in her place for such a public display of tastelessness, while they simultaneously fantasize that they were "there," on television gunning for the big deal. The prizes are right out of the suburban-middle-landscape catalogue: wall-to-wall carpeting, trash compactors, gas Bar-B-Qs, patio furniture, electric organs that play by themselves so you don't have to take lessons to be a musician, and self-polishing linoleum floor covering. "You have just won a replica of Ward Cleaver's house!" Applause.

The ultimate blending of the suburban-middle-landscape game show and that other daytime staple, the suburban-middle-landscape soap opera occurred in a queer, short-lived NBC program titled *Wedding Day*, aired in 1981. Critic John J. O'Connor called this program "the ultimate level of exploitation."[45] Far removed from the self-evident fantasy of the get-rich-quick game show, yet tied to the same mythic frame of reference, *Wedding Day* was a voyeuristic celebration of petit bourgeois mediocrity. It was *Goodbye Columbus* done with a straight face. Its attempt to provide a background of everyday life's realism for a ceremony of transition, a wedding rite, without any clear sense of the meaning of relations between people perhaps goes far to comment on the root of the contemporary malady of marriage failure in the larger society. When reduced to the status of soap opera, complete with painfully inept love poetry extracted from the most insipid greeting-card culture, the unoriginality of pecuniary culture is laid bare before us. The show, produced in association with the Osmonds, Donny and Marie, featured hosts Mary Ann Mobley, Miss America 1959, from Mississippi, and Cable News Network reporter Huell Howser, from Tennessee. The Southern charm associated with the civil society and its emphasis on traditional values is as self-consciously exuded as is the obvious discomfort of the participants, who reenact their bachelor party, bridal shower, and wedding ceremony in the television studio before a live studio audience, who applaud each successful stage. The ceremony is held on a revolving stage, which turns 180 degrees so the couple can exit to the reception and cut the cake. It is at this reception that, for making complete fools of themselves, they receive their reward—a water-skiing boat and a honeymoon trip to a secluded island. The cycle now completed, the payoff gathered in, the couple splits for a happily-ever-after life on the lake. We know, however, from the soap opera context that there will be rocky times ahead for our newlyweds. A stranger with more money—a mysterious physician with a skeleton in his closet—will enter and destroy this happy household. Meanwhile, the viewer can dream on of this elegant material life, which simultaneously attracts and repels and which one can never quite achieve no matter the effort.

Where did all this quest for prizes and brief electronic notoriety originate? One might trace the genre to its first highly successful program, *The Quiz Kids* of the radio era. A national favorite from mid-1940 through 1951 and on television until 1956, *The Quiz Kids* featured precocious children answering difficult questions. Like television's *College Bowl* spin-offs, knowledge was equated with memorization of facts and rapid recall under pressure—signifiers of rationality in the age of science and national competition and implicit in the myths of eternal progress and manifest destiny as they guided the outlook of a nation first at war and later in a Cold War. The radio quiz kids toured the country selling war bonds and entertaining the troops at military bases during World War II. The genre reached its peak in the 1950s, just before the quiz show scandals revealed the sham behind the glorification of American "genius." It was revealed that "brilliant" contestants on programs such as *Twenty One* and *The $64,000 Question* had been given answers in advance so that more popular contestants could dethrone the less popular champions and had faked their looks of intense concentration and perplexity to build dramatic suspense. The payoff was large, even in those years' dollars. With *The $64,000 Question* and similar programs thus exposed, the nation was forced to examine, if only briefly, television's lack of integrity and its representation of pecuniary social relations, in which the currency of exchange consisted of lies and deception. *The Quiz Kids* was back on television in 1980. The revival, produced at Boston television station WNAC, was syndicated in New York City and eight other markets. Five contestants, aged 7 to 14, participated on each show. The three with the top scores were called back the following week. In the true spirit of intellectual competition on television, the producers hoped "that, after a while, viewers will respond to the personality and intellect of the individual contestants and will root for some and against others."[46] Joel Kupperman, an original radio "Quiz Kid" who became a national celebrity and who in 1980 was teaching philosophy at the University of Connecticut, criticized the basic concept of the programs which "encourage people to come up with fast and superficial answers to questions."[47]

How can a television executive allow these programs to air on his or her station? The answer is twofold and simple. First, as a successful product of pecuniary society, a worshipper of the Great American Dream, and an inhabitant of the suburban middle landscape, the executive can accept these works of television as legitimate celebrations of the American spirit of competitiveness. Monty Hall and Stephan Hatos were obviously sincere when they thus defended *Let's Make a Deal*. The strength of the myth is, after all, the fact that it *is lived* and thus not transparent to those whose lives are deeply involved in its celebration and perpetuation. Second, in a medium "created for accountants," the genre makes ultimate good business sense. It cost as little as $50,000 to produce five episodes—an entire week's worth—of a game show for syndication. It cost a minimum of $200,000 per episode or $1 million to produce five episodes of an original situation comedy for syndication. This 20-to-one cost ratio lays the matter to rest.

THE GOSPEL ACCORDING TO THE BIBLE BOWL

"Coach" Jack Gray's television ministry originated in Tulsa, Oklahoma, a decidedly middle-class southwestern city exemplifying the new America of wealth and power derived from natural resources. Oral Roberts University and Roberts's City of Faith hospital, dedicated to finding a cure for cancer, are there. Oklahoma is a football state. The citizens are proud of their Oklahoma Sooners, for decades a major college football power appearing at least twice each year on national television. In the best traditions of both southern-style fundamentalism with its tent-show revivals and football with its intense competition and substantial pecuniary rewards for victory, Coach Jack offered us *The Bible Bowl* on CBN in the early 1980s.

This children's show featured two teams—"the bible boys" versus "the gospel girls"—who compete for prizes ranging from a five-dollar bill for a bible boy or gospel girl who correctly answers a question such as "Who walked on water?" to the grand prize, Coach Jack's "hunderd [sic] dollar bill!" Before the opening kick-off, Coach Jack sits in the Christian locker room and discusses the upcoming contest and the religious theme for the day with a cardboard robot that lights up. The kids, all neatly scrubbed, smiling, and eager to please Coach Jack and maybe win that five-dollar bill of his, jump up and down and shut up on command. To get the contest going, Jack asks one gospel girl to recite "The Pledge Allegiance [sic] to the Bible." The eager youngster stumbles through this task with Coach Jack's help. Jack reaches for his wallet and extracts a dollar bill, which he hands to the girl, who is very pleased. A tiny huckster resembling the Jimmy Joe Jeeter character on *Mary Hartman, Mary Hartman* does the breaks as Coach Jack prepares the halftime pitch, in which he sells the Bible Bowl board game for only twenty dollars. Later in the contest he takes a TV time-out to ask parents to send money so that he may continue his enlightened ministry, which brings so much joy to kids.

Coach Jack's message is clear: In the world of suburban-middle-landscape success, unquestioning obedience to dominant patterns of social control will produce pecuniary rewards. Believe in America, eternal progress, competition, and Jesus, and you will be a big winner. You win money, goods, trips, and even salvation by getting the right answers, which are not open to debate.

This rational world of the quick fix, of the person in himself, not for the group, has come to define the basis for contemporary social relationships in advanced capitalist America. The televangelist and the game show producer and host clearly reveal our own weaknesses to us, and for that perhaps we should be grateful—and, of course, send money.

NOTES

1. Edwin Diamond estimated there were 55 million "born-again" Christians in the United States in 1980. See Edwin Diamond, "God's Television," *American Film*, March 1980. Dick Dabney speculated there were perhaps as many as 80 million "conservative" Christians in 1980. Dabney did not define this term. See Dick Dabney, "God's Own Network," *Harper's*, August 1980. A 1979 Gallup survey, funded by 29 religious groups and quoted in John Mariani, "Television Evangelism: Milking the Flock," *Saturday Review*, February 3, 1979, found that 33 percent of the survey respondents considered themselves "born-again" Christians. This would place the numerical total at around 75 million Americans.

2. Russel Blaine Nye, *The Cultural Life of the New Nation* (New York: Harper and Row, 1960), p. 114.

3. Diamond, "God's Television," p. 32.

4. Wayne King, "Bakker, Evangelist, Resigns His Ministry over Sexual Incident," *New York Times*, March 21, 1987, p. 1.

5. William E. Schmidt, "TV Minister Calls His Resort 'Bait' for Christianity," *New York Times*, December 24, 1985, p. A8.

6. Ibid.

7. Jules Henry, *Culture Against Man* (New York: Random House, 1963), p. 62.

8. Dabney, "God's Network," p. 52.

9. Virginia Owens, *The Total Image, or Selling Jesus in the Modern Age* (Grand Rapids, MI: William B. Eerdmans, 1980), p. 37.

10. Dabney, "God's Network," p. 46.

11. Ibid., p. 38.

12. Cable News Network, "Televangelism," a special report with reporter Jim Clancy, 1981.

13. Mariani, "Television Evangelism," p. 25.

14. Ibid.

15. An excellent discussion of this overarching social theory is contained in Jeffrey K. Hadden and Charles E. Swann, *The Rising Power of Televangelism* (Reading, MA: Addison-Wesley, 1981).

16. Owens, *Total Image*, p. 47. We shall set aside for now the question of what to do with those found "unworthy" of initiation.

17. Dabney, "God's Network," p. 40.

18. Owens, *Total Image*, p. 62.

19. Diamond, "God's Television," p. 32.

20. Ibid.

21. *Hour of Power*, October 2, 1983.

22. Dabney, "God's Network," p. 40.

23. Mariani, "Television Evangelism," p. 23.

24. C. Wright Mills, *The Power Elite* (New York: Oxford University Press, 1956), p. 74.

25. Owens, *Total Image*, p. 67.

26. *Publisher's Weekly*, July 21, 1983, p. 66.

27. Michel Marriott, "The Devil Wore High Tops," *New York Times*, November 22, 1992, sec. 9, p. 10.

28. Owens, *Total Image*, p. 37.

29. Perry Miller and Thomas Johnson, *The Puritans* (New York: American Book Co., 1938), p. 209.

30. Thomas Paine, "The Rights of Man," in *Common Sense, The Rights of Man, and Other Essential Writings of Thomas Paine* (New York: Meridian/Penguin Books USA, 1984), p. 285.

31. Billy Graham, "TV Evangelism: Billy Graham Sees Dangers Ahead," *TV Guide*, March 5, 1983, p. 5.

32. Mariani, "Television Evangelism," p. 23.

33. Peggy Charren and Martin W. Sandler, *Changing Channels* (Reading, MA: Addison-Wesley, 1983), p. 102.

34. Data compiled from a variety of sources indicate that in 1983 there were

over 60 syndicated religious television programs, three major religious television networks (CBN, PTL, and Trinity), 38 full-time religious television stations, 66 cable systems owned by religious organizations, 1,400 Christian radio stations, and 125 pending low-power television applications submitted by the Radio and Television Commission of the Southern Baptist Convention.

35. Dabney, "God's Network," p. 36.

36. Cable News Network, "Televangelism."

37. Charren and Sandler, *Changing Channels*, pp. 154–55.

38. Ari Goldman, "Religion Notes," *New York Times*, November 21, 1992, p. 9.

39. Scott Eyman, "Chuck Barris," *Sunday Magazine*, October 12, 1980, p. 53.

40. Ibid.

41. Ibid.

42. Robert Lindsey, "School Is Back in Session for 'The Quiz Kids,' " *New York Times*, April 13, 1980, sec. 3, p. 37.

43. Karl E. Meyer, "The Gaming of America," *Saturday Review*, October 28, 1978, p. 37.

44. Ibid.

45. John J. O'Connor, "An Exploitation of the Fanciful," *New York Times*, June 21, 1981, sec. 2, p. D25.

46. Lindsey, "School Is Back," sec. 3, p. 37.

47. Ibid.

10

□ □ □ □ □ □

The TV Talk Show: *Commodifying the Individual Psyche*

Television is today's most powerful means of conferring status. In earlier chapters dealing with comedy and melodrama, we examined the roles of heroes central to fictional television narrative, namely, their function as models that provide viewers with clearly circumscribed rules of behavior. In the chapters on news and sport, we briefly examined the status of news anchors and correspondents, newsmakers, sports announcers, and athletes as television personalities. Whether we call these people heroes, television personalities, or celebrities, they all present us with a public persona that exceeds the boundaries of power, adventure, and glamour known to us through our everyday experience. We may worship them as ego ideals, seek to emulate their style of dress or coiffure or their mannerisms, or attempt to achieve an electronic status analogous to theirs, if only fleetingly. The concept of "media hero" has wide-ranging implications not only for the viewers entranced by the visible signs of success on television but also for the media heroes themselves who are brought under television's spell—trapped in an electronic hall of mirrors.

New York Times essayist Russell Baker clearly understood the nature of this television power, which he described in a poignant parable of inventor Harley Hatchfield's search for personal confirmation through television:

When Harley Hatchfield died the other day, the obituary writers all said he was a failure. I prefer to think of him as a dreamer on the finest American tradition. Though none of his dreams were realized, he never abandoned dreaming for the sour despair and self-pity into which lesser spirits withdraw from life's great adventure.

His final years were devoted almost entirely to schemes for getting himself televised. He had observed that with the aging of the present century, appearance on television had become the only persuasive evidence of an individual's existence.

He himself had come to doubt the existence of anyone who had not been on television.

"In Descartes' time," he told me, "a person could say, 'I think, therefore I am.' In our age anybody who thinks can only conclude that he is not, unless masses of people can see him on television and tell him yes, he is, too. In our age, Descartes would have said, 'I am televised, therefore I am.' "

This reasoning led Harley to doubt his own existence. . . .

Not surprisingly, Harley began dreaming of ways to get television to certify his existence. Study of the local news programs led him to conclude that the most certain way would be to arrange to have his wife and five children destroyed in a dreadful fire. In this event, he was fairly certain, the local stations would televise him looking distraught while a reporter asked, "How does it feel having your wife and five children burned to death here today?"

The difficulty was that Harley, being unmarried, did not have the essential wife and children. That led him to undertake his last big project: the development of a wife and five children constructed out of balsa wood, horse hair and ball bearings. When he finished them, however, he had become so fond of having them around the house and helping the children with their homework that he hadn't the heart to put them to the torch.

It was not until his death that the television cameras finally came. Attracted by the human interest angle of six balsa wood survivors mourning their loved one, the cameras finally granted existence to Harley, who no longer existed.[1]

The images and sounds captured on videotape or sent hurtling through space and into our living rooms, live, become the legitimizing agents of our time. The power of personal presence becomes at best ancillary to one's media power. This is true not only for advanced capitalist man and woman but also for precapitalist man and woman living in the shadows of modernization and technology.

Anthropologist and communications theorist Edmund Carpenter described the impact of electronic communications on the lives of rural New Guineans and Ojibwa Indians from the Lake Superior region of North America:

Electricity has made angels of us all—not Angels in the Sunday school sense of being good or having wings, but spirit freed from flesh, capable of instant transportation anywhere.

In New Guinea, when villagers ignore their leader, the government may tape-record his orders. The next day the assembled community hears his voice coming to them from a radio he holds in his own hand. Then they obey him.

Among the Ojibwa Indians, young people eagerly listen to tape recordings of their grandparents' stories, though they don't want to listen to the grandparents telling the same stories in person.[2]

"Televiso, ergo sum"—I am televised, therefore I am—is our new ontology. There exists an abundance of signs that support this theory of our electronic being. Where the answer to "What do you want to be when you grow up?" was once a doctor or a nurse, today it is a rock star or an astronaut or an anchorwoman—all people who owe a great debt to television for granting them electronic status and thereby assuring their success and fame. The Cartesian mind/body dualism today becomes a tape/body dualism. "Is it live, or is it Memorex?" is a moot question since we know that while these two states of being may be equivalent in presence, the latter is significantly more powerful than the former by virtue of its ubiquity and, as Carpenter pointed out, its otherworldliness. Desiring the power that television promises us, we begin to act out our lives as we think we would were we television personalities. The nature of the relationship between the viewer and the image, of course, helps marketing strategists regulate the flow of new commodities into the marketplace, which depends heavily on subtle shifts in lifestyle that are increasingly generated through both fictional and nonfictional media exposure. On a deeper level of commodification than material emulation, we find style working its way into the social relations delimiting political discourse. Chauncey Gardiner, the hero of Jerzy Kosinski's novel *Being There*, is an example of Marshall McLuhan's dictum that we become what we behold on our television screens. Gardiner, an illiterate menial, becomes a national political hero because he is an embodiment of all the television he has ever watched. Television, which with the garden he tended had constituted his entire life experience until his forced entry into the "real" world, framed the discourse available to him. He was pure substantive video feedback and thus, ironically, profoundly acceptable to a nation of what Kosinski termed "videots" who understood the television iconography on a cursory level. Chauncey was the perfect talk show guest, providing direct answers in sound bites that were nothing more than stale metaphors regarding the relationship of politics to gardening—in short, providing viewers with platitude camouflaged as profundity. Chauncey Gardiner lived and exuded the mythos of the American individual whose surface appearance of freedom masks the institutional control that commodifies and markets that appearance.

So far we have attempted to demonstrate that each television form contains elements of the exploitative—the mythic constructs that work to mask essences of actual lived social relations as they exist at any given time. In the television talk show, the myth of the individual frames much of the discourse that develops in this particular form. One manifestation of this myth is the American ideal of the "independent spirit"—one who acts and stands alone, who follows some solitary path outside the group, but who nevertheless operates within constraints imposed by the dominant culture.[3] The motorcycle traveller in the Kodak "America" commercial, discussed in chapter 3, exemplifies this character type. The myth admits certain character types as legitimate while excluding others.

In contemporary American culture the myth celebrates pragmatic "idea" persons. Those who produce unique utilitarian commodities such as gadgets that make everyday living easier; those who manufacture best-selling books and other profitable popular culture; and those who develop innovative advertising campaigns and new lifestyle designs are admitted and revered in commercial television's public celebration of importance. On the other hand, "pointy-headed" intellectuals—social critics and oppositional philosophers and artists—are generally excluded; when on rare occasion they are admitted, they are likely to be subjected to derision, which functions to reinforce the status of the acceptable "independent spirit." "Dreamers" are excluded in the name of practicality and populist conceptions of knowledge.

Increasingly in the 1980s and 1990s, with the emergence of what many critics have labelled "trash TV," individuals on the fringes—those who flout societal conventions of acceptable personal behavior in the domains of sexuality and violence—have become grist for the titillating late-afternoon television talk-show circuit, while other individuals, such as articulate sociologists, psychologists, and political observers, when admitted are attacked as "experts" lacking "common sense."

Of course, within any culture, there is never unanimity regarding who is a hero and who is a villain or fool. The alienated rebel who rejects and attacks conventional values with defiance or destructiveness (the Beats of the 1950s, the student radical underground and the revolutionary urban minority guerrillas of the 1960s, and the cults of working-class Punk in the 1970s and urban rappers in the 1980s are contemporary American examples) may be hero to repressed, disenfranchised urban street people, and villain or fool to respectable suburban bureaucrats or corporate executives. One thing is certain, that within the heroic pantheon exist dominant-culture heroes and minority-culture heroes, both providing models of behavior for those who acknowledge their heroic status and, by implication, their class position and politics. However, as mainstream television tends to restrict the discourse to that sanctioned by the dominant social strata, we find the myth of the individual more often circumscribing a compliant than a defiant political discourse. And when a defiant individual is included in the television-talk discourse, his or her function is generally a dramaturgical one—to "heat up" the conversation.

Television holds out the promise of ephemeral personal power and public status, but it reserves true power for itself as an apparatus that controls the drama of electronic existence. It grants people status as long as they advance its pecuniary ends.

Television talk repackages current fashion and dominant ideology for mass consumption. It lacks silence and contemplation (television, as nature, "abhors a vacuum"). It rejects intellectual complexity for emotional simplicity, and it substitutes notoriety for substance.

The television talk show is, above all, commerce—a finely tuned barter system. A prominent politician will appear and reap the public-relations benefits of addressing an audience substantially larger than any year's worth of nontelevision public speeches could reach, in exchange for the calculated risk that his or her extemporaneous speaking style may reveal inarticulateness or intellectual shortcomings (the risk of the latter is not great, however, as the host—unlike the competent journalist—will rarely, if ever, press substantive matters). A popular entertainer-celebrity will trade some intimate sexual or psychological revelation for a movie, album, or memoirs plug. Persons with advanced academic credentials who claim "expert" status offer mass-produced popular therapies in exchange for the immediate public adulation they would never achieve were their activities-of-the-mind carefully cultivated through intellectual rigor and years of observation and disciplined analysis. Authors sit through countless minutes of small talk, waiting their turns to take the stage in the "authors' ghetto" of the post-midnight segment of the network late-night talk show, in order to plug their latest tome and boost it toward success on the best-seller list. A regular citizen who, through some extraordinary or notorious act, has been admitted to ephemeral celebrity status will subject his or her motives and integrity to cursory public scrutiny—instance judgment by those not qualified to pass such judgment—and often even the host's ridicule in exchange for a fleeting moment of public recognition. The dramatic tension created by the possibility of the "dangerous revelation" holds the viewer's attention. However, the dangerous revelation will rarely be one of direct political or ideological import, but rather will be a titillating one restricted to the domain of personal impropriety or indiscretion.

This chapter will explore the ramifications of being "in the medium"—of flaunting one's individualism—especially in the arena of the talk show on which established celebrities from the entertainment, sport, literary, political, and lifestyle worlds of image marketing are thrown together with "ordinary folk" who personify the commercial version of the myth of individualism and themselves ascend to ephemeral celebrity status, to be used up and quickly discarded, in television's continual pecuniary search for the glamorous, the exotic, and the bizarre.

FORMS OF TELEVISION TALK

In his excellent study of the television talk genre, entitled *Television Talk*,[4] Bernard Timberg offers a systematic categorization of program types that comprise the form. A summary of Timberg's "Talk Chart" is presented below as a useful reference for our ensuing discussion. We will employ a somewhat different thematic breakdown; further, some "talk forms" have already been discussed elsewhere in this book.

Timberg divides television talk into four major categories—News Talk,

Entertainment Talk, Simulated Social Event Talk, and Sales Talk. News Talk includes (1) the "general interest hard news talk" of the expert panel (*Washington Week in Review*), the expert panel and news figure (*This Week with David Brinkley*), the magazine format on a single topic (ABC News's *Nightline*), the multiple-topic news magazine (*60 Minutes*), and the one-on-one host/guest interview (Bill Moyers's *A World of Ideas*); (2) "general interest soft news talk" on a single topic (*Donahue* and *The Oprah Winfrey Show*), the magazine format–multiple topic soft news talk (*Good Morning America* and *Today*), and the one-on-one, host/guest interview (*Larry King Live* and David Frost interviews); and (3) "special-interest news/information" (*Wall Street Week* on economics, *Siskel and Ebert* on film, and Dr. Ruth on personal psychology).

Entertainment Talk is characterized by informal celebrity host/guest talk, a hallmark of late-night talk programs (*The Tonight Show*, *The Letterman Show*, and *Arsenio Hall*). It has also been featured in comedy talk (*Fernwood 2-Night*) and game show talk (*You Bet Your Life* with Groucho Marx).

Simulated Social Event Talk includes the academic seminar, the manipulated encounter (*Candid Camera*), the ritualized encounter (*The Dating Game* and *Studs*), and the forensic event (*People's Court*).

Sales Talk includes infomercials, the "spontaneous talk" within commercials, and paid political advertising.

According to Timberg, these forms of television talk are united by "a set of talk show rules and principles." These include (1) the host's centrality and control of the show; (2) the programs' topicality—talk occurs in the present tense; (3) the host's private conversations in direct address with "millions of viewers as if they were one," creating a sense of intimacy; (4) the talk show's "commodity function" as a vehicle to hold its audience in the programming flow, which includes the advertising that makes the shows possible; and (5) a "conscious structuring and crafting of what seems spontaneous." The "performance" of the host and guests is paramount, in Timberg's view, providing the audience with a "pleasurable" experience. In many forms of television talk, a studio audience "serves to varying degrees as a surrogate for the viewing audience at home."

Most important to Timberg, television talk programs play a major role "in defining social, cultural, and political life in America." They became "powerful molders of public opinion in the 1980s," taking topics from the external social world and making them an integral part of the internal discourse of the talk programs.

About the latter assertion there can be little doubt. What do these gabfests—grounded, writes Timberg, in the chautauqua, vaudeville, and newspaper opinion and gossip columns—tell us about ourselves? The following examination of four clearly developed major television talk themes seeks to provide some answers to this question.

By far the predominant traditional television talk form, which has shown great staying power since its emergence in the early years of television, is the *entertainer-celebrity-talk-variety* form featuring comedy routines, musical numbers, and banal informal celebrity interviews, which are more properly classified as chitchat. All this is recorded on tape in a large television studio before a studio audience which applauds on cue. In this form, the guest is subservient to the pecuniary demands of the medium, which prevents substantive discourse (which producers and programmers believe would bore a mass audience), and especially discourse that is in opposition to dominant ideological frames. The only thing at stake in this form is the individual's claim to celebrity status—and that, rarely. Celebrity status itself is a given, not to be questioned. As C. Wright Mills noted, celebrities run interference for the "power elite," camouflaging the real locus of power in advanced capitalist society. To question celebrityhood would lead to questions regarding the social role of the television apparatus itself. In this form, entertainment is sacred, providing viewers release from the frightening events and less-than-desirable life conditions in their everyday experience. Fun is functional. Entertainers are elevated to the status of cultural heroes.

The form emerged on network television with *Tonight*, hosted by Steve Allen on NBC from 1954 to 1957. Allen and his resident company of singers and comedians kept the 90 minutes of frivolity moving briskly. He would open at the piano with a song, often his own composition. His "schtick" included person-on-the-street remotes from outside the NBC New York studios. While talk via the interview was not the major focus of the show, Steve Allen's *Tonight* show did set the tone for succeeding versions of *Tonight* that would use celebrity talk as an important viewer draw.

The Jack Paar Tonight Show, which ran on NBC from July 1957 to March 1962, like Allen's show, featured music and comedy. Paar's forte, however, was informal conversation. He became a sort of national antihero with some of his more controversial material. But the staple of this talk show was the amusing interview with the offbeat celebrity, notably Zsa Zsa Gabor and Cliff "Charlie Weaver" Arquette.

Of course the premier lighthearted talker was Johnny Carson, who took over *The Tonight Show* in October 1962 and was king of the genre for 30 years, finally retiring in the summer of 1992. Carson avoided the controversial guest. He was much less emotional than Paar, affecting instead a cool, detached midwestern persona. According to Timberg, Carson (and David Letterman, who followed *Tonight* on NBC in the 1980s with his offbeat late-night show) developed "the persona of a person from small town middle America who has adapted to the sophistication of big city America—Hollywood, show business, and the allures and absurdities of both the East and West coasts—without being overcome by it."[5] Carson's version of the late-night show, which began in New York, moved to Hollywood in 1971, the perfect backdrop for the stream of entertainment celebrities who paraded across the small screens of millions of sleepy American viewers.

Other, less notable representatives of the form included afternoon shows hosted by "crooners" Mike Douglas and Merv Griffin, both of whom went out of their way not to offend anyone.

Late Night with David Letterman began on NBC in 1982 as a replacement for Tom Snyder's *Tomorrow* program. Positioned as a "hip" youthful talk alternative for late-late-nighters, Letterman enjoyed a highly successful run on NBC for over a decade. In 1993, he headed for rival CBS to compete head-to-head with NBC's *Tonight Show*, now hosted by Jay Leno. Letterman's forte, "silly irreverence," has its television roots in the schtick of the best early years of *Saturday Night Live*.

The following account of a personal 1983 visit to a Letterman taping in New York City demonstrates the general ambience of talk Letterman style.

We are standing in a crowded, low-ceilinged hallway waiting to get in to NBC's small seventh-floor studio in Rockefeller Center. My connections with one of the show's writers got me "VIP" tickets. This was the "biggie." Show Number 246. The guests included the man of a thousand personalities and voices, Robin Williams, and reggae superstar Peter Tosh and his group. Outside with us were other VIP friends of the production staff, some of them obviously Robin Williams groupies. One particularly obnoxious older man kept chain-smoking Camel cigarettes, crushing the butts on the recently waxed floor, and making lewd adolescent comments to the female NBC pages, who did their best to maintain their composure and ignore him. At last the studio doors were opened and the VIPs were escorted in. The true VIPs get center seats, while the others get side-section seats. Never mind. One can see the action better on the overhead monitors anyway. The still-less-fortunate without VIP status get to watch the monitors in the NBC Green Room, and others in one of NBC's screening rooms where NBC execs normally screen programs. Seemingly thousands of others who wanted to see Williams and/or Tosh were turned away. I felt fortunate to be admitted to the inner circle this night.

Inside the studio, which looks so much larger on TV, are three studio cameras on pedestals and a portable camera that roves, handheld, picking up studio audience reaction shots that lend an air of informality to the tightly structured format. The production is highly professional, with carefully timed segments and commercial breaks.

We are all seated now. The show's announcer, Bill Wendell, does a short warm-up, and David Letterman comes out to offer a few lines for the warm-up as well. The Indiana-bred Letterman, tall and thin, wears his double-breasted suit well. This is no 1960s work-shirt George Carlin routine. It feels like a large late-night business, which it is. The guests are there to plug their latest releases: Williams, his new film with Walter Matthau, *The Survivors*, and Tosh, his latest recording. All is in apparent readiness. Director Hal Gurnee has the crew functioning like a Swiss watchworks.

The show is on. Letterman pulls out a giant, seven-foot goldfish from behind his desk; I sense shades of Steve Allen schtick—"schmock, schmock!" The diminutive Williams, looking like a little boy in a grown-up's suit, spends his allotted time bantering with Letterman in an "adult" discussion, which quickly wears thin, of the birthing process of his new baby. Williams, like most celebrity talk-show guests, is there merely to display himself for twenty minutes, plug his latest commodity, which is himself, pick up his paltry $431 (in 1983 the appearance fee), which is certainly not the inducement for appearance, and exit, stage left.

Despite the obvious professionalism of the production staff, this show broke down halfway through the taping, the first major technical failure in the show's brief history. Peter Tosh's reggae group had too much equipment to patch into NBC's studio board. For budgetary reasons NBC executives, I was told, refused to give Letterman an additional audio board earlier that afternoon. There was an inexorable delay as the technical staff tried to remedy the problem. The studio audience, perhaps wanting to see the "real" Robin Williams, responded "call out Robin" to Wendell's seemingly insincere question as to how they would prefer to wait out the delay. Wendell noted, matter-of-factly, "Robin left immediately after his segment. He had another engagement. He's a very busy man."

The highlight of the show was a periodic feature titled "stupid pet tricks," in which people parade their talented pets before a nation of bleary-eyed viewers in hopes that their pet's silly tricks, which were usually doomed to failure due to opening-night stage fright, would provide the nation comic relief while simultaneously skyrocketing them to ephemeral celebrityhood. There was the dog who smiles, but wouldn't. The parrot who walks through a box, but on this occasion just stared at the studio audience. The little poodle who sings, but had lost her voice. And the Afghan dog who barked whenever its master counted.

I left the studio after waiting in vain for the Tosh segment (which was finally taped about three hours later and edited together with the other material). I wondered what made *Late Night* any different from any of the dozen-or-so other late-night talkers from television history. All that remained in my mind were traces of commodity, schtick, display, and formatized midwestern informality. Perhaps I "just didn't get it."

Another talk form is the *visit-to-the-famous*, pioneered on television by Edward R. Murrow's *Person to Person*. In this talk form, celebrities, who ranged from heads of state to baseball heroes, allowed the television camera to enter their personal space—their homes—while the host would probe their minds and living spaces for a personal portrait that might reveal sides of their characters previously unknown to their public admirers.

The television camera provided the immediate visual element missing from the print portrait. In addition, Murrow's very popular *Person to Person* was live (Murrow had an almost childlike fascination with the technical capacities of video), which added a sense of drama to the event. *Person to Person* aired on Friday nights from 10:30 to 11:00 (EST) on the CBS television network from October 1953 to September 1961 (Charles Collingwood hosted the final two years of the series). Murrow electronically visited two celebrities each week. The celebrity would give Murrow and the television audience a tour of the house. Murrow actually conducted the interview from a CBS television studio (he thereby assumed a perspective similar to that of the viewer and avoided what might be construed to be the journalist's privileged position in this essentially one-way communication transaction). Murrow, who chain-smoked on the air—his trademark and ultimately the cause of his death—was "one of us." Murrow's guests included politicians such as former President Harry Truman, Senator John F. Kennedy, and Cuban leader Fidel Castro; actors and actresses Marilyn Monroe, Humphrey Bogart, Lauren Bacall, and Marlon Brando; authors John Steinbeck and Margaret Meade; opera singer Maria Callas; and sport hero Jackie Robinson, the first black major-league baseball player. While cinema stars Bogie, Bacall, and Monroe were very much at ease in front of the bulky cameras with their miles of cables strewn everywhere throughout the house, politicians still seemed nervous with the medium in those early years, although like the movie stars, our political leaders were eager for the exposure the new medium offered. Senator Jack Kennedy and his wife Jacqueline seemed shy and even awkward when they appeared on the program. Kennedy read a poem and talked about his life as a public figure and the sense of responsibility that a public servant must demonstrate. He and Jackie would grow up very quickly with the medium, and the medium, through its live qualities, would document the nation's sorrow only a few years later following Kennedy's assassination.

As was the case with the entertainer-celebrity-talk-variety form, the visit-to-the-famous form never questioned the institution of celebrityhood itself; it never asked, "Why, in this system of social relations, should this person be accorded such status?" Rather, the form merely reveled in the excitement of being admitted to the kingdom of the famous. Murrow opened the visit by asking his host, "May we come in . . . through the window . . . in this fashion?" True, the interviews were a step above the mindless chit-chat of the entertainer-celebrity-talk-variety form. A senator reading poetry assured that heightened status; no matter that the poetry may have been uninspired or the reading amateurish. Yet the incongruity of the hard-nosed reporter Murrow—this country's adversarial conscience in his *See It Now* confrontation with Wisconsin senator Joseph McCarthy and his *CBS Reports* "Harvest of Shame" exposé of the plight of our migrant workers—hosting meek celebrity interviews with the world's major public figures points to the strange amalgam of opinion and entertainment that, on a primary level, frames television's discursive structures. The basic promise of this talk form could permit a limited video probing of character in a manner consistent with the traditions of literary psychological and biographical criticism. Yet the televised form did not advance toward such revelation of character and motive because the discourse in which the human transaction was framed was television discourse—an underlying "one-to-many" communication pattern according to which the public figure was given a video soapbox to extol the Great American Dream that had led him or her to this very position of status and dominance. Celebrityhood, through such a vehicle, feeds back into itself, reinforcing its claim to importance.

More recent manifestations of this form find the celebrity coming to the television studio and engaging in a protracted conversation with the interviewer. Programs included PBS's *The Dick Cavett Show* (1979–1982) which featured nightly interviews with actors, authors, critics, and other public figures (in the early 1990s, Cavett's interview program returned on cable network CNBC); Chicago public television station WTTW's *John Callaway Interviews*; the late CBS Cable's *Signature*, hosted by Greg Jackson (who took his format to ABC's short-lived late-night show *The Last Word*, a follow-up to *Nightline*); and currently PBS's late-night *Charlie Rose*, produced by New York City's WNET/Thirteen. These programs feature the one-on-one interviewer form. Callaway's interviews were done in extreme close-up in a visual attempt to reveal character, while Jackson's interviews employed a Cubist video technique featuring a series of dissolves from a straight-on shot to a left and right-face profile of the interviewee, all done in close-up. Both approaches to visualization were strong and drew the viewer into the conversation. And these interviews were more contentious than those of earlier programs. Still, the interviewee controlled the talk from his expert position.

This form was carried to its extreme in a highly controversial 1977 case. David Frost's series of interviews with former President Richard Nixon was severely criticized for its unabashed use by Nixon as a vehicle to deny his complicity in the Watergate scandal. CBS and ABC, to their credit, turned down Nixon's request for a $1 million fee to do the interviews on grounds that this was "checkbook journalism." NBC News offered Nixon $400,000 and seemed willing to negotiate this figure upward, when Frost beat the network to the draw in 1976 and procured Nixon's services for $600,000 and 10 percent of the profits. The financing for the interviews, according to critic Les Brown, came in large part from "conservative West Coast businessmen who believed that Nixon had been wronged . . . and wanted him to have a forum to tell his side of the story."[6] Four 90-minute interviews were taped in Nixon's San Clemente, California, estate. One-hundred-fifty-five markets carried the syndicated interviews on a barter basis (i.e., Frost gave the program to the stations "free" in exchange for a certain number of national commercial slots on each program, which he would then sell to advertisers—in this case, six minutes were negotiated). The interviews were aired in 1977. The programs captured a large audience (45 million viewers for the first interview). While ostensibly a "news interview" program, the interviews caught the public imagination more as a human interest personality profile. Nothing new was learned about the structure of American government or its ideology. Little light was shed on the structural relationships that encourage such malfeasance. The very fact that Nixon agreed to "come out" lent a new legitimacy to his persona—the very act of the television appearance became his individual bold gesture. Far from a mea culpa, the interviews became tools for Nixon's self-promotion.

Three additional examples of the visit-to-the-famous form serve to demarcate the boundaries of television talk generally. The first, best characterized as a perversion, occurred on Tom Snyder's *Tomorrow* program. Snyder organized a video prison visit with convicted mass murderer Charles Manson. Snyder, trying to get to the bottom of the infamous matter of the Tate and LaBianca murders, took on the role of psychoanalyst, a role for which he was eminently unqualified. What emerged from this travesty of showmanship was a forced portrait of a paranoid, insignificant little man. The audience were invited to the prison as video voyeurs. When Snyder's visit was over, one came away with a sense of meaninglessness—not only with regard to the savage murders committed by Manson's cult but also with regard to the program itself. The interview with Manson was nihilistic and counterproductive. The audience had no greater insight into the influence of social structure on personality that may produce such persons as Manson; on the contrary, they may well have come away from the highly publicized program feeling helpless and fatalistic as they saw one "crazy" individual isolated from the social system and therefore from any possible control. Unlike Truman Capote's brilliant psychojournalistic investigation into the lives of mass murderers Richard Hickok and Perry Lee Smith, which resulted in the book and film *In Cold Blood,* Snyder's hit-and-run amateur psychoanalysis was ultimately a disservice to everyone except Manson, who had all his life sought individual status and finally achieved it with Snyder's help—"Televiso, ergo sum."

At the opposite pole we find two PBS series, produced 15 years apart, that featured conversations with some of the leading thinkers and artists of our time. Unlike Charles Manson, these were not household names. And that is precisely the point.

James Day's half-hour interview series, *Day at Night*, was produced by

Publivision, his independent production company, in 1973–74. *Day at Night* was syndicated to approximately 45 public television stations and aired on most of them five nights a week. Day, a former president of National Educational Television (NET) and general manager of station KQED in San Francisco, leased studio time from six major producing public television stations—WNET/Thirteen in New York City, WGBH in Boston, WETA in Washington, D.C., KQED, KCET in Los Angeles, and WTTW in Chicago—to conduct the interviews. His long list of prominent guests included scientist Dr. Jacob Bronowski, the host of the critically acclaimed series *The Ascent of Man*, science fiction writer Ray Bradbury, political activist and scholar Noam Chomsky, composer Aaron Copeland, architect I. M. Pei, leftist publisher I. F. Stone, psychiatrist Dr. Carl Menninger, and physicist Dr. Edward Teller, inventor of the hydrogen bomb.[7]

In 1988, Bill Moyers produced *A World of Ideas* for PBS. Broadcast over ten weeks, the 50 half-hour conversations allowed people to reflect, in Moyers's words, on "the ideas and values that are shaping America's future.[8] Moyers interviewed his guests in informal surroundings—their homes or the offices and laboratories in which they worked. Among Moyers's guests were Noam Chomsky (interviewed by Day 15 years earlier), leftist journalist Alexander Cockburn (see chapter 11 for an account of Cockburn's appearance on ABC News *Nightline*), novelist Joseph Heller, film producer David Puttnam, historian Henry Steele Commager, physicist Steven Weinberg, and environmental scientist Jessica Tuchman Mathews.

The series coincided with the 1988 presidential election campaign, and was intended to shift the public discourse away from the platitudes of media pundits commenting on presidential electoral politics and to, according to Moyers, "hold up the thought that there is much more being said out there than the policy debate is revealing."[9] The interviews were designed "to sketch the moral and ethical setting of the political contest." The irony of the series was that because scholars and scientists who have made significant advances in their often obscure disciplines rarely have access to the pervasive medium, television "fails in the presidential selection process in one very important respect: to produce a discussion worthy of democratic life."[10]

According to Moyers:

All communicators today in any field must be entertainers to a degree, and true intellectuals are reluctant to compete on those terms. The media don't want them anyway, unless they can speak in 30-second sound bites or two-minute to five-minute segments on one of the talk shows, or debate in strict oppositional format, a liberal on one side and a conservative on the other, which is a caricature itself of debate. So, many intellectuals find it distasteful or dishonest to perform under a label that has been put on them by the media.[11]

On the other hand, political candidates have reduced the national debate to "a series of slogans and vague pledges of goodness and virtue."[12]

An overriding theme emerging from the interviews in A World of Ideas is contemporary society's tendency toward frenetic activity in the pursuit of wealth and fame, undertaken without reflection about moral purpose. Historian Commager spoke of de Tocqueville's warning, in the early nineteenth century, about the strain of "individualism" that places selfish interest ahead of the larger interests of the society. Commager noted, "There was very little of that [thinking] in the 18th and much of the 19th century, because everybody depended on everybody else. We're still keeping the ideal of individualism, but we're not giving it the meaning it had."[13]

Moyers was convinced that Americans were not satisfied with the level of discourse surrounding political life (this was borne out in the public reaction during the 1992 campaign). He continues to hold firm to the belief that viewers want "a little wisdom, a little common sense, some guidance through the perplexities of modern life."[14] This is the least that television can offer.

Both Day at Night and A World of Ideas best exemplified the intelligent one-on-one interview. Their guests were highly intelligent individuals who refused to speak down to viewers. And the two hosts were respectful and well-informed.

A third traditional television talk form is the serious long-form–round-table discussion of substantive social and cultural issues with prominent political figures, intellectuals, and members of the creative community. (I am not including here the weekly Sunday news discussion programs such as This Week with David Brinkley, Meet the Press, or Face the Nation, on which individual dominant culture politicos are invited to provide the "party line" on some issue that headlines that particular week's news while correspondents stumble over one another in a self-conscious attempt to be aggressive and adversarial, but instead merely reveal their lack of intellectual acumen through their series of often banal questions, which come thinly disguised as challenges to their guests. These "public affairs" shows, while pure television talk, are discussed elsewhere in the context of "objective" newsgathering.) The long-form–roundtable studio talk form is closely related to its print counterpart, the symposium, in which a group of knowledgeable persons provide a variety of opinions on some topic of common interest. Debate, argumentation, and disagreement among individual thinkers who hold often highly disparate and nuanced viewpoints on the matter under consideration is the hallmark of this television talk form. Ideas rather than surface impressions, personal character or exigent political positions are the currency of this form. As such, its viewer popularity in the age of titillation and short attention span would not be expected to be very high, although its critical acceptance would.

An important program in this form in television's youthful years was David Susskind's *Open End*. Susskind, a producer of television drama for anthologies including *Kraft Theater, Armstrong Circle Theater,* and *Kaiser Aluminum Hour* and the critically acclaimed series drama *East Side/West Side*, created a critical tour de force in 1958 with *Open End*, which he both produced and hosted. The syndicated program introduced us to a new televisual form as we entered the final phases of the initial age of television program experimentation—the open-ended talk with no set time limit. The program ended when its host and guests ran out of energy. There was plenty of energy to go around. *Open End* featured such notable political discussants as Soviet premier Nikita Khrushchev and then vice president Richard Nixon, certainly not friends, as evidenced by the famous "Kitchen Debate" of 1959. Susskind was often challenging, sometimes abrasive, but always sincerely involved in his topics. His *Open End* displayed a serious commitment to the discussion of ideas and a respect for his audience, evidenced by his belief that provocative talk, freely unfolding, could sustain the interest of the concerned viewer. In fact, *Open End* must be considered an important model for the public-access talk program three decades later, with its emphasis on letting the conversation unfold unfettered by commercial television's time signature with its advertising constraints and its programmers' belief that viewers will quickly tire of thought. In the mid-1960s, *Open End* became *The David Susskind Show*, and its format was changed to a one-hour closed-ended discussion. As befell other television forms, notably anthology drama and the extended coverage of congressional hearings on issues of major public concern such as the Kefauver hearing on organized crime and the Army-McCarthy confrontation of 1954, talk was increasingly contained and packaged. The era of bold experimentation in live television was ending.

Other talk-show hosts would occasionally introduce truly contentious material, although not with the consistency or the depth of *Open End*. *The Jack Paar Tonight Show* had an occasional serious side. Paar used his program to crusade against Cuban dictator Batista prior to Castro's revolution. Paar, capable of outrage and petulance, walked out of NBC for a month following the network's censure of his famous "water-closet" joke. Tom Snyder's *Tomorrow* would on occasion tackle serious subjects such as drug abuse and draft dodging during the Vietnam War and would gather panels of psychologists and other experts from time to time to assess the contemporary social scene. But these ventures into the serious were exceptions to the main business of celebrity talk and the showcasing of "oddities" such as Snyder's visit to a nudist camp and his constant baiting of ordinary persons who were invited on the show because of some peculiar special interest they represented.

A fourth form of television talk might be best described as the *video-talk-trial*. Far from the world of entertainer-celebrities and experts, this is a world of common folk whose valiant exploits, despicable deeds, personal tragedies, bizarre inventions, and sometimes even their mere "commonness" earn them a brief moment under the kleig lights on the talk circuit. The binding agent in all these talk transactions is that of the end use of people as commodities—the folk are used up to attract an increasingly voyeuristic viewership.

The exploitation of inarticulate, camera-shy common folk as butts for the cynical talk-show comic's jokes flourished with the talk-game program *You Bet Your Life*, hosted by the immensely popular film comedian Groucho Marx. The game of answering trivia questions was but a backdrop to Marx's ridicule of the lifestyle, dress, and awkwardness of the contestants, who were paired in male-female teams. The program aired from 1950 to 1961 on NBC and has since reappeared throughout the country in a highly popular syndicated strip format. The contestants were amazingly good-natured (or docile) people, willing to endure Marx's insults in order to appear before the nation. This ostensibly harmless, all-in-fun abuse of the little guy set the trend for subsequent talk show discourse. The average working person was frequently portrayed in these settings as an "oddball"; his opinions, while perhaps interesting, were quaint if not "cracked." This was the view of the rural American we saw emerging in the rural-middle-landscape comedies of the 1960s—a childlike innocent not to be taken seriously.

In the most invidious manifestation of this talk form, the ordinary person, who through some extraordinary or outrageous personal act has become notorious, is paraded before millions of viewers as a surrogate defendant in a public video trial. The defendant must answer questions about his or her morality and values. The studio audience becomes both judge and jury and the talk-trial host, chimera-like, becomes one minute prosecutor and the next defense counsel. In all cases the guests appear of their own volition. They are not coerced by the production staff into appearing, although it might be argued that they are subconsciously coerced by the television apparatus itself through the implicit promise of fame, and perhaps a book and/or movie deal.

Early practitioners of this talk form, which emerged in the late 1960s, included Tom Snyder on NBC's *Tomorrow* and Joe Pyne and Les Crane on their syndicated talk shows. They would invite guests on the program, then bait them. Snyder would seek out people with odd inventions or aberrant social values and subject them to debates over their worth or their values. Pyne, a disabled war veteran, used his show to attack any liberal he could find, especially homosexuals and anti–Vietnam War protesters (Pyne was an excellent real-world model for the Archie Bunker character, although he was more sinister than the fictional bigot). Crane, on the other hand, sought out racists and other bigots for ridicule. No fun was intended in these dark displays of public antagonism. The shows, in a way, were seemingly little more than setups to show off the interrogatory acumen of their hosts; they were exercises in ego that traded on hapless people, many of whom were unprepared for the television pressure cooker.

In the late 1980s, two syndicated talk shows—*The Morton Downey, Jr., Show* and *Geraldo*—carried the video-talk-trial form to extremes. The former's progenitor was Joe Pyne; the latter's was Les Crane.

The Morton Downey, Jr., Show premiered in October 1987 as a live evening talk program on New York–New Jersey superstation WWOR. Downey's father, an Irish tenor, had hosted his own television show on NBC in 1949—a three-night-a-week musical show. Downey, Jr.'s show was a far cry from that of his father. Downey, Jr. chain-smoked on the air. His overt patriotism quickly attracted a cult following of young men. His trademark became his loud, abrasive style and his tendency to insult his guests. On a January 1988 program, "Downey wrapped an American flag around his bottom and told his Iranian guest to kiss it."[15] Downey, Jr. took on the role of "instigator," and his predominantly working-class youthful-male studio audience became his "assault team." The arrogant Downey, Jr. "physically threatened his guests, the women sexually, the men with 'wiping the floor up' with them. He shout[ed] down experts and orchestrate[d] his audience in a cacophony of hoots and grunts."[16] When an antiwar activist appeared on the show, Downey, Jr.'s studio audience drowned out his talk "not with an argument but a group singing of America the Beautiful."[17] Downey, Jr. would on occasion have an "expert guest" forcibly removed from the studio.

In May 1988, the show was nationally syndicated and enjoyed a brief period of popularity, but audiences grew tired of its abrasive style, and the show ended fourteen months later.

According to Carpignano et al., Downey, Jr. provided

a forum for the disenfranchised, especially young white men (working and lower middle class) who are not represented in the current knowledge-based commodity culture. . . . Downey provide[d] a forum for common sense (what workers have but what experts don't have) and reduce[d] the expert to just another member of the audience.[18]

If "common sense" is analogous to intolerance, then Carpignano et al. have a point.

Geraldo, an hour-long syndicated daytime talk program hosted by former ABC News correspondent Geraldo Rivera, also premiered in 1987.

Like the talk programs of his major rivals Oprah Winfrey, Phil Donahue, and Sally Jessy Raphael, Rivera's show had a participatory live studio audience and focused on a single topic each day.

In the early 1970s Rivera, trained as an attorney, had been an investigative reporter for WABC-TV in New York City. Half Puerto Rican and half Jewish, Rivera claimed he had been hired by the station to fill an "ethnic" niche on the local newscast. He first gained national attention when he sneaked a camera into the run-down Willowbrook State School for the mentally retarded in 1972. His exposé—he described how the school "smelled of filth, it smelled of disease and it smelled of death"—led to improvement of care for Willowbrook's residents. Rivera became a regular on the ABC network magazine program 20/20, but left ABC after the decision to cut a 20/20 segment on the personal life of Marilyn Monroe.

In April 1986, Rivera produced a nonnetwork live syndicated special program, "The Mystery of Al Capone's Vaults," which covered the opening of the Chicago mobster's long-hidden underground crypt. Hoping to find hidden treasure, Rivera uncovered nothing of value. However, because of its intense promotion, the program became the highest-rated syndication special in television history and led to the development of Rivera's talk show. Rivera's production company has been a major force in this genre, subsequently producing specials on drug abuse, AIDS and sex, the Mafia, and, yes, on Charles Manson. This form of programming spawned the plethora of "reality programming," including A Current Affair, America's Most Wanted, and Unsolved Mysteries, discussed elsewhere in this book.

Geraldo's aggressive guest-baiting produced one of the most notorious incidents in television history. During the November 1988 taping of "Teen Hatemongers," featuring representatives of racist youth organizations, a violent scuffle broke out and Rivera's nose was broken. Guests on the show included John Metzger of the White Aryan Resistance Youth and Roy Innis, national chair of the Congress of Racial Equality—a volatile mixture certain to produce high drama. This was not Innis's first pugilistic television experience. He had previously gotten into a fight on The Morton Downey, Jr., Show with the Reverend Al Sharpton, an outspoken black New York minister.

The Geraldo melee ensued after Metzger called Innis an "Uncle Tom." Metzger said to Innis, "I'm sick and tired of Uncle Tom here, sucking up and trying to be a white man." Innis stood up and began choking Metzger. Rivera, a former amateur boxer himself, and audience members joined the scuffle (this was "real" participatory TV), throwing chairs and punches and shouting epithets. Rivera was struck by a chair and punched in the nose by an audience member supporting Metzger. Rivera refused to go to the hospital, and instead finished taping the hour-long program after order had been restored and Metzger and other "teen hatemonger" guests were thrown out of the building by security guards.

Rivera did not press charges. After the brawl, he was quoted as saying, "These racist thugs are like roaches who scurry in the light of exposure." (Who provided the light?) Rivera added that he approved of Innis's actions: "If ever there was a case of deserved violence, this was it."[19]

After intense publicity prior to the airing of "Teen Hatemongers," a huge audience watched. In 18 major television markets, the program drew a 13.9 rating and a 39 share, "numbers virtually unheard of for daytime programs."[20]

While admitting that there are occasional excesses, Rivera defended his confrontational style of television talk: "At some point, even the ivory tower elite will recognize that an audience numbering in the tens of millions is not a lunatic fringe nor a gullible cult. It is America, and it is watching."[21]

The experts that Rivera and Downey, Jr. so disdain have a different take. Dr. Willard Gaylin, a psychoanalyst, sees such television programming reflecting "the coarsening and corrupting influence of modern urban life." Gaylin adds, "The deterioration of politeness and public manners is at a sufficiently rapid stage to be measurable within any one individual's experience."[22]

Some observers have attributed the success of such programs to people's need to vent anger at a system they feel powerless to change. Rivera uses this explanation to justify his programs which he believes empower people to speak out—to have their voices. The rationale of encouraging this behavior is a psychological theory that holds that unrestrained venting of anger is healthy. This, however, is no longer the prevailing view. According to Dr. Redford Williams, director of the Behavioral Medicine Research center at Duke University, research suggests instead that "overt expression of hostility, of contempt, of anger . . . has been found to be correlated with disease, especially high blood pressure and heart disease."[23]

THE NEW TALK

The video-talk-trial, as exemplified by *The Morton Downey, Jr., Show* and *Geraldo*, exhibits the worst traits of the "active" audience—shouting down "expert" guests and brawling in the television studio. The studio audience, often provoked by the host, becomes on such occasions an unruly mob, who defenders of the form nonetheless claim have been "empowered."

What we are categorizing as *new talk* on television, the primary examples of which are *Donahue*, *The Oprah Winfrey Show*, and *Sally Jessy Raphael*, also presupposes on "active" audience and eschews the sanctity of "expert" opinion (while still inviting experts to appear). The subjects explored on the new talk programs, like those on the video-talk-trial programs, frequently center on sexuality, forms of personal abuse often involving violence, women's feelings of insecurity or inadequacy in a male-centric social discourse, and alternative lifestyles considered by many to be taboo. The programs are often lurid and graphic. They frequently exhibit "participatory chaos, spectacular emotionalism." And they lack closure, instead offering "digressive wanderings of incident and coincidence without the conclusion by which one places things in perspective."[24] They reject, argues Masciarotte, "the classical strategies of knowledge construction, information gathering, proof through argumentation," that characterize a male discursive form that excludes women's voices.[25]

The format of these programs is essentially identical: a panel of guests appear to share their experiences with the studio audience and millions of viewers at home; specialists are often invited to interpret these experiences; the studio audience comments on the stage discussion and shares their own stories; viewers are invited to call in to do the same; and the host—the program's fulcrum—preaches and prods all the above-mentioned participants.[26]

These are primarily "women's" programs, operating in "the tradition of gossip."[27] Their time slots—midmorning, lunchtime, or late afternoon—are all housewife break times. The studio audience is largely comprised of women, students, and older men.

What most clearly distinguishes new television talk from the video-talk-trial is that, while not infrequently slipping into a "trial-like" atmosphere, new talk nevertheless encourages its audience to engage in a more "civil" form of conversation and to examine their own behavior and positions on the problems under examination. Rather than heaping abuse on the shows' guests, the studio audience and the viewers at home are often asked to tell their own related stories. Unlike Rivera and Downey, Jr., who assume the role of "instigators," Donahue assumes the role of "intermediary" while Winfrey takes on the role of "counselor" in their discursive positionings as hosts.[28]

New talk has roots in call-in radio, and especially a notorious early 1970s radio format known as "Topless Radio." However, new talk on television is anomalously positioned vis-à-vis Topless Radio, on the one hand drawing upon the radio format's titillating subject matter and on the other hand consciously rebelling against the overt sexism associated with its radio forerunner.

To place television's new talk in perspective, we will briefly examine Topless Radio. The pioneer program was *Feminine Forum*, hosted by Bill Ballance. Early in 1971, Ballance—a former all-night disk jockey—began *Feminine Forum* on KGBS-AM in Los Angeles. After twenty months, Ballance's show was the top-rated program in the nation's largest radio market. An estimated 400,000 people tuned in every day. By early 1973 there were an estimated fifty or sixty stations around the country programming daily radio shows in this format. The format was characterized by its focus on a single sexual topic each day; callers were not prescreened or pretaped, which would dampen spontaneity; only the caller's first name was revealed in order to protect the caller's privacy; the hosts were all men while the preponderance of the callers were women; and the target audience was described as "wives and mothers in their twenties." Storer Broadcasting, which owned KGBS, started versions of *Feminine Forum* on its five other A.M. radio stations in Cleveland, Detroit, Miami, Toledo, and New York City. Other media owners followed suit, including Metromedia-owned KNEW, San Francisco (with *California Girls*, hosted by Don Chamberlain); Fairchild's KLIF in Dallas with *The Dave Ambrose Show*; and WWDC's *Scott Burton Show* from the nation's capital. By the end of 1972, Ballance's show had become one of the hottest syndication properties in radio, handled by Dick Clark Radio Shows, Inc. (the "all-American" Dick Clark of *American Bandstand*). It had been placed in 22 markets, including four in Canada and one in Perth, Australia. Pilots for a Bill Ballance television show, to be handled by Clark, were "in the can."[29]

But the radio sex-talk form was not without its influential detractors. FCC Chairman Dean Burch, in a speech to the National Association of Broadcasters annual convention in Washington, D.C., in 1973, heralded the Commission's coming war against indecency in American life by saying, "If electronic voyeurism is what the authors of the Communications Act had in mind, I'll eat my copy."[30] The NAB shortly thereafter passed a resolution condemning "tasteless and vulgar program content." And on April 13, 1973, the FCC announced its intention to fine Sonderling Broadcasting Corporation's Oak Park, Illinois, radio station WGLD-FM $2,000 for airing its version of the sex-talk form—a program titled *Femme Forum*. The FCC invited Sonderling to appeal its fine through the judicial system so that a test case could be decided regarding indecency in broadcast programming, but Sonderling refused. Sonderling's refusal to pursue the matter was not an admission of guilt but rather a case of economic exigency. In fact, company president Egmont Sonderling said, WGLD's *Femme Forum* was a program dealing "with the problems of modern woman."[31] Ballance, who skyrocketed to fame on the strength of *Feminine Forum*, defended his work, claiming he helped women who "are conversationally intimate with me because they can't communicate with their husbands. The show brings out a lot of marital discord that has been simmering below the surface."[32] Ray Stanfield, manager of KGBS in Los Angeles, where it all began, said, "We do not have a sex-talk show on this station. We have a talented, clever interviewer on the air, talking to callers about man-woman relationships. Sex is an occasional by-product."[33] Despite Stanfield's clinical-sounding rationale, KGBS changed *Feminine Forum* to the *Bill Ballance Show* and cut the sex-talk, bending to FCC pressure.

Feminine Forum flourished during a period in which media had begun to open up, if usually quite tentatively, to the controversial content area of sexuality. *All in the Family* began its long CBS run in 1971. Richard Levinson and William Link's television film exploring the human relations of a homosexual father, *That Certain Summer,* had aired on ABC in November 1972. The daytime soap operas were becoming increasingly sexual. Sex manuals for the layperson led the lists of best-selling books. *Maude* developed a two-part episode on abortion (which received nearly two thousand viewer complaints). What made *Feminine Forum,* and "Topless Radio" generally, more offensive? Its defenders called this two-way talk "cathartic radio"—radio that asked listeners for personal experiences rather than political opinions. This was radio-as-therapy. Euphemism aside, underneath it all was a disingenuousness. Ballance and the other hosts seemed to prey upon the insecurities of these women who wanted so much to hear themselves talking, to confirm their being in the media-world. ("Please turn your radio down" has become the anthem of radio talk—a powerful symbol of the feedback of one ego talking and listening through the talk loop to itself—feeding one's desire for contact, masturbatory contact with one's own media image.) If these were mothers and wives in their twenties who, as Ballance himself noted, could not communicate with their husbands and were feeling isolated and confused, was this self-indulgent talk a legitimate outlet for their frustration? Was there any hope of resolution?

The content of the shows—one day oral sex, the next masturbation, the next the evils of miniskirts, the next the frequency, or lack thereof, of one's orgasms—seemed increasingly mundane as the months wore on. The content was much less intriguing than the very presence of these women whom we knew by first names only, but whose intimate lives we shared in the voyeuristic safety of our radio space. These intimate interludes were far from simple entertainment. When one would call and lay her sexuality on the line before 400,000 listeners, there would be the inevitable irascible next caller who would begin by chastising the hapless woman who had just opened up, calling into question the woman's morality or even her sanity. On occasion Ballance himself was not above deriding a caller for her narrow-mindedness or ignorance of a sexual subject. The program prided itself on its openness and sincerity—liberal, holier-than-thou buzzwords that easily disguised the callous pecuniary motivations behind this sex-talk. Like the contestants on television's *The $1.98 Beauty Show,* the women callers became audio prostitutes, selling images of their bodies but turning all the money over to the radio apparatus that hustled them on the airwaves. Beyond the practice of radio prostitution, however, was the trial-like atmosphere in which the talk took place. Women were judged by other women whom they had never before met or spoken to. The initial radio meeting was at best superficial—one event taken from a woman's entire experience and cast out on the airwaves as representing her. This unidimensional psychic and moral portrait is at best simplistic and probably quite misleading, given the ground rules of the talk.

What was gained and what was lost in this radio transaction? The stations made substantial profits from advertising revenues generated by these immensely popular programs. Millions of listeners were titillated, and maybe learned some new sexual techniques (one memorable program on oral sex discovered a woman who was revolted at the thought of fellatio until she discovered that putting peanut butter on her husband's genitals and licking it off made them both happy). The caller, under the protection of anonymity, achieved ephemeral celebrity status. She was an individual who held the media "floor" for three minutes or so—her thoughts counted and were part of the electronic discourse established by the number one radio show in L.A. Further, she could talk to a man. On the other hand, she had not begun to resolve the problem of her inability to talk with her husband, if Ballance's own assessment of the motivations of these women to call is granted. She had revealed intimate details of her life to a disinterested radio entertainer. And she helped legitimize the public media commodification of the isolated psyche. It is little wonder that women's organizations labelled Ballance as "the complete pig."

While Phil Donahue, unlike the sex-talk hosts, exudes integrity, his hour-long syndicated daytime talk program *Donahue* in its own way thrives upon revelation in an atmosphere often filled with severe cross-examination and incessant moralizing.

Donahue's rise to stardom occurred at the moment when Topless Radio was under intense scrutiny by FCC conservatives and was being attacked by liberal women's groups who had begun to organize for political action in the early 1970s. This fact likely contributed to the establishment of content boundaries and the liberal ideological positioning of his program in the emerging public debate on women's political agendas, as the role of women in the family and in the society began to change. Women's "private issues" were becoming social, and the social political.[34]

The Phil Donahue Show began in 1967 on WLWD-TV in Dayton, Ohio, and soon was syndicated nationally. In 1973, the program was retitled *Donahue* and moved to WGN-TV, Chicago. The program was highly successful, with carriage by 160 stations in the late 1970s. Donahue prepared a half-hour version for prime-access in 1979 and did interview features for NBC's *Today*. In 1982, he prepared an abbreviated 15-minute version of talk for ABC's *Late Night*. It seemed as if Donahue was omnipresent on the nation's television screens in the 1970s and 1980s—early morning, mid day, evening, and late night. He had unlocked the secret to immense video popularity.

The show initially featured celebrity interviews and discussions with experts on a variety of topical matters, but *Donahue* soon made "a complete break from the celebrity guest format and classical liberal debate . . . and turn[ed] on its own structuring strategy of consciousness-raising."[35] Women's issues came to dominate the program. According to Masciarotte, Donahue and the other new talk programs to follow his lead afforded women "the political gesture of overcoming their alienation through talking about their particular experience as women in society."[36] *Donahue* is generally recognized as the inventor of the new talk format in which "the studio audience was introduced as a major player."[37]

While the gender-empowerment arguments offered by defenders of *Donahue* and new talk generally have merit, one can make a convincing case that the program, like its radio sex-talk progenitor, uses women's intimate revelations to enhance its dramaturgy. No matter what their motivations, men and women with problems, who wish to share them with us through television, eagerly come to Donahue to open up their lives. The studio audience, at times resembling the Romans at a gladiatorial contest, cheers for or against a guest. And when the affair is over, one wonders what is gained, what lost.

The underlying feeling one carries away from *Donahue* is that of having just attended an intermixture of a group therapy session with people you have never before met but who seem genuinely deeply troubled and a rambling, undisciplined free-for-all discussion at a local PTA meeting. Critic William A. Henry III labelled *Donahue* the 1970s manifestation of the mid-1960s "common-man personality and topicality," which prospered to the extent that it "let the shameful tout their shamelessness."[38] Donahue prods and pokes, challenging his guests, then discreetly backs away. His feigned neutrality, camouflaged as "liberal tolerance" of the most aberrant behavior of the common folk, counteracts potential criticism of the program's flirtation with subject matter considered by many to be taboo. Like Ballance on radio, Donahue shifts the responsibility for moral judgment to members of his audience, those in the studio during the taping and occasionally the phone-in audience. Given limited information about the program's guests and lacking the necessary professional training to be able to properly evaluate the guests' motivations or to understand the complex questions of law that are often cursorily raised as they relate to a case, the audience nevertheless is called upon to interrogate the guest regarding his or her actions. This display of vox populi leaves one feeling uneasy. Masciarotte frames television's new talk positively as "an endless narrative of discomfort" that confronts the "balanced narrative of incorporation of the individual in the system."[39] The discomfort, however, can also be seen in a less sanguine light as an outcome of the program's sensationalized, voyeuristic exchange.

The guest, meanwhile, tries hard to persevere, to reiterate her conten-
tions. Donahue will defend her or empathize with her one moment, then,
in the interest of "balance," will turn on her, albeit with a cunning courtesy. As any lawyer will acknowledge, trials, even those involving a murder
suspect, can be deadly dull; but on television, they must become *Perry
Mason* adventures in discovery, fraught with intrigue and the constant
revelation of hitherto secret information.

A telling example of Donahue's new talk ambience was a program aired
in December 1977 in which Mrs. Francine Hughes appeared. Mrs. Hughes
had murdered her ex-husband (with whom she had reunited) out of fear,
she said, for her life and the lives of her children. Mr. Hughes had physically abused her for thirteen years. She tried to leave him but had nowhere to go; the police were of little help to her, and she did not know
of shelters for battered women. Her situation appeared increasingly hopeless. One night while Mr. Hughes was sleeping, she poured gasoline
around the bed, lit a match, and left. She was brought to trial. A jury
found her temporarily insane. Hughes's story was subsequently made into
a critically acclaimed 1984 DBOF, *The Burning Bed*, starring Farrah Faw-
cett.

Francine Hughes's admission to Donahue's circle of topicality was guaranteed by the verdict, which on the one hand seemed to permit justifiable
homicide by women victims of severe and persistent physical abuse and
on the other hand left the judicial floodgates ajar with the temporary
insanity verdict, clearly not an acquittal. In addition, the burning, the trial,
and the physical abuse constituted high drama.

Mrs. Hughes appeared with her lawyer. She did not seem remorseful
over the murder. Rather, she seemed tired and a bit withdrawn. She said
she wished only to share her experience with others. As the discussion
proceeded, Donahue and many in the studio and call-in audience tried to
get Mrs. Hughes to show some guilt, to be at least somewhat repentent.
In the next breath Donahue and others in the audience defended her
right to defend herself. Back and forth and back again. The studio audience became highly polarized, many cheering an audience member who
made an impassioned plea for women's rights, many others cheering an
audience member who insisted Mr. Hughes should have had some rights
as well, namely, rights to rehabilitation, and that his execution had negated those rights. By the program's midpoint, Mrs. Hughes began to fade
into the background, having served her purpose of stirring up the studio
audience and thereby guaranteeing heated confrontation.

What was learned from this talk? Nothing about the mechanisms of
existing support systems for victims of physical abuse such as secure shelters for battered women. Nothing about the intricacies of our legal system,
which allow a verdict of not guilty by reason of insanity. Nothing revealing
about the deep, highly individual emotional world in which Mrs. Hughes
had struggled for thirteen years. We received instead impressions, descrip-

tions of a murder; we were given a ticket to a group psychodrama that searches in vain for a universal emotional truth that doesn't exist, except on television—a psychodrama enacted by players on stage and in the audience. *Donahue* is serious business.

The Oprah Winfrey Show premiered in September 1986. Winfrey thereby became the first black woman to host a successful daytime talk show.[40] Winfrey began her television career as a news anchor in Nashville, Tennessee. In 1984 she became the host of a local Chicago talk show, *A.M. Chicago.* Within two months, her program overtook *Donahue* in Chicago's local ratings. Two years later, her show was syndicated nationally. Winfrey acquired ownership of the show in 1988 and founded her own production company.

What distinguishes Winfrey's new talk is its host's willingness to tell her own personal stories on the air "in order to cajole stories out of others."[41] She admitted on one program that she had been sexually abused as a child. According to Masciarotte, Winfrey made new talk "more emotional and less issue-oriented," rejecting Donahue's "sociological" and "liberal political" discourse in favor of "an emotionalism or affective talk."[42]

Winfrey's critics argue that her personality has eclipsed the program's "caring, informative, 'genuine' function," and that she has encouraged a "more vulgar, graphic, voyeuristic . . . exchange."[43] Defenders counter that while such charges may be credible, their inherently "negative evaluation" is misplaced. According to this rationale, Winfrey, a black woman in an oppressive political system, has offered other black women (and women generally) the "proud narcissistic gesture" of a "middle-class individuated subject" who is not embarrassed to display her emotions.[44]

The anomalies surrounding new talk are not easily resolved. In this primary "women's form" of television, women are empowered as they consciously relinquish their privacy as a social and ultimately political gesture. But there is a price: In the process, these women fuel the television apparatus that trades in sensationalist dramaturgy, encouraging ever-more titillating stories in the competitive quest for profit.

This is most evident in the case of the "talk show hoaxers."[45] Between 1986 and 1988 Tani Freiwald and Wes Bailey, two actors, appeared on *Sally Jessy Raphael, The Oprah Winfrey Show,* and *Geraldo.* On two of these, Freiwald claimed she was a trained sexual surrogate and Bailey claimed he was a married man suffering from impotence. They were both lying.

Freiwald, who subsequently appeared on *Sally Jessy Raphael* to do a mea culpa, said her talk show appearances provided her with "an improvisational challenge I couldn't pass up." Freiwald suggested that talk shows were mere entertainment: "If positive information is relayed to the public, that's a side benefit." Raphael clearly disagreed. She was visibly hostile to Freiwald during the follow-up program.

Raphael's staff apparently repeatedly called Dr. Dean C. Dauw, a Chicago sex therapist and frequent talk-show guest himself, to provide the show with guests suffering from sexual dysfunction. Freiwald, a part-time actress, worked as a manager in Dauw's office.

Freiwald first appeared on *The Oprah Winfrey Show* in November 1986 as "Barbara Hall," a married woman who hated sex. In July 1988, she and Bailey appeared on *Geraldo* as "Rebecca" and "George," the latter a middle-aged virgin who had been "cured" by Rebecca, a sex surrogate, according to Rivera in his introduction to the show.

Bill Boggs, producer of the defunct *The Morton Downey, Jr., Show*, called such guests "Exhibit A's—the cousins of cocaine sniffers, wives of child beaters." Boggs added that this type of guest is the most difficult to get on the program. Because of that, and because of the intense competition among talk shows, which compete head-to-head in late-afternoon time slots in many major markets, talk-show producers often take the first guests to agree to appear, relying on a single source and not cross-checking sources regarding the guests' credibility. *Geraldo*'s producers take a short cut in securing such guests, making them sign a release form stipulating that they will not make any remarks on the program that they believe to be false or defamatory. Apparently the producers feel their responsibility to their audience stops there.

Television's new talk form leaves many issues unresolved. Perhaps the most intriguing issue was raised by Jerzy Kosinski in *Being There*. Chauncey Gardiner, a simpleton-gardener who by circumstance became a media hero, had been invited to appear on a television talk show:

Chance turned on the TV. He wondered whether a person changed before or after appearing on the screen. Would he be changed forever or only during the time of his appearance? What part of himself would he leave behind when he finished the program? Would there be two Chances after the show: one Chance who watched TV and another who appeared on it?[46]

The experience of appearing on television talk shows must be both exhilarating and humbling. That experience is ultimately defined by the levels of meaning generated in the human exchanges that constitute the power of being in the media. The television talk program "often confuses notoriety with persuasive power, and visibility with impact."[47] When Chance exits the studio, he will leave behind traces of himself: his unintended metaphors linking his garden and world politics and economics, which come to symbolize his "quick mind" to gullible viewers suckled on platitudes, and his affability. When Mrs. Hughes exited the studio, she left behind traces of herself: her self-doubt hidden just beneath the veneer of her seeming remorselessness and her preoccupation with "sharing" her own confused world. The audience carries away traces of performances

that dish up emotion but provide no clear ground on which to seek answers to profound and complex questions of social relations.

The Winfrey brand of soul-searching group-psychotherapy is a delayed
video reaction to the self-help generation who seek solutions to complex
questions of personal identity in therapies of all kinds, including the ge-
neric quick-fix of pop psychology. It is but a short step from the "fix your
own plumbing" regimes of the 1950s, seen in those queer old books with
line drawings of gaskets and monkey wrenches, to the "fix your own head"
routines of the 1980s and 1990s. Television and radio have capitalized on
this trend.

"Psychological Radio" is a step beyond Bill Ballance's "Topless Radio."
Dr. Toni Grant, a radio psychologist from Syracuse University, took Ballance's job away from him at KABC radio in Los Angeles in 1978. She
was first in her time slot, with an average listenership of about 150,000 in
1982. Most of her listeners and callers were women. Dr. Grant insisted
she mainly provided information and did not make universal diagnoses or
prescribe universal remedies for psychological problems discussed with
individual listener/callers. But Dr. Peter Wish, a psychologist and a founding member of the Association for Media Psychology, which drafted
guidelines for media psychologists in 1982, argues that psychological radio
raises serious ethical issues regardless of the hosts' claims. Wish notes that
there is a tendency for the psychologist to become a media star; that
giving advice on the airwaves is distinct from providing therapy; that the
media psychologist, in talking to a caller, is working with minimal and
incomplete information on her "client"; that the media psychologist is
forced to make a snap judgment and a speculative, impersonal diagnosis;
and finally that there is a distinct danger that some listener will think he
has the same problem as the caller when he may not and may follow the
media psychologist's advice to the caller, which may not be appropriate
in his case.[48]

Psychological radio is entertainment pretending to provide a psychological service. The listener is the recipient of a one-way communication
while the client/caller is involved in a very limited two-way conversation
with the media psychologist. Some commentators claim that this talk form
is progressive because callers not only get psychiatric or medical advice
but also frequently offer encouragement and support for a previous caller,
thereby adding to an ongoing discourse.[49] Nonsense! This "discourse" is
phony. Without face-to-face, open confrontation, this is nothing but safe
media group therapy with no emotional strings attached. The caller who
does not like what she hears from the media psychologist or the next caller
can tune out (she has paid no money as an incentive to stay with the
therapy)—a response that probably in many cases produced the caller's
current psychological discomfort in the first place.

Psychological radio served as a model for psychological television, which has taken a variety of forms on the new specialized cable television networks. By the early 1980s, Cable Health Network had developed such psychological programs as *Take Charge*, featuring Lester Coleman, an upbeat media psychologist; *Human Sexuality*, with host Sharon Goldsmith, a half-hour interview show aired daily and featuring talks with "real people" about their sexual problems, all of which the host believes can be resolved by "relating"; and *Join the Group*, featuring twelve men and women in their 50s and 60s discussing psychological problems associated with aging such as fear of disease and dying, divorce, and children growing up and leaving the nest, and above all emphasizing people "coping." USA Network had *Sonya* with host Sonya Friedman interviewing people about their problems—a cross between *The Merv Griffin Show* and Dr. Joyce Brothers, the pioneer pop TV psychologist/talk-show maven.[50] Everyone is a "real person," "coping" and "relating" their way through the complexities of the late twentieth century. The only thing missing is sponsorship by a hot-tub manufacturer.

But enough of this pseudotherapeutic group commiseration. The ultimate psychological television is a direct one-to-one confrontation in the true realm of television psychodrama. Take, for example, "Dear John" video. A video service named Posterity Pix (because it specializes in videotaped reading of wills) tapes statements that people are reluctant (or afraid) to express in person but will put on tape. According to a *Time* magazine report, "One client could not work up the nerve to tell her husband face-to-face that she intended to leave him, so she taped a 'Dear John' message—and then left."[51]

Television talk, in this most blatant manifestation, is revealing, for we can clearly detect its form reduced to one person, cut off from meaningful human relationships, taking decisive action that produces the bold solution, leaving behind a video trace of her persona in a one-way communication. This is far from authentic communication as we once knew it. It is fatalistic and nihilistic. This is the true television talk—a video monologue without commitment—today's electronic mythic realm of the individual.

How far will television talk go? Until December 26, 1982, nothing seemed too outlandish for the form's appropriation. But that day, the boundaries of television talk were stretched to their limits. An Associated Press "News Digest" item speaks for itself:

People considering suicide would be the stars of a TV series proposed by a man who contends that the program, "Second Chance," would save lives.

"We'll set up a suicide hot line, and when a call comes in, we'll send out a psychiatrist or counselor to talk to that person, and we'll also send out a camera," Lawrence Schwab said. "The purpose is to talk the person out of suicide."

He said he is trying to recruit investors and make a pilot of the program.

The Suicide Prevention Center in Los Angeles has denounced the proposal as "potentially dangerous for suicidal persons seeking help."

The center issued a statement saying it could "provoke some individuals, who might have been helped, into actually killing themselves, and might attract others to act suicidally because of the publicity involved."

Asked if the program amounted to exploiting the miseries of would-be suicide victims, Schwab replied, "I'll get some money out of it, but not much. What I'm getting out of it is a fantastic sense of accomplishment and a chance to save lives.

"But certainly it's exploitation," he added. "Everything is exploitation. 'Captain Kangaroo' is exploitation. 'Laverne and Shirley' is exploitation. But this is not another one of these comedies or game shows. This is important."[52]

Second Chance turns the myth of the individual on its head. The potential suicide acts and stands alone, a solitary person outside the group. But he violates the unchallengeable moral constraints imposed by Western religion and common law and thus is branded the fool, to be pitied, not revered. He can be hero neither to the dominant culture nor to the oppositional culture, given the ground rules for this discourse (in the latter case because the potential suicide's action is divorced from any political context to which it might refer). His "worth" becomes his televisability— his value as a dramatic persona. His "life-and-death" struggle is ideally suited to television's dramatic desire for rudimentary moral conflict.

Rather than waste money on a media psychologist to attempt to talk the potential suicide out of committing the act on *Second Chance*, why doesn't the producer simply give the potential suicide a camera and recorder and let him become a "video poet," taping his own suicide note? Once a number of such messages are in the can, the producer can put those together that reflect a common theme, say, "No one understands my sensitivity," and edit them down to fit between the commercial breaks. Following the tapes, in the show's epilogue, the producer can come on camera, like Chuck Barris on *The Gong Show*, and tell the viewers who actually carried out the act and who didn't. That shall surely produce enough drama to go around.

NOTES

1. Russell Baker, "Televiso, Ergo Sum," *New York Times*, August 23, 1980, p. 23.

2. Edmund Carpenter, *Oh, What a Blow That Phantom Gave Me!* (Toronto: Bantam Books, 1973), p. 3.

3. Orrin E. Klapp, *Heroes, Villains, and Fools: The Changing American Character* (Englewood Cliffs, NJ: Prentice-Hall, 1962), pp. 43–45. Klapp sees the independent spirit functioning as a heroic model who offers a compensation for average people who are "tired of their roles and welcome a vacation."

4. Bernard M. Timberg, *Television Talk* (Austin, TX: University of Texas Press, forthcoming).

5. Timberg, unpublished manuscript of *Television Talk*. This idea was developed in greater detail in Bernard M. Timberg, "Television Talk and Ritual Space: Carson and Letterman," *Southern Speech Communication Journal* 52 (Summer 1987): 390–402.

6. Les Brown, *Encyclopedia of Television* (New York: Zoetrope, 1982), pp. 168, 308–309.

7. Conversation with James Day, New York City, June 30, 1993.

8. Richard Bernstein, "Moyers Designs a Talk Show for Thinkers," *New York Times*, September 11, 1988, sec. 2, p. 33.

9. Ibid.

10. Ibid.

11. Ibid.

12. Ibid.

13. Ibid., p. 45.

14. Ibid.

15. Alex McNeil, *Total Television*, 3d ed. (New York: Penguin Books, 1991), p. 521.

16. Paolo Carpignano, Robin Anderson, Stanley Aronowitz, and William Difazio, "Chatter in the Age of Electronic Reproduction: Talk Television and the 'Public Mind,'" *Social Text: Theory/Culture/Ideology* 25/26 (1990): 53.

17. Ibid.

18. Ibid., pp. 53–54.

19. "Geraldo Rivera's Nose Broken in Scuffle on His Talk Show," *New York Times*, November 4, 1988, p. B3.

20. Jeremy Gerard, "TV Notes: Hating and Ratings," *New York Times*, November 17, 1988, p. C30.

21. Geraldo Rivera, "TV's Wave of the Future," *New York Times*, December 16, 1988, p. A39.

22. Lena Williams, "It was a Year When Civility Really Took It on the Chin," *New York Times*, December 18, 1988, p. 1.

23. Ibid.

24. Gloria-Jean Masciarotte, "C'Mon Girl: Oprah Winfrey and the Discourse of Feminine Talk," *Genders* 11 (Fall 1991): 87.

25. Ibid., p. 91.

26. Ibid., p. 81.

27. Ibid., p. 89.

28. Carpignano et al., "Chatter," p. 47.

29. "Touchiest Topic on Radio Now: Talk about Sex," *Broadcasting*, March 19, 1973, pp. 118–121.

30. "Government and the NAB Close in on Sex Programs," *Broadcasting*, April 2, 1973, p. 27.

31. Ibid., p. 28.

32. "Sex on the Dial," *Newsweek*, September 4, 1972, p. 90.

33. "Touchiest Topic," p. 118.

34. Carpignano et al., "Chatter," p. 52.

35. Masciarotte, "C'Mon Girl," p. 90.

36. Ibid.

37. Carpignano et al., "Chatter," p. 47.

38. William A. Henry III, "From the Dawn of Gab: The Evolution of TV's Most Indigenous Form," *Channels*, May/June 1983, p. 43.

39. Masciarotte, "C'Mon Girl," p. 83.

40. McNeil, *Total Television*, p. 572.

41. Masciarotte, "C'Mon Girl," p. 86.

42. Ibid., pp. 93, 95–96.

43. Ibid., p. 93.

44. Ibid., p. 103.

45. Jeremy Gerard, "Talk-Show Hoaxers Face One of Their Victims," *New York Times*, September 8, 1988, p. C17.

46. Jerzy Kosinski, *Being There* (New York: Bantam, 1971), p. 51.

47. Henry, "Gab," p. 43.

48. Interview with Dr. Peter Wish, *ABC Nightline*, February 12, 1982.

49. Mary Pratt, "No, She Really Loves Eggs: Fighting It Out on Call-In Radio," *Tabloid*, Winter 1983, pp. 27–37.

50. Ross Wetzsteon, "Psychochatter: The Trend of the '80s," *Channels*, May/June 1983, pp. 49–51.

51. "Lights, Camera, Wills," *Time*, December 1981, p. 72.

52. Associated Press "News Digest" as reported in *The Athens (Ohio) Messenger*, December 26, 1982, p. B-6.

11

□ □ □ □ □ □

Toward an Oppositional Television

With rare exceptions, television network executives, program producers, writers, directors, actors, journalists, advertising agency people, commercial directors, and financiers ultimately respond to television as a business and the works of television as product. These are, by and large, men and women driven by the dream of "the good life"—the Great American Dream—a world of money, of freedom from the constraining regimes of ordinary everyday work and leisure, and of status. These men and women live the myth of eternal progress framed by the Protestant ethic: a vision of hard work and intense competition, with personal prestige and especially wealth the reward for the survivors. Their everyday lived experience is inevitably imprinted on the panorama of dominant centralized commercial television in the United States.

However, television, as Roger Silverstone has noted, is also a site of "struggle between competing discourses," as television's texts are "produced in and for societies full of contradictions and inequalities."[1] In earlier discussions we have noted those creators working in drama in mainstream prime-time commercial television (e.g., David Rintels, Abby Mann, and the writer/producer team of Richard Levinson and William Link) who have, with varying degrees of success, challenged the dominant industry definitions of acceptable "political" discourse. Most often, however, while they have fought hard for their beliefs, they have in the end accepted compromises dictated by cautious network programmers and standards and practices executives as preconditions for the funding and distribution of their creative efforts. Mann and Rintels in particular have bitterly and eloquently complained about the nature of the process.

Outside the domain of mainstream commercial television, creative space is occasionally provided for the expression of oppositional ideology, although as we shall see, constraints exist here as well. Oppositional ideology emerges, for example, in independently produced video documentary works addressing contemporary social problems related to both the material relations of work and the social relations of ethnic, racial, gender, sexual-orientation, political, religious, and economic groups; "antitelevision" performance art, such as the oppositional ideological "readings" of popular art texts and the siting of these texts in their economic contexts of production and dissemination, and truly two-way, "performer-viewer-performer" television conversation; and the revival and presentation of regional and local folk culture via video histories of cultural spokespersons who are often clearly marginalized (i.e., ignored) by dominant culture producers.

A major problem is that these forms are rarely foregrounded when they are presented. Rather, they remain lost in the background because of their lack of publicity (including pre-reviews in major print publications) and their inherently subordinate position as interlopers relegated to the outer reaches of public-access cable television channels.

One must place oppositional television work in context: What work, if any, is allowed on mainstream commercial and public television, and why? What work is automatically excluded, and what is the rationale for its exclusion? What programming apparatuses operate in the domain of oppositional television that may tend on occasion to duplicate the control mechanisms of dominant television? We will explore these and other questions in the following discussion of evolving trends in the development and restriction of oppositional television works. First, however, we must define our terms.

WHAT IS "OPPOSITIONAL"?

In an effort to maintain the privileged status of its class fraction, the dominant culture creates material desire and encourages consumption by incessantly parading the objects of an upper-middle-class lifestyle before viewers with lower economic, educational, and cultural capital; yet the economic structures inherent in advanced capitalism work to exclude most people from actually possessing such objects or attaining the status associated with them. A dialectic of seeming inclusion/actual exclusion is thus constructed through the creation of "spectacle" and the placement of the average viewer in the position of voyeur who desires and is allowed limited possession of lesser-quality "counterfeit" tokens of the prestigious lifestyle. This is accomplished, according to Andrew Britton, by "flattering the spectator with his or her familiarity with the forms and keepings of a hermetic entertainment 'world'."[2] The "narcissistic self-reference" of entertainment, writes Britton, produces "a certain kind of complicity with the spectator, a knowing sense of familiarity with the terms of the discourse." It is "a form of flattery." One is "in on something." It "makes

of the pleasures of communal feeling a cosy conspiracy of self-congrat-
ulation and spurious familiarity." This discourse requires little attention
and doesn't challenge the spectator. Entertainment thus "engineer[s]
structures of feeling which cannot be examined."[3] The function of entertainment is to induce a feeling among spectators that what is seen isn't
real and doesn't really matter. Distancing is thereby coopted. The spectator cannot reflect on the text and its production of meaning. There is
no alienation created by a disruption of the meaning-making process.

As noted repeatedly in this book, the dominant culture employs the
myth of eternal progress to provide closure for this process of cooptation.
According to Britton,

Throughout the history of its rule, the bourgeoisie has sought consistently to rationalize and depoliticise its own technical priorities by reference to the concept
of 'progress.' ... In fact, of course, 'progress' is never interest-free, and its agents
are far from being impersonal: in class societies, it always relates in some way to
an acceleration of the rate and scope of surplus-extraction by the ruling class.
     ... The fact that the bourgeoisie's 'progress'—that is, the unprecedented ex-
pansion of the forces of production which the rule of capital has produced—has
actually to be recovered for the general interest *by political means* is suppressed,
and history is seen as being borne towards equality by the sheer momentum of
human inventiveness.[4] (emphasis added)

The myth of eternal progress so evident in popular entertainment fiction
thus suppresses the history of class struggle, producing the "appearance
that the rights of the exploited have been 'granted.'"[5] In popular culture's
entertainment forms, we see "the spectacle of the technique of the future
defending the values of the past."[6]

Oppositional culture attempts to point out the inherent inequality of
this relationship and incite the viewer to act to break down the unequal
power of possession that holds those outside the power center in check.
On a formal, aesthetic level, it may employ Brechtian dramatic theory,
whose function "is not ... to remind the poor benighted spectator that
fictions are fictions, but to mobilize the dialectic ... for explicitly revolutionary purposes."[7] On a political level, oppositional culture encourages
the creation of desire and its transformation into *political action* that cannot be regulated in an unequal power relationship by the dominant culture, such as a desire for the political power of "community" to counteract
individual alienation and to secure a more equitable distribution of wealth,
guaranteed health protection, equal wages for equal work, and the like.

Dominant culture legitimizes those individuals who are wealthy and
ostentatious and wield power over others (the characters in *Dallas* are
excellent examples). Oppositional culture attempts to demonstrate how

that wealth was achieved and at whose expense and how it is being used to continue unequal class and status relationships.

Finally, dominant culture, in circumscribing the correct or "proper" alternative positions on issues—channeling resistance by providing an outlet for it—defuses truly oppositional positions. Thus *M*A*S*H*, as described earlier, is "antiwar" but not antipolitics. That is, *M*A*S*H* transcribes the horror of war into a personal revulsion through the characters of the cynical doctors. When the Korean War, and by implication Vietnam, is criticized, the critique centers on bureaucracy—the inability of the generals and civilian negotiators to end the interminable conflict. The politics that controls the discourse within which a war such as Korea or Vietnam comes to make sense to the American people is thereby defused. In a similar vein, the 1983 television movie *The Day After*, which depicted the results of a nuclear conflagration between the Americans and the Soviets, is "anti–nuclear war"—we see the devastation and individual misery all around. Lawrence, Kansas, the setting for this film, is blown back to the Stone Age. But *The Day After* is not anti–nuclear politics, for nuclear politics presupposes the survivability of the species, in whatever condition, and the film does the same. One of oppositional culture's most important and difficult tasks is to deconstruct what are presented as "proper" alternative political positions.

Countering the inherent imbalance of the power relationship between dominant television and oppositional television is a major undertaking that will need the highest levels of ideological commitment and staying power. Some tentative yet important examples of work in this vein can serve as models for future efforts.

Community-based video documentary works addressing contemporary community problems have, on occasion, been given air time on local public television stations and, on rare occasions, have gained access to national commercial television. An aesthetic premise, though certainly not a rule, of much if not most of this work is its rough-edged vérité style and technical unevenness. However, public television finds such work increasingly unacceptable as it goes after ratings like its commercial counterparts. While the rough-edged quality of the work can be an ideological advantage, that is, it can relate formal structure more authentically to content and context, it can also turn off viewers who are trained in dominant-television watching. Two important thrusts of this type of work bear close examination: (1) works made by workers themselves that address the material conditions of the work experience and (2) works made by community-based artists/documentarians that address the social and cultural conditions in the communities in which they live and work. As oppositional works, both types of work reveal commitment to an ideological position critical of an unjust contemporary social condition.

One important example of the first type of work is a videotape titled

Signed, Sealed, and Delivered, produced by striking postal workers with help from a number of community-based artist/documentarians. *Signed, Sealed, and Delivered* documents the struggle of postal workers in the New York City area to achieve safer working conditions in postal facilities and more humane consideration of their demands by postal officials. The tape, a combination of handheld black-and-white, handheld industrial-grade color, and local news footage, documents a wildcat strike by the postal workers over intolerable working conditions, the firing of the strikers, the death of a worker who was chewed up by an unsafe conveyor belt at the bulk-mail processing facility in New Jersey, and the attempts of workers to achieve justice through Congressional hearings on the working conditions that led to the death and the wildcat strike. The soundtrack features protest songs written especially for this videotape. A powerful, though aesthetically uneven document, it was aired on public television station WNET/Thirteen in New York City and submitted to video festivals around the country. *Signed, Sealed, and Delivered* demonstrates the use of the video camera as an important tool in workers' struggles.

The work of community-video documentarians such as John Alpert of Downtown Community Television Center (who has also done independent work for NBC News in Southeast Asia and Central America) is representative of the more significant community-based video documentary work being done today. This work also points to the subject matter required in order to receive widespread distribution.

With Rockefeller Foundation funding, Alpert's DCTV produced "Vietnam: Picking Up the Pieces," which was aired in 1978 as part of WNET's *Visa* series. The work, decidedly pro-Vietnam, describes the rebuilding and reeducation effort in a united Vietnam, as the former South Vietnamese are reintegrated into a society that labored continuously to eradicate prostitution, capitalist opportunism, drug addiction, adult illiteracy, and above all the emotional scars of a protracted war imposed on all the people of Vietnam from the outside, first by the French and later by the United States. Alpert's piece shows the new Vietnam succeeding, but with much rebuilding and social change remaining to be accomplished. Among the American legacies, Alpert points out toward the end of the piece, are 800,000 orphans, many with American fathers, who are now cared for by an order of Vietnamese nuns.

Alpert, working with NBC News, did a "Segment 3" on the nightly news program in which he followed the Sandinistas in Costa Rica as they attempted to overthrow Nicaraguan dictator Somoza. In a powerful interview with one Sandinista after a battle in which counterrevolutionary soldiers are killed, Alpert asks the Sandinista, "Is this victory?" The response: "We need notebooks and papers to write and read . . . and all we get is death." This segment does credit to the network news organization, which on occasion can rise above the political pressures of the dominant television ideological apparatus. Alpert, an independent, could gain the trust of the Sandinistas and the Vietnamese, who believed he could present their struggle without the dominant news frames distorting the story.

Downtown Community Television Center's work includes reports on poor people being evicted from their apartments in northern New Jersey to make way for the new upscale residents and their cooperatives and condominiums; drug addicts wandering the streets of New York City, stealing and shooting up; poor homesteaders in Philadelphia who were led to believe they could renovate abandoned houses and thereby become homeowners, but who in the end were deceived as the houses on which they spent so much time and love were put on the sheriff's auction block; and miners striking in South Dakota in an attempt to publicize occupational safety hazards. Many of these later tapes, while well-intentioned, are ideologically flawed. They take an oppositional stance but ignore debate. They become polemical, often lacking a clearly drawn political and social context. This tendency to focus on the emotions of the participants and beg the viewer for a reaction rather than to present a carefully reasoned argument against an institution and to convince the viewer of the intellectual validity of the oppositional position lessens these works' power to foster clearly conceived social change. Nevertheless, the works do exhibit commitment and encourage a response, even if that response is dissociated from the social context in which the work was constructed.

Alan and Susan Raymond's documentary *The Police Tapes* was produced in association with the Television Lab at New York City public television station WNET/Thirteen and first aired nationally on PBS in 1976 in a 90-minute version. It was subsequently shown on the ABC News *Close-Up!* documentary series in 1978 in an edited 50-minute version that cut out much of the violence and street language. This was the first independent video documentary ever aired on a national commercial television network.

The Police Tapes is an important example of the battle between the good intentions of the cultural workers who make the tape and the pressures, explicit or otherwise, which cause the ultimate defusion of oppositional work as it enters the dominant television apparatus. The work appears "oppositional," and some segments, taken by themselves, are clearly oppositional. Yet, taken in its entirety (in the 90-minute PBS version with which I am familiar), the work becomes not so much an indictment of the politics that maintains the ghetto as it is a celebration of police work (for this reason, its airing on ABC's *Close-Up!* is understandable). Yet, the black-and-white direct video technique and the subject matter—police wandering the streets of the 44th Precinct in the notoriously dangerous South Bronx area of New York City—lend the work a depressing quality and convince the viewer that "the system" has broken down. We see a Hispanic murder victim, killed during a robbery by two blacks,

lying in a pool of blood on the floor of a social club. We see a Latino boy
dead under a car, stabbed fourteen times in a family dispute. People in
the street are screaming. An officer yells, "Aw, . . . shut up!" We hear police describe the "trance-like state" of murderers and we hear police assert
that people with limited property will fight, and even kill, to defend it.
We hear talk of the "animals out there." We hear the officers continually
criticize the court apparatus for letting convicted felons back out on the
streets. We hear their frustration with plea-bargaining arrangements. Yet
we marvel at their restraint. There is no police brutality, no corruption,
no one at the precinct "on the take" or involved in selling drugs.

Like direct cinema/video work generally, *The Police Tapes* is absent a
narrator. Thus context is provided by the footage that is ultimately shot
and assembled in the final edit. As discussed earlier, direct cinema/video
work can be provocative, but it must "be there" to reveal crucial moments
of ideological conflict. *The Police Tapes* is important in revealing the stark
realities of ghetto life. It is not clear about causes, politics, or economics.
Its inherent drama will attract an audience (ABC surmised this), and its
aesthetic will seem provocative. Yet, beneath it all, its ideology is too easily
incorporated into the dominant conception of police work.

Ironically, *The Police Tapes* seems to have encouraged the development
of the incessant use of "reality" crime footage on the local nightly "action
news" broadcasts, the "real people and real crime" approach of Fox Television's series *Cops*, each episode of which documents one week in the
operations of the police force in a city, and the melodramatic recreations
of crimes on Fox Television's *America's Most Wanted*. All this demonstrates the short distance between the serious documentary on a lurid
subject and "tabloid television."

Other independently produced "political" documentaries cast their critical gaze on national and international subjects. The best of these point-
edly deconstruct the dominant television news frames, which not
infrequently mystify the events by omission or selective coverage. One
particularly well-crafted and provocative example is the three half-hour
segments of the 1987 documentary *Consuming Hunger*, produced by
Freke Vuijst and Ilan Ziv (Ziv directed and edited the documentary and
Vuijst was the correspondent). *Consuming Hunger* was distributed in
North America by the Catholic Foreign Mission Society of America,
Maryknoll Media Relations. The documentary's executive producer was
Michael Lavery, a Maryknoll lay missioner. Funding for the project was
secured from the Catholic Foreign Mission Society of America, Channel
Four (UK), the European Commission, and a Dutch foundation, Nation-
ale Commissie Voorlichting en Bewustwording Ontwikkelingssamenwerk-
ing.

The first 30-minute segment of *Consuming Hunger*, titled "Getting the
Story," focuses on television news coverage of the disastrous famine in

Ethiopia/Eritrea in 1983 and 1984. In the summer of 1983, David Kline, a freelance news producer who had learned of the impending famine from his contacts in international relief organizations, was assigned as a field producer by CBS News to go to Ethiopia and document the story. When he submitted his footage to CBS, it was turned down. CBS argued that the "images were not strong enough" for inclusion in the evening newscast, that Ethiopia "was not a Biafra." Kline was subsequently unable to convince any other television outlet to use the story. A British Visnews crew had preceded Kline by nearly four months, but Visnews was also unable to interest anyone in this story.

Fourteen months would pass before a Visnews crew, led by Visnews Africa Bureau Chief Mohamed Amin, and a British Broadcasting Corporation (BBC) correspondent, Michael Buerk, would gather footage of mass starvation so compelling that it could no longer be ignored. Visnews offered the story to NBC's London Bureau on October 23, 1984, following its airing on BBC's lunchtime newscast. The NBC bureau contacted New York news headquarters and described the story, pleading with NBC News executives to run the story on that evening's newscast. At first, little interest was shown in New York; but the London Bureau finally persuaded New York to take a satellite feed. When the images came across the newsroom monitors "there was dead silence," according to a senior NBC foreign producer. NBC "broke" the story in the United States, placing it in the final slot in that night's news hole. The lead story of that newscast: "President Reagan hackled at the University of Portland."

David Kline, who admits on camera that his footage was not as "dramatic," calls the Visnews/BBC pictures "almost Hollywood." Brian Winston, then Dean of the Pennsylvania State University School of Communication, argues that for disasters in the Third World to be considered news in the United States, their scope must be of "biblical" proportions. A sea of people huddled together in misery would constitute such a newsworthy scene. The Visnews/BBC pictures satisfied this criterion. Winston argues further that while NBC did ultimately deliver the story to viewers, it was framed as a human interest piece. There was no *structural location* of the famine in economic or political terms. As such, it existed at some "lower" location, according to Winston. "Getting the Story" concludes with Winston's discussion of the ethics of journalistic responsibility in this case. Winston argues that it would be naïve to hold any group of journalists alone responsible for the neglect of the Ethiopian famine. Rather, says Winston, blame for ignoring the developing tragedy must be collectively shared. The failure of the newsgatherers in this instance is simply the outcome of a long process—four centuries of lack of respect for Africa and Africans.

The second segment of *Consuming Hunger*, titled "Shaping the Image," examines television's role in providing famine relief to the Ethiopians.

NBC's transmission, in October 1984, of the Visnews/BBC story on the famine created a wave of sympathy for the victims throughout the United States. This was mirrored in other wealthy industrialized nations. Eight months later, on July 13, 1985, the "Live Aid" global media event and rock and roll concert was telecast to nearly two billion viewers worldwide by 13 communications satellites. *Consuming Hunger* places this media event in its sociopolitical and economic contexts.

"Shaping the Image" begins with a statement by James Oporio-Ekwaro, a Kenyan diplomat, charging that the United States's image of Africa, perpetuated by journalists, is the "Tarzan image"—an image of the "beggar continent" that permits the construction of a parallel image of "the white man coming to liberate Africa."

The documentary chronicles the activities of Christian outreach organizations such as World Vision that take celebrities to the camps in Africa in an effort to publicize the disaster. Father Elwood Keiser, producer of a DBOF on the crisis, *We Are the Children*, which focused on the lives of the Americans working in the Ethiopian refugee camps rather than on the Ethiopians themselves, argues that Americans trust celebrities and are intrigued by them. He adds, "I can get on the talk shows because of celebrities."

Father Keiser defended his DBOF to the *Consuming Hunger* producers this way:

If you're going to create a drama, you're going to have to create somebody the audience can identify with. The audience is going to identify with an American working in a refugee camp in Ethiopia more than it's going to be able to identify with the Ethiopians themselves. . . . This is entertainment.

Brian Winston condemns the images in both the news reports and the Christian outreach organizations' television programs as "dehumanized, masturbatory images." Winston argues that starving Africans became "objects without dignity." The images, Winston adds, ultimately allow Americans to feel good about their concern for these "objects."

"Shaping the Image" then turns to the "Live Aid" concert itself. Rock-and-roll critic Dave Marsh asserts that "Live Aid" deliberately misinformed the public. What was celebrated, Marsh adds, was rock and roll, not a solution to the crisis and the underlying problem.

AT&T, Kodak, Chevrolet, and Pepsi sponsored the "Live Aid" telecast. An AT&T executive is shown giving a corporate pitch extolling the public relations and marketing value of its sponsorship, major purposes of which were to demonstrate the sophistication of the company's telecommunications technologies and to promote the use of its "800 number." An AT&T commercial created especially for the event was disconcerting if not tasteless. It featured extreme close-ups of desperate famine victims ("objects of pity") intercut with the arrival of food relief airplanes and relief workers offering food to the grateful multitude. A specially rewritten version of the AT&T jingle "reach out and touch someone," used in many previous AT&T campaigns, provided the commercial's music bed. The new lyrics went like this: "Reach out and touch someone/*someone whose only hope is you . . .*" (emphasis mine). The AT&T executive called this an "excellent advertising buy."

The episode concludes, as it began, with diplomat Oporio-Ekwaro sitting in his rural Kenyan village. Oporio-Ekwaro argues that this should have been a story of African peoples helping each other. That never came out of either the news coverage or the "Live Aid" mega-event. Oporio-Ekwaro calls this a fundamental question of international power. It speaks to the imbalance of trade between the North and the South, he argues, adding that these are complex structural relationships. His final thoughts on the problem: "You cannot speak on equal terms unless you are free."

The final episode of *Consuming Hunger*, "Selling the Feeling," turns its attention to another media mega-event, "Hands Across America," staged in the United States on May 25, 1986. The event sought to provide a national catharsis to the problems of hunger and homelessness in America. The event was structured so that Americans who contributed $10 or more to fight hunger and homelessness would "reserve their place" in an unbroken chain of people holding hands from New York City to Los Angeles. Ken Kragan, Kenny Rogers's manager and organizer of the event, told supporters: "Hands Across America is the first time that you all and everyone in America can take an active role."

Like "Live Aid," "Hands Across America" featured a gallery of celebrities endorsing the project in promotional videotapes. Stuart Ewen, a professor of media studies at Hunter College in New York City, offers a telling on-camera critique of the "Hands" promotional videos, arguing that the event became another consumable item, framed and structured by its organizers and corporate sponsors, Citibank and Coca-Cola. The commercials produced by these sponsors in connection with the event, Ewen asserts, surrounded their products with a mood—a desire to consume. Their inspirational music was carefully linked with "family feel" products. (The theme song for "Hands" was created by Look & Co., who also created the theme music, sung by Kenny Rogers, for the mid-1980s Chrysler campaign "The Pride Is Back/Born in America.")

Stanley Aronowitz, a professor of sociology at the Graduate Center of the City University of New York, argues in the documentary that "Hands" is essentially a "middle-class effort" well tailored to the ideology of volunteerism advocated by the Reagan administration. Unfortunately, adds Aronowitz, "volunteerism purports to change the circumstances without organized political movement" and is thus bound to fail. Aronowitz asserts that for real change to occur, there must be consciousness-raising in connection with sustained action and a political program (e.g., the Civil Rights Movement). "Hands Across America" lacked the latter two elements.

Citibank, a major sponsor of this event, viewed "Hands" as a primary vehicle to help it remold its corporate image from one of a distant North-east corporate financial establishment to that of a "warm" nationwide "family" institution.

What did "Hands Across America" actually accomplish? National Co-alition for the Homeless spokesperson Robert Hayes put the best face on the event by speculating that "Hands" probably had some educational impact on some people. Some money was raised, some people were made better off, and some people had to at least think.

Ewen sees the event differently:

What we've got here is a parade of media stars which is being presented in certain ways as "the solution." . . . Instead of talking about social action and social trans-formation that might alter a society which now creates great wealth on the one hand and enormous poverty on the other, we view as a solution something that's offered to us by the world of the media. All the stars will come together—all these great individuals who we look at, who we admire, who to a certain extent we model our lives after, now join together. They're not individuals for a moment. They become part of a whole; we become part of that whole. We become part of the media event. And still nothing happens.

The documentary ends on a somber note. At a Moravian Church "drop-in center" in New York City sometime after the "Hands Across America" event, outreach program director Jennifer Barrows notes that many of the homeless and hungry were initially very enthusiastic about the idea be-hind the event but "lapsed into a somewhat cynical attitude" when they did not see concrete results. They saw "Hands" as "one more bit of hype." The final image is a scroll over the "Hands Across America" logo, which reads:

Hands Across America raised $32 million. After expenses, only $15 million re-mained.
This sum wouldn't pay for one night of shelter for the 2.5 million homeless Americans.

Some important general conclusions can be drawn from these provoc-ative documentary critiques of media and American society. Among them is the fact that media presentations tend to turn subjects into objects for our consumption and that we tend to discard them when the dramatur-gical narrative "work" is finished. These subjects-as-objects are "margin-alized." This marginalization takes shape as a cultural form (the media event). Subjects-as-objects represent "the other." In their depoliticized form, they are to be pitied but not respected. Above all, *Consuming Hun-*

ger asks the question, "Whose voices do we hear"? Those of the subjects of the news and the media mega-events? Or those of television's corporate sponsors? The views of the "victims" are rarely heard. Rather, we are given the views of journalists, relief workers, event organizers, and advertisers peering in from the outside, talking about the victimization of victims.

Consuming Hunger was aired on New York City public television station WNET/Thirteen and on the VISN cable program network. However, according to coproducer and director Ilan Ziv, it was twice turned down by PBS for national distribution.

In 1987, when it was first offered to PBS, Ziv was told that it was not timely—that "there was no longer a famine in Ethiopia." In 1992, as the famine in Somalia once again drew our attention to the Africans' misery, Ziv offered *Consuming Hunger* to PBS for a second time. Again it was rejected. The rationale for this second refusal, according to Ziv: *Consuming Hunger* was "too different from the situation in Somalia" and would take "too much time and money to update."[8]

The American mass audience was thereby denied access to one of television's most important provocative discussions of social relations in a global context. Not so the citizens of most other capitalist democracies. According to Ziv, *Consuming Hunger*'s first two episodes, in longer 45-minute versions, were aired nationally in Canada, the United Kingdom (on Channel Four), Sweden, Denmark, Germany, the Netherlands, Belgium, Italy, Switzerland, Ireland, Australia, and Japan. In addition, the European Community offered an English-language and French-language version, at no charge, to all television broadcasters in Africa. The documentary has had its widest distribution in the United States in educational institutions such as universities and high schools.

It is a "media event" in its own right when mainstream commercial television undertakes such a critical self-examination. Yet this did occur on the ABC News *Nightline* telecast of August 30, 1988, titled "What's Not News."[9] Its subject was American television news coverage of the Third World (the central question of *Consuming Hunger*'s "Getting the Story").

Ted Koppel, the program's regular host, anchored the telecast from ABC's Washington studios. Guests appearing in New York City were Ambassador Oumarou Youssouffou, executive secretary of the Organization of African Unity, and Lawrence Grossman, president of NBC News from 1984 to 1988 and former president of the Public Broadcasting Service. Guest Alexander Cockburn, a columnist for *The Nation*, appeared from San Francisco. Cockburn is one of the more radical, politically-left journalists writing in the United States today, and his appearance on the *Nightline* program was particularly surprising.

Koppel opens the program by questioning whether news media give adequate attention to tragic events—such as starvation and civil wars—occurring in the Third World. He notes critics' charges that Third World countries "are often treated as though they're not part of this world at all."

Following a background videotape narrated by ABC News correspondent James Walker, Koppel discusses the problem with Ambassador Youssouffou and Grossman.

Youssouffou points out that he is repeatedly told that American audiences are not interested in events in Africa except when there is a famine or other major tragedy. He compares the U.S. media's coverage of Africa with coverage of the hatching of a condor chick in California: "[T]hat egg got more coverage than the entire continent of 400 million people."

Grossman argues that journalists, and by extension, viewers, know very little about the Third World and consequently pay little attention to events occurring there.

Koppel questions the "ignorance" rationale, asking whether in fact money (the cost to send a reporter and camera crew to Africa to produce an in-depth story) and racism (the fact that a majority of Americans are white) are not major reasons for the media's lack of attention to the Third World.

Grossman asserts that money is not the issue. He argues that the reason NBC, for example, has only one correspondent stationed in Africa is that "the stories are so remote."

Koppel is unwilling to accept the ambiguity inherent in Grossman's argument, which deflects the politicized issue of racial bias by focusing instead on the politically neutral rationale of geographical and emotional "remoteness." After all, Grossman himself noted that NBC's single African correspondent was stationed in South Africa, which has a significant white population.

Koppel presses Ambassador Youssouffou for an explanation. Youssouffou responds that "racism is probably the more valid of the reasons, because obviously the money that American companies are making in Africa justifies the American networks investing money to cover stories in Africa."

Following a commercial break, Koppel brings *The Nation*'s Alexander Cockburn into the discussion, noting that Cockburn also writes for *The Wall Street Journal* and is on the editorial committee of *The New Left Review*. Cockburn proceeds to turn up the "political heat" of the discussion by locating the lack of news coverage of the Third World in the symbiotic relationship between the U.S. foreign policy establishment and mainstream newsgathering organizations:

Why do stories get on the network news, why do they get in the headlines of the papers? . . . The tempo is set . . . in Washington. It's set by the State Department. It's set by the White House. [F]or thirty years, when Somoza was running Nicaragua, . . . imprisoning people and torturing them and shutting up newspapers and killing people, you didn't hear much about it in the U.S. press, because he was basically "our guy," right? Now . . . you hear about Nicaragua on a daily basis.

Koppel acknowledges that Cockburn's analysis has "a certain reasonableness" and suggests that journalists may suffer from laziness. Grossman disagrees, returning to his earlier theme of journalists' ignorance of these remote areas.

Cockburn refuses to accept this rationale:

I don't think . . . lack of knowledge ever stopped a journalist from doing anything. . . . Let's take Afghanistan and South Africa. Now Afghanistan—the Soviets in Kabul city [say], "If we catch any journalist running around in Afghanistan unofficially, we'll shoot him." Right? So Dan Rather gets dressed up in a sheet and goes wandering around and it's great, he has dramatic shots, because that has been placed on the political agenda by the Reagan administration. . . . Then we go to South Africa, where the South Africans say, . . . "We're going to now control news." Now why didn't Dan Rather dress up in a sheet and start running around South Africa unofficially? The rules seem to be different, and I think . . . that agenda . . . has nothing to do with knowledge, it has nothing to do with expense, it's to do with that political agenda.

This installment of *Nightline* provides a powerful example of the kind of politically charged discourse that is so notably absent from the commerical television networks' standard public-affairs discussion programs. Cockburn, who is rarely seen on the mainstream small screen, skillfully challenged Grossman's depoliticized explanations of the problem—that journalists are just "regular folk" who are largely uninformed about events in the Third World because their audiences are not interesed in those events—by cleverly repoliticizing the context of journalistic agenda-setting.

"Antitelevision" performance is another important oppositional strategy. Paper Tiger Television, headquartered in New York City, has encouraged the development of this program form by distributing videotapes made by political artists to cable television access channels throughout the country. *Paper Tiger* videotapes, often exhibiting wit and political insight, offer an oppositional video "reading" or critique of the dominant culture's print and electronic media.

In one installment of *Paper Tiger Television*, Elayne Rapping "reads" romance novels. Rapping, sitting in a tacky Laundromat set, is folding clothes. In the background we see slides of a Laundromat alternating with covers from romances. Rapping offers a cogent feminist critique of the social relations depicted in these books. She highlights the fact that in these cover illustrations, as well as in the stories themselves, "Man is on top, woman is on the bottom." Rapping notes that Xerox and Scholastic Publications produce romances geared to 12-to-15-year-old girls. The stories, which present "sexual feelings" and "kissing," but no more, are really training manuals for the adulthood of "enormous consumer product spending" that is so prevalent as decor in the adult romances. While Rapping's reading flirts with a "rap," her preparation, obvious intelligence, sincerity, and the Laundromat setting make this engaging television. Unfortunately, it is still "one-way." Call-in audience response would intensify the effort by involving, for example, the viewer who reads romance novels.

Another form of "antitelevision" performance confronts the medium of its own turf. Coca Crystal's 1970s Manhattan cable public access weekly one-hour talk show *If I Can't Dance You Can Keep Your Revolution* directly confronted the centrist, stereotpyically Middle-American ambience of the television talk show. Crystal smoked a joint while she talked live with callers about politics.

Crystal's work exemplified the freedom of public access. So, too, in a different way, does the video performance of artist and critic Douglas Davis. Davis has worked to clarify the language of oppositional performance, of "performance-against-performance." In one piece, "How to Make Love to Your Television Set," Davis explores the meaning of talking back. Davis, a New York artist, had performed this work prior to being invited by Warner Cable in Columbus, Ohio, to perform it in the summer of 1979. Warner's QUBE cable system in Columbus had gained national attention as the first interactive cable television system in the United States, and artists were intrigued by the technology's communication potential. Subscribers to QUBE could respond to questions asked from the QUBE studios by pressing one of several buttons on a response console. They could also order up programs in a similar manner. Their responses and program selections were fed into a central computer at the cable head end. Davis wanted to use QUBE's interactive potential to engage in a more personal two-way communication than merely pressing buttons in response to questions. He would subject himself to the will of the viewer by following the viewer's phoned-in directions for his video performance in the studio.

The program was live. Anything could happen. In this way, a mutual trust could be built between the two human beings linked via television and telephone. But was QUBE ready for interaction in the human, rather than the computer sense of the term? Not quite. Davis was restricted to the talk-show format of Warner's *Columbus Alive* program. He was engaged in a brief discussion of his work and asked to do a brief demonstration of "interaction" (How, after all, does one demonstrate interaction? One merely interacts). The program's female host was television-pleasant and at first calm, although there was an atmosphere of apprehension in the studio and control room. What if someone asked Davis to do something outrageous? There were a few crank calls and a few calls from viewers who seemed intrigued by the possibility of directing the evolving discourse. Then an unexpected ideological breakthrough occurred. The host took another call. Although she didn't know it at the time, the caller was a male student in my television criticism class watching the performance from an off-studio viewing area. He wanted to break down traditional television performance barriers. He politely asked not Davis, but the host to "come over to the TV monitor in the studio and do what I ask." The host seemed to interpret the caller's gesture in sexual terms, not an unlikely response (Davis's performance piece was, after all, titled "How to Make Love to Your Television Set"). The student's warm sincerity was transformed by the voyeuristic, commodified television frame. Interaction was impossible in this context. The host was no longer in control of the discourse. She sensed her status as an "object," yet could not or would not relate that status to the larger realm of televised commodification.

To counter the distorted history offered by the national-centralized dominant television, many cable public-access channels have attempted to redirect attention to the vast wealth of regional and local history and culture—history and culture that speak directly in some cases, indirectly in others, of social struggle against racism, of the capitalist/labor struggle in the mines and fields and sweatshops, and of the rich heritage of the family as a social and work unit. Among the pioneers in this "video history" project are Austin Community Television (ACTV) in Texas and Appalshop in Kentucky. These organizations have compiled videotapes, films, and audiotapes of community elders who recall the social struggles and recount the development and maintenance of indigenous folk culture in their regions and communities. Each tape or film is a statement that links the present to its history via the eyewitness and thereby counters the tendency of dominant television to naturalize that history, that is, to render the past in terms of the power relationships of the present.

Until the early 1980s, the control by dominant television over the domain of electronic public art had remained unshaken. In the past decade, however, there has been increasing evidence of the erosion of popular support for commercial television. A report appearing in the April 13, 1983, edition of Variety revealed the results of a National Association of Broadcasters study of viewer attitudes. The results were overwhelmingly negative, according to Variety. Based on 500 in-depth interviews at home and 1,000 telephone interviews, the report found that people rated television less important in their lives than in 1977, less entertaining, and less of a technical marvel. Viewers saw television encouraging bad behavior and language. Half of the viewers surveyed said they were watching less television than in 1977, one-sixth the same amount, and only one-third more. More importantly, the drop-off in viewing was found across all demographic and socioeconomic groups. This indicated that traditionally heavy viewers in poorer socioeconomic classes were beginning to turn away from the system of constant electronic control to which they had been subjected for decades.

What has happened to produce such a response? While it certainly may be speculated that current dominant television fare is, on the whole, artistically vapid, the turning-away from television might also be attributed to a desire for discourse more relevant to the lives of viewers. The NAB study found that over 50 percent of the respondents said they wanted the new cable television technology for "participating in discussion or asking questions of political figures."[10] This strongly felt need for a serious political dialogue via television is highly encouraging. Cable television responded to this need in the 1980s via two channels of C-Span (Cable Satellite Public Affairs Network), which have demonstrated that articulate audience members can engage journalists and politicians in serious political discourse on extended live call-in programs dealing with complex policy questions. And, during the course of the 1992 presidential election campaign, politicians seemed to be responding to this shift in viewer attitudes regarding the importance of the medium of television in their lives. The electorate was engaged as active speaking subjects in two-way political communication to a degree not witnessed in the modern era of politics. They were no longer simply being "talked at." They were "talking back."

ART, IDEOLOGY, AND TECHNOLOGY

The increasing technological sophistication in electronics has resulted in the miniaturization of hardware and its increased portability, greatly expanded data storage capacity and ease of accessing data about our social milieu, better image resolution, and expanded person-machine interactive capability, all at increasingly affordable cost. The dream of a home information center is today a reality. While we have all this electronic technology at our disposal, however, we cannot neglect to question who establishes the information parameters for the software.

The most basic social manifestation of the electronics revolution is the proliferation of consumer-grade video recording and playback equipment. Relatively low-cost compared to broadcast-quality equipment and user-friendly, this video technology—single-chip color cameras, VCRs and video disc players, and powerful and highly portable personal computers—allows the viewer control of his or her video environment as an active programmer and program producer. While this emerging video system is important as an alternative to the dominant one-way, nonparticipatory television and while the business and leisure implications of the technology are profound, one cannot ignore the fact that the system still requires a substantial personal monetary investment and could well exacerbate the existing economic-class inequities in access to the production and reception of information.

The technology of electronic communication has permitted lower-cost production and distribution through an ever-increasing abundance of

available channels. The pent-up frustration of the enforced electronic silence of the many groups who were for years effectively closed out of our
electronic communications system now has an outlet, through public-
access cable television channels and electronic bulletin boards in personal
computer networks. Yet regardless of channel capacity, the cost to access
a channel and effectively to promote oppositional work so that it may
reach large numbers of viewers remains problematic. In addition to these
obvious cost problems, before we can assume an enlightened nation of
activist television workers, it is necessary to cultivate the true critical
viewer who would welcome the social and cultural debate offered in oppositional work. This book is one modest attempt in that direction.

CULTIVATING THE CRITICAL VIEWER

The critical viewer who sees "the fraudulence of a proposition in advertising," or the controlling myth of eternal progress through acquisitiveness operating in prime-time soap opera, or the overimportance
attached to the heroic splendid performer—whether athlete, politician, or
electronic preacher—is not likely to buy that product or complacently
stand outside the centers of capitalist power as the "correct" ideological
positions are circumscribed *for* him or her. The critical viewer is rather a
potential anarchist practicing, on one level, an ethics of resistance characterized by freedom, transgression, play, conflict, and serious cultural
negotiation and, in Jacques Ellul's words, embodying the notion that
"man accept *not* to do what he is capable of doing,"[11] namely, organizing
himself or herself, through technique, into an efficient, unthinking consuming machine. "Noise," considered to be dysfunctional in traditional
communications theory, is, according to this strategy, highly functional
because it serves to critique, through decidedly human acts of resistance,
a society of heteronomous alienated spectators whose history is manufactured by others for their consumption and who exist primarily through
products and outside the "web of human relations."[12] These acts of resistance, analogous to Michel de Certeau's notion of rearranging the furniture in a rented apartment, although important personal gestures of
defiance, will not however, in the longer term, threaten the stability of
advanced capitalism. Individuals must rather organize themselves into activist organizations with clear group goals, tactics, and strategies.

The individual critical viewer described above must, as a minimum first
step, fight neutralization by our culture's dominant institutions. Neutralization occurs naturally through a process of incorporation, of hegemonic
domination of entire ways of thinking and being. The educational institution, many critics argue, has become such an agent of incorporation.
British social critic Raymond Williams wrote that "Education transmits
necessary knowledge and skills, but always by a particular selection from

the whole available range, and with intrinsic attitudes, both to learning and social relations, which are in practice virtually inextricable."[13]

Bringing television and television studies into both the traditional and the nontraditional "classroom"—into our educational institutions via public television and community public and educational cable access channels—is clearly more than a reluctant act of admitting "popular art" into the established curricula of traditional educational structures. Television studies brings another set of critical strategies into cultural play, strategies that are extremely relevant to our everyday experience in which the pervasive medium of television has created a universe of discourse, a language of commonly shared symbols and commonly held beliefs that to a large degree frame the nature of our cultural negotiation. The culture critic must ask: In what manner does this negotiation occur in and outside the classroom? Is this negotiation confined by what Louis Althusser termed the Educational Ideological State Apparatus, in which the limiting and pervasive ideology of advanced capitalism encourages a view that the given material and social history is impenetrable and immutable? Or is it possible to open up the dominant ideology to serious critique, to the elaboration of residual and emergent oppositional ideologies and cultural formations,[14] encouraging the use of television as an important tool in the struggle for social change, change in which the inequities of social class stratification, the unequal distribution of the benefits of the "good life," and the condition of individual "unfreedom" will be redressed?

Clearly, the general character of cultural negotiation depends on the role of the individual teacher. Samuel Bowles and Herbert Gintis argue for the role of the teacher as social activist. Instead of encouraging naïve spontaneity, as in the "free school" environment, or student rebellion against harsh school authority, they argue that educators should instead highlight contradictions in the social system through the application of dialectical educational philosophy. They clearly delineate the ground for such a dialectic:

The struggle between working people and capital has its counterpart in educational conflict. . . . employers and other social elites have sought to use the schools for the legitimation of inequality through an ostensibly meritocratic and rational mechanism for allocating individuals to economic positions; they have sought to use the schools for the reproduction of profitable types of worker consciousness and behavior through a correspondence between the social relationships of education and those of economic life. On the other hand, parents, students, worker organizations, blacks, ethnic minorities, women and others have sought to use schools for their own objectives: material security, culture, a more just distribution of economic reward, and a path of personal development conducive not to profits but to a fuller, happier life.[15]

Television, with its powerful symbolic texts accessible to students of all backgrounds and classes, can prove quite useful by providing cultural material that highlights such a dialectic. Hard-hitting investigative social-activist community video documentary contains particularly relevant texts open to deconstruction, as does the best direct cinema/video work; but so too do the dominant television genres of comedy, melodrama, news, sport, electronic religion, game and talk programs, and commercials.

By engaging in serious critique, however, secondary and middle-school teachers, unlike their relatively protected university counterparts, may face overt political pressure from school principals, boards of education, and PTAs with vested interests in maintaining the dominant ideology. Thus the teacher must be able to overcome an "inner vulnerability," for, according to Jules Henry, "behind many intellectual failures is indeed a failure of nerve."[16] Nerve must be steady for the teacher to move beyond mere description of the way things are to an enlightened interpretation of why they are perceived to be that way, even if the explanation calls into question the very nature of the educational apparatus itself. Interpretation must occur in an educational environment open to the challenge of oppositional ideologies—an environment characterized by open enrollment, free tuition, no tracking that separates advantaged and disadvantaged students, and teachers who do not isolate themselves as unapproachable "professionals," but rather take active roles in counterhegemonic instruction by forming "alliances" with students, especially those from the working class, and by respecting students' insights developed through their prolonged and intensive television experiences.[17] While teachers who operate in this manner may be branded subversives, in fact they are upholding the ideals of enlightened education, which encourages active open debate of ideas and advocacy of principles by educated autonomous individuals.

NOTES

1. Roger Silverstone, "Television: Myth: Science: Commonsense," a paper presented to the International Communication Association Annual Conference, Chicago, Illinois, May 1986, pp. 6–7.

2. Andrew Britton, "Blissing Out: The Politics of Reaganite Entertainment," *Movie* 31/32 (Winter 1986): 4.

3. Ibid., p. 5.

4. Ibid., p. 12.

5. Ibid.

6. Ibid., p. 13.

7. Ibid., p. 6.

8. Conversation with Ilan Ziv, New York City, July 12, 1993.

9. ABC News *Nightline*, "What's Not News," August 30, 1988. Show #1897, printed transcript (New York: Journal Graphics, Inc., 1988), 7 pp.

10. David Bergmann, "In Search of the Hardcore Fan," *Variety*, April 13, 1983, p. 47.

11. Jacques Ellul, "The Power of Technique and the Ethics of Non-Power," in *The Myths of Information: Technology and Postindustrial Culture*, ed. by Kathleen Woodward (Madison, WI: Coda Press, 1980), p. 245.

12. Jan Pierre Dupuy, "Myths of the Informational Society," in *The Myths of Information*, p. 11.

13. Raymond Williams, *Marxism and Literature* (London: Oxford University Press, 1977), pp. 117–118.

14. Ibid., pp. 121–127. Examples include the residual ideology of rural "purity"—of community—in opposition to the personal isolation produced by urban industrial capitalism and the residual religious ideology of service to others without reward; both are areas the dominant culture has neglected or undervalued. An example of an emergent oppositional cultural form is the radical student and working-class press, which warns against, among other things, the incorporation of working-class lifestyles into popular advertising. This press has to date been unable to find an appropriate open distribution vehicle in American television, except for an occasionally progressive public-access cable channel. Radio, through community radio stations, has with some regularity opened its doors to such oppositional forms. One result of this openness was the lawsuit involving indecent language in the WBAI-Pacifica case.

15. Samuel Bowles and Herbert Gintis, *Schooling in Capitalist America* (New York: Basic Books, 1976), p. 101.

16. Jules Henry, *On Sham, Vulnerability and Other Forms of Self-Destruction* (New York: Vantage Books, 1973), p. 105.

17. Bowles and Gintis, *Schooling*, passim.

Selected Bibliography

An American Family. New York: Warner Paperback Library, 1973.

Arlen, Michael J. *The Camera Age.* New York: Farrar, Straus and Giroux, 1981.

———. *Thirty Seconds.* New York: Farrar, Straus and Giroux, 1979.

Barnet, Richard J., and Ronald E. Muller. *Global Reach.* New York: Simon and Schuster, 1974.

Barnett, Marvin. *Moments of Truth?* New York: Thomas Y. Crowell, 1975.

Barthes, Roland. *Mythologies.* Translated by Annette Lavers. New York: Hill and Wang, 1972.

Bellah, Robert N., et al. *Habits of the Heart: Individualism and Commitment in American Life.* Berkeley: University of California Press, 1985.

Benjamin, Burton. *Fair Play: CBS, General Westmoreland, and How a Television Documentary Went Wrong.* New York: Harper and Row, 1988.

Benjamin, Walter. "A Shory History of Photography." *Screen* 13:1 (1972): 5–26.

Berger, John. *Another Way of Telling.* With Jean Mohr. New York: Pantheon, 1982.

———. *Ways of Seeing.* London: British Broadcasting Company, 1972.

Bernays, Edward L., ed. *The Engineering of Consent.* Norman, OK: University of Oklahoma Press, 1955.

Bowles, Samuel, and Herbert Gintis. *Schooling in Capitalist America.* New York: Basic Books, 1976.

Boyer, Peter J. *Who Killed CBS?* New York: St. Martin's Press, 1988.

Britton, Andrew. "Blissing Out: The Politics of Reaganite Entertainment." *Movie* 31/32 (Winter 1986): 1–42.

Breen, Myles, and Farrel Corcoran. "Myth in the Television Discourse." *Communication Monographs* 49 (June 1982): 127–36.

Brooks, Peter. *The Melodramatic Imagination.* New Haven, CT: Yale University Press, 1976.

Brooks, Tim, and Earle Marsh, eds. *The Complete Directory to Prime Time Network TV Shows 1946–Present,* 5th ed. New York: Ballantine Books, 1992.

Brown, Les, ed. *Les Brown's Encyclopedia of Television,* 3d ed. Detroit: Gale Research, 1992.

———. *Televi$ion: The Business behind the Box*. New York: Harcourt Brace Jovanovich, 1971.

Campbell, Joseph. *The Hero with a Thousand Faces*. New York: Pantheon Books, 1949.

Campbell, Richard. *60 Minutes and the News: A Mythology For Middle America*. Urbana, IL: University of Illinois Press, 1991.

Carpenter, Edmund. *Oh, What a Blow That Phantom Gave Me!* Toronto: Bantam Books, 1973.

Carpignano, Paolo, Robin Anderson, Stanley Aronowitz, and William Difazio. "Chatter in the Age of Electronic Reproduction: Talk Television and the 'Public Mind.' " *Social Text: Theory/Culture/Ideology* 25/26 (1990): 33–55.

Chesebro, James W. "Communication, Values, and Popular Television Series—A Four Year Assessment." In *Television: The Critical View*, 2d ed., ed. Horace Newcomb, 16–54. New York: Oxford University Press, 1979.

Comstock, George. *Television in America*. Beverly Hills: Sage Publications, 1980.

de Certeau, Michel. *The Practice of Everyday Life*. Translated by Steven Rendall. Berkeley: University of California Press, 1984.

Dessart, George. "Of Tastes and Times." *Television Quarterly* 26:2 (1992): 33–41.

Eliade, Mircea. *Myth and Reality*. New York: Harper and Row, 1963.

Ellul, Jacques. *The Technological Society*. Translated by John Wilkinson. New York: Alfred A. Knopf, 1964.

Epstein, Edward Jay. *Between Fact and Fiction*. New York: Vantage Books, 1975.

———. *News from Nowhere*. New York: Vantage Books, 1973.

Espinosa, Paul. "The Audience in the Text: Ethnographic Observations of a Hollywood Story Conference." *Media, Culture and Society* 4 (1982): 77–86.

Feibleman, James K. *In Praise of Comedy*. New York: Horizon Press, 1970.

Fiske, John, and John Hartley. *Reading Television*. London: Methuen and Co., 1978.

Friendly, Fred. *Due to Circumstances beyond Our Control*. New York: Random House, 1967.

Fromm, Erich. *The Forgotten Language: An Introduction to the Understanding of Dreams, Fairy Tales and Myths*. New York: Rinehart and Co., 1951.

Frye, Northrop. *Anatomy of Criticism*. Princeton, NJ: Princeton University Press, 1957.

Gitlin, Todd. "Prime Time Ideology: The Hegemonic Process in Television Entertainment." In *Television: The Critical View*, 4th ed., ed. Horace Newcomb, 507–32. New York: Oxford University Press, 1987.

Hadden, Jeffrey K., and Charles E. Swann. *The Rising Power of Televangelism*. Reading, MA: Addison-Wesley, 1981.

Hall, Stuart. "The Rediscovery of 'Ideology': Return of the Repressed in Media Studies." In *Culture, Society and the Media*, ed. Michael Gurevitch et al., 56–90. London: Methuen, 1982.

———. "Signification, Representation, Ideology: Althusser and the Post-Structuralist Debates." *Critical Studies in Mass Communication* 2 (June 1985): 91–114.

Hallin, Daniel C. "Network News: We Keep America on Top of the World." In *Watching Television*, ed. Todd Gitlin, 9–41. New York: Pantheon, 1986.

Henry, Jules. *Culture against Man*. New York: Random House, 1963.

———. *On Sham, Vulnerability and Other Forms of Self-Destruction*. New York: Vantage Books, 1973.

Himmelstein, Hal. "Kodak's 'America': Images from the American Eden." *Journal of Film and Video* 41 (Summer 1989): 75–94.

———. *On the Small Screen: New Approaches in Television and Video Criticism.* New York: Praeger Publishers, 1981.

Huxley, Aldous. *Brave New World.* New York: Harper and Row, 1939.

Klapp, Orrin E. *Heroes, Villains, and Fools: The Changing American Character.* Englewood Cliffs, NJ: Prentice-Hall, 1962.

Kurtz, Bruce. *Spots: The Popular Art of American Television Commercials.* New York: Arts Communications, 1977.

Lahr, John. "Annals of Comedy: The Goat Boy Rises." *The New Yorker,* November 1, 1993, pp. 113–21.

Levinson, Richard, and William Link. *Stay Tuned.* New York: Ace, 1983.

Levi-Strauss, Claude. *The Raw and the Cooked.* Translated by John and Doreen Weightman. New York: Harper and Row, 1969.

Lifton, Robert Jay, ed. *America and the Asian Revolutions.* New York: Aldine, 1970.

———. *Home from the War: Vietnam Veterans—Neither Victims nor Executioners.* New York: Simon and Schuster, 1973.

Masciarotte, Gloria-Jean. "C'Mon Girl: Oprah Winfrey and the Discourse of Feminine Talk." *Genders* 11 (Fall 1991): 81–110.

McKibben, Bill. *The Age of Missing Information.* New York: Plume, 1992.

McLuhan, Marshall. *The Mechanical Bride.* New York: Vanguard, 1951.

McNeil, Alex. *Total Television,* 3d ed. New York: Penguin Books, 1991.

Miller, Perry, and Thomas Johnson. *The Puritans.* New York: American Book Co., 1938.

Mills, C. Wright. *The Power Elite.* New York: Oxford University Press, 1956.

Morley, David. *Family Television: Cultural Power and Domestic Leisure.* London: Comedia Publishing Group, 1986.

Newcomb, Horace. "On the Dialogic Aspects of Mass Communication." *Critical Studies in Mass Communication* 1 (March 1984): 34–50.

———. *TV: The Most Popular Art.* Garden City, NY: Anchor Press/Doubleday, 1974.

———, ed. *Television: The Critical View.* New York: Oxford University Press, 1987.

Nichols, Bill. *Ideology and the Image.* Bloomington: Indiana University Press, 1981.

Nye, Russel Blaine. *The Cultural Life of the New Nation.* New York: Harper and Row, 1960.

Owens, Virginia. *The Total Image, or Selling Jesus in the Modern Age.* Grand Rapids, MI: William B. Eerdmans, 1980.

Paine, Thomas. *Common Sense, The Rights of Man, and Other Essential Writings of Thomas Paine.* New York: Meridian/Penguin Books USA, 1984.

Phelan, John M. *Disenchantment: Meaning and Morality in the Media.* New York: Hastings House, 1980.

Postman, Neil. *Amusing Ourselves to Death.* New York: Penguin Books, 1985.

———. *Technopoly: The Surrender of Culture to Technology.* New York: Alfred A. Knopf, 1992.

Powers, Ron. *The Newscasters.* New York: St. Martin's Press, 1978.

Price, Jonathan. *The Best Thing on TV: Commercials.* New York: Penguin Books, 1978.

Real, Michael R. *Super Media: A Cultural Studies Approach.* Newbury Park, CA: Sage Publications, 1989.

Report of the National Advisory Commission on Civil Disorders. New York: Bantam, 1968.

Robinson, Michael J. "Future Television News Research: Beyond Edward Jay Epstein." In *Television Network News: Issues in Content Research,* eds. William Adama and Fay Schreibman, 197-211. Washington, DC: School of Public and International Affairs, George Washington University, 1978.

Ross, Alex. "The Politics of Irony." *The New Republic,* November 8, 1993, pp. 22-31.

Schultze, Quentin J. "The Mythos of the Electronic Church." *Critical Studies in Mass Communication* 4 (1987): 245-61.

Silverstone, Roger. "Narrative Strategies in Television Science—A Case Study." *Media, Culture and Society* 6 (October 1984): 377-410.

Slotkin, Richard. *The Fatal Environment: The Myth of the Frontier in the Age of Industrialization, 1800-1890.* Middletown, CT: Wesleyan University Press, 1985.

————. *Gunfighter Nation: The Myth of the Frontier in Twentieth-Century America.* New York: Atheneum, 1992.

————. *Regeneration Through Violence: The Mythology of the American Frontier, 1600-1860.* Middletown, CT: Wesleyan University Press, 1973.

Sontag, Susan. *On Photography.* New York: Delta, 1977.

Stein, Ben. *The View from Sunset Boulevard.* New York: Anchor Press/Doubleday, 1980.

Steinbock, Dan. *Television and Screen Transference.* Helsinki: Finnish Broadcasting Company, 1986.

Tamm, Goran, Hans Ingvar Hanson, and George N. Gordon. *Man in Focus: New Approaches to Commercial Communications.* New York: Hastings House, 1980.

Timberg, Bernard. *Television Talk.* Austin, TX: University of Texas Press, forthcoming.

Timberg, Bernard, and Hal Himmelstein. "Television Commercials and the Contradictions of Everyday Life: A Follow-Up to Himmelstein's Production Study of the Kodak 'America' Commercial." *Journal of Film and Video* 41 (Fall 1989): 67-79.

Tuchman, Gaye. "Consciousness Industries and the Production of Culture." *Journal of Communication* 33 (Summer 1983): 330-41.

Volosinov, V. N. *Marxism and the Philosophy of Language.* London: Seminar Press, 1973.

Williams, Raymond. *Marxism and Literature.* London: Oxford University Press, 1977.

————. *Television: Technology and Cultural Form.* New York: Schocken Books, 1975.

Wolfe, Tom. *The Electric Kool-Aid Acid Test.* New York: Bantam Books, 1969.

Woodward, Kathleen, ed. *The Myths of Information: Technology and Postindustrial Culture.* Madison, WI: Coda Press, 1980.

Index